MOUNT VERNON HIGH SCHOOL MEDIA CENTER

THE NEW SPANISH TABLE

EL XAMPANYET
Fundada el 1929
Ca l'Esteve
HAY
SIDRA
fresca.

THE NEW SPANISH TABLE

BY ANYA VON BREMZEN

FOOD PHOTOGRAPHY BY SUSAN GOLDMAN

MOUNT VERNON HIGH SCHOOL
MEDIA CENTER
8515 OLD MOUNT VERNON ROAD
ALEXANDRIA, VA 22309

WORKMAN PUBLISHING • NEW YORK

To B.Y.,
Who shared my journey

Copyright © 2005 by Anya von Bremzen
New food photography © 2005 by Susan Goldman

All rights reserved. No portion of this book may be reproduced—mechanically, electronically, or by any other means, including photocopying—without written permission of the publisher. Published simultaneously in Canada by Thomas Allen & Son Limited.

Library of Congress Cataloging-in-Publication Data
Von Bremzen, Anya.
The new Spanish table / by Anya von Bremzen.
Includes index.
ISBN-13: 978-0-7611-3994-2
ISBN-10: 0-7611-3994-X
ISBN-13: 978-0-7611-3555-5 (pbk.)
ISBN-10: 0-7611-3555-3 (pbk.)
1. Cookery, Spanish. I. Title.
TX723.5.S7V66 2005
641.5946-dc22 2005051806

Cover design: Paul Hanson
Book design: Lisa Hollander with Lori S. Malkin
New food photography: Susan Goldman
Author photo: Katie Dunn

Workman books are available at special discounts when purchased in bulk for premiums and sales promotions as well as for fund-raising or educational use. Special editions or book excerpts can be created to specification. For details, contact the Special Sales Director at the address below.

Workman Publishing Company, Inc.
708 Broadway
New York, NY 10003-9555
www.workman.com
Printed in the U.S.A.
First printing: October 2005
10 9 8 7 6 5 4 3 2 1

ACKNOWLEDGMENTS

This book is a tribute to the genius and generosity of Spanish cooks. It couldn't have been possible without their friendship, support, information, and recipes—not to mention the countless astonishing meals that I've enjoyed in Spain over the years. My heartfelt *gracias* to all the following people, as well as to those whom I may not have mentioned but whose kindness is deeply appreciated nonetheless.

Carles Abellan of Commerç 24; Las abuelas de Sils; Ferran Adrià and Juli Soler of El Bulli; Andoni Luis Adúriz of Mugaritz; Oscar Alberdi of Alberdi; Raúl Aleixandre of Ca' Sento; Josean Martínez Alija of Restaurante Guggenheim; Clara María de Amezúa; Felix and Susana Andres; Juan Mari and Elena Arzak of Arzak; Juanito Bayen of Pinotxo; Luis Bellvis; Martin Berasategui of Restaurante Martin Berasategui; Patxi Bergara of Bar Bergara; Xavier Canal of Pastisseria Canal; José Carlos Capel of El País; Pablo Carrington of Villa Soro; Gonzalo Córdoba of El Faro; Inma Crosas of Roig Robí; Quique Dacosta of El Poblet; José Ramón Elozondo of Aloña Berri; the Ferrer family of Freixenet; Xavier Franco of Saüc; Pedro Garcia; Maria Jesus Gil; Gabriela Llamas and Carlos Meier; Juan Llantada of Comunitat Valenciana; Laura Lorca; Pep Manubens of Cal Pep; Lourdes March; Francesc López and Jaume Marin of Patronat de Turisme Costa Brava; Quim Marques of Suquet de l'Almirall; Rodrigo Mestre; Alex Montiel and Iñaki Gulin of La Cuchara de San Telmo; Quim Monzo of El Quim de la Boqueria; Adolfo Muñez of Adolfo; Sonia Ortega of Spain Gourmetour; Quim Pérez of Quimet i Quimet; Lourdes Plana; Paulino Plata of Junta de Andalucía; Laura Robles of Casa Robles; Joan, Josep, and Jordi Roca of El Celler de Can Roca; Salvador Rojo of Salvador Rojo; Angeles Ruiz; Santos Ruiz; María Jose San Roman of Monastrell; David Solé i Torné of Barquet; Joan Torrens of Es Baluard; Roser Torres;

Mari Carmen Vélez of La Sirena, Jordi Vilá of Alkimia; Rosa Vilaseca of Hotel Sant Ferriol; Jaume Vidal of La Plaça.

I first started writing about Spain as a journalist, and I am sincerely grateful to Nancy Novogrod at *Travel+Leisure* and Dana Cowin at *Food&Wine,* and to their respective editorial teams, for all the amazing assignments over the years. As always, my agent, Jane Dystel, was unflappable, inexhaustible, and full of savvy and cheer, while her partner, Miriam Goderich, offered invaluable assistance with the proposal. *Mil gracias* to Pilar Vico for her years of friendship and for nurturing my passion for Spain. Thanks, too, to ICEX, Janet Kafka, and Holly Hansen and Karen MacKenzie for their support. All those recipe-testing marathons would have been utterly pointless without our friends who came to dinner, tasted the food, listened to my stories, and stayed up late drinking *orujo*. I also thank Melissa Clark for her crumbly treats, and Maricel Presilla for the seventeenth-century chocolate.

Because of the vision and brilliance of Peter Workman, being published by Workman is a writer's dream. To my editor, Suzanne Rafer, I'm grateful not just for whipping this book into shape, but for launching my entire food writing career more than fifteen years ago. Who knows where I'd be without her? Huge kudos to Lisa Hollander, Paul Hanson, and Lori Malkin for the dashing look of the book, and to Barbara Peragine for making it work; to Barbara Mateer for her unswerving attention to detail; to Katie Workman for her marketing genius; and to Sarah O'Leary and Jen Pare for their tireless publicity efforts. Susan Goldman, together with food stylists Mariann Sauvion-Grady Best and prop stylist Sara Abalan, made the book sparkle with fabulous food photography, and Leora Kahn found just the right scenics. Thanks, too, to Fred Rose of the Chelsea Ceramic Guild.

My mother, Larisa Frumkin, has taught me that food is a pleasure meant to be shared with others, even if my dinner parties are still nothing compared to hers. Her love is what calls me back home from Spain. My final *gracias* are to Barry Yourgrau, who shared in every stage of this project, from savoring the alchemical cooking of Ferran Adrià to washing the dishes after long, happy nights recipe-testing at our table.

CONTENTS

SALADS

SO FRESH, SO GOOD

PAGE 110

The Spanish take on salads: beautiful vegetables, simply dressed with the finest quality olive oil and vinegar. What could be better? Try Green Salad with Apricots and Hazelnuts, Mesclun with Figs, Cabrales, and Pomegranate, a Fava Bean Salad with Jamón and Fresh Mint, and a Roasted Pepper Salad so good that "addictive" is part of its name.

EGGS

MORE THAN BREAKFAST

PAGE 136

In Spain the egg is beloved—and more likely to show up at lunch or supper than first thing in the morning. The iconic Potato Tortilla. Tasty Eggs Over Smoked Bread Hash. A luxurious Wild Mushroom Revuelto in an Egg Carton. Use only the freshest, best-quality eggs for these heavenly dishes.

EMPANADAS

CANAPES, COCAS & MORE

PAGE 158

Canapés, *tostadas, cocas,* and empanadas—breads find their way onto the Spanish table in a remarkable array of tasty bites. Serve up Pastry Puffs with Roquefort and Apple Spread, Basque Triple Seafood Canapés, "Deconstructed" Tomato Bread, Galician Tuna Empanada with Melting Onions, and a crusty pizzalike Coca with Candied Red Peppers.

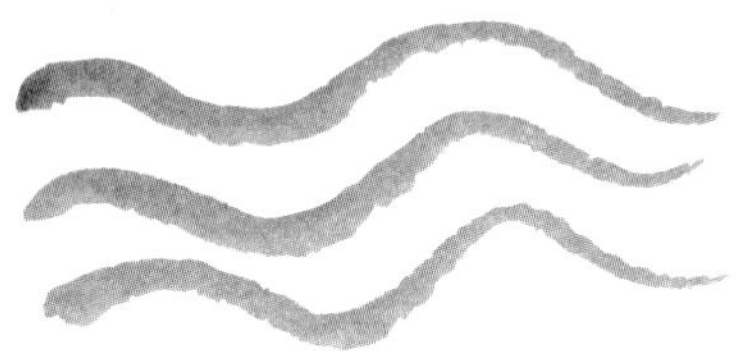

SEAFOOD

SOPHISTICATED SIMPLICITY

PAGE 184

Roasted Halibut on a Bed of Potatoes. Monkfish with Eggplant Allioli. Fresh Sardines with Garlic and Parsley. Seafood Stew in Romesco Sauce. Cadiz Clams with Spinach and Eggs. Incredibly fresh seafood is at the heart of the Spanish diet and translates into recipes that are welcome on any seafood lover's table.

MEAT

PORK, LAMB, AND BEEF

PAGE 228

Pork Tenderloin with Lightly Seared Strawberries. Salt-Baked Pork in Adobo. Braised and Glazed Pork Ribs with Applesauce. Pork is the number one meat with the Spanish, but they also make glorious lamb dishes (Lamb Shanks with Five Heads of Garlic) and beef dishes (Grilled Skirt Steak with Almond & Caper Salsa).

POULTRY

AND GAME

PAGE 270

Just wait until you try Grilled Chicken with Piquillo Gazpacho Sauce, Smothered Chicken with Vegetable Jam, and Lemon Chicken with Honey and Saffron. Plus Duck Legs with Prunes and Olives, Hunter's-Style Baked Quail in Escabeche, and a robust Rabbit Stew with a Touch of Chocolate.

BEANS AND POTATOES
RUSTIC ELEGANCE

PAGE 302

Originally thought of as poor man's cuisine, bean, legume, and potato dishes flourish in Spain. Enjoy Lentil and Wild Mushroom Hash with Poached Eggs, Chickpea Stew with Chorizo and Meatballs, White Bean and Clam Casserole, Pyrenean Potato and Kale Cake, Smoky Mashed Potatoes, and Wrinkled Potatoes with Spicy Chile Mojo.

RICE AND PASTA

PAGE 330

A Spanish cookbook without paella? Impossible. And this chapter includes a Classic Valencian Paella, a Black Paella with Squid, Mussels, and Peas, and a Paella with Pine Nut Meatballs, Sausage, and Potatoes. Plus there's a Toasted Pasta "Paella" with Shrimp and a Spanish take on Spaghetti and Clams in a Skillet.

VEGETABLES
LUXURIOUSLY PERFECT

PAGE 366

On Spanish tables, vegetables are frequently eaten as a first course rather than a side dish, and choices range from beautifully Batter-Fried Artichokes to Eggplant Ham and Cheese "Sandwiches" to Andalusian Spinach with Chickpeas to Zucchini "Boats" with Tuna and Roasted Tomatoes.

DESSERTS
THE GRAND FINALE

PAGE 396

Fragrant tarts, luscious mousses and ice creams, refreshing granitas—including one made with espresso and another with Campari and blood oranges—plus a full array of sensational chocolate treats like Adolfo's Warm Chocolate Soufflé Cakes, Chocolate Custards with a Citrus Cloud, and Hot Chocolate with Meringue Stars. Sensational!

VINOS
JOSE GARCIA
DELGADO

FALLING IN LOVE WITH SPAIN

T*he New Spanish Table* is the result of my two decades of travel in Spain, an exhilarating odyssey across one of the world's greatest foodscapes. The first time I visited the country was in the early eighties, as it was awakening from the isolation and destitution of the Franco years. I was instantly smitten with the regional rigor, the immense pull of traditions, the purity and warmth of the food culture. I became hooked on the rustic *asadores* of Castile where macho maestros roasted suckling lamb in wood-burning ovens. When I visited Valencia and Alicante expecting to find only one kind of paella, I stumbled upon whole cults devoted to rice. In the Basque country, I went crazy for *pinxtos,* the ornate local version of tapas. In Catalonia I marveled at the Mediterranean grace of the coastal *cocina* and at the intriguing inland combinations like salt cod with honey or rabbit with chocolate. In

Top left: The tile roof and tower of the colorful Casa Batlló, a flamboyant apartment house in Barcelona designed by Antoni Gaudí. *Top right:* At the end of the day, romance thrives at bars like Las Gabrieles. *Bottom left:* Spain's superchef Ferran Adrià enjoys a quiet moment on the terrace of his restaurant, El Bulli. *Bottom right:* The Guggenheim Museum in Bilbao, Frank Gehry's titanium-clad architectural tour de force.

Andalusia I ate my way through an encyclopedia of gazpachos and stayed up until *madrugada* (dawn) gulping sherry at smoky flamenco dives.

Besotted by Spain and its cuisine, I returned again and again—making pilgrimages to markets, fried fish shacks, and sausage shops; to countryside cider houses for fizzy apple brew and rare *chuletas*—T-bones, charred and thick as an airport novel; up to hilltop villages for roast baby pig with the crispest of skins; along rocky coastal roads to seafood hideaways for pristine langoustines and Europe's best salt-baked fish. Between meals I zipped from one crowded tapas bar to the next, comparing their crispy *patatas bravas* and garlicky shrimp. Addictive—but back in those days, Spain still had a one-note cuisine, elegant in its austerity but somehow lost in a time-warp.

Over the years, I have watched as Spain transformed itself from an almost archaic Mediterranean culture into a European capital of style and design. Yet despite its thrust into modernity, the country has kept globalization at bay, retaining the authenticity that seduced me in the first place. And something truly extraordinary has happened—fostered by a desire to break with the past: The boom that gripped Spanish cultural life after Franco, producing figures like filmmaker Pedro Almódovar, has taken hold in Spanish kitchens. "Eating well is part of our new freedom, it has made us feel modern," says my friend José Carlos Capel, the influential food critic for Madrid's *El País* newspaper.

REVOLUTIONARY CUISINE

New Spanish cuisine was conceived in the belle époque Basque resort of San Sebastián in the late 1970s. Impressed by the vibrant delicacy of revolutionary *nouvelle cuisine* across the border in France, a group of Basque chefs that included Juan Mari Arzak and Pedro Subijana decided to stage their own revolution. The result was *nueva cocina vasca,* or new Basque cuisine—a lighter, fresher, prettier, unapologetically modern style, both cutting edge *and* solidly grounded in Basque ingredients and traditions. It wasn't a coincidence that these first innovations took place in the Basque province of Guipuzcua, the most food-centric corner of Europe, that today boasts an improbably high concentration of Michelin stars. *Nueva cocina* soon spread across Spain, giving rise to new modern regional styles.

And then something radical happened. A self-taught Catalan genius named Ferran Adrià arrived on the scene. I had my first meal at Adrià's restaurant, El Bulli, in 1997, the year that he was awarded his third Michelin star and hailed by the great French chef Joel Robuchon as "the best cook on the planet." To get to El Bulli from the Catalan resort town of Rosas, I drove up the world's most treacherous, pot-holed dirt road. Though Adrià was already creating a stir in the food circles, El Bulli's whitewashed dining room was nearly empty when I arrived for lunch. (Today the restaurant gets around 300,000 early reservation requests and the chances of scoring a table without one are practically zero.) While enjoying aperitifs on the terrace, I looked down on a villa above a picturesque cove, inhaling the scent of Mediterranean fir trees. But that's where the familiar gave way to the uncanny.

My degustation menu unfolded in a series of edible whimsies, each dish a nose-thumbing to convention. Some of the *amuse-gueules*—a Parmesan ice-cream sandwich, a poached quail egg in a caramel cage—introduced the concept of dessert-as-dinner. Another Daliesque provocation was "smoke foam," a mousse made from water that had been smoked over burning wood. The rest of the meal? Egg-yolk sabayon with whipped cream and hazelnut vanilla sauce (a savory appetizer!). A garlicky ice cream of *ajo blanco* (an Andalusian almond gazpacho). Cuttlefish-and-coconut ravioli. Sardine roll-ups filled with raspberry froth ("*El señor chef* is in his 'foam' phase," a waiter confided). Eggplant ravioli stuffed with a yogurt mousse and caramelized with . . . Fisherman's Friend (a licorice cough lozenge). The finale was a sculptural contraption holding sublime and outrageous *petits fours.*

After lunch I had the good fortune to talk with Adrià for hours. I drove away completely under his spell, convinced that Europe's culinary future belonged to Spain. Almost every year I've returned to El Bulli in awe at Adrià's outrageously inventive thirty-course tasting menus that blend high design with groundbreaking scientific research. A self-proclaimed heir to Salvador Dalí, Adrià keeps developing his iconoclastic vocabulary, spending six months a year at his *taller* (laboratory) in Barcelona where he experiments with new dishes while El Bulli is closed for vacation.

THE ADRIA EFFECT

Ferran Adrià's influence in Spain—and beyond—can't be underestimated. He was the one who taught other chefs to create bewitching trompe l'oeil effects; to break down the boundaries between sweet and savory, hot and cold, liquid and solid; to refract ingredients into contrasting elements; to make use of such edible ephemera as savory ice creams, foams and bubbly airs, and hot and cold gelées. Most importantly, he taught chefs to re-examine traditional cooking methods through the prism of physics and chemistry. Today, the fanciful and often surreal fusion of cuisine and science is de rigueur in contemporary Spanish kitchens. In Gerona, for instance, two Michelin-starred brother chefs have been working with fragrance experts on desserts that replicate scents of famous perfumes (Lancôme as a final course). In Bilbao, with the help of a dairy scientist, the young chef at the Restaurante Guggenheim has created ephemeral riffs based on casein and curds. Spanish chefs are probing rice DNA to improve their paellas; using laser technology to perfect a grill pan; inventing futuristic vacuum distillers to extract colorless "flavor essences" from ingredients; applying liquid nitrogen to gazpachos; and poaching vacuum-packed food in a space-age bain marie originally used by biologists for heating vaccines. One chef even recruited a medical liver transplant specialist to help him improve his foie gras! It's as if the whole country were transformed into a giant poetically-touched food science lab. And if, in the past, Spanish cooks looked to France for new ideas, now even the most die-hard French snobs admit that for culinary adventure they cross the border to Spain. Welcome to the food mecca of the twenty-first century.

COOK THIS AT HOME

But who can tackle lab-perfect liquid nitrogen mojitos at home? Happily, visionary chefs like Adrià and Arzak and the Basque and Catalan culinary vanguard are only part of the story. Even the most experimental among Spanish chefs would be the first ones to acknowledge their debt to traditional cooking and to the luminous quality of local ingredients. It is this fusion of tradition and innovation that makes eating in Spain so thrilling right now. The divide between high and low, haute and homey, classic and iconoclastic, rustic and refined can be deliciously blurred. Owners of centuries-old tapas bars send their children for a *stage* (apprenticeship) at Michelin-starred meccas to pick up new cooking techniques. Avant-garde chefs, meanwhile, hang out at their favorite classic haunts, soaking up the rigorous simplicity of ingredient-driven *cocina popular.* In Spain, everyone eats at everyone else's restaurants and the country is united in its adoration of food.

So the exciting news for American home cooks is this: The same creative process that pushed Spain into the culinary stratosphere has transformed it into an epicenter of casual, thoroughly modern Mediterranean cooking—exquisite in its simplicity, yet often startling in its quiet inventiveness. Gazpachos these days come in a rainbow of flavors and colors, with arresting and varied textural flourishes. The modern tapas of San Sebastián are a showcase of what can be done with a piece of bread and a few simple ingredients. The range and creativity of desserts is unsurpassed. The presentations are fun and artistic yet simple enough to reproduce at home. Most importantly, each bite still feels fresh and new. While seemingly every culinary corner of France and Italy has been explored under a microscope, Spain remains an El Dorado with an immense untapped wealth of the kind of unfussy, elegant, alluring Mediterranean flavors we all swoon for these days. You want style? Spain's got style. You want simplicity? It's got simplicity. You want rustic slow-cooked bean or lamb casseroles to warm the soul in the winter—Spain has that, too.

It's impossible to resist the siren call of those Mediterranean-Moorish ingredients: aromatic splashes of olive oil, almonds and hazelnuts pounded into simple but emphatic sauces, garlic and parsley, piquillo peppers, tomatoes and saffron, pungent olives and anchovies, coarse sea salt and smoky paprika, lemons and bitter oranges. It's difficult not to admire the playful laid-back way the Spanish entertain. They make it all seem so simple, with an array of small tapas or a big earthenware *cazuela* placed on the table so that guests can help themselves while the hosts sit back and sip wine. Little wonder that Spanish lifestyle and way of eating is the envy of Europe.

ABOUT THE RECIPES

Recipes in *The New Spanish Table* are culled from different corners of Spain—Mallorca to Galicia to Extremadura—and I sincerely believe they do justice to the excitement and regional diversity of modern Spanish cuisine. Yet, it wasn't my aim to compile a comprehensive compendium of classic regional cooking. Instead the selection of dishes here reflects my personal travels and taste. If recipes from Catalonia and the Basque Country predominate, it's because I'm especially smitten with the foods of these regions. If the emphasis is on stylish, healthy, modern cuisine that romances seafood, vegetables, legumes, and olive oil, that's because I subscribe to this way of eating. Many recipes traveled perfectly and turned out like a dream in my New York kitchen. Other masterpieces I tasted in Spain got lost in translation. And for all my desire to convert cooks to far-out experimental Spanish techniques, I doubt that most are willing to tackle foam making and vacuum poaching at home. In the end, I found a way to deliver practical, accessible recipes without sacrificing excitement and authenticity.

Ranging from classic to creative, from traditional to trendy and back, the dishes here come from an extraordinary wealth of sources. Year after year I traveled through Spain, calling on my favorite chefs and discovering new talent as I reported on the country's astounding gastronomic developments for magazines such as *Food&Wine* and *Travel+Leisure.* I ate and took notes and asked for recipes that were *delicioso, estupendo, tremendo, genial,* and *fenomenal.* I got them from Michelin three-star luminaries like Ferran Adrià, Juan Mari Arzak, and Martin Berasategui; from mustachioed owners of obscure tapas bars in miniscule hamlets; from market vendors, taxi drivers, pig breeders, and winemakers' aunts. I've peered over the shoulders of rice specialists in Valencia, attended high profile avant-garde chefs' conferences, and spent hours interviewing prominent Spanish food writers, magazine editors, and restaurant critics. I visited cheesemakers, *cava bodegas,* paprika factories, and convents populated by sisters who bake like a dream.

Those looking for perfect renditions of traditional warhorses like gazpacho, paella, sangria, and tapas won't be disappointed. There are also plenty of fresh, easy fish recipes from the coast, hearty paprika-spiked bean and potato pots from the heartland, classic vegetable mélanges, and sweets from master bakers, grandmothers, and nuns. But cuisines evolve—and nowhere more so than in Spain. Next to classic tapas like *patatas bravas* and garlic shrimp, I've included New Wave creations such as tuna tartare with a date and almond sauce, and a truffled potato tortilla. Alongside traditional tomato gazpacho *The New Spanish Table* features creative chilled soups, such as cherry and beet gazpacho and a gazpacho sorbet. Fish recipes swing from fishermen's stews and shellfish pots to elegant restaurant dishes like scallops with candied lemon. For dessert, choose between a seventeenth-century hot chocolate or a twenty-first-century chocolate mousse startlingly accented with sea salt and olive oil. This is how Spain eats today. And no other country on Earth is better fed. *¡Buen provecho!*

THE REGIONS OF SPAIN

SPAIN AT A GLANCE

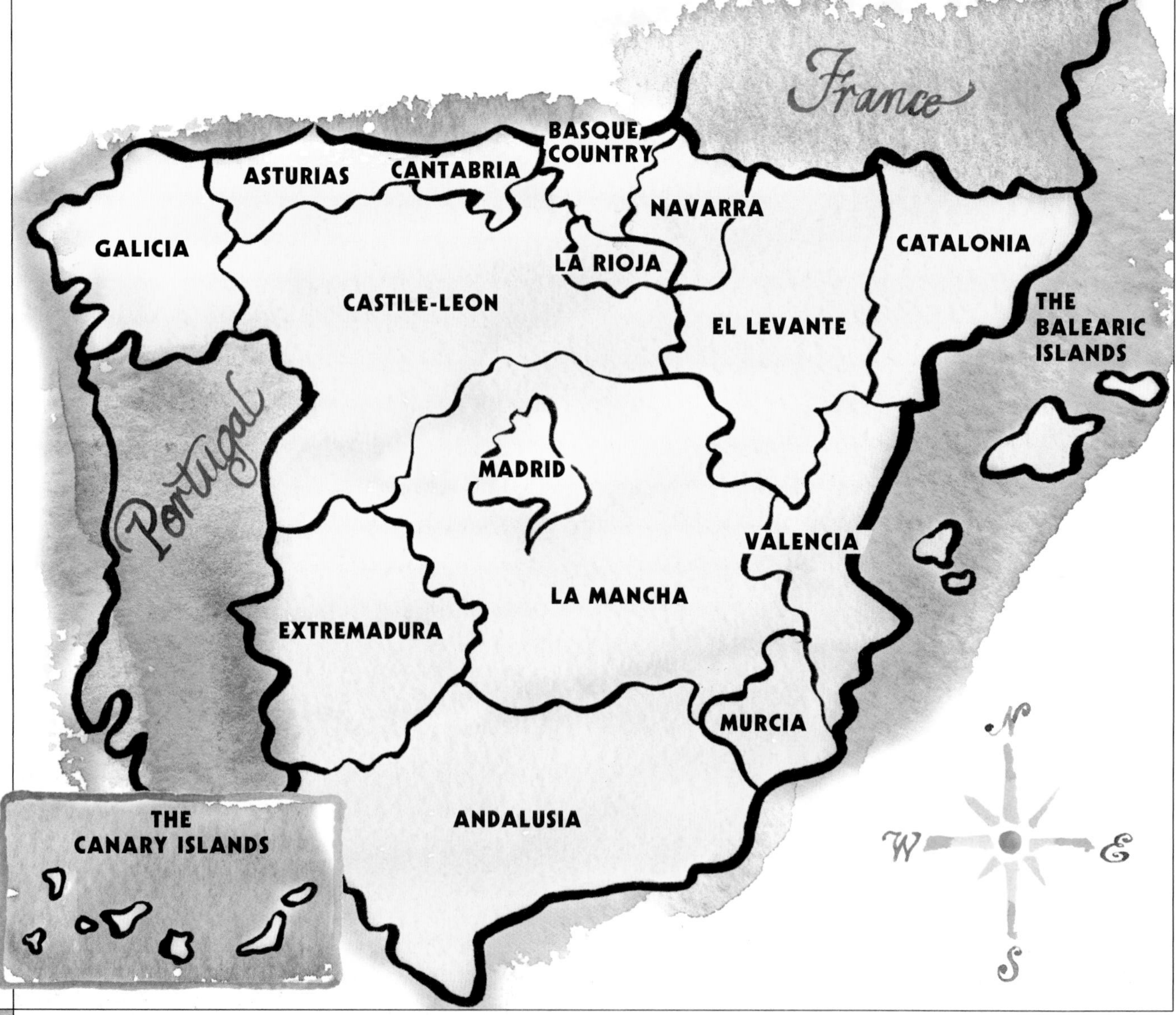

THE CENTRAL PLAINS

CASTILE-LEÓN

FAST FACTS

The ancient kingdom of Castilla y León today makes up Spain's largest autonomous region (Spain is divided into nineteen *comunidades autónomas,* which are subdivided into provinces). North and northwest of Madrid, this sweep of territory takes in parched plains, mountains and valleys, and hilltop castles and sleepy villages, as well as stunning historic towns like Burgos, Segovia, Salamanca, Avila, and León. To many Castile-León is the very cradle of modern Spanish culture. Although Madrid, Spain's worldly capital, is located within Castile, it has been given autonomous status.

FOOD

Classic Castilian cuisine is full of austere elegance, dominated by smoky *embutidos* (charcuterie), beans, lentils and chickpeas, garlic, and paprika. Macho meat reigns supreme here, especially suckling lamb and crisp-skinned baby pig roasted in wood-burning ovens.

The vineyards of Numanthia Termes in the up-and-coming Toro DO, in Castile, which is known for its bold reds.

Traditional specialties: *Lechazo* (roast suckling lamb); *cochinillo asado* (roast suckling pig); *cocido* (boiled dinner); bean and sausage *potajes* (stews); *albóndigas en salsa* (saucy meatballs); *gallina en pepitoria* (hen in almond sauce); tripe with chickpeas and sausages; *tortillas* and *revueltos* (filled omelets and scrambled eggs)

WINE

Located along the Duero river, Castile's Ribera del Duero DO (denomination of origin) is the source of Spain's most aristocratic, beautifully structured reds. From the Rueda DO in the province of Valladolid come crisp, well-balanced whites featuring the delightful verdejo grape. Castile's new wine powerhouse is the DO Toro, a hot, semiarid area around Zamora that produces big bold reds. Bierzo, another emerging wine region, has also been getting critical raves for its complex aromatic reds starring the local mencía grape.

Great Bodegas

Ribera del Duero DO: Alejandro Fernández (Pesquera); Emilio Moro; Vega-Sicilia (if you can afford it)
Rueda DO: Telmo Rodríguez (Basa), Bodegas Aldial (Naia); Marqués de Riscal; Angel Rodriguez (Martinsancho)
Toro DO: Fariña, Mauro; Numanthia Termes
El Bierzo DO: Dominio de Tares; Descendientes de J. Palacios (Corullón); Paixar

LA MANCHA

FAST FACTS

La Mancha (officially Castilla-La Mancha) is the vast windswept swath of Spain's central *meseta* where a certain Cervantes character famously battled the windmills. The Moors called it *manxa*—dry earth—because in Spain the rain does *not* often fall on the plain. This predominantly rural region of vineyards, olive groves, poppy fields—and many sheep—is also home to towns like Toledo, La Mancha's stunningly historic capital, and Cuenca, famed for its "hanging houses" dramatically etched into cliffs.

FOOD

Suffused with paprika, garlic and saffron, for which the region is famous, the sturdy cuisine of La Mancha has much in common with the food of Castile. As elsewhere in Spain, creative chefs here are reinventing regional flavors.

Traditional Specialties: *Pisto manchego* (a tomatoey vegetable stew); *sopa de ajo* (garlic and bread soup); *bacalao al ajo arriero* (a salt cod dish similar to brandade); *morteruelo* (warm game pâté); partridge either stewed or in *escabeche; migas* (fried bread bits); *marzipán; alajú* (a bread crumb, almond, and honey confection)

Left: The Archbishop's Palace in Toledo, the capital of Castilla-La Mancha. *Top right:* Dehesa, in Extremadura, is where the famous *ibérico* pigs graze before they become Spain's top ham.

WINE

As Europe's largest demarcated wine region, once known for bulk wines, today DO La Mancha is in the midst of a viticultural revolution. Airén, a local white grape, has traditionally predominated, but these days red varieties, such as cencibel (tempranillo), cabernet sauvignon, merlot, and syrah, often blended, are getting more and more play. The better new-wave La Mancha reds tend to be internationally styled but still possess plenty of *terroir.* Valdepeñas, a classic DO in southern La Mancha is likewise graduating from jug wines to quality reds.

Great Bodegas

Alejandro Fernández (El Vínculo); Finca Antigua; Finca la Estacada; Osborne

EXTREMADURA

FAST FACTS

A broad expanse of harsh but oddly majestic terrain, this western region bordering Portugal is Spain's own wild west. Extremadura is best known as the land of conquistadores, explorers who in the sixteenth century left their destitute hometowns to seek fortunes in the New World. The treasures they brought back fueled the construction of the churches and mansions in the cities of Trujillo and Cáceres. Mérida is another gem of a town notable for its ancient Roman remains and a striking Roman art museum designed by the architect Rafael Moneo. Extremadura's lush La Vera valley is one of the prettiest corners of Spain.

FOOD

With the same rough-hewn smoky identity as the cooking of Castile and La Mancha, *extremeño* is a

peasant cuisine, centered on pork, lamb, and game dishes and lots of dried peppers and leftover bread. The best-known regional products include *pimentón de la Vera,* Spain's inimitable smoked paprika; outstanding cheeses like Torta del Casar; and spectacular cured pork made from the prized *ibérico* pigs that feed on acorns in the local forests.

Traditional Specialties: Potatoes in *escabeche*; tomato and fig soup; *caldereta de cordero* (paprika-flavored lamb casserole); *frite* (lamb stews); *migas* (fried bread bits)

WINE

Still virtually unknown in America, the fruity reds from the Extemaduran DO of Ribera del Guadiana are gradually gaining a following among Spanish wine aficionados. Given the recent success of Spain's other formerly obscure wine-growing areas, this is a region to watch.

Great Bodegas

Marcelino Díaz; Martínez Payva; Viñas de Alange (Palacio Quemado)

THE NORTHERN COAST

BASQUE COUNTRY

FAST FACTS

Situated on the Cantabrian coast just west of the French border, the Basque Country—País Vasco in Spanish, Euskadi in Basque—is a land of pastoral hills swathed in eye-popping green and wide sandy beaches hugging the Bay of Biscay. Ferociously independent, the Basques are proud of their inscrutable tongue, Euskera, which has no known linguistic relatives, proud of the theories that claim them as Europe's most ancient ethnic group, and especially proud of their amazing cuisine. San Sebastián, Spain's epicurean capital, is also notable for its gorgeous shell-shaped bay called La Concha. Bilbao, formerly a sooty industrial seaport, has undergone a stunning urban renewal following the construction of the Guggenheim museum designed by Frank Gehry.

FOOD

Many Spanish gastronomic pilgrims call País Vasco mecca. Historically prodigious fishermen, shepherds and farmers, the Basques today enjoy one of Europe's highest standards of living and happily spend every last euro on food. Classic Basque dishes tend to be hearty and straightforward, featuring the highest-quality bacalao, pristine fish and shellfish, wild mushrooms, and bright dewy vegetables. But Basque Country is also the birthplace of Spain's *nueva cocina* and continues to be a hotbed of experimental gastronomic activity.

Traditional Specialties: *Bacalao al pil pil* (cod with garlic and an olive oil emulsion); *bacalao a la vizcaína* (cod in red pepper sauce); *marmitako* (bonito and potato stew); *merluza en salsa verde* (hake in green sauce); *chipirón encebollado* (squid in onion sauce); grilled turbot; *alubias de Tolosa* (red bean and smoked meats stew); *pastel vasco* (cream or cherry-filled tart)

Left: San Sebastián's 19th-century houses are majestically reflected in the Nervion river. *Top right:* The scenic village of Cahecho, in Cantabria, offers exquisite views of the majestic Pico de Europa mountains.

WINE

The traditional Basque Country wine is Txakolí, a simple but quaffable slightly pétillant white that goes perfectly with local seafood and *pintxos* (tapas). However, Rioja Alavesa—the Basque section of the Rioja wine region—supplies far more serious bottlings mainly featuring the classic Rioja grape, tempranillo.

Great Bodega

Txomín Etxaníz, for Txakolí (For Riojas, see La Rioja and Navarra)

ASTURIAS AND CANTABRIA

FAST FACTS

Located between the Basque Country to the east and Galicia to the west, Asturias and Cantabria share a beautiful stretch of the rocky Cantabrian coastline and a sizable chunk of the dramatically scenic Picos de Europa, one of Europe's last great mountain wildernesses. Asturias, with two major cities, Gijón and Oviedo, is a former kingdom famous for having never been conquered by the Arabs. (The Moors were bravely defeated here in the eighth century at the battle of Covadonga.) Although Cantabria's past is a bit less heroic, the region is the proud home of a priceless historic treasure: the Altamira caves, which are covered with breathtaking Paleolithic paintings more than 15,000 years old. Santander, Cantabria's fun seaside capital, is a major university town.

FOOD

Fishing, farming, sausage making, and some extremely serious cheese production in the Picos de Europa shape the cuisines of Cantabria and Asturias. Asturian is largely a mountain cuisine, highlighting beans and smoked pork, with seafood enjoyed mainly along the coast. The mild, hearty

Houses dot the vineyards of Arbi in the Rías Baixas.

cooking of Cantabria is bound to the sea, the source of anchovies, sardines, spider crabs, tuna, and hake.

Traditional Specialties: *Fabada* (bean and sausage casserole); *pote asturiano* (a stew of cabbage and smoked meats); chicken, chorizo, or hake braised in hard cider; *almejas a la marinera* (clams in wine sauce); *fabes con almejas* (white beans with clams); *arroz marinero* (seafood-studded rice); *arroz con leche* (rice pudding); *quesada pasiega* (cheese tart)

WINE

Asturias and Cantabria are the two Spanish regions without any serious winemaking tradition (the terrain isn't conducive to cultivating vines). They make up for it by drinking huge quantities of *sidra,* the fermented hard apple cider traditionally poured into wide glasses from great heights.

GALICIA

FAST FACTS

Occupying the country's northwestern corner, rainy green Galicia is miles away both in spirit and distance from the sun-splashed Spain of *toreros* and castanets (here they actually play bagpipes). A region with a Celtic heritage and landscapes that look more Irish than Iberian, Galicia has spectacular scenery: *rías* (fjordlike estuaries), lagoons, rocky coves, and lush swaths of emerald countryside dotted with stone crosses and *hórreos* (raised granaries). The Romanesque cathedral of Santiago de Compostela, Galicia's capital, attracts scores of pilgrims who walk there all the way from France along the Camino de Santiago, or Saint James Way.

FOOD

Seafood, usually cooked with minimum fuss, is Galicia's forte—from the prehistoric looking and stunningly expensive *percebes* (goose barnacles) to spider crabs, mussels, scallops, and exquisite Carril clams. The agriculturally minded region also has fabulous eggs, dairy products, potatoes, and Spain's greatest beef. *Grelos* (turnip greens) are omnipresent.

Traditional Specialties: Seafood and meat empanadas; *pulpo a feira* (paprika-dusted boiled octopus served on a wooden board); *caldo gallego* (a hearty white bean and smoked meat soup); *lacón con grelos* (cured ham with turnip greens); *filloas* (sweet crepes); *tarta de Santiago* (a tartlike almond cake)

WINE

Albariño, the elegant Galician white, is quite the star of the international wine world. Produced in the picturesque Rías Baixas area close to the Atlantic, albariños tend to be fresh tasting and faintly flowery—a perfect pairing for seafood. Overshadowed by the Rías Baixas, Ribeiro, Galicia's older and more traditional DO, is making a comeback with interesting bottlings made with native red and white grapes.

Great Bodegas
Rías Baixas DO: Fillaboa; Martín Códax; Pazo de Señorans
Ribeiro DO: Emilio Rojo

THE NORTHEAST INTERIOR

ARAGON

FAST FACTS

Rugged and remote, Aragon is surrounded by Castile and Navarra to the west, Catalonia to the east, and the Pyrenees to the north. It's famous for the mountain scenery in the north and its two royal residents—Catherine of Aragon, who was married to Henry VIII, and Ferdinand of Aragon, who together with his devoutly Catholic wife, Isabella of Castile, oversaw the defeat of the Moors at Granada and unified Spain in the fifteenth century. Zaragoza, the Aragonese capital, has a much-venerated basilica dedicated to the Virgin of the Pillar and an unbelievably happening bar scene.

FOOD

Aragonese cuisine is as delightfully bracing as its landscape, showcasing lamb, pork, olive oil, the delicious local Teruel ham, and trout from Pyrenean streams. Many dishes also feature the region's prized vegetables and fruit—especially peaches.

Traditional Specialties: *Ternasco asado* (roast lamb); chicken and lamb *chilindrón* (in a red pepper sauce); *magro con tomate* (fried smoked ham with tomato sauce); partridge with chocolate sauce; cardoons in almond sauce; *frutas escarchadas* (candied fruit dipped in chocolate); peaches in wine

WINE

Nobody took Aragon's wines seriously until the late nineties, when the DO Somontano, a region at the foothills of the Pyrenees, exploded onto the international scene. The combination of bold, intelligent, and decidedly modern wine-making and a cool mountain climate uncharacteristic of Spain results in elegant bottlings made from an unusual range of grapes: the indigenous alcañon, as well as gewürztraminer and chardonnay for whites, the traditional moristel, along with the not-so-classic merlot, cabernet savignon, and even pinot noir for reds.

Great Bodegas

Bodega Pirineos; Enate; Viñas del Vero

The Basilica of the Virgin of Pilar stands by the Ebro river in Zaragoza, the capital of Aragon.

Yuso Monastery, in the scenic town of San Millán de la Cogolla, La Rioja, is considered a birthplace of the Castilian language.

LA RIOJA AND NAVARRA

FAST FACTS

Northeast of Madrid lie the fertile agricultural regions of Navarra and La Rioja, where vines and vegetables are the two major industries. Both regions are traversed by the Camino de Santiago, an important Medieval pilgrimage route, and abound in Romanesque and Gothic churches and monasteries set amid gentle pastoral hillsides or in ancient walled towns. A major kingdom in the Middle Ages, today Navarra is famous for the raucous running of the bulls during the festival of San Fermin in Pamplona, its capital. La Rioja's fame is, of course, fueled by wine.

FOOD

The abundant *huertas,* or market gardens, of the lush Ebro valley supply Navarese and Riojan kitchens with extraordinary artichokes, asparagus, leeks, chard, tender lettuce hearts, and the delicate white beans called *pochas.* The vegetables show up in salads, fried in a light batter, or cooked into *menestras* (vegetable stews); they are also packed into gourmet jars and cans and sold all over Spain. Red peppers, both dried and fresh, are another signature staple, particularly piquillos, which can be either stuffed with seafood or meat or gently sautéed with garlic and olive oil. Potatoes make a frequent appearance, as do chorizo sausage, lamb, and bacalao.

Traditional Specialties: *Espárragos en vinagreta* (asparagus in vinaigrette); *menestra de verduras* (a mélange of stewed and fried vegetables); baby lamb chops grilled over vine cuttings; *patatas a la riojana* (potato and chorizo stew); white bean stew with quail; stuffed peppers

WINE

Rioja is Spain's most famous wine region. Its defining grape is the early-ripening tempranillo, which is frequently blended with grenache, mazuelo (carignan) and the aromatic graciano. Responding to competition from other emerging wine areas, Rioja's vintners are now offering wines in a range of styles, from the soft, light classic-style reds to richer, redder, fruitier new-wave bottlings. Rioja's citrusy whites should not be overlooked either—ditto wines from Navarra. Known mainly for its pleasant rosés, Navarra is successfully experimenting with more ambitious international-style wines made from French grape varieties.

Great bodegas

Rioja: Artadi; Contino; CUNE; Finca Allende; Marqués de Riscal; Martínez Bujanda; Montecillo; Muga; Remelluri; R. López de Heredia; Roda

Navarra: Guelbenzu; Julián Chivite; Otazu

THE MEDITERRANEAN

CATALONIA

FAST FACTS

"No, not Spanish, *Catalan*"—this rebuke echoes all over Spain's northeastern corner, startling a visitor primed for flamenco, sangria, and tapas. A country within a country, with its own language, complex history, and a wealth of artistic traditions, Catalonia—Catalunya to the natives—has more in common with neighboring France than with the arid, macho Castile. One can spend an eternity in Barcelona, the region's buoyantly cosmopolitan capital, admiring the brooding medieval quarter, the wacky architecture of Gaudí, and one of the world's greatest food markets, La Boqueria. But this would mean missing Catalonia's other attractions, among them ramshackle Romanesque churches surrounded by snow-capped Pyrenean peaks, some 250 miles of lyrical Mediterranean coastline, walled medieval villages, Roman ruins, and Dalí's outlandish museum in Figueres.

FOOD

Catalan food blends Roman, Arabic and even Italian influences into one of Europe's most distinct and emphatic cuisines, which today runs the gamut from rustic to ultra-refined. This is the turf of Ferran Adrià and his experimental disciples and of elegant modern-Mediterranean seafood *cocina.* Yet Catalan cooking is also about robust grills spiked with garlicky *allioli,* bracing rice dishes, rust-colored fisherman's stews, and inland casseroles in which seafood, poultry, or the beloved bacalao might be funkily paired with honey, dried fruit, or even chocolate. Barcelona's restaurant scene can give any world capital a run for its money.

Traditional Specialties: *Samfaina* (a kind of ratatouille); *escalivada* (grilled vegetables); rice casseroles; *rossejat de fideus* (toasted pasta casserole); duck with pears; rabbit with *allioli*; *mar i muntanya* (chicken and shellfish); *suquet* (seafood in tomato-based sauce); *romesco* (red pepper sauce with nuts); cannelloni; *cocas* (topped flatbreads); *crema catalana* (a sort of crème brûlee)

WINE

Wine-wise, Catalonia is a powerhouse. The wine world is abuzz over the big, dark, expensive reds from the once obscure Priorat region. Penedès, one of Spain's oldest wine-producing areas, is playing catch-up with its own new-style reds produced

Barcelona is home to one of the greatest markets in the world, La Boqueria.

alongside the more traditional rosés and dessert wines. Penedès is also famous for *cava,* a bubbly made by *méthode champenoise,* usually from a blend of three native grapes. Other Catalan DOs to watch are Ampurdán-Costa Brava, Montsant, and Tarragona.

Great Bodegas

Priorat DO: Costers del Siurana; Passanau; Alvaro Palacios; Clos Mogador; Clos Manyetes; Clos Erasmus

Penedès DO: Torres, Freixenet; Codorníu; Gramona

EL LEVANTE

FAST FACTS

The Levante (land of the rising sun) is the collective name for the provinces of Castellón,Valencia, and Alicante, plus the autonomous region of Murcia, which stretch along Spain's Mediterranean seaboard between Catalonia to the north and Andalusia to the south. The region is often called the garden of Spain, thanks to alluvial plains that support acres of extraordinary fertile farmland, rice paddies, and orange and almond orchards that have been cultivated since the time of the Arabs. Farming, fishing, and beach tourism are among the region's economic mainstays.

Valencia, Spain's flamboyant third largest city, is the home of paella—as well as a splendid cathedral which claims to possess the Holy Grail; the futuristic City of Arts and Sciences designed by architect Santiago Calatrava; and a fiery fiesta called Las Fallas.

FOOD

Paella, the gastronomic emblem of the Levante, is actually just one of its myriad scrumptious rice dishes. Seafood, almonds, artichokes, tomatoes, and peppers also show up in many local specialties. Salt curing fish has been a major business in the Levante since antiquity, and the pungent flavors of *mojama* (salted tuna) and anchovies remain as popular today as they were in Roman times. The region is also the source of *turrón* (almond and honey nougat) and *horchata,* a delightful milky summer refresher made from nutlike tubers called *chufas.*

Traditional Specialties: Paella; *arroz a banda* (seafood-flavored rice served in two courses); *arroz negro* (black rice); *arròs amb fesols i naps* (rice with beans, turnips, and meat); *fideuá* (pasta paella); *all-i-pebre de anguilas* (eel in garlic sauce); *caldero murciano* (Murcian rice and seafood casserole)

WINE

Levante reds are yet another recent Spanish success story, particularly the wines from the hot, dry Jumilla DO in Murcia. Here up-and-coming vintners are experimenting with bold mouth-filling reds made from syrah, along with more traditional grapes like monastrell (mourvèdre) and grenache. One of Spain's greatest dessert wines, Casta Diva, comes from Alicante.

Great Bodegas

Casa Castillo; Casa de la Ermita; Finca Luzón; Mustiguillo

Breathtaking vistas and moody skies are scenic features of the Levante.

THE SOUTH

ANDALUSIA

FAST FACTS

Ever seen tourist posters of Spain? That was probably Andalusia—the peninsula's sultry south, synonymous with flamenco and bullfighting, tapas and sherry, tiled patios scented with orange blossoms, historionic religious processions, and yes, mass-tourism that has pretty much ruined the beaches of the Costa del Sol. The legacy of the Arabs who ruled here for almost eight centuries is everywhere—in the blindingly white hilltop villages; in the flamenco music and the proverbially languorous lifestyle; in the architectural landmarks of Granada, Seville, and Córdoba, Andalusia's great cultural centers. Roughly the size of Portugal, with a landscape that takes in Atlantic and Mediterranean coasts as well as the high peaks of the Sierra Nevada, Andalusia often feels like its own planet.

FOOD

With its mosaic of tapas, coral-pink gazpachos, lacy fried fish, Jabugo ham, olive oil, and saffron-tinged seafood stews, Andalusian cooking is full of rustic pizzaz. Its Arab roots are evident in the liberal use of spices like cumin and confections rich in honey and nuts. Catholic nuns at Andalusian convents are still busy perfecting recipes for sweets, some of which go back to the fifteenth century.

Traditional Specialties: Gazpacho; *caracoles en salsa* (spicy snails); oxtail stew; *pescaíto frito* (fried fish); *espinacas con garbanzos* (spinach with chickpeas); *alboronía* (vegetable stew); *papas aliñas* (marinated potatoes); *yemas* (candied egg yolk confections); *pestiños* (sweet fried pastries)

WINE

Say Andalusia and one drink springs to mind: sherry. Most sherry bodegas are concentrated in the province of Cádiz, but the region's other DOs, such as Montilla-Moriles in Córdoba, and Málaga, around the city of the same name, also are the source of outstanding fortified wines.

Great Bodegas

Domecq; Emilio Lustau; Gonzalez Byas; Hidalgo (for manzanilla); Osborne

A horse ride along the waterfront in Sanlúcar de Barrameda, known for its sunsets and its manzanilla sherry.

THE ISLANDS

THE BALEARIC ISLANDS

FAST FACTS

The islands of Mallorca, Menorca, and Ibiza are moored in the azure Mediterranean waters off Spain's eastern coast. Closely related to Catalonia in language and culture, the Balearics have been visited by Phoenicians, Greeks, Romans, and Arabs, all of whom left their traces. (Pirates came, too.) Today the islands are colonized by vacationers who outnumber locals 15 to 1 in high season. White-washed Ibiza relishes its reputation as Europe's clubby summer playground. Mallorca with its secluded coves, beaches, and romantically lush interior has attracted celebrity couples like Chopin and George Sand, and Michael Douglas and Catherine Zeta-Jones, who even bought property. Menorca, formerly in British control, is the place to get away from the crowds.

FOOD

Although authentic island cuisine is being edged out by pizza parlors, those who stray off the tourist trail are rewarded with bold-flavored hyper-Mediterranean cooking that makes abundant and often surprising use of fish, olive oil, and the beautifully sweet local peppers and eggplants. The omnipresent pork shows up as *sobrasada*—the soft Mallorcan paprika-flavored sausage paste—and as lard, the secret behind the incredible crumbliness of sweet and savory island pastries, such as *cocas* and *cocarrois*. The sweet flavors that so often sneak into savory dishes are an Arab legacy.

Traditional Specialties: *Tumbet* (eggplant casserole); *sopes mallorquines* (bread and vegetable stew); *caldereta de langosta* (lobster stew); stuffed vegetables; *frit* (stir-fried offal); *arroz brut* (rice and pork casserole); *cocas* (topped flatbreads); *ensaimada* (coiled sweet bread)

WINE

Mallorca's viticulture dates back to the Romans. Today, thanks to a new breed of vintners who are reviving native grapes, its strong, spicy reds are a delicious surprise. Binissalem, the island's main DO, produces some excellent reds from local grapes like manto negro and callet, sometimes blended with cabernet sauvignon and tempranillo.

Left: There's great joy in a good grape harvest. *Top right:* Bananas grow in abundance on the Canary Islands.

Great Bodegas
Anima Negra; Finca Son Bordils

THE CANARY ISLANDS

FAST FACTS

Just seventy miles from the Moroccan coast and almost a thousand miles from mainland Spain, the exotic Canaries form an archipelago of seven volcanic islands. Searching for an Atlantic base after their discovery of America, Spaniards conquered the Canaries in the fifteenth century, subjugating the indigenous population, the Guanches (a mysterious people whose origins still puzzle scholars). Called the "Fortunate Islands" by the ancient Greeks, today the Canaries derive most of their income from tourists who flock here for the perpetual sunshine, beaches, and stunning volcanic landscapes.

FOOD

A fusion of Iberian, African, and Spanish-Caribbean influences—with a good dose of international tourist cuisine mixed in—Canarian cooking is lush with subtropical foodstuffs such as avocadoes, yams, pineapples, papayas, and the ubiquitous local bananas. Potatoes and tomatoes, planted here by Spaniards immediately following the discovery of the New World, also flourish in great profusion in the volcanic soil. Fish is abundant, and many dishes come accompanied by *mojos*—sprightly salsas made with mortar-pounded aromatics, such as garlic, chiles or herbs.

Traditional Specialties: *Gofio* (a kind of porridge made with toasted grain); *tortilla de platanos* (omelet with sliced bananas); *potaje de berros* (watercress soup); *puchero canario* (meat and chickpeas stew); *sancocho canario* (dried fish, potato, and sweet potato stew); *papas arrugadas* (salt-covered potatoes served with mojo); *quesadilla* (cheesecake)

WINE

Sweet Malvasia wine from the Canaries was known in Elizabethan England and praised by Voltaire. Despite the difficult climate and soil, the archipelago's vineyards are once again producing quality wines made from the white malvasia grape, as well as aromatic indigenous red grapes such as negramoll and listán negro.

Great Bodegas
El Grifo; Monje

THE NEW SPANISH TABLE

FROM LITTLE BITES AND BIG TASTES TO THE GRAND FINALE

TAPAS

LITTLE BITES, BIG TASTES

In a compulsively social country like Spain, the *tapeo*—tapas bar crawl—is a ritual of near-religious importance. And it isn't just the nibbling and the imbibing: In Spain, the *tapeo* embodies a whole worldview and a lifestyle.

From left to right: Bread and *jamón* are perennial favorites at tapas bars throughout Spain; Hauntingly beautiful Romanesque monasteries dot the Spanish countryside; Sardines, gently sauteed in olive oil, make a great tapa; La Mezquita, the great mosque of Cordoba, is a stunning example of Moorish architecture; *Below:* A selection of tapas: Crisp Potatoes with Spicy Tomato Sauce (page 69), Beet Leaves Stuffed with Morcilla (page 37), Tangerine-Marinated Olives (page 22)

The verb *tapear,* says the Sevillian tapas expert Juan Carlos Alonso, "is a broad concept that encompasses multiple actions: drinking, eating, chatting, strolling, greeting, seeing, being seen . . ." Indeed.

In its original form, the tapa (from the word *tapar,* to cover) was a free slice of cheese or *jamón* that topped a glass of sherry, thus protecting the drink from flies and dust. The tradition originated in the nineteenth century in Andalusia, the center of sherry production, where scorching summers make full meals unthinkable. Besides, a strong, fortified drink such as sherry fairly demands a snack. From these basic beginnings, the tapa evolved into a truly protean concept defined only by size and function: a bite to accompany drinks, normally eaten with one's hands, standing up. Place a portion of leftover stew in a small *cazuela* and you've got a tapa. Order a beer, chat up your neighbor, and it's a fiesta. No wonder the Spanish prefer hanging out in bars to entertaining at home.

Although Spain is presently in the grip of a *nueva cocina* revolution, old-school tapas bars happily remain true to themselves. Imagine a heart-stoppingly atmospheric tiled dive suffused with the musky scent of *jamones* (cured hams) hung from the ceiling. Its walls are plastered with bullfighting photos. Its floors are scattered with napkins, toothpicks, and olive pits. The crowds stand wall to wall, shoulder to shoulder, exchanging cracks with the countermen, who shout out orders for another round of briny anchovies or batter-fried bacalao. At classic bars all over Spain, standbys like *ensaladilla rusa* (a mayonnaise-drenched potato salad), *embutidos* (cured meats), cheese, and potato *tortillas* seem inescapable. But beyond these stereotypes, tapas vary dramatically from region to region and from bar to bar.

Meatballs, *patatas bravas* (potatoes with spicy tomato sauce), and cups of broth from *cocido* (boiled dinner) washed down with beer or vermouth on tap are the stuff of old Madrid *tabernas.* In the northwestern region of Galicia, the *tapeo* involves squares of seafood empanadas, paprika-dusted poached octopus slices known as *pulpo a feira,* and stubby glasses of albariño. *Sidra* (cider) is the drink in the mountainous Asturias region, accompanied by a wedge of stinky Cabrales cheese and a link of chorizo braised in more cider. In their Basque incarnation tapas are called *pintxos* and are almost always mounted on bread—fanciful canapés decorated with frilly mayonnaise borders and arrayed on bar counters like edible communion dresses. Andalusian bars seduce with a vast array of edibles, from small portions of stews or snails in a spicy

Tangerine-Marinated Olives (page 22)

sauce, to fried fish and delicacies like poached hake roe in a piquant *aliño* (marinade).

Spain's Mediterranean regions—Catalonia, Valencia, Alicante—don't have a long tapas tradition. But this is where you find the best *bares de producto*: ingredient-driven lunch and dinner counters that offer *raciónes* or *media raciónes,* full or half portions. Few things in life are more pleasurable than staking a perch at one of the counters at Barcelona's colorful Boqueria market and nibbling on flash-fired baby squid, as tiny as a pinky nail; just-picked fava beans with a fried egg on top; or the season's first asparagus.

Even within one region, bars tend to specialize: Some excel in fried stuff, like *croquetas,* others in griddled or skewered bites, yet others in *montaditos* (canapés). Certain bars draw crowds with their inexpensive portions of marinated carrots or roasted peppers, others with seafood delicacies like langoustines or goose barnacles for prices as steep as those at Tokyo's sushi bars. Some bars have menus, others have iron-lunged waiters who breathlessly recite the daily specials. Some lavishly display their wares on the counters; at other bars, each order emerges just-cooked from the kitchen. Wine bars and cheese bars, the breakfast bars of Seville and the beer bars of Madrid, bars out of central casting, and white neo-Moderne haunts with tapas artfully arranged in shot glasses, on skewers, and on spoons—at times, the entire country seems like one vast bar theme park.

Don't have a crowded, food-filled tapas bar on *your* street corner? Create one at home with the delicious tapas recipes that follow. *¡Olé!*

PICKLES, SPREADS, DIPS, AND NIBBLES

TANGERINE-MARINATED OLIVES

ACEITUNAS ALIÑADAS CON MANDARINA

Here's an enticing Moorish-inspired dish that I tasted in Alicante. It's a great, simple way to jazz up a bowl of olives. In Seville, a similar marinade would be made with the juice from bitter oranges—try it both ways. The longer the olives marinate, the tastier they get, so start ahead.

2 cups mixed cracked green olives
6 small garlic cloves, crushed with a garlic press
2 tablespoons grated tangerine zest
1/2 cup fresh tangerine juice
4 thin lemon slices, cut in half and seeded
3 to 4 tablespoons sherry vinegar, preferably aged
1/4 cup extra-virgin olive oil
2 small bay leaves
1/2 small dried chile, such as arbol, crumbled, or more to taste
1 medium-size pinch of ground cumin

Place the olives, garlic, tangerine zest and juice, lemon, vinegar, olive oil, bay leaves, chile, and cumin in a large glass jar or bowl and stir to mix well. Cover the jar and let the olives marinate overnight at room temperature, tossing occasionally. For a richer flavor, let the olives marinate for up to a week in the refrigerator. **MAKES ABOUT 2 CUPS**

SEVILLIAN MARINATED CARROTS

ZANAHORIAS ALIÑADAS

Spanish tapas bars can become legendary among locals for even the humblest of things—a great potato omelet, extra-fat caper berries. Las Golondrinas, a crammed, tiled institution in Seville's evocative Triana quarter, is a case in point. Its menu is varied, but the wall-to-wall crowds that gather there each evening all demand one thing: marinated carrots. Spiced in the Moorish manner with cumin and loads of garlic and swimming in a tangy puddle of lemon juice and aromatic olive oil, the carrot slices are indeed a treat. The bar also uses a similar *aliño* (marinade) for slices of cooked beets and roasted red peppers,

SEVILLE TAPEO

Sun-washed Moorish Seville, where Don Juan smirked and Carmen swirled, has always relished its role as the country's sherry-soaked fun central and bar paradise. And if in other regions a tapa is something to nibble on with a drink before lunch or dinner, *sevillanos* tend to turn the *tapeo* into a meal. This makes perfect sense in the summer, when the city resembles a furnace and nobody wants to sit down to a big, filling dinner. Besides, what could beat getting together with friends to shuffle from one crowded bar to the next? You grab a bite and a beer at each place. You run into more friends on the way. Suddenly, the *tapeo* turns into a street party.

Maestros of the frying pan, Sevillians rank their *frituras* at the top of the tapas chain. Floured fried slices of eggplant; tiny *puntillitas* (baby squid) that one can inhale by the dozens; *cazón en adobo* (dogfish in a tangy marinade); *tortillitas de camarones* (crunchy shrimp pancakes)—all emerge from the bubbling olive oil greaseless and as light as lace. Also in demand are the traditional stews, made in an *olla madre* (mother pot) and then apportioned into mini *cazuelas*. These include spinach with chickpeas; plump, saucy meatballs; potatoes in saffron; and the ubiquitous oxtail stew, found especially at bars near the Maestranza bullring crowded with bullfighting fans. Among cold tapas, *papas aliñas* (marinated potatoes) reign supreme, followed by *mojama* (cured tuna), *chacinas* (smoky charcuterie), and the country's tastiest olives and caper berries. And not to forget: the pitchers of coral-colored gazpacho that wait on bar counters during the summer; and *salmorejo,* gazpacho's thicker, creamier cousin, which often doubles as a dip.

My Seville lunchtime *tapeo* always centers on *calle* Gamazo, a narrow lane in the old city center, which has an improbable concentration of excellent bars. Here, hidden behind a century-old *ultramarino* (grocery store), is the spectacularly picturesque Casa Moreno, festooned with bullfighting paraphernalia and Holy Week posters of the virgin of Macarena, her doll-like face framed by a cascade of gaudy white lace. Wisecracking guys behind the long stainless-steel counter dispense dense, chewy smoked meats and warm, smoky chorizo sandwiches, slapping them onto pieces of waxed paper. Across the street, the macho bar Enrique Becerra beckons with mussels on toast, oxtail croquettes, and juicy mint-scented lamb meatballs. Next, I follow the *tapeadores* to the venerable pocket-size Casablanca, where the wall-to-wall crowd testifies to the excellence of its tapas-scaled seafood stews, extra-fluffy potato tortillas with whiskey sauce, and Seville's definitive *papas aliñas,* which impressed even King Juan Carlos. The last stop is Bodeguita Romero, where plates come draped with translucent slices of smoked bacalao, bread heaped with sea urchin caviar, and caper berries as big and juicy as grapes. And I would never—never—think of leaving without an order, or two, of *pringá*: a kind of Andalusian sloppy joe consisting of the solids from a boiled dinner (blood sausage, chorizo, root vegetables) mashed up and pressed into warm bread, like a *panino*. Time for a long siesta—followed by an evening *tapeo* in the Triana quarter across the Guadalquivir river.

and I invite you to follow its lead. Getting the actual recipe was out of the question; it's zealously guarded. But while not as transporting as the original, my version comes pretty close.

1 pound carrots (about $1\frac{1}{2}$ inches in diameter), trimmed and scraped
3 to 4 large garlic cloves, chopped
$1\frac{1}{2}$ to 2 teaspoons cumin seeds
2 teaspoons dried oregano
1 pinch of crushed red pepper flakes
1 tablespoon finely chopped fresh flat-leaf parsley, plus more for garnish
1 teaspoon coarse salt (kosher or sea)
$\frac{1}{2}$ cup plus 1 teaspoon fragrant extra-virgin olive oil
$\frac{1}{2}$ cup fresh lemon juice
$1\frac{1}{2}$ tablespoons best-quality red wine vinegar

1. Place the carrots in a large pot of boiling salted water and cook until crisp-tender, 8 to 10 minutes. Drain the carrots and let cool just enough to handle, then cut them into ¼-inch slices.

2. While the carrots are cooking, place the garlic, cumin, oregano, red pepper flakes, 1 tablespoon parsley, salt, and 1 teaspoon olive oil in a mortar and, using a pestle, mash them into a medium-fine paste. Whisk the lemon juice into the garlic paste.

3. Place the carrot slices in a glass bowl while they are still warm and pour the garlic paste over them. Add the vinegar and the remaining ½ cup olive oil and toss to mix. Cover the bowl with plastic wrap and let marinate for at least 6 hours or refrigerate overnight. The carrots can be refrigerated for at least a week. Let the carrots come to room temperature before serving, place in a serving bowl, and garnish with parsley. **SERVES 8 TO 10 AS A LIGHT TAPA**

SKEWERED!

Bites impaled on a stick are the most ubiquitous and beloved kind of tapa. They are called *banderillas,* after the colorful darts employed in bullfighting. Skewers of briny, appetite-stimulating things are ideal companions to *aperitivos* and can be put together in minutes at home. Keep in mind that these tapas should be rather small, to be eaten all in one bite. Use the ideas below, or experiment at your whim.

- A quartered artichoke heart, a cube of Roncal or Manchego cheese, and a cherry tomato
- A chunk of canned tuna sandwiched between pieces of a small pickled cucumber
- A cube of hard salami or chorizo, a pickled pearl onion, and a chunk of red bell pepper
- A hard-cooked egg quarter dabbed with mayonnaise, a poached shrimp, and a rolled-up anchovy
- A chunk of poached salmon, a piquillo pepper, and a cornichon
- A chunk of roasted green pepper, a rolled-up *boqueròn* (white anchovy), a cube of potato, and a pimiento-stuffed olive
- A cube of aged Manchego cheese and one of *membrillo* (quince paste), and a chunk of endive or radicchio
- A cube of honeydew melon and a rolled slice of serrano ham

Tangerine-Marinated Olives (page 22),
Smoky Fried Almonds (page 26),
Sevillian Marinated Carrots (page 22),
and Gilda (page 26)

GILDA
BASQUE SKEWERS

GILDA

The Gilda is a Basque bar classic: a spicy, briny skewer with alternating bits of aromatic fragrant pickled guindilla chiles, olives, and anchovies. Along with a stubby glass of Txakolí, the slightly fizzy local white, nothing quite hits the spot quite like the Gilda.

Locals know this, and consume them by the dozen. Said to be invented at a San Sebastián bar, the Gilda was named after Rita Hayworth's spicy performance in the 1946 film of the same name. The rest was history, and now Gildas are on practically every bar counter. Though not part of the classic recipe, squares of red bell pepper lend color and crunch. Serve Gildas with sherry or a light white wine, such as the Basque Txakolí or Portuguese Vinho Verde.

24 manzanilla olives (pimiento-stuffed are fine)
12 guindilla chiles (see Note)
12 best-quality oil-packed anchovy fillets, drained
12 red bell pepper squares (each about 3/4 inch)

Thread an olive onto a skewer. Add a guindilla chile, then an anchovy folded in half or thirds, followed by a square of red pepper, finishing with another olive. Repeat with the rest of the skewers. **MAKES 12 SKEWERS**

NOTE: Mildly spicy Basque guindilla chiles have a complex fragrance and are definitely worth seeking out. They're available at some specialty groceries and from mail-order sources—just Google "guindilla chiles." Otherwise, look for slender Italian pickled pale-green chiles that are about 3 inches long.

SMOKY FRIED ALMONDS

ALMENDRAS FRITAS

Roasted almonds are fine, but when the nuts are slowly fried in good olive oil they acquire a profoundly nutty character that is particularly Spanish. Tossed with sea salt and smoked paprika, they are practically addictive, especially if you use the fabulous marcona almonds. However, if you prefer to roast the nuts, spread them on a rimmed baking sheet and bake them in a 350°F oven for about 20 minutes, stirring them several times. Then toss them with the salt and paprika.

1 1/2 cups blanched almonds, preferably marcona
About 3/4 cup extra-virgin olive oil
1 1/2 teaspoons coarse salt (kosher or sea)
1/2 teaspoon smoked sweet Spanish paprika

1. Line a small baking sheet with paper towels. Place the nuts in an 8-inch skillet and add enough olive oil to come level with the almonds. Place the skillet over medium-high heat and heat until the oil begins to crackle gently. Reduce the heat to medium and continue cooking the nuts until they are light golden, about 5 minutes, stirring several times. Using a slotted spoon, remove the almonds from the oil and spread them on the paper towels to drain.

2. While the almonds are still warm, place them in a brown paper bag or another heatproof bag and add the salt and paprika. Close the bag and shake it to evenly coat the nuts. Transfer the almonds to a bowl and serve at once. **MAKES 1½ CUPS**

TAPAS TIPPLES

What you'll drink with your tapas depends on where in Spain your *tapeo* takes place. The custom of eating tapas originated in the sherry-producing area of Andalusia, so an ice-cold sip of fino or manzanilla (dry sherries) is a natural in these southern parts. In the Basque Country, the tipple is Txakolí, the slightly fizzy local white wine poured from arm's length to aerate it. In Asturias, you will have tapas with hard apple cider. The refreshing young white called albariño is served in small ceramic cups in the region of Galicia. And your flute will be filled with sparkling cava in Catalonia.

Okay, now forget all I said.

The most popular thing to drink with tapas all over Spain? A *caña,* meaning a small beer. In fact, my Andalusian friends insist that ordering sherry is a sure way to stand out as a foreigner. During a recent *tapeo* in the bars of Logroño, the capital of the wine-producing Rioja region, I was shocked to observe that beer orders outnumbered wine three to one. Considering that an average tapas bar crawl might involve some eight drinks, small glasses of beer make perfect sense in a country where getting slobbered in public is considered embarrassing. Splashed with some 7-Up or lemon soda, the *caña* becomes a *clara* (clear), or affectionately, a *clarita,* Spain's beloved summer refresher.

Add the same soda to a glass of cheap red wine and you've got *tinto de verano* (summer red), a hot-weather tipple much more popular in Andalusia than sangria, which tends to be dismissed as a tourist drink. My own Spanish bar favorite, especially at the über-traditional Madrid *tabernas,* is *vermú de grifo* (vermouth on tap) cut with soda. And though traditions die hard, these days one sees a new breed of wine bar opening all over the country, with a sophisticated choice of new-style wines by the glass.

For my *tapeos* at home, I usually avoid full-bodied new-wave reds, such as high-alcohol Priorats, and opt instead for lighter Rioja *crianzas* or rosés from Navarra. With seafood, a well-chilled albariño certainly hits the spot, as does the crisp Rueda white called verdejo or the festive, easy-drinking bubbly, *cava.* With predinner nibbles such as green olives, almonds, or anchovies, a fino or manzanilla is a natural.

Now about mixed drinks: Though the Spanish adore their *copas* and *cóctels*—especially the *cuba libre* (rum and Coke) and "gin tonic"—they have a strange habit of indulging in them after dinner, usually in glasses the size of a small chamber pot.

BLACK OLIVE, ANCHOVY, AND CAPER SPREAD

GARUM

In ancient Rome, *garum* was a pungent all-purpose condiment made from fermented anchovies, not unlike present-day Asian fish sauce. In modern Catalonia, the name refers to a spread similar to the French tapenade made of olives, anchovies, capers, sometimes mashed egg yolks, and either olive oil or softened butter. This recipe, flavored with rum and a touch of mustard, is adapted from one served at the Hotel Ampurdan in Figueres. The hotel is legendary for its robust Catalan cooking and credited with naming this spread *garum.* Try to find olives that are pungent, but not vinegary and briny. The spread is delicious on toasted baguette rounds or slices of grilled country bread. It also makes a fine accompaniment to grilled meat, chicken, or fish.

2 cups pitted black olives, such as niçoise (see Note)
4 anchovy fillets, chopped and mashed in a mortar or with a fork
2 tablespoons drained capers
1 large garlic clove, crushed with a garlic press
1 large hard-cooked egg yolk, mashed with a fork
2 tablespoons dark rum or brandy
1/2 teaspoon Dijon mustard
4 tablespoons fragrant extra-virgin olive oil
Grilled bread, toast, or breadsticks, for serving

Place the olives, anchovies, capers, garlic, egg yolk, rum, and mustard in a food processor and process in quick pulses to a medium-fine paste, scraping down the side of the bowl once or twice. Gradually add the olive oil, pulsing several times after each addition. Scrape the mixture into a bowl and let stand at room temperature for about 1 hour so that the flavors develop. Serve with grilled bread, toast, or breadsticks. The spread can be refrigerated, covered, for up to 2 weeks. **MAKES ABOUT 1 3/4 CUPS**

NOTE: If the only pitted olives you can find are Kalamatas, soak them briefly in cold water and use fewer capers and anchovies. To pit olives, place them in a plastic bag. Lay the bag on a flat surface, and crush them lightly with the flat side of a large knife, a mallet, or a heavy skillet. Then pick out and discard the pits.

CATALAN GUACAMOLE

GUACAMOLE A LA CATALANA

Barcelona might be as generously supplied with sushi joints as any other cosmopolitan city, but "fusion" cuisine of any kind is still regarded there with great suspicion. Witness the uproar that ensued when Juanito, the legendary proprietor of Bar Pinotxo in the Boqueria market, introduced a toasted canapé topped with an avocado spread on his menu. How could a place as iconically Catalan as Pinotxo dare to spread a tostada with a Mexican guacamole, the traditionalists cried out. Could this be the end of Catalan cuisine? None of it seemed to bother Juanito, who proudly plied regulars with his new concoction. Besides, his lemony avocado spread, bolstered with sherry vinegar, isn't exactly guacamole. Juanito serves it on long slices of toasted bread, topped with fat anchovies and sprinkled with chopped, briny black olives.

- 2 small garlic cloves, chopped
- 2 best-quality oil-packed anchovy fillets, drained and chopped
- 3 tablespoons minced fresh flat-leaf parsley
- 1 large pinch of coarse salt (kosher or sea)
- 1 1/2 tablespoons fragrant extra-virgin olive oil
- 1 tablespoon sherry vinegar, preferably aged
- 2 tablespoons fresh lemon juice, or more to taste
- 2 small ripe Hass avocados, pitted and diced
- 1 small ripe plum tomato, cut in half and grated on a box grater, skin discarded
- Toasted or grilled country bread, for serving

1. Place the garlic, anchovies, parsley, and salt in a mortar and, using a pestle, mash them into a paste. Whisk in the olive oil, vinegar, and lemon juice. Set the dressing aside.

2. Place the avocados in a bowl and, using a fork, mash them until completely smooth. Stir in the tomato and the dressing, then taste for seasoning, adding more lemon juice as necessary. Let the spread stand for 15 to 20 minutes for the flavors to meld, then serve with toasted or grilled bread. **MAKES ABOUT 1 1/2 CUPS**

ZUCCHINI, BELL PEPPER AND ONION JAM

PISTO

Every southern European culture has its own mixed vegetable spread: Provence has ratatouille, Sicily, caponata. In Spain, you find the Catalan *samfaina,* the Andalusian *alboronia,* and *pisto,* which is popular in the rest of the country, especially in La Mancha and the Basque Country. Similar to ratatouille but minus the eggplant, the flavor of *pisto* is sweeter because of the red bell peppers and onion. Serve it as a spread for bread or toast, a base for canapés, or with fried or poached eggs. The Basques use *pisto* in endless imaginative canapés made with everything from anchovies, to smoked salmon, to ham, to poached quail eggs.

- 1/3 cup extra-virgin olive oil, or more if needed
- 1 large white onion, finely chopped
- 2 medium-size zucchini, peeled and cut into fine dice
- 2 medium-size ripe red bell peppers, cored, seeded, and diced
- 1 small green bell pepper, cored, seeded, and diced
- 4 medium-size garlic cloves, crushed with a garlic press
- 3 large ripe tomatoes, cut in half and grated on a box grater, skins discarded
- 1/2 teaspoon best-quality red wine vinegar
- 1 pinch of sugar
- Coarse salt (kosher or sea) and freshly ground black pepper

1. Heat the olive oil in a large skillet over medium heat. Add the onion and cook until softened but not browned, about 7 minutes. Add the zucchini and the red and green peppers. Cook, stirring, until the vegetables soften, about 10 minutes, adjusting the heat so that the vegetables don't brown. Add a little more olive oil if the skillet looks dry. Stir in the garlic and cook for another minute. Add the tomatoes, reduce the heat to very low, and cook, covered, stirring often, until all the vegetables are very soft and the zucchini begins to disintegrate, 35 to 40 minutes. If the vegetables begin to stick to the skillet, add a tablespoon or so of water.

2. Add the vinegar and sugar to the *pisto,* then season it with salt and black pepper to taste. Let the *pisto* cool to room temperature, then serve. **MAKES ABOUT 2 CUPS**

TOASTED HAZELNUT ROMESCO DIP

ROMESCO DE AVELLANAS

I can't imagine a tapas bash without at least one dish accompanied by *romesco,* the famous pepper and nut sauce of the Catalan Tarragona province. In that region, one encounters dozens of variations on *romesco,* with ingredients that vary slightly, depending on how the sauce will be served. The version here—zesty with raw garlic, puckery with vinegar, and subtly spicy with dried chile—makes an ideal dip for crunchy green crudités, such as celery sticks, fennel sticks, or endive leaves. It is also delicious with grilled shrimp or poached or grilled asparagus, or simply smeared on a piece of grilled or toasted bread.

1 medium-size dried ñora pepper or ancho chile, stemmed, seeded, and torn into small pieces
2/3 cup hazelnuts, toasted and skinned (see page 267; see Note)
2 large garlic cloves, peeled
1 1/2 tablespoons toasted bread crumbs
1 small ripe plum tomato, chopped
1 tablespoon sweet (not smoked) paprika
1/8 teaspoon cayenne, or more to taste
6 tablespoons fragrant extra-virgin olive oil
2 tablespoons best-quality red wine vinegar, or more to taste
Coarse salt (kosher or sea)

1. Place the ñora pepper in a small heatproof bowl, add ½ cup very hot water, and soak until softened, about 30 minutes. Drain, setting aside the soaking liquid.

2. Place the hazelnuts in a food processor and pulse until they are ground medium-fine. Add the ñora pepper, ⅓ cup of its soaking liquid, and the garlic, bread crumbs, tomato, paprika, and cayenne, and process until fairly smooth but still with some texture from the nuts. With the motor running, drizzle in the olive oil until it is completely incorporated.

3. Scrape the sauce into a bowl, stir in the vinegar, and season with salt to taste. Cover the bowl with plastic wrap and let the sauce stand until the flavors meld, at least 30 minutes. Taste the sauce before serving, adding more vinegar and cayenne, if desired. The dip will keep, covered in the refrigerator, for up to 1 week. **MAKES ABOUT 1½ CUPS**

NOTE: To intensify the flavor of the hazelnuts, once they are toasted and skinned, you can fry them in 2 tablespoons olive oil until golden. Hazelnuts give a special character to the sauce, but fried almonds, or a mix of almonds and hazelnuts, are also delicious.

BACALAO HASH

BACALAO AL AJO ARRIERO

In the La Mancha region, cod *al ajo arriero*—or mule driver's style—refers to a bacalao and potato puree not dissimilar to the French *brandade.* In the Basque Country, *ajo arriero* is prepared with flaked cod that's slowly sautéed with onion, tomato, and peppers. It's often spread on bread as one of the region's favorite *pintxos* (tapas). At home, I mound it on bread or serve it as a chunky spread. Spooned on toast and topped with a poached egg, the hash also makes an excellent breakfast or brunch. This is one case where salt cod shouldn't be replaced by fresh, as the dish needs that nice pungent kick. Start at least a day ahead to give the bacalao a chance to soak.

6 ounces salt cod, soaked and cooked (see page 198), then drained
3 tablespoons fragrant extra-virgin olive oil, or more if needed
1 medium-size onion, finely chopped
3 large garlic cloves, minced
1/2 large green bell pepper, cored, seeded, and diced
6 to 7 piquillo peppers (from a can or jar), or 3 large pimientos, cut into strips
2 medium-size Yukon Gold potatoes (about 6 ounces each), peeled, boiled, drained, and diced
1/2 teaspoon sweet (not smoked) paprika
1/4 cup tomato sauce
1/2 teaspoon white wine vinegar or sherry vinegar
Coarse salt (kosher or sea) and freshly ground black pepper
2 tablespoons minced fresh flat-leaf parsley
Sliced crusty baguette, for serving

1. Flake the salt cod finely, discarding the bones, skin, and any tough bits.

2. Heat the olive oil in a large skillet over medium-low heat. Add the onion and garlic and cook, stirring, for 5 minutes. Add the green pepper and cook, stirring occasionally, until the onion and pepper are very soft, about 10 minutes, reducing the heat so they don't brown. If the skillet looks dry, add a little more olive oil, then stir in the flaked salt cod, piquillo peppers, and potatoes. Stir to mix well, then cover the skillet and cook for 5 minutes, stirring once or twice.

3. Add the paprika and stir for a few seconds. Stir in the tomato sauce, reduce the heat to very low, re-cover the skillet, and simmer until all the flavors are melded, 8 to 10 minutes. The cod hash should be nicely moist; if it isn't, add a little water and simmer for a few minutes longer. Stir in the vinegar and salt and black pepper to taste. Let the hash cool to warm or room temperature (the flavors will meld and develop further as it sits). Stir in the parsley and serve on or with bread. **SERVES 6 TO 8 AS A TAPA**

STUFFED, SKEWERED, STACKED

TUNA-STUFFED TOMATOES

TOMATES RELLENOS DE BONITO

The Cuchara de San Telmo tapas bar in San Sebastián is amazing. Its young chef/owners Iñaki Gulin and Alex Montiel have both worked at El Bulli, Ferran Adrià's outrageously inventive restaurant. But instead of applying their credentials and skill to someplace haute, they decided to open a simple neighborhood haunt serving restaurant food—at bar prices. Nothing there costs more than a few dollars but ah, the food: caramelized foie gras ravioli, shot glasses of ethereal chilled crab soup topped with tomato jam, amazing boned pork ribs glazed with balsamic vinegar (see page 238 for my adaptation). Here is one of Iñaki and Alex's simpler and most popular dishes, perfectly ripe skinned tomatoes filled with tuna mousse and presented in a bright-green puddle of parsley vinaigrette, with drizzles of aged balsamic vinegar. The chefs use *ventresca,* the prized tuna belly, for the filling, but good imported canned tuna will do just fine. The dish is as pretty as it is delicious, especially when served on an elegant white plate to show off the colors.

8 smallish vine-ripened tomatoes (about 2 1/4 pounds total; do not use beefsteak or plum tomatoes)
Coarse salt (kosher or sea)
1/4 cup best-quality red wine vinegar, plus more for sprinkling over the tomatoes
12 ounces imported solid oil-packed tuna, or 2 cans (each 6 ounces) Bumble Bee tonno in olive oil, drained and flaked into chunks
1/3 cup light olive oil for the filling, plus 1/2 cup for the vinaigrette
Freshly ground black pepper
1 packed cup chopped fresh flat-leaf parsley leaves, plus 8 whole parsley leaves for garnish
1 pinch of sugar, or more to taste
2 tablespoons syrupy aged balsamic vinegar, or 1/3 cup thin balsamic vinegar reduced over medium-high heat to 2 tablespoons

1. Using a vegetable peeler, peel the tomatoes. Slice the tops off and trim the bottoms so that the tomatoes will stand upright on a plate. Using a grapefruit spoon or a small coring knife, scoop out the pulp from the tomatoes, leaving about 1/8 inch of the shell and reserving the pulp. Arrange the tomatoes on a pretty white serving plate and sprinkle salt and a little red wine vinegar on the insides.

2. Finely chop the pulp from 4 of the tomatoes, setting aside the remaining tomato pulp for another use. Place the chopped pulp in a small sieve to drain off excess moisture.

3. Place the tuna in a food processor and pulse until a medium-fine puree forms. Scrape the tuna into a bowl and beat in ⅓ cup of the olive oil a little at a time. Stir in the drained chopped tomato pulp and season the filling with salt and pepper to taste. Scoop the filling into the tomatoes.

4. Place the parsley, the remaining ½ cup olive oil, ¼ cup red wine vinegar, and 2 tablespoons water in a blender and puree until very smooth. Season the parsley vinaigrette with salt, pepper, and sugar to taste and pour it around but not on the tomatoes. Drizzle the balsamic vinegar over the vinaigrette and serve. **SERVES 8 AS A TAPA, 4 AS A LIGHT LUNCHEON DISH**

GOAT CHEESE–STUFFED PIQUILLO PEPPERS

PIMIENTOS DE PIQUILLO RELLENOS DE QUESO DE CABRA

Simpler and somewhat less traditional than the Veal-Stuffed Piquillo Peppers on page 35, this version filled with goat cheese still makes a spectacular tapa. Basil oil adds a colorful, aromatic counterpoint, but can be omitted if you're in a hurry.

8 to 9 ounces herbed goat cheese, at room temperature
14 to 16 whole piquillo peppers (from a can or jar), and 2 piquillo peppers finely chopped
1 to 2 tablespoons of the liquid in which the piquillo peppers are packed
1/3 cup fragrant extra-virgin olive oil
4 large garlic cloves, thinly sliced
Fresh Basil Oil (optional; page 287), for drizzling

1. Preheat the oven to 350°F.

2. Place the goat cheese in a bowl, add the chopped piquillo peppers and their liquid, and mash them together. Stuff the whole piquillo peppers three-quarters full with the cheese mixture.

3. Place the olive oil and garlic in a large ovenproof skillet that can accommodate all the stuffed peppers in one layer and heat over medium-low heat until the garlic is very fragrant but not browned, 1 to 2 minutes. Add the stuffed peppers and cook for 1 minute on each side.

4. Transfer the skillet to the oven and bake until the peppers are hot and the cheese is very soft, about 15 minutes. (If the cheese oozes out, just push it back into the peppers with the back of a spoon.) Let the peppers cool to warm.

5. To serve, using a spatula, transfer the stuffed peppers to a large white serving platter and drizzle the garlic oil from the skillet over them. If desired, decoratively drizzle the basil oil on top and serve. **SERVES 6 TO 8 AS A TAPA**

PIQUILLO PEPPERS

Elegantly shaped, scarlet red, and supremely sweet with just a hint of heat and acidity, piquillo peppers are the caviar of capsicums. Fortunately, because these peppers are roasted, then packed flat in cans or in jars, piquillos travel perfectly well and can now be found at many American markets. In fact, piquillos prove that some preserved foods are indeed better than fresh. And once you discover them, there's no going back to ordinary roasted peppers.

Piquillos are adorable looking: small and triangular, with a characteristic peak that gives them their name. Grown in the vegetable-rich Navarra region, like a fine wine they have been given a denomination of origin, with the appellation of Lodosa, a small Navarrese village around which they are grown. Piquillo peppers are hand picked when perfectly ripe, slowly roasted over beechwood, which imparts a light smokiness, and then packed in their own sweet juices. Because they lose much of their water content during roasting, their flavor is amazingly concentrated: What you get is the essence of pepper.

Though it might seem that piquillos have held their place in the Spanish repertoire forever, their mass production dates back only to the 1970s, when they were popularized by modern Basque chefs. Today, you'll find them stuffed, baked, pureed, or sautéed at almost every Basque bar counter.

Kitchen uses for piquillo peppers are legion. Here are some of my favorites:

- Eaten straight from the jar, perhaps with a sprinkling of good olive oil, sherry vinegar, a touch of garlic and parsley or basil, and a little coarse salt
- Halved or quartered and tucked into grilled ham and cheese sandwiches
- Julienned and seasoned with a simple vinaigrette to be used as a bed for mozzarella or goat cheese, grilled seafood, or white or brown anchovies
- Slivered to decorate cream soups, stuffed eggs, or canapés
- Served as a side dish, briefly baked or sautéed over very low heat with lots of sliced garlic and olive oil. As you cook them, shake the pan slightly so that the oil emulsifies with their juices
- Diced or pureed and added to vinaigrettes
- Sliced and used as a garnish for salads or folded into scrambled eggs
- Pureed and added to a simple tomato sauce with a dash of vinegar and a pinch of sugar
- Heated with a little cream and chicken stock for a quick sauce

Of course, piquillos are a natural for stuffing. Cold piquillos are delicious filled with a salad of good canned tuna, roasted tomatoes, and a little mayo, or with a seafood or chicken salad. Hot, they are classically stuffed with chopped seafood, flaked cooked fish, or sautéed ground pork or veal. The filling usually begins with a béchamel sauce. Salt cod *brandade* also makes a terrific stuffing. Hot stuffed piquillos can be fried in a simple egg batter and baked, or simply baked with a drizzle of olive oil and some sliced garlic or with a sauce of their own pureed flesh.

VEAL-STUFFED PIQUILLO PEPPERS

PIMIENTO DE PIQUILLO RELLENOS DE CARNE

Stuffed piquillo peppers are enjoyed all over Spain, but nowhere are they more lovingly prepared than in the Basque Country, Navarra, and La Rioja. In these regions, the classic version usually involves a stuffing of seafood or meat that's been fluffed up with béchamel sauce. The filled peppers are fried briefly after being coated in a simple egg batter, then finished in a creamy sauce in the oven.

FOR THE PEPPERS:

4 tablespoons light olive oil, plus more for frying the peppers
1 medium-size onion, finely chopped
2 medium-size garlic cloves, minced
12 ounces ground veal
1 medium-size tomato, cut in half and grated on a box grater, skin discarded
Coarse salt (kosher or sea) and freshly ground black pepper
2 tablespoons all-purpose flour, plus more for flouring the peppers
2/3 cup whole milk
16 to 18 whole piquillo peppers (from a can or jar), drained
2 large eggs, beaten

FOR THE SAUCE:

2 tablespoons light olive oil
1/2 medium-size white onion, chopped
3 medium-size garlic cloves, minced
3 piquillo peppers (from a can or jar), chopped
1 large tomato, cut in half and grated on a box grater, skin discarded
2 teaspoons sweet (not smoked) paprika
1 pinch of hot paprika or cayenne
2/3 cup dry white wine
1/3 cup chicken stock or broth or water, or more if needed
3 tablespoons heavy (whipping) cream
1 teaspoon best-quality red wine vinegar, or more to taste
1 small pinch of sugar
Coarse salt (kosher or sea) and freshly ground black pepper
Finely minced fresh flat-leaf parsley or chives, for garnish

1. Make the peppers: Heat 2 tablespoons of the olive oil in a large skillet over medium-low heat. Add the onion and garlic and cook until completely softened but not browned, about 7 minutes. Add the veal, increase the heat to medium-high, and cook, mashing and breaking the meat up with a fork, until the veal is no longer pink, about 5 minutes. Add the tomato and cook, stirring, until the tomato is thickened and the pan juices are reduced, 5 to 7 minutes. Season the veal mixture with salt and black pepper to taste and set aside.

2. Heat the remaining 2 tablespoons olive oil in a medium-size saucepan over medium-low heat. Add the 2 tablespoons flour and stir for about 30 seconds to blend. Slowly pour in the milk, whisking constantly. Increase the heat to medium-high and cook, stirring, until the béchamel sauce thickens, 3 to 5 minutes. Season the sauce with salt and pepper to taste, then stir it into the veal mixture until thoroughly combined. Set the filling aside until cool enough to handle.

3. Stuff the piquillo peppers with the veal mixture; they should be quite full, but don't let the filling leak out from the ends of the peppers. Arrange the stuffed peppers on a plate, cover them loosely with plastic wrap, and refrigerate until the filling becomes firm, at least 2 hours or up to 24.

4. Spread flour on a large plate, place the eggs in a shallow bowl, and line a baking sheet with paper towels. Pour olive oil to a depth of ½ inch in a large skillet and heat it over medium-high heat until a little beaten egg dropped in it sizzles on contact. Roll a few stuffed peppers in the flour, shaking off the excess, then dip them in the egg, again shaking off the excess. Add the battered peppers to the hot oil and cook until golden, about 2 minutes per side. Using a slotted spoon, transfer the fried peppers to the paper towels to drain. Repeat with the remaining stuffed peppers, adjusting the heat so that the oil doesn't burn. The peppers can be prepared a day ahead up to this point and refrigerated, covered.

5. Make the sauce: Heat the olive oil in a medium-size skillet over medium-low heat. Add the onion and garlic and cook until softened but not browned, about 5 minutes. Add the chopped piquillo peppers and the tomato and cook, stirring, until the tomato is thickened and reduced, about 7 minutes, reducing the heat if necessary. Add the sweet and hot paprikas, stir for a few seconds, then add the wine and the chicken stock. Cook the sauce to reduce it slightly, 3 to 5 minutes. Add the cream and cook until heated through, about 1 minute. Let the sauce cool for a few minutes, then puree it in a blender until smooth. Scrape the sauce into a bowl, stir in the vinegar to taste and the sugar, and season the sauce with salt and pepper to taste. If the sauce seems too thick, dilute it with a little stock or water.

6. To finish preparing the peppers, preheat the oven to 425°F.

7. Spread half of the tomato sauce in a baking dish that can hold the peppers in one snug layer. Arrange the peppers on top and spread the remaining sauce over them. Bake the peppers and sauce until they are very hot, about 15 minutes. Remove from the oven and let cool for about 5 minutes. Serve garnished with parsley. **SERVES 8 AS A TAPA, 4 TO 6 AS A LIGHT MAIN COURSE**

VARIATIONS: Frying the piquillo peppers is traditional, but you can omit this step: Brush the stuffed peppers with oil and bake them in the tomato sauce. The recipe can be prepared ahead, in stages. Bake the peppers right before you are ready to serve.

While I've chosen a veal filling here, the dish is just as often prepared with salt cod or seafood. To make it that way, substitute 12 to 14 ounces seafood (flaked crab, finely chopped shrimp, chopped fresh fish, or a mixture), or presoaked poached, flaked salt cod for the veal. Cook the seafood briefly in the olive oil, then mix with the béchamel as described in Step 2.

BEET LEAVES STUFFED WITH MORCILLA

HOJAS DE REMOLACHA RELLENAS CON MORCILLA

At the Michelin three-star restaurant Arzak in San Sebastián, every *amuse-guele* arrives looking like a prettily wrapped gift. And although it's the height of bad manners to ask for seconds of a giveaway appetizer, the beet leaves stuffed with blood sausage and apples were so incredible I swallowed my pride, took a deep breath, and begged for more. The good news? The recipe turned out to be simple enough to reproduce at home. At Arzak, the beet leaf packages are served upright on a plate, accompanied by a silver spoon of tangy grapefruit vinaigrette to cleanse the palate. At home, you can serve them in a less showy way, arranging them flat on plates and spooning the grapefruit on the side. Even those who might feel unsure about blood sausage will be dazzled by it in this dish, with its sweet and tart counterpoint of apples and citrus. Feel free to use red chard leaves instead of beet leaves for the wrappers.

FOR THE VINAIGRETTE:

1 medium-size pink grapefruit
2 teaspoons honey
2 tablespoons cider vinegar
6 to 7 tablespoons light, flavorless oil, such as sunflower oil

FOR THE STUFFED BEET LEAVES:

8 ounces fully cooked blood sausage, such as Spanish morcilla without rice or boudin noir
2 to 3 tablespoons unsalted butter
1 large Granny Smith apple, peeled, cored, and grated
Coarse salt (kosher or sea) and freshly ground black pepper
12 large beet leaves, stemmed, tough center vein trimmed

1. Make the vinaigrette: Peel the grapefruit, making sure to remove all the bitter white pith. Finely chop the grapefruit, then place it and the honey in a small saucepan over medium-high heat. Cook until some of the juice evaporates, about 5 minutes. Stir in the vinegar and gradually whisk in the oil. Set the vinaigrette aside.

2. Make the stuffed beet leaves: Remove and discard the casings from the blood sausage and chop the meat finely. Melt 2 tablespoons of the butter in a medium-size skillet over medium heat. Add the apple and cook, stirring, until slightly softened, about 3 minutes (add more butter if the skillet looks dry). Add the blood sausage and salt and pepper to taste and cook, stirring, for 3 to 5 minutes. Cover the skillet and cook until the flavors blend, 3 to 4 minutes more.

3. Working in batches, steam the beet leaves in a large wide steamer set over boiling water until tender, about 1½ minutes. (Alternatively, the leaves can be blanched in boiling water for about 45 seconds and refreshed under cold running water.) Arrange the leaves flat in one layer on paper towels and blot off the excess moisture with another paper towel.

4. Place a spoonful of morcilla filling on the bottom third of a beet leaf, fold in the sides and the bottom of the leaf, and roll the leaf up spring roll fashion. Repeat with the remaining beet leaves and filling. Place two stuffed leaves on each of 6 pretty appetizer plates and spoon some vinaigrette on the side. Serve at once. **SERVES 6 AS A TAPA**

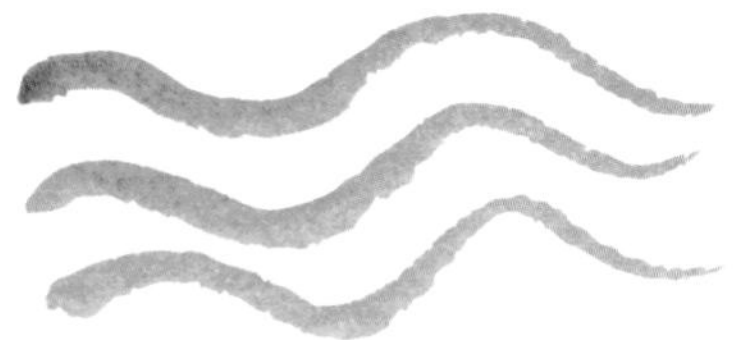

TUNA-STUFFED EGGS

HUEVOS RELLENOS DE ATUN

My Sevillian friend Lupe doesn't cook much, claiming that the hot climate isn't conducive to kitchen experiments. But she does have one passion: stuffed eggs—"the perfect light supper for a hot night," she insists. Lupe can make stuffed eggs a dozen different ways: with *jamón,* tuna, smoked salmon, anchovies, or sautéed mushrooms; spiked with capers and shallots; or with a red-hued filling of minced piquillo peppers. When she really wants to make a show of it, she covers her creations with a layer of mayonnaise and elaborate sprinkles of grated hard-cooked eggs. This is one of her recipes, sure to please anyone in need of a break from plain deviled eggs. The better quality the tuna and anchovies, the tastier the eggs.

- 6 large hard-cooked eggs, peeled and cut in half lengthwise
- 6 tablespoons imported solid oil-packed tuna or Bumble Bee tonno in olive oil, drained and finely flaked
- 2 tablespoons mayonnaise
- 1 tablespoon fresh lemon juice
- 2 tablespoons drained small capers, or 2 tablespoons chopped pimiento-stuffed olives
- Coarse salt (kosher or sea) and freshly ground black pepper
- 12 best-quality oil-packed anchovy fillets, drained
- Thin strips of piquillo peppers (from a can or jar), or roasted peppers
- Minced fresh flat-leaf parsley, for garnish

1. Place the egg yolks in a bowl and mash them well. Add the tuna, mayonnaise, lemon juice, and capers and stir to mix thoroughly. Season with salt and black pepper to taste.

2. Spoon the yolk mixture into the egg whites, spreading it slightly beyond the center hole (you may have more filling than you need). Loosely roll up an anchovy fillet, top a stuffed egg half with it, and tuck a piquillo pepper strip in the middle of the anchovy. Repeat with the remaining filled egg whites. Sprinkle parsley on top of the eggs and serve. **MAKES 12**

GRILLED SHRIMP WITH PEPPER CONFETTI

BROCHETAS DE GAMBA CON VINAGRETA

You know you are at a Basque tapas bar when you see seafood—pickled anchovies, mussels, shrimp—flourished with a colorful vinaigrette of diced green and red peppers, white onion, flavorful white wine vinegar, and mild olive oil. So festive, so delicious. Versatile, too. Try this Basque vinaigrette on chunks of good canned tuna, Basic Marinated Sardines (page 53), the white anchovies called *boquerones,* warm seared scallops, or steamed shelled mussels.

These shrimp brochettes are the specialty at Goiz Argi, a perpetually packed bar in San Sebastián's cobblestoned Parte Vieja. Like any proper *pintxo* (Basque tapa), the brochettes are served on pieces of bread, but since my house isn't a *pintxo* bar, I skip the starch. You can also poach the shrimp, thread them on skewers, spoon vinaigrette over them, and let them marinate lightly in the refrigerator for about two hours. The poached version doesn't use bacon.

FOR THE BASQUE VINAIGRETTE:

1/3 cup minced red bell pepper
1/4 cup finely minced green bell pepper
1/4 cup minced white onion
1 medium-size garlic clove, minced
1/4 cup light olive oil
3 tablespoons best-quality white wine vinegar

FOR THE SHRIMP:

1 teaspoon olive oil, plus more for brushing the shrimp
2 slices best-quality bacon
24 large shrimp, peeled and deveined, tails left on
Coarse salt (kosher or sea)

1. Make the Basque Vinaigrette: Place the red and green peppers, onion, garlic, olive oil, and vinegar in a bowl and stir to mix. Let stand for 30 minutes.

2. Prepare the shrimp: Heat the olive oil in a small skillet over medium heat. Add the bacon and cook until it is crisp and has rendered its fat, 3 to 5 minutes. Drain the bacon on paper towels. When cool enough to handle, finely crumble the bacon.

3. Soak 6 bamboo skewers in water for 30 minutes. Light the grill and preheat it to medium-high, or preheat the broiler.

4. Thread 4 shrimp on each skewer, brush them lightly with olive oil, and sprinkle salt over them. Grill or broil the shrimp until just cooked through, about 2 minutes per side, taking care not to overcook them. (The shrimp can also be seared on a griddle.)

5. Arrange the skewered shrimp on a serving plate, spoon the vinaigrette over them, and sprinkle the bacon on top. **SERVES 6 AS A TAPA, 3 AS A LIGHT MAIN COURSE**

SAN SEBASTIAN TAPEO

Standing at a tapas bar in the belle époque Basque resort of San Sebastián, I sometimes I feel as if I've fallen down a rabbit hole and emerged in some Epicurean Wonderland. Here's a platter laden with foie gras canapés drizzled with a sweet-tangy reduction of sherry vinegar. There's a tray of silvery anchovies decorated with a Technicolor vinaigrette of diced peppers. Beyond, a vast mound of porcini and chanterelle mushrooms exudes an expensive bosky perfume. In the impenetrable Basque tongue, the *tapeo* is called *txikiteo* (from *txikito,* a small tot of wine) and revolves around *pintxos* (small bites) and *zuritos* (small beers) or stubby glasses of Txakolí, the slightly *pétillant* local white wine. A glass, a nibble, a schmooze, then on to the next bar, comparing the merits of this rockfish mousse to that bacalao-stuffed piquillo pepper along the way. The food-obsessed Basques indulge in this ritual daily.

In their classic form, *pintxos* were simple morsels: a wedge of potato omelet or fried bacalao arranged on bread or a tangy, briny skewer called a Gilda. In the 1980s, however, bar owners began updating their brochettes and canapés with boutique ingredients, decorating them as if they were Fabergé eggs. Today, San Sebastián is known for the country's most creative small bites. Aloña Berri, in the bourgeois barrio of Gros, is a bar that pioneered the gourmet *pintxo*. Its small plates degustation menu leaves you wondering how it's possible for a plain neighborhood joint to serve food that belongs at a Michelin-starred restaurant. Like the killingly elegant dish composed of a spoon of grilled eggplant puree topped by an ethereal yogurt mousse, drizzled with aged balsamic vinegar, and paired with a shot glass of iridescent-green pea soup. "Modern Basque *pintxo* is the baroque apotheosis of tapa," a local food writer told me.

Though most counter displays at San Sebastián bars are almost pornographically lush, local gourmands insist that each bar excels only in particular items. In the moody, cobblestoned Parte Vieja (Old Town), Bar Martínez is renowned for its zucchini timbales stuffed with crab mousse, Bar Txepetxa is a tiny shrine to the anchovy, and Asador Ganbara specializes in wild mushroom dishes and smoky *jamón* stuffed into flaky mini croissants. Just down the road, but worlds away, is La Cuchara de San Telmo, where two young veterans of Ferran Adrià's El Bulli dish out innovative small plates that would dazzle even the most jaded food critics in New York or London. It's amazing what one can eat here for two dollars: caramelized foie gras ravioli; luxurious chilled crab soup dabbed with tomato marmalade; stupendous balsamic-glazed pork ribs, slow cooked, deboned, molded, and then flash grilled in a process that takes two days. La Cuchara, which advertises itself as a humble neighborhood bar, goes through at least 1,000 pounds of foie gras a year. Only in San Sebastián!

SCALLOPS WITH PISTACHIO VINAIGRETTE

BROCHETAS DE VIEIRAS CON VINAGRETA DE PISTACHOS

Inspired by a recipe of the great Basque chef Juan Mari Arzak, these brochettes make a super-stylish tapa. Though Arzak makes them with squid, I find that the pistachios in the vinaigrette perfectly echo the sweet nuttiness of scallops. The vinaigrette is also delicious with shrimp or squid.

- 1/2 cup Txakolí (a Basque white wine) or Portuguese Vinho Verde
- 2 tablespoons white wine vinegar
- 1 medium-size garlic clove, crushed with a garlic press
- 1 tablespoon minced shallot
- 2 teaspoons fresh lemon juice
- 1/3 cup light olive oil, plus more for brushing the scallops
- 1 small pinch of sugar
- Coarse salt (kosher or sea) and freshly ground black pepper
- 18 sea scallops
- A handful of baby lettuces, for garnish
- 2 tablespoons minced chives
- 1/3 cup lightly toasted unsalted pistachios (see page 267), finely chopped or coarsely ground

1. Place the wine in a small saucepan over medium-high heat and cook until reduced to about ¼ cup, 5 to 7 minutes. Transfer the wine to a bowl and whisk in the vinegar, garlic, shallot, and lemon juice. Gradually whisk in the olive oil, then season the vinaigrette with the sugar and salt and pepper to taste. Let the vinaigrette stand while you prepare the scallops.

2. Light the grill and preheat it to medium or preheat a ridged grill pan to medium-hot over medium heat.

3. Soak 6 bamboo skewers in water for 30 minutes. Pat the scallops dry with paper towels and lightly sprinkle salt and pepper over them. Thread the scallops on the skewers through the sides, placing 3 scallops on each skewer. Brush both sides of the scallops with olive oil.

4. Grill the scallops, working in batches if necessary, until just opaque inside and lightly browned on the outside, about 3 minutes per side.

5. To serve, place each skewer on a small appetizer plate and arrange a few lettuce leaves alongside. Stir the chives and the pistachios into the vinaigrette and dab some vinaigrette on the scallops. Serve at once. **MAKES 6**

EGGPLANT STACKS WITH TOMATO JAM

BERENJENAS CON MERMELADA DE TOMATES

Quimet i Quimet is a little Ali Baba's den of a tapas bar in Barcelona. Tiny, with every inch of wall space taken up by wine bottles, cans, and jars, it specializes in bites based on tinned gourmet products—the greatest tuna belly or anchovies ever packed in oil, boutique capers, seriously artisanal piquillo peppers. On a whim, Quim, the young owner, layers and drizzles, composing fanciful *montaditos* (canapés mounted on rusks) that never fail to amuse and surprise. One of his creations is these stacks of eggplant, anchovies, and shaved cheese, with unexpected sweet accents of Quim's famous tomato jam and syrupy aged balsamic vinegar. It is one of the best things to eat in Barcelona.

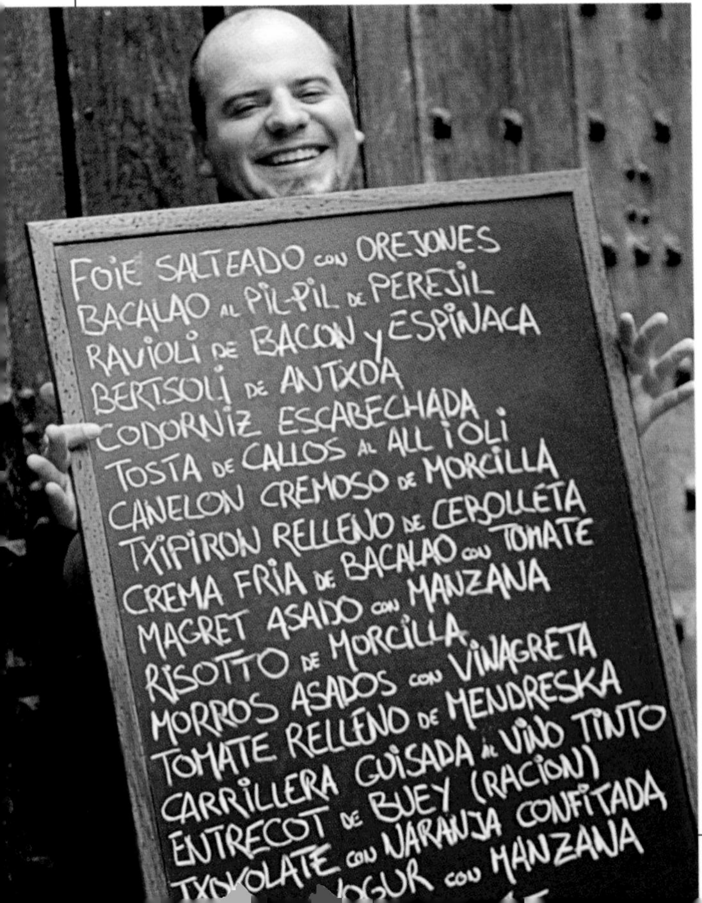

- 1 medium-size firm purple eggplant (about 1 1/4 pounds), trimmed and cut crosswise into 1/3-inch slices
- Coarse salt (kosher or sea)
- Olive oil, for brushing the eggplant
- 10 to 12 best-quality oil-packed anchovy fillets, drained
- Tomato Jam (page 390)
- Fragrant extra-virgin olive oil, for drizzling
- 3 tablespoons syrupy aged balsamic vinegar, or 1/3 cup thin balsamic vinegar reduced to 3 tablespoons
- 1 piece (3 to 4 ounces) aged Manchego or Parmesan cheese, preferably Parmigiano-Reggiano

1. Rub the eggplant slices generously with salt and place them in a colander. Let stand for 30 minutes. Rinse well and pat thoroughly dry with paper towels.

2. Preheat the broiler.

One of the owners of La Cuchara de San Telmo proudly displays a chalkboard with the day's tapas offerings.

3. Brush both sides of the eggplant slices generously with olive oil and arrange them on a large baking sheet. Broil the eggplant about 4 inches from the heat, turning once, until the slices are tender and golden brown, about 15 minutes. Let cool.

4. Arrange the eggplant slices on a serving platter and top each slice with an anchovy fillet, curling the fillet slightly. Dab some tomato jam on top and drizzle a little olive oil and vinegar over each slice of eggplant. Using a mandoline or a vegetable peeler, shave the cheese, then arrange the shavings on the eggplant. **SERVES 4 TO 6 AS A TAPA OR APPETIZER**

POTATO TOWERS WITH TUNA AND OLIVES

DELICIAS DE PATATAS, ATUN, Y ACEITUNAS

At Basque bars, when spicy, briny things aren't skewered, they are usually stacked into decorative towers held together with toothpicks. Bathed in a mild vinaigrette and fancifully arranged on big plates, these variations on the theme of anchovies, tuna, and olives are just what the doctor ordered to stimulate the appetite and soften the effects of alcohol. You can play with this recipe, substituting tomato slices for potatoes as a base or adding poached shrimp to the towers instead of, or in addition to, the anchovies. If you can't find piquillo peppers, omit them or use pimientos. These make a perfect starter to an alfresco summer luncheon.

3 all-purpose boiling potatoes, unpeeled
Coarse salt (kosher or sea)
4 large hard-cooked eggs, sliced
6 to 7 piquillo peppers (from a can or jar), or 3 to 4 roasted pimientos, each cut into 3 wedges
12 ounces imported solid oil-packed tuna, or 2 cans (each 6 ounces) Bumble Bee tonno in olive oil, drained and broken into 1-inch chunks
18 to 20 best-quality oil-packed anchovy fillets, drained
18 to 20 pimiento-stuffed manzanilla olives
Double recipe of Basque Vinaigrette (Step 1, page 39)

1. Place the potatoes in a medium-size saucepan, add cold water to cover them by 2 inches, and bring to a boil over medium-high heat. Reduce the heat to medium and cook the potatoes, partially covered, until they are completely tender when pricked with a skewer, about 30 minutes. Drain the potatoes. When just cool enough to handle, peel the potatoes and cut them into ¼-inch slices.

2. Place a potato slice on a large rimmed serving platter and sprinkle a little salt on it. Top the potato with an egg slice, a piquillo pepper wedge, a chunk of tuna, an anchovy, and an olive, lightly salting each layer before adding the next. Skewer the tower with a toothpick to hold it together. Repeat with the remaining ingredients. Pour the vinaigrette over the towers and let stand at room temperature for at least 1 hour or refrigerate, covered with plastic wrap, for up to 6 hours. Spoon vinaigrette over the towers two times as they stand. **MAKES 18 TO 20**

ALLIOLI!

Catalans are convinced that everything tastes better with *allioli,* the potent garlic mayonnaise that enlivens dozens of dishes, from paellas to shellfish to fritters to boiled potatoes to grills. And who can disagree? Dating back to ancient Rome—Pliny the Elder mentions a similar sauce in the first century A.D.—*allioli* takes its name from the words *all* (garlic), and *oli* (oil). Unlike Provençal *aioli,* a true Catalan *allioli* is made without eggs or lemon juice, the oil painstakingly whisked, drop by drop, into a paste of mortar-pounded garlic. Handmade *allioli* tends to be rather thick, with a glossy sheen and enough garlic to ward off an army of vampires. Such patience and skill are required to emulsify the sauce the old-fashioned way that these days even the staunchest traditionalists are embracing the egg-and-blender method. To temper the garlic's bite, modern chefs often blanch it, roast it, or sauté it in olive oil.

Some traditional *allioli* recipes contain honey, apples, or quince; when it comes to creative renderings, the sky's the limit. My friend Mari Carmen Velez from La Sirena restaurant in Alicante—a region where the sauce is much loved—is renowned for her new-wave *alliolis* spiked with passionfruit, raspberries, blood orange, almonds, seaweed, coffee, tea, avocado—even chocolate! Below you will find the classic blender version, plus a few fun variations.

One cup of *allioli* is enough for most recipes in this book. For dishes where you need more, I offer an alternative recipe, as the proportions and method vary slightly for larger amounts. *Allioli* takes no time to prepare, but if you don't have the ingredients or are unsure about using raw egg yolks, Mock Allioli prepared with store-bought mayonnaise is a good simple solution. All the *alliolis* should stand for a bit before serving—some for at least an hour, some for two hours. They all taste better if allowed to rest overnight, covered, in the refrigerator, and will keep that way for up to 3 days.

BASIC ONE-CUP ALLIOLI

2/3 cup extra-virgin olive oil
1/3 cup peanut or canola oil
4 large garlic cloves, minced
2 large egg yolks
4 teaspoons fresh lemon juice, or to taste
Coarse salt (kosher or sea)

Stir together both oils in a measuring cup with a spout. Place the garlic, egg yolks, and lemon juice in a blender and pulse until a coarse paste forms. With the motor running, add the oil in a slow, thin, steady stream. The mixture will be the consistency of a thick mayonnaise. Scrape the *allioli* into a bowl, and season with salt to taste, and more lemon juice, if desired. Let stand for at least 1 hour before serving, or cover and refrigerate if keeping longer. If the *allioli* seems too thick, thin it out with a little water before using. **MAKES JUST OVER 1 CUP**

BASIC TWO-CUP ALLIOLI

1 cup extra-virgin olive oil
1/2 cup peanut or canola oil
7 large garlic cloves, minced
2 large egg yolks
1 large whole egg
2 tablespoons fresh lemon juice, or more if needed
Coarse salt (kosher or sea)

Stir together both oils in a measuring cup with a spout. Place the garlic, egg yolks, whole egg, and lemon juice in a food processor and pulse until you have a fairly smooth paste. With the motor running, add the oil through the feed tube in a slow, thin, steady stream. The mixture will be the consistency of a thick mayonnaise. Scrape the *allioli* into a bowl and season with salt to taste, and more lemon juice, if desired. Let stand for at least 1 hour before serving, or cover and refrigerate if keeping longer. If the *allioli* seems too thick, thin it out with a little water before using. **MAKES JUST UNDER 2 CUPS**

MOCK ALLIOLI

- 1 cup store-bought mayonnaise (preferably Hellmann's)
- 2 tablespoons fresh lemon juice
- 4 large garlic cloves, crushed in a garlic press
- 3 tablespoons fruity extra-virgin olive oil
- Coarse salt (kosher or sea)

Put the mayonnaise in a bowl and whisk in the lemon juice, garlic, olive oil, and salt to taste. Let stand for at least 2 hours for the flavors to develop. **MAKES JUST OVER 1 CUP**

ALLIOLI VARIATIONS

ROASTED GARLIC ALLIOLI Cut off the top ½ inch from 1 medium-size head of garlic, exposing the cloves. Place the garlic cut side up in a small baking dish and brush with olive oil. Cover the dish with aluminum foil and bake the garlic at 375°F until tender, about 45 minutes. Cool, then squeeze the cloves from their skins. Substitute for fresh garlic in Basic One-Cup Allioli. Serve with paellas, fritters, or potato tortilla.

SWEET HONEY ALLIOLI Whisk ½ teaspoon honey into Basic One-Cup Allioli. Taste and add a little more honey, as necessary. Serve with pungent or salty dishes, such as Pear-Shaped Salt Cod Fritters La Sirena (page 67).

SMOKY PAPRIKA ALLIOLI Place 1 teaspoon mild smoked paprika, 1½ teaspoons tomato paste, and a pinch of cayenne in a small bowl. Stir in 2 tablespoons very hot water. Let cool, then whisk this mixture into Basic One-Cup Allioli. Serve with grilled meats or poultry or with fish cakes.

COLORFUL SAFFRON ALLIOLI Pulverize a medium-size pinch of saffron in a mortar, then steep it in 2 tablespoons very hot water; let cool. Whisk the saffron into Basic One-Cup Allioli. Add a little saffron *allioli* to seafood stews or serve it with grilled or fried fish.

ZESTY ORANGE ALLIOLI Whisk 3 tablespoons fresh orange juice and 1 tablespoon finely grated orange zest into Basic One-Cup Allioli. Refrigerate for at least 2 hours for the flavors to develop. Serve with grilled fish, shrimp, or chicken, or with roast duck.

NUTTY ALMOND ALLIOLI Whisk ⅓ cup finely ground almonds and a drop of almond extract into Basic One-Cup Allioli. Let stand for at least 2 hours for the flavors to develop. Stir a little into seafood stews or soups, or serve with grilled fish.

LA NUEVA TAPA

In a country where it's presently de rigueur for young chefs to collaborate with scientists and where the word *deconstruction* is uttered by chefs as routinely as it was at philosopher Jacques Derrida's graduate seminars, the verb *tapear* can be stretched quite far. Recently I got a taste of a truly futuristic *tapeo* while attending a cocktail party in Barcelona, given by the high priest of avant-garde cooking, Ferran Adrià.

In a scene out of a sci-fi flick, a blond assistant enveloped in clouds of hissing-cold vapors was immersing balls of pistachio paste in a cauldron of liquid nitrogen, a freezing agent that chills food in an instant. The Martian "Popsicles" emerged frozen solid on the outside and liquid inside. Across the room was a demonstration of "spherification." One of Adrià's favorite techniques, it involves liquid—fruit juice, vegetable puree—mixed with alginate (a kelp extract), then dropped into calcium chloride to form a delicate skin. I was handed a yellow ball on a porcelain spoon. It looked like an egg yolk and tasted like mango.

At another station, chefs used blowtorches to mold thin squares of caramel colored with gold powder around quail eggs. All around me, guests were gasping and gawking at Adrià's magic tricks posing as finger food: miniature loaf pans of frozen "air" flavored with Parmesan, gossamer cones filled with trout eggs and soy gelée. To drink? Hot-and-cold daiquiris and a glass of "spherified" beads with rum, coconut milk, pineapple, and cotton candy (a deconstructed piña colada).

"The tapa has come a long way since its original state: a morsel that came on or with bread and was eaten out of hand standing up," explains José Carlos Capel, Spain's top restaurant critic. "First you dropped the bread, then you started eating tapas sitting down with a knife and fork. Suddenly high-minded chefs started abandoning normal portions in favor of degustation menus of tapas-scaled bites." Adrià's progressions of thirty-plus tiny tastes at El Bulli sparked the small-plates revolution back in the '90s. In a culture already hooked on grazing, the trend spread like wildfire.

MOORISH KEBABS

PINCHOS MORUNOS

This tapa, found at bars all over Spain, is often singled out as an exemplary fusion dish: a Moorish (*moruno*) marinade applied to pork, the quintessentially Spanish meat that no Muslim would touch. Though it's romantic to think that the dish goes back to medieval Arab-Spanish culinary roots, more likely the idea for these brochettes was borrowed from North African immigrants. Either way, the kebabs are wonderful, and taste equally good made with pork, chicken, or lamb. At some bars, the seasoning is as simple as garlic and hot and sweet paprika; others use a more elaborate marinade that includes many spices. Because the marinade gives the meat so much zest, these *pinchos* are usually presented rather straightforwardly, without sauce. However, if you'd like to experiment with different combinations, serve the brochettes with Tangy Cilantro Mojo (page 235) or with Colorful Saffron Allioli (page 45). Feel free to thread cherry tomatoes, chunks of red bell pepper, or pieces of fruit, such as honeydew melon or green grapes, onto the skewers too.

- 2 tablespoons chopped onion
- 4 large garlic cloves, chopped
- 1 tablespoon smoked sweet Spanish paprika
- 1/2 teaspoon smoked hot Spanish paprika, or 1/4 teaspoon cayenne
- Coarse salt (kosher or sea)
- 1 teaspoon dried oregano
- 1 teaspoon black peppercorns
- 2 teaspoons dried thyme
- 1 teaspoon ground cumin
- 1/8 teaspoon ground cinnamon
- 1 bay leaf, crumbled
- 2 tablespoons best-quality white wine vinegar
- 2 tablespoons dry white wine (optional)
- 3 tablespoons olive oil, plus more for brushing the kebabs
- 1 1/2 pounds pork shoulder or tenderloin, leg of lamb, or chicken breasts or boneless skinless thighs, cut into 3/4-inch cubes

1. Place the onion, garlic, sweet and hot paprikas, 2 teaspoons of the salt, the oregano, peppercorns, thyme, cumin, cinnamon, bay leaf, vinegar, wine, (if using), and olive oil in a mini food processor and process to a paste.

2. Place the pork in a bowl and rub a little salt on it. Scrape the marinade into the bowl with the meat and toss to combine thoroughly. Cover the bowl and refrigerate the pork for 4 to 6 hours, tossing a few times. Let the meat come to room temperature before grilling.

3. Soak 16 bamboo skewers in water for 30 minutes. Light the grill and preheat it to medium-high or preheat a large ridged grill pan to medium-high over medium heat.

4. When ready to cook, thread the meat onto the skewers and brush it with a little olive oil. Cook the meat, brushing with olive oil and turning once, until it is just cooked through, 5 to 7 minutes. (If you are cooking lamb, and would like it medium-rare, don't cook it quite so long.) Serve the kebabs at once. **SERVES 8 AS A TAPA, 4 AS A LIGHT MAIN COURSE**

Located on the summit of Mount Benacantil, El Castillo de Santa Barbara overlooks the city of Alicante along the Costa Blanca.

Sizzling Garlic Shrimp

CAZUELITAS

SIZZLING GARLIC SHRIMP

GAMBAS AL AJILLO

There is a century-old tapas bar in Madrid called La Casa del Abuelo, a dim, miniscule place that serves sickly sweet jug wine and little else besides shrimp *a la plancha* and the house specialty—garlic shrimp. Sizzled slowly and patiently in small earthenware *cazuelas* while customers watch, the garlic shrimp offer a textbook example of how this classic tapa should taste. The Atlantic shrimp are ultrafresh and small, as they should be, and simmered so gently in olive oil that they come out just heated through rather than fried. The oil is of excellent quality, plentiful, and so suffused with garlic that people huddle around the bar dunking bread in what's left long after the shrimp are gone.

Even in less perfect renditions these garlicky shrimp are easy to love, making them one of Spain's most popular tapas. The secret to success is very fragrant olive oil that is not too heavy in texture, and a cooking vessel that conducts heat slowly and can be presented at the table so diners can dip in their bread. A *cazuela* is ideal, but you can also use an attractive, deep cast-enamel skillet. If by some rare chance you have any of the garlicky oil left over, toss it with pasta the next day.

1 1/4 pounds small shrimp, peeled and deveined
Coarse salt (kosher or sea)
1 cup fragrant extra-virgin olive oil
6 large garlic cloves, finely chopped
1/2 small dry red chile, such as arbol, crumbled
2 to 3 tablespoons minced fresh flat-leaf parsley
Country bread, for serving

1. Pat the shrimp dry with paper towels, then sprinkle salt over them.

2. Place the olive oil and garlic in a 10- to 11-inch earthenware *cazuela* and heat over medium-low heat until the oil shimmers and the garlic begins to sizzle gently. Cook until the garlic is very fragrant but not colored, 2 to 3 minutes, reducing the heat if necessary. Add the chile and stir for a few seconds. Add the shrimp and cook, stirring, until they just begin to turn pink, about 3 minutes.

3. Season with salt to taste, stir in the parsley, and cook for a few seconds longer. Serve the shrimp in the *cazuela* with plenty of bread alongside. **SERVES 4 OR 5 AS A TAPA, 2 OR 3 AS A LIGHT MAIN COURSE**

VARIATIONS: This dish can be made with large shrimp, in which case I like to cook them in their shells to preserve their texture. You can also prepare mushrooms, clams, or small pieces of chicken the same way.

MUSSELS WITH CHORIZO

MEJILLONES CON CHORIZO

While in America the pairing of shellfish and sausage represents a vision of Spanish cuisine, the combination is actually more typical of Portuguese cooking. Yet chorizo and mussels make such a delicious and easy crowd-pleasing tapa, I felt it would be a crime to pass it up. Serve the mussels in an earthenware *cazuela* as a tapa with plenty of bread for mopping up the sauce, or try them over spaghetti (see Variation).

2 tablespoons extra-virgin olive oil
6 to 7 ounces sweet Spanish-style chorizo sausage, cut in half lengthwise, then into medium-thin slices
6 medium-size garlic cloves, sliced
1 1/2 cups chopped canned tomatoes
1/2 small dried red chile, such as arbol, crumbled
2 cups Shrimp Shell Stock (page 356), or 1 1/4 cups clam juice diluted with 3/4 cup water
1 medium-size pinch of saffron, pulverized in a mortar and steeped in 2 tablespoons very hot water
1 teaspoon best-quality red wine vinegar
1 medium-size pinch of sugar
Coarse salt (kosher or sea)
2 pounds mussels, scrubbed well and debearded right before using
1/4 cup minced fresh flat-leaf parsley, for garnish
Country bread, for serving

1. Heat the olive oil in a wide, heavy pot over medium heat. Add the chorizo and cook, stirring, until lightly browned and beginning to crisp, 4 to 5 minutes. With a slotted spoon, transfer the chorizo to a bowl. Add the garlic to the pot and cook until golden and crisp, 2 to 3 minutes. With a slotted spoon, transfer the garlic to the bowl with the chorizo.

2. Spoon off all but 1 tablespoon of the oil from the pot, then add the tomatoes and the chile. Cook over medium-low heat until the tomatoes are well-reduced and lightly caramelized, about 7 minutes, stirring occasionally. Add the shrimp stock, increase the heat to medium-high, and bring to a boil. Reduce the heat to low, add the saffron, and simmer, covered, to blend the flavors, about 10 minutes. Add the vinegar, sugar, and salt to taste.

3. Add the mussels to the pot, cover, and cook over medium-high heat, shaking the pot occasionally, until the mussels open, 5 to 7 minutes. Remove and discard any of the mussels that don't open. Stir in the reserved chorizo and garlic. Transfer the mussels to an earthenware *cazuela* or another rustic serving dish, sprinkle with the parsley, and serve with slices of country bread. **SERVES 4 TO 6 AS A TAPA**

VARIATION: If you'd like to serve the mussels with pasta, increase the amount of olive oil to 4 tablespoons and don't drain it off; decrease the amount of shrimp stock to 1½ cups. You'll need 12 ounces of cooked spaghetti to serve 4 to 6.

ASTURIAN CHORIZO IN HARD CIDER

CHORIZO A LA SIDRA

Along with *fabada* (the heroic bean and pork casserole), chorizo braised in hard cider pretty much defines the cuisine of the rugged, mountainous Asturias region. At good country taverns—in Asturias these are called *chigres*—the chorizo is likely to be made in house, as is the cider. After a good hike in the mountains, there is nothing I'd rather eat. Asturian cider is fermented, which renders it pretty acidic. If you can't find hard cider at a good liquor or specialty store, use beer with a dash of apple juice. The chorizo is also delicious braised in *cava,* dry sherry, or red wine, and you can prepare pork sausage this way as well.

1 pound sweet Spanish-style chorizo sausage
1 tablespoon olive oil
About 1 cup dry hard cider
1 small bay leaf
Country bread, for serving

Prick the chorizo all over with the tines of a fork. Heat the olive oil over medium heat in a deep skillet that can hold the chorizo snugly. Add the chorizo and lightly brown them all over, 2 to 3 minutes. Drain off all the fat from the skillet. Add enough cider to come about halfway up the chorizo and bring to a boil. Add the bay leaf, reduce the heat to low, and simmer, covered, turning the chorizo several times, until they are cooked through, 20 to 25 minutes. Cut the chorizo into thick slices and serve with plenty of bread. **SERVES 6 TO 8 AS A TAPA**

SAFFRON-FLAVORED CLAMS AND POTATOES

PATATAS CON ALMEJAS

A saffron-hued broth redolent with garlic and parsley, and filled with clams, bright roasted peppers, and potatoes—this dish pushes all the right buttons.

Harvesting saffron in Consuegra, La Mancha's saffron capital, is back-breaking work.

Spooned into small *cazuelas* or bowls, this makes a stewy tapa typical of Andalusia. A big bowlful is a fantastic first course or a light main dish. Double the recipe and you have a crowd-pleasing party dish. You'll be making it often.

4 tablespoons extra-virgin olive oil
2 large garlic cloves, minced, plus 5 small whole garlic cloves
1/2 large white onion, finely chopped
1 Italian (frying) pepper, cored, seeded, and diced
2 pounds Yukon Gold potatoes, peeled and cut into 1/2-inch dice
1 large, ripe tomato, cut in half and grated on a box grater, skin discarded
1 1/2 cups bottled clam juice
1 large pinch of saffron, pulverized in a mortar and steeped in 3 tablespoons very hot water
2 medium-size roasted red bell peppers (see page 385), chopped
Coarse salt (kosher or sea) and freshly ground black pepper
1/3 cup chopped fresh flat-leaf parsley
1/3 cup dry white wine
2 pounds small Manila clams, scrubbed well

Flowerpots often decorate the whitewashed Moorish-style houses in Arcos de la Frontera, one of Andalusia's "white cities."

1. Heat 3 tablespoons of the olive oil and the minced garlic in a heavy 4- to 5-quart pot over medium heat. Add the onion and cook until it begins to soften, about 5 minutes. Add the Italian pepper, reduce the heat to low, and cook until the pepper softens, about 5 minutes. Add the potatoes and cook, stirring, for 2 to 3 minutes. Add the tomato and continue cooking, stirring occasionally, until the juices thicken slightly, 5 minutes. Add the clam juice and enough water to cover the potatoes by ½ inch and bring to a boil, skimming. Stir in the saffron, the roasted peppers, and salt and black pepper to taste. Reduce the heat to low, cover the pot, and simmer until the potatoes are very soft but not quite falling apart, about 20 minutes. Stir and lightly skim the mixture occasionally, adding a few tablespoons of water if necessary to maintain the level of liquid in the pot.

2. While the potatoes are cooking, heat the remaining 1 tablespoon olive oil in a small skillet over medium heat. Add the 5 whole garlic cloves and cook until the garlic is golden and crisp, 3 to 4 minutes. Using a slotted spoon, transfer the garlic to a mini food processor and add the parsley. Pulse until finely chopped, but not pureed.

3. Place the wine in a wide pot and bring to a boil over medium-high heat. Add 2 teaspoons of the parsley mixture and the clams. Cover the pot and let the clams steam until they open, 4 to 7 minutes. Discard any unopened clams.

4. Stir the remaining parsley mixture into the potato mixture. Gently stir in the clams and their liquid, taking care not to crush the potatoes. Cook over medium heat until the flavors meld, 1 to 2 minutes. Spoon the stew into bowls and serve at once.

SERVES 8 AS A TAPA, 4 AS A MAIN COURSE

SEAFOOD TO START

BASIC MARINATED SARDINES

SARDINAS ALIÑADAS

Silvery marinated sardines are one of the great pleasures of eating in Spain. And they are extremely easy to prepare at home, provided you know where to get very fresh ones. If your fishmonger is an affable type, ask him to clean and bone the sardines for you. Otherwise, it isn't hard to do at home; you'll find instructions below. Essentially a form of ceviche, the fresh sardines marinate in vinegar until they turn opaque and are "cooked" by the acid. Then, they can be served with nothing more than a sprinkling of minced flat-leaf parsley and garlic or with the colorful Basque Vinaigrette (Step 1, page 39). You can make a raspberry vinaigrette, another intriguing dressing, by pureeing a cup of raspberries in a blender with a quarter cup of red wine vinegar and straining it through a sieve. I often serve the sardines on thin slices of sourdough toast, with a few arugula leaves and thinly sliced figs. They're also great with grapes and balsamic vinegar ice cream (see page 55).

6 medium-size (each 3 to 4 ounces) very fresh sardines
About 3/4 cup white wine vinegar (see Note), or more if needed
About 1/3 cup fragrant extra-virgin olive oil

1. To clean and bone the sardines, remove the scales from the fish by gently scraping them with a small dull knife under cold running water. Cut off and discard the heads, then, using a small sharp knife, carefully make a slit along the bellies. Gut and clean the fish under cold running water. Grab on to the top of the spine of a sardine and pull it out quickly, trying not to remove too much of the flesh around it. Repeat with the remaining sardines. Cut each sardine in half to make two fillets and, if you feel small bones, trim the sides of the fillets. Rinse the fillets under cold running water and pat them dry with paper towels.

2. Arrange the sardine fillets skin side down in one layer in a shallow glass dish and add enough vinegar to cover them. Cover the dish with plastic wrap and let the sardines marinate in the refrigerator until they turn white, 6 to 8 hours depending on their size, turning them several times. Drain off the vinegar and pour the olive oil over the fillets. Let them come to room temperature before serving. **MAKES 12 FILLETS**

NOTE: In Spain, a mild, flavorful white wine vinegar is usually used to marinate fish. If your vinegar seems too strong, dilute it with a little water or use rice vinegar or lemon juice instead.

SANGRIA!

Even those snooty Spaniards who shrug sangria off as a tourist drink would certainly change their mind upon tasting the sexy potions mixed by Alex Ureña, the gifted chef at Suba, a lounge-restaurant in New York. Red, white, or rosé, Alex's sangrias will add pizzazz to any tapas bash. Each of the recipes below will make a medium-size pitcher and serve six. Double, triple, or quadruple the recipes, but watch out—this is potent stuff.

FRUITY RED SANGRIA

1 bottle (750 milliliters) inexpensive dry Spanish red wine, such as Vina Borgia Grenache
1/2 cup triple sec
1/4 cup brandy, preferably Spanish
1 1/2 cups fresh orange juice
1/4 cup Simple Syrup (recipe follows) or superfine sugar, or more if needed
About 1 1/2 cups diced fruit, such green apples (peeled) and thin-skinned oranges and lemons (diced with their peels)
Ice cubes
Chilled club soda

Mix together the wine, Triple Sec, brandy, orange juice, simple syrup, and fruit in a medium-size pitcher. Refrigerate for 4 to 6 hours to macerate the fruit in the wine. When ready to serve, add the ice cubes, and club soda to taste. Taste for sweetness, adding more syrup, as necessary.

SIMPLE SYRUP

3/4 cup sugar
1/2 cup water

Place the sugar and water in a small saucepan and bring to a simmer over medium heat, stirring to dissolve the sugar. Simmer for 3 to 4 minutes. Alternatively, combine the sugar and water in a microwave-safe container and microwave on high for 4 minutes. Refrigerate to cool completely. **MAKES ABOUT 3/4 CUP**

ROSE-RASPBERRY SANGRIA

2 cups raspberries
1 bottle (750 milliliters) inexpensive Spanish róse wine, such as Señorío de Sarría rosado
1/2 cup triple sec
1 cup fresh orange juice
3/4 cup POM pomegranate juice
2 tablespoon fresh lemon juice, or more if needed
3 tablespoons Simple Syrup (see above), or to taste
1 1/2 cups diced strawberries and thin-skinned lemons (diced with their peels)
Ice cubes

1. Place the raspberries in a blender and pulse to puree. Place a fine-mesh sieve over a medium-size pitcher and pour the puree into the sieve, straining it to remove the seeds.

2. Add the wine, triple sec, orange juice, pomegranate juice, lemon juice, simple syrup, and fruit to the pitcher and mix together. Refrigerate for 4 to 6 hours to macerate the fruit in the wine. When ready to serve, add the ice cubes. Taste and add more lemon juice or syrup, as necessary.

WHITE WINE–PEAR SANGRIA

1 bottle (750 milliliters) inexpensive dry Spanish white wine, such as Muga Rioja Blanco
2 cups pear nectar
1/3 cup Beefeater Wet Gin (or substitute dry gin)
1/4 cup peach schnapps
3 tablespoons Simple Syrup (see facing page) or superfine sugar, or more if needed
2 to 3 tablespoons fresh lemon juice, or more if needed
1 1/2 cups diced mixed fruit, such as peeled Golden Delicious apples, pears, and peaches
Ice cubes

Mix together the wine, pear nectar, gin, peach schnapps, simple syrup, 2 tablespoons of the lemon juice, and fruit in a medium-size pitcher. Refrigerate for 4 to 6 hours to macerate the fruit in the wine. When ready to serve, add the ice cubes. Taste, adding more lemon juice or syrup, as necessary.

SARDINES WITH BALSAMIC VINEGAR ICE CREAM

SARDINAS CON HELADO DE VINAGRE DE MODENA

A sprightly salad of green grapes and a small scoop of sweet-tart vinegar ice cream to cleanse the palate make a sensational counterpoint to the rich, buttery flesh of marinated sardines. This memorable combination of flavors was inspired by a dish at Hisop restaurant in Barcelona, where it's made with sparkling fresh *caballa* (mackerel) that is marinated briefly in olive oil. It works beautifully with sardines as well, and you can also try it with thin slices of fatty sashimi-quality tuna or tuna tartare. (Fish that's good enough to be eaten raw doesn't need to marinate in the lemon juice; all it requires is a drizzle of good olive oil and a sprinkling of coarse sea salt.) The chefs at Hisop make their own vinegar ice cream, but doctoring store-bought vanilla is a cool, easy option (the dish is also delicious without the ice cream). The fish in the Basic Marinated Sardines recipe needs to marinate for six to eight hours, so plan accordingly.

- 1 cup green seedless grapes, sliced
- 2 tablespoons fresh lemon juice, or more if the grapes are very sweet
- 1 tablespoon fragrant extra-virgin olive oil
- 3 tablespoons finely chopped shallots
- 1/4 cup finely minced fresh flat-leaf parsley
- About 1 cup best-quality vanilla ice cream
- 2 tablespoons syrupy aged balsamic vinegar, or 1/3 cup thin balsamic vinegar reduced over medium-high heat to 2 tablespoons
- 6 Basic Marinated Sardines (12 fillets; page 53)

1. Place the grapes, lemon juice, olive oil, shallots, and parsley in a glass bowl and toss to mix. Let the grape salad stand for 30 minutes.

2. Place the ice cream in a bowl and let stand until just soft enough to stir, 5 to 10 minutes. Stir the vinegar in gently but thoroughly, cover the bowl with plastic wrap, and refreeze the ice cream until firm, 20 to 30 minutes.

3. To serve, arrange 2 sardine fillets on a plate and spoon some grape salad on top. Scoop some ice cream into a shot glass or a tiny cup and place it on the plate. Repeat with the remaining sardines, grape salad, and ice cream. To eat, take a bite of sardine with the grape salad, followed by a teaspoon of the ice cream. **SERVES 6**

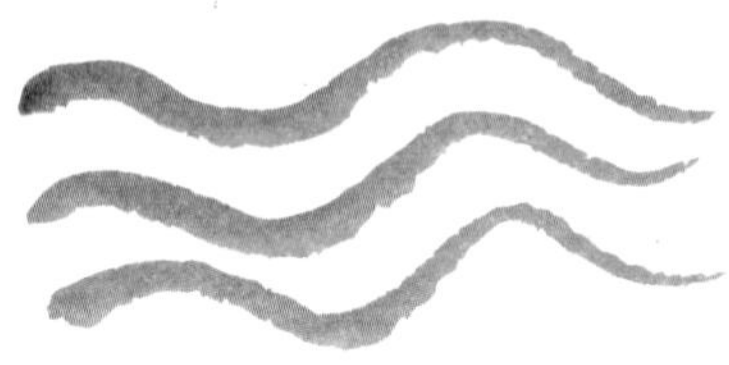

SALMON WITH SALMON ROE AND VANILLA OIL

SALMON A BAJA TEMPERATURA CON HUEVOS DE SALMON Y ACEITE DE VAINILLA

This dish is a knockout, a truly inspired juggling of three distinctive flavors. What's key here is the salmon's texture—extraordinarily silky and almost creamy, achieved by cooking the fish on a plastic-wrapped plate in a very low oven (a home simulation of *sous vide,* or vacuum-packed cooking). Carles Abellan, the progressive Barcelona chef who created the dish, poaches his salmon with oil before cooking. The method here (suggested by New York chef David Bouley) achieves the same texture without the oil. The resulting fish retains the bright pink color of raw salmon but is cooked through. (Don't worry about putting plastic wrap in the oven—at such a low temperature, it shouldn't burst or melt.) Combined with drizzles of vanilla-infused oil and juicy salmon eggs, the dish is as impressive as any fancy three-star restaurant appetizer. The vanilla oil can become habit-forming. Use it to add an intriguing dimension of flavor to such sweet shellfish as crab, lobster, scallops, or shrimp. And it's delicious stirred into mashed potatoes.

FOR THE VANILLA OIL:

- 1 1/2 best-quality vanilla beans
- 1/2 cup light-bodied, flavorless cooking oil, such as grapeseed or sunflower oil

FOR THE SALMON:

1 1/2 pounds extremely fresh skinless center-cut salmon fillets (at least 1 inch thick)
Vegetable oil, for brushing the salmon
Coarse salt (kosher or sea)
4 to 5 ounces salmon roe

1. Make the vanilla oil: Scrape the seeds from the vanilla beans into a small microwave-safe glass bowl. Add the oil and the vanilla pods and heat in a microwave oven on high power for 45 seconds. Then cover the bowl with aluminum foil and let the oil infuse at room temperature for 4 to 6 hours. Remove the vanilla pods. The oil will keep for several days stored at room temperature in a clean jar.

2. Prepare the salmon: Preheat the oven to 180°F.

3. Cut the salmon fillet lengthwise into 2 pieces and place on a well-oiled heatproof plate. Brush the fish with a little vegetable oil and sprinkle a little salt over it. Wrap the plate tightly in a double layer of sturdy plastic wrap and place it on a baking sheet. Bake for 13 to 15 minutes. Check after about 7 minutes. If for some reason the plastic wrap has burst, wrap another piece over the plate. When done, the salmon won't look cooked through, so just go by the number of minutes.

4. Remove the salmon from the oven, unwrap it, and let cool to room temperature, loosely covered with a sheet of clean plastic wrap.

5. To serve, blot the salmon dry with a paper towel and slice it crosswise into medium-thin slices. Arrange 3 or 4 slices on pretty appetizer plates and drizzle some vanilla oil on and around the salmon. Spread a little salmon roe on top of each slice of salmon, then serve at once. **SERVES 6 TO 8 AS A TAPA**

MACKEREL IN QUICK ESCABECHE

CABALLA EN ESCABECHE

Here's chef Ferran Adrià's delicious quick take on the classic Spanish dish *escabeche.* Though classic *escabeches* normally marinate for many hours, this fish is good to eat right away. Serve plenty of bread to sop up the tasty marinade. And feel free to try the recipe with other oily fish, such as bluefish or sardines.

4 Spanish mackerel fillets (each about 8 ounces), each cut in half crosswise
Coarse salt (kosher or sea) and freshly ground black pepper
All-purpose flour, for dusting the fish
1/2 cup fragrant extra-virgin olive oil
8 thick asparagus stalks, trimmed
4 medium-size garlic cloves, peeled and lightly crushed
1 jar (6 1/2 ounces) marinated artichokes, drained
2 bay leaves
1/4 teaspoon smoked sweet Spanish paprika
1/2 cup sherry vinegar, preferably aged
Country bread, for serving

1. Season the fish with salt and pepper and let stand for 5 to 10 minutes. Dust the fish very lightly with flour, shaking off the excess.

2. Heat 2 tablespoons of the olive oil in a large nonstick skillet over medium-high heat. Add the fish and cook, turning once, until brown and crisp, about 5 minutes per side. Transfer the fish to a deep platter and pour off the oil from the skillet.

SHERRY

Banish the image of that dusty bottle of cream sherry in your grandmother's cupboard. Good dry sherry—*Jerez* in Spanish—is one of the world's sexiest drinks, an ideal companion to tapas. The wine is named after the town of Jerez de la Frontera, where most of it is produced and where viticulture has flourished since the time of Phoenicians in the twelfth century B.C. The sherry grapes, predominantly Palomino, as well as the sweet Pedro Ximénez, grow in the area's unique chalky soil called *albariza,* which soaks up winter rain like a sponge, and feeds the deep, craggy roots of the vines throughout the hot, arid summers. After the grapes are picked, crushed, and fortified with grape spirits, the liquid is placed in wooden casks, where the wine may develop a characteristic covering of yeast called flor (flower) on its surface. Flor intensifies the wine's flavor, keeping it crisp and dry. Sherry that develops flor will be labeled fino; sherry that doesn't will be left to oxidize and will be sold as oloroso. Next, the sherry undergoes a complex maturing and blending process known as the solera, in which some of it is blended at regular intervals with wine from an older barrel and then topped up with a younger wine. This ensures consistency and leaves consumers free from having to worry about particular vintages. Bottled sherry comes in the following categories:

FINO (meaning "fine") is light, dry, straw-colored, and delicate. It's usually fortified to about 15 percent alcohol. (Pale cream sherry is a sweetened fino.)

MANZANILLA is the incomparable fino-style sherry produced in the picturesque seaside town of Sanlúcar de Barrameda, which has an Atlantic microclimate believed to lend manzanilla its irresistible crisp-dry salty tang.

AMONTILLADO, another member of the fino family, is aged longer in the solera system and left to oxidize after it loses its flor, which accounts for its amber color, deep nuttiness, and brassy richness. Amontillado, which should really be enjoyed dry, is often sweetened for export. Its alcohol content is higher than that of a fino.

OLOROSO (meaning "fragrant") is a dark amber, wonderfully walnuty, rich sherry with a high degree of alcohol (about 20 percent). Olorosos don't develop flor and take longer to mature than finos. While olorosos are also frequently sweetened (and labeled cream sherry), the best examples are dry.

PALO CORTADO is the much prized, complex maverick sherry that begins life as amontillado, then "mutates" into an oloroso, sharing the best characteristics of both. A special treat, it's worth seeking out.

PEDRO XIMENEZ, or PX, is the raisiny-sweet unctuous dessert sherry made from Pedro Ximénez grapes, which are traditionally dried in the sun.

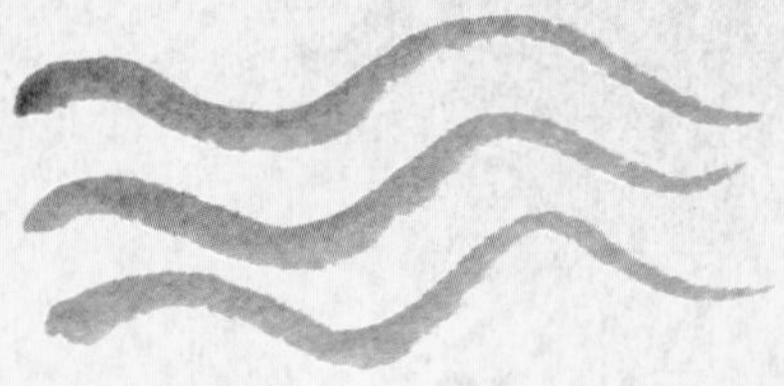

3. Add the remaining 6 tablespoons olive oil to the skillet and heat over medium heat for a few seconds. Add the asparagus, garlic, artichokes, and bay leaves and cook until the asparagus is golden and just tender, 5 to 6 minutes.

4. Remove the skillet from the heat, add the paprika and vinegar, and pour the vegetable mixture over the fish. The fish will be ready to serve after about 15 minutes; for a more pickled taste, it can be marinated longer, anywhere from 2 to 24 hours. Refrigerate the fish if marinating it longer than 2 hours and let come to room temperature before serving the fish with country bread. **SERVES 6 TO 8**

TUNA TARTARE WITH DATES AND TOMATOES

TARTAR DE ATUN CON DATILES Y TOMATES

Inspired by a recipe from the gifted La Rioja chef Francis Paniego, this brilliant dish will seduce even people who think they've OD'd on tuna tartare. Intensely Mediterranean, with a surprising sweet touch of dates, it is extremely simple to make but does require terrific ingredients: sashimi-quality tuna, aromatic tomatoes with a lively acidity, and your loveliest, fruitiest olive oil. The creamy, garlicky almond sauce elevates the dish to further heights, but if you are in a hurry the tartare is also delicious with nothing more than a drizzle of olive oil.

- 3 medium-size, ripe but firm tomatoes, peeled with a vegetable peeler, seeded, and diced
- 4 to 5 medium-size dates, finely diced
- 7 tablespoons fragrant extra-virgin olive oil, plus more for drizzling on the tuna
- 1 1/2 teaspoons best-quality white wine vinegar
- 6 to 7 ounces sashimi-quality tuna, finely diced
- Flaky sea salt, such as Maldon
- 2 tablespoons slivered fresh basil
- Creamy Almond Sauce (recipe follows)

1. Place the tomatoes and dates in a bowl, separating the date pieces with a fork so they don't clump together. Toss with 2 tablespoons of the olive oil and the vinegar and let stand for about 20 minutes.

2. Place the tuna in another bowl, toss it with a pinch of salt, rubbing the salt lightly into the fish. Add the tuna to the tomato mixture and stir in the remaining olive oil and the basil.

3. To serve, press a quarter of the tuna mixture in a small cup, such as an espresso cup or a ¼- or ⅓-cup measuring cup, then unmold it onto a pretty serving plate. Repeat with the remaining tuna mixture. Spoon some of the Creamy Almond Sauce around each tartare. Drizzle a little olive oil over both the sauce and the tuna. Sprinkle sea salt on top of the tuna tartares and serve at once. **SERVES 4**

CREAMY ALMOND SAUCE

SALSA DE AJO BLANCO

In the last few years, it has become fashionable among Spanish chefs to serve *ajo blanco* (the Andalusian almond gazpacho) as a sauce for seafood. It's an inspired idea. Just remember, you'll need to make the sauce at least a half hour before you plan on serving it, to allow the flavor to develop.

- 1/2 slice white sandwich bread
- 1/3 cup blanched almonds, finely ground in a food processor
- 1 tablespoon sherry vinegar, preferably aged, or more to taste
- 1/4 cup fragrant extra-virgin olive oil
- 1 medium-size garlic clove, crushed with a garlic press
- Coarse salt (kosher or sea)

1. Crumble the bread into a small sieve and run cold water over it for a few seconds, until the bread almost dissolves. Drain well.

2. Place the bread in a blender along with the almonds, 3 tablespoons cold water, and the vinegar and process to a paste. With the motor running, drizzle in the olive oil, as if making mayonnaise.

3. Scrape the almond mixture into a bowl, add the garlic, and season with salt to taste. Cover the bowl with plastic wrap and let the sauce stand for at least 30 minutes for the flavors to develop. Just before serving, taste the sauce and add a little more vinegar if you think it needs more kick. If the sauce seems too thick, thin it with cold water until it has the consistency of a thin mayonnaise. This sauce will keep for 2 days, covered, in the refrigerator. **MAKES ABOUT 1/2 CUP**

GRATINEED OYSTERS WITH SPINACH

OSTRAS GRATINADAS CON ESPINACAS

These showstopping oysters and spinach, with a lush cap of bubbling gratinéed saffron hollandaise, are a specialty at Aloña Berri, a wonderfully creative tapas bar in San Sebastián. The owner, José Ramón Elizondo, says that it's his Basque take on oysters Rockefeller.

- 1 tablespoon extra-virgin olive oil
- 2 small garlic cloves, chopped
- 6 cups firmly packed fresh baby spinach, rinsed, drained, and chopped
- Coarse salt (kosher or sea)
- 12 large oysters, shells well scrubbed
- 2 small or 1 jumbo egg yolk
- 1 tablespoon fresh lemon juice, or more to taste
- 6 tablespoons (3/4 stick) cold unsalted butter, cut into small pieces
- 1 small pinch of saffron, pulverized in a mortar and steeped in 2 teaspoons very hot water
- 2 or 3 lemon wedges, for serving
- About 3 cups kosher salt, for serving

1. Heat the olive oil in a large skillet over medium heat. Add the garlic and stir until fragrant, about 30 seconds. Add the spinach, increase the heat to medium-high, and cook until just wilted, 2 to 3 minutes. Season the spinach with salt to taste, transfer it to a bowl, and let cool while you prepare the oysters. (The spinach can be prepared up to a day ahead. Cover and refrigerate.)

2. Shuck the oysters, straining their liquor into a bowl. Carefully remove the oysters from their shells, reserve the deep bottom shells, and discard the top shells. (Or you can ask your fishmonger to shuck the oysters; request that as much of the oyster liquor as possible remains with the oysters.) Rinse the bottom shells well and dry them.

3. Place the egg yolks and lemon juice in a small bowl and whisk to mix. Fill a medium-size skillet halfway with water and bring to a simmer. Place the yolk mixture and the butter in a small saucepan and set it in the skillet. Reduce the heat to a minimum, so that the water in the skillet is just below a simmer. Stir the butter mixture with a wooden spoon until the butter just melts. Using a whisk, whisk the sauce continuously until it thickens, about 1 minute. Do not overcook or let the sauce get too hot or it will curdle. Scrape the sauce into a bowl and stir in the saffron. Season with salt to taste and add a little more lemon juice, if you like.

4. Preheat the broiler.

5. Spread the kosher salt on a broiler-proof platter to a depth of ½ inch, covering the platter completely. Place a little spinach in each oyster shell, sprinkle a little of the oyster liquor over it, and add a squeeze of lemon juice, then place an oyster on top. Top with about 1 teaspoon of the hollandaise sauce. Repeat with the remaining oysters and shells, nestling the filled shells in the salt.

6. Broil the oysters about 4 inches away from the heat until the sauce is bubbling and browned in spots, about 2 minutes. Serve at once. **MAKES 12**

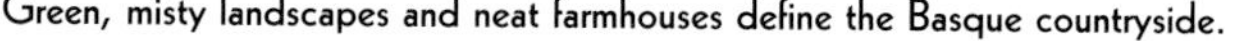

Green, misty landscapes and neat farmhouses define the Basque countryside.

PLANNING A TAPAS BASH

Tapas can be as simple as small plates of store-bought olives, anchovies, fried almonds, chorizo slices, and quartered piquillo peppers passed around with predinner drinks. Or they can make up a whole colorful meal or buffet of small dishes. If you want to go the latter route, try presenting a varied menu that combines something fried really crunchy and something baked; something briny and something mild; something saucy or salady and something dry. Because at Spanish bars tapas are usually served consecutively, each on its own plate, I always urge my friends to try one thing after another, rather than mix all the flavors and dishes on one plate. (They never listen.)

Any tapas bash should begin with a trip to the market for Spanish cheeses, olives, marcona almonds, anchovies, and dry-cured chorizo or good salami. Then pick a few recipes from this chapter, a salad, some canapés or an empanada, one of the tortillas in the egg chapter, perhaps a meatball dish, and saucy mussels or clams. In addition, here are ten more tapas ideas so simple they don't really require proper recipes.

- Boiled diced potatoes with chopped red onion, piquillo peppers, chunks of good tuna, loads of good olive oil, and a splash of sherry vinegar

- *Boquerones* (white anchovies) on a bed of julienned piquillo peppers or pimientos, drizzled with reduced balsamic vinegar and sprinkled with parsley

- Cubes of Manchego cheese marinated in olive oil with aromatic herbs, such as thyme and rosemary

- Simple seafood kebabs brushed with olive oil that has been flavored with garlic and *pimentón,* grilled or broiled, and served with Toasted Hazelnut Romesco Dip (page 30) or Colorful Saffron Allioli (page 45)

- Smoked salmon slices rolled around a salad of cooked salmon tossed with diced apples and cornichons, shredded lettuce, and mayo; served on endive spears

- Steamed mussels, cooled and served on the half shell, drizzled with a vinaigrette of olive oil and white wine vinegar, a sprinkling of diced red, green, and yellow bell peppers, and parsley

- Dates stuffed with marcona almonds, Cabrales cheese, or small chunks of chorizo, wrapped in bacon and baked or broiled until crisp (turning them once)

- Lightly steamed fat asparagus stalks, wrapped in piquillo pepper halves, then in serrano ham slices, and grilled, griddled, or broiled for a few minutes

- Green grapes rolled in goat cheese, coated in coarsely chopped toasted almonds, and chilled for about 1 hour

- Grilled or roasted fig halves wrapped in serrano ham slices or topped with a smear of Cabrales

- A smear of Cabrales on dried figs that have been macerated in port wine and drained

FRIED AND TRUE

BLUE CHEESE AND DATE CROQUETTES

CROQUETAS DE DATILES Y ROQUEFORT

It's a pleasure to go around the La Boqueria market in Barcelona tasting and comparing the *croquetas* served at the various lunch counters. While the spinach, pine nut, and raisin croquettes at Quim de la Boqueria are sublime, my prize goes to Bar Pinotxo for its crisp Roquefort and date fritters. Their combination of sweetness and pungency is fabulous. This is my adaptation of the dish.

5 medium-size pitted dates
Boiling water
4 tablespoons (1/2 stick) unsalted butter
Olive oil
5 tablespoons all-purpose flour, plus more for breading the croquettes
1 1/2 cups whole milk
4 ounces blue cheese, such as Roquefort or Cabrales, finely crumbled (about 1 cup)
2 or 3 gratings of nutmeg
Coarse salt (kosher or sea) and freshly ground white pepper
2 large eggs
About 2 cups fine dry white bread crumbs, for breading the croquettes

1. Place the dates in a small heatproof bowl, add boiling water to cover, and let soak until softened, 10 to 15 minutes. Thoroughly drain the dates, then mince them.

2. Melt the butter in 5 teaspoons of the olive oil in a large skillet over medium-low heat. Add the flour and cook, stirring, until a smooth paste forms, about 1 minute. Increase the heat to medium-high and gradually add the milk, whisking constantly, until the mixture is completely smooth, about 1 minute. Add the blue cheese and the minced dates and stir until the cheese is completely melted. Reduce the heat to low and stir the mixture with a wooden spoon until it begins to pull away from the side of the skillet, 3 to 5 minutes. Grate in the nutmeg and season with salt and white pepper to taste. Scrape the croquette mixture into a well-oiled shallow bowl that is 6 to 7 inches in diameter and has straight sides. Let cool to room temperature, place a piece of plastic wrap directly on top of the croquette mixture, and chill until firm, at least 3 hours. (The croquette mixture can be prepared up to a day ahead.)

3. Place some flour in a shallow bowl; beat the eggs in a second shallow bowl; and place the bread crumbs in a third shallow bowl. Arrange the bowls in that order for easy breading. Lightly flour your hands, then break off a scant tablespoon of the croquette mixture. Lightly roll it in the flour, shaking off the excess, then roll it gently between your hands to form an oval. (Alternatively, you can invert the croquette mixture onto a cutting board and using a floured knife cut the croquettes into 1-inch cubes.) Dip the croquette in the beaten egg, then dip it generously in the bread crumbs. Transfer the croquette to a small baking sheet. Repeat with the remaining mixture. Croquettes rolled in bread crumbs will keep in the refrigerator, covered, for at least a day; see the last paragraph in the box on the facing page.

4. Set a small rack over a baking sheet and line it with a double thickness of paper towels. Pour olive oil to a depth of 1 inch in an 8-inch skillet and heat it over medium-high heat to 350°F; when hot, a croquette placed in the oil will sizzle on contact. Fry the croquettes, 6 or 7 at a time, until deep golden on all sides, turning once and adjusting the heat so the oil doesn't burn. Using a slotted spoon, transfer the fried croquettes to the paper towels to drain. Once all the croquettes have been fried, serve them immediately. **MAKES ABOUT 3 DOZEN**

TRUFFLED TURKEY AND WILD MUSHROOM CROQUETTES

CROQUETAS DE PAVO Y SETAS TRUFADAS

These are classic turkey *croquetas* elevated to the realm of the sublime by the addition of wild mushrooms and truffle oil. Fried food just doesn't get any better. White and black truffle oils are sold at many gourmet markets; though they may seem expensive, they're actually quite a bargain, since a little goes a very long way. This is a terrific way to utilize Thanksgiving leftovers, but if you don't have roast turkey on hand, you can use good-quality sliced deli roast turkey instead.

- Olive oil
- 1/3 cup finely chopped onion
- 4 ounces mild-flavored wild mushrooms (such as porcini, oyster, or chanterelles), wiped clean with a damp paper towel and finely chopped
- 1 cup finely shredded cooked turkey or chicken
- 4 tablespoons (1/2 stick) unsalted butter
- 1/3 cup all-purpose flour, plus more for breading the croquettes
- 1 1/2 cups whole milk
- Coarse salt (kosher or sea) and freshly ground black pepper
- 3 gratings of nutmeg
- 1/2 teaspoon white or black truffle oil, or more to taste
- 2 large eggs
- About 2 cups fine dry white bread crumbs

1. Heat 2 tablespoons of the olive oil in a small skillet over medium-low heat. Add the onion and cook until limp but not brown, 3 to 5 minutes. Add the mushrooms and cook over medium-high heat, stirring, until they have released and reabsorbed their liquid, 4 to 5 minutes. Add the turkey and stir for another minute or so, adding a little more olive oil if the skillet looks dry. Remove the skillet from the heat and set it aside.

2. Melt the butter in 2 more tablespoons of olive oil in a large skillet over medium-low heat. Add the

CROQUETAS CALLING

The Spanish are addicted to *croquetas* (croquettes), those perfectly crisp fried shells with a silky, oozy béchamel center. "*Croquetas* are a genius fusion of a classic French sauce with the Spanish art of frying," says my friend José Carlos Capel, the food critic for *El País* newspaper. "It must have been some ingenious cook in the late nineteeneth century who discovered that you can fry pieces of leftover béchamel," Capel adds. From then on, croquettes entered the repertoire of bourgeois Spanish home cooks. These days, they are a staple both at home and at countless tapas bars all over the country. When done well, there's almost nothing I'd rather eat.

The secret to a *croqueta* with an almost liquid interior is to make the béchamel sauce rather thin (3 tablespoons flour per 1 cup milk is a good proportion). Then, the mixture needs plenty of chilling time to become firm enough to be shaped, breaded, and fried. Thrifty *abuelas* (grandmothers) flavor their *croquetas* with shredded leftover meats from a *cocido*—a boiled dinner—or with roast turkey or chicken, but the possibilities are almost infinite. To make about three dozen croquettes, start with a béchamel base made with 2 tablespoons olive oil and 4 tablespoons butter, 5 tablespoons flour, and 1 1/2 cups milk (see the recipe on the facing page for detailed instructions). You can stir a heaping cup of any of the following into this béchamel base.

- Shredded leftover poultry, diced serrano ham, and a little minced parsley
- Shredded roast pork or lamb or leftover stew and diced piquillo peppers
- Chopped cooked seafood or finely flaked fish or salt cod (for the béchamel, use half milk, half fish stock or clam juice)
- Finely chopped wild mushrooms sautéed in olive oil with garlic, parsley, and a dash of dry sherry
- Finely chopped Spinach with Raisins and Pine Nuts (page 388)
- A combination of flaked cooked salmon, chopped smoked salmon, and about 3 ounces cream cheese
- A combination of shredded Manchego, Cheddar, or Gruyère; Parmesan; and diced pimientos

You can add any grated cheese of your choice; diced cooked vegetables, such as potatoes, carrots, or broccoli; such spices as paprika, cayenne, or nutmeg; and fresh or dried herbs to any of these fillings. For the béchamel, instead of using all milk, try adding half milk and half stock, the flavorful juices from roast poultry or meat, or a little wine.

Once the batter is well chilled, traditionally home cooks shape *croquetas* into balls, ovals, or cylinders with the help of two teaspoons. A speedier method is to chill the béchamel in a well-oiled straight-sided dish (the layer should be at least 1/2 inch thick), then invert it onto a cutting board and cut it into rectangles or squares. Or the chilled béchamel mixture can be rolled out into ropes, then cut into cylinders. *Croquetas* can be shaped and breaded way ahead of time. However, before frying them, check for cracks in the breading, lest the filling leak out. Cracks can be fixed by rolling the cracked croquette in more bread crumbs.

flour and cook, stirring, until a smooth paste forms, about 1 minute. Increase the heat to medium-high and gradually add the milk, whisking constantly, until the mixture is completely smooth, about 1 minute. Add the turkey mixture and stir until the mixture is thick and begins to pull away from the side of the skillet, about 5 minutes. Season with the salt, pepper, nutmeg, and truffle oil to taste. Scrape the croquette mixture into a well-oiled shallow bowl that is 6 to 7 inches in diameter and has straight sides. Place a sheet of plastic wrap directly on top of the croquette mixture and chill until firm, at least 3 hours. (The croquette mixture can be prepared up to a day ahead.)

3. Place some flour in a shallow bowl; beat the eggs in a second shallow bowl; and place the bread crumbs in a third shallow bowl. Arrange the bowls in that order for easy breading. Wet your hands lightly, then break off a scant tablespoon of the croquette mixture. Lightly roll it in the flour, shaking off the excess, then roll it gently between your hands to form an oval. (Alternatively, you can invert the croquette mixture onto a cutting board and, using a floured knife, cut the croquettes into 1-inch cubes.) Dip the croquette in the beaten egg, then dip it generously in the bread crumbs. Transfer the croquette to a small baking sheet. Repeat with the remaining croquette mixture. Croquettes rolled in bread crumbs will keep in the refrigerator, covered, for at least a day; see the last paragraph in the box on page 65.

4. Set a small rack over a baking sheet and line it with a double thickness of paper towels. Pour olive oil to a depth of 1 inch in an 8-inch skillet and heat it over medium-high heat to 350°F; when hot, a croquette placed in the oil will sizzle on contact. Fry the croquettes 6 or 7 at a time, until deep golden on all sides, turning once and adjusting the heat so the oil doesn't burn. Using a slotted spoon, transfer the fried croquettes to the paper towels to drain. Once all the croquettes have been fried, serve them immediately. **MAKES ABOUT 3 DOZEN**

BLACK-AND-WHITE CALAMARI FRITTERS

CALAMARES A LA ROMANA REBOZADAS CON SU TINTO

Of the delicious multitude of seafood fritters I tasted in Spain, these stand out as the most dramatic and memorable—the sort of dish that instantly provokes gasps of excitement. For one, the beer batter is so light that tempura seems leaden in comparison. But the real surprise here is the colors: a batter hued jet-black by squid ink, with snow-white *calamares* hiding inside. This is one of many scandalously delicious creations of Quim Marquéz, a Barcelona chef who can work miracles with just one or two simple flavors at his restaurant El Suquet de l'Almirall. Quim extracts ink from the squid himself, but the plastic packets of squid ink imported from Spain are a fine, labor-saving option. Quim recommends serving the fritters with Roasted Garlic or Colorful Saffron Allioli (page 45); they are just as good with lemon wedges or on their own. If you don't have squid ink, the fritter will still be delicious without it.

- 1/2 pound cleaned squid, patted thoroughly dry
- Coarse salt (kosher or sea)
- 3/4 cup all-purpose flour
- 3/4 teaspoon baking powder
- 1 large egg, beaten
- 3/4 cup cold lager-style beer
- 3 to 4 packets (each 4 grams/.14 ounce) squid ink (about 1 teaspoon total; see Note)
- Olive oil, for frying
- Allioli (page 44), or lemon wedges, for serving

1. Cut the squid bodies into ⅓-inch-wide rings. Rub all the squid with a little salt and let stand while you prepare the batter. Set a small rack over a baking sheet and line it with a double thickness of paper towels.

2. Sift the flour and baking powder together into a large bowl. Gradually whisk in the egg and beer, whisking until the batter is completely smooth. Whisk in ½ teaspoon salt and enough squid ink to color the batter a purplish dark gray.

3. Pour olive oil to a depth of 1½ inches in a large, deep skillet and heat it over medium-high heat to 360°F; when hot, batter placed in the oil will sizzle on contact. Add a third of the squid rings to the batter and stir until completely coated. Using a fork, remove the squid rings from the batter, shaking off the excess. Place the battered squid in the hot oil and fry until the batter is puffed up and the squid is just cooked through, 1 to 1½ minutes per side. As you cook, lower the heat as needed so that the squid has a chance to cook through without the batter burning. Using a slotted spoon, transfer the fried squid to the paper towels to drain. Repeat with the remaining squid rings. Serve immediately with *allioli* or lemon wedges. **SERVES 6 AS A TAPA, 4 AS A LIGHT FIRST COURSE**

NOTE: As the intensity of the ink can vary, use as many packets as you need to get a very dark batter. If the ink inside the packets seems a little congealed, warm the packets in a pot of hot water.

PEAR-SHAPED SALT COD FRITTERS LA SIRENA

PERITAS DE BACALAO LA SIRENA

Spanish cooks can usually make good salt cod fritters in their sleep. But those made by Mari Carmen Vélez, the feisty chef at La Sirena restaurant in Alicante, are in a league of their own. Not only are hers impeccably fluffy and crisp; they are also adorable—shaped like tiny pears. Little wonder that the tapas bar at La Sirena is always mobbed.

MADRID TAPEO

When it comes to *tapeos,* Madrid has a split personality. There is the Madrid of the fast-talking, street-smart, tripe-loving *castizos*—pure-blood, working-class *madrileños* who are the Spanish answer to British cockneys. (This is a city that was once famous for its profusion of populist taverns where the aristocracy rubbed shoulders with *toreros* and flamenco musicians.) Then there is the *pijo,* or yuppie Madrid, which favors fast cars, designer labels, and haute cuisine tapas served up in modish surroundings in the upmarket barrio of Salamanca. And there's everything in between: The Madrid of blue-blooded *señoras* who decorously nibble on salmon canapés at the neo-rococo Café de Oriente. The Madrid of gypsies who scarf down *jamón* after-hours at the legendary flamenco haunt, Casa Patas. The melting pot Madrid, with its Asturian, Galician, Andalusian, and Basque taverns, Irish pubs, Moroccan joints, and Cuban cocktail bars.

Madrid's *castizo* old center remains a trove of dark, battered *tabernas, tascas,* and beer halls, with their well-worn zinc counters, tiled walls, macho meatballs, griddled pig's ears, and vermouth on tap. Searching for the crispest, lightest batter-fried bacalao, I fight the dense crowds that spill onto the pavement of Casa Labra, a haunt famous as much for its salt cod as for being the birthplace of the Spanish socialist party. The broth from a *cocido* (boiled dinner), a popular lunchtime pick-me-up, is fortifying and perfectly clear at Lhardy. Upstairs there's an early nineteenth-century restaurant straight out of an old master painting; downstairs, a small deli dispenses its consommé from an ornate silver samovar, along with dainty savory puff pastries displayed in glass cases. Then, off for a taste of the legendary "smashed" eggs with french fries at the bar of Casa Lucio, a blue-chip *taberna* where members of Spain's royal family might be dining within the pass-the-salt range of couples in faded jeans. Other signature Madrid tapas all have their bars. For garlicky shrimp there's the miniscule century-old Casa del Abuelo. The definitive *patatas bravas,* with a spicy, smoky tomato sauce, can be found at the loud, overlit Las Bravas. And in Los Austrias—the Hapsburg heart of Madrid—new-wave bars are luring young crowds with boutique cheeses, charcuterie, and fancy wines by the glass.

1 pound medium-size Yukon Gold potatoes, unpeeled
½ pound boneless salt cod, soaked and cooked (see page 198), then drained
Basic One-Cup Allioli (page 44) or Mock Allioli (page 45)
1 tablespoon finely minced fresh flat-leaf parsley
Coarse salt (kosher or sea)
1 large egg, beaten
Olive oil or mild vegetable oil, for frying
About 24 pieces of parsley stem (each 1 inch long)
Lemon wedges (optional), for serving

1. Place the potatoes in a large saucepan, add cold water to cover by 2 inches, and bring to a boil over medium-high heat. Reduce the heat to medium and cook the potatoes, partially covered, until they are completely tender when pierced with a skewer, about 30 minutes. Drain and let cool.

2. Shred the salt cod finely with your fingers, removing and discarding any bones.

3. When the potatoes are just cool enough to handle, peel them and grate on the large holes of a box grater into a large bowl. Add the salt cod and, using a fork, stir the cod and the potatoes together until the mixture is thoroughly combined (do not overmix or the potatoes will release too much starch). Stir in 2 tablespoons of the *allioli,* then taste for seasoning, adding a little salt, if necessary. Add the egg and stir to mix thoroughly. Refrigerate the salt cod mixture, covered, for 1 hour.

4. Wet your hands slightly and shape the salt cod mixture into 1½-inch balls. Place the balls on a plate, pressing them down to flatten one side slightly, then pat them into a pear shape.

5. Pour olive oil to a depth of 1 inch in a large, heavy skillet and heat it over medium-high heat to 360°F; when hot, a bit of salt cod mixture placed in the oil will sizzle on contact. Fry a few fritters in the oil, flat side first, until golden brown on all sides, about 1½ minutes total. Using a slotted spoon, transfer the fritters to paper towels to drain. Repeat with the remaining fritters. Once all the fritters are fried, insert a parsley stem in the narrow end of each. Serve immediately with *allioli* and lemon wedges, if desired. **MAKES 22 TO 24**

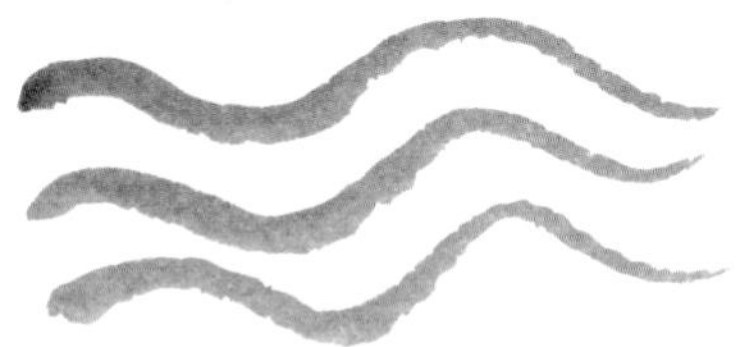

CRISP POTATOES WITH SPICY TOMATO SAUCE

PATATAS BRAVAS

Ladies and gentlemen, here is one of Spain's most definitive tapas. *Bravas*—fierce—refers to the spicy tomato sauce, for which there are as many recipes as there are tapas bar owners. My version was inspired by the smooth, smoky, *pimentón*-tinged sauce at Las Bravas, a bar that's been doing a booming *patatas bravas* business in Madrid for over a century. In the Catalan manner, I drizzle my *bravas* with both the tomato sauce and garlicky *allioli* mayonnaise, which makes the dish insanely delicious. At good bars, the cubed potatoes are deep-fried twice, first in coolish oil and then in very hot oil to crisp them. I present an easier option, using small red potatoes that are parboiled, cut into quarters, and crisped in the oven. Serve them skewered on toothpicks.

16 small red potatoes (1½ to 2 inches in diameter)
3 to 4 tablespoons extra-virgin olive oil
Coarse salt (kosher or sea)
Spicy Tomato Sauce (recipe follows)
About ¼ cup any Allioli (pages 44 to 45), thinned with 1 to 2 tablespoons water

Crisp Potatoes with Spicy Tomato Sauce and Allioli (pages 69, 44)

1. Place the potatoes in a large saucepan, add cold water to cover by 2 inches, and bring to a boil over medium-high heat. Reduce the heat to medium and cook the potatoes, partially covered, until they are completely tender when pierced with a skewer, about 20 minutes. Do not overcook. Drain and let cool. When just cool enough to handle, cut them into quarters.

2. Preheat the oven to 475°F.

3. Place the quartered potatoes, 3 tablespoons of the olive oil, and some salt in a bowl and toss to coat evenly, adding more oil, if needed. Be careful not to crush the potatoes. Spread the potatoes in a single layer on a large rimmed baking sheet and bake, turning once, until crisp and browned, about 45 minutes.

4. Arrange the potatoes on a serving platter and generously drizzle Spicy Tomato Sauce and *allioli* over them. **SERVES 4 TO 6**

SPICY TOMATO SAUCE

SALSA DE TOMATE PICANTE

I've purposely proportioned this recipe so that you'll have some left over. It keeps for several days and is delicious with just about anything.

- 4 1/2 teaspoons olive oil
- 1 small onion, minced
- 3 garlic cloves, chopped
- 3/4 teaspoon smoked sweet Spanish paprika
- 1/4 teaspoon ground cumin
- 1 medium-size pinch of crushed red pepper flakes
- 1 can (15 ounces) peeled plum tomatoes, chopped, with their liquid (about 1 1/2 cups)
- 2 teaspoons distilled white vinegar
- 1 large pinch of sugar
- Coarse salt (kosher or sea)
- Tabasco sauce

Heat the olive oil in a heavy medium-size saucepan over medium-low heat. Add the onion and garlic and cook until limp but not browned, 3 to 5 minutes. Add the paprika, cumin, and red pepper flakes and stir for a few seconds. Add the tomatoes with their liquid and ½ cup water and bring to a simmer. Cover the saucepan and simmer until the tomatoes have cooked down to a puree, 15 to 20 minutes, stirring occasionally and adding a little more water if the sauce seems too thick. Add the vinegar and sugar. Season the sauce with salt and Tabasco sauce to taste and remove it from the heat. Let the sauce cool for a few minutes, then puree it in a blender. Let the sauce cool to room temperature, taste it again, and add more salt and/or Tabasco as necessary. Stored in a clean jar, with a film of olive oil on top, the sauce can be refrigerated for up to a week. Let it return to room temperature before using. **MAKES ABOUT 1¾ CUPS**

WANDERING CADIZ

I could easily spend the rest of my days in Cádiz, a raffish whitewashed Andalusian city strung out along a thin three-mile-long peninsula that extends into the Atlantic like a gaunt, outstretched arm. Cádiz is the place to perfect the art of the *paseo,* joining the crowds of sailors, lovers, and older *gitanas* for a panoramic amble by the bay; to linger over brandy-laced coffee on a palm-shaded plaza; to wander the narrow streets in the echo of babbling locals who lean perilously out of the windows to gawk at the passersby.

Another one of the city's great pleasures is *tortillitas de camarones,* lacy-crisp pancakes made with *camarones,* miniscule crustaceans of the shrimp family. The pancakes are believed to have been invented by a local lady known as the *guapa de churros* (fried crullers belle) and were originally prepared with chickpea flour and sold at *churrerías,* or cruller joints. Over time, *tortillitas* became one of the most famous dishes of the Cádiz province and are now enjoyed as a tapa all over Andalusia and beyond.

CRISP SHRIMP PANCAKES FROM CADIZ

TORTILLITAS DE CAMARONES

In Cádiz, the shrimp are mixed into the pancake batter while still live and in their delicate shells. If you use ordinary shrimp, the intense marine smack and some of the crunch will be missing, but the pancakes are still a delight when prepared at home. These days, the original chickpea flour is mostly replaced by the coarse wheat flour used for coating fried fish (a mixture of all-purpose and semolina flour is a good substitute). For the pancakes to come out greaseless, the oil has to be very hot; for them to be crisp rather than spongy, it is important to quickly spread the batter out in the pan so it is as thin as possible.

6 ounces medium-size shrimp, shells and tails removed and set aside, shrimp chopped medium-fine
Coarse salt (kosher or sea)
1/2 cup all-purpose flour
1/2 cup chickpea flour (available at Indian groceries), or 1/2 cup medium to coarse semolina
3 tablespoons grated onion
2 tablespoons minced fresh flat-leaf parsley
Olive oil, for frying

1. Place the shrimp shells and tails in a small saucepan with 2 cups water and bring to a boil. Cover the saucepan, reduce the heat to low, and simmer for 10 minutes. Remove from the heat and let cool completely. Strain the shrimp liquid into a bowl and discard the shells.

2. Rub the chopped shrimp with a little salt and let stand while you mix the batter. Sift together the all-purpose flour, chickpea flour, and 1 teaspoon salt in a bowl. Whisk in 1¼ cups of the shrimp liquid, setting the rest aside. Whisk the batter until it is fairly smooth. Add the onion, parsley, and shrimp

and stir to mix evenly. Cover the bowl with plastic wrap and refrigerate the batter for 2 to 4 hours. Let come to room temperature before frying.

3. Whisk 4 to 6 tablespoons of the reserved shrimp liquid into the batter, using enough to give it the consistency of medium-thin pancake batter.

4. Set a small rack over a baking sheet and line it with a double thickness of paper towels. Pour olive oil to a depth of ½ inch in a medium-size skillet and heat it over medium-high heat to 375°F; when hot, a piece of batter placed in the oil will sizzle on contact. Place a heaping tablespoon of the batter in the oil and immediately flatten the batter with the back of a spoon to form a thin pancake about 2½ inches in diameter. Repeat with 4 more tablespoons of batter. Fry the pancakes until crisp and golden brown, 30 to 50 seconds per side, then using a slotted spoon, transfer them to the paper towels to drain. Repeat with the remaining batter, frying 5 or 6 pancakes at a time. (If you like, you can keep the finished pancakes warm in a 300°F oven until all the batter is cooked.) The pancakes are best straight from the frying pan, but you can also make *tortillitas* ahead and reheat them for 5 to 7 minutes in a 475°F oven before serving.

MAKES 20 TO 22

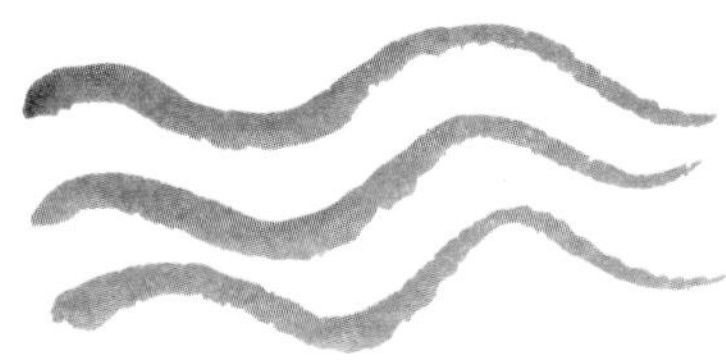

RESTAURANT

SOUPS

FROM COZY TO COOL

I encountered Iberian soup in its most basic form while cooking one afternoon with a group of grandmothers in the Catalan village of Sils. One of them grabbed half a loaf of stale bread and crumbled it into a pot. She added water; she tossed in a few mint leaves. Intently and patiently, she stirred the soup with a long wooden stick until the bread all but dissolved into the liquid, swelling and forming a porridge. "Sopa de menta cura la venta" (mint soup cures the stomach), she intoned, swirling an egg into the soup to thicken it. Then she splashed in some olive oil. *Basta.* Maybe it was the taste of the good country loaf or the special aroma of the freshly pressed oil. Or was it the fact that the egg had been laid just that morning? No matter

Top left: Juan Mari Arzak and his daughter Elena in the kitchen of their three-star Restaurante Arzak in San Sebastián. *Top right:* Peppers, here drying on a string, will add a touch of color and flavor to many Spanish dishes. *Bottom left:* Cadaques, the idyllic whitewashed resort on Catalonia's Costa Brava, is a longtime favorite vacation spot for artists. *Bottom right:* Crusty bread, fresh every day, makes just the right accompaniment to soup.

which, four simple ingredients added up to one of the most deliciously nourishing things I can remember—a taste I have never been able to replicate in my own kitchen. Spanish cuisine is full of such miracles.

The frugal Mediterranean combination of bread and water—often replaced these days by light stock or broth—still forms the basis for many traditional Spanish soups. We're talking about classic Castilian garlic soup with its dusky additions of cured ham and *pimentón.* Or the delicious Extremaduran tomato soup poured over thick, toasted bread slices and unexpectedly garnished with figs. Or the Catalan wild mushroom soup to which bread pureed with the broth lends a special smooth creaminess. And gazpacho? Though most Americans associate it with the New World, tomato, bread, olive oil, and vinegar are actually the only constant ingredients in the endless regional permutations of this Andalusian summer refresher.

Rich, hearty potages that veer into stews are another popular soup genre. These are likely to be thickened with potatoes or legumes instead of bread and flavored with *hueso añejo* (a smoky ham bone) and sausages or, during Lent, bacalao. Not to forget the coastal fishermen's soups, the velvety vegetable and legume purees, or the strong consommé that normally precedes a *cocido* (boiled dinner). Rustic they might be, but traditional Spanish soups are rarely stodgy or bland, deriving their earthy sophistication from a layering of flavors: a fruity swirl of olive oil, a green flourish of parsley, a mortar-pounded mixture of fried garlic, nuts, and yes, bread.

As you move into the *nueva cocina* territory, soups become vibrant, smooth, and adventurous. Often you savor them topped with foam or a crunchy contrasting garnish. Or they'll be deconstructed into two textures or temperatures and served in a shot glass as an *aperetivo.* A scoop of saffron ice cream and some crisp fried basil turn a simple squash puree into something unexpected and magical. A tomato gazpacho is transformed into a refreshing sorbet enlivened with a tart-sweet reduction of vinegar. Whether it's a hearty slurp of tradition or a dainty sip of innovation, there's no better way to start a meal than with a Spanish soup.

HOT SOUPS

ROASTED SQUASH SOUP WITH SAFFRON ICE CREAM

SOPA DE CALABAZA ASADA CON HELADO DE AZAFRAN

The Roig Robí restaurant in Barcelona has a devoted clientele of intellectuals and artists (one of Spain's greatest modern artists, Antoni Tàpies, designed its menu). Under the watchful eyes of Mercé Navarro and Inma Crosas, a mother and daughter team who cook like angels, the food, for all its modern touches, remains deeply soulful and utterly Catalan. Their soup is a case in point. A velvety, satisfying pumpkin puree, it comes with an imaginative garnish of saffron ice cream and deep-fried basil—a truly arresting contrast of hot and cold, smooth and crisp, sweet and savory. Catalan pumpkins have a delicious sweet, dense flesh; here a mixture of butternut squash and sweet potatoes serves as a good substitute. Roig Robí makes its own saffron ice cream, but stirring some saffron-steeped milk into store-bought vanilla ice cream does the trick easily. Ladle the soup into beautiful glass or stark white bowls and prepare for compliments.

1 medium-size butternut squash (2 to 2 1/2 pounds), cut in half lengthwise
Fragrant extra-virgin olive oil
2 medium-size sweet potatoes (about 1 pound), scrubbed
1 small pinch of saffron, pulverized in a mortar
2 tablespoons hot milk
About 1 cup best-quality vanilla ice cream
10 to 12 large unblemished basil leaves, patted dry (see Note)
1 medium-size onion, finely chopped
2 to 3 teaspoons finely grated orange zest
4 cups chicken stock or broth, or more if needed
1/3 cup heavy (whipping) cream
Course salt (kosher or sea) and freshly ground black pepper

1. Preheat the oven to 400°F.

2. Scrape the seeds from the squash, brush the cut side with a little olive oil, and set it on a baking sheet lined with aluminum foil, cut side down. Wrap the sweet potatoes individually in aluminum foil and place them on the same baking sheet. Bake the squash and sweet potatoes until they feel completely tender when pierced with a skewer, about 1¼ hours.

3. While the vegetables bake, prepare the ice cream: Steep the saffron in the hot milk for 15 minutes, then let cool completely. Place the ice cream in a bowl and let stand until just soft enough to stir, 5 to 10 minutes. Stir the saffron milk in gently but thoroughly, cover the bowl with plastic wrap, and refreeze the ice cream until firm, 20 to 30 minutes.

4. Make the fried basil: Pour olive oil to a depth of 1 inch in a small, deep skillet. Heat it over medium heat to 360°F; when hot, a basil leaf dropped in the oil will sizzle on contact. Deep-fry the basil leaves 3 or 4 at a time until crisp, about 45 seconds, transferring them with a slotted spoon to drain on paper towels.

5. Let the squash and sweet potatoes cool until manageable. Remove and discard the squash skin and any browned bits. Peel the sweet potatoes. Cut the vegetables into medium-size chunks.

6. Heat 1½ tablespoons olive oil in a soup pot over low heat. Add the onion and orange zest and cook until soft but not browned, 5 to 7 minutes. Stir in the baked squash and sweet potatoes and the chicken stock and cook, partially covered, until the vegetables almost disintegrate, about 10 minutes, shaking the pot occasionally. Working in 2 or 3 batches, puree the soup in a blender until completely smooth, adding a little more chicken stock to each batch if it seems too thick. Return the soup to the pot, add the cream, and cook until heated through, about 5 minutes. Season with salt and pepper to taste.

7. To serve, let the saffron ice cream soften at room temperature for 2 to 3 minutes. Ladle the soup into bowls or tumblers, top each with a small serving scoop of ice cream (I use a melon baller for this), and top the ice cream with a fried basil leaf. Drizzle a little olive oil over each portion and serve immediately. **SERVES 8**

NOTE: The basil must be completely dry before frying, otherwise the olive oil will splatter like mad. Although you will only need 8 basil leaves, fry extra in case any crumble during frying.

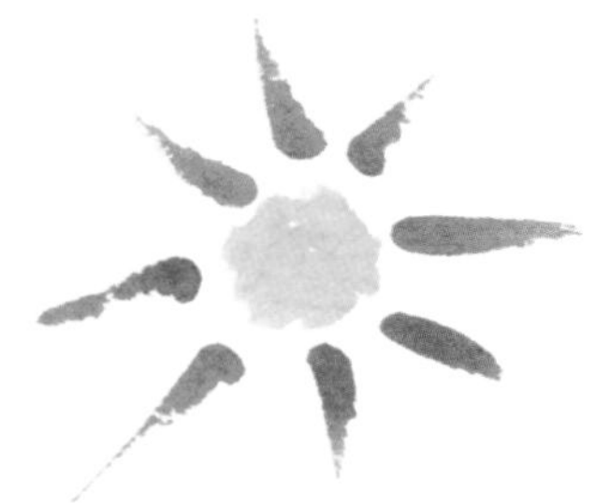

TOMATO AND BREAD SOUP WITH FRESH FIGS

SOPA DE TOMATE CON HIGOS

Bread and tomato soups are a Mediterranean staple—think, for instance, of the Tuscan *pappa al pomodoro.* What makes this *sopa* from Extremadura unique is the way it is eaten: topped with fresh sliced figs or green grapes. This recipe is from Jarandilla de la Vera, an extraordinarily fertile section of northern Extremadura renowned for its fruit, which the locals happily mix into savory dishes such as soups and salads. Use the ripest tomatoes you can find, preferably ones from the farmers' market, and make sure they are completely soft and cooked down before adding the stock. If you don't have fresh figs, you can serve the soup with sliced green grapes instead.

- 1/4 cup fragrant extra-virgin olive oil, plus more for serving
- 1 medium-size onion, finely chopped
- 1 medium-size green bell pepper, cored, seeded, and diced
- 4 large garlic cloves, finely chopped
- 2 pounds ripe, fleshy tomatoes, such as beefsteak or very ripe plum tomatoes, peeled and chopped
- 1 teaspoon smoked sweet Spanish paprika
- 2 to 2 1/2 cups chicken stock or broth, or vegetable broth
- 1 medium-size pinch of sugar, or more if needed
- 1 dash of red wine vinegar, or more if needed
- 1 tablespoon chopped fresh oregano
- 3/4 teaspoon cumin seeds
- 6 black peppercorns
- 1 large pinch of coarse salt (kosher or sea), or more if needed
- 3 slices (1/2 inch thick) dense country bread from a large round loaf, very lightly toasted
- 4 green or purple figs, cut in half vertically and sliced, or 2/3 cup sliced seedless green grapes

1. Place the olive oil in a heavy 4-quart saucepan, preferably nonstick, and heat over medium heat. Add the onion and cook, stirring, until softened, 2 to 3 minutes. Add the green pepper, cover the pan, and reduce the heat to low. Cook the vegetables until soft, about 10 minutes, stirring occasionally. Stir in half of the garlic and cook for another minute.

2. Stir the tomatoes into the vegetable mixture, increase the heat to medium-high, and cook, stirring occasionally, until the tomatoes reduce to a thick puree, 25 to 30 minutes, adjusting the heat so that the tomatoes don't stick to the bottom of the pan. Add the paprika and 2 cups of the chicken stock, stir to mix, then let come just to a simmer; don't let the soup boil. Add the sugar and vinegar and simmer for 6 to 8 minutes, skimming if necessary. If the soup seems a little too thick, add the remaining ½ cup chicken stock.

3. While the soup is cooking, place the remaining garlic and the oregano, cumin seeds, peppercorns, and salt in a mortar and, using a pestle, mash them into a paste. Add a little liquid from the soup to the mortar to rinse it out, then stir the contents into the soup. Let the soup cook until the flavors blend, 2 to 3 minutes, then taste for seasoning, adding more sugar, vinegar, and salt as necessary. Turn the heat off and let the soup cool for about 10 minutes.

4. To serve, cut the slices of bread in half. Place each half bread slice in a soup bowl and ladle the soup over it. Top each serving of soup with a few fig slices and drizzle a little olive oil over them. **SERVES 6**

ROASTED VEGETABLE SOUP WITH ANCHOVY TOASTS

CREMA DE HORTALIZAS ASADAS CON ANCHOAS

In this recipe, from Barcelona chef Xavier Franco, roasted vegetables are blended into a delicious cream and eaten warm or at room temperature with a garnish of slivered olives and garlicky anchovy toasts. Spanish red peppers and even onions have an almost candied sweetness not found in their American counterparts. To approximate the flavor, I add a bit of sugar and vinegar to the soup, not for a sweet-sour effect but to heighten the taste.

- 6 medium-size ripe fleshy red bell peppers, cored, seeded, and cut in half lengthwise
- 3 medium-size ripe tomatoes, cut in half
- 8 large garlic cloves, peeled, plus 2 garlic cloves crushed with a garlic press
- 6 tablespoons fragrant extra-virgin olive oil
- 1 medium-size eggplant, pricked in several places with the tip of a knife
- 1 small red onion, cut into thick wedges
- 3 cups hot chicken stock or broth, or more if needed
- Coarse salt (kosher or sea) and freshly ground black pepper
- 1 teaspoon best-quality red wine vinegar or sherry vinegar, preferably aged, or more to taste
- 1 large pinch of sugar, or more to taste
- 12 slices (1/2 inch thick) from a dense, skinny baguette
- 6 best-quality oil-packed anchovy fillets, drained
- 1/4 cup slivered pitted black olives, such as niçoise or cured green olives
- 2 to 3 tablespoons minced fresh flat-leaf parsley

1. Preheat the oven to 425°F.

2. Place the red peppers, tomatoes, and 8 whole cloves of garlic in a large bowl, add 1 tablespoon of the olive oil, and toss to coat. Arrange the vegetables on a large, well-oiled baking sheet, placing tomatoes and peppers skin side up. Place the eggplant on another well-oiled baking sheet. Wrap the onion wedges in aluminum foil and place them on the baking sheet with the eggplant. Bake the vegetables until the peppers and tomatoes are very tender, about 30 minutes, switching the position of the baking sheets halfway through. Remove the baking sheet with the peppers, tomatoes, and garlic from the oven and continue to bake the eggplant and onion until tender, about 10 minutes longer. Leave the oven on.

3. While the eggplant finishes baking, place the peppers in a bowl, cover it with plastic wrap, and let stand. When the eggplant and onion have finished baking, peel the peppers, then scoop out the pulp from the eggplant and discard the skin. Coarsely chop all the vegetables. Working in three batches, puree the vegetables in a blender until medium-fine, adding 1 cup chicken stock per batch. Transfer the pureed vegetables to a large bowl, adding a little more stock if the soup seems too thick. Season the soup with salt, black pepper, vinegar, and sugar to taste. Let the soup cool slightly while you prepare the anchovy toasts.

4. Place the bread slices on a baking sheet and bake until lightly golden and slightly crisp, 3 to 4 minutes per side.

5. Place the anchovies in a mortar or a small bowl and, using the pestle or the back of a wooden spoon, mash them well. Stir in the 2 crushed garlic cloves and whisk in 3 tablespoons of the olive oil. Spread the anchovy mixture on the toasted bread.

6. To serve, ladle the soup into serving bowls and swirl some of the remaining 2 tablespoons of olive oil into each serving. Sprinkle the olives and parsley over the soup, then top each serving with 2 anchovy toasts. **SERVES 6**

CASTILIAN GARLIC SOUP

SOPA DE AJO

What gazpacho is to Andalusia, *sopa de ajo* is to the plains of Castile and La Mancha—a dish that started life as a poor man's porridge but that's gone on to achieve status as the region's gastronomic symbol. Garlic, bread, smoky paprika, *jamón,* poached egg, and olive oil (which has replaced the more traditional lard) team up to produce a boldly flavored and quintessentially Spanish potage filling enough for a one-bowl meal.

Tradition dictates that the soup be presented in individual earthenware *cazuelas*; if you don't have these, use nicely rustic ceramic bowls or crocks.

6 tablespoons fragrant extra-virgin olive oil, or more if needed
10 medium-size garlic cloves, 6 sliced and 4 crushed with a garlic press
1 piece (4 ounces) serrano ham or prosciutto, finely diced
3 slices (1/2 inch thick) day-old dense country bread without crusts, from a medium-size round loaf, cut into 1 1/2-inch squares
2 teaspoons smoked sweet Spanish paprika
5 cups chicken stock or broth
Coarse salt (kosher or sea) and freshly ground black pepper
4 Poached Eggs (page 156); see Note
4 teaspoons finely minced fresh flat-leaf parsley (optional), for garnish

1. Heat the olive oil in a heavy 4-quart saucepan over low heat. Add the sliced garlic and the ham and cook, stirring, until the garlic is very fragrant but not browned, 4 to 5 minutes. Add the bread and cook, stirring to coat the bread with oil, 2 to 3 minutes, adding a little more olive oil if the pan looks dry. Off the heat, sprinkle in the paprika, and toss the bread well to coat it evenly. Return the pan to the heat, add the stock, increase the heat to medium, and simmer until the bread swells but still holds its shape, about 7 minutes.

2. Season the soup with salt and pepper to taste, add the crushed garlic, and cook for 1 minute. Ladle the soup into four warmed soup crocks or ceramic bowls. Using a slotted spoon, transfer a poached egg to each soup bowl and garnish with parsley, if desired. Serve at once. To eat, break the poached egg, stirring the yolk into the soup; the egg will cook slightly from the heat and thicken the broth. **SERVES 4**

NOTE: Classically, the eggs are poached right in the soup, but they can be poached ahead of time. Once added to the soup they will warm through from the heat of the broth. In some versions the eggs are fried or broken into the soup crocks and baked. And there are practical home cooks who suggest breaking an egg into each serving of soup and microwaving it for about 1¼ minutes.

Castroeriz, Burgos, lies along the St. James' Way, one of Europe's most important pilgrimage routes.

GARBANZO CREAM WITH HAM CRACKLINGS

CREMA DE GARBANZOS CON JAMON CRUJIENTE

Contemporary chefs all over Spain are enamored with chickpea purees, topping the humble legume with such luxury stuff as foie gras, *cigalas* (langoustines), sautéed fresh porcini mushrooms, or more traditionally, coins of fried blood sausage. While Spanish chickpeas are creamy and nutty, the dried legumes found in America are usually not much of an improvement on the canned stuff. So, I offer a quick version of the soup, using canned garbanzos, which are greatly improved by a simmer in a bacon-infused broth. The smooth, earthy puree makes an ideal backdrop for any number of garnishes, such as the smoky *pimentón*-infused oil and crisped diced *jamón* offered here. You can also top the soup with parsley oil (its color will contrast nicely with that of the paprika oil), crisp-fried chorizo slices, small piles of sautéed wild mushrooms, or shrimp stir-fried with garlic and olive oil. The soup is equally great as a sit-down first course or as a kind of predinner "shot," passed around in tumblers or espresso cups.

Garbanzo Cream with Ham Cracklings

5 tablespoons fragrant extra-virgin olive oil
1 heaping teaspoon smoked sweet Spanish paprika
1 medium-size onion, chopped
1 medium-size carrot, diced
1 small leek, white part only, well rinsed and sliced
3 medium-size garlic cloves, chopped
3 cups canned chickpeas (garbanzo beans; from two 15-ounce cans), plus 1 cup of their liquid
2 cups chicken stock or broth, or more if needed
1 piece (6 to 8 ounces) smoky slab bacon
Coarse salt (kosher or sea)
1 piece (2 ounces) serrano ham or prosciutto, finely diced
Parsley Oil (optional; page 353)
2 tablespoons minced fresh flat-leaf parsley
Tiny Olive Oil Croutons (optional; page 90)

1. Make the paprika oil: Heat ¼ cup of the olive oil in a very small skillet or saucepan over low heat. Remove the pan from the heat, stir in the paprika, and let the oil infuse for 30 to 45 minutes. When ready to use, spoon off the oil into a small bowl, leaving the paprika in the skillet. You'll have more oil than you need for the garbanzo soup; set the rest aside for drizzling on other dishes.

2. Heat the remaining 1 tablespoon olive oil in a heavy, medium-size soup pot over medium-low heat. Add the onion, carrot, leek, and garlic and cook, stirring, for 2 to 3 minutes. Cover the pot and cook the vegetables until softened but not browned, 5 to 7 minutes. Add the chickpeas and their liquid, the chicken stock, and bacon and bring to a boil, skimming. Cover the pot, reduce the heat to very low, and cook for 30 minutes.

3. Remove the pot from the heat and let the soup stand, covered, for 10 minutes. Remove and discard the bacon or save for another use. Working in two batches, puree the soup in a blender until very

PIMENTON: SPAIN'S SMOKY ESSENCE

La Chinata *pimentón* was a study in different shades of red: the vast rust-colored stacks of dried peppers, the bright-ocher pyramids of ground paprika, the shiny dark-crimson tins in which the product is packaged. Even the workers in their red jumpsuits resembled peppers. My friend Gabriela brought me to La Chinata so I could learn more about the production of one of the most essential Spanish ingredients, *pimentón de la Vera.* This indispensable paprika lends a reddish hue to myriad Spanish regional stews, imparts an earthy smokiness to chorizo, and decorates the classic Galician octopus dish, *pulpo a feira.* The center of its production is the extraordinarily fertile La Vera, a section of the Cáceres province in the western Spanish region of Extremadura.

Gabriela's friend, the *pimentón* expert Julia Gonzales Serrano, whisked us around the factory reciting pepper lore. In 1493, Columbus brought capsicum peppers back from his second American voyage. Local legend holds that he presented them along with other edible curiosities to the Catholic monarchs Isabella and Ferdinand at the Guadalupe monastery not far from La Chinata. The peppers, Julia declared, were an instant hit with the monks, who began spreading the word to brothers at other monasteries in the region. It was the monks of the nearby Yuste monastery who are credited with inventing the technique of drying and smoking the pimientos that now grow in La Vera in such profusion.

Sifting through a heap of the smooth smoky-red powder, Julia explained what makes the local paprika so unique (*pimentón de la Vera* was the world's first pepper to be awarded denomination of origin status). The process begins with unblemished, vine-ripened fruit that's harvested by hand in the fall. Next comes the laborious task of drying the peppers over smoldering oak or holm oak for up to two weeks, during which time they are hand turned every twenty-four hours. This slow, patient smoking is the secret to *pimentón's* unmistakable tangy, leathery punch and aroma.

Once the smoked peppers arrive at the mills, such as those of La Chinata, they are sorted into three types: *dulce* (sweet), *agridulce* (bittersweet), or *picante* (hot). Last but not least, the peppers are ground. Whereas as other paprikas might get no more than a quick whizz, *pimentón de la Vera* is painstakingly pulverized for eight to nine hours in temperature-controlled stone mills in a process specially engineered to bring out the peppers' natural flavors and pigments. That's how *pimentón* gets its velvety, powdery texture that dissolves so easily in soups and stews. La Chinata—which incidentally makes La Vera's most prized *pimentón*—produces two-hundred tons of paprika per year. In Spain there's no such thing as too much *pimentón.*

smooth, then return to the pot, adding a little more chicken stock if you'd like the soup to be thinner. Season with salt to taste.

4. Place a heavy, medium-size skillet over medium-high heat (do not use a nonstick skillet) and heat until very hot, about 1 minute. Add the ham and cook (without oil), stirring, until it turns crisp, about 3 minutes. (If the ham bits begin to pop out of the skillet, cover it.) Transfer the ham to a bowl and let stand for 5 minutes; it will crisp further.

5. Reheat the soup, if necessary, then ladle it into soup plates or wide tumblers. Drizzle the paprika oil decoratively over the soup and sprinkle the crisp ham, parsley, and Parsley Oil and croutons, if using, on top. Serve at once. **SERVES 6**

ROSA'S WILD MUSHROOM SOUP WITH GARLIC SHOOTS

SOPA DE SETAS CON AJOS TIERNOS

Rosa Vilaseca, the accomplished Catalan country cook who gave me the recipe for Rosa's Roast Chicken and Wild Mushroom Casserole with Red Wine (see page 273), contributed this equally hearty mushroom soup. In the rustic tradition followed pretty much all over Spain, the soup is thickened with bread (just like Andalusian gazpacho). Both the *picada* of crushed garlic and almonds and the use of garlic shoots are characteristic of Catalan cooking. Look for garlic shoots at farmers' markets or Chinese supermarkets. If you don't find them, you can substitute julienned scallions (use the white and some of the green parts) or julienned leeks, plus three cloves of minced garlic (in addition to the garlic that's in the *picada*). Cream is not part of Rosa's recipe and has little use in the Catalan kitchen, but add it if you'd like to lighten the color of the soup. Because the soup is so rich and bosky tasting, I like to pass small portions of it before dinner in small, pretty glasses.

6 cups chicken stock or broth, or more if needed
1/2 ounce dried porcini mushrooms
3 tablespoons light olive oil
1 medium-size onion, finely chopped
4 to 6 garlic shoots, trimmed and chopped
2 tablespoons (1/4 stick) unsalted butter, or more if needed, cut into small pieces
12 ounces assorted delicate fresh mushrooms (chanterelles, oysters, morels, and/or stemmed shiitakes), wiped clean and chopped
1 large ripe tomato, cut in half and grated on a box grater, skin discarded
Coarse salt (kosher or sea) and freshly ground black pepper
2 slices (1/2 inch thick) day-old country bread from a medium-size round loaf, crusts removed
1/3 cup heavy cream (optional)
12 to 14 blanched almonds, toasted (see page 267) and chopped
3 medium-size garlic cloves, chopped
2 tablespoons chopped fresh flat-leaf parsley
Minced fresh chives, for garnish

1. Place 1 cup of the chicken stock in a small microwave-safe bowl and heat in the microwave on high power for 2 minutes. Add the porcini and soak until softened, about 30 minutes. Drain the porcini in a small sieve lined with a coffee filter or cheesecloth, reserving the soaking liquid. Finely chop the porcini.

Wild mushrooms make for an attractive window display.

SERVE SOUP RIGHT

The most important soup lesson I gleaned from Spain's modern restaurants had to do with presentation. There's nothing wrong with a rustic bowl or an earthenware *cazuela,* especially for a family lunch. But even the simplest potage acquires an aura of sophistication when ladled into a cool tumbler, a cappuccino cup, a minimalist white or glass bowl, or a dish with an unusual shape. My own favorites include triangular and jellyfish-shaped white bowls (spoils from a Crate & Barrel sale) and the wide, stubby wine and cider glasses that are available cheaply at every *ferretería* (hardware store) in Spain.

Portions also matter. Rather than overwhelm guests with large servings, why not pass soup around in shot or martini glasses, or espresso cups, as a predinner teaser? Squat glass votive candle holders are also great for the job. Served this way, and sprinkled with a few interesting garnishes, even a plain vegetable puree becomes a showstopper.

2. Heat the olive oil in a heavy-bottomed soup pot over medium-low heat. Add the onion, garlic shoots, and the chopped porcini and cook until the onion is soft but not browned, 5 to 7 minutes. Add the butter and the fresh mushrooms and cook, stirring, until the mushrooms cook down and release their liquid, about 5 minutes, adding a little more butter if the pot looks dry. Add the tomato and cook until thickened and reduced, 5 to 7 minutes more. Stir in the remaining 5 cups chicken stock and bring to a simmer. Reduce the heat to low, cover the pot, and simmer the soup for about 30 minutes, occasionally skimming the fat off the top. Add salt and pepper to taste.

3. Turn off the heat, add the bread to the soup, and let it soak for 10 minutes. Working in batches, coarsely puree the soup in a blender and return it to the pot. If the soup seems too thick, add a little more stock. Stir in the cream, if using.

4. Place the almonds, garlic, and parsley in a mini food processor and pulse until ground. Rinse out the processor bowl with a little of the soup, then stir the contents into the soup pot. Let the soup come to a simmer over low heat and cook until warmed through, 2 to 3 minutes. Ladle the soup into bowls and serve with chives sprinkled on top. **SERVES 6**

MORNING-AFTER VEGETABLE AND SAUSAGE SOUP

POTAJE DE VERDURAS

Early in the morning, before customers descend on Barcelona's La Boqueria market, a crowd of vendors and chefs gathers around the counter of Bar Pinotxo for breakfast. Some quickly scarf down a tostada rubbed with tomatoes and olive oil; others grab one of the vegetable *tortillas* (omelets) arrayed on the counter. But you always know the patrons who are recovering from a night out on the town—they are the ones fortifying themselves with Pinotxo's thick vegetable soup with sausage and lacing their coffee with brandy or strong anisette.

Of course, you don't have to be hungover to love this soup loaded with La Boqueria's beautiful vegetables. Its taste is somewhat reminiscent of an Italian minestrone, but with such Catalan flavorings as *sofrito* of leeks, tomatoes, and garlic; blood sausage, and chickpeas. If you can't find or don't like blood sausage, use chorizo or a good, smoky kielbasa or linguica. Sometimes the cook at Pinotxo also adds *fideo* noodles. Since the soup's flavor improves on standing, I recommend making it a day ahead. If it thickens too much, thin it out with some water or broth.

- 2 tablespoons olive oil
- 1 large leek, white part only, chopped
- 4 medium-size garlic cloves, minced
- 2 medium-size tomatoes, cut in half and grated on a box grater, skin discarded
- 3 quarts (12 cups) chicken stock or broth, or more if needed
- 2 medium-size carrots, cut into medium-size dice
- 8 ounces diced pumpkin or yellow squash
- 8 ounces diced daikon radish or turnip
- 2 small zucchini, diced
- 2 medium-size all-purpose boiling potatoes, diced
- 4 loosely packed cups chopped spinach or Swiss chard
- 6 ounces morcilla or other blood sausage or sweet Spanish-style chorizo, or 8 ounces kielbasa or linguica
- 1 can (15 ounces) chickpeas (garbanzo beans), drained
- 1 can (15 ounces) small white beans, drained
- 1 piece (3 to 4 ounces) serrano ham, prosciutto, or smoky boiled ham, diced
- Coarse salt (kosher or sea) and freshly ground black pepper
- 1/4 cup minced fresh flat-leaf parsley, for garnish

1. Heat the olive oil in a 5-quart soup pot over medium-low heat. Add the leek and garlic and cook until the leek softens, about 5 minutes. Add the tomatoes and cook, stirring occasionally, until thickened and reduced, about 5 minutes. Add the chicken stock, increase the heat to medium-high, and bring to a simmer. Skim thoroughly and add the carrots, pumpkin, daikon, and zucchini. Reduce the heat to medium-low and simmer, covered, to soften the vegetables, 20 minutes. Add the potatoes and spinach, bring the liquid back to a simmer, skim, and cook, partially covered, to soften the potatoes, another 15 minutes.

2. Blanch the sausage in boiling water for 2 minutes, then drain and slice it. (If you are using kielbasa or linguica, there's no need to blanch it.) Add the sausage to the soup along with the chickpeas, beans, and ham. Return the soup to a simmer and skim it. Continue cooking, partially covered, until some of the vegetables are falling apart and the flavors have melded, about 20 minutes longer. Skim the soup one final time, if necessary. Add a little more stock if the soup seems too thick and stir it vigorously if you'd like the texture to be creamier. Season with salt and pepper to taste. Let the soup rest for about 10 minutes, then serve it with the parsley sprinkled on top. **SERVES 8 TO 10**

POTATO SOUP WITH FRIED ALMONDS

SOPA DE PATATAS Y ALMENDRAS

This easy recipe was passed on to me by Laura Lorca, the niece of the great Spanish poet Federico García Lorca. Laura, who directs the Lorca foundation in Granada, told me, "I know it's a dish Federico would have loved, because it's so Andalusian." In its most frugal version, Laura explained, this popular soup from Granada is just fried almonds, garlic, potatoes, and water. To enrich it one can add chicken stock and/or *jamón*—which I've done here. It's one of those elemental dishes that fairly screams Spain.

- 1 1/2 pounds Yukon Gold potatoes
- 1/4 cup extra-virgin olive oil
- 1/2 cup whole blanched almonds
- 6 large garlic cloves, peeled
- 1/3 cup (about 2 ounces) finely diced serrano ham or prosciutto
- 4 cups chicken stock or broth, or more if needed
- Coarse salt (kosher or sea) and freshly ground black pepper
- 1 medium-size pinch of saffron, pulverized in a mortar
- 2 teaspoons sherry vinegar, preferably aged, or more to taste
- 2 tablespoons minced fresh flat-leaf parsley
- Dense country bread, for serving

1. Cut the potatoes into irregular chunks by inserting the tip of a small, sharp knife into a potato and twisting it until a 1½-inch chunk comes out. Repeat until the entire potato is cut up, then continue with the remaining potatoes; set aside.

2. Heat the olive oil in a heavy 3-quart saucepan over medium heat. Add the almonds and garlic and cook, stirring, until golden, 4 to 5 minutes, adjusting the heat so the oil doesn't burn. Using a slotted spoon, transfer the almonds and garlic to a bowl. Add the ham to the pan and stir for 1 minute. Add the potatoes and cook, stirring, for another minute. Add the chicken stock and bring to a boil, skimming. Reduce the heat to medium-low and simmer the soup.

3. Meanwhile, place the almond and garlic mixture in a mini food processor and grind it. If you like almond bits in your soup, grind the mixture somewhat coarsely; otherwise, grind it fine. Add all but about 2 tablespoons of the ground nut mixture to the saucepan with the potatoes. Season with salt and pepper to taste.

4. Steep the saffron in a few tablespoons of the simmering soup for 2 minutes, then add it to the pan. Simmer the soup, partially covered, until about half of the potatoes have disintegrated, about 35 minutes. Skim the soup a couple of times as it cooks and add a little more chicken stock if the soup seems too thick.

5. When ready to serve, check the texture of the soup. If you'd like it creamier, break up some of the potatoes with a sturdy spoon; if you'd like it thinner, add a little more chicken stock. Add 2 teaspoons vinegar to the remaining 2 tablespoons ground almond mixture and stir it into the soup. Add the parsley and cook for another minute. Taste for seasoning, adding a little more vinegar if necessary. Serve the soup with bread. **SERVES 4**

FENNEL, POTATO, AND MUSSEL SOUP

CREMA DE HINOJO Y PATATAS CON MEJILLONES

The recipe for this elegant Catalan soup is adapted from one created by the Michelin three-star chef Santi Santamaría of El Racó de Can Fabes restaurant. To me, its aromas recall blissful walks in the hills above Costa Brava, with the scents of wild fennel and the sea. The velvety fennel cream is delicious on its own, but what really transforms the soup are the simple but expressive finishing touches: a swirl of delicate olive oil, the tiny croutons, and the fragrant accent of mint. Rather than serve big portions in bowls, I like passing small glasses of the soup before dinner. Served this way, it makes a perfect start to a festive occasion, such as a Thanksgiving or Christmas dinner party.

- 7 cups Fish Stock (page 108), or 4 cups bottled clam juice diluted with 3 cups water
- 1 cup dry white wine
- 1 bay leaf
- 2 pounds mussels, scrubbed well and debearded right before cooking
- 2 tablespoons fragrant extra-virgin olive oil, plus more for drizzling
- 1 small onion, finely chopped
- 2 medium-size garlic cloves, sliced
- 2 medium-size fennel bulbs, trimmed (set aside some fronds for garnish) and coarsely chopped
- 1 pound Yukon Gold potatoes, peeled and diced
- Coarse salt (kosher or sea) and freshly ground white pepper
- Tiny Olive Oil Croutons (page 90), for garnish
- Finely slivered fresh mint, for garnish

1. Place the fish stock, wine, and bay leaf in a large pot and bring to a boil over medium-high heat. Reduce the heat to medium-low and simmer the broth for about 10 minutes. Add the mussels and increase the heat to high. Cover the pot and cook until the mussels open, about 5 minutes. Remove and discard any mussels that do not open. Strain the broth through a sieve lined with cheesecloth into a large bowl, setting aside the broth and the mussels separately and discarding the bay leaf. When the mussels are cool enough to handle, remove them from their shells and discard the shells. Place the mussels in a bowl, pour a little broth over them to keep them moist, cover with aluminum foil, and set aside until ready to use in Step 4. (Refrigerate the mussels if you are cooking them ahead of time. They'll keep for up to 6 hours.)

A secluded old stone house sits among the hills in Girona province, famous for its hearty cuisine.

TINY OLIVE OIL CROUTONS

When bread isn't used to thicken Spanish soup, it often finds its way into the bowl in the form of crisp croutons. You can always make croutons in the oven, but little ones fried in good olive oil are an especially good crunchy treat. To make the bread easier to cut into cubes, freeze it for twenty minutes. Stored in an airtight container, the croutons will keep for several days.

About 3 tablespoons extra-virgin olive oil, or 2 tablespoons (1/4 stick) butter, melted
1/3 cup 1/4-inch bread cubes

For fried croutons: Heat the extra-virgin olive oil in a small skillet over medium heat until a bread cube dropped in the oil sizzles on contact. Add the bread and cook, stirring, until crunchy and golden brown, 1 to 1 1/2 minutes. Using a slotted spoon, transfer the croutons to a plate lined with paper towels to drain.

For baked croutons: Preheat the oven to 350°F. Toss the bread cubes with 2 tablespoons extra-virgin olive oil or melted butter. Spread the bread cubes out on a rimmed baking sheet and bake until browned, 5 to 8 minutes.

2. Heat the 2 tablespoons olive oil in a clean pot over medium-low heat. Add the onion and garlic and cook, stirring occasionally, until translucent, about 5 minutes. Add the fennel and potatoes, cover, and cook until the fennel begins to soften, about 7 minutes, stirring occasionally. Set aside 1 cup of the strained broth and keep it hot. Add the remaining broth to the fennel mixture. Increase the heat to medium-high and bring to a boil, skimming. Cover the pot, reduce the heat to medium-low, and simmer until the potatoes and fennel are very tender, about 30 minutes.

3. When the vegetables have finished cooking, working in two batches, puree them in a blender together with their cooking liquid. Return the puree to the pot and season the soup with salt and white pepper to taste. Add enough of the remaining reserved broth to thin the mussel soup to the desired consistency (you may not need all of it). Reheat the soup, if necessary.

4. Ladle the soup into tumblers or bowls and add some mussels to each portion. Drizzle a little olive oil over each portion, add a few croutons, and sprinkle fennel fronds and mint on top. Serve at once. **SERVES 6 TO 8**

SEAFOOD SOUP WITH NOODLES

SOPA DE ALMEJAS Y GAMBAS CON FIDEOS

Quick to make, this excellent, easy soup is essentially a liquid version of *fideuá,* the Spanish-Mediterranean pasta paella studded with seafood. And like *fideuá,* it's delicious with a little garlic mayonnaise stirred into the broth. You can serve it as a one-dish meal (as you would a filling Asian noodle soup) or in smaller portions as a first course.

- 2 tablespoons extra-virgin olive oil
- 1 medium-size onion, finely chopped
- 4 medium-size garlic cloves, minced
- 1 small red bell pepper, cored, seeded, and cut into thin strips
- 1 small green bell pepper, cored, seeded, and cut into thin strips
- 1 cup canned crushed tomatoes with their juice
- 8 cups Fish Stock (page 108), or 5 cups bottled clam juice diluted with 3 cups water
- 1/4 cup dry white wine
- Coarse salt (kosher or sea) and freshly ground black pepper
- 1 medium-size pinch of saffron, pulverized in a mortar and steeped in 3 tablespoons very hot water
- 1 1/2 cups broken-up fideo noodles or thin spaghetti
- 2 dozen small clams, scrubbed well
- 6 ounces medium-size shrimp, shelled and deveined
- 3 tablespoons minced fresh flat-leaf parsley, for garnish
- Allioli (page 44), for serving

1. Heat the olive oil in a heavy 4-quart saucepan over medium-low heat. Add the onion and garlic and cook until the onion has softened, about 5 minutes. Add the red and green peppers and stir for 3 minutes. Cover the pan, reduce the heat to low, and cook until the peppers are very soft, about 7 minutes, adding a little water if the pan looks dry. Add the tomatoes, increase the heat to medium, and cook until the tomatoes thicken, about 5 minutes. Stir in 7 cups of the fish stock and the wine and bring to a simmer, skimming. Season with salt and black pepper to taste. Then add the saffron, reduce the heat to medium-low, and cook, uncovered, for 10 minutes, skimming a few times if necessary.

2. Increase the heat to medium-high, add the noodles, and cook until just al dente, about 5 minutes, adding some or all of the remaining 1 cup fish stock if the soup seems too thick. Add the clams, cover the pan, and cook for 2 minutes. Stir in the shrimp and continue to cook, covered, until the clams open and the shrimp turn pink, 2 to 3 minutes. Discard any unopened clams. Serve the soup with the parsley sprinkled on top and accompanied by the *allioli.* **SERVES 6 AS FIRST COURSE, 3 OR 4 AS A MAIN COURSE**

BASQUE LEEK, POTATO, AND COD CHOWDER

PORRUSALDA

Taking its name from the word *puerro,* or leek, *porrusalda* is a soup beloved by the Basques. And while theirs is a culture famous for its men-only gastronomic societies—where guys take turns cooking for one another—somehow *porrusalda* is a dish that always evokes mother or grandmother. Most renditions of *porrusalda* include bacalao, which gives it a savory smack and an unmistakeably Basque identity. However, because really good bacalao is so hard to come by, I use fresh cod and add slivers of salty smoked whitefish at serving time. The results are completely delicious. I thank Oscar Alberdi, the great bacalao specialist of Bilbao, for this recipe. Oscar's tip: Save the briny liquid from canned vegetables, such as artichokes or asparagus, and add it to soups instead of or along with stock.

1 piece cod fillet (about 1 pound), pin bones removed
4 tablespoons coarse salt (kosher or sea), plus more for seasoning the soup
3 tablespoons olive oil
4 medium-size leeks, white and pale green parts only, sliced 1/2 inch thick
1 small onion, chopped
4 medium-size garlic cloves, sliced
3/4 pound pumpkin or calabaza, cut into 1-inch cubes
3 medium-size Yukon Gold potatoes, peeled
3/4 cup dry white wine
6 cups Fish Stock (page 198), or 3 cups bottled clam juice diluted with 3 cups water or with liquid from canned vegetables
4 to 6 ounces sliced smoked whitefish or salmon, torn into slivers
Minced fresh flat-leaf parsley, for garnish
Fragrant extra-virgin olive oil, for drizzling

1. Rub the cod on both sides with the 4 tablespoons salt and let stand while you prepare the soup.

2. Heat the olive oil in a large, heavy soup pot over medium heat. Add the leeks, onion, garlic, and pumpkin, cover the pot, and cook, stirring occasionally, until the leeks are soft but not browned, about 10 minutes.

3. While the vegetables are cooking, cut the potatoes into irregular chunks by inserting the tip of a small, sharp knife into a potato and twisting it until a 1-inch chunk comes out. Repeat until the entire potato is cut up, then continue with the remaining potatoes, adding them to the pot with the leeks. Increase the heat to high, add the wine and fish stock, and bring to a gentle boil. Skim, reduce the heat to medium-low, cover the pot, and simmer the soup until the pumpkin and potatoes are very tender and beginning to disintegrate, about 25 minutes. Stir the soup vigorously with a wooden spoon to give it a creamy texture and season with salt to taste.

4. Rinse the cod under cold running water and cut it into 4 to 6 pieces. Add the cod to the soup and cook until it just begins to flake, about 5 minutes. Remove the soup from the heat and let stand, covered, for 5 to 7 minutes.

5. To serve, divide the slivered whitefish among soup bowls and ladle the soup over it. Sprinkle parsley on top, drizzle a little extra-virgin olive oil over the soup, and serve. **SERVES 4 TO 6**

VARIATIONS: If you'd like to make *porrusalda* with salt cod, soak the cod following the instructions on page 117, then tear it into pieces and add it to the soup in Step 4. Cook the soup over very low heat for about 10 minutes, then let it stand off the heat for 10 minutes before serving.

For a vegetarian version, omit the fish altogether and substitute vegetable stock for the fish stock.

GALICIAN WHITE BEAN SOUP

CALDO GALLEGO

Caldo gallego, a bracing, nourishing white bean potage, has become something of an ambassador of Spanish cuisine abroad, thanks to the scores of Galician immigrants who settled in the Americas in the early twentieth century. The greens customarily used for this soup are called *grelos* (a kind of turnip green)—one quintessential Galician sight is of old women carrying huge baskets of *grelos* on their heads as they return from the market. The consistency of the soup varies slightly from cook to cook, but it is usually brothy rather than thick. The traditional Galician version also includes *unto,* a lightly smoky lard, alas unavailable in the States.

1 large (1 pound) meaty smoked ham bone or smoked ham hock
1 veal shank (about 1 pound)
6 to 7 ounces smoky slab bacon
2 small onions
2 small carrots, peeled
Coarse salt (kosher or sea) and freshly ground black pepper
1 1/2 cups dried white beans, such as Great Northern or navy beans, soaked overnight in cold water and drained, or quick soaked (see page 309)
6 ounces sweet Spanish-style chorizo sausage
3 medium-size all-purpose boiling potatoes, cut into 1 1/2-inch cubes
3 cups shredded turnip greens, mustard greens, kale, or collard greens (from 1 bunch; see Note)
Fragrant extra-virgin olive oil, for drizzling

1. Place the ham bone, veal shank, bacon, onions, and carrots in a large soup pot and add 3 quarts (12 cups) water. Bring to a boil over high heat, skimming. Reduce the heat to low and season with salt and pepper to taste. Cover the pot and simmer until the veal shank is tender, about 1½ hours.

2. Remove the onions and carrots from the broth and discard them. Remove the ham bone, veal shank, and bacon. When cool enough to handle, pull the meat off the bones of the ham bone and the veal shank, removing and discarding the fat and gristle. Tear the meat into bite-size pieces and set aside. Discard the bones. Remove the extra fat from the bacon. Chop the bacon and set it aside with the ham and veal. (If you prefer not to use the bacon, simply discard it.)

3. Skim the fat from the broth. (The broth can be prepared up to 2 days ahead, chilled, and then degreased.) Add the beans and bring to a boil over medium-high heat, skimming. Cover the pot and simmer the soup until the beans are almost tender, about 1¼ hours.

4. Add the chorizo and potatoes and cook until the potatoes are almost tender, about 15 minutes. Add the greens and simmer for another 15 minutes. Add the reserved ham, veal, and bacon, if using, and cook just until heated through. If you want the soup to be a little thicker, spoon out a ladleful of beans and potatoes, mash them, and return them to the pot. Using a slotted spoon, remove the chorizo from the soup, slice it, and return it to the pot. Taste for seasoning, adding more salt and pepper as necessary. Ladle the soup into bowls, drizzle some olive oil on top, and serve. **SERVES 6 TO 8**

NOTE: If using turnip or mustard greens, blanch them in boiling water for 1 minute to remove the bitterness, then refresh them under cold running water (you do not need to do this if you are using kale or collard greens).

SILKY-TEXTURED CHICKEN SOUP WITH MINI MEATBALLS

SOPA DE MINI ALBONDIGAS DE TIA LOLA

Tía Lola is a wonderful cook (see box, facing page). Her chicken soup gets its silky texture from rice flour and is afloat with small, juicy meatballs. This is comfort food par excellence. The meatballs can be prepared ahead and the soup put together right before serving. Try to use good homemade chicken stock here, or failing that, chicken broth from a carton rather than a can.

2 slices white sandwich bread, crusts removed
1/2 cup milk
1/2 pound ground pork shoulder (preferably freshly ground and not too lean)
1 large egg white, beaten until frothy
3/4 teaspoon coarse salt (kosher or sea)
1 large pinch of white pepper
1 medium-size pinch of freshly grated nutmeg
Flour, for coating the meatballs
2 tablespoons olive oil, or more if needed
9 cups best-quality chicken stock
7 tablespoons rice flour (available at Asian groceries and some supermarkets)
Minced fresh chives or flat-leaf parsley, for garnish

STOCK OPTIONS

Let's face it: These days nobody makes chicken stock at home, what with so many decent options available in the supermarket. The same goes for Spain, where many a recipe given to me by home cooks included *un cubito de caldo* (a stock cube). When it comes to commercial chicken broths, what comes in cartons is better than the canned kind, which can taste rather metallic. Swanson is my favorite among the nationally available brands.

Although fish stock is always better strong and homemade (see the recipe on page 108), bottled clam juice diluted with water is an acceptable stand-in. So are the cartons of fish stock now available at many supermarkets and the frozen fish fumet (concentrated stock) carried by many fishmongers. I often doctor store-bought fish stock by boiling it down a little with sautéed shrimp shells and a few mussels and/or clams.

Most commercial beef stock tends to be yucky stuff, although cartons are definitely better than cans. The good news is that you'll hardly need it for recipes in this book.

1. Place the bread and milk in a bowl and let soak for 10 minutes. Drain, squeeze out some of the excess liquid, then finely crumble the bread.

2. Place the crumbled bread and the pork, half of the beaten egg white (discard the rest), salt, white pepper, and nutmeg in a bowl. Gently knead the pork mixture with your hands just until all the ingredients are thoroughly combined.

3. Spread a thin layer of flour on a large plate. Wet your hands, then break off a little piece of the pork mixture and shape it into a ball about cherry size. Repeat with the remaining pork mixture. Coat the meatballs very lightly in the flour, shaking off the

excess and gently tossing the meatballs between your hands to give them shape. As you work, place the coated meatballs on a small baking sheet.

4. Heat 1 tablespoon of the olive oil in a large, preferably nonstick skillet over medium heat. Add as many meatballs as will comfortably fit in the skillet and reduce the heat to low. Cook the meatballs until cooked through but not browned, about 5 minutes, shaking the skillet and turning the meatballs so they cook on all sides. Using a slotted spoon, transfer the cooked meatballs to a clean baking sheet lined with paper towels. Add the remaining tablespoon of olive oil to the skillet and cook the rest of the meatballs in the same fashion. (The meatballs can be prepared up to 1 day ahead and refrigerated, covered.)

5. Set aside about ⅓ cup of the chicken stock. Place the remaining stock in a 4-quart saucepan, bring it to a boil over high heat, and cook until reduced to 6 cups, about 25 minutes.

6. Place the rice flour in a bowl, add the reserved ⅓ cup chicken stock, and whisk until completely smooth. Slowly whisk the rice flour mixture into the reduced stock, whisking constantly for a few minutes to prevent lumps from forming. Let the soup thicken slightly, then gently stir in the meatballs and cook until warmed through, 1 to 2 minutes. Ladle the soup into bowls and serve garnished with chives or parsley. **SERVES 6 TO 8**

LUNCH WITH TIA LOLA

You are probably familiar with the cool, frosted bottles of Freixenet *cava*. Amazingly for a high-tech winery that produces the world's largest volume of sparkling wine, Freixenet remains resolutely family-run. And each day, the numerous members of the Ferrer clan gather for lunch around the table of Tía Lola—aka Dolores Ferrer. Everyone's favorite aunt, Tía Lola occupies spacious quarters above the bodega in the Catalan *cava*-producing town of Sant Sandurní d'Anoia. Now in her eighties, she is a woman who lives for her family and has three passions in life: cooking, religion, and soccer. The sort of domestic genius who spends an eternity making huge quantities of *sofregit* (Catalan *sofrito*), she peels and grinds almonds for *panellets* (marzipan-like confections) and puts up enough diced tomato *conservas* for the whole winter. The Freixenet workers pack these for her in elegant *cava* bottles. She also oversees the family *huerta,* which supplies her kitchen with green beans, cauliflower, and escarole. Hunched over her fancy wood-fired stove, Tía Lola listens to live soccer coverage on the radio, religiously keeping up with Catalonia's favorite sport so as to better relate to the boys in the family.

No one ever bothers to inform Tía Lola how many people will be coming to lunch. She just makes enough food for everyone: rich fish soups, plump meatballs smothered in homemade tomato sauce, the baked cheesy pasta that the kids love so much, and always a seafood paella on Thursdays. One day I had the pleasure to lunch with the Ferrers in Tía Lola's palatial dining room. On the menu that day was the entire family's favorite dish—a velvety-smooth chicken soup thickened with rice flour and topped with the tiniest, tastiest pork meatballs. The recipe begins on the facing page.

COLD SOUPS

CLASSIC GAZPACHO

GAZPACHO SEVILLANO

Here is the coral-pink Sevillian gazpacho that most foreigners are familiar with. Ripe, gorgeous tomatoes; excellent olive oil (preferably Andalusian hojiblanca); and a good aged (*reserva*) sherry vinegar make the soup unforgettable. It's as good as classic gazpacho gets! Although the original mortar-pounded gazpachos were probably rather coarse in texture, modern Spanish cooks like their soup silky smooth. I suggest using a food processor to puree the vegetables, then switching to a blender to achieve a velvety texture. OK, so you might have to rinse an extra utensil, but the payoff is worth it, and the blender sure beats the tedious traditional method of forcing the vegetables through a fine sieve.

Chilled Herbed Pea Soup (page 106),
Almond Gazpacho with Figs and Edible Flowers (page 103),
and Cherry and Beet Gazpacho (page 101)

FOR THE SOUP:

2 cups cubed day-old country bread, crusts removed
2 medium-size garlic cloves, chopped (see Note)
1 small pinch of cumin seeds or ground cumin
Coarse salt (kosher or sea)
3 pounds ripest, most flavorful tomatoes possible, seeded and chopped
2 small Kirby (pickling) cucumbers, peeled and chopped
1 large Italian (frying) pepper, cored, seeded, and chopped
1 medium-size red bell pepper, cored, seeded, and chopped
3 tablespoons chopped red onion
1/2 cup fragrant extra-virgin olive oil
1/2 cup chilled bottled spring water, or more as needed
3 tablespoons sherry vinegar, preferably aged, or more to taste

FOR THE GARNISHES:

Finely diced cucumber
Finely diced peeled Granny Smith apple
Finely diced slightly under-ripe tomato
Finely diced green bell pepper
Tiny Olive Oil Croutons (page 90)
Slivered small basil leaves

1. Place the bread in a bowl, add cold water to cover, and let soak for 5 to 10 minutes. Drain the bread and squeeze out the excess liquid.

GAZPACHO

If paella defines the Levante region and paprika-hued garlic soup represents Castilla–La Mancha, then gazpacho is the edible emblem of Andalusia. Although the smooth, zesty salad-soup is easy to love, I didn't appreciate its genius until one torrid June in Seville. By 11 A.M. the temperature had climbed to 105°F, the entire city was hiding indoors, and my body went into heat shock. Eating was simply out of the question. Except for gazpacho—filling yet light with an acidity that somehow combated the heat. I guzzled it down by the gallon, and to this day I refer to gazpacho as my "summer survival soup."

Most Americans imagine gazpacho as something rust-red, possibly chunky, and likely to contain celery and tomato juice. A real gazpacho is none of these things. True, there are plenty of versions based on tomatoes; yet to understand gazpacho is to remember that its defining ingredient is actually bread. That's what gives the soup body, and that creamy richness. Bread is what makes gazpacho into a meal rather than just a sip. And it was the foundation of the earliest gazpacho, pounded with water, vinegar, salt, garlic, and olive oil in a wooden tub called a *dornillo.* Although the arrival of the tomato from the New World revolutionized gazpacho, many regional versions still remain white, based on nuts or simply water, garlic, and bread.

The word *gazpacho* most likely derives from the Mozarabic *caspa,* which means fragments (referring to the broken-up bread), or from the Hebrew *gazaz* (to break into pieces). The origins of the dish itself could well date back to the Romans who roamed in antiquity what is now Andalusia and had a special fondness for bread gruels and vinegared foods. Though tomatoes and peppers were introduced to Spain in the 1500s, these "exotic" ingredients took several centuries to gain acceptance. Even as late as the mid-eighteenth century, Juan de la Mata, author of *Arte de Reposteria,* describes a gazpacho commonly called *capon de galera* as a frugal porridge of crustless bread, garlic, vinegar, oil, and anchovy bones.

Gazpacho truly came into its own in the early nineteenth century as the main summer sustenance of workers who labored in the sweltering Andalusian olive groves, cork forests, and wheat fields. The Sevillian food historian Juan Carlos Alonso describes how in the morning, before heading to work, the *campesino* packed his day's meal: a hide flask of olive oil and vinegar and another of water, a paper packet of salt, stale bread, plus a few vegetables and the indispensable mortar and pestle used for making his lunch. Gazpacho acquired cachet when Eugenia de Montijo, the Andalusian-born wife of Napoleon III, introduced it to France in the 1850s. Romantic poets and travelers who fell for the exotic allure of Andalusia spread the word further.

Today the map of Andalusia is a veritable quilt of gazpachos. The most familiar, creamy-pink version comes from Seville. A tomato-less *ajo blanco* (literally white garlic), an alluring Moorish cream based on ground almonds and served with a cooling accent of green grapes or apples, is the traditional gazpacho of Málaga. Also in Málaga one finds a soup called *gazpachuelo,* which is not a cold soup but a light mayonnaise-based seafood chowder. *Salmorejo,* the gazpacho of Córdoba, resembles its Sevillian cousin but is thicker and creamier. In some parts of the province eggs and fried bread are added.

And so it goes: the *gazpacho tostao* (with toasted bread and Seville orange juice) in Cañete la Real, near Ronda; gazpachos with fresh green fava beans in the province of Granada; the green gazpachos with lettuce and herbs enjoyed in the mountains of Huelava. And did I mention the hot, game-based gazpachos of La Mancha, the stewlike *gaspatxos* of Alicante, and the *nueva cocina* gazpachos—deconstructed into granitas, *sorbetes, espumas,* and gelées? The variations are endless and I invite you to experiment.

2. Place the garlic, cumin, and ½ teaspoon salt in a mortar and, using a pestle, mash them to a paste.

3. Place the tomatoes, cucumbers, Italian and red peppers, onion, soaked bread, and the garlic paste in a large bowl and toss to mix. Let stand for about 15 minutes. Working in two batches, place the vegetable mixture in a food processor and process until smooth, adding half of the olive oil to each batch. Once each batch is finished, puree it finely in a blender, then transfer it to a large mixing bowl.

4. When all the gazpacho has been pureed, whisk in the spring water and vinegar. It should have the consistency of a smoothie. Taste for seasoning, adding more salt and/or vinegar as necessary. Refrigerate the gazpacho, covered, until chilled, about 2 hours. Serve the soup in glass bowls or wineglasses with the garnishes. **SERVES 8**

NOTE: If making the gazpacho a day ahead, do not add the garlic more than 2 to 3 hours before serving, or it may overwhelm other flavors.

CREAMY CORDOBAN GAZPACHO

SALMOREJO

The Cordoban version of gazpacho, called *salmorejo,* is a cream with a texture that falls somewhere between a dip and a soup. It's a wonderful accompaniment for crudités or a pile of poached shrimp and is delicious as a sauce. But more often than not it is served in individual bowls, with the traditional garnishes, as a savory warm-weather cream to be eaten with a spoon.

- 2 1/2 cups cubed or torn day-old country bread, crusts removed
- 2 pounds ripest, most flavorful tomatoes, seeded and diced
- 1 medium-size Italian (frying) pepper, cored, seeded, and chopped
- 2 medium-size garlic cloves, chopped (see Note, this page)
- 1/2 cup fragrant extra-virgin olive oil, plus more for drizzling
- 1 1/2 tablespoons sherry vinegar, preferably aged, or more to taste
- Coarse salt (kosher or sea)
- 2 large hard-cooked egg whites, finely chopped, for garnish
- 1 piece (2 ounces) serrano ham or prosciutto, slivered or finely diced, for garnish

1. Place the bread in a bowl, add cold water to cover, and let soak for 5 to 10 minutes. Drain and squeeze out the excess liquid.

2. While the bread is soaking, place the tomatoes in a sieve set over a bowl and let them drain for 5 to 10 minutes.

3. Place half of the drained tomatoes, Italian pepper, and garlic in a food processor and process until smooth. Transfer the tomato mixture to a blender and blend until very smooth, 1 to 2 minutes. With the motor running, add ¼ cup of the olive oil in a slow stream, as you would when making mayonnaise. Pour the tomato mixture into a mixing bowl and repeat with the remaining tomatoes, Italian pepper, garlic, and ¼ cup olive oil. Whisk the vinegar into the tomato mixture and season it with salt

to taste. Cover the bowl with plastic wrap and refrigerate the soup for at least 2 hours or overnight for the flavors to develop.

4. To serve, place the *salmorejo* in bowls or shot glasses and invite the diners to garnish their portions with drizzles of olive oil, chopped egg white, and ham. Leftover *salmorejo* makes a great dip for poached or grilled seafood. **SERVES 6 IN BOWLS, 12 IN SHOT GLASSES**

SALMOREJO

ANDALUCIA'S OTHER TOMATO AND BREAD MASTERPIECE

During the torrid Andalusian summer, *salmorejo* is appreciated as much as gazpacho. What distinguishes *salmorejo* from its relative is the absence of water, onions, and cucumbers, as well as a higher proportion of bread, which makes for a lusher, creamier texture. Each cook insists on a different ratio: Some suggest it should be one to one (one pound of tomatoes to one pound of bread). In my recipe, borrowed from Jaylu, my favorite restaurant in Seville, I use a quarter pound of bread to two pounds of tomatoes. To me, the texture is ideal.

The quality of the tomatoes is of utmost importance—they should be sweet and fragrant but also have a lively acidity. Adding vinegar is delicious but not necessarily traditional; it's mostly used in *porra,* the version of *salmorejo* from the Andalusian city of Antequera near Seville. In some versions, especially those from Córdoba, a raw egg yolk is blended with the other ingredients. The classic garnishes are chopped hard-cooked egg whites and diced or slivered *jamón,* but other possibilities include small chunks of canned tuna, small poached shrimp, diced cooked potatoes, and/or chopped tomatoes and onions. As a tapa, I like serving *salmorejo* in shot glasses topped with a poached or grilled shrimp on a skewer. Once you learn how to make the soup, you'll discover that its uses are almost endless—a perfect summer refresher!

STRAWBERRY AND FENNEL GAZPACHO

GAZPACHO DE FRESAS E HINOJO

This innovative, cooling gazpacho with a fragrant accent of strawberries is from my friend Adolfo Muñoz, host of a daily TV cooking show, caterer to Spanish celebrities, winemaker, and chef-owner of Adolfo, the best restaurant in Toledo. The flavors here are perfectly balanced, Adolfo says, and the berries snap them into focus so you don't need vinegar. However, if you feel the soup could use an extra kick, feel free to add some good sherry vinegar.

CHERRY AND BEET GAZPACHO

GAZPACHO DE CEREZAS

Adapted from a soup prepared by Andalusia's greatest young chef, Dani García, this dramatic gazpacho has a gorgeous pastel pink hue, the result of adding ripe cherries and beets to the usual base of tomatoes and bread. Pistachios, mint, and diced cucumber make a simple and sophisticated garnish. For something sublime, I suggest that you try this topped with a small scoop of Minty Granita (page 447) or green apple sorbet. If fresh cherries are out of season, try the sour cherries that come in jars, imported from eastern Europe.

Freshly picked cherries are a common sight in Extremadura, Spain's cherry capital.

1 cup cubed day-old country bread, crusts removed
2 pounds ripest, most flavorful tomatoes, seeded; 2 tablespoons finely diced, for garnish, the rest chopped
2 pounds strawberries, hulled; 2 tablespoons finely diced, the rest chopped
1 large green bell pepper, cored and seeded; 2 tablespoons finely diced, the rest chopped
1/4 medium-size fennel bulb; 2 tablespoons finely diced, the rest thinly sliced
1/4 cup extra-virgin olive oil, plus more for drizzling
1 1/4 cups chilled bottled spring water
2 medium-size garlic cloves, crushed with a garlic press
Coarse salt (kosher or sea)

1. Place the bread in a bowl, add cold water to cover, and let soak for 5 to 10 minutes. Drain the bread and squeeze out the excess liquid.

2. Place the soaked bread and the chopped tomatoes, strawberries, green pepper, and fennel in a large bowl. Toss to mix and let stand for 15 minutes. Working in two batches, place the vegetable mixture in a food processor and process until smooth, adding half of the olive oil to each batch. Once each batch is finished, puree it finely in a blender, then transfer it to a large mixing bowl. Add the spring water and garlic (the gazpacho should have the consistency of a smoothie). Season the soup with salt to taste and refrigerate it, covered, until chilled, about 2 hours.

3. Meanwhile, place the finely diced tomato, strawberries, green pepper, and fennel in a bowl and toss to mix.

4. Spoon the diced tomato mixture into shallow bowls and ladle the chilled gazpacho on top. Drizzle olive oil over the surface and serve. **SERVES 8**

DANI GARCIA'S SOUP SORCERY

People visit the Andalusian city of Ronda to admire the perfect proportions of one of Spain's oldest bullrings and to gasp at the vertiginous Tajo gorge, which has sent many a Romantic poet into a tizzy. Me? I went there to taste what Dani García, a sweet teddy bear of a chef, was up to at his restaurant Tragabuches. Dani—who has since moved to a restaurant in Marbella—is already renowned in Spain as the father of new-wave gazpacho, producing dozens of futuristic riffs on the Andalusian classic.

My soup tasting at Tragabuches was exhilarating. There was *ajo blanco,* a white almond gazpacho, poured around a floppy shrimp and caviar *raviolo*—the seemingly disparate flavors held together by tiny threads of candied angel hair squash. *Gazpachuelo* (a hot fish soup) resembled an eye-popping still life in white (squid), black (potatoes mashed with squid ink), and red (candied tomato), moistened with an earthy-sweet cuttlefish broth. As an homage to the New World, an avocado gazpacho came garnished with frozen corn dust. The best? A shocking-pink beet and cherry gazpacho, with a funky backdrop accent of anchovies mediated by the smokiness of cured *queso de Ronda* sorbet. It was the soup of the century.

In his quest to perfect the science of chilling, Dani is now working with a university scientist to explore the culinary uses of liquid nitrogen. In his kitchen, this high-tech freezing agent accounts for such edible miracles as olive oil "carpaccio" (flash-frozen sliced olive oil that melts in the mouth) or a crisp frozen foam of poached quail eggs, with a texture akin to a savory frozen meringue.

1 medium-size beet (6 to 7 ounces), stemmed
1 3/4 pounds ripest, most flavorful tomatoes, seeded and chopped
2 cups pitted Bing cherries (see Note)
1 medium-size Italian (frying) pepper, cored, seeded, and chopped
1 medium-size Kirby (pickling) cucumber, peeled and chopped
3 tablespoons chopped red onion
2 medium-size garlic cloves, crushed with a garlic press
Coarse salt (kosher or sea)
1 3/4 cups cubed day-old country bread, crusts removed
1/2 cup fragrant extra-virgin olive oil, plus more for drizzling
4 to 6 tablespoons sherry vinegar, preferably aged, or more to taste
About 1 1/4 cups chilled bottled spring water
3 to 4 tablespoons coarsely chopped green pistachios and/or Minty Granita (page 447), for garnish
1/4 cup diced peeled cucumber, for garnish
Finely slivered mint leaves, for garnish

1. Preheat the oven to 400°F.

2. Wrap the beet in aluminum foil, place it on a small baking sheet, and bake until it feels tender when pierced with a skewer, about 1 hour. Unwrap the beet and rinse it under cold running water. Slip off and discard the skin; let the beet cool completely, then dice.

3. Place the diced beet and the tomatoes, cherries, Italian pepper, cucumber, onion, and garlic in a large bowl and toss to mix. (If you are making the gazpacho a day ahead, do not add the garlic more than 3 hours before serving, so it does not overwhelm the other flavors.) Sprinkle a little salt over the beet mixture, toss, and let stand for 10 to 15 minutes.

4. Place the bread in a bowl, add cold water to cover, and let soak for 5 to 10 minutes. Drain the bread, squeeze out the excess liquid, and add the bread to the beet mixture.

5. Working in two batches, place the beet mixture in a food processor and process until smooth, adding half of the olive oil and half of the reserved sour cherry juice, if using, to each batch. Once each batch is finished, puree it finely in a blender, then transfer it to a large mixing bowl. Add the vinegar, whisk to mix, then taste for seasoning, adding more vinegar as necessary. Add enough spring water to thin the gazpacho to the consistency of a smoothie. Season with salt to taste and refrigerate the gazpacho, covered, until chilled, about 2 hours. Serve the soup in glass bowls or martini glasses, garnished with pistachios, cucumber, and mint, and drizzles of olive oil. **SERVES 8 TO 10**

NOTE: To substitute imported pitted sour cherries, drain 2 cups cherries, setting aside ⅓ cup of the liquid to add to the gazpacho in Step 4.

ALMOND GAZPACHO WITH FIGS AND EDIBLE FLOWERS

AJO BLANCO CON HIGOS

Ajo blanco, literally white garlic, is a smooth almond and garlic gazpacho popular in the province of Málaga. Containing no tomatoes or other vegetables, it is essentially an almond and olive oil emulsion diluted with ice water and enlivened by vinegar. Very Moorish tasting and completely original, *ajo blanco* is classically garnished with peeled green muscat grapes. Modern chefs, however, use *ajo blanco* as a blank canvas. Here, inspired by the *ajo blanco* I tasted at a small restaurant in Valencia, the garnishes include a veritable bouquet of baby lettuces, fresh figs, and edible flowers. Following the modern Spanish tradition, the garnishes are arranged in soup bowls and the gazpacho is poured around them as guests look on. The dish is gorgeous, dramatic, and fabulously delicious.

2 1/2 cups cubed day-old country bread, crusts removed
1 cup whole blanched almonds, finely ground in a food processor
2 medium-size garlic cloves, crushed with a garlic press
1/2 teaspoon coarse salt (kosher or sea), or more to taste
About 1 1/2 cups chilled bottled spring water
1/3 cup fragrant light extra-virgin olive oil
1 1/2 tablespoons sherry vinegar, preferably aged, or more to taste
2 cups baby lettuces of different colors
1 cup edible flowers, broken into petals
3 fresh Black Mission figs, quartered
Tiny Olive Oil Croutons (page 90)

1. Place the bread in a bowl. Add cold water to cover and let soak for 5 to 10 minutes. Drain the bread, squeezing out the excess liquid, then crumble the soaked bread into a blender.

2. Add the almonds, garlic, salt, and 1 cup of the spring water to the blender and puree until a smooth paste forms. With the blender running at the highest speed, drizzle the olive oil through the feed tube until emulsified.

GAZPACHO GARNISHES

Admittedly, elaborately garnished gazpachos are more of a formal restaurant thing. At home and in neighborhood bars, most people drink the cold soup from a glass just like a smoothie. But this isn't to say that gazpacho's smooth creaminess doesn't invite all kinds of playful toppings. The most traditional restaurant garnish consists of diced vegetables and sometimes tiny croutons. Slivered herbs, such as basil and mint, are another good way to add a refreshing note. Ditto diced fruit, such as green apple, melon, or seedless grapes cut in half. More adventurously, gazpachos are magical when topped with a scoop of savory ice cream, tart sorbet, or an herbal granita. Aromatic, infused green oils, such as basil or parsley oil, make another terrific flourish, as does a simple swirl of fruity olive oil or a drizzle of syrupy aged balsamic vinegar. And don't forget seafood: A small pile of crabmeat; a nice plump seared, poached, or grilled scallop or shrimp; a sweet nugget of lobster; or a small zesty jolt of seviche, if you happen to have some on hand, would all be welcome.

3. Scrape the almond mixture into a large bowl. Whisk in the vinegar and the remaining ½ cup spring water. The consistency should be that of very thick cream or very thin mayonnaise. Taste for seasoning, adding a little more vinegar and/or salt as necessary. Transfer the soup to a pretty glass pitching and refrigerate it, covered, for at least 2 hours to allow the flavors to develop.

4. To serve, pile small heaps of the lettuce in the middle of soup bowls and top each with flower petals, 2 fig quarters, and some croutons. Bring the pitcher to the table and pour the soup around the lettuce and figs in each bowl. **SERVES 6**

SPICY GAZPACHO SORBET WITH BALSAMIC DRIZZLES

SORBETE DE GAZPACHO CON VINAGRE DE MODENA

Adventurous savory ice creams and sorbets are one of the hallmarks of Spanish *nueva cocina.* And what lends itself better to the ice cream maker than gazpacho? This version gets an extra punch from hot sauce and vodka. I can't think of anything more vibrant and fun to start off a summer meal. Scooped into martini glasses, it forms a whimsical "soup course" that can be passed around in small glasses at a cocktail party. Or—as is often done in Spain—it can accompany shellfish or fish. How about serving gazpacho sorbet in a shot glass or on a porcelain spoon topped with a raw oyster or clam, a grilled shrimp, or a rolled-up anchovy? Or pair a scoop of the sorbet with grilled slices of rare tuna or tuna tartare.

Because the sorbet contains very little sugar (which normally acts as a stabilizer), it will freeze solid and crystallize somewhat if left in the freezer for too long. Try not to freeze the sorbet for more than two to three hours; if you must make it further ahead, leave it out at room temperature for twenty to thirty minutes before serving.

FOR THE SORBET:

5 very ripe but firm tomatoes (about 1 1/2 pounds), seeded and chopped
1 cup cubed day-old country bread, crusts removed
1 envelope unflavored gelatin (2 1/4 teaspoons)
1/4 cup chopped red bell pepper
1/4 cup chopped green bell pepper
1/4 cup chopped celery
2 tablespoons chopped red onion
1 small garlic clove, crushed with a garlic press
1/4 cup chilled vodka
2 tablespoons light corn syrup
1/4 cup fragrant extra-virgin olive oil
2 tablespoons sherry vinegar, preferably aged
2 teaspoons Tabasco sauce, or more to taste

FOR THE GARNISHES:

2 tablespoons syrupy aged balsamic vinegar, or 1/3 cup thin balsamic vinegar reduced over medium-high heat to 2 tablespoons and cooled
Fragrant extra-virgin olive oil
Finely diced peeled Granny Smith apple
Finely diced red bell pepper
Finely diced cucumber
Finely slivered fresh mint

1. Make the sorbet: Place the tomatoes in a sieve set over a bowl and let them drain for 10 to 15 minutes.

2. Place the bread in a bowl, add cold water to cover, and let soak for 5 minutes. Drain the bread and squeeze out the excess liquid.

3. Place the gelatin in a small bowl, sprinkle 1 tablespoon of cold water over it, and let stand for 5 minutes. Add 3 to 4 tablespoons very hot water and stir until the gelatin is completely dissolved.

4. Place the drained tomatoes, soaked bread, dissolved gelatin, red and green peppers, celery, onion, garlic, vodka, corn syrup, olive oil, sherry vinegar, and Tabasco sauce in a bowl and toss to mix. Working in two batches, place the tomato mixture in a food processor and process until smooth. Once each batch is finished, puree it finely in a blender, then transfer it to a mixing bowl. Refrigerate the gazpacho, covered, until very cold, 2 to 3 hours.

5. Stir the gazpacho, then freeze it in an ice cream maker following the manufacturer's instructions. Transfer the gazpacho sorbet to a plastic container and place it in the freezer for about 2 hours—but not much longer or the sorbet will crystallize. (If making the sorbet ahead, let it stand a room temperature for about 30 minutes before serving.)

6. Scoop the sorbet into large shot glasses or small martini glasses. Drizzle a little balsamic vinegar and olive oil over each serving, then sprinkle some of the diced apple, red pepper, and cucumber and mint on top. **SERVES 8**

An ornate window featured on a home in Marbella, one of Spain's most exclusive summer escapes

WATERMELON AND TOMATO SOUP

SOPA DE SANDIA Y TOMATES

Want a soup that's even simpler than a gazpacho and just as refreshing during the dog days of summer? Here's a recipe from Hisop, an impossibly stylish small restaurant in Barcelona, whose playful chefs Guillem Pla and Oriol Ivern are enamored of soups made with raw vegetables and fruit. "Liquid salads" is what they call them, insisting they have to be made fresh and served right away. The effect is somewhere between a soup and smoothie. In Spain, the blending is done in a miraculous kitchen gadget called a Thermomix (see box, page 108) which produces unbelievably smooth purees. As with gazpachos, I use both a food processor and a blender, but you can certainly get away with just the food processor. For garnish, I like just a touch of slivered basil, but you can play with the soup, topping it with Tiny Olive Oil Croutons (see page 90), with julienned mint and/or fresh ginger, or with edible flowers.

- 4 cups cubed, seeded, ripe but firm watermelon
- 1 pound ripe, fleshy tomatoes, seeded and chopped
- 2 tablespoons fresh lemon juice, or more to taste
- 1/2 cup diced celery
- 1/4 cup fragrant extra-virgin olive oil, plus more for drizzling
- Coarse salt (kosher or sea) and freshly ground black pepper
- Finely slivered basil, for garnish

1. Working in two batches, puree the watermelon, tomatoes, lemon juice, celery, and 1/4 cup olive oil in a food processor. Transfer the watermelon mixture to a blender and puree until it is very smooth and frothy.

2. Season the soup with salt and pepper to taste and add more lemon juice, if desired. Ladle the soup into pretty glasses, drizzle olive oil on top, and serve right away, sprinkled with basil. **SERVES 6**

CHILLED HERBED PEA SOUP

SOPA DE YERBAS FRESCAS

Martin Berasategui, the Basque superchef of the eponymous restaurant near San Sebastián, heads an incredibly successful restaurant group that includes the avant-garde restaurant at the Guggenheim in Bilbao, as well as the even more avant-garde Mugaritz, headed by chef Andoni Luis Adúriz. Berasategui is coauthor of a lovely cookbook called *El Mercado en el Plato*—the market on your plate. While the food at his restaurants is too complicated for regular home cooks, the book is filled with sophisticated but practical recipes. This is my adaptation of one, a divine chilled soup made with fresh peas and a gardenful of herbs, plus cheese for body and tang. Feel free to vary the herbs according to what's in your garden or at the farmer's market.

1 tablespoon unsalted butter
5 tablespoons fragrant extra-virgin olive oil, plus more for drizzling
2 small leeks, white part only, thinly sliced
2 cups chicken stock or broth
3 1/2 cups frozen baby peas (from two 10-ounce boxes), thawed
2 cups finely chopped iceberg lettuce
3 tablespoons chopped fresh tarragon
1/2 cup chopped fresh basil
1/3 cup chopped fresh chervil or parsley
1/3 cup chopped fresh chives, plus more for garnish
1/4 cup chopped fresh mint
5 ounces mild goat cheese or cream cheese
Coarse salt (kosher or sea) and freshly ground white pepper

1. Melt the butter with 1 tablespoon of the olive oil in a medium-size saucepan over medium-low heat. Add the leeks and cook until soft but not browned, 5 to 7 minutes. Add the chicken stock and 3 cups water, increase the heat to high, and bring to a boil. Add the peas and lettuce, reduce the heat to medium-low, and simmer until the vegetables are bright green and tender, 3 to 4 minutes.

2. Drain the vegetables, setting aside their cooking liquid. Run the vegetables under cold water to stop the cooking process, then let the vegetables and cooking liquid cool.

3. Place the cooked vegetables, the tarragon, basil, chervil, ⅓ cup chives, the mint, goat cheese, remaining 4 tablespoons olive oil, and 3 cups of the reserved cooking liquid in a large bowl and stir to combine. Working in two batches, puree the mixture in a blender until completely smooth and frothy, about 1 minute. Transfer the puree to a large bowl and whisk in the remaining cooking liquid.

4. Season the soup with salt and white pepper to taste, and refrigerate it covered, until chilled, at least 3 hours. Serve the soup in pretty glasses, garnished with chives and drizzled with olive oil. **SERVES 6**

CHILLED POTATO AND BACON SOUP

SOPA FRIA DE PATATA Y BEICON

Here is another elegant chilled soup from Basque chef Martin Berasategui, this one made with salt-baked potatoes and bacon-infused cream, blended together into a luscious, extra-smooth potion. Shavings of white summer truffles make it truly luxurious, but if that's too much of an indulgence, use just the truffle oil. Baking the potatoes on a bed of salt gives them a faint smokiness and a nicely concentrated flavor. However, you can also boil them in their skins until tender, then drain and peel them before mashing them with the cream.

1 1/2 to 2 cups kosher salt, plus more coarse salt (kosher or sea) for seasoning the soup
1 1/2 pounds Yukon Gold potatoes
2 cups heavy (whipping) cream
1 1/2 cups chicken stock or broth
6 to 7 ounces smoky slab bacon, cut into 3 or 4 pieces
Freshly ground white pepper
White truffle oil
1 small white truffle (optional), shaved with a mandoline or a vegetable peeler
Minced fresh chives or chervil, for garnish

TOOL ENVY

The texture of Spanish cooking changed forever when Ferran Adrià popularized a kitchen gadget called the Thermomix. Now, not only every chef but also many middle-class home cooks have one in their kitchen. Made by a German company called Vorwerk, this space-age kitchen slave with a monster motor can perform a shocking number of tasks. It blends, whips, and kneads. It measures and weighs; it chops, pulverizes, simmers, and steams. And it performs most of these things brilliantly. Warm emulsions—cooked right in the machine—are creamier than anything you've tasted before. Gazpachos come out improbably silky and foamy. Ice creams are airy and smooth. Got a grand? Thermomix might now be available near you (try thermomix.com). As for me, while I wait for the price to come down, I use my prehistoric food processor and blender, in combination, to approximate these twenty-second-century textures.

1. Preheat the oven to 375°F.

2. Place a layer of kosher salt in a large, heavy ovenproof skillet (preferably cast-iron). Prick the potatoes with a fork, then arrange them on top of the salt. Bake the potatoes, turning them once, until they feel completely tender when pierced with a skewer, about 50 minutes. Let cool.

3. While the potatoes are baking, place the cream, chicken stock, and bacon in a medium-size saucepan and bring to a simmer. Cover the saucepan and let cook over very low heat for 10 minutes. Remove the saucepan from the heat and let the cream infuse, covered, for about 40 minutes. Strain the cream mixture into a bowl, discarding the bacon.

4. When the potatoes are just cool enough to handle, cut them in half, scoop out the flesh, and place it in a bowl, discarding the skins. Mash the potatoes finely with a potato ricer or a sturdy fork. Working in two batches, puree the potatoes in a blender, adding half of the bacon-infused cream to each batch. Run the blender in quick pulses, pureeing the potatoes just until smooth; do not overblend them or they will become gummy. Transfer the potatoes to a bowl, season them with salt and white pepper to taste, and chill for 3 to 4 hours.

5. To serve, divide the soup among glasses or bowls, drizzle truffle oil over each portion, and garnish with a few slices of truffle, if using, and the chives. Serve at once. **SERVES 6 TO 8**

FISH STOCK FOR SOUPS, RICES, AND SEAFOOD DISHES

CALDO DE PESCADO

A good strong fish stock will lend a special marine smack to a number of soups, seafood dishes, and rices in this book. While you can always doctor a mixture of bottled clam juice and water with a few mussels and shrimp shells, real fish stock is easy to make and will keep for a long time in the freezer. You don't need expensive fish to make stock: Just ask your fishmonger for fish trimmings, such as heads, tails, and frames. Black bass, grouper, rock cod, halibut, and especially the gelatinous monkfish tails will all work, but avoid oily fish like salmon or bluefish. For extra flavor, I like to toss in a couple of blue crabs and some mussels, as well as cheap small fish like porgy, mullet, whiting, or ocean perch. Chinatown fish markets—if there's one in your area—are a good source of inexpensive, but very fresh, fish.

2 tablespoons olive oil
12 large garlic cloves, unpeeled and smashed
1 large onion, chopped
1 large carrot, chopped
4 pounds fish frames, heads, and tails, thoroughly rinsed under cold running water, gills trimmed and discarded
1 pound inexpensive small fish (see headnote), cleaned, gutted, and scaled (optional)
3 large plum tomatoes, coarsely chopped
1 cup dry white wine
10 mussels, scrubbed and debearded right before using (optional)
2 blue crabs (optional)
4 large parsley sprigs
Coarse salt (kosher or sea) and freshly ground black pepper

1. Heat the olive oil in a large heavy soup pot over medium heat. Add the garlic, onion, and carrot and cook, stirring, until the garlic is fragrant and the vegetables begin to soften, 6 to 7 minutes. Add the fish frames, whole fish, and the tomatoes, cover, and cook until the fish is opaque and the tomatoes have thrown off some of their juices, 8 to 10 minutes. Add 11 cups water and the wine, increase the heat to high, and bring to a boil, thoroughly skimming off the foam. Add the mussels and crabs, if using, and the parsley. Season with salt and pepper to taste, reduce the heat to low, and simmer, uncovered, until the stock is flavorful, about 30 minutes. If you'd like stronger-tasting stock, reduce it over medium-high heat for about 10 minutes longer.

2. Strain the stock through a fine sieve into a clean pot or bowl, pressing on the solids to extract as much liquid as possible. Discard the solids, taste the stock, and adjust the amount of salt and pepper. If using the stock right away, skim off as much fat as you can. Otherwise, place the stock, covered, in the refrigerator and remove the fat when chilled. The stock will keep in the refrigerator for up to 4 days and can be frozen for up to 3 months. **MAKES 10 TO 12 CUPS**

SALADS

SO FRESH, SO GOOD

It's odd that Spain, a country where vegetables and greens burst with flavor, hasn't developed a serious salad tradition. I always ask friends why one so rarely sees *ensaladas* at traditional restaurants. They always respond that

From left to right: Harvesting organic produce by hand; An array of tapas awaits a crowd of hungry customers; Boutique lettuces, such as baby lollo rosso, are gaining popularity in Spain; A traditional hut stands out in Tarragona's Delta del Ebro Natural Park.

beautiful vegetables dressed with good olive oil are so common at home, nobody wants to pay for them when dining out. Clearly Spain isn't the place for elaborately composed concoctions cloaked in fanciful vinaigrettes—you don't even find these at creative modern restaurants. And unlike the United States with its filling lunch salads, France with its bracing bistro appetizer *salades,* or Italy with its custom of serving peppery greens at the end of a meal, Spain doesn't really afford salad a fixed role at the table. The notion of a salad here tends to be improvisational. Just toss together *verduras* or greens, delicious diced boiled potatoes, and/or roasted peppers. Throw in some tuna, anchovies, or hard-cooked eggs, if you fancy. Dress with lots of aromatic oil and a flavorful vinegar. Then, enjoy at whim, as a snack, lunch, or tapa. I like this approach!

Where Spanish salads do come into their own is at tapas bars. First among tapa salads is the omnipresent *ensaladilla rusa,* or Russian salad, which combines diced cooked vegetables, tuna, and a creamy mayonnaise dressing. A good *ensaladilla*—such as the one in this chapter from Estrella de Plata in Barcelona—is a dish to behold. Another counter classic is the Andalusian *papas aliñas* (dressed potatoes), a simple salad that sings. Also ubiquitous and shockingly good are the juicy roasted red pepper concoctions (known as *zorongollo, asadillo,* or *mojete*), which sometimes contain tangy, fishy things like bacalao or salt-cured tuna. Here I offer two versions: one classic, the other creative, both sensational. And it's worth mentioning the curious family of tomato-based chopped salads—*pipirrana, piriñaca,* or *trempó* in Mallorca—which are left to sit for a while to release juices. The result is an intriguing cross between a cold soup and a salad, related to gazpacho and perfect for dunking bread into.

One region in Spain that takes salads seriously is Catalonia, where you can sample such masterpieces as *xató* (curly greens with bacalao, anchovies, and *romesco* dressing) and *escalivada* (a scrumptious mélange of grilled vegetables), as well as leafy greens imaginatively paired with fruit and nuts. But even here, the maxim is: Keep it simple. Which is probably the highest respect one can pay to great greens and vegetables.

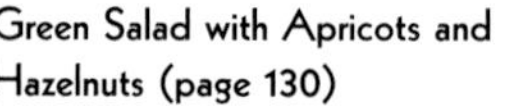

Green Salad with Apricots and Hazelnuts (page 130)

THE BEST RUSSIAN SALAD

ENSALADILLA RUSA, ESTRELLA DE PLATA

I'm not sure how the Russian potato salad (called Olivier in its native country) became a world staple, showing up as a part of a Korean appetizer spread, finding its way into the Turkish meze assortment, and becoming one of the most beloved tapas of Spain. But being Russian, I can testify that in Spain *ensaladilla rusa* is even more popular than it is in its homeland. Spain's tastiest *ensaladilla,* hands down, is served at Estrella de Plata, a stylish tapas bar in Barceloneta, Barcelona's old fishermen's quarter. Even my mother—who claims that *her* Russian salad is the world's greatest—was sufficiently smitten to ask the chef, Dídac López, for the recipe. In addition to the cooked potatoes, carrots, and peas found in the Russian version, his features tuna and roasted red peppers, plus a wonderfully piquant touch of green olives and anchovies in the mayonnaise dressing. All the ingredients are partially mashed, so the texture is halfway between a salad and a spread (at Estrella de Plata it's served with thin bread rusks). Bring the salad on a picnic, serve it as part of a tapas buffet, or just enjoy it as a light lunch with cold meat or cold cuts.

FOR THE SALAD:

3 medium-size Yukon Gold potatoes, cut in half
1 large carrot, cut in half crosswise
1 small turnip, cut in half
About 3 ounces green beans, trimmed
1 cup cooked green peas
6 ounces imported solid oil-packed tuna, or 1 can (6 ounces) Bumble Bee tonno in olive oil, drained and flaked with a fork
2 roasted red bell peppers (see page 385; from a jar is fine too), diced
3 hard-cooked eggs; 2 finely chopped, 1 grated

FOR THE DRESSING:

20 pimiento-stuffed green olives
6 to 7 best-quality oil-packed anchovy fillets, drained and chopped
1/3 cup mayonnaise (preferably Hellmann's), or more to taste
2 tablespoons fresh lemon juice
Coarse salt (kosher or sea) and freshly ground black pepper

1. Make the salad: Place the potatoes, carrot, and turnip in a medium-size saucepan. Add water to cover by 2 inches, bring to a boil over medium-high heat, then reduce the heat to medium-low and simmer, partially covered, until all the vegetables feel tender when pierced with a skewer, about 15 minutes for the carrot and turnip, and a little longer for the potatoes. As the vegetables become soft, use a slotted spoon to transfer them to a bowl. Take care not to overcook. Bring the water back to a boil, add the green beans, and cook until tender, about 5 minutes (they should be neither al dente nor overcooked). Drain the beans, blot them dry with paper towels, and set aside. Let the vegetables cool to room temperature.

2. Peel the potatoes, carrot, and turnip, then cut them into small dice and transfer to a mixing bowl.

ODE TO A CAN OF TUNA

One of the greatest meals of my life? Canned tuna—for real! It was summer and my friend and I were in San Sebastián, staying at the villa of our friend, the Michelin three-star chef Juan Mari Arzak. Arzak himself was off in Madrid, cooking for the wedding of Crown Prince Felipe, heir to the Spanish throne. Unable to face another haute restaurant meal, we decided to stay in for dinner and raid our host's fridge. Well, the refrigerator of a world-famous chef looks like this: *empty,* save for a few forlorn cans of foie gras, Iranian caviar, and enough bottled water to put out a forest fire. But down in Arzak's cellar amid dusty bottles of wine and pieces of old kitchen equipment, we discovered a treasure: a shelf lined with cans of piquillo peppers and tuna. We grabbed one of each, settled on a terrace overlooking the overgrown garden, and uncorked a bottle of Rioja *reserva.* The piquillo peppers were so ripe, red, and sweet it was like eating a perfect fall day. The tuna was more rich and buttery than any foie gras or *toro,* delicate but possessing the concentrated intensity of a confit. We ate in the twilight practically moaning with pleasure, periodically running down to the cellar to fetch more cans.

When I told Arzak that his tuna was the best thing in the world, he exploded with laughter. "Hombre, por supuesto [man, of course]," he hooted, "do you realize what you ate?" The fish was *ventresca,* the exquisite belly section of the season's first rod-caught tuna, packed in some unbelievable olive oil and canned especially for Arzak. (The peppers were of a similarly exalted quality.) "Sure, my tuna is the best meal in the world," Arzak kept mumbling all day.

Arzak's attachment to his tuna is nothing if not Spanish; only in Spain would a cutting-edge chef wax rhapsodic about something that comes in a *can.* This is because Spanish canned goods are so special. Even the average canned bonito one finds at supermarkets tends to be great, making our flavorless water-packed fish taste like cat food in comparison. And when you get to *ventresca,* this stuff is better than caviar (and costs about as much). The good news is that Spanish tuna is getting increasingly easy to find at American specialty food stores or by mail. Look for *bonito del norte* (literally Northern Beauty), which is a rich, moist albacore tuna from the Cantabrian sea. Good canned bonito is caught by rod, cleaned and filleted by hand, boiled, and canned in olive oil, a process that renders it silky and delicate. As for *ventresca,* if you see it, grab as many cans as you can afford. It just might be the best thing you'll ever taste.

Cut the green beans into ¾-inch lengths and add them to the bowl with the diced vegetables. Then add the peas, tuna, roasted peppers, and the 2 chopped eggs. Using a sturdy fork, mash the salad until it has a chunky-creamy consistency.

3. Make the dressing: Place the olives, anchovies, 2 tablespoons of the mayonnaise, and 3 tablespoons water in a blender and process until a medium-fine paste forms. Stir the olive mixture into the salad. Place the remaining mayonnaise and the lemon juice in a small bowl and whisk to mix, then stir into the salad. Season with salt and black pepper to taste. If you'd like the salad to be moister, add a little more mayonnaise. Cover the bowl with plastic wrap and let the salad stand for about 2 hours. (You can make the salad up to 1 day ahead. Refrigerate it and let it come to room temperature before serving.) To serve, spoon the salad on a shallow serving dish and garnish it with the grated egg. **SERVES 8 TO 10 AS A TAPA, 4 TO 6 AS A SIDE DISH**

ANDALUSIAN POTATO SALAD

PAPAS ALIÑAS

You'd be crazy to go to an Andalusian tapas bar and not order *papas aliñas* (marinated potatoes). These are shallow bowls of diced yellow potatoes tossed with sweet white onions, green peppers, and sometimes tomato and tuna, then generously bathed with good olive oil and sherry vinegar. Like many a classic tapa, it is a simple but fundamental dish on which a bar's reputation depends. Bar Casablanca, a venerable Seville tapas counter, has my favorite version—and many *sevillanos* agree. The secret is the texture; the potatoes are slightly mashed rather than diced so they absorb the dressing better. Another secret is to use the best possible olive oil and be generous with it.

3 medium-size Yukon Gold potatoes (1 1/2 to 1 3/4 pounds total)
1 small sweet white onion, finely diced
1 large Italian (frying) pepper, cored, seeded, and finely diced
1 large vine-ripened tomato, peeled, seeded, and finely diced
3 to 4 tablespoons minced scallion
1/2 cup fragrant extra-virgin olive oil
6 to 7 tablespoons sherry vinegar, preferably aged
Coarse salt (kosher or sea)
Minced fresh flat-leaf parsley, for garnish

1. Place the potatoes in a medium-size saucepan, add enough cold water to cover them by 2 inches, and bring to a boil over medium-high heat. Reduce the heat to medium and cook the potatoes, partially covered, until they are completely tender when pricked with a skewer, 30 to 35 minutes. Drain the potatoes. When just cool enough to handle, peel the potatoes and cut them into very fine dice.

2. Place the diced potatoes and the onion, Italian pepper, tomato, scallion, ⅓ cup of the olive oil, and 6 tablespoons of the vinegar in a bowl and stir to mix. Season with salt to taste. Toss everything together, crushing the potatoes slightly, so that they are half mashed. Let the salad stand for about 2 hours to absorb the dressing. Taste and add more vinegar as necessary.

3. To serve, spread the potato salad on a serving plate, sprinkle parsley on top, then drizzle the remaining oil over it. **SERVES 8 AS A TAPA**

MOLDED TUNA AND ROASTED PEPPER SALAD

MILHOJAS DE ATUN Y PIMIENTOS

Salads of tuna, tomatoes, and roasted peppers are as abundant in Spain as tuna with mayo is in the United States. Of all the versions I've sampled—and there've been *lots*—this one stands out as the most scrumptious. It is a specialty at one of my favorite Madrid tapas bars, La Castela, in the upmarket residential area around Retiro Park. Every morsel at La Castela is fabulous, from the tostadas of Cabrales cheese and duck ham (*jamón de pato*) to the richly flavored braised beef cheeks. But this molded tuna masterpiece, layered with slightly sweetened tomatoes and dolled up with basil and black olive purees, is what I order again and again.

Serve it as a part of a tapas spread or as a luncheon salad with grilled country bread and have the recipe ready to hand out to guests. (They always ask!) The basil puree and the tomatoes can be prepared a day or even two ahead (the tomatoes need to sit about an hour). For molding the salad I use a pie plate, but you can experiment with a loaf pan or bowl, or make individual portions using ramekins or soufflé cups.

5 tablespoons best-quality olive oil, plus more for brushing the peppers
2 pounds ripe red tomatoes, peeled, seeded, and diced
4 1/2 teaspoons sugar
3 tablespoons sherry vinegar, preferably aged, or best-quality red wine vinegar
Coarse salt (kosher or sea)
6 large roasted red bell peppers (page 385), cut into thin strips
3 tablespoons store-bought black olive paste (see Note)
12 ounces imported solid oil-packed tuna, or 2 cans (each 6 ounces) Bumble Bee tonno in olive oil, drained and flaked into chunks
Fresh Basil Oil (page 221)

1. Heat 1 tablespoon of the olive oil in a large skillet over medium-high heat. Add the tomatoes and cook, stirring gently, until reduced slightly, 6 to 7 minutes. Stir in the sugar, and 2 tablespoons of the vinegar and season with salt to taste. Cook the tomatoes until the flavors blend, about 1 minute. Using a slotted spoon, transfer the tomatoes to a sieve set over a bowl and let the liquid drain for a few minutes. Let the tomatoes cool completely.

2. Meanwhile, place the roasted peppers in a bowl and add 1 tablespoon of the olive oil, the remaining 1 tablespoon vinegar, and a little salt and toss to mix. Let stand for about 30 minutes.

3. Place the olive paste and the remaining 3 tablespoons olive oil in a small bowl and whisk to mix.

4. Assemble the salad: Line a 9-inch pie plate with plastic wrap, leaving some overhanging in two places. Arrange half of the roasted peppers on the bottom of the pie plate, scatter half of the tuna on top, drizzle a little basil oil over it, and top with half of the tomato mixture. Top with layers of the remaining pepper strips, tuna, and tomato mixture, drizzling some of the basil oil very lightly over the layers. Place a large serving plate on top of the pie plate, invert it, and remove the pie plate and plastic wrap. Drizzle a little of the basil oil and the olive paste mixture over the top of the salad. Decoratively drizzle the remaining basil oil around the salad (you might not need all of it) and dot it with the remaining olive paste mixture. Serve the salad at once. **SERVES 8**

NOTE: Small jars of black olive paste are available in specialty food markets. If you can't find any, substitute tapenade.

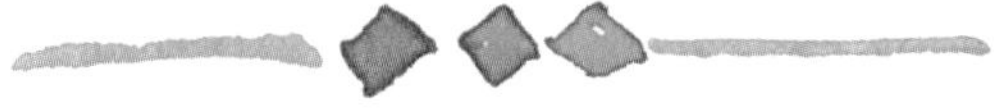

WARM SALAD OF COD AND ORANGES

ENSALADA TIBIA DE BACALAO CON NARANJAS

This salad is another contribution to this book from the great Toledo chef Adolfo Muñoz. Lyrically Mediterranean and terrifically tasty, this is Adolfo's sophisticated take on *remojón*, a traditional Andalusian salad of salt cod and oranges. In the states it is nearly impossible to find the fat loin of bacalao, which tastes even better than fresh cod when reconstituted, so I suggest you cure your own fresh cod in sea salt. It's very easy to do but does take an hour, so plan ahead.

1 pound center-cut skinless cod fillet
Coarse salt (kosher or sea)
4 medium-size navel oranges
6 tablespoons fragrant extra-virgin olive oil
Freshly ground black pepper
2 to 3 teaspoons fresh lemon juice (optional)
4 cups mesclun, rinsed and dried
1/2 cup small basil leaves
1/2 medium-size red onion, quartered and thinly sliced
1/4 cup minced red bell pepper
1/4 cup minced green bell pepper

1. Place the cod in a shallow bowl and pat salt all over it. Cover the bowl with plastic wrap and refrigerate for 1 hour.

2. Peel the oranges with a small, sharp knife, removing all the bitter white pith. Working over a

Warm Salad of Cod and Oranges

sieve set over a bowl, cut in between the membranes to release the orange sections into the sieve. Set aside the orange membranes. Let the orange sections drain.

3. Make the salad dressing: Squeeze the juice from the orange membranes into another bowl and add the juice that drained from the orange sections. Measure ¼ cup, and discard the rest or set aside for another use. Whisk 2 tablespoons of the olive oil into the orange juice and season the dressing generously with salt and black pepper. Taste the dressing and, if it seems too sweet, add lemon juice to taste.

4. Pat the cod dry with paper towels, taking care to remove any excess salt. Heat the remaining ¼ cup olive oil in a large skillet over medium-low heat. Add the cod and cook, turning once and shaking the pan, until the cod is just cooked through and starts to separate into large flakes, about 10 minutes. Transfer the cod to a plate.

5. Place the mesclun and basil leaves in a large bowl and toss with 2 tablespoons of the dressing. Divide the greens among serving plates and top with the orange sections and cod, separating the flakes slightly. Scatter the onion and red and green peppers over the salads, drizzle the remaining dressing on top, and serve. **SERVES 6 TO 8**

OCTOPUS CONFIT AND SAFFRON POTATO SALAD

ENSALADA DE PULPA CONFITADA CON PATATAS AL AZAFRAN

I love octopus every which way, but no dish has impressed me more than this one. I tasted it at Saüc, a Barcelona restaurant where a modest décor belies truly poetic and quietly ambitious modern Catalan cooking. The octopus was amazingly tender, paired with meltingly delicious saffron potatoes and dabbed with an intense tomato-onion reduction. The dish seemed simple, but when the chef, Xavier Franco, started explaining, I realized how much thought and technique had gone into it. Octopus can be rubbery even when boiled for a long time. The secret to a silky texture, Xavier explained, is cooking it very slowly, covered in olive oil. The result is a sort of confit. His potatoes were cooked in saffron oil twice at different temperatures. Dressing the salad was a Catalan *sofregit,* or *sofrito*—a mixture of tomatoes and onions—cooked for hours into an intensely flavorful jam. I've adapted the recipe to the home kitchen, but even with shortcuts it is still an exceptional salad. Try it warm or at room temperature, either as part of a tapas spread, as a first course, or even as a light main course. If you feel like tossing a few halved cherry tomatoes into the dish, go right ahead.

1 octopus (about 2 pounds; see Note), thawed if frozen
6 unpeeled medium-size garlic cloves, lightly smashed
About 1 1/2 cups olive oil, or more as needed
2 pounds Yukon Gold potatoes, peeled and cut into 1/2-inch cubes
2 cups chicken stock or broth
1 medium-size pinch of saffron, toasted and pulverized in a mortar
4 to 5 cups arugula leaves, rinsed and dried
1 to 2 tablespoons fragrant extra-virgin olive oil
Coarse salt (kosher or sea) and freshly ground black pepper
Sofrito Vinaigrette (recipe follows)
2 to 3 tablespoons minced fresh flat-leaf parsley

1. Preheat the oven to 250°F.

2. Cut the tentacles from the octopus and discard the head. Bring a pot of salted water to a boil and blanch the tentacles for 2 minutes. Drain, rinse under cold running water, and pat dry with paper towels. Place the octopus in a deep flameproof baking dish or ovenproof skillet that can hold it in a single snug layer. Scatter the garlic among the pieces of octopus and add enough olive oil to completely cover the octopus. Place the baking dish on the stove over low heat and bring the oil to a simmer. Cover the baking dish with aluminum foil and bake the octopus until extremely tender, 3½ to 4 hours. Let the octopus cool to warm. (The octopus can be prepared up to 3 days ahead and refrigerated, covered. Rewarm over low heat before serving.)

3. Place the potatoes in a saucepan that will hold them snugly. Add the chicken stock and enough cold water to cover the potatoes by 1½ inches. Bring to a boil over medium-high heat. Steep the saffron in 3 tablespoons of the hot cooking liquid for 2 to 3 minutes, then pour it into the potatoes. Cover the saucepan and cook the potatoes over low heat until tender but not mushy, about 12 minutes. Drain the potatoes and cool to warm or to room temperature. (The saffron broth can be reserved for another use, such as cooking rice.)

4. Place the arugula and extra-virgin olive oil in a mixing bowl and toss to mix. Season lightly with salt and pepper.

5. Drain the octopus, discarding the garlic. Blot the octopus dry with paper towels to remove excess oil, then cut it into ¾-inch pieces. Place the potatoes and the octopus in a bowl and gently toss them, taking care not to crush the potatoes. Stir the vinaigrette well, add it to the potatoes and octopus, and gently toss to mix. Line a large serving platter with the arugula leaves or divide the arugula among

A chef about to cook a giant octopus in Galicia, where it's considered a delicacy

dinner plates, if serving individual portions. Mound the octopus salad on top and sprinkle parsley over it. **SERVES 6 OR 7 AS A FIRST COURSE, 8 TO 10 AS A TAPA**

NOTE: If you are not an octopus fan or can't easily find it, try the salad with steamed shelled mussels or another seafood.

SOFRITO VINAIGRETTE

This versatile vinaigrette is delicious tossed with warm potatoes, string beans, or white beans, as well as with seafood. It needs to be made about an hour before you plan to use it.

- 1/2 cup fragrant extra-virgin olive oil
- 1/4 cup finely chopped red onion
- 3 large garlic cloves, minced
- 3 tablespoons finely diced red bell pepper
- 2 tablespoons finely diced Italian (frying) pepper
- 1 large, slightly under-ripe plum tomato, peeled with a vegetable peeler, seeded, and finely chopped
- 1/2 cup best-quality red wine vinegar
- 1 large pinch of sugar, or more to taste

Heat the olive oil in a small saucepan over low heat. Add the onion, garlic, and red and Italian peppers and cook for about 2 minutes to soften, stirring. Stir in the tomato, vinegar, and sugar. Taste for sweetness, adding more sugar as necessary, and cook for another minute. Remove the vinaigrette from the heat, season it with salt and pepper to taste, and let stand for 1 hour. **MAKES ABOUT 1 1/2 CUPS**

CURLY GREENS WITH TUNA AND ANCHOVIES

XATO

Ramon Parellada, a prominent Barcelona restaurateur, gave me this recipe for the legendary Catalan salad *xató* years ago, and I've been happily enjoying it ever since. I intentionally make extra *romesco* dressing here: Once you've tasted it on the *xató,* try what's left over on other substantial salads, based on chicken or seafood, or spoon it on grilled poultry, fish, or meat. It tastes good on just about anything.

A proper *xató* features salt cod prepared *esqueixada*-style—soaked and eaten raw torn into pieces. As it is almost impossible in this country to find bacalao good enough to eat uncooked, I use smoked whitefish or salmon or simply leave the cured fish out altogether. (For more about *xató,* see the facing page.)

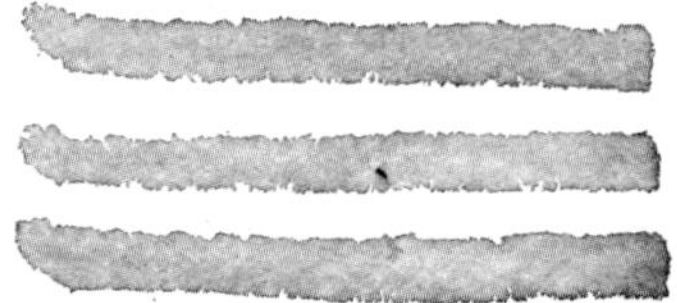

2/3 cup plus 2 tablespoons fragrant extra-virgin olive oil
1/3 cup cubed day-old country bread, crusts removed
15 blanched almonds
4 large garlic cloves, chopped
6 ounces imported solid oil-packed tuna, or 1 can (6 ounces) Bumble Bee tonno in oil, flaked
2 medium-size ripe tomatoes, blanched, peeled, and chopped
1 large vinegar-packed pimiento, chopped
1 tablespoon sweet (not smoked) paprika
1/8 teaspoon cayenne, or more to taste
1/3 cup best-quality red wine vinegar
Coarse salt (kosher or sea) and freshly ground black pepper
8 to 9 cups frisée (curly endive) or tender escarole leaves, rinsed, dried, and torn into bite-size pieces
15 arbequina or niçoise olives, or a mixture of your favorite black and green olives
12 best-quality oil-packed anchovy fillets, drained
4 ounces cold-smoked whitefish or smoked salmon (optional), torn into slivers

1. Heat the 2 tablespoons olive oil in a small skillet over medium heat. Add the bread and almonds and cook until golden brown, 2 to 3 minutes. Using a slotted spoon, transfer the bread and almonds to a food processor.

2. Add the garlic to the food processor and process until the mixture is finely ground. Add 2 tablespoons of the tuna and the tomatoes, pimiento, paprika, cayenne, and vinegar and process until smooth. With the motor running, drizzle the 2/3 cup olive oil through the feed tube; the dressing will emulsify. Scrape the dressing into a bowl and season with salt and black pepper and more cayenne to taste. Let stand for 30 minutes for the flavors to develop.

3. Place the frisée on a large serving platter and drizzle some of the dressing over it. Scatter the remaining tuna over the frisée. Decoratively arrange the olives, anchovies, and whitefish, if using, on top. Serve the salad with additional dressing on the side.

SERVES 6 AS A FIRST COURSE OR LIGHT MAIN COURSE

XATÓ-MANIA

Xató is the Catalan answer to *salade niçoise:* a bold-flavored, refreshing mix of curly greens, olives, and salted fish. Popular in the winter months, *xató* is distinguished by its *romesco* dressing, a garlicky mortar-pounded mix of tomatoes, peppers, and nuts. (Make the recipe on the facing page, and you'll understand why it has a cult following.) Everything about *xató* is just right: the perfect way in which the robust, puckery sauce clings to the delicate jagged greens; the briny layer of olives and anchovies; the substantial presence of tuna and bacalao. So popular is the salad in the wine-producing Penedès area south of Barcelona that it boasts its own fiesta, called *xatonada.* During the feast, normally held at carnival time, everyone in the hamlets and villages gathers on plazas around long wooden tables to consume thousands of portions of *xató,* accompanied by *cava* or Penedès red wine. The festivities usually culminate in a competition of Mestres Xatonaires, *xató* masters. In addition, this salad-mad area features a *xató* route, along which some one hundred restaurants offer their versions.

Traditionally *xató* is prepared with escarole, which is left to "wilt" for a while in the dressing, but frisée is also delicious. I've substituted whitefish or smoked salmon for the bacalao, since finding top-quality salt cod is difficult.

ANDALUSIAN RICE, SHRIMP, AND FAVA BEAN SALAD

ENSALADA DE ARROZ CON GAMBAS Y HABAS

Andalusian home cooking abounds in zesty, unfussy recipes that can be whipped up in the scorching summer heat without breaking a sweat. This salad is a perfect example. Served along with Tuna-Stuffed Eggs (page 38), it makes a great simple alfresco meal. Many versions of this salad also include chunks of canned tuna and chopped hard-cooked eggs, so feel free to play around.

- 1 cup long-grain rice
- 10 ounces small shrimp, peeled and deveined
- 1 1/2 cups fresh shelled fava beans (about 1 1/2 pounds unshelled, see Note)
- 2 medium-size ripe but firm tomatoes, peeled with a vegetable peeler, seeded, and chopped
- 1 medium-size red onion, finely chopped
- 1 medium-size red bell pepper, cored, seeded, and diced
- 4 to 5 tablespoons drained small capers
- 2/3 cup finely chopped fresh flat-leaf parsley, or more to taste
- 6 tablespoons fragrant extra-virgin olive oil
- 1/4 cup fresh lemon juice, or more to taste
- 3 tablespoons sherry vinegar, preferably aged
- Coarse salt (kosher or sea) and freshly ground black pepper

1. Bring a large pot of salted water to a boil. Add the rice, let the water return to a boil, and stir the rice a few times. Reduce the heat to medium and cook the rice until it is tender, 15 to 17 minutes. Drain and keep warm.

2. Meanwhile, bring a medium-size saucepan of water to a simmer. Add the shrimp and cook for 30 seconds. Turn off the heat and let the shrimp steep for 1½ minutes. Drain the shrimp in a colander, then rinse them under cold running water to prevent them from overcooking.

3. Bring a pot of water to a boil, then add the fava beans and cook until just tender, 2 to 4 minutes. Drain the fava beans in a colander and place it under cold running water until the beans are cool enough to handle. Gently peel the skins off the beans. Let the beans cool to warm.

4. While the rice is still warm, transfer it to a large bowl. Add the shrimp, fava beans, tomatoes, onion, red pepper, capers, parsley, olive oil, lemon juice, and vinegar and toss to mix. Season with salt and black pepper to taste and add more lemon juice, if desired. Cover the salad with plastic wrap and refrigerate it for 2 to 4 hours. Let the salad return to room temperature, then taste for seasoning, adding a little more lemon juice, if desired, and serve. **SERVES 6**

NOTE: You can substitute 1 cup shelled edamame (soybeans) or 1 cup baby lima beans for the fava beans. Let them thaw if frozen. The soybeans will be done after boiling for 3 to 5 minutes. The lima beans will need to boil for about 5 minutes.

FRISEE SALAD WITH "BURNT" GARLIC VINAIGRETTE

ESCAROLA A L'ALL CREMAT

Vegetables or fish dressed with warm garlicky olive oil and topped with garlic chips can be found in many regions of Spain, from Andalusia to the Basque Country to Catalonia. The Catalans call these "burnt" garlic dishes, and they cook the garlic to a deep brown. This robust bistro-style salad was inspired by one served at Cal Pep, a lunch counter dearly loved by everyone in Barcelona. The proprietor, "Pep" Manubens, suggests including anything from sausage, to cold cuts such as *jamón,* to good-quality canned tuna in the salad. It's also delicious with leftover roast chicken or turkey.

- 5 tablespoons fragrant extra-virgin olive oil
- 6 ounces sweet Spanish-style chorizo sausage, sliced
- 7 to 8 medium-size garlic cloves, thickly sliced
- 3 tablespoons sherry vinegar, preferably aged
- Coarse salt (kosher or sea) and freshly ground black pepper
- 7 to 8 cups frisée (curly endive), rinsed, dried, and torn into bite-size pieces

1. Heat 1 tablespoon of the olive oil in a medium-size skillet over medium heat. Add the chorizo and cook until warmed through but not browned, about 1 minute per side. Using a slotted spoon, transfer the chorizo to a plate lined with a paper towel.

2. Heat the remaining 4 tablespoons olive oil in a small skillet over low heat. Add the garlic and cook, stirring, until deep-brown but not burnt, 8 to 10 minutes. Remove the skillet from the heat and, using a slotted spoon, transfer the garlic to another plate lined with a paper towel. Stir the vinegar into the skillet (stand back, as the oil might splatter) and season the dressing with salt and pepper to taste.

3. Place the frisée and chorizo in a mixing bowl and lightly season them with salt and pepper. Add the dressing, toss to coat evenly, and transfer the salad to a large serving platter. Scatter the garlic over the salad and serve at once. **SERVES 4 OR 5**

FRISEE WITH PEARS AND HONEYED LARDONS

ENSALADA DE ESCAROLA CON JAMON Y PERAS

Whenever you come across a savory dish that includes pears, you can safely bet that the recipe is from Catalonia, perhaps from the

Pyrenean Puigcerdá region, famous for its divinely delicious pears. This recipe is inspired by one from Can Ventura, a restaurant in an area that, due to a fluke of history, is within the French border but is governed by Spain. Its cuisine offers the best of the two cultures. Essentially a variation on the French bistro salad called *frisée aux lardons,* this smoky-sweet-tangy salad includes pancetta *lardons* (a stand-in for Catalan mountain bacon), caramelized with honey and vinegar, and pears that flavor both the salad and the vinaigrette. (Though not part of the original version, you can also add shavings of aged Manchego cheese or Parmesan to the mix.) Accompanied by Catalan Tomato Bread (page 165), it makes a delicious first course served before any number of the Catalan dishes you'll find in this book.

- 1 piece (5 to 6 ounces) pancetta, diced medium-fine
- 4 1/2 teaspoons honey
- 2 tablespoons best-quality red wine vinegar, plus 1/4 cup for the dressing
- 2 small ripe but firm pears, peeled, cored, and cut into 1/2-inch dice (see Note)
- 1/4 cup fragrant extra-virgin olive oil
- Coarse salt (kosher or sea) and freshly ground black pepper
- 7 to 8 cups frisée (curly endive), rinsed, dried, and torn into bite-size pieces

1. Place the pancetta in a small skillet over medium-high heat and cook until it begins to render its fat, about 2 minutes. Reduce the heat to medium and continue cooking until the pancetta is lightly browned. If there is too much fat in the skillet, pour some off. Add the honey and 2 tablespoons of the vinegar, stirring until the honey dissolves. Cook until the vinegar evaporates and the pancetta is evenly coated with the honey mixture. Turn off the heat and let the pancetta cool a little.

2. Place 3 to 4 tablespoons of the diced pear and the remaining ¼ cup vinegar in a blender and puree. Scrape the puree into a bowl and whisk in the olive oil. Season the dressing generously with salt and pepper to taste.

3. Place the frisée in a bowl, add the caramelized pancetta and the remaining diced pears, and toss to mix. Stir in enough of the dressing to coat the frisée lightly (you may not need all of the dressing). Taste for seasoning, adding more salt and/or pepper as necessary, and serve at once. **SERVES 4 TO 6**

NOTE: If you dice the pears ahead of time, sprinkle them with lemon juice to prevent discoloration.

LENTIL SALAD WITH CHORIZO AND JAMON CRISPS

ENSALADA TIBIA DE LENTEJAS CON CRUJIENTE DE JAMON Y CHORIZO

Gutsy, smoky, and wonderful, this salad is substantial enough for a light main course and perfect for parties. The best lentils for the job are the green French du Puy lentils or the Spanish pardina lentils, but regular brown lentils are also delicious. The tomatoes add a fresh counterpoint to the salad, and for this dish I prefer peeling them raw with a vegetable peeler rather than blanching them first, which tends to make them mushy. Choose tomatoes that aren't overly ripe. You'll need a small cheesecloth bag to hold the onion, garlic, and herbs while the lentils cook.

- 1 small onion
- 3 medium-size garlic cloves, peeled
- 3 fresh flat-leaf parsley sprigs, plus 1/4 cup chopped parsley
- 1 bay leaf
- 1 cup green or brown lentils (see Note), rinsed and picked over
- Extra-virgin olive oil
- 1/2 pound sweet Spanish-style chorizo sausage, diced medium-fine
- 2 ounces thinly sliced serrano ham or prosciutto
- 2 tablespoons sherry vinegar, preferably aged
- 1 tablespoon best-quality red wine vinegar
- 1 tablespoon chicken stock or broth, or water
- 1 teaspoon honey
- Coarse salt (kosher or sea) and freshly ground black pepper
- 3 medium-size firm tomatoes, peeled, seeded, and chopped
- 1/4 cup finely sliced scallions, both white and green parts

1. Place the onion, garlic, parsley sprigs, and bay leaf in a double layer of cheesecloth and tie it shut.

2. Place the lentils in a medium-size saucepan and add enough cold water to cover them by 3 inches. Bring to a boil over high heat. Skim the foam off thoroughly, add the cheesecloth bag, and reduce the heat to low. Simmer until the lentils are tender, 15 to 18 minutes. Drain the lentils. (If you are making the lentils ahead, toss them with a little olive oil. They will keep for up to 2 days, covered, in the refrigerator. Let them come to room temperature before continuing with the recipe.)

3. Heat 1 tablespoon olive oil in a medium-size skillet over medium-high heat. Add the chorizo and cook, stirring, until nicely browned and beginning to crisp, about 5 minutes. Using a slotted spoon, transfer the chorizo to paper towels to drain and keep warm.

4. Pour olive oil to a depth of ½ inch in a small skillet and heat over medium heat until almost smoking. Add the ham slices, one at a time, and cook until shriveled and crisp, about 30 seconds, transferring the cooked slices to paper towels to drain.

5. Place 3 tablespoons olive oil, the sherry vinegar, red wine vinegar, chicken stock, and honey in a small microwave-safe bowl and stir to mix. Microwave on high power for 30 seconds, then season the vinaigrette with salt and pepper to taste.

6. Place the drained lentils, chorizo, tomatoes, chopped parsley, scallions, and warm vinaigrette in a large bowl and toss to mix. Crumble the crisp ham slices into medium-size pieces, toss some with the salad, scatter the rest on top, and serve. **SERVES 4 TO 6**

NOTE: If you are using Spanish pardinas, they will need to soak overnight before being cooked. Goya brand pardinas do not need to be soaked, despite what it says on the package.

A SPANISH OLIVE OIL SAMPLER

No ingredient is more fundamental to Spanish cooking than olive oil, which ranges from an inexpensive, everyday fat for frying to pricey elixirs reverentially drizzled on langoustines or swirled into soups. Having supplied the Roman empire with the bulk of its oil in antiquity, Spain never looked back and today produces some whopping 50 percent of the world's olive oil. Although most Spanish oil comes from the Andalusian provinces of Jaén and Córdoba, other regions, especially Catalonia, are playing catch-up with boutique products that can give Tuscany or Liguria a run for their olives. Generally, the dry Andalusian heat results in oils that are smooth, golden, and fruity, with just a hint of the peppery bite we associate with Tuscan oils. But with so much variety, it's best not to generalize. Likewise, one should retire the notion that there's such a thing as generic, all-purpose olive oil. Both chefs and home cooks these days choose their olive oil depending on how they plan to use it (frying, sautéing, drizzling, dressing a salad) and on the flavor they desire (fruity, peppery, smooth, astringent, delicate, robust). As I write this, I have some eight different Spanish olive oils arrayed on my kitchen counter: Each has its own nuance, texture, and color.

The effect of a specific olive variety on the character of its oil is not unlike that of a particular grape on its wine. Spain boasts more than 260 olive cultivars, with a scope of flavors and fragrances that reflect the diversity of the country's geography. Though it's impossible to keep track of them all—especially since so many olive oils are blends of different varieties of olive—here's an introduction to the best-known olives and their oils.

ARBEQUINA From Catalonia and Aragon The suave oil from the small, delicate arbequina olives is herbaceous and fruity, with intimations of almonds and artichokes, and an attractive bitterness on the finish. It has a smooth texture, a heady fragrance, and a color that ranges from gold to muted green. Arbequina oils are young, fragile, and fresh tasting—not really suitable for cooking. Use them on salads, as a final touch for grilled fish or tender green vegetables, or for moistening toasted or grilled bread. The nutty, light-bright fruit is Catalonia's best-loved table olive.

CORNICABRA From Toledo and Ciudad Real in Castilla La Mancha The oil from these ancient horn-shaped olives—*cornicabra* means goat horn—is sweet-bitter-pungent, well balanced, and velvety textured, with a greenish-gold hue. Oil from riper cornicabra olives is reminiscent of avocado, with which it deliciously pairs. Use cornicabra oil straight from the bottle on gazpachos, in warm potato or bean salad, or for braised green vegetables, sautéed fish or chicken, or *escabeches.*

EMPELTRE From Bajo Aragon, Tarragona, and the Balearic Islands Light, mild, faintly sweet, and vividly fruity, this pale-golden oil has notes of apples and almonds and just a faint hint of pepper. Because of its sweetness, empeltre oil is great for blending with other varieties of olive oil. By itself, it's delicious in salad dressings, in uncooked marinades, or drizzled over asparagus. Like arbequina, this oil is delicate and unstable. It's best used raw (don't cook in it) and stored in a cool dark place.

HOJIBLANCA From Seville, Málaga, and Córdoba *Hojiblanca* olives have been around since antiquity, producing oils that can range rather widely in flavor but generally tend to be pleasantly bittersweet, fruity,

and lightly peppery, with a note of almonds. As it can withstand chilling, this stable oil is perfect for gazpachos. It's also good for frying and sautéing. And it's terrific for baking—both sweet and savory. The plump, round fruit also shows up as a popular black table olive.

PICUAL From the Andalusian provinces of Jaén, Córdoba, and Granada A high-yield variety, picuals comprise some 50 percent of all Spanish olives and are prized for their reliability and versatility. Picual oil is rather robust, peppery, fresh tasting, and pleasantly bitter. Because it's so stable, this is an excellent cooking oil, whether you're deep-frying, sautéing, braising vegetables, or cooking potatoes. It's also delicious in vinaigrettes made with sherry vinegar. Picual oil is often blended with other varieties, such as hojiblanca.

PICUDO From Córdoba, Jaén, Granada, and Málaga The pointed end of the fruit—*picudo* means prominent peak—accounts for the name of this olive, which generally makes a sweet, light, well-balanced oil with floral hints of apples and tropical fruit. Use it to drizzle on mild, delicate dishes, with buttery salad greens, and fruit gazpachos, and when baking sweets or frying fish.

WARM WHITE BEAN AND HAM SALAD

ENSALADA DE ALUBIAS BLANCAS Y JAMON

Inspired by a recipe given to me by the renowned Madrid recipe developer María Jesús Gil, this easy salad is pure comfort food. Serve it as a tapa or a light supper or lunch, and delight in how a handful of diced, musky *jamón* and a colorful, garlicky bell pepper vinaigrette can transform a simple can of white beans. Though black beans aren't particularly Spanish, they are also excellent served with the warm pepper vinaigrette.

- 2 cans (each about 15 ounces) cannellini or Great Northern beans, with their liquid
- 1/2 cup chicken stock or broth
- 1/2 cup fragrant extra-virgin olive oil
- 6 medium-size garlic cloves, minced
- 1 piece (4 ounces) serrano ham or prosciutto, finely diced
- 1/2 small dry red chile, such as arbol, crumbled
- 1/2 cup finely diced red bell pepper
- 1/2 cup finely diced green bell pepper
- 1 small plum tomato, diced
- 1/2 cup minced fresh flat-leaf parsley
- 1 tablespoon sherry vinegar, preferably aged, or more to taste
- Coarse salt (kosher or sea) and freshly ground black pepper

1. Place the beans, their liquid, and the chicken stock in a medium-size saucepan and bring to a simmer over medium heat. Cover the saucepan, reduce the heat to very low, and simmer until the beans are warmed through and no longer al dente but are not mushy, 7 to 8 minutes. Drain the beans, setting aside 2 tablespoons of the cooking liquid, and place them in a bowl.

2. While the beans are cooking, heat the olive oil in a small saucepan over medium-low heat. Add the garlic and cook, stirring, until very fragrant but not browned, 1 to 2 minutes. Add the ham and chile and cook for another 2 to 3 minutes. Add the red and green peppers and cook until they just begin to soften, 2 to 3 minutes. Stir in the tomato and cook until it softens slightly but still holds its shape, 2 minutes. Remove the saucepan from the heat and stir in the parsley, vinegar, and the reserved bean cooking liquid. Taste for seasoning, adding more vinegar as necessary. Stir the dressing into the beans and season with salt and black pepper to taste. Let the salad cool to warm, 10 to 15 minutes, then serve.

SERVES 6

SHERRY VINEGAR

Vinagre de Jerez is the aristocrat of the vinegar world. Vivid and well structured, with a penetrating, lasting astringency, it has the nutty notes characteristic of sherry and the complex bouquet of a fine wine. Sherry vinegar gives special vigor to salad dressings, makes awesome glazes and marinades, and lends an inimitable brightness to Andalusian gazpachos.

Like its mother wine, *vinagre de Jerez* comes from the Jerez region of Andalusia, specifically the sherry-producing centers of Jerez de la Frontera, Sanlúcar de Barrameda, and El Puerto de Santa María, a triangle of towns that today make up the DO (*Denominación de Origen*) of *vinagre de Jerez.* Sherry vinegar starts by injecting good-quality sherry wine with a bacteria that converts the alcohol into acetic acid. Once it begins to ferment, the vinegar undergoes the same solera aging process as the wine sherry: Younger vinegars are added to older ones, progressing through a series of stacked oak barrels filled with vinegars of various ages. American oak barrels, previously used for aging sherry, contribute character to the vinegar; the process of transferring it from barrel to barrel increases the oxygenation that imparts complexity and a dark amber color. *Reserva* (reserve) sherry vinegars are aged for at least two years, and it isn't uncommon to find vinegars matured for up to thirty years. The longer the vinegar ages, the higher the acidity, but with a good vinegar high acidity means a taste that is concentrated rather than sour. Profoundly aged boutique sherry vinegars are becoming widely available in the United States, and for a fraction of what you'd pay for an old balsamic vinegar. (I mean the real *balsamico,* not a supermarket counterfeit.)

At times sherry vinegar can be used interchangeably with red wine vinegar, but remember that it has a personality all its own. It's sharper and more intense than the average wine vinegar, and not always right for dishes that call for, say, a lighter white wine vinegar. And don't forget that Spanish vinegar production isn't limited to *vinagre de Jerez.* Look for vinegars made from *cava* and the absolutely extraordinary chardonnay and cabernet vinegars called Forum, adored by contemporary Spanish chefs.

CATALAN GRILLED VEGETABLE SALAD

ESCALIVADA

Eating this dish in Catalonia, I always quietly gasp at how utterly magical plain grilled vegetables can taste. I had ascribed my gasps to the quality of the Catalan peppers, onions, and eggplants, but when I made *escalivada* at home, the magic remained. *Escalivada*—or *escalibada*—is from *escalivar,* or to cook in ashes, which is how the dish is traditionally prepared. Though today many Catalans roast the vegetables in a hot oven, to me this misses the point, as smokiness is an essential flavor component. In summer, the vegetables can be grilled on a grate until charred and soft or cooked whole directly in glowing coals, then peeled. When cooking indoors, I char the eggplants right on a gas burner and broil the rest of the vegetables while the eggplants cook. Torn into pieces and moistened with olive oil, the vegetables blend into a luscious savory marmalade, which can be served as a tapa, a relish with grilled meats, or a salad, perhaps topped with a few fat anchovies or a sprinkling of chopped black olives. *Escalivada* also makes a delicious topping for *coca* (Catalan pizza) or Catalan Tomato Bread (page 165).

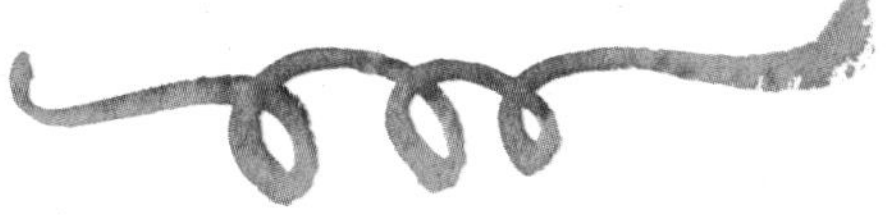

1 large very ripe red bell pepper, cut in half, cored, and seeded
3 medium-size firm but ripe tomatoes, each cut into 6 to 8 wedges
1 medium-size red onion, cut in half, each half cut into 5 or 6 wedges
3 tablespoons fragrant extra-virgin olive oil, plus more for brushing the vegetables
3 slender Asian eggplants (no longer than 6 to 7 inches)
1 medium-size garlic clove, crushed with a garlic press
$4^1/_2$ teaspoons best-quality red wine vinegar, or more to taste
Flaky sea salt, such as Maldon
1 to 2 tablespoons minced fresh flat-leaf parsley

1. Preheat the broiler.

2. Flatten the red peppers slightly so that they lie flat and place them on a large, well-oiled broiler pan. Arrange the tomatoes, cut side up, and onion on the same pan and brush all the vegetables with olive oil. Broil the vegetables until they are soft and charred, about 15 minutes for the onion, a few minutes longer for the tomatoes and red peppers, transferring the vegetables to a platter as they finish cooking. When all the vegetables are done, place the peppers in a bowl, cover it with plastic wrap, and let steam for 15 minutes.

3. While the vegetables are broiling, place a small flameproof rack, such as the rack from a toaster oven, directly over a gas burner and set the heat to medium. Place the eggplants on the rack over the flame and cook until soft and charred all over, 7 to 8 minutes, turning often so they all cook evenly. (If the eggplants begin to leak, wipe off the area around the burners as soon as the eggplants are done. Keep an eye on the eggplants at all times, being aware of any stray sparks. Using tongs, transfer the eggplants to a plate and let cool enough to handle.

4. Peel the red peppers and tear them into strips. Peel the eggplants, remove and discard the stems, and tear the flesh into long strips. Decoratively arrange the eggplants, peppers, tomatoes, and onion wedges on a platter, alternating the various vegetables.

5. Place the 3 tablespoons olive oil, the garlic, and vinegar in a small bowl and whisk to mix. Pour the dressing over the vegetables, sprinkle with salt and parsley, and let stand for about 1 hour before serving. **SERVES 4 TO 6**

GREEN SALAD WITH APRICOTS AND HAZELNUTS

ENSALADA CON FRUTAS SECAS

Carmelitas restaurant is Barcelona's favorite art-world haunt, overflowing at lunchtime with hipster *artistes,* gallerists sporting the latest fashion in eyewear, and sundry other bohemians. The menu is stylish, unpretentious, and impeccably tasty, and one of the perennial favorites is a salad that shows off the Catalan taste for dried fruit and nuts. This is my adaptation. The perfect greens for this salad are frisée, baby arugula, mâche, bite-size pieces of Belgian endive, and bits of radicchio. It is always better to create your own salad mixture, but in a pinch you can make do with store-bought mesclun. I like the apricots to be slightly chewy, but if you prefer, you can soak them in a warm sherry or a not-too-dry white wine. Use your best olive oil.

- 1/2 cup finely slivered dried apricots, or more to taste
- 1/2 cup hazelnuts, toasted (see page 267), skinned, and coarsely chopped
- 10 to 12 cups mesclun, rinsed and dried
- 3 tablespoons best-quality red wine vinegar
- 1 tablespoon fresh orange juice
- 1/2 teaspoon honey
- 1/4 cup fragrant extra-virgin olive oil
- Coarse salt (kosher or sea) and freshly ground black pepper

1. Set aside a couple of tablespoons of the apricots and hazelnuts for garnish. Place the remaining apricots and hazelnuts, and the mesclun, in a large salad bowl and gently toss to mix.

2. Place the vinegar, orange juice, and honey in a small bowl and whisk until the honey dissolves.

3. Carefully toss the salad with the olive oil until the leaves are evenly coated. Add the vinegar mixture and toss until evenly distributed. Season with salt and pepper to taste, sprinkle the reserved apricots and hazelnuts on top, and serve at once. **SERVES 6**

MESCLUN WITH FIGS, CABRALES, AND POMEGRANATE

ENSALADA CON HIGOS, CABRALES Y GRANADA

Pretty and fruity-tart, this salad is equally delicious as a first course or after a meal in lieu of a cheese course. You can use raw figs, but broiling them intensifies their flavor and adds an interesting smoky note. As a variation, try hazelnut or walnut oil in the dressing.

1 medium-size pomegranate
1/2 teaspoon honey
4 1/2 teaspoons fresh lemon juice
4 1/2 teaspoons best-quality red wine vinegar
2 tablespoons minced shallots
1/4 cup fragrant extra-virgin olive oil
Coarse salt (kosher or sea) and freshly ground black pepper
10 purple figs, trimmed and quartered lengthwise
8 to 10 cups loosely packed mesclun, rinsed and dried
1/4 cup toasted pine nuts (see page 267)
2 to 3 ounces Cabrales or other blue cheese, crumbled

1. Cut the pomegranate into quarters. Remove the seeds from 3 pomegranate quarters and place them in a bowl, picking out and discarding any pieces of membrane. Working over a sieve, press the juice from the remaining pomegranate quarter into a second bowl. Whisk in the honey, lemon juice, vinegar, and shallots, then slowly whisk in the olive oil. Season the dressing generously with salt and pepper to taste and let stand while you prepare the figs.

2. Preheat the broiler.

3. Arrange the fig quarters, cut side up, on a broiler pan. Broil the figs until they look a little caramelized and lightly charred, about 5 minutes.

4. Place the broiled figs, pomegranate seeds, mesclun, and pine nuts in a bowl and gently toss to mix. Add enough dressing to lightly coat the mesclun and season the salad with salt and pepper to taste. Gently toss in the cheese and serve at once.

SERVES 4 TO 6

THE ADDICTIVE ROASTED PEPPER SALAD

ZORONGOLLO

Here is a dish I never tire of—sweet roasted bell peppers in a soupy marinade of chopped or grated tomatoes, vinegar, and good olive oil, perfect for dipping bread into. Enjoyed basically everywhere in Spain south of Madrid, the salad is called *zorongollo* and sometimes includes boiled potatoes, tuna, or bacalao. In Andalusia, it goes by the name of *pimientos aliñados* (dressed peppers) and is often featured as part of a tapas spread. By any name, it's one of the world's great basic dishes, wonderful as a tapa, a side dish salad, or a topping for grilled chicken or fish.

- 4 large roasted ripe red bell peppers (see page 385), cut into medium-size strips
- 4 large roasted green bell peppers (see page 385), cut into medium-size strips
- 2 medium-size vine-ripened tomatoes, cut in half and grated on a box grater, skins discarded
- 1/2 medium-size sweet white onion, cut into quarters and thinly sliced
- 1/3 cup fragrant extra-virgin olive oil
- 3 tablespoons sherry vinegar, preferably aged, or more to taste
- Coarse salt (kosher or sea)
- 4 medium-size garlic cloves, finely chopped

1. Place the roasted red and green peppers, the tomatoes, onion, olive oil, and vinegar in a mixing bowl and toss to mix. Season with salt to taste and add more vinegar if the salad is not tart enough. Let the salad stand at room temperature for at least 1 hour for the flavors to develop.

2. To serve, place the salad on a shallow serving dish and sprinkle the garlic over it. Leftovers will keep for up to 2 days, covered, in the refrigerator.
SERVES 6 TO 8 AS A TAPA OR SIDE DISH

GAZPACHO SALAD

COJONDONGO

I had always wanted to find an authentic version of gazpacho in its preliquid form: a salad of tomatoes, peppers, cucumbers, onion, and bread, dressed with vinegar, garlic, and olive oil. I had no luck in Andalusia, the birthplace of cold gazpacho, but in neighboring Extremadura—a region where the gazpachos are normally hot and feature game and where bread makes its way into almost every dish—I hit the jackpot. The salad, called *cojondongo,* which I encountered in an anonymous village tapas bar, was every bit as good as I had hoped for. It's a cooling, nourishing peasant dish,

Beautiful organic green peppers ready for market

traditionally made by shepards from provisions they carried with them to the pastures. The version I tasted also featured green grapes, since it is common in parts of Extremadura to add fruit to salads and other savory dishes. Though not entirely authentic, slivered mint or basil is delicious in this. To make the salad dressier and more modern, feel free to use different colors and types of heirloom tomatoes.

- 2 1/2 cups cubed day-old dense country bread (1-inch cubes)
- 2 medium-size garlic cloves, chopped
- 1 large pinch of coarse salt (kosher or sea)
- 1 small pinch of cumin seeds
- 3 tablespoons sherry vinegar, preferably aged, or best-quality red wine vinegar, or more to taste
- 1/3 cup fragrant extra-virgin olive oil
- 1 1/2 pounds very ripe but firm tomatoes, cut into 3/4-inch cubes
- 2 small Kirby (pickling) cucumbers, peeled and diced
- 1 large Italian (frying) pepper, cored, seeded, and diced
- 1/2 cup finely chopped white onion
- 1/2 cup seedless green grapes, cut in half
- About 1/2 cup slivered fresh mint or basil (optional)

1. Preheat the oven to 350°F.

2. Arrange the bread cubes in a single layer on a large rimmed baking sheet and bake until they are just beginning to turn golden, 8 to 10 minutes, stirring once. Let the bread cubes cool.

3. Place the garlic, salt, and cumin in a mortar and, using a pestle, mash them into a paste. Add the vinegar and olive oil and whisk to mix.

4. Place the toasted bread and the tomatoes, cucumbers, Italian pepper, onion, grapes, and mint, if using, in a large bowl and toss to mix. Add the dressing to the salad and toss to combine well. Let the salad stand for 5 to 10 minutes before serving to allow the bread to soak up the dressing. **SERVES 4**

SPANISH SALAD, ANYONE?

I always hold my breath when ordering an *ensalada mixta* (mixed salad) in Spain. Even at respectable restaurants, I've been subjected to discolored iceberg lettuce tossed with canned peas, beets, and corn. At other times, though, especially in *vegetable-happy* Navarra, Rioja, or the Basque Country, the *ensaladas* were truly memorable mélanges of famously buttery Tudela lettuce hearts, boutique canned vegetables like white asparagus and piquillo peppers, and the much-prized canned tuna belly. These are the kinds of salads that I turn to at home again and again.

Spanish cooks tend to take the notion of *mixta* literally, blending raw and cooked vegetables and some form of protein—but keeping the dressing basic and on the side. Start with tender hearts of delicate lettuce, such as green leaf or Boston, and a few spears of endive, if you wish, and arrange them on a platter. Scatter quartered hard-cooked eggs and wedges of ripe, aromatic tomatoes on top. Then, decorate the salad with strips of piquillo peppers and good canned white asparagus, chunks of oil-packed tuna and/or anchovy fillets, or with strips of serrano ham instead of the fish. If you feel like tossing in some boiled green beans, artichoke hearts from a jar, or grated carrots, go right ahead. Sprinkled with sea salt and served with cruets of beautiful olive oil and aged red wine vinegar, *ensalada mixta* is one of the greatest simple lunches I know.

WILD ARUGULA AND ARTICHOKES

ENSALADA DE RUCULA Y ALCACHOFAS

The bar Nou Manolín in the seaside Mediterranean city of Alicante is a place I could happily settle into and never leave. A perfect *bar de producto* (an ingredient-driven dining bar), it specializes in seafood *a la plancha* and seasonal vegetables arrayed lavishly on the counter. Anything they prepare with artichokes—whether it's crisp fritters with an accent of sea salt or artichokes braised slowly in aromatic oil—is outstanding. One day I fell for a simple, elegant salad of wild, bitter greens called *llitsons,* thinly sliced raw artichokes, and shaved raw porcini mushrooms accented with lemon and oil. While regular arugula—the smaller and younger the better—will work fine in place of *llitsons,* try seeking out wild arugula. Available at some farmers' markets and specialty food stores, it has very small jagged leaves and an especially vivid peppery taste that's similar to that of *llitsons.* Shaved fennel can also be added to the mix, though that's more Italian than Spanish. And if you can get fresh porcini, well, *fenomenal!*

- 4 large button mushrooms, wiped clean and stemmed
- 2 1/2 tablespoons fresh lemon juice, plus more to taste
- 3 medium-size artichokes (about 1 1/2 pounds total), pared down to the heart (see page 370)
- 1 lemon, cut in half
- 3 to 4 tablespoons fragrant extra-virgin olive oil
- 2 small bunches wild arugula or very young arugula, stemmed, rinsed, and dried
- Coarse salt (kosher or sea) and freshly ground black pepper

1. Using a mandoline or a vegetable peeler, slice the mushrooms paper-thin and toss them with 1 tablespoon of the lemon juice. Let marinate for about 30 minutes.

2. Rinse the artichoke hearts and pat them dry with paper towels. Using a mandoline, a vegetable peeler, or a very sharp knife, slice the artichokes paper-thin. As you work, rub the cut sides with a lemon half to keep the artichoke from discoloring. Toss the artichokes with the remaining lemon juice and 1 tablespoon of the olive oil and let marinate for about 30 minutes.

3. Place the arugula in a salad bowl and season it with salt and pepper to taste. Toss the arugula with just enough of the remaining olive oil to lightly coat the leaves. Add the sliced mushrooms and artichokes and toss to mix. Taste the salad for seasoning, adding a little more lemon juice and salt and/or pepper as necessary. Serve the salad at once. **SERVES 4**

FAVA BEAN SALAD WITH JAMON AND FRESH MINT

AMANIDA DE FAVES AMB MENTA

In Italy, springtime fava bean salads are usually tossed with shaved Pecorino cheese. In Catalonia, the complementary ingredients are smoky-sweet slivered cured *jamón* and a bright accent of mint. Though the salad may sound traditional, it was actually "invented" by the legendary Catalan chef Josep Mercader and is now copied all over the region. If shelling and peeling fresh favas seems like too much of a chore, use shelled soybeans, which need no peeling.

3 cups shelled fresh fava beans (about 3 pounds unshelled), or 3 cups shelled soybeans (edamame), thawed if frozen
1 1/2 cups shredded tender escarole or iceberg lettuce leaves
2 to 3 ounces thinly sliced serrano ham or prosciutto, torn into thin slivers
1/3 cup shredded fresh mint
2 large shallots, finely chopped
Coarse salt (kosher or sea) and freshly ground black pepper
1/4 cup fragrant extra-virgin olive oil
2 tablespoons sherry vinegar, preferably aged, or best-quality red wine vinegar
2 tablespoons fresh lemon juice
1/2 teaspoon Dijon mustard
1 small garlic clove, crushed with a garlic press

1. Bring a pot of water to a boil, add the fava beans, and cook until just tender, 2 to 4 minutes. Drain the fava beans in a colander then place it under cold running water until the beans are cool enough to handle. Gently peel the skins off the beans.

2. Place the fava beans, escarole, ham, mint, and shallots in a bowl and toss to mix. Season with salt and pepper to taste.

3. Place the olive oil, vinegar, lemon juice, mustard, and garlic in a small bowl and whisk to mix. Toss the dressing with the salad. Taste for seasoning, adding more salt and/or pepper as necessary, and serve at once. **SERVES 4 TO 6**

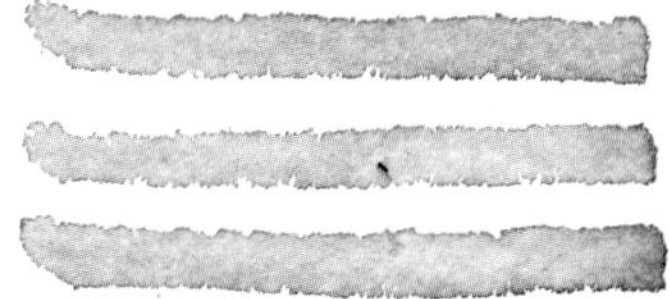

La Favorita
Fundada en 1946
MANTEQUILLAS
QUESOS

EGGS

MORE THAN BREAKFAST

What would happen to Spanish cuisine if the egg suddenly disappeared? The idea is too shocking to even consider, as there are times when the entire Spanish diet seems to revolve around yolks and whites. Fried in lots of olive oil until the edges are sizzled crisp but the yolk is still runny, *huevos fritos* are an essential meal, taken at any time of the day, either alone or on top of everything from sautéed baby squid to the season's first fava beans or peas. For *once* (a midmorning snack), the *huevo* shows up as a tall, fluffy *tortilla,* the cakelike omelet without which most tapas bars would instantly go out of business. A fancy restaurant lunch could begin with

Top left: A reservoir is a welcome relief in the typically arid landscape of Extremadura. *Top right:* Gaudí's colorful mosaic tiles decorate a bench in Park Güell, Barcelona. *Bottom left:* Old-fashioned Spanish shops such as this one often carry amazingly fresh eggs. *Bottom right:* A monastery along St. James' Way.

a poached egg served over a potato velouté with a shaving of truffles. Bar suppers might feature a stirringly good *revuelto*—eggs gently scrambled withother ingredients (the word means flipped over).

The egg in Spain goes high and low, haute and humble, universally adored by all. As all of Madrid knows, King Juan Carlos's favorite dish is *huevos rotos* (smashed eggs) with french fries at a taberna called Lucio. Three-star Michelin chef Juan Mari Arzak once confessed to me that the only thing he bothers making at home is *revuelto*. The renowned food critic Rafael García Santos famously organizes a yearly *tortilla de patata* competition in San Sebastián, where the potato omelets are dissected and judged as if they were the latest culinary haute couture. And Andoni Luis Adúriz, one of Spain's most creative young chefs, takes the egg so seriously that he has spent two years researching the chemistry of coagulation to conclude that for an ideal poaching, an egg should be just a few hours old and cooked at exactly 65°C (147°F)—sort of like a warm bath—for precisely 55 minutes. Today Adúriz's 65°C egg is among the country's most copied dishes.

As I said, the Spanish *really* like eggs.

In large measure, the egg's cult appeal is due to that fact that Spain is a formerly agrarian culture where the dining habits still remain close to these roots. There is also the egg's natural beauty, nutrition, and symbolism. The quality of Spanish eggs helps too. Even those from a corner store tend to be excellent. And when you get a *huevo* from a free-range, naturally fed barnyard hen, with its compact, flavorful, bright-saffron yolk, all you need to do is crack it into the pan to reach heaven. As the dishes in this chapter will demonstrate, eggs in Spain aren't just for breakfast.

POTATO TORTILLA

TORTILLA DE PATATAS

Here it is: Spain's most iconic, most popular dish, *tortilla de patata,* prepared in the classic way. Which is to say, the potatoes are first cooked in plenty of aromatic olive oil and drained before being mixed with the eggs and fried into a fat, fluffy omelet. Served as a light luncheon, with a salad of perfectly ripe tomatoes and a glass of Rioja, this is one of life's great simple pleasures. And you can't beat it as a tapa. Some Spanish cooks in the States add a pinch of saffron to their *tortillas* to simulate the bright yellow color of Spanish egg yolks.

3 medium-size Yukon Gold potatoes (about 1 1/2 pounds), peeled and quartered lengthwise
Coarse salt (kosher or sea)
1 1/4 cups extra-virgin olive oil
1 small onion, quartered and thinly sliced
6 large, very fresh eggs, preferably organic
2 tablespoons chicken stock or broth

1. Using a food processor, slice the potato quarters thinly crosswise, then pat thoroughly dry with paper towels. Rub potato slices with salt.

2. Heat the olive oil in a large, heavy skillet over medium-high heat until very hot, about 3 minutes. Reduce the heat to medium-low and add the potatoes in even layers. Cook, stirring occasionally, to prevent the potatoes from sticking and browning, until they are half-cooked, about 7 minutes. Stir in the onion, reduce the heat to low, and cook the potatoes until all of them are soft, about 15 minutes more. Using a slotted spoon, transfer the potatoes and onion to a colander set over a bowl and let them drain thoroughly. Set aside 2 tablespoons of the cooking oil and strain the rest for another use. Season the potatoes with salt.

3. Place the eggs, chicken stock, and a couple of pinches of salt in a large mixing bowl and beat until just scrambled. Gently stir in the potato mixture. Mash and stir the egg mixture gently with a fork to crush the potatoes just a little and mix them up well with the eggs. Let stand for about 10 minutes.

4. Heat 5 teaspoons of the reserved olive oil in a heavy 8-inch skillet, preferably nonstick, over medium-high heat until it is just beginning to smoke. Pour the egg mixture into the skillet and flatten the potatoes with a spatula until the top is fairly even. Reduce the heat to medium-low. Cook, moving and shaking the skillet, running a thin spatula around the edge and sliding it into the middle so that some of the egg runs under. Cook the *tortilla* in this fashion until the top is a little wet but not liquid, 6 to 8 minutes. Run the thin spatula under the *tortilla* to make sure that no part of the bottom is stuck to the skillet. Top the skillet with a rimless plate slightly larger than the skillet and, using oven mitts, quickly invert the *tortilla* onto the plate. If the skillet looks dry, add a little more olive oil. Carefully slide the *tortilla* back into the skillet, uncooked side down. Shake the skillet to straighten the *tortilla* and push the edges in with the spatula. Reduce the heat to very low and cook the *tortilla* until a toothpick inserted in the center comes out dry, 3 to 4 minutes.

TORTILLA DE PATATAS, SPAIN'S EGG MASTERPIECE

All it takes is three ingredients: eggs, potatoes, and olive oil. It's delicious hot, warm, or cold. It can be enjoyed for breakfast, lunch, or supper. And it makes an ideal tapa or snack. No wonder that in Spain, *tortilla de patata,* a plump, moonlike, potato-filled omelet, basks in such universal devotion—its image deserves to be emblazoned on the country's flag. When good, a *tortilla de patata* is about the most satisfying thing you can eat.

In Spanish, *tortilla* means a flat cake (in Mexico the same word came to describe the indigenous corn flatbreads). Though the term has been applied to omelets in Spain since the seventeenth century, the *tortilla* recipes found in historical cookbooks are for French-style omelets, without potatoes. The potato version probably emerged in the late eighteenth century, when the spud, which the *conquistadores* brought from the Andes around 1570, finally gained full acceptance. According to one legend, *tortilla de patata* was "invented" during the first Carlist War, a battle for the Spanish crown fought between 1833 and 1839. A famished general, goes the myth, dropped by an inn in the Navarra region and was treated to a wondrous dish improvised by the innkeepers with the staples from their war-ravaged larder: potatoes and eggs. (Scholars are skeptical of this story, pointing out that *tortilla de patata* had already been mentioned in an 1817 text that describes the foodstuffs of Navarra.) It is also possible that the very first potato omelet was flipped even earlier in Galicia, a region that pioneered the cultivation of the tuber. Either way, by the mid-nineteenth century, the potato omelet was a widely popular dish called *tortilla de patata* or *tortilla española,* to distinguish it from the French omelet.

These days, every Spaniard can make a pretty decent *tortilla* blindfolded; it's the sort of recipe that seems encoded in the national DNA. And while each cook brings a subtle personal touch to the dish, the most common version is a fat, round *tortilla,* loaded with olive-oil-fried potatoes, left to cool, then cut into wedges or squares. Of course, serious *tortilla* fanatics dismiss the make-ahead version as, well, lazy. For an exalted omelet experience, they'll send you to Galicia, a region famous for its *tortillas de patatas,* thanks to the quality of its potatoes and farm-fresh eggs, and the skill of its cooks. There, at good tapas bars the *tortilla* is always made to order. Not necessarily thick, it has a runny interior that forms a delicious foil for the potatoes, which are fried until very soft with a suggestion of crispness around the edges. This is the *tortilla* elevated to an art form.

Invert the *tortilla* again, as before, to cook on the first side for another minute.

5. Invert the *tortilla* onto a serving plate and pat the top with a paper towel to get rid of excess oil. Let it cool a little, then cut the *tortilla* into wedges and serve warm or at room temperature. To serve as a tapa, cut the *tortilla* into squares and serve with toothpicks. **SERVES 6 TO 8 AS A TAPA, 4 AS A LIGHT MAIN DISH**

TRUFFLED TORTILLA

TORTILLA TRUFADA

Dressed up with a few drops of truffle oil, sautéed mushrooms, and caramelized onions, the basic potato *tortilla* gets transformed into a Wow! restaurant-style dish that will leave your guests swooning. It's best served just slightly warm.

- 1/2 cup extra-virgin olive oil, or more if needed
- 4 ounces oyster mushrooms, trimmed, wiped clean with a damp paper towel, and finely chopped
- 2 medium-size onions, quartered and thinly sliced
- 2 medium-size (about 1 pound) boiled Yukon Gold potatoes, quartered and thinly sliced
- Coarse salt (kosher or sea) and freshly ground black pepper
- 5 large, very fresh eggs, preferably organic
- 2 tablespoons chicken stock or broth
- 3/4 teaspoon white or black truffle oil

1. Heat 1 tablespoon of the olive oil in a large skillet over medium-high heat. Add the mushrooms and cook, stirring, until they are lightly browned and have released and reabsorbed their liquid, 4 to 5 minutes. Using a slotted spoon, transfer the mushrooms to a bowl.

2. Wipe out the skillet and add another 2 tablespoons olive oil. Add the onions and cook over medium heat, stirring occasionally, until they are very soft and lightly caramelized, about 15 minutes. If the skillet looks dry as the onions cook, sprinkle in a little water, and adjust the heat so that the onions don't burn. When the onions are done, add another 3 tablespoons of the oil to the skillet, then add the potatoes. Cook over low heat, stirring very gently, until the ingredients are mixed and the potatoes are infused with the oil, 2 to 3 minutes, adding more oil if the potatoes look dry. Transfer the mixture to the bowl with the reserved mushrooms and gently stir to combine. Season with salt and pepper to taste and let cool completely. (The potato mixture can be prepared up to this stage a few hours in advance.)

3. Place the eggs, chicken stock, and a few pinches of salt in a large mixing bowl and beat until the eggs are just scrambled. Add the potato mixture and the truffle oil and mix until well combined. Let stand for about 10 minutes.

4. Heat about 5 teaspoons of the remaining olive oil in a heavy 8-inch skillet, preferably nonstick, over medium-high heat until it is just beginning to smoke. Pour the egg mixture into the skillet and flatten it with a spatula until the top is fairly even. Reduce the heat to medium-low. Cook, moving and shaking the skillet, running a thin spatula around the edge and sliding it into the middle so that some of the egg runs under. Cook the *tortilla* in this fashion until the top is a little wet but not liquid, about 6 minutes. Run the spatula under the *tortilla* to make sure that no part of the bottom is stuck to the skillet. Top the skillet with a rimless plate slightly larger than the skillet and, using oven mitts, quickly invert the *tortilla* onto the plate. If the skillet looks dry, add a little more olive oil. Carefully slide the *tortilla* back into the skillet, uncooked side down. Shake the skillet to straighten the *tortilla* and push the edges in with the spatula. Reduce the heat to

very low and cook the *tortilla* until a toothpick inserted in the center comes out dry, 3 to 4 minutes. Invert the *tortilla* again, as before, and cook on the first side for another minute.

5. Invert the *tortilla* onto a serving plate and pat the top with a paper towel to get rid of excess oil. Let cool a little, then cut the *tortilla* into wedges and serve warm or at room temperature. To serve as a tapa, cut the *tortilla* into squares and serve with toothpicks. **SERVES 6 AS A TAPA, 3 OR 4 AS A LIGHT MAIN COURSE**

TORTILLA WITH CHORIZO, POTATOES, AND ALLIOLI

TRUITA TREMPERA

This omelet is so delicious! Filled with chorizo, potatoes, and sautéed onion, it is covered with a layer of garlicky *allioli* mayonnaise that brings all the flavors together under a piquant cap. This *tortilla—truita* in Catalan—is the proud creation of the venerable bar Cal Pep in Barcelona. They call it a "tricky" omelet, presumably because *allioli* in a *tortilla* is so unexpected. It's excellent as a tapa and even better as a light supper or luncheon dish.

About 7 tablespoons extra-virgin olive oil, or more if needed
1 small onion, quartered and thinly sliced
6 to 7 ounces sweet Spanish-style chorizo sausage, cut into medium-size dice
2 medium-size Yukon Gold potatoes (about 1 pound total), boiled, cooled, peeled, and cut into fine dice
7 large, very fresh eggs, preferably organic
4 1/2 teaspoons chicken stock or broth
Coarse salt (kosher or sea) and freshly ground black pepper
4 to 5 tablespoons Allioli (page 44)

1. Heat 4 tablespoons of the olive oil in a large skillet over medium-low heat. Add the onion and cook until soft but not browned, about 5 minutes. Add the chorizo and cook for 2 minutes, stirring. Add the potatoes, stir to coat them with the olive oil, cover the skillet, and cook to blend the flavors, about 5 minutes, stirring once. Using a slotted spoon, transfer the potato mixture to a bowl and let cool.

2. Place the eggs, chicken stock, and a few pinches of salt in a large bowl and beat until just scrambled. Add the eggs to the chorizo mixture and mix until well combined. Season with pepper to taste.

3. Heat 2 tablespoons of the olive oil in a heavy 10-inch skillet, preferably nonstick, over medium-high heat until it is just beginning to smoke. Pour the egg mixture into the skillet and flatten it with a spatula until the top is fairly even. Reduce the heat to medium-low. Cook, moving and shaking the skillet, running a thin spatula around the edge and sliding it into the middle so that some of the egg runs under. Cook the *tortilla* in this fashion until the top is a little wet but not liquid, 6 to 8 minutes.

TORTILLA DE PATATAS

According to Ferran Adria

Ferran Adrià, the genius chef of El Bulli, has done quite a few far-out things to eggs in his life. One of the creations he is most pleased with, however, involves . . . a bag of potato chips. Galicians, who are the great *tortilla de patata* masters, Adrià notes, like their omelets with *patatas* a little bit crisp. To simulate the effect and eliminate the task of frying the potatoes, Adrià fills potato *tortillas* with chips. Though this isn't the kind of dish you'll ever eat at El Bulli, the simple idea has become a great hit with Spanish home cooks. Adrià suggests using fresh olive-oil-fried potato chips from a *churrería* (the fried cruller shops that also sell bags of chips). But even good-quality supermarket chips, such as Lay's, work fine. Just avoid chips that are too thick, flavored, or oversalted.

To make Adrià's potato chip *tortilla,* use two 1-ounce bags of potato chips for every four eggs. Crush them slightly into the beaten eggs and let them sit for five to ten minutes. Then make the *tortilla* following the recipe on page 139.

4. Run the thin spatula under the *tortilla* to make sure that no part of the bottom is stuck to the skillet. Top the skillet with a rimless plate slightly larger than the skillet and, using oven mitts, quickly invert the *tortilla* onto the plate. If the skillet looks dry, add 2 teaspoons of the remaining olive oil. Carefully slide the *tortilla* back into the skillet, uncooked side down. Shake the skillet to straighten the *tortilla* and push the edges in with the spatula. Reduce the heat to very low and cook the *tortilla* until a toothpick inserted in the center comes out dry, 3 to 4 minutes. Invert the *tortilla* again, as before, and cook the first side for another minute.

5. Invert the *tortilla* onto a serving plate and pat the top with a paper towel to get rid of excess oil. Let the *tortilla* cool for about 10 minutes and then spread the *allioli* over it. The *tortilla* can be served warm or at room temperature, cut into wedges. To serve as a tapa, cut the *tortilla* into squares and serve with toothpicks. **SERVES 6 AS A TAPA, 4 AS A LIGHT MAIN DISH**

TORTILLA WITH POTATOES, ARTICHOKES, AND PEPPERS

TORTILLA DE PATATAS, ALCACHOFAS Y PIMIENTOS DE PIQUILLO

One day, dying from hunger in my tiny rented Madrid apartment with half a kitchen, I improvised this *tortilla* using jars of artichokes and piquillo peppers and a leftover boiled potato. It was so incredibly good I've been making it ever since. Serve it as a snack, a tapa, or a light lunch for two.

TORTILLA TECHNIQUE

Though cooking the perfect *tortilla de patata* takes a bit of practice, once you get the knack, it's the easiest thing in the world—and a whole lot of fun. It's a dish you'll be making again and again. Here are some pointers. (You'll find a recipe for *tortilla de patatas* on page 139.)

THE POTATOES AND THE EGGS To make a *tortilla de patata* you need moderately starchy potatoes. In Spain they mostly use Kennebecs, a sort of all-purpose variety, but I find that the trusted and true Yukon Golds work best in the States. Start by cutting the potatoes into thin, uniform slices, then fry them in plenty of olive oil. Infusing the potatoes with the olive oil is what gives the *tortilla* its inimitable flavor and fragrance. (While Spanish cooks consider using boiled potatoes a crime, sometimes I cheat by sautéing boiled slices in olive oil; the trick works for me.) Once fried, scrupulously drain the potatoes of any excess oil, mix them with the beaten eggs, and let them sit a little while so that they meld properly. *Tortilla* "specialists" insist that overbeating the eggs makes for a dry omelet. However, adding a little chicken broth to the eggs will make the *tortilla* super *jugosa* (juicy).

THE FRYING Ready to fry the *tortilla?* Choose a deep, heavy skillet, preferably a nonstick one. The classic size is eight inches in diameter. Once you've mastered a smaller omelet, you can increase the ingredients and make *tortillas* as large as you want. You'll also need a sturdy plate without a rim—one that's slightly larger than the skillet—for when it's time to flip the *tortilla* over. Let the oil in the skillet get hot before you pour in the egg and potato mixture so that the bottom of the omelet can begin to set instantly. Then, keep shaking and moving the skillet, running a spatula or knife under the eggs so they have no chance to stick. As you cook, adjust the heat so that the center of the omelet sets without the bottom burning. When the uncooked side is no longer liquid, but *is* still wet and jiggly, you're ready for the dramatic *vuelta*—the flip!

LA VUELTA Before flipping the *tortilla* over, always check that no bits of the omelet are stuck to the skillet; that way, the omelet will come out in one piece. Wearing oven mitts, place the rimless plate over the skillet, holding it firmly with your left hand (if you are right-handed). With your other hand, grab the skillet handle and invert the *tortilla* onto the plate in a quick steady motion. Bits of *tortilla* stuck to the skillet? Remove them and tuck them into the top of the *tortilla* while it's still on the plate. To cook the other side, slide the *tortilla* back into the skillet, shaking it to straighten the *tortilla* out in its pretty round shape and tucking the edges under with a spatula.

How do you know when a *tortilla* is done? Well, Spaniards prefer their *tortillas* slightly—or very—runny, but they have those incredible Spanish eggs. Your best bet is to cook the *tortilla* until a toothpick inserted in the center comes out clean. Flip the *tortilla* over once or twice more for the best-looking omelet—and because flipping is fun. Then, turn it out on a serving plate and wait for at least ten minutes before cutting into it. I like the *tortilla* best when it's just slightly warm.

THE FLAVORS *Tortillas de patatas* are excellent made with only potatoes and eggs. They're even better when you add onions. Beyond that, you can flavor the *tortilla* with just about anything. Some ingredients to try:

- Diced chorizo or ham
- Strips of roasted or fried red bell peppers
- Peas, cooked artichokes, or sliced cooked asparagus
- Cooked wild mushrooms
- Truffle shavings

Of course, *tortillas* don't always include a potato filling. They can be made with a single vegetable or a combination or with such ingredients as salt cod and peppers. The Spanish *tortilla,* you see, is one of the world's most versatile dishes.

About 4 tablespoons olive oil, plus more if needed
1/2 medium-size onion, quartered and thinly sliced
1 large boiled Yukon Gold potato, quartered and thinly sliced
3 marinated artichoke hearts (from a can or jar), rinsed, patted dry, and thinly sliced
1/4 cup sliced piquillo peppers or roasted red bell peppers (see page 385)
4 large, very fresh eggs, preferably organic
2 tablespoons chicken stock or broth
Coarse salt (kosher or sea)

1. Heat 2 tablespoons of the olive oil in a medium-size skillet over medium heat. Add the onion and cook until limp but not brown, 3 to 5 minutes. Add the potato and cook, stirring gently, for 5 minutes. Stir in the artichokes and piquillo peppers and cook, stirring, for another 2 to 3 minutes. Using a slotted spoon, transfer the vegetable mixture to a bowl and let cool completely.

Tortilla with Potatoes, Artichokes, and Peppers (page 143) and Grilled Asparagus with Honey and Sherry Vinegar (page 373)

2. Place the eggs, chicken stock, and a few small pinches of salt in a medium-size bowl and beat until just scrambled. Add the potato mixture and mix until well combined. Let stand for about 10 minutes.

3. Heat 5 teaspoons of the remaining olive oil in a heavy 8-inch skillet, preferably nonstick, over medium-high heat until it is just beginning to smoke. Pour the egg mixture into the skillet and flatten it with a spatula until the top is fairly even. Reduce the heat to medium-low. Cook, moving and shaking the skillet, running a thin spatula around the edge and sliding it into the middle so that some of the egg runs under. Cook the *tortilla* in this fashion until the top is a little wet but not liquid, about 5 minutes.

4. Run the thin spatula under the *tortilla* to make sure that no part of the bottom is stuck to the skillet. Top the skillet with a rimless plate slightly larger than the skillet and, using oven mitts, quickly invert the *tortilla* onto the plate. If the skillet looks dry, add a little more olive oil. Carefully slide the *tortilla* back into the skillet, uncooked side down. Shake the skillet to straighten the *tortilla,* and push the edges in with the spatula. Reduce the heat to very low and cook the *tortilla* until a toothpick inserted in the center comes out dry, 3 to 4 minutes.

5. Invert the *tortilla* onto a serving plate and pat the top with a paper towel to get rid of excess oil. Let it cool a little, then cut the *tortilla* into wedges and serve warm or at room temperature. To serve as a tapa, cut the *tortilla* into squares and serve with toothpicks. **SERVES 4 TO 6 AS A TAPA, 2 AS A LIGHT MAIN DISH**

SALT COD AND GREEN PEPPER TORTILLA

TORTILLA DE BACALAO

My idea of heaven? Eating fat, juicy salt cod *tortillas* at crowded Basque *sidrerías,* the traditional cider houses up in the countryside. The fancier *sidrerías* serve thick *chuletas* (steaks) and an assortment of cooked dishes. But at the no-frills rustic ones—usually big eating halls with long wooden tables that are only open during the fresh cider season in March—customers are content with plates of *jamón* and *queso* and their beloved *tortilla de bacalao.* The classic cider house version of this *tortilla* is made to order and eaten warm, fluffy, and a little runny. The version here can be served as a light main course, with a green salad, or as a tapa, cut into wedges or squares. The cod needs to soak overnight, so plan ahead.

- 1/2 cup plus 3 tablespoons olive oil
- 1 large white onion, quartered and sliced
- 1 large green bell pepper, cored, seeded, and thinly sliced
- 6 to 7 ounces salt cod, soaked and cooked (see page 198), then drained, bones and hard bits removed
- Coarse salt (kosher or sea)
- 6 large, very fresh eggs, preferably organic
- 2 tablespoons chicken stock or broth

1. Heat the ½ cup olive oil in a large skillet over medium-high heat. Add the onion and green pepper and cook until the onion is translucent, about 5 minutes. Reduce the heat to low, cover the skillet, and cook, stirring occasionally, until the onion and pepper are meltingly soft, about 12 minutes. Add the salt cod and cook for 5 minutes, flaking it with a fork. Taste for seasoning and, depending on the saltiness of the cod, add salt as necessary. Transfer the salt cod mixture to a sieve set over a small bowl and let it cool and drain for about 25 minutes. (The salt cod mixture can be prepared a day ahead and refrigerated, covered. Bring to room temperature before continuing with the recipe.)

2. Place the eggs, chicken stock, and a few small pinches of salt in a medium-size bowl and beat until just scrambled. Add the salt cod mixture and mix until well combined. Let stand for about 10 minutes.

3. Heat 2 tablespoons of the remaining olive oil in a heavy 8-inch skillet, preferably nonstick, over medium-high heat until it is just beginning to smoke. Pour the egg mixture into the skillet and flatten it with a spatula until the top is fairly even. Reduce the heat to medium-low. Cook, moving and shaking the skillet, running a thin spatula around the edge and sliding it into the middle so that some of the egg runs under. Cook the *tortilla* in this fashion until the top is a little wet but not liquid, 6 to 8 minutes.

4. Run the thin spatula under the *tortilla* to make sure that no part of the bottom is stuck to the skillet. Top the skillet with a rimless plate slightly larger than the skillet and, using oven mitts, quickly invert the *tortilla* onto the plate. If the skillet looks dry, add a little more olive oil. Carefully slide the *tortilla* back into the skillet, uncooked side down. Shake the skillet to straighten the *tortilla* and push the edges in with the spatula. Reduce the heat to very low and cook the *tortilla* until a toothpick inserted in the center comes out dry, 3 to 4 minutes. Invert the *tortilla* again, as before, and cook on the first side for another minute.

5. Invert the *tortilla* onto a serving plate and pat the top with a paper towel to get rid of excess oil. Let it cool a little, then cut the *tortilla* into wedges and serve warm or at room temperature. To serve as a tapa, cut the *tortilla* into squares and serve with toothpicks. **SERVES 8 AS A TAPA, 4 AS A LIGHT MAIN DISH**

SANTA'S FARM-FRESH ASPARAGUS TORTILLA

TORTILLA DE ESPARRAGOS DE SANTA

Santa is a small, sturdy farmwoman from Extremadura who grows insanely delicious raspberries and blueberries, and sometimes cooks traditional meals for my friend Gabriela. This *tortilla* was part of a lunch she prepared when I visited. It's essentially just a skilletful of delicate, sautéed asparagus bound with a few farm-fresh eggs. If you'd like some extra kick, you can sauté the asparagus with a handful of finely diced serrano ham or prosciutto or add some slivered mint to the cooked asparagus mixture.

- 4 tablespoons extra-virgin olive oil, plus more if needed
- 1/2 cup finely chopped white onion
- 2 medium-size garlic cloves, minced
- 1 pound medium-thin asparagus, well trimmed and thinly sliced
- 5 large, very fresh eggs, preferably organic
- 2 tablespoons chicken stock or broth
- Coarse salt (kosher or sea)
- 1/4 cup slivered fresh mint (optional)

1. Heat 3 tablespoons of the olive oil in a large skillet, preferably nonstick, over medium heat. Add the onion and garlic and cook, stirring, until the onion is limp but not brown, 3 to 5 minutes. Add the asparagus and cook, stirring occasionally, until the asparagus is tender and has lost its crunch but is still bright green, 5 to 6 minutes. Transfer the asparagus mixture to a bowl and let cool completely. (The recipe can be prepared up to this stage a day in advance.)

2. Place the eggs, chicken stock, and a few small pinches of salt in a medium-size bowl and beat until just scrambled. Add the asparagus mixture and the mint, if using, and mix until well combined. Let stand for about 10 minutes.

3. Heat the remaining 1 tablespoon olive oil in a heavy 8-inch skillet, preferably nonstick, over medium-high heat until it is just beginning to smoke. Pour the egg mixture into the skillet and flatten it with a spatula until the top is fairly even. Reduce the heat to medium-low. Cook, moving and shaking the skillet, running a thin spatula around the edge and sliding it into the middle so that some of the egg runs under. Cook the *tortilla* in this fashion until the top is a little wet but not liquid, 3 to 5 minutes.

4. Run the thin spatula under the *tortilla* to make sure that no part of the bottom is stuck to the skillet. Top the skillet with a rimless plate slightly larger than the skillet and, using oven mitts, quickly invert the *tortilla* onto the plate. If the skillet looks dry, add a little more olive oil. Carefully slide the *tortilla* back into the skillet, uncooked side down. Shake the skillet to straighten the *tortilla* and push the edges in with the spatula. Reduce the heat to very low and cook the *tortilla* until a toothpick inserted in the center comes out dry, 2 minutes. Invert the *tortilla* again, as before, and cook on the first side for another minute.

5. Invert the *tortilla* onto a serving plate and pat the top with a paper towel to get rid of excess oil. Let it cool a little, then cut the *tortilla* into wedges and serve warm or at room temperature. To serve as a tapa, cut the *tortilla* into squares and serve with toothpicks. **SERVES 6 AS A TAPA, 4 AS A LIGHT MAIN DISH**

FLOWER MARKET EGGPLANT TORTILLA SANDWICH

TORTILLA DE BERENJENAS, MERCAT DE LA CONCEPCION

To research Catalan recipes for this book, I rented an apartment in Barcelona that had a balcony overlooking Gaudí's eccentric Sagrada Família cathedral. The best place for breakfast nearby was the vast Concepció flower market, with a food counter where vendors gathered for hearty Catalan stews or vegetable omelets. Every morning I'd perch at the counter, surrounded by the extravagant scents of roses and lilies, and order the same thing: a stupendous sandwich of tomato-rubbed bread, smeared with a little garlic mayonnaise and topped with an eggplant omelet and some roasted green pepper. It was the breakfast of champions. Feel free to use split, toasted focaccia instead of the baguette.

- 2 medium-size green bell peppers, cored, cut in half, and seeded
- Extra-virgin olive oil
- 1 slender Asian eggplant (7 to 8 ounces), peeled and cut crosswise into 1/3-inch-thick slices
- Coarse salt (kosher or sea)
- 5 large, very fresh eggs, preferably organic, beaten together with a large pinch of salt
- 2 pieces (each 10 inches long) crusty French bread, or focaccia, split horizontally
- 1 ripe tomato, cut in half
- 2 to 3 tablespoons Allioli (page 44)

1. Preheat the broiler.

2. Place the green pepper halves skin side up in a broiler pan, crush them lightly with your hand, and brush them with olive oil. Broil the peppers until they are soft and charred in spots, about 15 minutes. Transfer the peppers to a bowl, cover it with plastic wrap, and let stand for 10 minutes. Peel the peppers and cut each half in half.

3. Place the eggplant in a colander and generously sprinkle salt over it. Let stand for 30 minutes. Rinse off the salt and pat the eggplant thoroughly dry with paper towels.

4. Heat 3 tablespoons olive oil in a 10-inch nonstick skillet over medium heat. Add as many eggplant slices as will fit in one layer. (Save any extra eggplant for another use.) Cook the eggplant until soft and golden, 3 to 5 minutes per side, adding olive oil, 1 teaspoon at a time, if the skillet looks dry (resist adding too much oil). Pour the eggs over the eggplant and cook until the bottom is set, about 3 minutes, loosening the *tortilla* with a thin spatula. Reduce the heat to very low, cover the skillet, and cook until the top is set, 2 to 3 minutes longer. Using the spatula, loosen the *tortilla* from the skillet and slide it onto a plate. Cut the *tortilla* into wedges.

5. Preheat a ridged grill pan over medium-high heat.

6. Brush the cut sides of the bread with olive oil and grill cut side down until lightly charred and crisp, about 45 seconds. Rub the cut sides of the tomato halves over the cut sides of the bread. Place the bottom half of a piece of bread on a work surface and spread some of the *allioli* on it. Arrange *tortilla* and green pepper wedges on top, then cover with the top half of the bread. Cut the sandwich in half. Repeat with the remaining bread, *allioli,* and *tortilla* and green pepper wedges. Serve the sandwiches right away. **SERVES 4 AS A LIGHT MAIN DISH**

EGGS OVER SMOKY BREAD HASH

MIGAS CON HUEVOS

In formerly destitute central and southern Spain (Castile, La Mancha, Extremadura, Andalusia), recipes for leftover bread are legion. Today, although the poverty is long gone, *migas* remain one of the most cherished tastes. The word *migas* means crumbs, and the dish is a kind of fried bread hash usually flavored with smoky meats and paprika, plus such original additions as grapes, raisins, radishes, or pomegranate seeds for a fresh counterpoint to the dense smoked flavors. Classically, *migas* are made with day-old country bread, which is dampened with a little water, wrapped in cloth, and left for several hours. (To simplify things, in this recipe I sprinkle the bread with water as it fries.) The damp bread is added to a skillet of hot oil, then stirred and crumbled until the liquid evaporates. The resulting "crumbs" are completely wonderful, especially with fried or poached eggs.

3 tablespoons extra-virgin olive oil, or more if needed
4 medium-size garlic cloves, thickly sliced
1 piece (2 ounces) pancetta or smoky bacon, diced
1 piece (2 to 3 ounces) serrano ham or prosciutto, diced
4 ounces sweet Spanish-style chorizo sausage, diced
4 cups day-old dense country bread, torn into very small pieces
1 1/2 teaspoons smoked sweet Spanish paprika
1/4 cup seedless green grape halves
Coarse salt (kosher or sea); optional
4 Spanish Fried Eggs (page 156), or Basic Poached Eggs (page 156)

1. Heat the olive oil in a large nonstick skillet over medium-low heat. Add the garlic and cook until very fragrant and lightly golden, 2 to 3 minutes. Using a slotted spoon, transfer the garlic to a bowl. Add the pancetta, ham, and chorizo to the skillet and cook, stirring, until lightly browned, 3 to 4 minutes. Using a slotted spoon, transfer the meat to the bowl with the garlic.

2. Add the bread to the skillet and stir to coat with the oil, adding a little more oil if the skillet looks dry. Sprinkle about ½ cup water evenly over the bread, using just enough to moisten it. Cook the bread, stirring, breaking it up, turning it with a spatula, and scraping the bottom of the skillet until the bread is no longer moist and is golden and crisp in spots, about 10 minutes. It should resemble coarse crumbs. If the skillet looks dry, add a little more olive oil. Add the paprika to the skillet and stir for a few seconds. Return the garlic, pancetta, ham, and chorizo to the skillet, add the grapes, and stir to distribute all the ingredients evenly. Cook, stirring, for 1 to 2 minutes. Taste for seasoning, adding salt if necessary. Remove the hash from the heat and keep warm until ready to serve.

3. Divide the hash among four plates, top with the eggs, and serve right away. **SERVES 4 AS A BREAKFAST OR BRUNCH DISH**

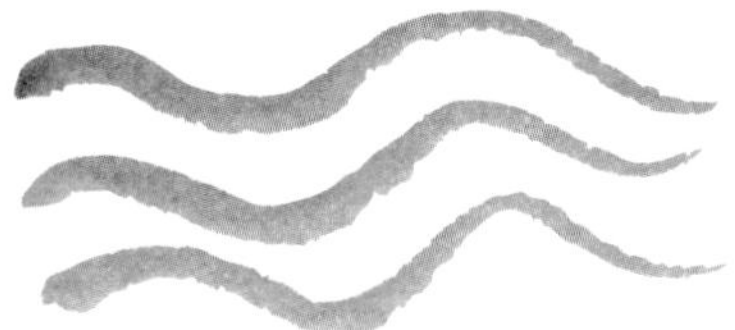

BAKED EGGS ON RED PEPPER RAGOUT

HUEVOS AL HORNO CON PIPERRADA

Piperrada, the sweet, luscious Basque bell pepper ragout, is an ideal partner for eggs. Though most commonly the eggs are scrambled into the peppers, here they bake in ramekins on top of the *piperrada,* with a round of toasted baguette tucked in the bottom. The result is one of the tastiest brunch dishes imaginable. The ragout can easily be beefed up with diced chorizo or serrano ham, which should be cooked with the peppers. You can prepare the ragout ahead; reheat it before adding the eggs. For a larger crowd, just double the recipe.

3 tablespoons extra-virgin olive oil
1 large white onion, quartered and sliced
2 red bell peppers, cored, seeded, quartered lengthwise, and thinly sliced crosswise
3 medium-size garlic cloves, crushed with a garlic press
1 large ripe tomato, finely chopped
1/4 cup chicken stock or broth, or more if needed
Coarse salt (kosher or sea)
4 slices (1/2 inch thick) of baguette, toasted
4 large, very fresh eggs, preferably organic
Minced fresh flat-leaf parsley, for garnish

1. Preheat the oven to 400°F.

2. Heat the olive oil in a medium-size skillet over medium heat. Add the onion and red peppers and cook, stirring, until softened, about 10 minutes, adjusting the heat so the vegetables don't brown. Add the garlic and tomato and cook, stirring, for 2 to 3 minutes. Add the chicken stock, cover the skillet, and cook until the vegetables are very soft, about 20 minutes, stirring occasionally and adding a little more stock if the skillet looks dry. If there is too much liquid in the skillet by the time the vegetables are done, increase the heat to high for a few seconds to reduce the liquid slightly. Season the *piperrada* with salt to taste.

3. Place baguette rounds on the bottom of four ¾-cup ramekins or soufflé cups. Spoon equal portions of the *piperrada* on top of each bread round and even out the top with the back of a spoon. Break an egg into each ramekin, being careful not to break the yolk, and sprinkle it lightly with salt. Set the ramekins on a small baking sheet and bake until the

THE ELEGANT EGG

On my bookshelf sits a fascinating Spanish cookbook with a bright-yellow cover. In it, the country's most creative chefs pay homage to the *tortilla de patatas,* with recipes that take such basic ingredients as potatoes and eggs where they've never ventured before. Ferran Adrià contributes ravioli in which a gossamer "dough" of crunchy potatoes encloses a semiliquid poached egg. Sergi Arola, the young superstar chef of La Broche restaurant in Madrid, weighs in with nests fashioned from blue potatoes sautéed in the fat of *ibérico* pig, filled with an egg yolk, and accompanied by tomato sorbet and, of all things, toasted bread foam! Jean-Louis Neichel, of the Barcelona restaurant Neichel, reinvents the *tortilla* as a crisp potato tart, dolled up with sautéed foie gras and Périgord truffles and topped with a fried egg. And Basque chef Pedro Subijana presents his own futuristic take on the omelet: frozen sliced egg sandwiched between crunchy paper-thin potato rectangles miraculously encrusted with herbs. *Señores y señoras,* the potato *tortilla* has come a long way.

eggs are just set, 10 to 15 minutes. Carefully transfer the ramekins to serving plates and let them cool for about 5 minutes. Sprinkle a little parsley on top and serve. **SERVES 4 AS A BRUNCH DISH**

ASPARAGUS AND ARTICHOKE FLANS

FLANES DE ESPARRAGOS Y ALCACHOFAS

Inspired by a dish I tasted in the vegetable-rich Navarra region, these flans make a lovely first course for a festive spring dinner. I like them served straight from the ramekins, but for a fancier presentation you can turn them out onto dinner plates. To do this, you will need to line the bottom of the dishes with rounds of buttered waxed paper. Run a sharp knife around the finished flans, then invert them.

- 1 pound asparagus, tough lower parts of the stalks trimmed
- 5 teaspoons olive oil, plus more for frying the ham
- 2 packages (each 9 ounces) frozen artichoke hearts, thawed and blotted dry
- 2 medium-size garlic cloves, minced
- 3/4 cup heavy (whipping) cream
- 3/4 cup grated Manchego cheese, Pecorino Romano, or good Parmesan
- 3 tablespoons unsalted butter, at room temperature
- 1/2 teaspoon coarse salt (kosher or sea)
- 4 large, very fresh eggs, preferably organic, beaten well
- 6 thin slices (about 2 ounces total) serrano ham or prosciutto

1. Bring water to a boil in the bottom of a wide steamer. Add the asparagus, cover the steamer, and cook until tender but still bright green, 5 to 8 minutes depending on the thickness. Remove the asparagus from the steamer, pat it dry with paper towels, and chop it. Set the asparagus aside to cool.

2. Heat 2 teaspoons of the olive oil in a medium-size skillet over medium-low heat. Add the artichokes and garlic and cook until the artichokes are soft, about 7 minutes; don't let the artichokes brown. Remove the artichokes from the heat and let cool before proceeding. (The asparagus and artichokes can be prepared up to this stage 1 day in advance.)

3. Position an oven rack in the lower third of the oven, then preheat the oven to 325°F. Butter six ¾-cup soufflé dishes or ramekins. Set the dishes in a baking dish that can hold them snugly.

4. Working in two batches, puree the asparagus and the artichokes and garlic in a blender or food processor until smooth, adding half of the cream, cheese, and butter, and ¼ teaspoon of the salt to each batch. Scrape the puree through a sieve into a large mixing bowl. Add the eggs and whisk until the mixture is well combined.

5. Evenly divide the egg mixture among the prepared soufflé dishes. Add enough hot water to the baking dish to reach halfway up the sides of the dishes. Bake the flans until a skewer inserted in the center comes out clean, 40 to 50 minutes.

6. While the flans are baking, make the ham crisps. Pour olive oil to a depth of ½ inch and heat it over medium-high heat; when hot, a piece of ham placed in the oil will sizzle on contact. Place 3 slices of ham in the hot oil and cook, stirring gently to submerge the ham, until it is crisp, about 1 minute. Using a slotted spoon, transfer the fried ham to paper towels to drain. Repeat with the remaining slices of ham.

7. When the flans are done baking, carefully remove the soufflé dishes from the baking dish and let cool on a rack for 5 minutes. Spear each flan with a ham crisp and serve at once. **SERVES 6 AS A FIRST COURSE OR BRUNCH DISH**

SHRIMP AND ASPARAGUS REVUELTO

REVUELTO DE GAMBAS Y ESPARRAGOS

Simple but pristinely wonderful, *revuelto* (a kind of scrambled eggs) is a dish for which good Spanish restaurants charge dearly—and customers happily pay, knowing that a few good ingredients well prepared add up to much more than the sum of their parts. Taste it, and you will agree. The best versions of this *revuelto* feature matchstick-thin *espárragos trigueros* (wild asparagus), but any flavorful seasonal asparagus will work as well. As it has to cook very quickly, make sure you trim away all the woody parts. The *revuelto* is also excellent made with leek or garlic shoots. (For more about *revueltos,* see page 157.)

3 tablespoons olive oil
1 large garlic clove, minced
1/2 cup thinly sliced asparagus (4 to 6 stalks, well trimmed)
4 to 6 ounces peeled small shrimp
5 large, very fresh eggs, preferably organic
Coarse salt (kosher or sea) and freshly ground white pepper

1. Heat 2 tablespoons of the olive oil in a 12-inch skillet, preferably nonstick, over medium heat. Add the garlic and asparagus and cook, stirring, for 1 minute. Add the shrimp and cook, stirring, until the shrimp just turn pink and the asparagus is bright green and tender, 1 to 2 minutes.

2. Add the remaining tablespoon of olive oil to the skillet. Reduce the heat to medium-low and

DALI DOES EGGS

From the outlandish sculptures of giant eggs crowning Dalí's museum in his former home town of Figueres, Catalonia, to the gravity-defying fried egg suspended on a string in his painting *Fried Egg on the Plate Without the Plate,* the humble *huevo* occupied a prime place in Salvador Dalí's oeuvre. Eggs appealed to the artist's scrambled imagination because of their smooth round surfaces, their sexual connotations, and the strange, formal contrast between their raw and cooked states. Dalí's pal, the surrealist filmmaker Luis Buñuel, once recalled that "Salvador Dalí seduced many ladies, particularly American ladies, but these seductions usually consisted of stripping them naked in his apartment, frying a couple of eggs, putting them on the women's shoulders, and, without a word, showing them the door." Ouch.

Wild Mushroom Revuelto
in an Egg Carton

break the eggs into the skillet, leaving enough space between each egg so the yolks don't run together. As soon as the egg whites turn opaque, about 20 seconds, vigorously stir and scramble the eggs with a wooden spoon or a spatula until they are barely set, 45 seconds to 1 minute. (Do not let the eggs overcook!) Spoon the eggs onto plates while they are still a little wet. They will continue to set on the way to the table. Season with salt and a touch of white pepper and serve at once. **SERVES 2 OR 3**

WILD MUSHROOM REVUELTO IN AN EGG CARTON

REVUELTO DE SETAS

Carles Abellan, chef-owner of Comerç 24, a designer tapas bar in Barcelona, is nuts about eggs, treating them to all kinds of whimsical preparations. His *revueltos*—sometimes featuring truffles, other times caviar or cèpes—are presented in hollowed-out eggshells nestled in an egg carton. The trick is wonderfully simple to reproduce at home; all you need is a cardboard egg carton that holds six eggs. It never fails to bring smiles to people's faces, making an adorable little tapa. For a more casual meal, the *revuelto* is delicious served on plates with a simple green salad, though you will probably want to double the recipe. If you happen to have truffle oil, a few drops will make the *revuelto* truly luxurious.

6 jumbo brown eggs
3 tablespoons extra-virgin olive oil, or more if needed
2 medium-size garlic cloves, crushed with a garlic press
6 ounces assorted wild and cultivated mushrooms (porcini, chanterelles, cremini, oyster, and/or morels), trimmed, wiped clean with a damp cloth, and finely chopped
1 tablespoon minced fresh chives
Coarse salt (kosher or sea) and coarsely ground black pepper

1. Prepare the egg cups: Hold an egg, pointed end up, in the palm of your hand. Invert an empty spice bottle on top of the egg and secure it with the thumb and forefinger of that hand. With the other hand, using a heavy wooden spoon, hit the bottom of the spice bottle. The shock will create a crack around the top of the egg. Remove the top of the eggshell and discard it. Pour the egg into a bowl. Repeat with the remaining eggs, placing 2 more eggs in the bowl, setting the remaining eggs aside for another use. You will need 6 eggshell cups for serving but only 3 eggs for the *revuelto*. Rinse the eggshells under warm running water. Turn them upside down on paper towels to dry, then place the empty shells in a 6-egg cardboard carton.

2. Heat 2 tablespoons of the olive oil in an 8- or 10-inch nonstick skillet over medium heat. Add the garlic and cook for 1 minute. Add the mushrooms, raise the heat to medium-high, and cook, stirring, until they have released and reabsorbed their liquid, about 5 minutes, adding a little more olive oil if the skillet looks dry. Stir in the chives and season with salt and pepper to taste.

3. Reduce the heat to medium-low. Add the remaining tablespoon of olive oil to the skillet. Working quickly, pour the 3 eggs into the skillet. As soon as the egg whites turn opaque, about 20 seconds, vigorously stir and scramble the eggs with a wooden spoon or spatula until they are barely set, 45 seconds to 1 minute. (Do not let the eggs overcook!) Quickly spoon them into the prepared eggshells. They will continue to set on the way to the table. Serve at once, with little cocktail forks. **SERVES 6 AS A TAPA IN THE EGGSHELL CUPS, 2 AS A FIRST COURSE SERVED ON A PLATE**

BASIC POACHED EGGS

HUEVOS ESCALFADOS

Though not particularly Spanish, my favorite egg-poaching method produces foolproof eggs without any fancy egg-poaching gadgets. A very Spanish way of serving these would be over cooked baby peas or tender fava beans sautéed with a little *jamón* or with garlicky sautéed mushrooms, Smoky Bread Hash (page 150), or in Castilian Garlic Soup (page 81).

4 large, very fresh eggs, preferably organic
1 tablespoon vinegar (any kind is fine)

Carefully break the eggs into 4 small egg cups, measuring cups, or coffee cups. Fill a medium-size skillet with water to a depth of 2 to 3 inches, add the vinegar, and bring to a steady simmer over low heat. Lower a cup with an egg sideways into the simmering water so that the lip of the cup is slightly submerged in the water. Slide the egg carefully into the water and repeat with the remaining eggs. When the water returns to a simmer, cover the skillet tightly, turn off the heat, and let the eggs sit for exactly 4 minutes for medium-runny eggs. If making ahead, use a slotted spoon to transfer the eggs to a bowl. Gently resubmerge the eggs in simmering water for a few seconds to warm through before serving. **MAKES 4 EGGS**

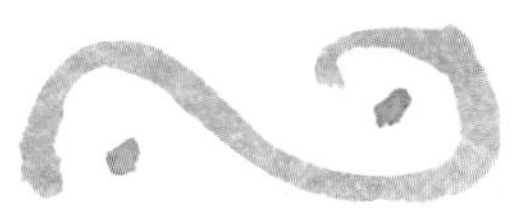

THE SPANISH FRIED EGG

HUEVOS FRITOS

For the Spanish, an ideal fried egg is one that has been fried in lots of very hot olive oil and has a lightly crisped, puffed-up white and a juicy, runny yolk that bursts in a bright-orange explosion when you puncture it with a fork. Cooked this way, the egg is deliciously different from the American diner-style sunny-side-up, particularly if you use fine olive oil and very fresh organic eggs. The recipe here is for one egg, but you can fry as may as you can fit in your skillet. With toasted dense sourdough, this is my favorite midday snack.

ALL SCRAMBLED

The Fine Art of the Revuelto

As crazy as the Spanish are about *tortillas,* they are equally fond of *revueltos,* creamy scrambled eggs served for lunch or supper at countless tapas bars and restaurants all across the country. Unlike American scrambled eggs, which are about *eggs,* Spanish *revueltos* center on the ingredients that flavor them. The texture is smooth, light, and fluffy: Delicate moist curds barely jell around ingredients like leeks and shrimp, sautéed wild mushrooms, onions, and bacalao—even french fries!

The basic principle of a *revuelto* couldn't be simpler: Start with an ingredient or two—shrimp, onion, and/or mushrooms, for example—sautéed in good olive oil. Add eggs, scramble vigorously, serve at once. But while a *revuelto* requires less know-how than a *tortilla,* technique *is* important here as well. And the quality of the eggs makes all the difference. Each cook has his or her own trick. Many people break the eggs right into the skillet, but some beat them very lightly first. Some cook their *revueltos* over fairly high heat; others use a pan set in a skillet of simmering water so the eggs can't scorch. The different methods produce similar results. The most important thing to remember is this: Work as quickly as you can so the eggs come out of the pan not quite set. They will continue to cook in their residual heat on their way to the table. The scrambling process should take less than a minute. If the eggs in the skillet look done, they are already overcooked and will land on the table dry. Once out of the pan, a *revuelto* should be served in an instant.

Wild mushrooms, garlic shoots, wild asparagus, mashed blood sausage, and shrimp or langoustines are some of the most popular *revuelto* flavorings in Spain. But do try the delicious combinations I offer here. Just remember to cook the ingredients in olive oil before the eggs go in the pan (with a little garlic, if you wish). And because eggs are by nature delicate and somewhat bland, make sure everything else is well seasoned.

- Sliced leeks and diced serrano ham
- *Pisto* (Zucchini, Bell Pepper & Onion Jam; see page 29)
- Diced chorizo and piquillo peppers
- Sliced asparagus and oyster mushrooms
- Bacalao and sautéed green peppers
- Potatoes and diced pancetta
- Delicate-flavored mushrooms and small shrimp

1/4 cup extra-virgin olive oil
1 large, very fresh egg, preferably organic
Coarse sea salt, such as Maldon

Heat the olive oil in an 8-inch skillet, preferably nonstick, over medium-high heat until almost smoking. Break the egg into the skillet, being careful not to puncture the yolk. Reduce the heat to medium-low and cook until the white is puffy, sizzled, and set, but the yolk is still runny, gently loosening the white from the skillet with a thin metal spatula and pouring hot olive oil over the yolk. The egg should be done in about 45 seconds. Using a thin slotted spatula, lift the egg out of the skillet, gently shaking off the excess oil. Transfer the egg to a plate. **MAKES 1 EGG**

EMPANADAS, CANAPES, COCAS & MORE

Despite its central role in the culture, by itself Spanish bread may appear unremarkable. Plain, sturdy, and somewhat underseasoned, it comes alive when paired with other ingredients—especially the traditional garlic and olive oil. Topped with anything from a few coins of chorizo to seared

From left to right: In Spain, olive oil is consumed by the gallon (or jug!); A Galician baker displays her pork-filled empanadas fresh from the oven; It is haunting landscapes like this one that draw crowds to Mallorca; A jovial chorizo vendor with plenty of the popular sausage.

foie gras or *angulas,* the astronomically expensive baby eels, bread forms the basis for countless canapés and tostadas (Spain's bruschetta) so fundamental to any *tapeo.* Brushed with olive oil and perhaps smeared with frothy tomato pulp, *pan* is a breakfast mainstay, while the *bocadillo* (a sandwich roll) is the snack that fuels most Spanish days.

As for yesterday's bread, it seems to find its way into half of Spain's traditional dishes, from gazpacho and *sopa de ajo* to *torrijas* (Spanish french toast) and *migas,* the delicious fried crumbs found on so many tables in Andalusia and Extremadura. Cubed, fried, and pounded in a mortar with nuts and/or garlic, bread thickens stews and sauces, such as Catalonia's famous *romesco.* For Spaniards, every last crumb counts.

In its more evolved version, bread becomes empanadas, rustic but elegant Galician pies, thick with fillings that ooze sautéed onions and peppers and, usually, seafood (the word is derived from *en pan,* or in bread). Or seductive *cocas* (think pizzas with a difference) that are sold in the bakeries of the Spanish Mediterranean, from Catalonia to the Balearics to Alicante.

This chapter is somewhat of a tapas extension. Most of the recipes here function best as appetizers, snacks, cocktail nibbles, or light luncheon dishes. For your tapas bash, here are irresistible canapés from the best tapas bar in San Sebastián, where food-on-bread veers into haute cuisine territory. As for toast smeared with melted dark chocolate, drizzled with olive oil, and sprinkled with salt, it's one of these recipes that should be labeled "dangerously addictive."

CANAPES WITH ANCHOVIES AND ROASTED BELL PEPPERS

PINTXOS DE ANCHOAS Y PIMIENTOS

Here's a recipe for one of my favorite canapés at Bar Bergara in San Sebastián (page 164). This colorful, savory confection includes green and red bell peppers, as well as two kinds of anchovies, regular brown ones and vinegar-pickled white *boquerones.* Also featuring potatoes and eggs, the canapés are filling enough for a light mid-day meal. If you can't find *boquerones,* use all brown anchovies; the canapés will still have plenty of color.

1 large roasted red bell pepper (see page 385), cut into 1-inch-thick strips
1 large roasted green bell pepper (see page 385), cut into 1-inch-thick strips
1 tablespoon extra-virgin olive oil, plus more for brushing the peppers
1 tablespoon sherry vinegar, preferably aged
8 diagonal slices (1/4 inch thick) baguette (see Note), lightly toasted
1 to 2 tablespoons mayonnaise
8 thin slices hard-cooked egg (from 2 eggs)
8 thin slices boiled potato (from 1 medium-size all-purpose boiling potato)
8 white anchovy fillets (boquerones en vinagre), drained
8 best-quality oil-packed brown anchovy fillets, drained
Minced fresh flat-leaf parsley, for garnish

Place the red and green pepper strips, olive oil, and vinegar in a bowl and toss to mix. Lightly spread a baguette toast with mayonnaise. Place a slice of egg on one end of the toast and a slice of potato on the other end. Layer a strip of red pepper and a strip of green pepper side by side over the egg and potato, trimming them as necessary to fit. Top the red pepper strip with a white anchovy fillet and the green pepper strip with a brown anchovy fillet. Repeat with the remaining slices of bread. Sprinkle the canapés with parsley and serve. **MAKES 8 SUBSTANTIAL CANAPES**

NOTE: Look for a thick baguette, one that's about 2 inches in diameter. Slice it very thin, on a diagonal; each slice should be about 5 inches long.

BASQUE TRIPLE SEAFOOD CANAPES

PINTXOS DE CHATKA, SALMON, Y ANCHOAS

Owners of Basque *pintxo* bars love constructing elaborate canapés, piling up various ingredients, especially seafood. One of the staples includes surimi—mock crab legs, known in the Basquelands as *chatka.* Mixed with mayo and a

CANAPES

Colorful, tasty, easy to eat—Spanish-style canapés, tostadas, and *bocadillos* (sandwiches) are impossible to resist. For lunch, cocktails, or as a predinner nibble, here are a dozen ideas from tapas bars around Spain.

- Baguettes halved lengthwise, then sliced, toasted or grilled, and topped with smoked whitefish (a stand-in for smoked bacalao), thin orange slices, sliced pitted black olives, and drizzles of fruity olive oil
- Grilled cheese sandwiches made with brioche slices, fresh mozzarella, thin grilled asparagus, and a touch of truffle oil
- Baguettes halved lengthwise, then sliced and topped with serrano ham, anchovies, roasted green pepper, and sprinkles of grated Emmental cheese, briefly passed under a broiler
- Baguette rounds with Best Russian Salad from Barcelona (page 113), topped with poached shrimp
- Toasted white bread triangles topped with *Pisto* (Zucchini, Bell Pepper & Onion Jam, page 29), white anchovies, drizzles of syrupy reduced balsamic vinegar, and minced parsley
- Toasted baguette rounds with Cabrales cheese, sprinkled with finely diced Granny Smith apple and chopped toasted walnuts
- Open-faced sandwiches of piquillo pepper and boiled ham, with a relish of minced capers and cornichons
- Boiled purple potato rounds topped with chunks of lobster and a dab of Saffron Allioli (page 45)
- Toasted baguette rounds with Brandada (page 326), roasted green pepper strips, and minced parsley
- Slices of Classic Potato Tortilla (page 139) topped with crème fraîche and salmon roe
- Toasted baguette rounds with Black Olive, Anchovy, and Caper Spread (page 28), sliced marinated artichokes, goat cheese, and piquillo peppers
- Toasted rolls with sliced grilled chorizo, roasted red peppers, lettuce, and *allioli* (page 44)

few piquant additions, surimi makes one of the favorite bases for canapés topped with smoky fish, in this case both salmon and anchovies. The result is a sensational predinner bite. If you want to be classy, substitute lump crab meat, though it isn't as authentic.

1 cup shredded surimi (mock crab legs) or lump crabmeat
3 tablespoons minced red onion
3 1/2 tablespoons mayonnaise (preferably Hellmann's)
1 tablespoon fresh lemon juice
1/2 teaspoon ketchup
1 dash Tabasco sauce
Coarse salt (kosher or sea)
16 diagonal slices (1/4 inch thick) crusty baguette (see Note)
16 thin slices smoked salmon (about 6 ounces total)
16 best-quality oil-packed anchovy fillets, drained
Minced fresh flat-leaf parsley, for garnish

1. Place the surimi, onion, mayonnaise, lemon juice, ketchup, and Tabasco sauce in a small bowl and stir to blend. Taste for seasoning, adding more Tabasco sauce as necessary, and salt to taste.

2. Spread the surimi mixture on the baguette slices. Arrange a slice of salmon on each, trimming it to fit, then top with an anchovy fillet. Garnish with parsley and serve. **MAKES 16 SUBSTANTIAL CANAPES**

NOTE: Look for a thick baguette, one that's about 2 inches in diameter. Slice it very thin, on a diagonal; each slice should be about 5 inches long. If you wish, lightly toast the bread.

DAINTY BASQUE EGG AND HAM SANDWICHES

TRIANGULITOS

This recipe from Goiz Argi tapas bar in San Sebastián proves that the Basques can turn even something as simple as a toasted white bread sandwich into a visual treat. Filled with egg and ham salad and decorated with shredded lettuce, grated hard-cooked egg, and poached shrimp, these sandwich triangles look as frilly and festive as cakes. They are delicious, too. Serve them as a tapa, a luncheon sandwich, or for an afternoon tea party. You will need large toothpicks or seven-inch wooden skewers for holding the sandwiches together.

3 large hard-cooked eggs
2 medium-size ripe tomatoes
2 ounces (3 to 4 slices) boiled ham, finely chopped
2 large leaves green-leaf lettuce, finely shredded
3 tablespoons mayonnaise (preferably Hellmann's), plus more for decorating the sandwiches
1/4 teaspoon Dijon mustard
Coarse salt (kosher or sea)
8 slices white bread, toasted
8 medium-size poached shrimp

1. Finely chop 2 of the eggs and place them in a medium-size bowl. Grate the remaining egg on the large holes of a box grater and set aside.

2. Cut 1 of the tomatoes in half, finely chop 1 of the halves, and add it to the eggs in the bowl. Thinly slice the remaining tomatoes and set aside.

3. Place the ham and half of the shredded lettuce in the bowl with the eggs and tomato. Add the mayonnaise, mustard, and salt to taste and stir until well combined.

4. Arrange 4 slices of the toasted bread on a work surface and spread each with the egg mixture. Top with a slice of toast and spread a thin layer of mayonnaise over each sandwich. Arrange the tomato slices in a single layer on top of the mayonnaise, trimming them to fit. Cut each sandwich in half diagonally to form triangles.

5. Transfer the sandwiches to a pretty serving platter and sprinkle with the remaining shredded lettuce and the grated egg. Top each triangle with a poached shrimp and secure it with a toothpick or a small skewer. Serve at once. **MAKES 8 SANDWICH HALVES TO SERVE 4 FOR LUNCH OR 8 AS A TAPA**

CANAPES WITH PIQUILLO PEPPER AND ANCHOVY REVUELTO

PINTXOS DE ANCHOAS EN REVUELTO

Among the most sought-after *pintxos* at Bar Bergara in San Sebastián are canapés topped with a *revuelto* (egg scramble; see page 157) of sweet piquillo peppers and anchovies. They're so delicious that the regulars seem to inhale them by the half dozen. Though Patxi Bergara, the owner, makes his *pintxos* with fresh anchovies, substituting salted anchovies adds an interesting savory twist. Serve these for brunch and watch them vanish. The eggs are also delicious on their own.

2 tablespoons extra-virgin olive oil
2 medium-size garlic cloves, thinly sliced
8 piquillo peppers (from a can or jar), drained and diced
8 or 9 best-quality oil-packed anchovy fillets, drained and cut into 4 pieces each
4 large, very fresh eggs, preferably organic
Coarse salt (kosher or sea), if needed
12 slices (1/2 inch thick) crusty baguette
2 roasted green bell peppers (see page 385), cut into thin strips, or minced fresh flat-leaf parsley, for garnish

1. Heat the olive oil in a medium-size nonstick skillet over medium-low heat. Add the garlic and stir until fragrant, about 1 minute. Add the piquillo peppers and cook, stirring, for about 2 minutes. Add the anchovies and cook for another minute. Break the eggs into the skillet, leaving enough space between the eggs so the yolks don't run together. As soon as the egg whites turn opaque, about 20 seconds, vigorously stir and scramble the eggs with a wooden spoon or spatula until they are barely set,

BAR BERGARA'S AMAZING CANAPES

Bar Bergara in San Sebastián is the Tiffany of *pintxo* (tapas) bars—a place where the canapé died and went to heaven. Sporting frilly chive garlands, grated egg sprinkles, and Technicolor bell pepper confetti, Bergara's bread-based *pintxos* preen atop their Villeroy & Boch plates like Lilliputian wedding cakes. I try an adorable canapé piled with a custard-soft *revuelto* of piquillo peppers and fresh anchovies (see this page), decorated with crisscrossed fried green pepper strips. Then I reach for a *pintxo* called *arco iris* (rainbow): nuggets of bacalao mounted on bread slathered with *pisto* (a vegetable spread) and topped with piped mashed potatoes. Festive egg white confetti and a single fat anchovy adorn a canapé of sliced seafood pâté. A luscious salad of the local spider crab is stuffed into flaky mini croissants. Tartlets emerge from the kitchen filled with duck gizzards and Armagnac-caramelized apples.

So baroque and elaborate are the offerings here that it takes the owner, Patxi Bergara, and several assistants, four hours to assemble the counter display. "An ideal *pintxo* should be impeccably fresh, visually pleasing, and small enough to be eaten in no more than two bites," Bergara explains. It should also be low in price, he adds, otherwise people will simply go elsewhere. "You should put a Do Not Touch sign on your *pintxos*," I tell Bergara, sad that his gorgeously assembled counter will soon be ravaged by hungry mobs. He laughs and hands me a pastry boat filled with seared foie gras and grapes.

but still look a little wet, 45 seconds to 1 minute. Do not let the eggs overcook; they will continue to set on their way to the table. Taste for seasoning, adding salt as necessary.

2. Spoon the eggs onto the baguette slices. Decorate the canapés with green pepper strips, arranging them in a crisscross pattern, or sprinkle parsley over them. Serve warm. **MAKES 12 CANAPES**

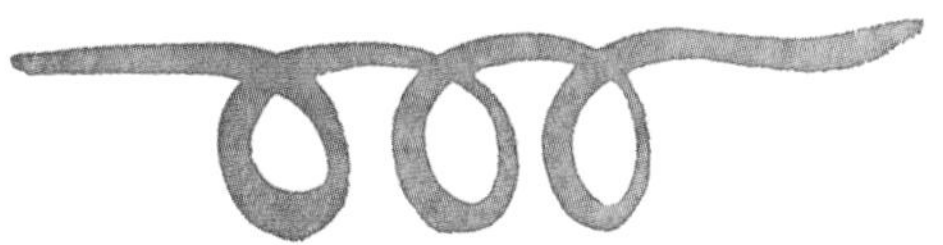

CATALAN TOMATO BREAD

PA AMB TOMAQUET

Here is my favorite version of Catalan tomato-rubbed bread, based on the *pa amb tomàquet* at Paco Meralgo, a modern tapas bar in Barcelona famous for the dish. Choose a baguette that's dense, chewy, and not too skinny, rather than a fluffy and crusty one. Or use half-inch-thick slices from a round loaf of country bread. (Sourdough is not very Catalan but *is* delicious.) Serve the bread as a tapa, either on its own or topped with an anchovy, cheese, or cured ham. It's also wonderful as an accompaniment to saucey, olive oil–based dishes.

1 piece (9 to 10 inches long and at least 2 inches in diameter) dense, chewy baguette, cut in half lengthwise
Fragrant extra-virgin olive oil
2 fat garlic cloves (optional), cut in half
1 large ripe but firm tomato, cut in half crosswise
Coarse salt (kosher or sea)

1. Light the grill and preheat it to medium or preheat the broiler.

YOU SAY TOMATO, CATALANS SAY PA AMB TOMAQUET

Whether it's breakfast, lunch, tapas, or dinner, a Catalan meal is pretty much unimaginable without a slice of country bread rubbed with a tomato half and drizzled with fruity olive oil. A snack born out of poverty—what could be more basic and cheap than bread and tomatoes?—*pa amb tomàquet* has achieved the status of a Catalan national dish. Eaten on its own or topped with *jamón,* cheese, anchovies, or just about anything else, *pa amb tomàquet* is essential and simple. It also provokes endless debates: Should the bread be toasted, grilled, or just slightly stale? Does the olive oil go on before or after the tomato? (Some say it needs two layers.) What kind of tomato is best, the sturdy half-green winter tomato or the ripe tomato of summer? And, it needs to be noted that a purist's conception of good tomato bread doesn't leave room for garlic (which isn't to say that it's not delicious). Classicists also frown on the practice followed by many restaurants of brushing the bread with frothy grated tomato pulp: To them it must be rubbed with a whole real tomato half.

2. Brush the cut side of each baguette half very lightly with olive oil and rub it with garlic, if using. Grill or broil the bread until golden, about 45 seconds, watching out that it doesn't burn around the edges.

3. When the bread is just cool enough to handle, rub the cut side of each half with the cut side of a tomato half, pressing down on the tomato to extract some of the pulp. Drizzle more olive oil over the bread and sprinkle it with salt. Cut each baguette in half on the diagonal into roughly 1¼-inch pieces and serve at once. **SERVES 4**

"DECONSTRUCTED" TOMATO BREAD

PA AMB TOMAQUET "DECONSTRUIDO"

It was all but inevitable that something as ubiquitous and basic as tomato bread would get *nueva cocina* treatment in the hands of avant-garde chefs. Spain's most famous "deconstructed" tomato bread was devised by Ferran Adrià, who translated the idea into tiny, ethereal pastry balls injected with tomato water and olive oil by means of a syringe. Less radical cooks play with the idea by taking the elements apart and reconfiguring them in new ways. The following recipe is the "deconstructed" tomato bread from Alkimia, a Barcelona restaurant run by the ever-creative Jordi Vilà. As an *amuse-guele,* Vilà often fills stylish martini glasses with toasted bread cubes tossed with olive oil and foamy tomato pulp and topped with slivers of dense, smoky salami. It's a terrific idea. For a larger crowd, I like to serve this in Chinese porcelain spoons as a bite-size hors d'ouevre.

3 large ripe tomatoes, cut in half, seeded, and grated on a box grater, skins discarded
Coarse salt (kosher or sea) and freshly ground black pepper
1 small pinch of sugar (optional)
1 dash of red wine vinegar (optional)
1/4 cup fragrant extra-virgin olive oil, plus more for drizzling
2 cups 1/2-inch bread cubes, from day-old dense country bread (see Note)
1/4 cup slivered fresh basil
3 to 4 slices good-quality imported dried salami or Italian sopressata, cut into slivers

1. Preheat the oven to 400°F.

2. Place the grated tomatoes in a large bowl and season with salt and pepper to taste. Taste the tomatoes; if they seem a little bland, add the sugar and vinegar to heighten the flavor. Stir in ¼ cup of the olive oil.

3. Spread the bread cubes on a rimmed baking sheet and bake until golden and crisp, about 5 minutes, tossing halfway through the cooking.

4. Add the toasted bread cubes and the basil to the tomatoes and toss to mix. Immediately spoon the bread and tomato mixture into martini glasses or large shot glasses, top with the salami, and drizzle olive oil over it. Serve at once, before the bread gets soggy. **SERVES 6**

NOTE: To facilitate cutting small bread cubes, place the bread in the freezer for 20 to 30 minutes.

CHOCOLATE TOSTADA WITH OLIVE OIL AND FLAKY SALT

TOSTADA DE CHOCOLATE CON ACEITE DE OLIVA

"This is one of those recipes that changes your life!" my friends told me when they tasted this unusual toast for the first time. Combining bread, melted dark chocolate, salt, and olive oil is a Catalan tradition that goes back to the days of rationing and speaks to the Catalan love of mixing the sweet and the savory. *Nueva cocina* chefs have been having great fun with these flavors, but the original tostada, born out of deprivation, is still the best thing. Try it, and you'll see chocolate in a completely new light. Serve the tostada for breakfast, afternoon tea, or at the end of the meal when the dessert is long finished but guests are still gathered around the table drinking wine.

- 5 to 6 ounces best-quality bittersweet chocolate (at least 70 percent cacao), grated
- 1 piece (9 to 10 inches long and at least 2 inches in diameter) dense, chewy baguette, cut in half lengthwise
- Fragrant extra-virgin olive oil
- Flaky sea salt, such as Maldon

1. Preheat the broiler.

2. Place the chocolate in the top of a double boiler and melt it over simmering water.

3. Brush the cut side of each baguette half very lightly with olive oil. Broil the bread until golden, watching out that it doesn't burn around the edges. (Alternatively, you can toast the bread.)

4. Spread the cut side of each baguette half with the melted chocolate, lightly drizzle a little olive oil over the chocolate, and judiciously sprinkle it with salt. Cut each baguette half on the diagonal into roughly 1¼-inch pieces and serve at once. **SERVES 4 TO 6**

PASTRY PUFFS WITH ROQUEFORT AND APPLE SPREAD

HOJADRE DE ROQUEFORT

For all the wealth of home-grown products available to Spanish tapas bar owners, it's French Roquefort cheese that they seem to cherish the most. From Madrid to Bilbao to Seville, Roquefort canapés are a perennial favorite with the crowds. In this easy, elegant Basque *pintxo,* a Roquefort and apple spread and a sprinkling of toasted walnuts top baked puff pastry squares. (Of course, you could use Cabrales cheese, but Roquefort is, in fact, more Spanish.) The canapés tend to vanish in the time it takes to say *gracias,* so make lots.

4 1/2 teaspoons unsalted butter
1 large apple, such as Gala, Golden Delicious, or Jonagold, peeled, cored, and finely diced
1/2 pound Roquefort or Cabrales cheese, at room temperature, crumbled
1/3 cup heavy (whipping) cream
2 tablespoons medium-dry sherry
Olive oil, for oiling the baking sheet
All-purpose flour, for dusting the work surface
1 sheet frozen puff pastry, thawed
About 1/2 cup finely chopped lightly toasted walnuts (see page 267)

1. Melt the butter in a medium-size skillet over medium heat. Add the apple and cook, stirring, until soft, 7 to 8 minutes, adding a little water to the skillet if it looks dry and adjusting the heat so the apple doesn't brown.

2. Place the cooked apple and the Roquefort, cream, and sherry in a food processor and pulse until medium-smooth. Scrape the mixture into a bowl, cover it with plastic wrap, and refrigerate for 1 hour to firm up the mixture.

3. Place an oven rack in the center of the oven and preheat the oven to 425°F. Lightly brush a 17- by 11-inch baking sheet with olive oil.

4. Lightly flour a work surface, then roll the puff pastry out to a roughly 16- by 11-inch rectangle. Transfer it to the oiled baking sheet. Prick the pastry all over with the tines of a fork and bake it on that center rack until golden brown and cooked through, 15 to 17 minutes. If the pastry has puffed too much, gently press it down with your hand once it is cool enough to handle. Transfer the pastry to a rack to cool completely.

5. Right before serving, spread the pastry evenly with the Roquefort and apple mixture and sprinkle the walnuts on top. Using a long sharp knife, cut the pastry into rectangles, about 2 by 1½ inches, and transfer to a platter. Serve at once. **MAKES ABOUT 30 PUFFS**

MANCHEGO CHEESE CRACKERS WITH MARCONA ALMONDS

GALLETAS DE QUESO MANCHEGO CON ALMENDRAS

These "you just can't stop eating them" crackers are from my friend, food writer Melissa Clark, who, while not Spanish, is the best baker I know. With a bowl of Tangerine-Marinated Olives (page 22) and a glass of icy, bone-dry sherry, they make a perfect *aperitivo* for company, hard as it is to resist the urge to horde every single one for yourself.

4 tablespoons (1/2 stick) unsalted butter, softened
1 cup (about 1/4 pound) grated Manchego cheese
1 1/4 cups all-purpose flour
1/2 teaspoon salt, plus more for the egg wash
1 large egg
About 40 blanched almonds, preferably marcona

1. In the bowl of an electric stand mixer fitted with the paddle attachment, cream the butter with the cheese until well combined. Scrape down the side of the bowl and add the flour and salt. Mix on low speed until the dough just comes together.

2. Turn the dough out onto a piece of plastic wrap and form it into a log 1½ inches in diameter. Wrap the dough log in the plastic and refrigerate it until firm, at least 1 hour or up to 4 days (the dough can also be frozen for up to 1 month).

3. Place an oven rack in the center of the oven and preheat the oven to 350°F. Line two baking sheets with parchment paper or nonstick liners.

4. Slice the dough into ¼-inch-thick coins and place them on the prepared baking sheets, leaving 1 inch between each. Place the egg and a large pinch of salt in a bowl and beat to mix. Brush the crackers with this egg wash, then press an almond on top of each cracker. Bake on the center rack until the crackers are golden and firm, about 15 minutes. Transfer the crackers to a wire rack to cool. Packed in an airtight container, the crackers will keep for several days. **MAKES ABOUT 40 CRACKERS**

BIKINI "PIZZA"

"PIZZA" BIKINI

Bikini is what Catalans call grilled cheese (don't ask me why), and the combination here of thinly sliced mushrooms, sun-dried tomatoes, and mozzarella tucked inside grilled bread comes courtesy of El Bulli's chef, Ferran Adrià. The flavors remind him of pizza. Admittedly, it's a pretty international recipe. Then again, the Catalans are a pretty cosmopolitan bunch, and *bikini* is something of a favorite snack in Barcelona.

- 8 slices best-quality sourdough bread or white bakery bread
- 8 ounces buffalo mozzarella, sliced
- 1/2 cup drained oil-packed sun-dried tomatoes, 4 teaspoons of their oil reserved
- 4 small white mushrooms, thinly sliced
- 4 large basil leaves
- 2 tablespoons extra-virgin olive oil

1. Arrange 4 slices of the bread on a work surface and place 1 or 2 mozzarella slices on top of each. Arrange the tomatoes on top, followed by the mushrooms. Drizzle 1 teaspoon of the tomato oil over the mushrooms on each sandwich and top with a basil leaf. Top each sandwich with a slice of bread.

2. Heat a griddle over medium heat.

3. Brush the sandwiches with the olive oil. Place them on the griddle and top with a heavy pan or grill press. Cook, turning once, until the bread is golden and crisp and the cheese is melted, 8 to 9 minutes. Cut into halves or quarters and serve at once. **SERVES 4**

SPANISH CHEESE PRIMER

Along with the ubiquitous Manchego and the terrifically smelly blue Cabrales, some outstanding Spanish cheeses are finally making their way to a cheesemonger near you. Although it would take a whole book to do justice to the delights of Spanish cheese making, the ten *quesos* here are a good start. Look for them at a good cheese store or specialty food shop, or order them by mail (see page 461).

CABRA AL VINO The name of this young goat cheese from the southeastern Murcia region translates as drunken goat (or more literally goat with wine). The cheese is soaked in the tannic *doble pasta* red wine for up to three days, resulting in a distinctive purplish rind. Inside, Cabra al Vino is pleasantly mild, smooth, and bone white, with a lovely hint of milk and fruit. I love serving it with sliced strawberries.

CABRALES Here's one of Spain's better-known culinary exports: a rich blue cheese from the mountainous northern Asturias region. (It's named after the town of Cabrales in the northern spur of the dramatic Picos de Europa mountain range.) This artisanally produced cheese is gutsy, complex, and almost wild—you can smell it from miles away—but often has a surprising sweetness in the finish. Unlike some other blues, which are injected with mold, Cabrales develops its own natural blue veining in the cold, humid caves where it matures for at least three months. Most commonly it is made with raw cow's milk; sometimes goat's and ewe's milk are blended in. Treat Cabrales as you would any other blue cheese: crumbled on salads, smeared on toasted bread and sprinkled with walnuts, or paired with crisp apples for dessert (a typically Asturian combo). Once you've tried Cabrales, don't miss the other outstanding blue cheese from Picos de Europa: Gamonedo and the milder Valdeón.

GARROTXA From the Garrotxa province of Catalonia, cushioned with fragrant Mediterranean woodland, comes this round, semisoft goat cheese with an attractive bluish gray rind. Creamy and white, aged in natural caves for at least twenty days, it's appreciated for its velvety texture and suggestive hints of wild mushrooms, herbs, and nuts. The production of Garrotxa was begun in the 1970s by a group of visionary urban professionals-turned-farmers who had a dream of reviving traditional cheese making. Today it is one of Spain's best-loved *quesos*.

IDIAZABAL This is the signature farmhouse cheese of the verdant Basque hills. In the past it was produced by shepherds using lamb rennet and hung to drain on chimneys to

The breast-shaped tetilla from Galicia is one of Spain's most famous cheeses.

acquire a smoky character. Made from the raw milk of the long-fleeced Latxa and Carranzana sheep, Idiazábal has a somewhat dense, buttery texture and a flavor that's rich, nutty, and faintly piquant. Most Idiazábal available in this country is lightly smoked (usually over a local wood, such as hawthorn), which gives it a special rustic appeal. Fabulous for melting (try it in the Creamy Basque Smoked Cheese Risotto on page 352), Idiazábal is delicious on a piece of grilled country bread teamed with a sweet-smoky piquillo pepper. Or have it for dessert with a pear compote (such as the topping for the Blue Cheese & Pear Tart, page 408).

MAHON This outstanding cow's milk cheese, a specialty of the northernmost Balearic island of Menorca, comes in hefty, cushionlike blocks, shaped by placing the curd in pieces of cloth and twisting and knotting the corners together. Young Mahón is buttery, nutty, and tangy; as the cheese ages, it acquires a sophisticated, slightly rancid piquancy and a crumbly texture that recalls Parmesan. In Spain, Mahón is almost as popular as Manchego. It's traditionally served sliced, drizzled with olive oil, and sprinkled with black pepper and herbs.

MAJORERO Majorero is made on the exotic island of Fuerteventura in the Canaries, fewer than one hundred miles from Africa. Inside its ocher-colored rind, with its distinctive imprint of braided palm fronds, is a semisoft to hard cheese made with the rich milk of the hardy Majorera goats who scour the forbidding volcanic terrain for lichen. Many connoisseurs consider aged Majorero the best goat cheese in Spain, for its beautifully nuanced nutty-fruity-lemon flavor. Frequently the rind is treated with attractive notes of toasted corn flour, which further enhances it.

MANCHEGO Mentioned by Cervantes in *Don Quixote,* Manchego is produced from the milk of Manchega-breed ewes, who graze on the arid planes of the central La Mancha region. Spain's best-known cheese varies in quality; when good it is rich, oily-textured and vaguely briny, with the long finish of a noble wine. Manchego can be fresh, seimcured, or cured, and aged anywhere from two months to more than a year. The mature cheese develops a crumblier texture and a salty complexity. Marinate cubes of semicured Manchego in olive oil and herbs, and serve it with drinks alongside marcona almonds and green olives. Aged Manchego makes a terrific last course; it's classically paired with *membrillo* (quince paste), honey, or dried figs.

RONCAL From the Navarra region, close to the French border, this exciting raw sheep's milk cheese is somewhat similar to Manchego but drier and even earthier, with a musty suggestion of gaminess that evokes hay and sheep. Roncal is delicious with *membrillo* or cherry preserves, Tomato Jam (page 390), plump medjool dates, or grated on pasta.

TETILLA Named for its evocative breast shape—*tetilla* means nipple—this semisoft cow's milk cheese comes from the lushly green, rainy northwestern Galicia region. Surrounded by a waxy yellow rind, the interior is elastic and creamy with the texture of Muenster and a buttery, subtly grassy taste. It's great as a table cheese or for melting on sandwiches. San Simón, a similar—but rather more interesting—Galician cheese is also worth seeking out.

TORTA DEL CASAR This disk-shaped semisoft cheese from the Extremadura region is produced largely from the milk of merino sheep. Following an ancient practice, a local thistle is used in place of rennet to coagulate the unpasteurized milk, giving Torta del Casar its exotic, floral-herbal bitterness. As the cheese matures and ripens, it becomes spectacularly oozy and sensuous, with a terrific complexity. Traditionally, Torta is warmed in the oven ever so slightly, the top rind is cut off, and the insides are scooped out with a spoon. This is my favorite cheese in the world, expensive but worth every cent. A similar, but somewhat less stunning, cheese from Extremadura is la Serena.

MOORISH CHICKEN AND NUT PIE

PASTELA MORUNA

This is one of my favorite recipes of all times, a swooningly good pie, clearly related to the Moroccan *bastila,* but not nearly as sweet, rich, and time-consuming. *Pastela moruna* is a specialty at many bakeshops in the bewitching Andalusian city of Granada, and local food historians like to say that the recipe was made by the Moorish aristocracy of the Alhambra palace and then kept alive in convents by nuns. Romantic as that sounds, it's more likely to have been borrowed from the city's sizeable North African community. Because I make *pastela* for every possible occasion, I've come to rely on store-bought rotisserie chicken for the filling. If you purchase the puff pastry, too, the pie is a cinch to make.

3 tablespoons olive oil, or more if needed
1 large onion, quartered and thinly sliced
1/2 cup chicken stock or broth, plus more for sprinkling on the onion
3 cups skinned chicken, torn into bite-size pieces (from 1 medium-size rotisserie chicken)
1 tablespoon sweet (not smoked) paprika
1/2 teaspoon ground cumin
3/4 teaspoon ground ginger
1/4 teaspoon ground cinnamon
1/8 teaspoon cayenne
2 plum tomatoes, chopped
1/3 cup dark raisins
Coarse salt (kosher or sea)
All-purpose flour, for dusting the work surface
2 sheets frozen puff pastry, thawed
1/4 cup lightly toasted pine nuts (see page 267)
1/4 cup lightly toasted slivered almonds (see page 267)
1 large egg yolk
1 1/2 teaspoons milk
Confectioners' sugar, for dusting the pie

1. Heat the olive oil in a large skillet over medium-high heat. Add the onion and cook until it begins to soften, 3 to 5 minutes. Reduce the heat to low and cook until the onion is very soft but barely browned, about 15 minutes, stirring occasionally and adding a little more olive oil and 1 to 2 teaspoons of the chicken stock if the skillet looks dry. Stir in the chicken and cook for 1 minute. Add the paprika, cumin, ginger, cinnamon, and cayenne and stir for a few seconds. Add the ½ cup chicken stock, the tomatoes, and raisins, cover the skillet, and cook for 12 to 15 minutes. The filling should be soft and moist; if it seems a little too wet, increase the heat to high for a few seconds so the liquid reduces. Season the filling with salt to taste and let it cool completely. The filling can be prepared up to a day ahead and refrigerated, covered.

2. Place an oven rack in the center of the oven and preheat the oven to 375°F. Lightly brush a 17- by 11-inch baking sheet with olive oil.

3. Lightly flour a work surface. Using a floured rolling pin, roll out 1 sheet of puff pastry to a roughly 18- by 12-inch rectangle. Transfer it to the oiled

Moorish Chicken and Nut Pie

baking sheet. Roll out the remaining sheet of puff pastry to a rectangle that is slightly smaller than the first. Spread the filling evenly over the pastry on the baking sheet, leaving about 1 inch bare along each of the 4 edges. Sprinkle the pine nuts and almonds evenly on top. Cover the filling with the second pastry rectangle. Fold the edges of the bottom crust up over the top and crimp them decoratively.

4. Place the egg yolk and milk in a small bowl and whisk to mix. Brush the top of the pie with this egg wash. Using a sharp knife, make slits all over the top crust to allow steam to escape.

5. Bake the pie on the center rack until golden brown and baked through, 30 to 35 minutes. Let the pie cool until slightly warm or room temperature. Dust very lightly with confectioners' sugar, cut it into squares, and serve. **SERVES 12 AS A TAPA, 6 TO 8 AS A LIGHT MAIN COURSE**

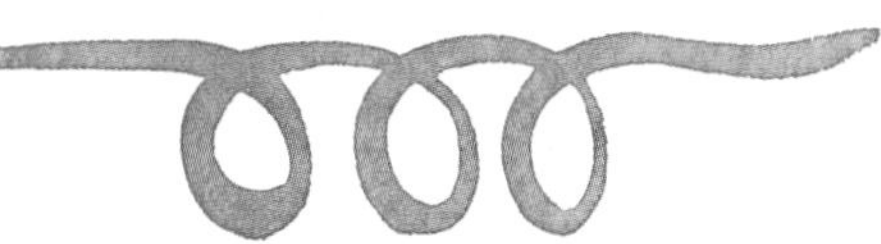

GALICIAN TUNA EMPANADA WITH MELTING ONIONS

EMPANADA GALLEGA DE ATUN

One of my favorite Galician empanadas features good canned tuna, tons of slowly cooked onions and bell peppers, and the pungent accent of green olives to balance the oniony sweetness. Tuna is the simplest option, but you can use this recipe as a blueprint for any Galician seafood empanada, using flaked, cooked, white-fleshed fish, sardines, or sliced raw scallops, for example.

In Galicia empanadas are often made with a wheat or cornmeal dough purchased from a bakery or with puff pastry. The wonderfully flaky—and remarkably easy—olive oil and yeast dough you'll find here comes from a baker who sells her pies at a market in the medieval town of Pontevedra. This empanada tastes even better when made a day ahead and gently reheated.

1/3 cup extra-virgin olive oil, plus more if needed
2 medium-size garlic cloves, minced
2 large white onions, quartered and thinly sliced
3 large red bell peppers, cored, seeded, and thinly sliced
1 medium-size green bell pepper, cored, seeded, and thinly sliced
1 large ripe tomato, peeled, cut in half, and grated on a box grater, skin discarded
2 teaspoons sweet (not smoked) paprika
1 small pinch of saffron threads, pulverized in a mortar and steeped in 2 tablespoons very hot water
18 ounces imported solid oil-packed tuna, or 3 cans (each 6 ounces) Bumble Bee tonno in olive oil, drained and flaked thoroughly with a fork
3 tablespoons minced fresh flat-leaf parsley
Coarse salt (kosher or sea) and freshly ground black pepper
3/4 cup thinly sliced pitted manzanilla olives
All-purpose flour, for dusting the work surface
Olive Oil and Saffron Pastry (recipe follows)
1 large egg yolk
1 1/2 teaspoons milk

1. Place the olive oil in a large skillet over medium heat. Add the garlic and cook for 1 minute. Add the onions and cook until translucent, about 5 minutes. Add the red and green peppers and cook until they begin to soften, 7 to 8 minutes, adding a little more olive oil if the skillet looks dry. Reduce the heat to low and cook, stirring occasionally, until the vegetables are very soft but not brown, about 12 minutes. Add the tomato, paprika, and saffron, cover the skillet, and simmer over very low heat, stirring occasionally, until the vegetables are reduced to a jamlike consistency, about 15 minutes. Let the vegetable mixture cool, then stir in the tuna and parsley. Season with salt and black pepper to taste.

A restaurant owner shows off a fresh delivery of seafood and pimientos.

EMPANADA: THE TRIUMPH OF THE GALICIAN OVEN

In her fascinating book *America's First Cuisines,* food historian Sophie Coe describes a legendary banquet given by the Spanish conquistador Hernán Cortés in Mexico City in 1538. The pièce de résistance, we learn, was gargantuan empanadas brought out at the end of the meal. Ladies were invited to dig in first, and when the crusts were broken live rabbits and birds leapt out onto the table. The chronicler who recorded this extravaganza was awestruck, as well he should have been.

In Spanish the word *empanada* means "in dough" and describes glorious (if not always Cortésian) pies with savory fillings enclosed in bread dough, short pastry, or puff pastry. Though turnover-shaped South American empanadas are better known in this country, these smaller pies (called *empanadillas* in Spain) are just the offspring. Their progenitor—a handsome large pie, as thick as a book and oozing a filling of fish or pork sweetened with masses of onions—remains the mother of all empanadas. They're an obsession in Galicia, a misty-green, northwestern corner of Spain.

Spanish historians believe that the empanadas of yore were akin to sandwiches: large round breads (probably stale), split horizontally and piled with some kind of filling. These empanadas became a veritable fast-food industry in medieval Galicia, sold to pilgrims walking the long Way of St. James from France to the Galician capital of Santiago de Compostela, where the saint's relics are kept in its cathedral. You can still find such sandwichlike "pies" in remote parts of Galicia, and if you look closely, you'll spot them depicted on the sculpted relief adorning the twelfth century Pórtico de la Gloria, the Romansque entrance to the splendidly florid cathedral.

Fillings for large Galician empanadas always start with *zaragallada,* a delicious mixture of onions and peppers, sometimes flavored with tomatoes and saffron, cooked down in ample amounts of olive oil to an almost candied sweetness and jamlike consistency. To this base cooks add steamed and shelled mussels, salt cod or sardines, oysters or clams, thinly sliced scallops, chopped cooked octopus, or something meaty, like pork, chorizo, or game.

Today empanadas are the pride of any *gallego* baker or home cook, and an excuse for endless fiestas and contests where empanadas turn up as fantastical bread sculptures adorned with baroque decorations of heraldic symbols, towers, or flowers.

The empanada filling can be prepared up to a day ahead and refrigerated, covered.

2. Place an oven rack in the center of the oven and preheat the oven to 375°F. Lightly brush a 17- by 11-inch baking sheet with olive oil.

3. Lightly flour a work surface. Using a floured rolling pin, roll out the larger pastry ball to a roughly 19- by 12-inch rectangle. Transfer it to the oiled baking sheet; it will overhang the edge slightly. Roll out the remaining pastry to a rectangle that is slightly smaller than the first. Spread the filling evenly over the pastry on the baking sheet. Scatter the olives evenly on top. Cover the filling with the second pastry rectangle. Fold the edges of the bottom crust up over the top and crimp them decoratively.

4. Place the egg yolk and milk in a small bowl and whisk to mix. Brush the top of the empanada with this egg wash. Using a sharp knife, make several slits all over the top crust to allow steam to escape.

5. Bake the empanada on the center rack until golden brown and baked through, about 45 minutes. Cover the empanada loosely with a clean kitchen towel and let cool until slightly warm or room temperature before serving. **MAKES 1 LARGE EMPANADA; SERVES 12 TO 14 AS A TAPA, 8 AS A LIGHT MAIN COURSE**

OLIVE OIL AND SAFFRON PASTRY

MASA PARA EMPANADAS

I adore this dough. It's easy to knead, easy to roll out, deliciously short, and good for just about any savory pastry or pie. It can be made a day ahead and refrigerated, wrapped loosely in plastic.

- 1 teaspoon active dry yeast
- 1/2 teaspoon sugar
- 2/3 cup lukewarm water (105° to 115°F)
- 4 tablespoons (1/2 stick) unsalted butter, melted
- 1/2 cup extra-virgin olive oil
- 1 large egg, beaten
- 1 large pinch of saffron threads, toasted, pulverized in a mortar, and steeped in 3 tablespoons very hot water
- 2 scant teaspoons salt
- 3 1/2 to 3 3/4 cups all-purpose flour

1. Place the yeast, sugar, and water in a large bowl, stir to mix, and let stand until foamy, about 10 minutes. Whisk in the butter, olive oil, egg, saffron, and salt, and mix well with a wooden spoon. Stir in 3½ cups of the flour, 1 cup at a time, stirring well after each addition.

2. Turn the dough out onto a floured work surface and knead until it is smooth and elastic, about 5 minutes, kneading in the remaining ¼ cup flour if the dough feels sticky. The dough will be oily and pliable. Divide the dough into two parts, one slightly larger than the other. Shape into two balls, place in a buttered bowl, cover loosely with plastic wrap, and let stand for 20 minutes. The dough will rise only slightly. The dough can be refrigerated, covered in plastic wrap, for up to 24 hours. Let it return to room temperature before using. **MAKES ENOUGH DOUGH FOR 1 LARGE EMPANADA**

LENTEN EMPANADA WITH SALT COD AND GOLDEN RAISINS

EMPANADA DE BACALAO CON PASAS

During Lent in Spain, salt cod takes the place of meat in all kinds of terrific dishes. This empanada, with its marvelous play of the sweet and the salty, is delicious made either with store-bought puff pastry or with the Olive Oil and Saffron Pastry on the facing page. It takes a little effort but the results are to die for. Serve it for a light lunch along with a green salad or as a tapa, cut into small squares. The salt cod needs to soak for at least twenty-four hours, so plan accordingly.

- 1 pound boneless salt cod, soaked and cooked (see page 198), then drained
- 1/3 cup olive oil, plus more if needed
- 4 large garlic cloves, minced
- 2 medium-size white onions, quartered and thinly sliced
- 2 medium-size green bell peppers, cored, seeded, and thinly sliced
- 1 large red bell pepper, cored, seeded, and thinly sliced
- 2 teaspoons sweet (not smoked) paprika
- 1 small bay leaf, crumbled
- 6 canned tomatoes, chopped, plus about 2 tablespoons of their juices
- 3/4 cup golden raisins
- 1/4 cup dry white wine
- Coarse salt (kosher or sea) and freshly ground black pepper
- Fresh lemon juice (optional)
- All-purpose flour, for dusting the work surface
- 2 sheets frozen puff pastry, thawed, or Olive Oil and Saffron Pastry (facing page)
- 1/3 cup minced fresh flat-leaf parsley
- 1 large egg yolk
- 1 1/2 teaspoons milk

1. Pat the salt cod dry with paper towels. Flake the cod into small pieces, removing any bones or hard bits. Set the cod aside.

2. Heat the olive oil in a large skillet over medium heat. Add the garlic, and cook for 1 minute. Add the onions and cook until translucent, about 5 minutes. Add the green and red peppers and cook, stirring, until they begin to soften, 7 to 8 minutes, adding a little more olive oil if the skillet looks dry. Reduce the heat to low, and cook, stirring occasionally, until the vegetables are very soft but not brown, about 12 minutes. Add the paprika, bay leaf, and tomatoes and their juices, and stir for 1 to 2 minutes. Add the raisins and wine, cover the skillet, and simmer over very low heat, stirring occasionally, until the vegetables are reduced to a jamlike consistency, about 15 minutes. Let the vegetable mixture cool, then stir in the salt cod. Season the filling with salt and black pepper to taste, adding a little lemon juice if it needs a touch of acidity. The empanada filling can be prepared up to a day ahead and refrigerated, covered.

3. Place an oven rack in the center of the oven and preheat the oven to 375°F. Lightly brush a 17- by 11-inch baking sheet with olive oil.

4. Lightly flour a work surface. Using a floured rolling pin, roll out 1 sheet of puff pastry to a roughly 18- by 12-inch rectangle. Transfer it to the oiled baking sheet; it will overhang the edge slightly. Roll out the remaining sheet of puff pastry to a rectangle that is slightly smaller than the first. Spread the filling evenly over the pastry on the baking sheet. Sprinkle parsley evenly on top. Cover the filling with the second pastry rectangle. Fold the edges of the bottom crust up over the top and crimp them decoratively.

5. Place the egg yolk and milk in a small bowl and whisk to mix. Brush the top of the empanada with this egg wash. Using a sharp knife, make slits all over the top crust to allow steam to escape.

6. Bake the empanada in the center rack until golden brown and baked through, about 30 minutes

for puff pastry, 45 minutes for Olive Oil and Saffron Pastry. Once the empanada has been removed from the oven, if you've used Olive Oil and Saffron Pastry, cover the empanada loosely with a clean kitchen towel (if you've used puff pastry, don't cover it). Let the empanada cool until slightly warm or room temperature. Cut it into squares and serve. **MAKES 1 LARGE EMPANADA; SERVES 12 TO 14 AS A TAPA, 8 AS A LIGHT MAIN COURSE**

COCA WITH CANDIED RED PEPPERS

COCA CON PIMIENTOS ROJOS CARAMELIZADOS

For sipping wine and watching the crowds go by, few bars in Spain are more enjoyable than Vinya del Senyor in Barcelona. Considering its location—right in the shadow of the fourteenth-century Santa Maria del Mar church, in the city's most touristy area—the offerings are truly outstanding: interesting wines by the glass, first-rate cheeses, boutique charcuterie. The most curious and addictive thing on the menu is the *coca* (a Spanish-Mediterranean pizza), baked with a Mallorcan topping of sweetened red peppers that are dusted with confectioners' sugar. The result is a delicious, intriguing cross between a dessert tart and a savory pizza. And there is nothing I'd rather eat with a glass of crisp, chilled rosé.

Because I'd sooner hang out sipping wine than slave in the kitchen, I've adapted this recipe to use store-bought pizza dough and roasted peppers from a jar—with excellent results. (For best results buy the dough from a pizzeria.) If the confectioners' sugar topping seems too unorthodox, feel free to omit it—but not without trying it first!

2 tablespoons olive oil, plus more for brushing the coca
1 medium-size white onion, quartered and thinly sliced
4 cups thinly sliced drained roasted peppers in oil (from four 14- to 16-ounce jars)
5 tablespoons granulated sugar
2 tablespoons sherry vinegar, preferably aged, or best-quality red wine vinegar
Coarse salt (kosher or sea)
All-purpose flour, for dusting the rolling pin
1 pound store-bought pizza dough, thawed if frozen
Confectioners' sugar, for dusting the coca

1. Heat the 2 tablespoons olive oil in a large skillet over medium-low heat. Add the onion and cook until limp but not browned, 5 to 7 minutes, stirring occasionally. Add the roasted peppers and cook for about 5 minutes, stirring. Add the granulated sugar, vinegar, and 2 tablespoons water and stir until the sugar dissolves. Cover the skillet, reduce the heat to low, and cook until the liquid is reduced, about 10 minutes, stirring from time to time. Season with salt to taste and let the pepper mixture cool completely.

2. Place an oven rack in the center of the oven and preheat the oven to 450°F. Lightly brush a 17- by 11-inch baking sheet with olive oil.

3. Lightly flour a work surface. Using a floured rolling pin, roll out the dough so it is roughly as large as the baking sheet. Transfer it to the oiled baking sheet and brush it with olive oil. Spread the filling evenly on top.

4. Bake the *coca* on the center rack until it is light golden and baked through, 18 to 20 minutes. Let the *coca* cool to warm (or make the *coca* ahead, which actually adds to its flavor; reheat it gently before serving). Cut the *coca* into rectangles (I use sturdy kitchen scissors for this), dust it very lightly with confectioners' sugar, and serve at once. **MAKES 1 LARGE COCA; SERVES 12 AS A TAPA**

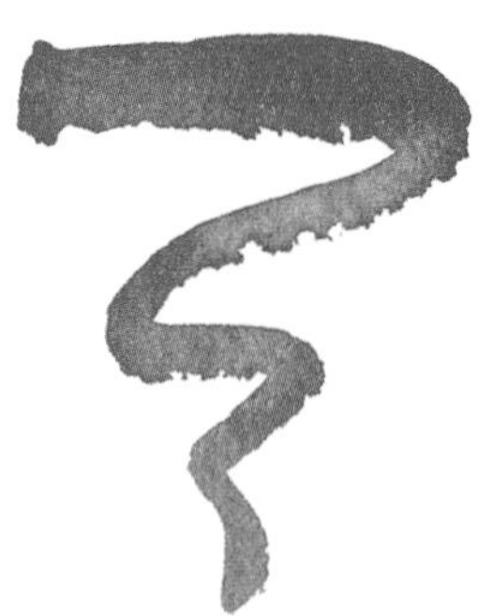

COCA WITH HONEYED ONIONS AND PINE NUTS

COCA DE CEBOLLA CON MIEL Y PIÑONES

The recipe for this incredible flatbread was demonstrated to me by my favorite Mallorcan chef, Joan Torrens, at his restaurant Es Baluard. Harking back to medieval Arab cooking, the intriguing mix of sweet and savory flavors here is typical of the island's cuisine. Joan prebakes the *coca* dough briefly so that the topping doesn't render it soggy. To soften the onions and get rid of some of their bitterness, he rubs them with salt and lets them sit (you'll need to allow about an hour for this). Once you're ready to bake the *coca,* make sure to rinse the onions well and thoroughly squeeze the water out. See the Variations to turn this *coca* into a savory one, made with anchovies.

- 4 large sweet white onions (about 3 pounds total), cut in half and very thinly sliced
- Coarse salt (kosher or sea)
- 1/4 cup plus 2 to 3 tablespoons extra-virgin olive oil
- All-purpose flour, for dusting the work surface
- Joan's Coca Dough (recipe follows)
- 1/4 cup plus 1 to 2 tablespoons honey, preferably rosemary honey
- 1 tablespoon best-quality red wine vinegar
- 1/3 cup dried currants
- 2 tablespoons finely minced fresh rosemary
- 1/2 cup pine nuts

1. Place the onions in a sieve and massage about 1 tablespoon salt into them. Place the sieve over a bowl and let stand for about 1 hour.

2. Place an oven rack in the center of the oven and preheat the oven to 425°F.

3. Generously brush a 17- by 11-inch baking sheet with olive oil. Lightly flour a work surface. Using a floured rolling pin, roll out the dough so that it's roughly as large as the baking sheet. Transfer it to the oiled baking sheet. Prick the dough all over with the tines of a fork and bake it on the center rack until half done, about 15 minutes.

4. While the crust is baking, rinse the onions well under cold running water. Thoroughly press the slices of onion hard against the sieve to get rid of the excess moisture. Add ¼ cup of the honey to the onions in the sieve, massaging it into the onions and pressing against the sieve to squeeze out more moisture. Transfer the onions to a bowl and add the vinegar, currants, rosemary, and ¼ cup of the olive oil.

5. When the dough is half baked, spread the onion mixture evenly on top. Drizzle 1 to 2 tablespoons of honey over it, then scatter pine nuts on top. Bake the *coca* for 20 minutes, drizzle with the remaining olive oil, then continue baking until the onion is lightly golden and has lost most of its crunch, 15 to 20 minutes longer.

6. Cover the *coca* with a clean kitchen towel and let it cool for about 30 minutes, then cut it into squares and serve. The *coca* can be baked ahead and served the next day; it will taste even better. **MAKES 1 LARGE COCA; SERVES 12 AS A TAPA**

VARIATIONS: To turn this *coca* into a more savory onion-and-anchovy flatbread, follow the recipe but omit the honey, vinegar, and currants. After spreading the onion topping on the dough, top it with drained, oil-packed anchovy fillets (you'll need 20 to 24 fillets). Or toss some chopped anchovies into the onion topping before spreading it on the *coca*. Alternatively, the onion *coca* can be topped with thin slices of pork sausage, julienned salami, or cleaned, fresh sardine fillets before baking.

JOAN'S COCA DOUGH

MASA PARA COCAS DE JOAN

The traditional *coca* dough of Mallorca is made with lard and is incredibly rich—delicious but hardly what the doctor ordered. It often includes a yeast starter. In his typical fashion, chef Joan Torrens has modernized the recipe, using olive oil and a touch of beer.

- 1/3 cup lager-style beer
- 1/2 cup light olive oil
- 1 large egg, beaten
- 2 teaspoons coarse salt (kosher or sea)
- 2 3/4 to 3 1/4 cups all-purpose flour

1. Place the beer, olive oil, egg, salt, and ⅔ cup water in a large bowl and whisk to mix. Add 2¾ cups of the flour, ½ cup at a time, mixing well after each addition. Knead the dough briefly in the bowl to incorporate all the stray flour.

2. Turn the dough out onto a floured work surface and knead until smooth and elastic, about 5 minutes, kneading in enough of the remaining ½ cup flour for the dough not to stick to your hands. (If the dough still sticks after all the remaining flour has been incorporated, oil your hands and continue kneading.) The dough will be pliable and slightly oily. Shape the dough into a ball, place it in a well-oiled bowl, cover it with plastic wrap, and let stand while you prepare the *coca* filling. **MAKES ENOUGH FOR ONE 17- BY 11-INCH COCA**

COCA WITH A TOMATO SALAD

COCA DE TRAMPO

On its own, *trampó* (or *trempó*) is a classic Mallorcan salad of finely diced tomatoes, sweet onion, and pepper made soupy with good olive oil and some vinegar, and often eaten with a spoon and bread for dipping. Drained, it's frequently used for topping flatbreads, making for one of the island's most popular *cocas*. The *trampó* is delicious plain, but you can also cap it with anchovy fillets or add some chopped black olives to the mix. Once it's baked, squares of *coca* make a great base for a slice of good cheese or ham.

Chopping the vegetables fine to the point of mincing is important here—besides being traditional, it also helps the topping bake through faster.

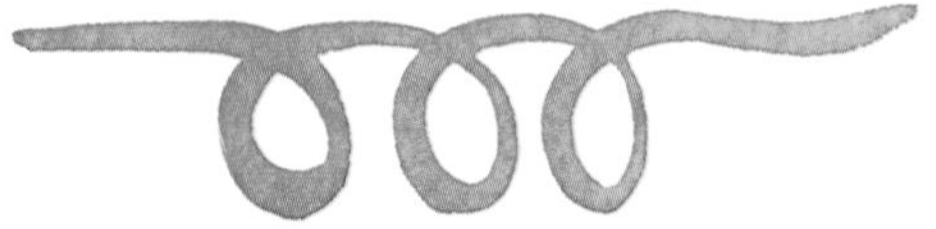

- 1 1/2 pounds ripe sweet tomatoes, peeled, seeded, and diced as finely as you can
- 1 pinch of sugar (optional)
- 1 dash of red wine vinegar (optional)
- 1 medium-size white onion, diced as finely as you can
- 2 medium-size Italian (frying) peppers, cored, seeded, and diced as finely as you can
- 1 large red bell pepper, cored, seeded, and diced as finely as you can
- 1/4 cup fragrant extra-virgin olive oil, plus more for drizzling over the coca
- 6 medium-size garlic cloves, crushed with a garlic press
- Coarse salt (kosher or sea) and freshly ground black pepper
- All-purpose flour, for dusting the work surface
- 1 pound store-bought pizza dough, thawed if frozen

1. Place the tomatoes in a fine sieve and let them drain for 20 minutes. Transfer the tomatoes to a large mixing bowl and taste them: If they are too acidic or seem to lack flavor, add the sugar and/or vinegar to heighten the flavor.

2. Add the onion, Italian peppers, red pepper, olive oil, and garlic and toss to mix. Season with salt and black pepper to taste. Let the *trampó* stand for at least 15 minutes.

3. Meanwhile, place an oven rack in the center of the oven and preheat the oven to 425°F.

4. Generously brush a 17- by 11-inch baking sheet with olive oil. Lightly flour a work surface. Using a floured rolling pin, roll out the dough so it is roughly as large as the baking sheet. Transfer it to the oiled baking sheet. Prick the dough all over with the tines of a fork and bake it on the center rack until half done, about 12 minutes.

5. Remove the *coca* crust from the oven. Take a handful of the *trampó* and press it against a fine sieve to squeeze out the excess moisture, then spread the *trampó* over the dough. Repeat with the remaining *trampó,* spreading it over the crust in a thick, even layer. Bake the *coca* until the vegetables are soft and lightly charred, about 30 minutes. Halfway through baking, drizzle a little olive oil over the vegetables.

6. Let the *coca* cool to room temperature, then cut it into squares and serve. **MAKES 1 LARGE COCA; SERVES 12 AS A TAPA**

bonito
7€
CEUTA
PIEZA
Hueva
Merluza
Extra
5500 ptas Kilo
Mojama
Almadraba
27.05 €
4.500 ptas Kilo
Marrajo
de barca
7000 ptas Kilo
bonito
larache
15.03 € Limpio
2500 ptas Kilo

CARMEN

SEAFOOD

SOPHISTICATED SIMPLICITY

The Spanish seafood experience goes something like this: You enter a nautically themed dining room swathed in dark, gleaming wood and make your way to an open-air terrace overlooking a working harbor. Around you, men in striped shirts are sucking the sweet, briny juices from shrimp heads. Platters of salt-grilled whole fish, piles of saucy clams, and kettles of seafood stews are rushed out of the kitchen, landing on tables occupied by large, unruly families. Finally, the proprietor approaches your table. He carries himself with the gravitas of a heart surgeon—discussing your order as if your entire well-being depended on it. A few seafood *croquetas* and bacalao fritters to start—check. Half a dozen *almejas de Carril,* the astronomically expensive Galician clams, eaten raw without as much as a squeeze of lemon—double check. Do

Top left: A fisherman along the Costa Brava takes the time to mends his nets. *Top right:* Porto Colom, a small traditional fishing village in Mallorca, has managed to keep its old-world charm despite the growing tourist trade. *Bottom left:* Dry-cured fish is a favorite of shoppers at a Valencia market. *Bottom right:* An old fishing boat in for repairs on Andalusia's Costa del Sol.

you want your *camarones*—translucent shrimp, heads and all—boiled or *a la plancha?* Alas, the kitchen just ran out of turbot. A butterflied sole grilled over a wood fire instead? You nod yes to all, knowing that you might have to wager your inheritance on this meal.

It doesn't matter. Side orders? Nah. At the best Spanish seafood restaurants, there's no room for side dishes or garnishes; no elaborate sauces; no frills. What you get is an austerely elegant meal of sublime *materia prima,* possibly a glass of brandy on the house, and a Havana *puro,* if you happen to smoke.

A peninsula flanked by the Atlantic, Cantabrian, and Mediterranean seas, Spain boasts more than 3,000 miles of coastline and some of the world's most prodigious fishing fleets. What comes out of its waters is so extraordinary, and treated by cooks with such savvy and care, that at times it seems like all my travels in Spain can be summed up as a collage of great seafood meals. I close my eyes, thinking of a *chiringuito* (a seafood shack) on an Andalusian beach: the dime-size purple-shelled clams called *coquinas,* the salty pungency of the air, the crunch of fried baby squid. Then my thoughts turn to Sanlúcar de Barrameda. Three things draw visitors to this sherry-producing Andalusian town where the Guadalquivir river empties into the Atlantic. One is manzanilla, the queen of dry sherries, with a unique salty tang. Two is *langostinos,* the fat, succulent prawns that rank among the country's most sought-after crustaceans. Three is the chance to savor the two together at sunset at one of the restaurants on the water's edge, watching the blazing red sun slowly sink into the Atlantic.

Galicia conjures up images of grilled sardines with new potatoes, wooden boards of sliced octopus dusted with paprika, glasses of fresh albariño, and mounds of *percebes,* or goose barnacles, which look like strange prehistoric claws and explode with warm marine juices when you break them apart. A Basque seafood repast revolves

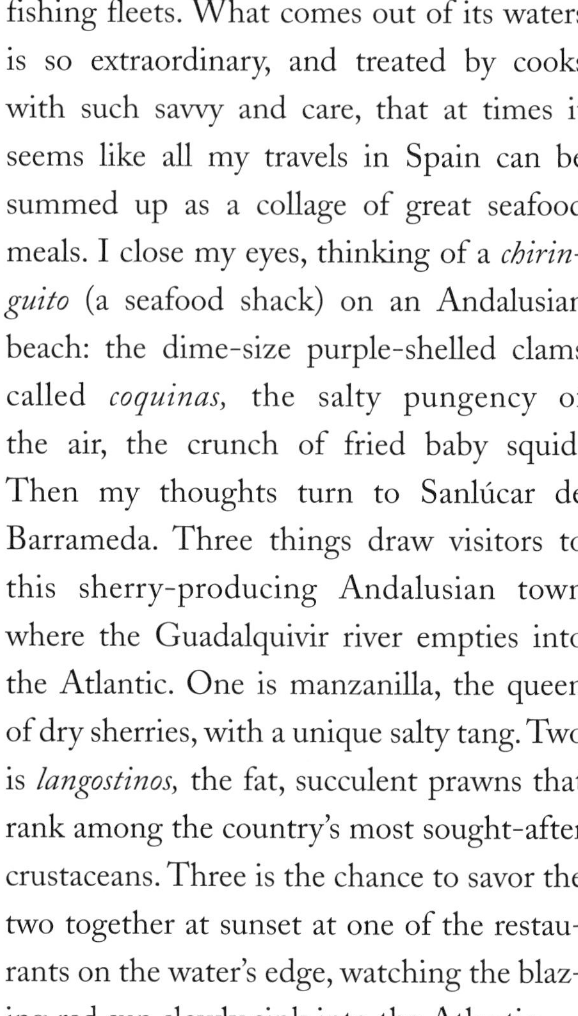

Clams in Olive Oil with Jamón and Pine Nuts (page 223)

around line-caught hake in a delicate *salsa verde, kokotxas* (hake cheeks) fried in the lightest of batters, anchovies bathed in garlicky olive oil, and—always—a magnificent whole grilled turbot. Say Valencia and Catalonia, and I imagine the messy fishermen's stews called *suquets* and seafood bobbing in kettles of terra-cotta-colored *romesco,* a sauce so delicious one could happily drown in it.

Wherever you go in Spain, you find bacalao—salted dried cod—recipes for which could fill many volumes. Modern Spanish cooks may be fanatical about freshness, yet it was preserved fish—anchovies, salt cod, cured tuna, and the various *escabeches*—that formed the backbone of the country's traditional diet. Today these flavors are as sought after as ever.

When it comes to seafood, sophisticated simplicity is the mantra in contemporary Spanish kitchens. Rather than waste time on complicated constructions and fancy garnishes, Spanish chefs are pushing the envelope by devising novel techniques designed to bring out the fish's flavor and texture. Delicate hake might be submerged in olive oil and poached at a radically low temperature, emerging from the pan moister than any fish you've tasted before. Bacalao, which can overcook and toughen in a nanosecond, could be poached *al vacío* (vacuum-packed) in a high-tech bain-marie, so that it has all the succulence of fresh fish. Sauces may be thickened with flavorless, colorless agar-agar (Asian gelatin), whipped into diaphanous foams and "airs," or reimagined as infused broths or gelées.

From robust fish and potato dishes traditionally prepared aboard trawlers, to kettles of shellfish flavored with garlic and olive oil, to quick but sophisticated modern creations, the recipes in this chapter are a seafood lover's delight.

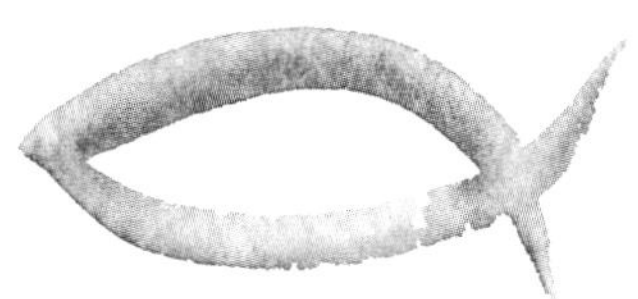

FISH

ROAST COD IN RED BELL PEPPER BROTH

BACALAO EN CALDO DE PIMIENTOS ASADOS

This is my take on a fetching dish I tasted at Kukuarri, a restaurant in San Sebastián that belongs to the empire of Michelin three-star Basque chef Martin Berasategui. There, it was prepared with a beautifully moist loin of salt cod, but fresh cod makes a better substitute than the dried-out bacalao most commonly available in the States. The flavors here are minimalist and memorable: a great piece of fish and a grilled scallion spear afloat in a rust-colored broth infused with broiled red peppers. The recipe calls for straining out the peppers, but if you like you can add some to the broth. Or, toss the peppers with some sherry vinegar and good olive oil and use them on sandwiches or grilled chicken or fish. The pepper broth can be prepared ahead and reheated.

1 small dried pimiento choricero or ancho chile, stemmed and seeded
4 large red bell peppers, cored, seeded, and cut in half lengthwise
3 tablespoons extra-virgin olive oil, plus more for brushing the vegetables
4 fat scallions, trimmed, with 2 1/2 inches of green
1 small onion, chopped
2 cups Fish Stock (page 108) or store-bought fish stock, or 1 1/2 cups bottled clam juice diluted with 1/2 cup water
1 tablespoon sherry vinegar, preferably aged
1 large pinch of sugar, or more to taste
1/2 cup chopped fresh flat-leaf parsley
4 medium-size garlic cloves, chopped
4 thick skinless cod fillets (each about 1 inch thick; about 2 pounds total)
Coarse salt (kosher or sea)

1. Preheat the broiler.

2. Place the *pimiento choricero* in a small bowl, add very hot water to cover, and let soak while you broil the red peppers and scallions.

3. Arrange the red peppers on a broiler pan lined with aluminum foil and brush lightly with olive oil. Broil the peppers until they are soft and charred, about 12 minutes. Transfer the peppers to a bowl, cover with plastic wrap, and let stand for 15 minutes (leave the broiler turned on). While the peppers are standing, place the scallions on the broiler pan, brush them lightly with olive oil, and broil until soft and lightly charred, about 3 minutes per side. Transfer the scallions to a plate and set aside.

4. Peel the broiled peppers and chop them coarsely. Drain the *pimiento choricero*. Heat 1 tablespoon of the olive oil in a medium-size saucepan over medium heat. Add the onion and cook until limp but not browned, about 7 minutes. Add the

pimiento choricero and red peppers and stir for 1 minute. Add the fish stock and bring to a simmer. Add the vinegar and sugar, cover the saucepan, and reduce the heat to low. Simmer for 20 to 25 minutes to infuse the broth. Taste for seasoning, adding more sugar as necessary. Strain the broth into a bowl through a fine sieve, pressing on the peppers to extract as much liquid as possible. Puree ½ cup of the strained peppers in a blender with a little of the strained broth. Stir the pureed pepper mixture into the remaining strained broth. Save the rest of the strained peppers for another use. The pepper broth can be refrigerated, covered, for up to 1 day.

5. Preheat the oven to 500°F.

6. Place the parsley and garlic in a mini food processor and finely chop them. Scrape the parsley mixture into a small bowl and stir in the remaining 2 tablespoons olive oil. Season the cod generously with salt. Arrange the cod on a small oiled baking sheet and spread some of the parsley mixture on top of each fillet. Bake the cod until it just flakes when prodded with a fork, 10 to 12 minutes.

7. While the cod is baking, reheat the pepper broth. To serve, place each cod fillet in a shallow soup plate with a grilled scallion and pour about ½ cup of the pepper broth around it. Serve at once.
SERVES 4

A fisherman cleans his catch along the Costa del Sol.

MALLORCAN BRAISED GROUPER

AMFOS A LA MALLORQUINA

Those seeking truly authentic Mallorcan cuisine, uncorrupted by the tastes of the northern European tourists who descend on the island in droves, should head to Es Baluard restaurant in Palma. Here, chef Joan Torrens lovingly preserves old recipes, modernizing them slightly but always staying true to the vibrant simplicity of the local traditions. One of his signature dishes is this fish, slowly braised in the oven on a bed of potatoes and capped with a mouthwatering ragout of red and yellow bell peppers, tomatoes, and chard. Currants and pine nuts, which are used liberally in Joan's kitchen, add the Moorish accent characteristic of Mallorcan cuisine. In fact, the dish brings to mind the food of Sicily—another cuisine that melds

Mediterranean and Arab flavors to seductive effect. The recipe is a bit more involved than just plonking fish in the oven, but the result is a marvelous one-dish meal that requires nothing more than a salad of peppery greens.

- 5 tablespoons extra-virgin olive oil, plus more for drizzling over the fish
- 1 medium-size white onion, quartered and thinly sliced
- 5 medium-size garlic cloves, sliced
- 2 teaspoons sweet (not smoked) paprika
- 1/4 teaspoon crushed red pepper flakes
- 2 roasted red bell peppers (see page 385), cut into strips
- 2 roasted yellow bell peppers (see page 385), cut into strips
- 2 large vine-ripened tomatoes, peeled, seeded, and chopped
- 2 1/2 cups chopped Swiss chard (leaves only)
- 1 medium-size bunch flat-leaf parsley (leaves only), chopped
- 1 bay leaf
- 1/3 cup dry white wine
- 1/3 cup dried currants
- 4 thick grouper steaks (about 2 pounds total; see Note)
- Coarse salt (kosher or sea) and freshly ground black pepper
- All-purpose flour, for dusting the fish
- 4 large Yukon Gold potatoes (about 2 pounds total), boiled and sliced 1/4 inch thick
- 1/4 cup pine nuts

1. Heat 4 tablespoons of the olive oil in a large skillet, preferably nonstick, over medium-low heat. Add the onion and garlic and cook until soft but not browned, about 7 minutes. Add the paprika and red pepper flakes and stir for a few seconds. Add the roasted red and yellow peppers and the tomatoes, increase the heat to medium, and cook until the tomatoes begin to release their juice, about 5 minutes. Stir in the chard and parsley and cook, stirring, just until they wilt. Add the bay leaf, wine, and currants and bring to a simmer. Reduce the heat to medium-low and cook until the vegetables are softened and the flavors blended, 5 to 7 minutes. The vegetable mixture can be prepared ahead and refrigerated, covered, for 1 day.

2. Preheat the oven to 300°F.

3. Rub the fish steaks generously with salt and black pepper. Heat the remaining 1 tablespoon olive oil in a large skillet over medium heat. Dust the fish lightly with flour, add it to the skillet, and sear for about 30 seconds on each side. Transfer the fish steaks to a plate.

4. Set out an earthenware casserole or a deep ceramic or glass baking dish in which the fish steaks will fit snugly in a single layer. Arrange the potato slices in the casserole in one layer, overlapping them slightly. Sprinkle salt on the potatoes, then arrange the fish on top.

5. Remove the bay leaf from the vegetable mixture and discard it. Season the vegetable mixture with salt to taste, then spoon it evenly over the fish, along with its pan juices. Drizzle olive oil over the vegetables and sprinkle with pine nuts. Bake the fish steaks until they are very tender, 45 to 50 minutes depending on their thickness. Let the fish and vegetables cool for about 10 minutes, then serve straight from the casserole. **SERVES 4**

NOTE: If grouper is unavailable, you can substitute another firm saltwater fish, such as monkfish, mahimahi, or halibut. If you want to use fillets, they need to be thick; reduce the baking time by about 15 minutes.

BASQUE HAKE & CLAMS IN SALSA VERDE

MERLUZA CON ALMEJAS EN SALSA VERDE

Whenever Basques talk about food—which is pretty much all the time—the conversation always turns to *merluza* (hake) in *salsa verde,* perhaps the most iconic dish in the País Vasco. Which restaurant has the most definitive version? Which stall at the fish market offers the freshest *merluza,* a mild, delicate fish in the cod family? Should you add flour to thicken the parsley-flecked sauce or let the natural gelatin in the fish's skin do the job?

Line-caught *merluza* is the pride of Basque fishermen. *Salsa verde* makes the perfect foil for it and the clams, both of which need to be handled gently. It's a soupy sauce that allows the seafood to cook at a low temperature, preserving its moistness. While *salsa verde* is distinctive, its flavor doesn't overpower the fine taste of the fish. *Merluza*—called either hake or by its Spanish name—is becoming increasingly available in the States. If you can't find it, use another delicate but not overly flaky fish, such as cod, scrod, or sea bass.

4 hake, cod, or sea bass fillets (each about 1 inch thick and 6 ounces), preferably with the skin
Coarse salt (kosher or sea) and freshly ground white pepper
1/4 cup light olive oil
2 teaspoons all-purpose flour, plus more for dusting the fish
5 medium-size garlic cloves, minced
1/3 cup finely minced fresh flat-leaf parsley
1/4 cup dry white wine
1 cup Fish Stock (page 108) or store-bought fish stock, or 2/3 cup bottled clam juice diluted with 1/3 cup water
12 small littleneck clams, scrubbed
2/3 cup frozen baby peas, thawed
Crusty bread, for serving

1. Rub the fish with salt and white pepper and let stand for 15 minutes.

2. Heat the olive oil in a 10-inch earthenware *cazuela* or a deep, heavy skillet over medium-low heat. Dust the fish very lightly with flour and cook it for 30 seconds on each side. Transfer the fish to a plate. Add the garlic and half of the parsley to the *cazuela.* Cook, stirring, until the garlic is very fragrant but not browned, about 1 minute. Add the 2 teaspoons flour and stir for another 30 seconds. Add the wine and the fish stock, increase the heat to medium-high, and cook the sauce, stirring, until it thickens a little, about 2 minutes.

3. Return the fish to the *cazuela.* If the fillets have skin, arrange them skin side down. Reduce the heat to low and cook for 2 minutes. Using a spatula, turn the fish over, then add the clams and peas. Cover the *cazuela* and cook, shaking the *cazuela,* until the fish just flakes when prodded with a fork and the clams open, 4 to 7 minutes more. Stir in the remaining

A BASQUE SEAFOOD EPIPHANY

Gastronomy to the Basques is what love is to the French and soccer to the Brazilians—a subject that permeates every nook and cranny of the collective unconscious. Basque cuisine is dense with tradition, wedded to both the land and the sea. Think pure, singular flavors and an extreme level of ingredient worship. From the misty slopes come farmhouse cheeses such as Idiazábal, iridescent-green peas, and an amazing profusion of mushrooms. The Cantabrian sea yields pristine langoustines, tender-fleshed hake, anchovies, and the sweetest, tiniest *chipirones,* or baby squid. From a nation whose navigating and fishing skills took them to Newfoundland's Grand Banks possibly even before Columbus discovered America, Basques take fish fetishism to a whole new level. Here markets display the day's catch—sea bream, bonito, sole, turbot—arranged on faux sea shells in theatrically illuminated marine still lifes. Here, every kindergartner knows that a hake (line-caught, of course) cooked above a precise temperature is ruined forever.

"The only way we ate fish was off the boat," says my friend Manu. "Next day we threw it out because for us it wasn't fresh." Manu, who is the son of a hake fisherman and is married to chef Elena Arzak, is explaining all this at Kaia. A venerable seafood mecca in the fishing village of Getaria, Kaia has a fetching view of the tangle of boats in the harbor below as well as its own live fish tanks. The great French chef Michel Bras called Kaia's *cigalas* (langoustines) the world's greatest ingredient. I agree, prying their exquisite, pearlescent flesh from the shells. Fresh anchovies caught just minutes ago land on the table gently sautéed in a puddle of delicate olive oil. Tasting a little like oysters but meatier, *kokotxas*—the much-venerated hake's cheeks—are flash fried in the lightest of egg batters to just seal in their delicate succulence. "This food might seem simple," Manu muses, "but preparing it perfectly takes immense skill." Then he stops talking, picking out tender nuggets of flesh from the head of a majestic grilled turbot.

parsley. Taste the sauce for seasoning, adding salt and/or white pepper as necessary. You can serve the dish straight from the *cazuela* or transfer it to a deep serving dish. Serve with bread to sop up the sauce. **SERVES 4**

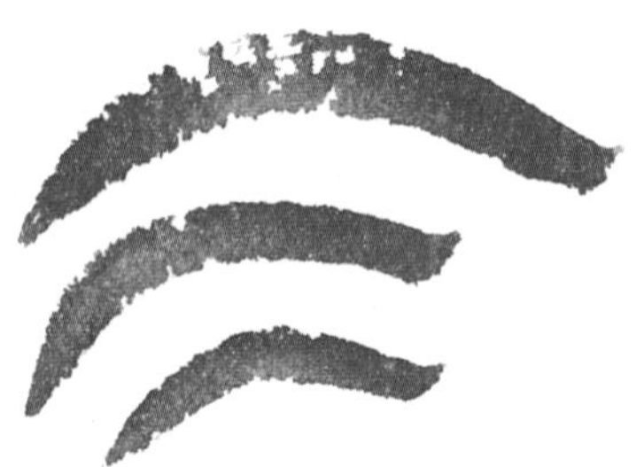

ROASTED HALIBUT ON A BED OF POTATOES

"MERLUZA" AL HORNO CON PATATAS

Here's a recipe from Xavier Franco, a Barcelona chef who truly understands fish. This one is

Xavier's slightly tweaked version of a popular Basque dish that dresses fish with a *refrito* of fried garlic, chile, good olive oil, and vinegar. The fish comes out delightfully tangy and savory, with the sliced potato layer soaking up all the yummy juices. Because the *merluza* (hake) called for in the original recipe isn't easy to find, I substitute halibut. Other firm white-fleshed fish, such as sea bass, turbot, or tilefish, will also work. So will salmon; it isn't particularly Spanish but it *is* incredibly good when prepared this way.

4 skinless halibut fillets (each about 8 ounces)
Coarse salt (kosher or sea) and freshly ground black pepper
1 pound medium-size Yukon Gold potatoes, peeled
About 1/3 cup fragrant extra-virgin olive oil
8 large garlic cloves, thinly sliced
1 small dried red chile, such as arbol, crumbled
2 tablespoons sherry vinegar, preferably aged
Minced fresh flat-leaf parsley, for garnish

1. Preheat the oven to 500°F.

2. Rub the halibut with salt and pepper and let stand while you prepare the potatoes.

3. Place the potatoes in a saucepan. Add salted water to cover by 2 inches and bring to a boil. Cook the potatoes until they just begin to feel tender when pierced with a skewer, 25 minutes or longer depending on their size. Do not overcook. Drain the potatoes and let cool enough to handle, then, using an oiled knife, cut them into slices between ¼- and ⅛ inch thick. Generously coat a 10-inch ovenproof skillet with olive oil (a cast-iron skillet is ideal or use a similar-size baking pan). Arrange the potatoes in a slightly overlapping layer on the bottom. Sprinkle the potatoes with salt.

4. Place ⅓ cup olive oil and the garlic in a small skillet and heat over medium-low heat until the oil simmers and the garlic just begins to take on color, about 2 minutes. Add the chile and stir for 15 seconds. Using a slotted spoon, transfer the garlic and chile to a bowl. Add the vinegar to the skillet and *immediately* cover it, as the oil will splatter. Cook, covered, for the flavors to blend, 2 minutes, turn off the heat, and let stand until the oil stops popping against the lid.

5. Pour some of the vinaigrette over the potatoes and scatter some of the fried garlic and chile over them. Arrange the halibut fillets on the potatoes, pour the remaining vinaigrette on top, and scatter the remaining garlic and chile over them. Bake the fish until it just flakes when tested with a fork, 10 to 12 minutes depending on the thickness. Sprinkle the parsley on top and serve. **SERVES 4**

MONKFISH WITH EGGPLANT ALLIOLI

RAPE GRATINADO CON ALLIOLI DE BERENJENAS

This lovely ultra-Mediterranean recipe comes by way of my favorite Mallorcan chef, Joan Torrens. Although he uses salt cod loin, monkfish also makes an excellent choice. The fish is gratinéed after roasting under a hat of smoky grilled eggplant *allioli,* then served with a compote of yellow bell peppers. Spinach with Raisins and Pine Nuts (page 388) would add a splash of green to the presentation. If you like, both the *allioli* and the peppers can be prepared ahead.

- 2 tablespoons extra-virgin olive oil, plus more for brushing the fish
- 4 medium-size ripe yellow bell peppers, cored, seeded, quartered, and thinly sliced
- 2 medium-size garlic cloves, minced
- 2 tablespoons dry white wine
- 4 monkfish fillets (each about 1 inch thick and 8 ounces), trimmed of all membranes and gray bits
- Coarse salt (kosher or sea)
- Eggplant Allioli (recipe follows)

1. Preheat the oven to 450°F.

2. Heat the olive oil in a large nonstick skillet over medium-high heat. Add the yellow peppers and garlic and cook, stirring, until the peppers begin to soften, 2 to 3 minutes. Add the wine, reduce the heat to low, cover the skillet, and cook until the peppers are very soft, about 25 minutes, stirring occasionally.

3. Meanwhile, rub the monkfish with salt, brush it generously with olive oil, and let stand for 10 minutes. Place the fish on a baking sheet and bake until it is cooked through and feels firm to the touch, about 15 minutes.

4. Change the oven setting to broil. Generously top each fish fillet with Eggplant Allioli and broil about 3 inches away from the heat until the *allioli* is browned, 2 to 3 minutes. To serve, spoon the peppers and their cooking liquid onto plates and top with a fish fillet. **SERVES 4**

EGGPLANT ALLIOLI

ALLIOLI DE BERENJENAS

Charring the eggplant right on a gas flame gives it an extra smokiness. However, you can also cook the whole eggplant under a broiler until soft and charred, about seven minutes per side. If cooking the eggplant directly over the flame, watch out for flare-ups. The egg in this *allioli* remains uncooked, so it should be of the highest quality.

- 1 purple Asian eggplant (about 6 ounces)
- 3 large garlic cloves, chopped
- 1 small, very fresh egg, preferably organic
- 2 tablespoons fresh lemon juice
- 3/4 cup extra-virgin olive oil, or more if needed
- Coarse salt (kosher or sea)

1. Place a small flameproof rack, such as the rack from a toaster oven, directly over a gas burner and set the heat to medium. Place the eggplant on the rack over the flame and cook until soft and lightly charred all over, about 7 minutes, turning the eggplant often so that it cooks evenly. (If the eggplant begins to leak, wipe off the area around the burners as soon as it is done.) Using tongs, transfer the eggplant to a plate and let cool enough to handle. Peel the eggplant, discarding the stem, and chop coarsely.

2. Place the chopped eggplant in a blender, add the garlic, egg, and lemon juice, and puree until smooth. With the motor running, gradually drizzle ¾ cup of the olive oil through the feed tube; the *allioli* will emulsify. If the *allioli* isn't quite thick enough, add a little more olive oil. Scrape the *allioli* into a small bowl and season it with salt to taste. Let it stand for about 30 minutes for the flavors to develop. **MAKES ABOUT 1 CUP**

SALMON WITH FAVA BEANS AND FRESH FENNEL

SALMON CON HABAS Y HINOJO

If I had my way, I'd salt bake every fish and meat known to man, so outstanding are the results. In this recipe—adapted from Spain's great chef, Juan Mari Arzak—you spread a salt crust on the skin of the salmon, then remove the skin after the fish is broiled. The fish skin protects the salmon from being over exposed to the heat. Serving the fish with a refreshing warm vinaigrette of fava beans, citrus, and fennel makes for a ravishingly pretty presentation. Fava bean salad is also delicious with white-fleshed fish, such as sea bass, and is great cold over poached or steamed salmon. For best results, Arzak recommends using wild salmon.

NIFTY TRICKS: COOKING IN A BAG, THE NEW WAY

The method known as *al vacío* in Spain and *sous vide* in France is all the rage in Spanish kitchens. This technique entails poaching fish, meat, or vegetables vacuum-packed in a plastic bag. The results are miraculous: an ingredient that has a startlingly voluptuous texture and a vibrantly natural taste. Unlike poaching directly in water, the method intensifies, rather than leaches away, the flavor. Like poaching in olive oil, the method is carried out at very low temperatures (normally 145°F or below). At such temperatures, ingredients like a whole leg of baby lamb or a suckling pig can be cooked for as long as thirty-six hours and come out supple-textured yet meltingly soft. Joan Roca, the endlessly inventive Catalan chef at El Celler de Can Roca, one of Spain's most innovative restaurants, is so obsessed with this method that he invented a poaching device called a Roner. A futuristic bain-marie that looks like a stainless steel drawer and cooks at highly controlled, precise temperatures, the Roner was inspired by a similar device used in medical labs for cooking vaccines. Call it science-fiction cuisine!

1 cup shelled fresh fava beans (about 1 1/2 pounds unshelled), or 1 cup shelled soybeans (edamame), thawed if frozen
3 tablespoons minced fresh fennel, plus 1 to 2 tablespoons torn fennel fronds
1 medium-size shallot, minced
Grated zest of 1 lemon
2 tablespoons sherry vinegar, preferably aged
2 tablespoons fresh lemon juice
6 tablespoons fragrant extra-virgin olive oil
1/3 cup coarse salt (kosher or sea), plus salt for the vinaigrette
Freshly ground black pepper
1 large egg white, beaten
4 salmon fillets, preferably wild (each 6 to 7 ounces), with their skin
1/4 cup coarsely chopped roasted cashews
1 tablespoon minced fresh chives

1. Bring a pot of water to a boil, then add the fava beans and cook until just tender, 3 to 5 minutes. Drain the fava beans in a colander, then place it under cold running water until the fava beans are cool enough to handle. Gently peel the skins off the beans and set the beans aside. (If you are using soybeans, there is no need to peel them.)

ARZAK AND NEW BASQUE CUISINE

The Spanish food revolution began in the late 1970s, in San Sebastián, when a group of Basque chefs set out to modernize their sturdy bourgeois cooking. Inspired by the nouvelle cuisine movement across the border in France, they came up with *nueva cocina vasca,* an inventive, light style, radically original in form but solidly Basque in substance: traditional ingredients reconfigured into new dishes; forgotten recipes reimagined without flour or cream. In just a few years the movement swept across Spain and became the nation's default haute cuisine, paving the way for Ferran Adrià's innovations. Everyone from this group went on to stardom: Pedro Subijana, the chef at Michelin two-star Akelarre; Karlos Arguiñano, Spain's answer to Emeril Lagasse. But the name Juan Mari Arzak—the man who in 1989 gave the country one of its earliest three-star Michelin restaurants—is mythical.

Arzak presides over his namesake restaurant in San Sebastián, a bastion of Basque *alta cocina* that started life more than a century ago as his grandmother's roadside *taberna.* Arzak is larger than life, quick to laugh, and possesses the high energy and common touch of a great politician. Though he hobnobs with royalty and celebrities (Spain's royal family are his fans), he insists that his most important clients and critics are the local farmers and fishermen who save up for a Sunday lunch. Can a visionary three-star Michelin restaurant be populist? Arzak is. Young couples in T-shirts mingle with Armani'ed bankers in the cozy dining room attended by matronly waitresses. The food is as experimental as any in Spain—Juan Mari's co-chef is his forward-thinking daughter, Elena—yet it delivers the sort of visceral pleasure one associates with small back-road bistros.

One of the signature dishes, pumpkin and squid ravioli, arrives hidden beneath a murky black squid ink gelée that dissolves under a stream of warm broth poured tableside to reveal the Day-Glo orange disks underneath. The stunt is visually riveting, but what lingers is the sweet, earthy intensity of the pumpkin and squid broth. Another conceptual joke is a lamb chop concealed in a tissue-thin layer of *café con leche* (which has been baked between two Silpat pan liners) that gradually melts into the pan juices. Along with the punch line, one can savor this planet's loveliest, rosiest piece of meat. Oysters and potato confit arrive at the table in a gauzy, crinkled veil of rice cellophane. *Morcilla* (blood sausage) and apples are trapped between slices of extravagantly colorful tropical fruit called pitahaya. And yet for all the magic tricks and technical somersaults, Arzak's food somehow remains as soulfully Basque as *bacalao al pil-pil* (salt cod in a garlic emulsion). There's no other chef on earth who can pull this off.

2. Place the fennel, shallot, and lemon zest in a medium-size bowl and toss to mix. Add the vinegar, lemon juice, and olive oil and whisk to combine. Season the vinaigrette with salt and pepper to taste. Let the vinaigrette stand for 1 hour or longer for the flavors to develop.

3. Preheat the broiler and oil a broiling pan.

4. Place the ⅓ cup salt and the egg white in a bowl and stir until a paste forms, adding a little water if necessary. Place the salmon on the broiling pan, skin side up, and spread the salt paste over the skin. Broil the salmon about 5 inches away from the heat until just cooked though, about 6 minutes.

5. While the fish is baking, heat the vinaigrette in

a small saucepan or in a microwave oven until warm but not piping hot, about 30 seconds.

6. Let the salmon cool for 2 to 3 minutes. Using a small spatula, remove and discard the salt and skin, wiping off any salt that clings to the fish. Place the fish on dinner plates. Stir the fava beans, cashews, chives, and fennel fronds into the vinaigrette and spoon some over each salmon fillet. Serve at once. **SERVES 4**

PAVIA SOLDIERS

SOLDADITOS DE PAVIA

Impeccably crisp fried salt cod in a light batter is a fixture at tapas bars in Andalusia and Madrid, the sort of dish on which an establishment's reputation rests. I've been enjoying it for years, but the name had always puzzled me. What could be the connection between bacalao and the 1525 battle of Pavia (a Lombardian town) in which the soldiers of the Spanish king Carlos V defeated the French? When I asked food historian and critic José Carlos Capel about this, first he explained that the name refers not to the battle but to the Pavia hussars, a nineteenth-century Spanish regiment. Originally, cod that was fried in its saffron-hued batter was decorated with strips of red peppers and resembled their regiment's uniforms. Cooks abandoned the pepper decoration a long time ago, but the name stuck.

While we were on the subject, Capel cautioned that the success of *soldaditos de Pavia* depends on good olive oil brought to the right temperature and nice moist pieces of salt cod. If you find thick, stellar-quality bacalao, by all means use it, soaking it as directed on page 199 (it will take at least twenty-four hours). Otherwise, liberally seasoned fresh cod works fine. Serve *soldaditos* as a tapa or as a light main course with a green salad. If you use the same batter with shrimp, you'll have *gambas en gabardina* (shrimp in gabardine), another delicious and wildly popular dish.

1 pound best-quality salt cod, soaked (see page 199) and drained, or 1 pound skinless fresh cod or scrod fillets, cut crosswise into 1 1/2-inch pieces
Coarse salt (kosher or sea)
Fresh lemon juice, for sprinkling on the fish
Sweet (not smoked) paprika
1 cup all-purpose flour, plus more for dusting the fish
3/4 teaspoon baking powder
3/4 cup chilled club soda or seltzer
1 large egg, separated
2 tablespoons olive oil, plus more for frying the fish
1 medium-size pinch of saffron, pulverized in a mortar, steeped in 2 tablespoons very hot water, and cooled
Lemon wedges (optional), for serving

1. If using fresh cod, pat it thoroughly dry with paper towels and sprinkle it generously with salt. Rub the fish with lemon juice and just a little paprika, cover it with plastic wrap, and let stand while you prepare the batter.

SALT COD WORSHIP

As much as the Spanish revere fresh seafood, it's the salted, dried Nordic fish that they regard as a kind of totem. Which is why one day I found myself hurrying down a narrow street in Bilbao, looking for Alberdi, the temple to that most esteemed local ingredient: bacalao. In the restaurant's kitchen, the chef and owner, Oscar Alberdi, stood towering over the stove. He placed a pristine, fleshy slab of desalted cod in warm garlicky olive oil and started gently shaking the earthenware *cazuela*. Through some strange alchemy, the gelatin in the fish's skin began to emulsify with the oil, forming a smooth lemon-hued sauce. This was *bacalao al pil-pil,* the most famous Basque dish (its name is a typically onomatopoeic Basque term for the splashing of codfish in oil). Over lunch, which included *porrusalda* (leek, bacalao, and potato chowder), *bacalao al pil-pil,* and *bacalao a la vizcaína* (with a sweet-spicy sauce of dried peppers and sautéed onions), Oscar and I reviewed the bacalao lore.

It was the Vikings who discovered how to air-dry cod. But medieval Basques perfected the method by applying the salt-curing techniques they had previously employed for whale meat, making the cod last longer and taste better. In search of cod banks, the Basques ventured as far as Newfoundland most probably before Columbus stumbled on the Americas. Perhaps the world's earliest venture capitalists, the Basques turned the bacalao trade into a huge global business, aided by Catholicism, with its endless litany of meatless days. The practical need for preserving fish is long gone. But bacalao remains as vital to Spanish cooking as ever, eaten often at home (especially during Lent) and proudly served up at avant-garde Michelin-starred restaurants, where it's likely to be poached in olive oil or *al vacío* (vacuum-packed) at a very low temperature. Cooked with care, desalted reconstituted bacalao is a treat: moist, plump, and falling apart in big, luxurious flakes.

Once abundant and cheap, these days good bacalao can cost more than fresh fish. This is not unreasonable when you consider that the best salt cod has all the succulence of fresh cod, plus that faint saline smack and a slightly gelatinous, supple texture the Spanish adore. All over Spain, but especially in Catalonia and the Basque Country, numerous bacalao shops display vast arrays of different grades and cuts, from the cheaper tail end and trimmings, to the pricey fat loin, to cheeks, and even innards. The most prized bacalao comes from Scandinavia. "The bacalao I buy could be Norwegian, fished by Icelanders on the Faeroe Islands," Oscar said. "Exact provenance isn't important. What matters is the quality of the salt and the precision of the curing techniques, such as the right temperature and humidity."

Alas, it's all but impossible to find bacalao of this quality in the United States. And because most of the codfish recipes in this book rely on fish that should be fleshy and moist, well-seasoned fresh cod is a better choice than the thin, desiccated bacalao readily available here. However, if you find thick, top-quality bacalao, do use it for the cod recipes in this chapter. Fresh fish is great but bacalao is, well, a world unto itself.

HANDLING AND COOKING SALT COD

CHOOSING

The best places to look for top-grade bacalao are Italian and Portuguese markets and fishmongers; choice bacalao loin can also be mail ordered from Tienda.com. When buying bacalao, look for thick, white, supple, boneless pieces that don't appear overly desiccated. Ideally, the pieces should be at least 3/4 inch thick. Goya bacalao packed in plastic bags—get one labeled codfish, not pollock—is quite reliable, easy to find, and doesn't require more than twenty-four hours of soaking.

DESALTING

Depending on the grade of the fish and the salting method used, bacalao can take anywhere from twenty-four hours to two days to desalt properly. To desalt bacalao, place it in a wide bowl, add cold water to cover by two inches, cover the bowl with plastic wrap, and place it in the refrigerator. Let soak for twenty-four hours, changing the water four or five times. If the fish still seems too salty after twenty-four hours, soak it longer, continuing to change the water.

The best way to tell if it's ready is to break off a small piece and taste it (the fish is fully cured and perfectly safe to eat). It should taste pleasantly salty but not overly so. If the salt cod still seems overly salty to you and you don't have the patience to soak it longer, you can cook it in milk instead of water to draw out some of the salt.

COOKING

It is important to cook salt cod very gently; otherwise it becomes tough and rubbery. To cook, place the drained fish in a wide saucepan, add fresh water to cover by two inches, and bring the water to a simmer over medium heat. As soon as the water comes to a simmer (do not allow it to boil), reduce the heat to very low and simmer the fish for one minute. Take the saucepan off the heat, cover, and let the salt cod stand in the liquid for about twenty minutes, or slightly longer for thicker fillets. The fish is ready when it flakes easily when prodded with the tip of a knife. Drain the fish and, using tweezers, pick out any small bones. Then proceed with the instructions in the individual recipes. If the recipe calls for the fish to be flaked, pick out more bones and tough bits from the salt cod as you flake it.

2. Place the 1 cup flour, the baking powder, and ½ teaspoon salt in a large bowl and whisk to mix. Add the club soda, the egg yolk, the 2 tablespoons olive oil, and the saffron and whisk until the batter is completely smooth. Let the batter stand for 20 to 30 minutes.

3. Place the egg white in a small bowl and whisk until frothy, then whisk it into the batter. Spread a thin layer of flour on a large plate. Lightly dip the cod in the flour, shaking off the excess.

4. Line a small rack with a double layer of paper towels and set it over a baking sheet. Pour olive oil to a depth of 1½ inches in a deep, heavy saucepan and heat it over medium-high heat to 360°F; when hot, a piece of batter placed in the oil will puff on contact. Using a fork, dip a piece of fish in the batter until well coated, thoroughly shake off the excess, and place the fish in the hot oil. Dip 3 or 4 more pieces of fish into the batter, and then place them in the oil. Fry the fish until it is golden brown, crisp, and cooked through, about 2 minutes per side. Using a slotted spoon, transfer the fried fish to the rack to drain. Repeat with the remaining fish, then serve at once, with lemon, if desired. **SERVES 4 OR 5 AS A TAPA, 2 OR 3 AS A LIGHT MAIN COURSE**

FRESH SARDINES WITH GARLIC AND PARSLEY

SARDINAS AL AJO Y PEREJIL

One of the Basques' favorite ways to treat just-caught anchovies is to butterfly them, then gently cook them in fragrant olive oil that, with the addition of garlic and parsley, turns into a delectable sauce. During the anchovy season in May, you can enjoy the small fish prepared this way at humble tapas bars and fancy restaurants alike. Here in the States, if you can find fresh anchovies—and don't mind cleaning them—by all means use them in this recipe (you'll need about one pound). Sardines are equally delicious prepared this way. I describe how to clean them, but if you prefer, ask the fishmonger to clean, bone, and butterfly the sardines for you. The secret to keeping the flesh of the fish nicely moist is not letting the temperature of the oil rise to the point where it shrivels the skin. If you like an acidic kick, add a splash of white wine vinegar or lemon juice to the oil once you turn off the heat.

- 8 smallish fresh sardines (about 1 pound)
- Coarse salt (kosher or sea)
- 3/4 cup fragrant extra-virgin olive oil (do not use an assertive peppery oil)
- 4 large garlic cloves, minced
- 3 to 4 tablespoons minced fresh flat-leaf parsley
- Crusty bread, for serving

1. To clean and bone the sardines, remove the scales from the fish by gently scraping them with a small dull knife under cold running water. Cut off and discard the heads, then, using a small sharp knife, carefully make a slit along the bellies. Gut and clean the fish under cold running water. Grab the top of the spine of a sardine and pull it out quickly, trying not to remove too much of the flesh around it. Butterfly the sardine by opening it up like a book. If you feel small bones, trim the sides of the fillets. Repeat with the remaining sardines. Rinse the sardines under cold running water, pat them dry with paper towels and lightly sprinkle salt over them.

2. Heat the olive oil in a large skillet over low heat for about 30 seconds. Add the sardines and cook until they just turn opaque, 30 to 45 seconds per side. Using a slotted spatula, transfer the sardines to a rimmed serving dish. Add the garlic to the olive oil and stir until it is very fragrant but not browned, about 1 minute. Stir in the parsley and cook for about 15 seconds, then pour the olive oil over the sardines. Serve at once with bread to mop up the garlic oil. **SERVES 4 TO 6 AS A TAPA, 2 OR 3 AS A LIGHT MAIN COURSE**

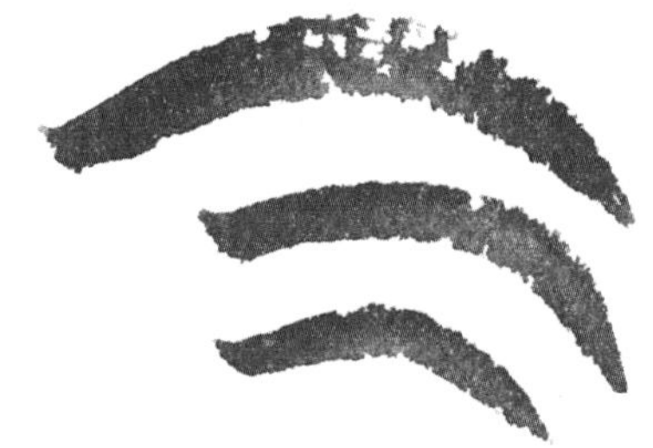

SALT-BAKED SEA BASS WITH TOMATO VINAIGRETTE

LUBINA A LA SAL CON VINAGRETA DE TOMATES

One of the great pleasures of eating at seafood restaurants in coastal Spain is watching the waiters rush to and fro ceremoniously bearing platters of whole fish baked in an armor of sea salt to be filleted with great pomp at the table. Quintessentially Mediterranean, this method of cooking seals in the fish's sweet flavor. And, since the salt crust is removed at serving time, the fish isn't salty in the least. The warm cherry tomato vinaigrette is the perfect accompaniment.

- Extra-virgin olive oil
- 3 cups kosher salt
- 5 large egg whites, lightly beaten
- 1 whole sea bass (about 2 pounds), cleaned and scaled (see Note)
- 4 medium-size garlic cloves; 3 smashed with the flat side of a knife, 1 minced
- 2 fresh flat-leaf parsley sprigs, plus 1 tablespoon finely chopped parsley leaves
- 2 lemon slices, cut in half
- 1 pinch of saffron threads, crumbled
- 1 small shallot, minced
- 3/4 cup halved cherry tomatoes
- 2 tablespoons chicken stock or broth
- 1 tablespoon sherry vinegar, preferably aged
- Freshly ground black pepper

1. Preheat the oven to 425°F.

2. Line a baking sheet with parchment paper and lightly coat the paper with olive oil. Place the salt and egg whites in a large bowl and stir until evenly moistened. The paste should just hold together. If it doesn't, sprinkle in a little water. Place the fish on the prepared baking sheet and fill the cavity with the smashed garlic, parsley sprigs, and lemon slices. Pat the salt mixture all over the top and sides of the fish to completely cover it. Bake the fish until cooked through, about 25 minutes.

3. Meanwhile, heat 2½ teaspoons olive oil in a small skillet over low heat. Add the saffron and cook for 5 minutes. Add the shallot and minced garlic and cook, stirring occasionally, until fragrant, about 2 minutes. Add the cherry tomatoes and cook until slightly softened, about 3 minutes. Add the chicken stock and cook just until the tomatoes begin to break down, about 3 minutes longer. Remove the skillet from the heat. Add the vinegar and chopped parsley and season with pepper to taste.

Salt-Baked Sea Bass with Tomato Vinaigrette

4. To serve, using a wooden spoon, tap the salt crust to crack it and lift it off the fish in large pieces. Carefully remove the fish skin. Run a knife along the backbone of the fish to separate the top fillet, then lift it off the bones. Remove the bones, and transfer the filleted fish to plates. Top with the tomato vinaigrette and serve right away. **SERVES 2**

NOTE: Here I recommend salt baking a 2-pound sea bass to serve two. For a larger crowd, either bake two fishes or one larger one, increasing the cooking time 4 to 5 minutes for each additional pound.

SWORDFISH WITH THYME-SCENTED ASPARAGUS

PESCADO A LA BRASA CON ESPARRAGOS

The scents of honey, orange, and thyme instantly evoke the Mediterranean. This easy, lyrical recipe is from Saüc, one of my favorite restaurants in Barcelona. The owner, Xavier Franco, prepares it with gorgeous loins of monkfish. It's hard in this country to find monkfish that's high-quality enough to be so simply grilled, so I've substituted swordfish. (Grilled or seared scallops or shrimp would also be delicious prepared this way.) The drizzle of fruity olive oil and sprinkling of salt at the end may seem like an afterthought, but their effect is transformational—so get out your best olive oil and flaky sea salt. The amount of honey needed will depend on the tartness of the oranges. Start with a tablespoon and add more until you get a nice balance of sweet and tart.

4 swordfish steaks (each about 1 inch thick and 6 ounces)
Coarse salt (kosher or sea) and freshly ground black pepper
Fragrant extra-virgin olive oil
2/3 cup fresh orange juice (from 4 to 6 oranges)
2 tablespoons fresh lemon juice
1 to 2 1/2 tablespoons floral honey, such as orange blossom honey
2 small garlic cloves, crushed with a garlic press
1 1/2 pounds thin asparagus, trimmed
1/2 cup Fish Stock (page 108), store-bought fish stock, or bottled clam juice
1 tablespoon minced fresh thyme
Flaky sea salt, such as Maldon

1. Rub the swordfish with salt and pepper, brush it generously with olive oil, and let stand until ready to use.

2. Place the orange and lemon juices in a small saucepan over medium-high heat and cook until reduced to ⅓ cup, 10 to 12 minutes. Reduce the heat to low, whisk in 1 teaspoon of the honey, and taste the orange sauce; it should be nicely sweet and tart. If it is too tart, add more honey. Let the sauce cook for another minute. Season the sauce with salt to taste and keep warm until ready to serve.

3. Light the grill and preheat it to high or preheat the broiler.

4. Grill the swordfish on an oiled grate positioned 5 inches above the glowing coals, or broil it, until just cooked through, 3 to 4 minutes per side.

The fish is done when it just flakes when prodded with a fork. Transfer the fish to a plate and cover it with aluminum foil to keep warm.

5. Heat 1½ teaspoons olive oil in a large skillet over high heat with the garlic. Add the asparagus and cook, tossing, for 1 minute. Add the fish stock and thyme and bring to a boil. Cover the skillet and cook the asparagus until it is bright green and crisp-tender, 3 to 5 minutes. Transfer the asparagus to a plate. Continue to cook the fish stock mixture until it is reduced and syrupy, 3 to 5 minutes. Divide the asparagus among 4 plates and drizzle the fish stock mixture on it. Arrange a fish steak on each plate and drizzle the orange sauce over the asparagus and the fish. Drizzle a little olive oil over each serving and sprinkle sea salt on top. Serve at once. **SERVES 4**

GRILLED TUNA WITH SALMOREJO SAUCE

ATUN A LA BRASA CON SALMOREJO

The restaurant La Montería is one of Madrid's great little gems. In the bar section up front, for just a few euros you can indulge in delicacies like crisp-fried sweetbreads and a swooningly good warm partridge salad. In the back, there is a small bistro, for which my friend Miguel dreams up simple but surprisingly creative dishes. Miguel's Andalusian roots show in this tuna dish with its refreshing *salmorejo* sauce, a sort of dense gazpacho, and the earthy accent of frizzled leeks. Miguel uses the luxurious *ventresca,* or bonito belly, but regular tuna is also delicious prepared this way. The sauce is best when made in advance so the flavor can ripen—plan accordingly.

FOR THE SALMOREJO SAUCE:

1 pound (2 to 3) beautiful ripe tomatoes, peeled, seeded, and chopped
2 slices day-old sandwich bread, crusts removed
1/4 cup diced Italian (frying) pepper, or green bell pepper
2 tablespoons chopped red onion
2 small garlic cloves, crushed with a garlic press
1/4 cup fragrant extra-virgin olive oil
2 tablespoons sherry vinegar, preferably aged, or more to taste
Coarse salt (kosher or sea) and freshly ground black pepper

FOR THE TUNA AND LEEKS:

1/2 cup olive oil, plus more for brushing the fish
2 medium-size leeks, white and some tender green parts, trimmed and cut into 2-inch-long julienne
Coarse salt (kosher or sea)
6 tuna steaks (each about 5 ounces)
Freshly ground black pepper

1. Make the *salmorejo* sauce: Place the tomatoes in a sieve or colander and let drain for about 10 minutes. Meanwhile, place the bread in a small bowl, add cold water to cover, and let soak for 5 minutes. Drain the bread and squeeze out the excess liquid.

2. Place the soaked bread and drained tomatoes and the Italian pepper, onion, and garlic in a food processor and process until smooth. With the motor

running, drizzle the olive oil through the feed tube. Push the sauce through a fine sieve set over a bowl, pressing on it with the back of a large spoon and scraping the bottom of the sieve (or puree the sauce in a blender). Add the vinegar and stir to mix. Taste for seasoning, adding salt and black pepper to taste and more vinegar if desired. Let the sauce stand for at least 2 hours at room temperature for the flavors to develop. (The *salmorejo* sauce can be refrigerated, covered, for up to 2 days. Let it return to room temperature before serving.)

3. Prepare the tuna and leeks: Heat the ½ cup olive oil in a medium-size saucepan over medium heat until it shimmers; when hot, a piece of leek will sizzle on contact. Working in two batches, cook the leeks, stirring, until golden and crisp, 3 to 4 minutes. Using a slotted spoon, transfer the leeks to paper towels to drain. Lightly sprinkle the leeks with salt and set aside.

4. Light the grill and preheat it to high or preheat a ridged grill pan over medium-high heat.

5. Rub the tuna steaks with salt and black pepper and brush with a little olive oil. Grill the tuna steaks until nicely charred, 2 to 3 minutes per side for medium-rare. Slice the tuna into medium-thick slices.

6. To serve, divide the *salmorejo* sauce among 6 small bowls or egg cups. Place each bowl of sauce in the center of a dinner plate. Fan the tuna slices out around the bowls of sauce and top them with some frizzled leeks. **SERVES 6**

MEDITERRANEAN FISH IN ZUCCHINI JACKETS

PESCADO EN CAMISA DE CALABACIN

Adapted from a dish served at a country restaurant near Valencia, this zucchini-wrapped fish with a black olive vinaigrette is as virtuous as it is delicious. And it's easy, to boot. In Valencia, it's made with the firm-fleshed *pez limón* (a kind of amberjack), but many other fish—sea bass, pompano, sole—work well in this preparation. Choose the longest zucchini you can find, so that the slices can wrap comfortably around the fish fillets.

Marinas, where lucky owners harbor their boats, are a common sight along the Mediterranean coast.

FOR THE VINAIGRETTE:

7 tablespoons extra-virgin olive oil
2 medium-size garlic cloves, minced
2 small plum tomatoes, peeled, seeded, and finely diced
1/4 cup chopped pitted black olives, such as niçoise or Gaeta
2 best-quality oil-packed anchovy fillets, drained and minced
1 scallion, white and some green parts, trimmed and minced
1/2 teaspoon grated lemon zest
2 tablespoons sherry vinegar, preferably aged
1 tablespoon fresh lemon juice
Coarse salt (kosher or sea) and freshly ground black pepper
3 tablespoons minced fresh flat-leaf parsley

FOR THE FISH:

2 long zucchini
6 skinless pompano, sole, or sea bass fillets (each 6 to 7 ounces)
Coarse salt (kosher or sea) and freshly ground black pepper
Fresh lemon juice

1. Make the vinaigrette: Heat 1 tablespoon of the olive oil in a small skillet over medium-low heat. Add the garlic and stir until fragrant, about 1 minute. Add the tomatoes and cook, stirring, until they soften a little but still hold their shape, about 2 minutes. Transfer the tomatoes to a bowl and stir in the olives, anchovies, scallion, lemon zest, vinegar, and lemon juice. Slowly, whisk in the remaining 6 tablespoons olive oil. Season the tomato vinaigrette with salt and pepper to taste and let stand for at least 30 minutes so the flavors can meld.

2. Prepare the fish: Using a vegetable peeler, slice the zucchini lengthwise into paper-thin slices. Season the fish with salt and pepper and lightly sprinkle with lemon juice. Lay some of the zucchini slices vertically on a work surface. Center a fish fillet crosswise near the top of the row of zucchini and roll it over to wrap it in the slices. Repeat with the remaining fish and zucchini (you may not need all of the zucchini).

3. Pour water to a depth of 2 inches into a wide steamer and bring to a boil over medium-high heat. If you don't have a wide Chinese-style steamer, you can steam the fish on a rack set over a large skillet. Place the zucchini-wrapped fish in the steamer or on the rack, seam side down. Cover the steamer or skillet and steam until the zucchini is bright green and the fish is opaque throughout, 7 to 10 minutes depending on the thickness of the fish. To check for doneness, you can lift up a zucchini slice and prod the fish with the tip of a knife.

4. Using a slotted spatula, carefully transfer the zucchini-wrapped fish fillets to plates, gently shaking off the excess moisture. Let the fish cool for about 5 minutes. Add the parsley to the tomato vinaigrette and whisk to recombine. Decoratively dab some of the vinaigrette on top of each portion of fish and pass the rest in a bowl. **SERVES 6**

BAKED FISH WITH ROMESCO POTATOES

PESCADO AL HORNO CON ROMESCO Y PATATAS

Can Sole, a famous old seafood restaurant in Barcelona's fishermen's quarter, has the world's grumpiest service, but I forgive them. Their bacalao croquettes set the gold standard, and the anchovies are supremely fat and buttery. As for the salt cod, which is baked over potatoes in *romesco* sauce and gratinéed with garlic mayonnaise—it's nothing short of a masterpiece. This is my approximation of Can Sole's recipe, using well-seasoned fresh scrod in lieu of bacalao. The *romesco,* potatoes, and *allioli* can be made ahead, so all you have to do is bake the dish right before serving. The one-dish meal is so perfect for a large dinner party I've given amounts that will feed a crowd. You can easily make less, saving the rest of the *romesco* sauce for later.

FOR THE ROMESCO SAUCE:

3 dried ñora peppers, or 2 dried ancho chiles, stemmed, seeded, and torn into small pieces
6 sun-dried tomatoes, coarsely chopped
1 1/2 cups boiling Fish Stock (page 108), store-bought fish stock, or 1 cup bottled clam juice diluted with 1/2 cup water, plus more for thinning the sauce, if necessary
1/3 cup extra-virgin olive oil
3 slices (1/2 inch thick) baguette
7 large garlic cloves, cut in half crosswise
1/4 cup blanched almonds
1/3 cup hazelnuts, toasted (see page 267) and skinned
1 medium-size onion, chopped
2 cups chopped ripe tomatoes
1 teaspoon sweet (not smoked) paprika
1 pinch of cayenne
1 1/2 teaspoons sherry vinegar, preferably aged, or more to taste
Coarse salt (kosher or sea) and freshly ground black pepper

FOR THE POTATOES AND FISH:

2 pounds large Yukon Gold potatoes
2 tablespoons extra-virgin olive oil
2 1/2 pounds fish fillets (about 3/4 inch thick), such as scrod, cod, haddock, or halibut, cut into serving portions
Coarse salt (kosher or sea) and freshly ground black pepper
1 1/2 cups Allioli (page 44)

1. Make the *romesco* sauce: Place the ñora peppers and sun-dried tomatoes in a small heatproof bowl. Add 1½ cups of the fish stock and let soak until soft, about 30 minutes. Transfer the ñora peppers and tomatoes with their soaking liquid to a blender and finely puree them, then set aside.

2. Heat the olive oil in a small skillet over medium heat until almost smoking. Add the bread and garlic and cook until deep golden and crisp, about 3 minutes. Using a slotted spoon, transfer the bread and the garlic to a bowl. Add the almonds and hazelnuts to the skillet and cook until the nuts are golden, 2 to 3 minutes, adjusting the heat so the oil doesn't burn. Using a slotted spoon, transfer the nuts to the bowl with the bread and garlic.

3. Spoon about 4 teaspoons of the garlicky oil into a medium-size skillet and heat over medium heat (set aside the remaining garlicky oil). Add the onion and cook, stirring, until softened, about 7 minutes. Add the tomatoes, increase the heat to medium-high, and cook until thickened and reduced, 5 to 7 minutes longer. Add the paprika and cayenne and stir for a few seconds. Let the tomato mixture cool a little.

4. Break the fried bread into pieces and place them in a food processor along with the fried garlic and nuts, and process until finely ground. Add the

tomato and onion mixture, the pureed ñora pepper mixture, 1 tablespoon of the garlicky oil, and ¼ cup water to the processor bowl. Puree until completely smooth. Scrape the *romesco* sauce into a bowl and stir in the vinegar. Season the sauce with salt and black pepper to taste and add a little more vinegar, if desired. The sauce can be used right away but is best when prepared a day ahead so the flavors can develop (store, covered, in the refrigerator). Discard the remaining garlicky oil.

5. Prepare the potatoes and fish: Place the potatoes in a saucepan, add salted water to cover by 2 inches, and bring to a boil. Cook the potatoes until they just begin to feel tender when pierced with a skewer, about 30 minutes. Do not overcook. Drain the potatoes and let cool enough to handle. If making ahead, wrap in plastic and store in the refrigerator for up to 1 day. Use an oiled knife to cut the potatoes into slices ¼ inch thick.

6. When ready to assemble the dish, heat the olive oil in a large skillet over medium heat. Add the *romesco* sauce and bring to a simmer over high heat. Reduce the heat to medium-low, and cook the sauce, stirring, until it is fragrant and turns a shade or two darker, 2 to 3 minutes. If the sauce seems too thick to bake the fish in, thin it with a little fish stock or water. Season the sauce with salt and black pepper to taste.

7. Preheat the oven to 425°F.

8. Set out a deep, attractive, flameproof baking dish that can hold the fish in a single layer. Spoon some of the *romesco* sauce into the dish and arrange the potato slices on top in a single layer, overlapping them slightly. Season the fish generously with salt and black pepper, then arrange it on top of the potatoes. Spoon the remaining *romesco* sauce evenly over the fish. Bake until the sauce is very hot and the fish just begins to flake, 12 to 15 minutes or slightly longer depending on the kind of fish. Do not overcook.

9. Change the oven setting to broil. Remove the fish from the oven and spread the *allioli* evenly over the top. Broil close to the heat until the *allioli* is browned in spots, 2 to 3 minutes. Let the dish cool for a few minutes, then serve it using a sturdy spatula and a spoon. **SERVES 8**

BASQUE FISHERMEN'S STEW

MARMITAKO

Like Catalan *suquet,* American cod chowder, or Marseille's bouillabaisse, *marmitako* is a classic fishermen's stew. Traditionally prepared on makeshift stoves aboard tuna boats on the icy Bay of Biscay, *marmitako* consisted of the day's catch combined with sturdy shipboard provisions like potatoes, onions, and *pimientos choriceros,* the region's smoky-sweet, fleshy dried peppers. (Before these ingredients were brought from the Americas, *marmitako* consisted of tuna, water, pork fat, and stale bread.) The name is from *marmitekua,* or *marmita,* the stew pot used for cooking the fish. Luis Irízar, the legendary Basque cooking teacher who gave me this recipe, insists that the secret to a good *marmitako* is "breaking" rather than cutting the potatoes, so that they release more starch and properly thicken the stew. *Pimientos choriceros* or the Spanish ñora peppers are available through some mail-order sources (see page 461), or you can substitute ancho chiles. Sun-dried tomatoes aren't traditional in *marmitako*, but I add them for extra depth of flavor. Like any Spanish stew, this one is delicious served with grilled or toasted country bread.

- 2 dried pimientos choriceros, ñora peppers, or ancho chiles, stemmed, seeded, and torn into small pieces
- 4 to 5 plump sun-dried tomatoes
- 1 1/2 pounds medium-size Yukon Gold potatoes, peeled
- 1/4 cup extra-virgin olive oil
- 1 small white onion, finely chopped
- 1 medium-size red bell pepper, cored, seeded, and diced
- 1 medium-size green bell pepper, cored, seeded, and diced
- 3 large garlic cloves, minced
- 2 medium-size ripe tomatoes, peeled, seeded, and chopped
- 1/3 cup dry white wine
- About 3 cups Fish Stock (page 108) or store-bought fish stock, or 2 cups bottled clam juice diluted with 1 cup water
- Coarse salt (kosher or sea) and freshly ground black pepper
- 1 1/2 pounds boneless bonito or bluefin tuna, cut into 1-inch cubes
- 3 to 4 tablespoons minced fresh flat-leaf parsley
- Grilled or toasted dense country bread, for serving

1. Soak the *pimientos choriceros* and sun-dried tomatoes in 1 cup very hot water until soft, about 30 minutes. Using a blender, puree the *pimientos* and tomatoes with their soaking liquid. Set the tomato-chile paste aside.

2. Meanwhile, cut the potatoes into irregular chunks by inserting the tip of a small sharp knife into a potato and twisting it until a 1½-inch chunk comes out. Repeat until the entire potato is cut up, then continue with the remaining potatoes. Set them aside.

3. Heat the olive oil over medium-high heat in a heavy 4- to 5-quart saucepan. Add the onion and the red and green peppers and cook, stirring, until the vegetables begin to soften, about 5 minutes. Cover the saucepan, reduce the heat to low, and cook until the peppers are very soft, 10 to 12 minutes longer, stirring once or twice. Stir in the garlic and cook for another minute. Add the tomatoes and potatoes and cook, stirring, for about 5 minutes. Add the reserved tomato-chile paste, the wine, and 2½ cups of the fish stock, increase the heat to high, and bring to a boil, skimming. Reduce the heat to medium-low and cook, partially covered, until the potatoes are very tender and some are just beginning to fall apart, about 30 minutes. If the sauce seems too thick, add some or all of the remaining ½ cup fish stock and return the sauce to a simmer. Season the sauce with salt and black pepper to taste.

4. Rub the tuna cubes gently with salt and add them to the sauce. Cook, shaking the pot gently, until the fish is just cooked through, about 5 minutes. Season the stew with salt and pepper to taste, sprinkle with parsley, and serve in soup bowls with bread. **SERVES 4 TO 6**

SPAIN'S BEST CATCH

With its Mediterranean and Cantabrian coasts, Spain boasts some of the world's greatest fish. Here are some that you will encounter.

ANCHOAS (anchovies), members of the *pescado azul* (bluefish) family, are difficult to find fresh in the States. If you see them, grab them! Fresh anchovies are heavenly butterflied (if you can stand all the work) and sautéed very gently in olive oil with plenty of garlic. They are also a treat rolled in coarse flour and fried.

ANGULAS (elvers) are the ultimate Basque delicacy, more revered than, and just as expensive as, caviar. The baby eels are tiny, like short, skinny linguine strands. They're normally cooked for mere seconds in garlicky olive oil. You may find them to be an acquired taste, but don't tell that to the Basques.

ATUN (tuna) in Spain usually refers to the red-fleshed bluefin tuna. The best catch is *atún de almadraba,* trapped off the Andalusian coast (near Cape Trafalgar) in a vast network of nets (*almadraba*) suspended from buoys, a fishing method that goes back at least two thousand years.

BESUGO (red bream), *dorada* (gilthead bream), and their numerous cousins, make up the sea bream family, much appreciated in Spain. Baked *besugo* is a typical Christmas Eve dish in Madrid; *dorada* is great baked in salt. Porgy or red snapper make fine substitutes.

BONITO (albacore) from the Cantabrian sea is the mainstay of the Spanish canning industry. But its ivory flesh is also wonderful fresh, particularly the *ventresca,* the wildly expensive buttery part around the belly.

LENGUADO (Dover sole), the best of which comes from the Bay of Biscay, is a much-loved flatfish with sweet, moist flesh. At good seafood restaurants, *lenguado* is likely to be small and served whole *a la espalda:* butterflied, grilled on the *parrilla,* and presented on its back, drizzled with lemon juice and olive oil.

LUBINA (sea bass) is the aristocrat of the fish world: Lean, firm, stark white, it's beautiful as a fillet and even better when roasted whole, either in salt (see page 201) or on a bed of sliced lemons. Even if I just want a fillet, I prefer buying a whole fish and having the fishmonger bone it; this way I know it's perfectly fresh. Don't substitute Chilean sea bass, which is in danger of being overfished and should be avoided.

MERLUZA (European hake) is Spain's *numero uno* favorite, especially prized when line caught. Sweet, snow-white, delicate yet not mushy, it's prepared most classically in *salsa verde* (see page 191) but it's also great baked, fried in an egg batter, or gently sautéed at a low temperature, covered in olive oil. You can find hake at some better fish stores, as well as at Korean fish markets, although it won't match the flavor of Spanish *merluza*. Or, substitute cod or scrod.

RAPE (monkfish) is hugely popular along Spain's Mediterranean shores. Known as poor man's lobster, it has a firm flesh that stands up well to roasting and doesn't fall apart when cooked in traditional soupy stews, such as *suquet*. Its gelatinous tail and big, ugly head add oomph and body to many a fish stock.

RODABALLO (turbot) is a deepwater flatfish that reigns supreme on Spain's northern coast, from the Basque Country to Galicia. Sweet, meaty, and wonderfully rich, it tastes like halibut from the fourth dimension. *Rodaballo* is divine when grilled whole, Basque style, finished with a vinegar glaze that offsets its richness.

SEAFOOD STEW IN ROMESCO SAUCE

ROMESCO DE PEIX

There are as many *romesco* sauces as there are cooks, each tailored to the particular food with which it's served. The principal ingredients—dried ñora pepper, fried bread and garlic, nuts, and tomatoes—may be consistent, but their proportions and the other ingredients vary, resulting in a wealth of different nuances. This recipe for the sauce, based on one by David Solé i Torné, the great *romesco* specialist from Tarragona, makes a brothy one, perfect for a mixed seafood extravaganza. Roasted tomatoes produce a flavor that's deep and concentrated, while the unexpected use of grated chocolate lends an intriguing touch, subtly adding even more depth.

This version features monkfish, clams, squid, and, for a rustic touch, unpeeled shrimp. Dig in with your fingers and mop up all the delicious sauce with crusty bread. And feel free to vary the assortment of seafood—mussels, different types of fish, and lobster would all be good choices. (For more about *romesco,* see the facing page.)

FOR THE ROMESCO SAUCE:

3 medium-size ripe tomatoes, cut in half
12 large garlic cloves
Coarse salt (kosher or sea)
7 tablespoons extra-virgin olive oil, plus more for drizzling over the tomatoes
3 dried ñora peppers or 2 dried ancho chiles, stemmed, seeded, and torn into small pieces
2 slices (1/2 inch thick) baguette
2/3 cup blanched almonds
2/3 cup dry white wine
1/4 cup chopped fresh flat-leaf parsley, plus more for garnish
2 teaspoons sweet (not smoked) paprika
1 small pinch of crushed red pepper flakes, or more to taste
4 1/2 teaspoons grated bittersweet chocolate
About 2 cups Fish Stock (page 108) or store-bought fish stock, or 1 1/2 cups bottled clam juice diluted with 1/2 cup water
Freshly ground black pepper

FOR THE SEAFOOD:

1 1/2 pounds monkfish, cut into 2-inch chunks
Coarse salt (kosher or sea)
1/3 cup dry white wine
3 dozen small clams, such as Manila or littleneck, scrubbed
3/4 pound cleaned squid, bodies cut into 1/3-inch rings, tentacles cut in half if large
12 to 15 ounces large shrimp, preferably in their shells
Crusty bread, for serving

1. Make the *romesco* sauce: Preheat the oven to 400°F.

2. Place the tomatoes and 6 of the garlic cloves in a roasting pan, sprinkle them with salt, and drizzle olive oil over them. Bake until soft and lightly charred, about 40 minutes. Let the tomatoes and garlic cool slightly, reserving any juices in the pan.

TARRAGONA: RUINS AND ROMESCO

The coastal Mediterranean city of Tarragona, some sixty miles southwest of Barcelona, has many things to recommend it to a visitor. Formerly the principal outpost of the Roman empire on the Iberian peninsula, Tarragona is a trove of Roman ruins, among them a handsome amphitheater, a beautifully preserved aqueduct, and imposing stone walls. Tarragona also has a very fine Romanesque-Gothic cathedral, pretty beaches, and a quaint old fishermen's quarter called El Serallo. The city's principal attraction, however, is gastronomic. I'm talking about *romesco,* a ruddy, nutty, garlicky sauce that flourishes here as something of an edible life force. "I don't think there are many cities that have, in addition to an incomparable past, a splendorous present and a uniquely beautiful location, a sauce of their own," wrote Catalan writer and gastronome Josep Pla.

To learn more, I booked a table at a Tarragona restaurant called Barquet. Its *romesco*-obsessed owner, David Solé i Torné, features the sauce in practically every dish and has even written a book on the subject. David believes that the etymological roots of *romesco* lie in the medieval mozarabic word *rumiskal,* which means "to mix things together." Originally, the term described some kind of fish stew, but it gradually evolved to refer to this uber-Mediterranean sauce. Some of *romesco's* defining ingredients—mortar-pounded garlic, nuts, and sometimes bread—feature in scores of medieval Catalan recipes and continue to form the base for another famed Catalan sauce, the *picada*. What changed the *romesco* forever was the introduction of tomatoes and peppers from the New World. Today most versions include the mild, fleshy dried chiles called *pebrots de romesco,* fried almonds and/or hazelnuts, always garlic, sometimes tomatoes and bell peppers, and often vinegar and olive oil. *Romesco,* David explains, functions in two different ways. One is as a hot soupy stew base for fish (classically monkfish). This is the traditional celebratory *romesco de peix*—also known as *romescada*—the stuff of countless fishermen's fiestas. The other *romesco* is an *aliño,* a cold table sauce that can dress raw vegetables and greens, boiled potatoes, fried rabbit, cold meat, egg tortillas . . . in short, just about anything.

According to David, *romesco* comes in infinite versions. My meal at Barquet was perfect proof of its versatility. An impeccable salad of white asparagus, shaved mushrooms, and bitterish endive was dabbed with a *romesco* that was sprightly and sharp, with a pronounced taste of raw garlic and toasted hazelnuts. In the next dish, plump snails, the sauce was rounder and sweeter, featuring, this time, poached garlic, lots of tomatoes, nuts, and a touch of sugar. For the classic hot *romesco* stew of monkfish and potatoes, the *romesco* base of fried chiles, onion, almonds, and bread was diluted with strong white wine and fish stock, giving it an entirely different character. Up next was an *arroz meloso* (soupy rice in a paella pan) made with tuna, squid, and a *romesco*-based broth (David's own invention, of which he seemed especially proud). How about a dessert *romesco*? I proposed. David chuckled and promised to work on it.

3. While the tomatoes are baking, place the ñora peppers in a small bowl. Add 1 cup very hot water and let soak until soft, about 30 minutes. Transfer the peppers and their soaking liquid to a blender and finely puree them, then set aside.

4. Heat 5 tablespoons of the olive oil in a small skillet over medium heat until almost smoking. Add the bread and the remaining 6 garlic cloves and cook until deep golden and crisp, about 3 minutes. Using a slotted spoon, transfer the bread and garlic to a

THE ETHEREAL ANDALUSIAN FISH FRY

Every time I approach the Andalusian port cities of Cádiz or Málaga, my pulse quickens in anticipation of a meal from a *freiduría,* a fry shop specializing in fish. The best ones are holes-in-the-wall suffused with the aroma of seafood and olive oil. Gripped by indecision, I'm likely to idle by the counter. What will it be? A dozen thimble-size *puntillitas* (baby squid), a lacy pile of miniscule whitebait, a tangy *cazón en adobo* (marinated dogfish)? Or perhaps something larger and a little more noble—say, a *pijota* (small hake)? Inevitably, I settle for a *variado* (an assortment). Then, salivating, I tote my paper-swaddled booty to the nearest outdoor café on a palm-fringed plaza. A glass of icy, dry fino sherry in front of me, finally I dig in. The fish tastes of the sea and good olive oil; light, crunchy, and utterly greaseless. I order more sherry, wistful that it will be a long time before I eat fried fish like this again.

The world's largest producers of olive oil, Andalusians have been frying for centuries. Under the Moors (those great cultivators of olive trees), the region had so many stalls selling deep-fried Moorish pastries and fish on the coast that strict laws had to be passed regulating the number of the locales and the quality of their wares. Today, frying fish is an Andalusian birthright.

Though batter is used in some dishes, the essential Andalusian fish fry is simplicity itself: just freshly caught fish, salt, flour, and oil. Of course, there are secrets. Number one: the flour, which is coarsely milled and yellowish and sold in Spain as *harina para freír,* flour for frying. It's not available in the States, but semolina, either coarse or medium fine, is just right instead. Mixing all-purpose flour and coarse cornmeal is also an option, even if the corn gives fried fish an inflection of the American South. The dredging technique is likewise noteworthy. Andalusian *fritura* maestros place lots of flour in a deep bowl and set a sieve over it. In a scooping motion, they dip the fish deep into the flour, then shake off the excess in the sieve. It's best if the fish is a little moist, so the flour sticks better.

Now, the oil. The notion that extra-virgin olive oil has a low smoke point and is therefore unsuitable (or even unhealthy) for frying is a bit of a myth. It all depends on the specific variety. While you'd never use the delicate Catalan arbequina oil to fry, stable extra-virgin oils such as picual or cornicabra produce the world's best fried food. Miguel Palomo of Alhucemas, a restaurant legendary for its *frituras,* insists that using top-grade extra-virgin olive oil is the only way to fry fish. If cost is of concern (you'll need three to four cups for the job), go with oil labeled virgin or simply olive oil. Me? I normally fry in two parts Goya extra-virgin and one part peanut oil. For the fish to come out crisp and greaseless the oil needs to be at least 360°F but not higher than 375°F, so keep a thermometer handy. A deep, snug saucepan is best for the job, and it should never be overcrowded with fish.

But which fish? Andalusians will fry anything that swims, but the best choice for a mixed fry is this: very small fish, like fresh anchovies, tiny smelts, or miniscule whitebait (look for these at Chinese markets). Slightly bigger whole gutted and cleaned saltwater fish, such as red mullet, baby flounder, and small red snapper or whiting. Chunks of *cazón en adobo* (marinated dogfish or shark). And squid—preferably tiny and whole, but larger ones can be cut into rings.

Accompaniments? Andalusians normally serve *nada,* not even lemons (asking for *limón* implies that the fish isn't quite fresh). But feel free to offer a simple green salad dressed with lemon and olive oil. To drink: ice-cold beer, fino sherry, or a light young white wine. Pure heaven.

bowl. Add the almonds to the skillet and cook until golden, 2 to 3 minutes, adjusting the heat so the oil doesn't burn. Using a slotted spoon, transfer the almonds to the bowl with the bread and garlic. Set the skillet aside; you'll use some of the cooking oil in the *romesco* sauce.

5. Break the fried bread into pieces and place them in a food processor, along with the fried garlic and almonds, and process until finely ground. Add the roasted tomatoes and garlic and any juices from the roasting pan, the pureed ñora peppers, 2 tablespoons of the garlic frying oil, the remaining ⅓ cup of wine, the ¼ cup parsley, the paprika, and red pepper flakes (start with a small pinch and add more if you'd like your sauce a little hotter) to the processor bowl. Puree until completely smooth. You can finish making the *romesco* sauce right away, but it is best when prepared 1 day ahead up to this stage so that the flavors can develop. Store, covered, in the refrigerator. Discard the remaining garlicky oil in the skillet.

6. Heat the remaining 2 tablespoons olive oil in a heavy, attractive, 4- to 5-quart casserole over medium heat. Add the *romesco* sauce and bring to a simmer. Add the chocolate, reduce the heat to medium-low, and cook, stirring, until the sauce is fragrant and turns a shade or two darker, 2 to 3 minutes. Scrape the bottom of the casserole so the chocolate doesn't stick. Add another ⅓ cup wine and 1½ cups of the fish stock, reduce the heat to low, and simmer, uncovered, to blend the flavors, about 10 minutes. Taste for seasoning, adding salt and black pepper as necessary.

7. Prepare the seafood: Season the monkfish generously with salt and add it to the simmering *romesco* sauce, adding a little more fish stock if the sauce doesn't seem liquid enough. Simmer the fish until almost cooked through, about 5 minutes.

8. While the fish is simmering, heat the wine in a wide pot over medium heat. Add the clams, cover the pot, and cook the clams until they open, 5 to 7 minutes.

9. When the monkfish has cooked for 5 minutes, add the squid to the *romesco* sauce and cook for 2 minutes. Add the shrimp and cook until they turn pink, 3 to 5 minutes. Check the fish; if it hasn't completely cooked, simmer it for a few more minutes.

10. Discard any clams that haven't opened, then gently stir the clams and their cooking liquid into the *romesco* sauce. If you'd like the sauce to be soupier, add a little more fish stock. Sprinkle parsley on top and serve with bread for dunking. Don't forget to set out finger bowls and empty bowls for the shells. **SERVES 6**

ANDALUSIAN FISH FRY

PESCADO FRITO A LA ANDALUZA

What you'll find here is less a specific recipe than a general technique for frying fish the way Andalusians do. You can use several different kinds of fish for a mixed fry or just fry up one kind of seafood or fish. Calamari, for instance, comes out spectacular when prepared this way, as do tiny fish, like whitebait and smelts; they're terrific as a tapa. For slightly larger whole fish, I love small snapper, baby flounder, and small whiting, but you can use whatever looks good and fresh at the fish market. Fillets and small, thin fish steaks are fine too, as long as they are not too flaky or thin. And don't miss the *cazón en adobo* (marinated shark), either as part of the mixed fry assortment here or on its own. The amounts I've given make a mixed fish fry for four, but again, be flexible with the choice and quantity of fish. When frying, I like to start with the squid and tiny fish, so guests have something to nibble on while the larger fish cooks. For more about Andalusian fish fries, see the box on page 212.

FOR THE SHARK IN ADOBO:

1 pound boneless shark or swordfish, cut into 1 1/4-inch chunks
Coarse salt (kosher or sea)
3 medium-size garlic cloves, crushed with a garlic press
1 teaspoon sweet (not smoked) paprika
3/4 teaspoon ground cumin
1 1/4 teaspoons dried oregano
1/8 teaspoon cayenne
3 tablespoons best-quality white wine vinegar
1 tablespoon dry white wine (optional)

FOR THE REST OF THE FISH FRY:

1/2 pound cleaned squid
Coarse salt (kosher or sea)
4 ounces whitebait (optional)
12 fresh anchovies or very small smelts, gutted and cleaned
4 small whole fish (each 6 to 8 ounces), such as baby flounder, red mullet, red or white snapper, or whiting, scaled, gutted, and cleaned, heads removed
4 to 5 cups olive oil (not extra-virgin) for frying
3 to 4 cups semolina, preferably medium or coarse ground (see Note)
Lemon wedges and/or Allioli (page 44), for serving (optional)

1. Make the shark in adobo: Place the shark in a bowl and rub it generously with salt. Place the garlic, paprika, cumin, oregano, cayenne, vinegar, and wine, if using, in a small bowl and stir to mix. Pour this marinade over the shark and toss to coat evenly. Refrigerate the shark for 4 to 6 hours, tossing occasionally. Let the shark come to room temperature before cooking. Using paper towels, blot the excess marinade off the shark before coating it with flour to fry.

2. Prepare the rest of the fish fry: Using paper towels, thoroughly blot the excess moisture off the squid (otherwise it will splatter like crazy when fried). Cut the squid bodies into rings about 1/3 inch wide. Cut any large tentacles in half. Rub the squid generously with salt and set it aside. Rub the whitebait, if using, with salt and set it aside separately.

3. Rinse the anchovies and the larger whole fish under cold running water and gently shake off the excess water. Place the fish on a baking sheet or a large platter and rub generously with salt (unlike

Fresh sardines, ready for plenty of garlic and parsley (see page 200)

squid, it's best if the fish is left slightly wet, so the flour adheres better).

4. Preheat the oven to 300°F.

5. Line a rack with a double thickness of paper towels and set it over a large baking sheet. Pour olive oil to a depth of 2 inches in a deep saucepan, or a small wok about 10 inches in diameter, and heat it over medium-high heat to 360°F. While the oil is heating, place the semolina in a deep bowl. Place half of the squid in the semolina, scooping under the squid and piling the semolina on top. Set a fine sieve over the bowl of semolina, place the floured squid in the sieve, and gently shake the sieve, letting the excess semolina fall back into the bowl. When the oil reaches 360°F, add the squid to the pan, standing back in case it splatters. Fry the squid until golden, crisp, and tender, about 3 minutes, adjusting the heat so that the oil doesn't burn, and turning the squid once or twice. While the first batch of squid is frying, flour the remaining squid. Using a slotted spoon, transfer the fried squid to the paper towels to drain. Let the oil return to 360°F (a few seconds) before adding the second batch of squid. Once all the squid is drained, place it on a baking sheet and put it in the oven to keep warm until ready to serve.

6. Flour and fry the remaining fish, preferably in the following order: whitebait, 3 to 4 minutes per batch; anchovies or smelts, 3 to 6 minutes per batch, depending on their size; the marinated shark, 2 to 3 minutes per side; and, finally, the larger whole fish, about 4 minutes per side. As you fry, don't overcrowd the pan, let the oil reheat briefly before adding each new batch of fish, and adjust the temperature so that it doesn't exceed 375°F. Transfer each batch of fried fish to the rack to drain briefly, then place it on a baking sheet and put it in the oven to keep warm. Even better, serve the fish as soon as it comes out of the pan.

7. If you have been keeping the fish warm in the oven, once all of it has been fried, arrange the calamari and whitebait on separate serving dishes and place the rest of the fish on a large platter. Serve with lemon wedges and/or *allioli,* if desired. **SERVES 4**

NOTE: If you can't find semolina at the supermarket, try a specialty food store or Middle Eastern grocery.

CRISP-FRIED FLOUNDER IN A POTATO CRUST

LENGUADO FRITO EN COSTA DE PATATAS

Salvador Rojo, who presides over a stylish namesake restaurant in Seville, changed my life when he suggested coating fried fish in instant mashed potato flakes! Though coarsely milled flour is the classic coating in Andalusia, to achieve perfection these clever flakes deliver a light crust similar to that of the fashionable Japanese *panko* crumbs, with the added benefit of the lovely taste of potatoes. Although I particularly like this nifty "breading" with delicate fish such as flounder or sole, it works with just about any fish—as well as for shrimp, scallops, and thin chicken or pork cutlets. For the breading to stick properly, press it on well and make sure your oil is sufficiently hot; otherwise, the potato flakes tend to fall off.

1 1/2 pounds flounder fillets, cut crosswise into 2-inch pieces
Coarse salt (kosher or sea)
About 2 1/2 cups instant mashed potato flakes
3 large egg whites
Olive oil, for frying
Lemon wedges or Allioli (page 44), for serving (optional)

1. Rub the pieces of flounder generously with salt and let stand for 10 minutes.

2. Place the mashed potato flakes in a large bowl and crumble them thoroughly with your fingers. Place the egg whites in a shallow bowl and beat them until frothy. Set a small rack over a baking sheet that's been lined with a double layer of paper towels.

3. Pour olive oil to a depth of about 1½ inches in a large, deep skillet, and heat it to 360°F; when hot, a piece of bread placed in the oil will sizzle on contact. Dip a piece of flounder in the egg whites, then press both sides into the potato flakes to coat them. Repeat with a few more pieces of fish. Fry 5 or 6 pieces of fish in the hot oil until deep golden, about 1½ minutes per side. Using a slotted spoon, transfer the fried fish to the prepared rack and baking sheet set up to drain. Repeat with the remaining fish, then serve at once, with lemon wedges or *allioli,* if desired. **SERVES 6 AS AN APPETIZER, 4 OR 5 AS A LIGHT MAIN COURSE**

SHELLFISH

SALT-COOKED SHRIMP

GAMBAS A LA SAL

Already hooked on salt-cooked fish, I was intrigued to discover this ingenious shrimp-cooking method at a restaurant near Valencia. It involves cooking whole shrimp in their shells in a cast-iron skillet on a bed of salt, which heats the crustaceans gently and evenly, leaving them with plenty of savor. (Anyone who truly loves shrimp knows that they are best when cooked in their shells to preserve the flavor and juices.) When the shrimp are of impeccable quality, as they are on coastal Spain, no sauce is necessary. But if you like, make a simple vinaigrette with a third of a cup of fruity olive oil, the juice of one lemon, two crushed garlic cloves, and a few tablespoons of minced parsley. Don't forget finger bowls and empty bowls for the shells.

- 1½ to 2 cups coarse salt (kosher or sea)
- 1 pound large unshelled shrimp, preferably with the heads on, patted dry
- Fragrant extra-virgin olive oil, for serving (optional)
- Lemon wedges, for serving (optional)

Spread the salt evenly on the bottom of a heavy 12-inch skillet, preferably cast iron. Heat the skillet over medium-high heat until the salt is very hot and almost beginning to smoke. Place half of the shrimp on the salt and cook for 3 to 4 minutes. Using tongs, turn the shrimp over and continue cooking until the shrimp are just cooked through, about 3 minutes longer. Transfer the shrimp to a plate and cook the remaining shrimp in the same way (the second batch may take less time to cook, since the salt will be very hot). Let the shrimp cool just enough to handle, then gently wipe off any excess salt with paper towels. Serve the shrimp with olive oil and lemon wedges, if desired. **SERVES 4**

MARI CARMEN'S SCALLOPS WITH CANDIED LEMON

VIEIRAS CON LIMON CONFITADO DE MARI CARMEN

The last time I ate at La Sirena, a restaurant in Alicante that I adore, the chef, Mari Carmen Vélez, offered an unforgettable scallop dish. Presented in stark white soup bowls, the fat, seared scallops came in a delightful sweet-tart broth strewn with a bright confetti of diced zucchini, pumpkin, and mushrooms. "But what gives the dish that unusual citrusy kick and mystique?" I wanted to know. Candied lemon peel was the answer. Adapted to a home kitchen, the scallops make a showstopping first course. They are also simple to make, as you can use high-quality store-bought candied lemon instead of making your own. If you'd like to serve the dish as a main course, just increase the number of scallops to six per person.

- ⅓ cup diced zucchini (¼-inch dice)
- ⅓ cup diced yellow pumpkin, butternut squash, or calabaza (¼-inch dice)
- ¼ cup diced red bell pepper (¼-inch dice)
- ¼ cup diced cleaned, unblemished white mushrooms (¼-inch dice)
- 3 heaping tablespoons minced high-quality candied lemon or citron
- 6 tablespoons fresh juice from a tart-sweet orange
- 2 tablespoons fresh lemon juice
- 16 large sea scallops
- Coarse salt (kosher or sea) and freshly ground black pepper
- 2 tablespoons extra-virgin olive oil
- ¼ cup Fish Stock (page 108) or store-bought fish stock, or chicken stock or broth
- 1 teaspoon white wine vinegar, or more to taste
- 1 teaspoon balsamic vinegar

1. Place the zucchini, pumpkin, red pepper, mushrooms, and candied lemon in a large bowl and toss to mix. Add the orange and lemon juice, toss, and let the vegetables stand for about 30 minutes.

2. Pat the scallops dry with paper towels and season with salt and black pepper. Heat 1 tablespoon of the olive oil in a very large skillet over high heat until almost smoking. Working in two batches, cook the scallops until golden brown and opaque throughout, about 2 minutes per side. Transfer the cooked scallops to a plate and cover with aluminum foil to keep warm.

3. Heat the remaining 1 tablespoon olive oil in a medium-size skillet over medium heat. Add the diced vegetables and their soaking liquid and cook until they just begin to soften slightly but are still bright colored, about 1½ minutes. Add the fish stock and cook until warm, about 1 minute. Add the wine and balsamic vinegars, season with salt and black pepper to taste, and remove the sauce from the heat.

4. Divide the scallops among elegant soup plates and spoon the vegetables and some liquid around them. Serve at once. **SERVES 4 AS A FIRST COURSE**

SCALLOPS WITH GARLIC CREAM AND TOMATO JAM

VIEIRAS CON CREMA DE AJO Y MERMELADA DE TOMATES

This modern Catalan way of preparing seafood is not only great for scallops; it's also fabulous for many different types of seafood, from shrimp to lobster to fish fillets, such as turbot or sea bass. The contrast of tastes—the smooth garlicky cream and olive oil emulsion and the sweetened roasted tomatoes—is truly attention grabbing.

14 medium-size garlic cloves; 12 lightly smashed and 2 minced
1 cup heavy (whipping) cream, or more if needed
1/3 cup bottled clam juice, or chicken stock or broth
6 tablespoons extra-virgin olive oil
Coarse salt (kosher or sea)
24 large sea scallops
Freshly ground black pepper
Tomato Jam (page 390)

1. Place the smashed garlic cloves, cream, and clam juice in a small, heavy saucepan over medium heat and bring to a simmer. Reduce the heat to low and cook, partially covered, until the garlic feels completely soft when poked with a skewer, 10 to 12 minutes. If the cream mixture has reduced in volume, add enough cream to make about 1 cup. Let the garlic cream cool for a few minutes, then transfer it to a blender and puree until smooth.

2. Place 4 tablespoons of the olive oil and the minced garlic in a small, deep skillet over medium-low heat. Stir until the garlic is very fragrant but not browned, 1 to 2 minutes. Add the garlic cream and whisk until the sauce is emulsified. Continue cooking, stirring from time to time, until the sauce thickens a little, about 3 minutes. Season the sauce with salt to taste, remove it from the heat, and keep warm.

3. Pat the scallops dry with paper towels and season them with salt and pepper. Heat the remaining 2 tablespoons olive oil in a very large skillet over high heat until almost smoking. Working in three batches, cook the scallops until golden brown and opaque throughout, about 2 minutes per side. Transfer the cooked scallops to a plate and cover with aluminum foil to keep warm.

4. To serve, spread the garlic cream on 4 plates and arrange 6 scallops on top of each. Dab the scallops with the Tomato Jam and serve at once. **SERVES 4**

LOBSTER AND MONKFISH SUQUET

SUQUET DE LLAGOSTA I RAP

Suquet is a cousin of bouillabaisse, an essential, soupy stew and a classic in the regions of Catalonia and Valencia. Its name comes from the Catalan *suquejar,* or to throw off juice. Like bouillabaisse, it originated as a fisherman's meal, prepared on boats from potatoes, seawater, and small gelatinous rockfish that wouldn't fetch top money at markets but were excellent for flavoring broth. These days *suquet* can be as simple as a single kind of fish, some broth, a tomato or two, and a *picada* of minced garlic and parsley. Or it can get a bit more elaborate, prepared with a whole host of seafood and a fancier *picada.* Either way, the soul of a good *suquet* is a strong fish stock traditionally made with lots of small rockfish, a monkfish head, and other Mediterranean critters. Away from the Mediterranean shores, I suggest using clam juice infused with lobster shells. Or, you can make *suquet* with large shrimp instead of lobster, using the shells for the stock. In addition to the monkfish here (or in its place), sea bass, tilefish, snapper, or halibut are all welcome. So are clams and mussels. And, don't forget the *allioli,* which gives the dish a great garlicky smack.

2 live lobsters (1 1/2 pounds each)
1/4 cup plus 1 tablespoon extra-virgin olive oil
8 medium-size garlic cloves; 6 left whole and 2 chopped
4 cups bottled clam juice, diluted with 1 1/2 cups water
1 cup dry white wine
1/4 cup cubed day-old country bread
1/4 cup blanched almonds
1 large onion, chopped
4 large ripe tomatoes, peeled, seeded, and chopped
4 medium-size Yukon Gold potatoes, peeled and cut into 3/8-inch-thick slices
1 1/2 to 2 pounds monkfish fillets, cut into 2-inch chunks
Coarse salt (kosher or sea)
3 to 4 tablespoons minced, fresh flat-leaf parsley
Almond or regular Allioli (page 44), for serving

1. Bring a very large pot of salted water to a rolling boil. Plunge the lobsters into the water, heads first. Cook, uncovered, for 10 minutes. Using tongs, transfer the lobsters to a large bowl or baking dish and let cool until manageable. Working over a bowl to catch the juices, remove the meat from the tails and claws, place it in a bowl, and set aside. Do not discard the shells. Remove and discard the tomalley. If there is any roe, set it aside with the meat. Crack the body and claw shells slightly.

2. Place 1 tablespoon of the olive oil and the chopped garlic in a large pot over medium heat and cook for about 1 minute. Add the body and claw shells and cook, stirring, for 3 to 4 minutes. Add the clam juice and wine and bring to a boil. Reduce the heat to medium-low and cook, uncovered, for about 15 minutes to extract all of the flavor from the shells.

Strain the stock, discarding the solids. (The recipe can be prepared 1 day ahead up to this point. Cover and refrigerate the lobster meat and stock separately.)

3. Heat the remaining ¼ cup olive oil in a heavy 4-quart saucepan over medium heat until almost smoking. Add the bread and the 6 whole garlic cloves and cook until the bread is deep golden and crisp, about 3 minutes. Using a slotted spoon, transfer the bread and the garlic to a mini food processor. Add the almonds to the saucepan and cook until golden, 2 to 3 minutes, adjusting the heat so the oil doesn't burn. Using a slotted spoon, add the almonds to the food processor. Run the food processor until the fried bread, garlic, and almonds are finely ground. Set the *picada* aside.

4. Add the onion to the saucepan and cook over low heat until softened, 6 to 7 minutes. Add the tomatoes and cook, stirring, until they are thick, dark, and reduced, about 20 minutes, periodically adding a little lobster stock to the pan if they begin to stick or burn. Stir in the potatoes and cook for 1 to 2 minutes. Add the lobster stock and bring to a boil over high heat. Reduce the heat to medium and cook until the potatoes are half cooked, 7 to 8 minutes. Rub the monkfish generously with salt, add it to the pan, and cook until just cooked through, about 8 minutes.

5. When the fish is just cooked through, add the *picada* to the saucepan, then rinse out the processor bowl with a little liquid from the stew and add this as well. Add the reserved lobster meat to the stew and cook until it is just warmed through. Stir in the parsley and let the stew stand for about 5 minutes. Ladle the stew into bowls and serve with the *allioli* on the side. **SERVES 4 TO 6**

SEARED SQUID IN RED, GREEN, AND BLACK

CHIPIRON A LA PLANCHA EN ROJO, VERDE, Y NEGRO

Griddled squid served with peeled diced tomatoes, basil oil, and a vinaigrette tinted with squid ink is incredibly fashionable among Spanish cooks. This isn't surprising—the simple combination of flavors is hard to beat, and the dish looks as striking as it tastes. Packets of squid ink are increasingly available at better fish stores, or you can order them by mail (see page 461). Look for the smallest squid you can find. It's important that the squid sear in a griddle without releasing their liquid and stewing (for tips, see "Searing Squid" on page 222). Squeeze bottles, available from many cookware shops, are a great tool for drizzling the squid ink vinaigrette and the basil oil.

1 1/2 pounds very small squid, cleaned but left whole (see Note)
Coarse salt (kosher or sea)
6 tablespoons fragrant extra-virgin olive oil, plus more for tossing with the squid
2 ripe but firm plum tomatoes, peeled, seeded, and finely diced
2 tablespoons best-quality red wine vinegar
1 pinch of sugar
4 packets squid ink (each 4 grams /.14 ounce), warmed in hot water if the ink has congealed
Freshly ground black pepper
2 medium-size garlic cloves, crushed with a garlic press
2 tablespoons minced fresh flat-leaf parsley
Fresh Basil Oil (page 287), for serving

1. Place the squid in a bowl. Rub it lightly with salt and toss it with a little olive oil. Let stand for 30 minutes.

2. Place the tomatoes, 1 tablespoon of the olive oil, 1½ teaspoons of the vinegar, and the sugar in another bowl. Toss to combine, then season with salt to taste. Let stand until ready to use.

3. Place the squid ink in a small saucepan and whisk in the remaining 4½ teaspoons vinegar and 4 tablespoons of the olive oil. Season the squid ink vinaigrette with salt and pepper to taste and bring to a simmer over medium-low heat, stirring. Keep the vinaigrette warm until ready to use.

4. Blot the squid dry with paper towels. Lightly oil a large griddle and heat it over high heat for about 5 minutes. Working in three or four batches, cook the squid, stirring, until lightly charred and tender, about 3 minutes. Transfer all the cooked squid to a bowl. Add the garlic and parsley and the remaining 1 tablespoon olive oil and toss to coat evenly.

5. To serve, place some squid on a plate and spoon some of the tomato mixture on top. Decoratively drizzle some of the squid ink vinaigrette and the basil oil around the squid. Repeat with the remaining squid. Serve at once. **SERVES 4 AS A FIRST COURSE**

NOTE: If the squid you find are longer than 2 inches, cut the bodies into ⅓-inch rings. Slice large tentacles in half.

GRILLED RAZOR CLAMS WITH WHITE TRUFFLE OIL

NAVAJAS A LA PLANCHA CON ACEITE DE TRUFA BLANCA

Nothing describes "Spanish seafood treat" better than a plate of razor clams, all chewy sweetness and brininess. Seemingly, it's a dish you can't improve upon . . . unless, like chef Quim Marqués of the Barcelona seafood restaurant El Suquet de l'Almirall, you add a touch of genius—white truffle oil for an extra dash of exotic earthiness. Razor clams are an obsession in the American Pacific Northwest, available there from April to early fall. In other areas, look for them at Chinese seafood markets or by mail order. If you can't find them, this simple but luxurious recipe is great made with regular clams, such as littlenecks or Manilas.

SEARING SQUID

There are few things more delicious than *chipirón a la plancha,* squid seared on a hot, flatiron griddle. When cooked properly—a procedure that takes just a few minutes—the squid comes out kissed by the fire and beautifully tender. However, when the searing goes wrong, the squid ends up stewing in its own juices, looking pallid, and tasting tough. Here's how to do it right.

First choose your utensil. Lacking a *plancha,* my favorite searing surface is a paella pan. Because the pan is so large, there is less chance of overcrowding the squid. Plus, as the surface is so thin, it heats very quickly. If you don't have a paella pan, use a large seasoned cast-iron skillet or a griddle pan. A wok or a Mexican *comal* are fine, too.

When searing squid, the crucial thing is not to put too much into the pan, lest it release too much liquid and sweat rather than sear. To sear a pound of squid properly, you'll need to do it in four or five batches. Make sure to blot the squid thoroughly dry with paper towels before cooking. Heat the pan until it's red-hot; this will take three to five minutes. The amount of oil should be minimal: Either wipe the pan with an oiled paper towel before heating it or toss the squid with a little oil right before searing.

Seared squid is delicious with nothing more than a wedge of lemon. It's divine on a bed of arugula with a drizzle of *allioli,* perhaps one flavored with saffron or roasted garlic. As for the *plancha* technique, it's ideal for cooking many different things—unpeeled shrimp, scallops, clams, small sardines, asparagus, oyster mushrooms, baby lamb chops—you name it.

18 large razor clams, or 30 small littleneck, cherrystone, or Manila clams, scrubbed
1 small bottle white truffle oil
Coarse salt (kosher or sea) and freshly ground white pepper
Finely minced fresh flat-leaf parsley

1. Light the grill and preheat it to high.

2. Rinse the clams under cold running water, pat dry with paper towels, and chill until ready to use.

3. When ready to cook, place the clams on the hot grill, close the cover, and cook until the clams have opened, about 3 minutes. Start checking the clams after 2 minutes, removing the ones that are open. Take care not to overcook the clams or their delicate meat will turn rubbery. (If you are using small clams, grill them in 2 or 3 batches.)

4. When all of the clams are done, transfer them to a platter, discarding any unopened ones. Put your thumb over the opening of the bottle of truffle oil so that only a trickle comes out and drizzle a little oil over the meat of the clams. Sprinkle the parsley judiciously on top and serve at once. **SERVES 6 AS A FIRST COURSE**

CADIZ CLAMS WITH SPINACH AND EGGS

ALMEJAS CON ESPINACAS

El Faro in Cádiz is one of Spain's legendary fish restaurants. Its proprietor, Gonzalo Córdoba, runs a tight ship. Here he is, receiving a shipment of fish so fresh it still jumps. There he is plying a table of regulars with an old Pedro Ximénez sherry and boasting about his ethereally crisp *tortillas de camarones* (shrimp fritters) to a German couple. And finally he's urging everyone to try his famous *almejas*: clams cooked in a deliciously messy sauce of spinach, brandy, and scrambled eggs. Gonzalo's secret ingredient here is the pureed fish soup that lends the sauce roundness and depth. The lobster bisque that's sold at many fancier food stores is the ideal option; failing that you can use Campbell's cream of shrimp soup or bottled clam juice diluted with a little water. Though Cádiz is a long way from Hong Kong, there is something Cantonese in the expressive simplicity of the dish—not to mention the belief that everything tastes better with eggs.

About 10 ounces fresh spinach, stemmed and rinsed but not dried
3 tablespoons fragrant extra-virgin olive oil
4 medium-size garlic cloves, finely minced
2 pounds Manila or small littleneck clams, scrubbed
4 tablespoons good-quality brandy, preferably Spanish
1/2 cup store-bought seafood or lobster bisque, or 1/3 cup Campbell's Cream of Shrimp Soup whisked together with 2 to 3 tablespoons water, or 1/3 cup clam juice diluted with 3 tablespoons water
2 large eggs, beaten
Coarse salt (kosher or sea) and freshly ground white pepper
Crusty bread, for serving

1. Cook the spinach in the water clinging to its leaves in a large pot over medium heat until just wilted, about 2 minutes. Drain the spinach in a sieve, pressing gently to get rid of the excess moisture. Coarsely chop the spinach and set it aside.

2. Heat the olive oil in a large, wide pot or wok over medium-low heat. Add the garlic and cook until it is very fragrant but not colored, about 2 minutes. Add the clams and the brandy, increase the heat to medium-high, and cook until the brandy is reduced to about 1 tablespoon, 1 minute. Add the seafood bisque, cover the pot, and steam the clams until they open, 4 to 7 minutes depending on their size. Discard any unopened clams.

3. Add the wilted spinach to the pot and toss it with the clams for about 1 minute. Using a large spoon, push the clams and spinach to the side of the pot. Reduce the heat to low, add the eggs, and stir, scrambling the eggs until they just begin to set, 45 seconds to 1 minute. Toss the clams with the eggs and season the dish with salt and white pepper to taste. Transfer to a bowl along with all the cooking liquid and serve at once with bread. **SERVES 4 AS A FIRST COURSE**

CLAMS IN OLIVE OIL WITH JAMON AND PINE NUTS

ALMEJAS CON ACEITE DE OLIVA, JAMON Y PIÑONES

What timing—the day I finished testing chef Quim Marqués's exquisite recipe for razor clams with truffle oil (see page 222), Quim himself arrived in New York from Barcelona for a guest

stint at Solera restaurant. On his menu was a dish of clams "poached" in olive oil together with pine nuts and bits of serrano ham. Once again, I was wowed: three simple flavors, each with its own elusively sweet aftertaste, combined in a dish that lingered for days in my memory. When I tried making it for a dinner party, *knockout* was the word that came out of everyone's mouth. And the dish is ridiculously easy, to boot. For best results use a lovely olive oil and good pine nuts, preferably imported from the Mediterranean, not from China. You'll want plenty of bread to mop up the sauce. Any leftover sauce is delicious tossed with pasta.

1 1/4 cups fragrant extra-virgin olive oil
2 small garlic cloves, sliced
2/3 cup pine nuts
1 piece (3 ounces) serrano ham or prosciutto, finely diced
2 pounds small clams, such as Manilas or littlenecks, or cockles, scrubbed
2 to 3 tablespoons minced fresh flat-leaf parsley
Crusty bread, for serving

Heat the olive oil and garlic in a wide earthenware *cazuela,* a very large, heavy skillet, or a wide casserole over medium heat. Add the pine nuts and ham and cook, stirring, until the nuts just begin to color, about 2 minutes. Add the clams, cover the *cazuela,* and cook until the clams open, 4 to 7 minutes depending on their size, shaking the pan occasionally. Discard any clams that don't open. Serve the clams directly from the *cazuela* or spoon them into bowls, adding plenty of the cooking liquid to each bowl. Sprinkle the parsley on top and serve with plenty of bread. **SERVES 4 AS A FIRST COURSE**

Clams in Olive Oil with Jamón and Pine Nuts

CLAM AND ARTICHOKE CAZUELA

ALMEJAS CON ALCACHOFAS

Clams and artichokes is a truly ingenious Spanish pairing: The particular sweetness of both ingredients mingles in the mouth in a most delightful way. Found on the menu of many Spanish seafood restaurants during the artichoke season, the dish should really be called artichokes with clams, rather than the other way around, since the chokes constitute the principal flavor. Fresh, young artichokes make all the difference, but if these are out of season, go ahead and use frozen artichoke hearts. The dish is usually served as a first course, with bread to dunk in the sauce.

3 medium-size artichokes, pared down to the hearts (page 370)
1 lemon, cut in half
1/4 cup fragrant extra-virgin olive oil
2 medium-size garlic cloves, minced
2 teaspoons all-purpose flour
1/3 cup dry or medium-dry sherry
2/3 cup Fish Stock (page 108) or store-bought fish stock, or 1/3 cup bottled clam juice diluted with 1/3 cup water
12 to 16 medium-size littleneck clams, scrubbed
Coarse salt (kosher or sea) and freshly ground white pepper
2 to 3 tablespoons minced fresh flat-leaf parsley
Crusty bread, for serving

NIFTY TRICKS: POACHING IN OLIVE OIL

At modern Spanish restaurants these days, your fish order is likely to be *confitado en aceite de oliva*. This means gently cooked in a bath of olive oil. Prepared this way, fish comes out amazingly silky and moist and not at all oily. A low cooking temperature is the key to this method: In Spain it's never higher than 65°C (about 150°F), just below the point at which the proteins in the fish begin to dry out. Great candidates for this smart, simple technique are very fresh halibut, sea trout, salmon, snapper, or cod fillets, and sashimi-quality tuna loin. It's best if the fish is cut into 1-inch-thick, 6- to 7-ounce portions, and is at room temperature. The olive oil should ideally be aromatic and rather light in texture; it can also be cut with a lighter, flavorless oil, such as sunflower or peanut oil. For even more flavor, before cooking the fish, infuse the oil with aromatics, such as unpeeled lightly smashed garlic cloves, sprigs of thyme or rosemary, citrus peel, or even a stick of vanilla (this is delicious with flaky white-fleshed fish, such as cod). To do this, cook the oil with the aromatics over low heat for about 15 minutes, then either strain it before adding the fish, or leave the aromatics in.

To submerge a single layer of 1-inch-thick fillets you'll need 3 to 4 cups of oil. Use a saucepan in which the fish will fit snugly so you don't waste oil. Pour the oil in the saucepan and heat it over low heat until it registers about 150°F on a candy thermometer. Add the fish and adjust the heat to maintain a temperature of about 130°F. It will take about 15 minutes for cod or halibut to be done, less for rare tuna or salmon. But, if you leave the fish in longer, no problem: At such a low temperature, it's unlikely to overcook. Blot the oil off the fish before serving. Another method is to heat the oil, pour it over the fish to cover, and bake in a 225°F oven for about 30 minutes.

Oil-poached fish is best served with an acidic counterpoint, such as Tomato Vinaigrette (page 201), Black Olive Vinaigrette (page 205), or a sprightly raw tomato or cucumber salsa. Or you can simply dress it with fresh olive oil and a dusting of Maldon (flaky) sea salt. Shrimp, scallops, or lobster also taste incredible when prepared this way. Try it—the texture of olive oil–poached seafood will come as a revelation!

1. Drain the artichoke hearts and pat them dry with paper towels. Cut each artichoke heart into 6 wedges, rubbing them with the cut edge of a lemon half so they don't discolor.

2. Heat the olive oil in a medium-size earthenware *cazuela* or a deep skillet over medium-low heat. Add the artichokes and the garlic, cover the *cazuela,* and cook, shaking the *cazuela* occasionally, until the artichokes are tender, 7 to 10 minutes. Using a large spoon, push the artichokes to one side of the *cazuela,* add the flour to the oil, and stir to blend. Add the sherry and fish stock, increase the heat to medium-high, and cook, stirring, until the sauce thickens a little, 3 to 4 minutes. Add the clams, cover the *cazuela,* and cook, shaking the *cazuela* occasionally, until the clams open, 4 to 7 minutes, depending on their size. Discard any unopened clams. Season the sauce with salt and white pepper to taste and stir in the parsley. Serve the dish straight from the *cazuela* or transfer to a rustic serving dish. Serve with bread.

SERVES 4 AS A FIRST COURSE

TARRAGONA MUSSELS

MEJILLONES A LA MARINERA

Tarragona, the ancient Roman city in Catalonia, has a quaint nineteenth-century fishermen's quarter called El Serallo, with a small working harbor crowded with fishing boats and a slew of restaurants where locals indulge in seafood cuisine. One of the best places to lunch here is La Puda. Here the specialty is a great pile of mussels with a wonderful, sassy tomato sauce enriched by a *picada* of fried garlic and nuts that lends a straightforward dish a hint of toasty complexity. The sauce through Step 1 can easily be prepared a day ahead—in fact it tastes better that way. Then it only takes a few minutes to steam the mussels in the reheated sauce right before serving.

1/4 cup extra-virgin olive oil
6 medium-size garlic cloves, cut in half
10 blanched almonds
8 hazelnuts, toasted (see page 267) and skinned
1 medium-size onion, diced
1/2 dried red chile (such as arbol), crumbled, or 1/4 teaspoon crushed red pepper flakes
1 1/2 cups finely chopped canned tomatoes, 1/4 cup of their juices reserved
1 pinch of sugar
1/3 cup dry white wine
About 2 1/2 cups Fish Stock (page 108) or store-bought fish stock, or 1 1/2 cups bottled clam juice diluted with 1 cup water
3 pounds mussels, scrubbed and debearded
Coarse salt (kosher or sea) and freshly ground black pepper
1/4 cup chopped fresh flat-leaf parsley
Grilled or toasted country bread, for serving

1. Heat the olive oil in a large, wide pot over medium-low heat. Add the garlic, almonds, and hazelnuts and cook, stirring, until golden, 2 to 3 minutes. Using a slotted spoon, transfer the garlic, almonds, and hazelnuts to a bowl and set aside. Add the onion to the pot and cook, stirring occasionally, until translucent, about 5 minutes. Add the chile and stir for 30 seconds. Add the tomatoes (but not their juices) and sugar, increase the heat to medium-high, and cook until the tomatoes thicken and reduce, about 5 minutes. Stir in the wine, 2 cups of the fish stock, and the ¼ cup tomato juices. Cover the pot, reduce the heat to very low, and simmer the tomato sauce for 30 minutes. The tomatoes will have dissolved and the sauce will be flavorful. Add additional stock if it seems too thick.

2. Meanwhile, place the fried garlic, almonds, and hazelnuts in a mini food processor and pulse until finely ground. Add the garlic mixture to the tomato sauce. Cook, stirring, until well blended, about 1 minute.

3. Add the mussels to the pot, cover it, raise the heat to medium-high, and bring the sauce to a boil. Cook the mussels, shaking the pot occasionally, until they open, 5 to 7 minutes. Discard any unopened mussels. Season with salt and black pepper to taste, sprinkle the parsley over the mussels and sauce, then serve in soup bowls with the bread. **SERVES 4 TO 6**

MEAT

PORK, LAMB, AND BEEF

Spain is Europe's most macho country: Where else would you see old blue-haired señoras nibbling on ham canapés while gleefully watching a *torero* being bested by a bull? And eating meat—prodigious amounts

From left to right: Trevélez, located on Spain's highest mountain, is where air-cured serrano ham is produced; A shop in Mallorca overflows with plenty of staples, including sausages of all types; A restaurant owner holds a plate heaped with *cocido* (boiled dinner), one of Spain's most emblematic dishes, and majestic Alcazar in Segovia is one of her most picturesque castles.

of it—has always been seen as an expression of the culture's vigor. *Madrileños* make weekend excursions to old Castilian towns like Segovia and Sepúlveda to savor stupendous roast suckling lamb and pig. Andalusian bullfighting aficionados indulge in rich, long-braised oxtail stews at old *taurino* taverns during bullfighting season. Basque and Galician grill houses ply beef lovers with two-pound rare rib steaks, while many restaurants in La Rioja serve little more than sublime baby lamb chops grilled over vine cuttings. And the entire country is mad for *cocido,* a delicious orgy of boiled meats, sausages, and tender chickpeas preceded by a strong, clear broth.

Above all, Spain is a nation of pork eaters, a preference with deep historical roots. From the eighth century to the fifteenth, much of the Iberian Peninsula was dominated by Muslims. When the last Moorish kingdom fell, all Muslims and Jews who refused to convert were expelled by orders of the Catholic monarchs, Isabella and Ferdinand. Suspicious of false converts and infidels, Catholic authorities saw eating pork—a meat forbidden by Jewish and Muslim laws—as an affirmation of Christian faith. No doubt you've heard of the Inquisition? Fearing persecution, converts hung sausages or hams on their doors or carried pork bones with them on their travels. "Spanish cooking reeks of garlic and Catholicism," notes a Spanish writer.

Spain's penchant for pork has economic underpinnings as well. The *matanza*—the fall slaughter of the family hog—was central to rural life. For days, entire villages labored around the clock, transforming every inch of the pig into hams, sausages, salt-cured ribs, blood puddings, and lard. To this day, the hog is valued in Spain as much for fresh meat as for smoky charcuterie: the luxurious cured *ibérico* ham, chorizos powered with paprika, dark, rich blood sausages, and the aristocratic cured loin. You know you're in Spain when you enter a bar and see a huge ham dangling from a rafter.

Trailing right behind pork, Spanish lamb tends to be gorgeous: young, pale pink, lush meat tasting sweetly of the grasses on which the sheep grazed. At temples of modern cuisine I've tasted lamb in a gauzy veil of espresso; lamb vacuum-cooked at a low temperature and presented in a sherry broth laced with candied lemon; lamb served with an intriguing sheep's milk foam. In this chapter, traditional dishes—lamb braised with dried and fresh peppers or baked with five heads of garlic—mingle with contemporary preparations, such as baby lamb chops with a sweet marmalade of piquillo peppers or Ferran Adrià's rack of lamb roasted in a crust of pistachios.

Travelers to Spain often ask where the beef is. One answer—visit a Basque or Galician steak house. But while presently northern Spain produces some excellent beef, Spain is not known for its cattle pastures. It's a culture more interested in raising bulls for *corridas* than for red meat. Not to say that you won't find delicious beef recipes here, including smoky Asturian beef stew with beans and succulent steak with Cabrales butter. And meatballs! Balls of minced meat bound with eggs can be found in the recipe books of Al-Andalus and are appreciated today just as much as they were in the thirteenth century. Some things never change.

PORK

CATALAN BRAISED PORK SHOULDER WITH DRIED FRUIT

PORC GUISAT AMB FRUITA SECA

Moist, slow cooking brings out the best in a humble cut like pork shoulder, making it fit for the most festive occasions. The sauce, enhanced with dried fruit and a whiff of cinnamon, is classically Catalan. Try to get best-quality organic dried cherries and apricots, ones that have some tartness. If you're using ordinary dried fruit, you might want to reduce the amount slightly, so the dish doesn't come out overly sweet. Alternatively, you can add a splash of red wine vinegar to the sauce at the end. The dish is best made ahead; cool the pork in the sauce and slowly reheat it. Spinach with Raisins and Pine Nuts (page 388) makes an ideal accompaniment. For a savory counterpoint, I also like Smoky Mashed Potatoes from Extremadura (page 323) alongside.

1 boneless pork shoulder roast, such as Boston butt (about 4 pounds; see Note), trimmed of excess fat
Coarse salt (kosher or sea) and freshly ground black pepper
2 medium-size garlic cloves, crushed with a garlic press
2 to 3 tablespoons light olive oil
1 medium-size onion, chopped
1 fat carrot, diced
1 cup peeled pearl onions, thawed if frozen
1/4 cup kirsch or brandy
2 cups full-bodied dry red wine with a lively acidity
1 cup beef or chicken stock, or broth
3/4 cup pitted dried sour cherries
1/2 cup dried apricots, preferably Californian, halved or quartered if large
1 large bay leaf
1 small piece of cinnamon stick
2 fresh rosemary sprigs

1. Preheat the oven to 325°F.

2. Using kitchen string, tie the pork shoulder crosswise, spacing the ties 1 inch apart. Rub the pork generously with salt and pepper and the garlic.

3. Heat 2 tablespoons of the olive oil in a 5- to 6-quart flameproof casserole or Dutch oven over high heat until almost smoking. Add the pork and cook until richly browned on all sides, about 8 minutes total. Add the remaining oil while the pork browns, if the casserole looks too dry. Transfer the pork to a bowl. Add the chopped onion, carrot, and pearl onions to the casserole and brown well, 6 to 7 minutes. Add the kirsch and cook over high heat until it is reduced to about 1 tablespoon, about 1 minute. Add the wine, beef stock, cherries, apricots, bay leaf, cinnamon stick, and rosemary sprigs

Pork Tenderloin with Lightly Seared Strawberries

and bring to a boil, scraping the bottom of the casserole to dislodge the brown bits. Season the sauce with salt to taste.

4. Return the pork to the casserole. Cover the casserole tightly and transfer it to the oven. Bake the pork, turning it once or twice, until it is very tender and an instant-read meat thermometer registers 165°F, about 1½ hours.

5. Transfer the pork to a plate and cover it with aluminum foil to keep warm. Remove and discard the bay leaf, cinnamon stick, and rosemary sprigs. Transfer the casserole to the stove top and cook the sauce over high heat until it is slightly syrupy, 3 to 5 minutes.

6. Remove the string from the pork and discard it. Cut the pork into slices and arrange on a serving platter. Pour the sauce over the pork and serve. **SERVES 6**

NOTE: If you prefer, this recipe is also great made with a 2- to 3-pound boneless pork loin, which should be cooked until it registers 150°F on a meat thermometer (it will take about 45 minutes).

PORK TENDERLOIN WITH LIGHTLY SEARED STRAWBERRIES

SOLOMILLO DE CERDO CON FRESAS

Playing off the tart-sweet-aromatic flavors of sherry vinegar and seared strawberries, this modern Spanish dish is outstanding—as sophisticated and striking as it is easy to make. The amount of sugar you use will depend on how sweet you'd like the sauce and the tartness of your sherry vinegar. The strawberries likewise need some acidity; choose berries that are fragrant and seasonal but just a touch underripe. They should be tangy-sweet and seared very briefly. The pork is best when slightly pink and moist; a meat thermometer is indispensable here.

2 pork tenderloins (each about 1 pound)
Coarse salt (kosher or sea) and freshly ground black pepper
About 2 tablespoons crumbled dried rosemary
2 tablespoons olive oil, plus more for brushing the griddle
10 to 12 large aromatic but firm strawberries, hulled and sliced
1/3 cup chicken stock or broth or water
1/2 cup sherry vinegar, preferably aged
2 to 4 teaspoons sugar
Flaky sea salt, such as Maldon, for garnish
Minced fresh chives, for garnish

1. Rub the pork generously with salt, pepper, and rosemary. Heat the olive oil in a large, heavy skillet over medium-high heat. Add the pork and cook until richly browned on all sides, about 6 minutes total. Reduce the heat to medium-low and cook the pork, turning several times, until it is tender and an instant-read meat thermometer registers 155°F, about 15 minutes. Transfer the pork to a cutting board and let rest, covered with aluminum foil, while you prepare the strawberries and the sauce. The internal temperature will rise as the meat stands. Set the skillet aside; you'll use it to make the sauce.

2. Rub an unridged rimmed griddle pan or a large, heavy skillet with an oiled paper towel and heat until almost smoking. Add the strawberries and sear for about 45 seconds, turning once. They should be cooked until slightly softened but should not release too much juice.

3. Add the chicken stock to the skillet in which the pork cooked and place it over medium-high heat, scraping the bottom of the skillet to dislodge the brown bits. Cook until the stock is almost syrupy, about 3 minutes. Add the vinegar and 2 teaspoons of the sugar and continue cooking until the sauce is almost thick enough to coat a spoon, 3 to 5 minutes longer. After about 1½ minutes, taste the sauce and add more sugar to taste if it seems too tart.

4. Cut the pork into thick slices and arrange them decoratively on dinner plates. Spoon some seared strawberries beside the meat and drizzle the sauce on and around the meat and the strawberries. Sprinkle flaky salt over the pork and garnish it with chives. Serve at once. **SERVES 4 OR 5**

SALT-BAKED PORK IN ADOBO

LOMO EN ADOBO A LA SAL

The zesty *adobo* marinade in this recipe is a blend of smoky *pimentón,* garlic, oregano, and parsley that's straight from the Spanish heartland. While *adobo* pork is usually sliced and fried in oil or lard, baking the pork in a salt crust produces a fabulously moist, tender, and original dish, minus the fat. Because the salt acts as a kind of pressure cooker, start checking the temperature of the meat after it has baked for about thirty-five minutes. The Tangy Cilantro Mojo goes perfectly with the pork, which is delicious hot, warm, or cold.

6 large garlic cloves, chopped
3 tablespoons chopped fresh flat-leaf parsley
2 tablespoons chopped fresh oregano, or 2 teaspoons dried oregano
1 tablespoon smoked sweet Spanish paprika
1 teaspoon hot paprika or cayenne
1/2 teaspoon black peppercorns
3 tablespoons best-quality white wine vinegar
1 tablespoon olive oil
1 pork loin (2 1/2 to 3 pounds)
3 cups coarse kosher salt
5 large egg whites, beaten
Tangy Cilantro Mojo (recipe follows), for serving

1. Place the garlic, parsley, oregano, sweet and hot paprikas, peppercorns, vinegar, and olive oil in a mini food processor and process until a coarse paste forms. Place the pork in a glass bowl and rub the spice paste all over it. Cover the pork with plastic wrap and refrigerate it for 4 to 6 hours. Let it come to room temperature before baking.

2. Preheat the oven to 375°F.

3. Place the salt and egg whites in a large bowl and stir until evenly moistened. The paste should just hold together. If it doesn't, sprinkle in a little water.

4. Line a rimmed baking sheet with aluminum foil and place the pork on it. Coat the pork completely with the salt paste. Bake the pork until cooked through, about 35 minutes. To test for doneness, insert an instant-read meat thermometer through the salt crust into the center of the loin; it should register 155°F. If it's not quite there yet, bake the pork 7 to 10 minutes longer.

5. Transfer the pork to a cutting board and let it rest for 5 minutes. Using a wooden spoon, tap the salt crust to crack it and lift it off in large pieces. Using a paper towel, gently wipe off any excess salt from the meat. Cut the pork into slices and serve with the Tangy Cilantro Mojo. **SERVES 6**

TANGY CILANTRO MOJO

Spicy and tangy, this sauce is inspired by the ubiquitous mortar-pounded *mojos* of the Canary Islands. It makes a terrific accompaniment to roasts or cold meats. If you want the sauce hot, leave the seeds in the serrano pepper.

1 1/2 cups fresh cilantro leaves, coarsely chopped
5 medium-size garlic cloves, chopped
1 green serrano pepper, seeded (optional) and chopped
2 teaspoons dried oregano leaves
1 teaspoon freshly ground black pepper
1/2 cup best-quality white wine vinegar
1/3 cup light olive oil
Coarse salt (kosher or sea)

Place the cilantro, garlic, serrano pepper, oregano, black pepper, vinegar, and olive oil in a blender. Add ¼ cup water and pulse to a medium-fine puree. Season with salt to taste. Transfer the sauce to a bowl and let stand until the flavors develop, about 30 minutes. **MAKES ABOUT 1 1/2 CUPS**

GYPSY PORK STEW

ESTOFADO DE CERDO A LA GITANA

Light but full-flavored, this stew of pork and spring vegetables touched with mint is a perfect treat for a cold April day. The recipe is adapted from a delightful book called *La Cocina Gitana de Matilde Amaya—Matilde Amaya's Gypsy Cooking*. The author, Matilde, is the wife of the flamenco guitarist Juan Carmona (aka Habichuelo or Bean) and mother of Juan and Antonio, members of the popular band Ketama. In the *cocina pobre* tradition, this is more of a vegetable ragout flavored with meat than a meaty stew. You can serve it with rice, but the best accompaniment is a slice of dense country bread, grilled, rubbed with garlic, and brushed with olive oil.

1 3/4 pounds pork shoulder (Boston butt), cut into 1-inch cubes
Coarse salt (kosher or sea) and freshly ground black pepper
1 3/4 cups shelled fresh fava beans (about 2 pounds unshelled), or 1 3/4 cups frozen baby lima beans (from a 10-ounce package), thawed
4 tablespoons olive oil
4 large artichokes pared down to the heart (see page 370) and quartered, or 1 package (9 ounces) frozen artichoke hearts, thawed
1 piece (3 to 4 ounces) serrano ham or prosciutto, finely diced
1 medium-size onion, chopped
4 large garlic cloves, chopped
1 teaspoon sweet (not smoked) paprika
4 canned peeled tomatoes, chopped, with 1/4 cup of their juice
2 1/2 cups chicken stock or broth
1 cup dry white wine
1 pinch of sugar
1 medium-size pinch of saffron, pulverized in a mortar and steeped in 3 tablespoons very hot water
2 medium-size Yukon Gold potatoes, peeled and cut into 1-inch chunks
1/4 cup slivered fresh mint leaves

1. Preheat the oven to 350°F.

2. Rub the pork generously with salt and pepper and let stand for 15 minutes.

3. Bring a pot of water to a boil, then add the fava beans and cook until just tender, 2 to 4 minutes. (If you are using lima beans, there is no need to precook them. Add them in Step 5.) Drain the fava beans in a colander and place it under cold running water until the beans are cool enough to handle. Gently peel the skins off the beans and set the beans aside.

4. Heat the olive oil in a 5-quart ovenproof pot over medium-high heat. Working in two batches, brown the pork lightly all over, about 5 minutes per batch. Using a slotted spoon, transfer the pork to a bowl. Add the artichoke hearts to the pot and cook until lightly browned, about 3 minutes. Using a slotted spoon, transfer the artichokes to another bowl and set aside. Add the ham to the pot and cook, stirring, for about 1 minute. Add the onion and garlic and cook until softened but not browned, about 5 minutes. Add the paprika and stir for a few seconds. Add the tomatoes with their juice and the chicken stock, wine, and sugar and bring to a boil, scraping the bottom of the pot to dislodge any brown bits. Stir in the saffron. Return the browned pork to the pot.

5. Bake the pork, covered, for 1 hour. Add the potatoes and bake until they are almost tender, about 25 minutes. Stir in the artichokes and bake, covered, for 10 minutes, then add the fava beans and continue baking until the pork and the vegetables are very tender, 10 minutes more. The stew should be a little soupy, but if you like a little thicker sauce, uncover the pot, increase the oven temperature to 400°F, and let the stew bake for 5 to 10 minutes longer.

6. Remove the stew from the oven and let it rest, covered, for about 15 minutes. Sprinkle the mint on top before serving. **SERVES 4 TO 6**

HAM I AM

Jamón ibérico is the pig's proudest moment—a cured ham so luxurious and unique the Spanish venerate it as if it were a religious cult or a pleasure-inducing drug. Who can blame them? Not even Italy's best prosciutto or Spain's own formidable serrano ham can come close to *ibérico,* with its ultrasilky texture, its deep purple-red hue, its dusky-sweet-salty-fatty-funky mystique. It's to porcine products what Château Pétrus or Vega-Sicilia Unico is to the grape universe. It's a delicacy that ranks up there with Iranian caviar and Périgord truffles.

What sets *ibérico* ham apart is the hog, the black-bristled, boarlike *ibérico* pig that is descended from an ancient Iberian race. Eager to meet these elusive porkers, I roamed the bucolic countryside of western Andalusia and Extremadura for years. One day I saw them. It was dusk, and my friend and I were driving on a deserted back road in Jabugo, where some of Spain's best ham is produced. In the distance, we spotted a herd of black, long-snouted pigs grazing lazily in their fenced-off field. We approached them. Suddenly, the pigs turned into monsters—scratching wildly against the fence and emitting such hellish oinks and squeals we felt catapulted into a scene from Dante's *Inferno*. We ran.

Anyway, back to the ham . . . Breed and feed are what contribute to the pigs' sublime flavor. While *ibérico* hogs eat very little in summer, from October to February they are let loose in *dehesas,* sylvan pastures covered with oak trees. The trees provide wild acorns—the pigs' favorite food. During the winter fattening stage, they gobble up some twenty pounds of acorns a day, increasing up to 60 percent in weight. Thanks to a combination of the acorn diet and exercise, the meat acquires gorgeous streaks of luxurious ivory fat. The fat has the unique nutty flavor of sun-ripened acorns and coats the mouth with a long-lasting aftertaste of pure pleasure. *Jamón ibérico de bellota* is the label given to the tiny fraction of hams from hogs fattened only on acorns. After the hogs meet their fate, the hind legs are salted and cured according to centuries-old artisanal methods; aging takes fourteen to thirty-six months at carefully controlled temperatures. Besides *jamones,* the pigs yield delicacies like chorizo, *paleta* (forelegs), and *lomo* (boneless loin). Fresh *ibérico* pork meat is quite a treat.

The consumption of *ibérico* ham is a highly ritualized business. Most decent tapas bars have yellow waxy *jamones* hanging from the rafters. Yet true connoisseurs favor establishments where the owner not only chooses hams from the most respected producers (Joselito, for instance) but also goes himself to the factory to handpick his wares. The ham is carved into precise rectangular slices by hand with a special long razor-sharp knife, usually wielded by a guy who's been doing this for most of his adult life. The ham is served at room temperature, sometimes on lightly warmed plates. The best—the only!—way to eat it is unadorned, with bread on the side.

Long banned in this country by the USDA, *ibérico* ham is finally due to legally arrive in the United States in 2007 or 2008. Get on a waiting list! And while you wait, consider serrano ham. Meaning from the mountains—cool mountain air is essential for the curing—*serrano* is the generic term applied to dry-cured Spanish hams. When not labeled *ibérico* (less than 10 percent of Spain's hams are), serrano ham will likely come from white pigs not fed on acorns. But the meat is still exquisite. Somewhat similar in texture and taste to *prosciutto di Parma,* it's considered superior because of its lean suppleness and depth of flavor. High-quality sliced serrano ham (usually labeled *reserva*) is a must at any good tapas bash. Use lesser-quality serrano ham for cooking; it's an essential flavor in many of the recipes in this book.

PIGS POSSESSED

"They return from the woods at night, of their own accord, and without a swine's general. On entering the hamlet, all set off at a full gallop, like a legion possessed with devils, in a handicap for home, into which each single pig turns, never making a mistake. We have more than once been caught in one of these pig-deluges, and nearly carried away horse and all."

—TRAVEL WRITER RICHARD FORD, 1830s

BRAISED AND GLAZED PORK RIBS WITH APPLESAUCE

COSTILLA DE CERDO LACADA

Slowly cooked until they fall apart at the mere touch of a fork, these ultradelicious ribs are crisped with a glaze of reduced balsamic vinegar. The recipe is from La Cuchara de San Telmo, an innovative tapas bar in San Sebastián where small, neat slabs of ribs make a substantial tapa. In a process that takes two days, the owners slow-cook the ribs for many hours, let them cool in the liquid, debone them completely, then press them into a mold for twenty-four hours so the meat forms a kind of terrine. I've simplified the procedure considerably (my version is extremely easy and takes far less time), while keeping the essence intact. Flaky sea salt is a small but important final touch to offset the sweet-tart glaze.

4 to 5 pounds baby back pork ribs
Coarse salt (kosher or sea) and freshly ground black pepper
1 cup dry red wine
2 pounds (about 4) Golden Delicious or Gala apples, peeled, cored, and chopped
2 tablespoons fresh lemon juice
1/4 cup beef stock or broth
2/3 cup balsamic vinegar
3 tablespoons soy sauce
2 tablespoons Worcestershire sauce
3 tablespoons honey
1 tablespoon sunflower oil
1 large bunch watercress, stemmed, rinsed, and dried, for serving
Flaky sea salt, such as Maldon, for serving

1. Preheat the oven to 425°F.

2. Rub the ribs generously with salt and pepper and arrange them in one layer on a very large roasting pan, cutting them into two slabs if necessary. Bake the ribs for 15 minutes, then reduce the oven temperature to 275°F and add the wine to the pan. Cover and seal the roasting pan very tightly in a double layer of aluminum foil and bake the ribs until the meat comes apart easily when you prod it with a fork, about 4½ hours.

3. While the ribs are baking, make the sauce: Place the apples, lemon juice, and ¼ cup water in a large saucepan and bring to a boil over medium-high heat, stirring from time to time. Reduce the heat to low, cover the saucepan, and cook until the apples are almost falling apart, about 25 minutes. Let the apples cool slightly, then place them in a food processor and process until a coarse puree forms.

4. Remove the ribs from the oven; increase the oven temperature to 425°F. When the meat is cool enough to handle, gently pull out the bones (they will slip out easily) and scrape off the excess fat. Cut the ribs into 8 to 12 pieces and, using a spatula, transfer them to a large baking sheet lined with aluminum foil.

5. Make the glaze: Place the beef stock, balsamic vinegar, soy and Worcestershire sauces, and honey in a medium-size saucepan. Bring to a boil over medium heat, stirring, and boil until the glaze is syrupy and has reduced to about ⅓ of a cup, about 12 minutes. Whisk in the sunflower oil.

6. Brush the ribs all over with the glaze and bake until caramelized, about 10 minutes, watching that the ribs don't burn (start checking after 5 minutes). If you'd like them more caramelized, pass them under a broiler for a few minutes, at least 6 inches away from the heat.

7. When ready to serve, reheat the applesauce on the stove top or in a microwave oven before serving. Line a large serving platter with watercress. Using a spatula, transfer the ribs to the platter and season them judiciously with flaky salt. Serve at once with the warm applesauce. **SERVES 4 TO 6**

LAMB

SEVEN HOUR LEG OF LAMB

GIGOT DE XAI A LES SET HORES

Who said that roast lamb must be rare? Mouthwatering recipes for slow-cooked lamb abound in the Mediterranean and are becoming increasingly popular in the States. Few, however, deliver the moist, you-can-eat-it-with-a-spoon meat of this one. The best slow-cooked lamb I've ever eaten was at Les Cols, a stunning restaurant in the Pyrenees where a space-age décor happily coexists with incredible neotraditional Catalan cooking. Fina Puigdevall, the chef-owner, cooks the lamb *al vacio*—vacuum-packed in plastic in a type of high-tech bain-marie. This didn't seem practical for home kitchens, so I've adapted Fina's technique, slowly roasting the lamb tightly bundled in aluminum foil in a very low oven, with a little liquid to release steam and keep the meat wonderfully moist. For a crisp crust, the lamb is browned at a high temperature before being served. The cooking time here is pretty approximate: The lamb will be delicious after about six and a half hours and can easily cook for as long as eight.

1/2 cup crumbled mixed dried herbs, such as rosemary, thyme, and mint
2 tablespoons cracked black pepper
3 tablespoons coarse salt (kosher or sea)
8 medium-size garlic cloves, crushed with a garlic press
Olive oil
1 leg of lamb (7 to 8 pounds; see Note), trimmed of all but a thin layer of fat
1 cup dry red or white wine

1. Preheat the oven to 450°F.

2. Place the herbs, pepper, salt, and garlic in a bowl and add enough olive oil to make a spreadable paste. Spread the herb paste all over the lamb and set it in a large roasting pan. Bake the lamb for 20 minutes, then reduce the oven temperature to 275°F. Pour 1 cup water into the roasting pan and cover and seal the pan very tightly with a double layer of aluminum foil. Bake the lamb for 3 hours. Uncover the pan and carefully pour out the liquid (there will be quite a lot). Set the liquid aside. Add the wine to the pan, cover it again with aluminum foil, return the lamb to the oven, and continue roasting for 3½ hours more.

3. Increase the oven temperature to 475°F. Uncover the lamb and carefully pour the liquid that has accumulated in the roasting pan into the reserved pan juices. Return the lamb to the oven and bake, uncovered, until the top is nicely browned and crisp, about 20 minutes.

4. Meanwhile, skim the fat from the pan juices, transfer them to a medium-size saucepan, and boil over high heat until reduced by one third, about 10 minutes.

5. Remove the lamb from the oven and let rest for about 10 minutes. Cut it into thick slices, place these on a platter, drizzle some of the reduced pan juices on top, and serve with the remaining pan juices on the side. **SERVES 8 TO 10**

NOTE: If you want to prepare a 5- to 6-pound shank half of a leg of lamb, reduce the cooking time to about 5 hours. A whole unboned lamb shoulder also lends itself wonderfully to this cooking method.

BRAISED LAMB SHOULDER WITH TWO WINES

CORDERO CON DOS VINOS

Adolfo Muñoz, the Toledo chef who created this recipe, is also a winemaker—which means that the guy *really* knows about cooking with wine. For braising the lamb in this rustic but elegant recipe, he uses white wine, which doesn't overshadow the flavor of the meat. After the lamb is cooked, he makes a red wine reduction from his syrah Pago del Ama to add depth to the sauce. Though your butcher might not necessarily have lamb shoulder on display, if you call ahead and ask, most will happily reserve one for you. Moist and tender, it's the ideal cut for braising.

ADOLFO—THE MAN OF LA MANCHA

Most tourists come to Toledo to gaze at the florid Gothic cathedral, visit El Greco's house, gorge on marzipan (a local specialty that goes back to the days of the Moors), and hastily soak up nine hundred years of Spanish history—a melding of Muslim, Jewish, and Christian cultures. Me? I traveled there to meet Adolfo Muñoz, owner of one of Spain's best restaurants, Adolfo. The introduction came from my friend José Carlos Capel, the revered food critic of the newspaper *El País*. "Not only will you eat and drink stupendously," Capel promised, "you'll also meet a remarkable character: a great chef, host of a daily cooking show, caterer to Spanish celebrities, winemaker, and olive grower." I packed my bags.

Walking down Toledo's cobblestoned lanes flanked by ocher facades with an occasional arabesque arch or latticework window, I finally reached Adolfo. Muñoz greeted me at the door with a vigorous handshake. Minutes later we were heading a few blocks up a moonlit street to his wine cellar. Wine cellars can be a musty yawn, but not Muñoz's. It isn't just that the collection of bottles includes complete verticals of cult Spanish labels like L'Ermita and Pingus. The cellar itself is amazing, a ninth-century house, once owned by a Jewish family, that later served as an ancient water-storage facility. "In Toledo everybody is an archaeologist by default," Muñoz said, pointing to a hearth used for baking bread and marzipan—1,100 years ago.

Adolfo, Muñoz's restaurant, started life as an *asador* (a rustic roast house) more than a quarter century ago, gradually evolving into one of the most sophisticated kitchens in Spain, highlighting regional ingredients such as saffron, oil made with cornicabra olives, Manchego cheese, and Alto Tajo truffles. The delicious results are dishes like a new-wave Strawberry and Fennel Gazpacho (page 100), a light Warm Salad of Cod and Oranges (page 117), the incredible Braised Lamb Shoulder with Two Wines (page 240), and ethereal Adolfo's Warm Chocolate Soufflé Cakes with Thyme Ice Cream (pages 418 and 437). King Juan Carlos once declared Adolfo's partridge to be the best in Spain. Julio Iglesias is another fan.

Not content just to wear a chef's toque, Muñoz also makes wine: a ripe, fruity red called Pago del Ama, which elegantly blends syrah grapes with cabernet and merlot. The next afternoon, Muñoz took me to his wine estate near his house, high in the hills above Toledo. I don't think I've ever seen a prettier spot. Centered around a *cigarral*—a traditional villa—the plot was lush, with grapevines and olive groves, juniper bushes and three-hundred-year-old oak trees. Scattered about were a few *tinajas,* huge earthenware jugs that have been used for fermenting and storing wine in the area since Roman times. As the setting sun bathed everything in a golden-pink light, Muñoz pointed to the vista of Toledo below. Perched on a craggy bluff across the river Tagus, the delicate cathedral spire and the somber towers of the *alcazar* (fortress) rose above a jumble of houses with terra-cotta roofs spilling down the hill. This could well be, he mused, the vantage point from which El Greco had painted his masterpiece *View of Toledo*.

1 boneless lamb shoulder roast (about 6 pounds)
Coarse salt (kosher or sea) and freshly ground black pepper
1/4 cup plus 2 tablespoons extra-virgin olive oil
2 bottles (each 750 milliliters) light dry white wine, such as albariño, pinot grigio, or muscadet
2 large fresh rosemary sprigs
2 large fresh thyme sprigs
2 large fresh sage sprigs
2 large fresh marjoram sprigs
1 1/2 cups dry red wine, such as syrah

1. Preheat the oven to 325°F.

2. Using kitchen string, tie the lamb shoulder crosswise, spacing the ties 1 inch apart. Rub the lamb generously with salt and pepper. Heat ¼ cup of the olive oil in a very large flameproof roasting pan set over 2 burners at medium heat. Add the lamb and brown it all over, about 5 minutes per side. Transfer the lamb to a large plate and pour off all the fat from the roasting pan.

3. Return the lamb to the roasting pan, add the white wine and 1 quart water, and bring to a boil over high heat. Add the rosemary, thyme, sage, and marjoram, cover the lamb with parchment paper, then cover the roasting pan with aluminum foil. Braise the lamb until the meat is very tender, 2½ to 2¾ hours, turning it halfway through.

4. Transfer the lamb to a cutting board and cover it with aluminum foil. Carefully pour the braising liquid into a large saucepan and skim off the fat. Bring the braising liquid to a boil over high heat, occasionally skimming off any foam, until it is reduced to about 4 cups, about 30 minutes.

5. Meanwhile, place the red wine in a medium-size saucepan and bring to a boil over high heat. Cook until reduced to about ⅔ cup, about 7 minutes. Strain the reduced lamb braising liquid into the red wine reduction, discarding the herb sprigs. Add the remaining 2 tablespoons olive oil and boil over high heat until reduced to about 2½ cups, 10 to 15 minutes. Season the sauce with salt and pepper to taste.

6. Remove the string from the lamb roast and discard it. Slice the lamb ½ inch thick and transfer it to plates. Ladle the sauce over the lamb and serve right away. **SERVES 8 TO 10**

LAMB SHANKS WITH FIVE HEADS OF GARLIC

JARRETE DE CORDERO CON CINCO CABEZAS DE AJO

It was at a country luncheon in the Aragon region that I first tasted these lamb shanks. They had a deep burnished flavor and came with whole garlic heads that had been cooked with the meat—plus there was more garlic flavoring the delicious pan juices. The combination of roasting and braising is a winning one, eliminating the fuss of browning the meat and contributing rich roasty notes. The pan juices are thin but extremely flavorful, more like *jus* than sauce. Large chunks of lamb shoulder, with some bone and trimmed of most fat, would also be good here.

Lamb Shanks with Five Heads of Garlic

- 4 large, meaty lamb shanks (about 1 1/4 pounds each)
- Coarse salt (kosher or sea) and freshly ground black pepper
- 1 large onion, cut in half, each half cut into 4 or 5 wedges
- 2 small, slender carrots, cut into chunks
- 5 small heads of garlic; 4 heads with the outer layer of skin removed, 1 head separated into cloves, each clove peeled and lightly smashed
- Olive oil
- 1 large fresh rosemary sprig
- 3/4 cup dry white wine
- About 1 1/2 cups chicken stock or broth

1. Preheat the oven to 475°F.

2. Rub the lamb generously with salt and pepper. Choose a heavy, deep, flameproof baking dish that can hold the lamb and vegetables in one snug layer and can be tightly covered. Scatter the onion, carrots, and smashed garlic cloves on the bottom of the dish, season them with salt and pepper, and toss with some olive oil. Brush the lamb shanks all over with olive oil and place them on top of the vegetables. Tuck the heads of garlic and the rosemary sprig between the lamb shanks and brush them with a little more olive oil.

3. Bake the lamb shanks, uncovered, turning once, until the meat and the vegetables are nicely browned, about 45 minutes. Check after 25 minutes, and if the vegetables in the bottom of the baking dish are beginning to burn, add a little water and reduce the oven temperature to 425°F.

4. After 45 minutes, add the wine to the baking dish and enough chicken stock to come about halfway up the meat (the garlic heads should stick out from the liquid). Cover the baking dish tightly (if it doesn't have a close-fitting lid, seal it with a double layer of aluminum foil) and reduce the oven temperature to 325°F. Bake the lamb shanks until they are extremely tender and begin to pull away from the bone, about 2 hours. Turn the shanks once or twice as they bake and add more chicken stock, if necessary, to maintain the level of liquid.

5. Transfer the lamb, vegetables, and garlic heads to a serving platter. Skim the fat off the pan juices, then transfer the juices to a sauceboat or a small pitcher. If you'd like the sauce to be thicker, place the baking dish over medium-high heat and cook until the sauce is reduced to the desired consistency. **SERVES 4**

FERRAN'S RACK OF LAMB WITH PISTACHIO PESTO

CARRE DE CORDERO CON PISTACHOS

Here's a quick and elegant recipe, adapted from Ferran Adrià's cookbook *Cocinar en Casa* (*Cooking at Home*). Though something as conventional as rack of lamb will never, ever find its way to the hyper-experimental kitchen of his restaurant, El Bulli, in this recipe Adrià demonstrates his ability to turn a few simple ingredients into much more than the sum of their parts. The pancetta is a substitute for Spanish bacon, but if it's unavailable regular bacon will also work, keeping the meat nicely moist as it roasts.

$1/3$ cup raw unsalted pistachios
1 tablespoon fresh thyme leaves
1 $1/2$ teaspoons chopped fresh rosemary
$1/3$ cup extra-virgin olive oil
Coarse salt (kosher or sea) and freshly ground black pepper
1 rack of lamb (about 1 $1/2$ pounds; 8 chops), frenched
6 thin slices pancetta, cut into 1-inch-wide strips
8 scallions, white and tender green parts, trimmed

1. Preheat the oven to 400°F.

2. Place the pistachios, thyme, and rosemary in a mini food processor. Add half of the olive oil and process to a paste. Season with salt and pepper to taste. Pour half of the pistachio pesto into a small bowl, stir in the remaining olive oil, and set aside to use as a sauce.

3. Spread some of the remaining pistachio pesto all over the lamb. Place the strips of pancetta between the bones and wrap it around the meat, leaving the bones exposed. Spread the rest of the pistachio pesto over the pancetta and place the rack in a medium-size roasting pan. Bake the lamb until an instant-read meat thermometer registers 130°F, about 40 minutes for medium-rare.

4. Transfer the lamb to a cutting board and let it rest for 5 minutes. Spoon 1 teaspoon of the rendered pancetta fat into a medium-size skillet and heat over high heat. Add the whole scallions and cook until softened and browned in spots, about 4 minutes.

5. Cut the rack of lamb into 4 servings of 2 chops each and arrange on plates, along with the scallions. Drizzle the pistachio pesto sauce all around the chops and serve at once. **SERVES 4**

SHEEP THRILLS

Spaniards might have the world's most evolved modern cuisine, yet their palates remain uncorrupted by globalization. Not for them are overwrought menus that span the globe in the course of one meal. What appeals to their purist taste is the quality of ingredients and the rigor of preparation. And they love making food pilgrimages—clocking in miles to sample famous regional specialties at their source. Topping all Spanish food journeys is the quest for *lechazo,* the roast suckling lamb that's to the parched plains of Old Castile what barbecue brisket is to central Texas. Rafael García Santos, a prominent food critic, calls *lechazo* the gastronomic banner of Spain.

Lechazo is the speciality of *asadores,* or roast houses, normally dark, burnished taverns, suffused with the scent of smoldering coals from the vaulted adobe brick ovens where the lamb roasts. Some *asadores* start you off with grilled chorizo, blood sausage, and roasted pepper, and there's always a salad. But lamb's the thing. Though shepherding has always been a way of life in Castile, in the last century wool-producing merino sheep gave way to the Churra breed—slender long-legged animals that yield milk and meat. The sheep for *lechazo* are a few weeks old, weigh about fifteen pounds, and have fed exclusively on their mother's milk. A regular order for two is a whole quarter, preferably a front one, which has plusher meat and crisper bones. The roasting is done in unglazed earthenware *cazuleas* with minimal seasoning: perhaps a smear of lard to keep the skin extra crunchy, lots of salt, and splashes of water that turn into light, amber juices as the lamb roasts. The *lechazo* is a thing of beauty, with sweet, white buttery flesh soft enough to eat with a spoon, tasting subtly of the wild grasses on which the mother sheep grazed. On top is a thin sheet of crackling skin; in your glass, a young, slightly coarse Ribera del Duero red produced somewhere down the road. No distance is too far to travel for such a meal.

LAMB CHOPS WITH PIQUILLO PEPPER MARMALADE

CHULETILLAS DE CORDERO CON MERMELADA DE PIMIENTOS DE PIQUILLO

I can smack my lips forever thinking about the incredible baby lamb chops of La Rioja. Almost as tiny as lollipops, with sweet white meat, they are either fried until crisp or grilled *al sarmiento*—over aromatic vine cuttings. Usually you get an order of slowly sautéed piquillo peppers to start or as a side dish. But here, cooked down to a marmalade with garlic, rosemary, and a touch of orange, the peppers make a delicious relish for the meat. If you can't find piquillos, use four large roasted red bell peppers, store-bought or roasted as directed on page 385.

FOR THE PIQUILLO PEPPER MARMALADE:

2 tablespoons extra-virgin olive oil
1/2 medium-size onion, cut in half and thinly sliced
3 medium-size garlic cloves, thinly sliced
8 large piquillo peppers (from a can or jar), cut into strips, plus 1 tablespoon of their oil
2 teaspoons grated orange zest
2 tablespoons fresh orange juice
1 fresh rosemary sprig
1 small bay leaf
1 teaspoon sherry vinegar, preferably aged
Coarse salt (kosher or sea) and freshly ground black pepper

FOR THE LAMB CHOPS:

8 rib lamb chops (about 1 inch thick)
Coarse salt (kosher or sea) and freshly ground black pepper
1 tablespoon crumbled dried rosemary leaves
2 tablespoons extra-virgin olive oil
3 medium-size garlic cloves, crushed with a garlic press

1. Make the piquillo pepper marmalade: Heat the olive oil in a small skillet over medium-low heat. Add the onion and cook until soft but not colored, 3 to 4 minutes. Add the garlic and cook, stirring, for 1 minute. Add the piquillo peppers and cook for 3 minutes. Add the piquillo pepper oil, orange zest, orange juice, rosemary, bay leaf, and 2 tablespoons water. Reduce the heat to very low, cover the skillet, and cook until the peppers are soft, about 10 minutes, stirring occasionally. Add a little more water if the skillet looks dry. Remove and discard the rosemary sprig and bay leaf and stir in the vinegar.

A flock of sheep in the Basque country—their milk will be used for the delicious cheese Idiazábal.

Season with salt and black pepper to taste. Let the marmalade cool to warm.

2. Light the grill and preheat it to medium-high.

3. Make the lamb chops: Rub the chops generously with salt and pepper and the dried rosemary. Place the olive oil in a shallow dish and stir in the garlic. Add the lamb chops and turn to coat with the garlic oil. Grill the chops until cooked to taste, about 4 minutes per side for medium-rare. Place 2 chops on each of 4 serving plates and top with some piquillo marmalade. Serve at once. **SERVES 4**

MALLORCAN LAMB STEW WITH DRIED FRUIT

CORDERO A LA MALLORQUINA

The Arab legacy in the cuisine of the Balearic Islands can be so pronounced that some dishes transport you straight to Morocco with their sweet-spicy flavors. A case in point is this stew enriched with dried fruit and honey, adapted from a recipe by Manuel Vázquez Montalbán, a great Catalan food writer. Of course, a bonus not encountered in Muslim cuisines is the brandy and wine that lend the dish oomph. And the *picada* of ground nuts and sweet spices added at the end is characteristic of Spain's northern Mediterranean. The ingredient list might be long, but the recipe itself is straightforward and simple. Serve the stew with couscous, rice, or new potatoes.

3 to 4 tablespoons olive oil
2 medium-size onions, diced
2 medium-size green bell peppers, cored, seeded, and diced
2 medium-size garlic cloves, minced
3 pounds boneless lamb shoulder, cut into 1 1/2-inch chunks
Coarse salt (kosher or sea) and freshly ground black pepper
All-purpose flour, for dusting the lamb
1/2 cup brandy
2 cups full-bodied dry red wine
2 1/2 cups chicken stock or broth, or water
16 to 18 pitted prunes
1/3 cup golden or brown raisins
16 toasted blanched almonds (see page 267)
1/2 tea biscuit, such as a Maria, or 1 Ritz cracker, crumbled
1 large pinch of cinnamon
1 large pinch of saffron, crumbled
1 small pinch of ground cloves
1 teaspoon brown sugar
1 tablespoon honey
1 1/2 tablespoons best-quality red wine vinegar
1/3 cup toasted pine nuts (see page 267), for garnish
Slivered fresh mint, for garnish

1. Preheat the oven to 325°F.

2. Heat 1½ tablespoons of the olive oil in a large skillet over medium heat. Add the onions, green peppers, and garlic and cook until softened and slightly browned, about 7 minutes, adding a little more olive oil if necessary. Using a slotted spoon, transfer the onion mixture to a large bowl.

3. While the onions and peppers are cooking, season the lamb generously with salt and black pepper. Spread a thin layer of flour on a large plate, then lightly dust the lamb with it. Heat 1½ tablespoons of the olive oil in a 5-quart ovenproof casserole over medium-high heat. Working in two or three batches, brown the lamb all over, transferring the browned pieces to the bowl with the onion mixture. Add the brandy to the casserole, increase the heat to high, and cook for 30 seconds, scraping the bottom of the casserole to dislodge any brown bits. Add the wine and chicken stock and bring to a boil. Return the lamb to the casserole, add the onion mixture, and stir to mix evenly. Season with salt and pepper to taste.

4. Cover the casserole and bake the lamb for 1 hour. Stir in the prunes and raisins and continue baking until the meat is very tender, 45 minutes to 1 hour longer.

5. Meanwhile, place the almonds, tea biscuit, cinnamon, saffron, cloves, and brown sugar in a mini food processor and process just until the almonds and biscuit are ground. Scrape the almond mixture into a small bowl. Add 3 to 4 tablespoons of the hot lamb cooking liquid and the honey and vinegar to the almond mixture. Stir until the honey dissolves.

6. Place the casserole with the lamb on the stove over low heat. Push the meat to one side with a large spatula and stir the almond mixture into the sauce, then stir the meat back into the sauce, coating it evenly. Cook until the flavors meld, 3 to 4 minutes. Let the stew rest, covered, for 5 to 10 minutes, then sprinkle with the pine nuts and some mint and serve. **SERVES 8**

LAMB WITH DRIED AND FRESH RED PEPPERS

CORDERO AL CHILINDRON

Where would Spanish cuisine be without the New World's tomatoes and peppers? This is a good question to contemplate over a warming bowl of *chilindrón,* a dish associated with the Navarra region but also popular in nearby La Rioja, as well as in parts of Aragon and the Basque Country. Nobody can pinpoint where the name *chilindrón* comes from—it is also used for a card game—and everyone argues over whether an authentic *chilindrón* should or should not include tomatoes. The main flavor here comes from a combination of red bell peppers and the dried smoky-sweet *pimientos choriceros* (or anchos, if you can't find the authentic item). Some versions of the stew include serrano ham or potatoes, and *chilindrón* is also popular (and delicious) prepared with chicken.

- 4 pimientos choriceros (see page 384), or 3 ancho chiles, stemmed, seeded, and torn into pieces
- 1 cup boiling chicken stock or broth, plus 1 cup room-temperature stock
- 5 tablespoons extra-virgin olive oil
- 3 large onions, finely chopped
- 2 medium-size fleshy red bell peppers, cored, seeded, and cut into strips
- 2 1/2 pounds boned lamb shoulder, cut into 1 1/2-inch chunks
- Coarse salt (kosher or sea)
- All-purpose flour, for dusting the lamb
- 1/2 cup dry white wine
- 3/4 cup chopped canned tomatoes, with about 1/4 cup of their juice
- Freshly ground black pepper
- 4 medium-size garlic cloves, minced
- 1 teaspoon black peppercorns
- 1 tablespoon best-quality red wine vinegar
- 3 tablespoons finely minced fresh flat-leaf parsley, for garnish

1. Place the *pimientos choriceros* in a heatproof bowl, add the 1 cup boiling chicken stock, and soak until the peppers are soft, about 30 minutes. Place the peppers and their soaking liquid in a blender and blend to a very smooth puree, then set the puree aside.

2. Heat 3 tablespoons of the olive oil in a large skillet over medium-low heat. Add the onions and cook until softened but not browned, 10 to 12 minutes. Stir in the red peppers and cook for 5 minutes, stirring. Cover the skillet, reduce the heat to low, and continue cooking until the onions and peppers are very soft, about 15 minutes longer, adding a tablespoon of water from time to time if the skillet looks too dry.

3. While the onions are cooking, season the lamb generously with salt. Spread a thin layer of flour on a large plate, and lightly dust the lamb with it. Heat the remaining 2 tablespoons olive oil in a heavy 5-quart casserole over medium-high heat. Working in batches, brown the lamb all over, about 5 minutes per batch, transferring the browned pieces to a bowl.

4. Once all the lamb has been browned and removed, add the wine, the remaining 1 cup chicken stock, the tomatoes with their juice, and the pepper puree to the casserole. Bring to a boil over medium-high heat, scraping the bottom of the casserole with a wooden spoon to dislodge the brown bits. Add the onion mixture, stir to mix, and return the lamb to the casserole. Season with salt and black pepper to taste. Cover the casserole, reduce the heat to low, and cook until the lamb is tender, 1½ to 1¾ hours, stirring often, as the stew tends to stick to the bottom. Alternatively, the lamb can be braised in a 325°F oven, in which case you don't need to stir it. (Braised in the oven, the juices are more concentrated, so you might want to add an extra ½ cup stock.)

5. Place the garlic, peppercorns, and a pinch of salt in a mortar and, using a pestle, crush them into a paste. Add the vinegar, then stir the paste into the stew. Cook until the flavors blend, 2 to 3 minutes. Taste for seasoning, adding more salt and/or pepper as necessary. Serve the stew at once, sprinkled with the parsley. **SERVES 4 TO 6**

BEEF AND VEAL

COCIDO: SPAIN'S FAMOUS BOILED DINNER

COCIDO

Cocido is a big multi-ingredient feast that will feed an army—soup, meat, vegetables—and still leave leftovers. The ingredients list and instructions might look involved, but there's not much more to it than throwing a bunch of stuff in a pot.

Spanish cooks tend to be militantly chauvinistic about their *cocidos,* insisting that *their* region, province, city, neighborhood, or household makes the best. Not being bound by regional rules, I have the freedom to combine the best features of *cocidos* from all around Spain. In the Catalan manner, a hefty veal knuckle flavors the broth, giving it depth. From the Alicante region, I've borrowed deliciously delicate meatballs studded with pine nuts and subtly scented with lemon peel. The thin noodles belong to Castile, while green beans (instead of the usual cabbage) are an Andalusian touch. Call it a composite *cocido.*

This recipe makes a rather large amount, so you can enjoy the yummy dishes made with *cocido* leftovers (see page 254 for some dishes to make with them).

FOR THE MEATS, CHICKPEAS & BROTH:

2 small bay leaves

1 teaspoon black peppercorns

6 medium-size garlic cloves, lightly smashed

2 fresh flat-leaf parsley sprigs

1 1/2 cups dried chickpeas, soaked overnight and drained (not quick soaked)

2 pounds veal shanks or knuckles, rinsed well

1 pound beef marrow bones or knucklebones, rinsed well

1 piece (6 ounces) serrano ham or prosciutto

1 piece (1/2 pound) smoky, meaty slab bacon

2 pounds boneless beef shin, shank, chuck (preferably arm or shoulder), or brisket

1 chicken (about 3 1/2 pounds), rinsed well a nd trimmed of excess fat

1 large carrot, scraped

1 large onion stuck with a few cloves

12 ounces sweet Spanish-style chorizo sausage

6 ounces morcilla or other blood sausage (see Notes)

FOR THE MEATBALLS (OPTIONAL):

1 slice white sandwich bread, crust removed

1/4 pound ground pork

1/4 pound chicken or turkey sausages, casings removed

1 large egg, beaten

1/4 cup pine nuts

1/2 teaspoon grated lemon zest

1/2 teaspoon salt

1/2 teaspoon freshly ground black pepper

A few gratings of nutmeg

1 medium-size pinch of ground cinnamon

1 1/2 tablespoons minced fresh flat-leaf parsley

Alicante's magnificent Explanada de España, with its palm trees and cafés, is well designed for a Spanish favorite, the *paseo*—an evening stroll.

FOR THE VEGETABLES AND SOUP:

About 2 pounds small new potatoes, scrubbed

Coarse salt (kosher or sea)

1 1/4 pounds green beans, trimmed

1 cup fideo noodles or thin vermicelli, broken into 1-inch lengths

FOR SERVING:

Minted Tomato Vinaigrette (recipe follows)

A green salad dressed with lemon juice and extra-virgin olive oil

1. Prepare the meat, chickpeas, and broth: Place the bay leaves, peppercorns, garlic, and parsley sprigs in a small piece of cheesecloth and tie it closed. Wrap and tie the chickpeas in a large square piece of cheesecloth, so you can easily remove them later.

2. Place the veal shanks, beef bones, serrano ham, bacon, beef shin, and chicken in a very large, heavy stockpot. Add 4½ quarts (18 cups) water and bring to a boil over high heat. Thoroughly skim off the foam. Add the cheesecloth bags of herbs and chickpeas and the carrot and onion and bring back to a boil, skimming. Cover the pot, reduce the heat to low, and simmer for 1 hour (the liquid should barely bubble). Using a slotted spoon, transfer the chicken to a large bowl and cover it with aluminum foil. Cook the broth for another 45 minutes, then transfer the ham and bacon to the bowl with the chicken. The beef and bones should still be in the pot.

3. Meanwhile, bring about 2 quarts water to a boil. Add the chorizo and blood sausage and blanch for 2 minutes. Using a slotted spoon, transfer the sausages to the pot with the beef. Keep the water in which you blanched the sausages at a simmer.

COCIDO OPTIONS

When making *cocido,* feel free to be flexible about the specific ingredients and amounts. The meatballs are delicious but optional. To flavor the broth, you'll need some good gelatinous bones and something smoky, like serrano ham, bacon, salt pork, pancetta, or a ham bone. The best meat is a marbled cut, like shin or chuck, but you can use oxtails, short ribs, a two-pound hunk of pork shoulder, and/or a small, meaty veal breast. Poultry can be a whole chicken or just a few thighs. For the vegetables—besides the obligatory chickpeas and potatoes—consider cabbage, pumpkin, or leeks. If Spanish chorizo and *morcilla* (blood sausage) are unavailable, use good pork and/or chicken sausages. Many Spanish cooks insist that the chorizo and *morcilla* sausages "corrupt" the taste of the broth and should be cooked separately. Personally, I like the flavor they impart to the cooking liquid, but purists can cook them in the pot with the vegetables.

4. Make the meatballs, if using: Place the bread and a little of the liquid from the meat pot in a small bowl and let soak for a few minutes. Drain, squeeze out the excess liquid, and finely crumble the bread. Finely chop enough of the reserved bacon to measure ¼ cup; set the remaining bacon aside. Place the chopped bacon, bread, ground pork, chicken sausages, egg, pine nuts, lemon zest, salt, pepper, nutmeg, cinnamon, and parsley in a food processor. Pulse until well combined but not minced or pureed. Scrape the mixture into a bowl. Wet your hands, then shape the meatball mixture into 2½-inch ovals, gently tossing them between two cupped hands to give them shape. Add the meatballs to the simmering water and cook for 2 minutes. Using a slotted spoon, transfer the meatballs to the pot with the beef and bones. Simmer until the beef shin is extremely tender, 45 minutes. The total cooking time for the meat should be 2½ to 3 hours. (The *cocido* can be prepared to this point 1 day in advance; see Notes, page 255.)

5. While the beef and meatballs are simmering, prepare the vegetables and soup: Place the potatoes in a large pot and add cold water to cover by 4 inches. Bring to a boil over high heat, add salt, reduce the heat to medium-low, and cook, partially covered, until the potatoes are almost tender, about 15 minutes. Add the green beans to the pot and cook until the potatoes and beans are very tender, about 7 minutes. Drain the vegetables and transfer them to a large serving platter, leaving room for the chickpeas. Carefully remove the cheesecloth bag with the chickpeas from the meat pot. Working over a sieve, cut the bag open to release the chickpeas. Add the chickpeas to the vegetable platter. Sprinkle the vegetables with a little of the hot broth from the meat pot, season them with salt, and keep warm, covered with aluminum foil.

6. Skim off as much fat as you can from the broth in the meat pot. Line a sieve with cheesecloth. Ladle by ladle, strain about 8 cups of the broth through the cheesecloth-lined sieve into a clean pot. (Figure on about 1 cup broth per person.) Bring the strained broth to a boil over medium-high heat. Add the noodles and cook until just tender, about 7 minutes.

7. While the noodles are cooking, using a slotted spoon remove and discard the bones, carrot, onion, and cheesecloth bag of herbs from the meat pot. Return the reserved chicken, ham, and bacon (all or what remains, if you used some in the meatballs) to the pot and cook until warmed through.

EVERY SPANIARD LOVES A BOILED DINNER

Paella belongs to Valencia and gazpacho to Andalusia, while *fabada* is the specialty of Asturias. *Cocido,* however, is truly Spain's national dish, a one-pot feast enjoyed in every part of the country. Most *cocidos* include sturdy vegetables, legumes, and an assortment of meats and charcuterie ranging from modest to regal. Simmered in water for hours, they yield two courses: first, a rich amber broth with pasta or rice, then platters of meats and vegetables. Meaning boiled, *cocido* is the offspring of the mythical *olla podrida,* or rotten pot (see page 317), the mother of all Spanish one-dish meals. While the exact composition varies somewhat from region to region, the essence of a *cocido* remains the same: a hearty multi-ingredient pot that was once weekly fare but these days is mainly served for special occasions and always eaten for lunch.

Catalan *cocido, escudella i carn d'olla* (*escudella* means bowl) is a Christmas tradition. Besides the prerequisite chickpeas and bacony things, it has veal, mild *butifarra* sausages, big fluffy meatballs *(pilotas),* and a broth afloat with pasta shells called *galets.* An Andalusian *cocido* consists of *berzas* (vegetables such as cardoons, pumpkin, and chard) and *pringá* (a collective term for meats like blood sausage, chorizo, bacon, and pork), with a broth tinted yellow by saffron and often speckled with mint. In the Mediterranean Alicante, the pot might contain turkey along with extra-succulent meatballs scented with cinnamon and grated lemon peel and wrapped in cabbage leaves. In a Galician *cocido* you will find salt-cured pork ribs, pork shoulder, and possibly turnip greens. In the Canary Islands, corn on the cob, tropical tubers, pears, and seven different meats flavor the pot. And don't forget the scrumptious *cocido maragato* of the Castilian province of León, which is served in reverse order, starting with meat, progressing to vegetables, and ending with soup. As for the meatballs that feature in so many *cocido* recipes—variously called *bolas, relleno, pelotas, farcedures*—one could write a whole book about these!

In Madrid, *cocido* remains a grand luncheon tradition maintained by old institutions like Lhardy. There you indulge in it surrounded by somber oil paintings, ornate cupboards laden with what looks like church silver, and frail old couples who vigorously devour blood sausage and tripe. And there's La Bola, an ancient folksy *taberna* where the smoky (and very heavy) *cocido* simmers over hot coals and is served in potbellied earthenware jugs. The three courses of classic *cocido madrileño*—broth with fine noodles, chickpeas and vegetables, and finally meats—are known as *sota, caballo,* and *rey.* These can be roughly translated as jack, queen, and king, meaning that the dishes you're dealt get more noble as the meal moves along. And when the huge heaps of vegetables and meats are gone, you fall into a *cocido*-induced stupor. Siestas were invented for dishes like this.

8. Using a slotted spoon, transfer the chicken, sausages, meatballs, bacon, ham, beef, and veal to a big bowl. Keep the broth in the meat pot hot. Cut or slice all the meats, sausages, chicken, and meatballs into serving pieces, removing and discarding any gristle and bones. Arrange the meats on a large platter, sprinkle with hot broth from the meat pot, and keep warm, covered with aluminum foil.

9. Serve the *cocido*: Ladle the soup and the noodles into shallow soup bowls and serve this first. Follow it with the meat and the vegetables platter, accompanied by Minted Tomato Vinaigrette and a pitcher of hot broth from the meat pot for moistening the meat and the vegetables. Follow with salad to cleanse the palate. **SERVES 8 WITH LEFTOVERS**

COCIDO: A SECOND TIME AROUND

Cocido is a big hearty family feast meant to be enjoyed for a Sunday lunch and then provide light meals for days to come. Not surprisingly, *cocido* leftovers are legion. Here are seven favorite ways of using them.

BAKED RICE: For Spaniards, rice baked in the rich *cocido* broth is the ultimate comfort food. Heat a couple of tablespoons of olive oil with a few minced garlic cloves in a medium-size casserole and stir for a minute. Add a large grated tomato, cook for a few minutes more, then add some paprika. Stir in 1 cup short-grain Spanish rice or Italian risotto rice along with some chickpeas from the *cocido* and diced chorizo and blood sausage. Add 2 cups of strained *cocido* broth, some minced parsley, and a pinch of crumbled saffron; bring to a boil. Cover and bake in a 400°F oven until the rice is tender, about 18 minutes. Uncover, and let stand for 10 minutes before serving.

CROQUETTES: The first thing a Spanish cook will do with *cocido* leftovers is make delicious crispy, fluffy *croquetas*. Shred, mince, and mash enough of the beef, chicken, veal, chorizo, and potatoes from the *cocido* to measure 1 heaping cup. Then make croquettes, following the recipe on page 64, omitting the mushrooms and truffle oil.

HASH: This is an Andalusian specialty called *ropa vieja,* or old clothes (in Cuba, the name describes a shredded flank steak braised in tomato sauce). Heat a couple of tablespoons of olive oil in a skillet with a few cloves of minced garlic. Add some chopped meats, sausages, and vegetables from the *cocido* and stir for a few minutes. Add 1 to 2 tablespoons of tomato sauce and a little *cocido* broth and let simmer for a few minutes more. Sprinkle with parsley and serve with fried or poached eggs—my favorite breakfast!

OMELET: *Tortilla de ropa vieja* was an unforgettably succulent specialty at Bar Astelena in San Sebastián. Alas, the bar has closed, but the recipe lives on. Thinly slice 2 medium-size yellow onions and cook them in olive oil over low heat until very soft but not browned. Transfer to a bowl and let cool, then toss with 2 cups of shredded beef, veal, and chicken from the *cocido*. In a separate bowl, beat 6 large eggs. Stir the eggs into the meat mixture, add some minced parsley, 2 tablespoons of *cocido* broth, and salt. Fry the tortilla as directed in the Potato Tortilla recipe (page 139).

Even chefs need an occasional coffee break.

PRINGA: The very best thing one can order at an Andalusian tapas bar is a *pringá:* a toasted *chapata* roll filled with mashed-up meats and sausages from a *cocido* and cooked in a press. Mince skinned blood sausages and chorizo, bacon, ham, and a bit of veal or beef from the *cocido* and fry them briefly in a little olive oil, moistening them with a little broth. Split a small, dense flat roll (an Italian *ciabatta* is best), brush it with olive oil, and toast or griddle it split side down. Fill the roll with the meat mixture, sprinkling on a little hot sauce or some julienned piquillo pepper, if you wish, then heat in a sandwich press. If you don't have a sandwich press, you can improvise one by placing a flat plate weighed down with something heavy, like a 28-ounce can of tomatoes or beans, on top of the sandwich.

SALAD: *Cocido* leftovers also make a tasty salad called *salpicón*. Shred or dice about 3 cups of beef, chicken, and veal from the *cocido*. Add a handful of cooked chickpeas and some diced boiled potatoes and string beans. Toss with thinly sliced red onion and lots of minced parsley. Dress with a good olive oil and some sherry vinegar or red wine vinegar.

TERRINE: Tear or cut the beef, chicken, bacon, and ham from the *cocido* into enough bite-size pieces to measure 2 cups. Toss in some capers and chopped cornichons, diced boiled potatoes and string beans, a handful of cooked chickpeas, lots of minced parsley, 2 to 3 tablespoons of lemon juice; and 2 crushed garlic cloves. Line a 4-cup loaf pan with plastic wrap, leaving some overhang, and place the mixture in it.

Place a packet of gelatin and 2 tablespoons of cold water in a small saucepan to soften. Add 2 cups of strained *cocido* broth and heat, stirring to dissolve the gelatin. Let cool slightly, then pour the gelatin mixture over the meat mixture. Cover with aluminum foil, chill until set, and unmold onto a plate. Serve for supper with an assortment of mustards and a salad of peppery greens.

NOTES: If blood sausage is unavailable, increase the amount of chorizo to 18 ounces or substitute 6 ounces of fresh pork or turkey sausages for them.

I suggest preparing the *cocido* a day ahead through Step 4, so you can strain and degrease the broth for the soup at your leisure. Let the *cocido* cool down a bit, then ladle out 8 cups of the broth from the meat pot. Strain it through a cheesecloth-lined sieve into a storage container. Cover and refrigerate. Pick through the meat pot, discarding the bones, the bag of herbs, and the vegetables. Remove the chickpea bag, wrap it in aluminum foil, and refrigerate. Prepare the meats as described in Step 8, return them to the remaining broth in the meat pot, and store, covered, in the refrigerator. The next day, continue with the recipe, degreasing and reheating the 8 cups of broth separately from the broth in the meat pot. Reheat the bag of chickpeas in the pot with the meat, and add them to the vegetable platter as described in Step 5.

MINTED TOMATO VINAIGRETTE

VINAGRETA DE TOMATE A LA MENTA

This refreshing Andalusian-inflected sauce is delicious on grilled or boiled meat. Make it up to four hours ahead so the flavors can meld.

- 1 pound ripe but firm tomatoes, blanched, peeled, and chopped
- 6 tablespoons extra-virgin olive oil
- 7 to 8 tablespoons best-quality red wine vinegar
- 2 large garlic cloves, chopped
- 1/2 teaspoon cumin seeds
- 1 large pinch of salt, or more to taste
- 1 teaspoon dried mint

1. Place the tomatoes in a mini food processor and pulse until minced but not pureed. Scrape into a bowl and stir in the olive oil and the vinegar.

2. Place the garlic, cumin, and salt in a mortar and, using a pestle, mash them into a paste. Add 3 to 4 tablespoons cold water and stir into the tomato mixture. Add the mint and taste for seasoning, adding salt to taste. Let stand for at least 30 minutes for the flavors to develop. Serve with the *cocido*. **MAKES ABOUT 1 1/2 CUPS**

ASTURIAN BEEF STEW

GUISO DE TERNERA A LA ASTURIANA

Whenever you see a recipe for a folksy dish that features turnips, meat, and smoked porkstuffs, you can pretty much bet it's from the mountainous region of Asturias. This stew is great rib-sticking fare for a cold winter night.

- 3 pounds well-marbled beef chuck, cut into 1 1/2-inch chunks
- Coarse salt (kosher or sea) and freshly ground black pepper
- 3 tablespoons olive oil
- 4 ounces best-quality smoky slab bacon or pancetta, cut into medium-size dice
- 1 medium-size white onion, chopped
- 5 large garlic cloves, minced
- 2 fat carrots, diced
- 2 tablespoons all-purpose flour
- 3/4 cup dry white wine
- 3 cups chicken stock or broth
- 1 cup dried white beans, such as cannellini or navy beans, soaked overnight and drained or quick soaked (see page 309)
- 6 canned plum tomatoes, chopped, plus 1/3 cup of their juice
- 12 ounces turnips (2 medium-size), peeled and cut into 1-inch chunks (see Notes)
- 4 cups chopped, well-rinsed turnip greens, tough stems removed (see Notes)

1. Preheat the oven to 300°F.

2. Season the meat generously with salt and pepper. Heat 1 tablespoon of the olive oil in a heavy, wide 5-quart ovenproof casserole over medium-high heat. Add half of the beef to the casserole and brown on all sides, about 10 minutes. Using a slotted spoon, transfer the browned beef to a bowl. Add 1 tablespoon of olive oil to the casserole. Brown the remaining beef, then transfer it to a bowl.

3. Add the remaining 1 tablespoon olive oil and the bacon to the casserole, reduce the heat to medium, and cook, stirring, until the bacon begins to render its fat, about 2 minutes. (If it seems to be rendering too much fat, spoon some off.) Add the onion, garlic, and carrots, increase the heat to medium-high, and cook, stirring, until the vegetables begin to brown, about 8 minutes. Add the flour and stir for a few seconds. Gradually add the wine, stirring to combine thoroughly with the flour, then add the chicken stock. Bring to a boil, scraping the bottom of the casserole to dislodge the brown bits.

4. Return the meat and any accumulated juices to the casserole and add the beans and the tomatoes with their liquid. Return to a boil, skim if necessary, then season with salt and pepper to taste. Cover the casserole and bake for 2 hours. Stir in the turnips and 1 cup water and bake until the meat and the beans are very tender, 30 to 50 minutes longer.

5. Bring a pot of water to a boil. Add the turnip greens and blanch until wilted and just tender, 2 minutes (sturdier greens such as kale or collards will take a little longer). Drain the greens in a colander, pressing against them to squeeze out excess moisture.

6. Taste the stew for seasoning, adding more salt and/or pepper as necessary. Stir the greens into the stew and let rest for about 5 minutes before serving.
SERVES 6

NOTES: Turnip greens are sold on their own at some markets or you can simply snip a bunch off turnips or daikon radish. If they're not available, use another sturdy green, such as mustard greens, kale, or collard greens.

Not a turnip fan? Substitute a pound of potatoes cut into wedges.

Sol y Sombra, in Seville's evocative Triana quarter, is among the city's favorite bars.

MEATY OXTAIL STEW TORERO STYLE

RABO DE TORO

Enjoyed all over the country, the macho, full-bodied dish *rabo de toro* is most closely associated with Andalusia, a region particularly crazy for bullfighting. Connoisseurs insist that the best time to indulge in oxtail stew is the day after a *corrida*, and that it should be ordered at a *taurino* tavern near a bullring, where it will be prepared with the tail of a fallen bull. By eating it, one absorbs some of the heroic bravery of the animal—at least that's the theory.

Long, slow cooking is the secret to a good oxtail stew. "Just put the pot on the stove and forget it exists," suggested one cook in Seville. Spanish oxtails are incredibly meaty and rich; if you can't find excellent oxtail, try short ribs. The dish is best prepared ahead; that way you can easily skim off the fat and the flavors get a chance to develop. My favorite side dish for this is the Potato and Onion Gratin with Allioli (page 320).

- 4 1/2 to 5 pounds meaty oxtails
- Coarse salt (kosher or sea) and freshly ground black pepper
- All-purpose flour, for dusting the oxtails
- 4 to 5 tablespoons olive oil
- 1 large onion, chopped
- 5 medium-size garlic cloves, chopped
- 2 medium-size carrots, diced
- 1 small leek, white part only, rinsed thoroughly, cut in half lengthwise, and sliced
- 4 to 5 ounces cremini or portobello mushrooms, wiped clean with a damp paper towel and coarsely chopped
- 1 teaspoon sweet (not smoked) paprika
- 1/2 cup brandy, preferably Spanish
- 1 small bay leaf
- 1 fresh thyme sprig
- 2 1/2 cups full-bodied dry red wine
- 1 1/2 cups chicken stock or broth
- 1 1/2 cups plum tomatoes, chopped, with 1/2 cup of their juice

1. Place the oxtails in a large bowl and season generously with salt and pepper. Spread a thin layer of flour on a plate and, working in batches, dust the oxtails with flour.

2. Heat 2 tablespoons of the olive oil in a heavy 5- to 6-quart casserole over medium-high heat. Working in batches, brown the oxtails all over until richly browned, 8 to 10 minutes per batch, transferring the browned oxtails to a large bowl.

3. Add 2 tablespoons of the olive oil and the onion, garlic, carrots, leek, and mushrooms to the casserole. Cook until the vegetables are softened and browned, about 7 minutes, adding the remaining oil and adjusting the heat so the bottom of the casserole doesn't burn. Add the paprika and stir for a few seconds. Add the brandy, scraping the bottom of the casserole to dislodge the brown bits. Add the bay leaf, thyme, 2 cups of the wine, the chicken stock, and tomatoes and bring to a boil, skimming any foam off the surface. Season with salt to taste, then return the oxtails and their accumulated juices to the casserole. Reduce the heat to very low, cover the casserole, and simmer until the oxtails are very tender, 2½ to 3 hours. (The stew can be prepared to this point up to 1 day ahead and stored, covered, in the refrigerator.)

4. Skim as much fat as possible off the top of the stew, then, if it has been refrigerated, reheat it slowly. Using a slotted spoon, transfer the oxtails to a large bowl. Add the remaining ½ cup wine to the casserole, increase the heat to high, and cook until the pan juices are nicely thickened, 12 to 15 minutes. Return the oxtails to the casserole, turning them to coat with the pan juices, and cook until heated through, 1 to 2 minutes. Transfer to a serving bowl and serve. **SERVES 6**

GRILL GRAILS

If in Castile you go to an *asador* to indulge in roast lamb, in the Basque Country *asadores* are grill restaurants specializing in fish at the shore and meat in the hinterlands. The meat to eat at an *asador* is *chuleta:* a heroic rib chop cut from a Galician or Danish cow. And one of the best places to eat it is Casa Julián in the town of Tolosa. You enter through a fabulously ramshackle garage, claim one of the six tables, and watch the burly, mustachioed proprietor tend to his bovine masterpieces sizzling on a specially constructed sloped grill. The indelible aroma of fatty, dark-juiced expert grilling wafts over you from just feet away. Then the steak lands on your table—beautifully rare, thick as *War and Peace,* profoundly charred, and gorgeously crusted with salt. There are no heaped fries or hash browns in sight, no salads chockablock with tomatoes and onions, no steak sauce. Casa Julián, in fact, serves only four things: steak, stalks of white Navarra asparagus as big as cigar tubes, fruity-sweet sheets of roasted piquillo peppers, and some of Spain's best *ibérico* ham. With a dusty bottle of Rioja *reserva* for company.

Casa Julián's steak is pretty transcendent, but the region's greatest *asador* is Etxebarri in the village of Axpe. Etxebarri is Spain's premier *restaurante de producto:* with each morsel of food brought by the grill to its ultimate expression, a state of almost surreal perfection. It's to a rustic grill house what Einstein is to your high school physics teacher. Víctor Arguinzoniz, the owner, grew up on a farm with the aromas of woodsmoke; in his youth he eked out a living gathering firewood. In his quest to push barbecue to a higher plane, he makes his own charcoal from various woods—oak for fish; old vines for meat—and invents new techniques and equipment, such as a movable rack used to regulate the food's distance from the smoldering coals. Each millimeter counts; each new dish brings a distinct nuanced smokiness. The *chuleta* here, aged for three weeks, and grilled by a novel technique that cooks both sides simultaneously—is as much a miracle of engineering as it is an awe-inspiring slab of protein.

GRILLED T-BONES WITH CABRALES BUTTER

CHULETONES CON MANTEQUILLA DE CABRALES

Making a trip to a country *asador* (grill restaurant) that specializes in T-bone steaks is a sacred ritual in the Basque Country. It goes without saying that the dish is only as good as the meat: If you want something transcendent, get dry-aged prime T-bones. Can't find Cabrales cheese for the butter? Use Roquefort, which is one of the most popular cheeses in Spain. Serve this steak with grilled or roasted red peppers, simple sautéed greens, such as spinach or chard, and a baked potato—all of which taste delicious with a pat of the Cabrales butter. A bottle of good Ribera del Duero is fairly obligatory.

4 tablespoons (1/2 stick) unsalted butter, at room temperature
6 tablespoons Cabrales cheese or Roquefort, finely mashed
Coarse salt (kosher or sea) and freshly ground black pepper
4 T-bone steaks (about 12 ounces each)
1 tablespoon extra-virgin olive oil
Flaky sea salt, such as Maldon

1. Place the butter and Cabrales in a small bowl, stir to blend, and season to taste with salt and pepper. Place the Cabrales butter on a piece of plastic wrap, shape it into a log, and wrap it in the plastic. Refrigerate until firm, about 1 hour.

2. Place the steaks in a large, shallow dish and rub them generously with salt and pepper and the olive oil; let stand for 30 minutes.

3. Light the grill and preheat it to medium-high.

4. Grill the steaks until done to taste, about 5 minutes per side for medium-rare. (An instant-read meat thermometer inserted diagonally into the thickest part of a steak but not touching the bone will register 125°F for medium-rare.)

5. Transfer the grilled steaks to a platter and let rest for about 5 minutes. Cut the Cabrales butter into 4 slices. Top each steak with a piece of butter and serve with a small bowl of flaky sea salt alongside. **SERVES 4**

VARIATION: Steaks are also delicious cooked *a la plancha*—seared in a dry cast-iron skillet or griddle that's been preheated over high heat for 6 to 7 minutes (turn off your smoke alarms). If you're searing rather than grilling, I recommend a boneless cut, such as rib eye, as the bone in a T-bone prevents the meat from searing evenly. Sear the steaks without crowding them for 3 to 4 minutes per side.

GRILLED SKIRT STEAK WITH ALMOND & CAPER SALSA

FALDA DE TERNERA CON VINAGRETA DE ALMENDRAS Y ALCAPARRAS

Though grilled skirt steak isn't particularly Spanish—the huge popularity of Argentinean steak houses in Spain notwithstanding—this one, with its zestful salsa of almonds, olives, capers, and parsley, does taste Iberian. The salsa, inspired by a recipe from the great Basque chef Juan Mari Arzak, is also delicious on grilled chicken or firm fish, such as swordfish.

FOR THE SALSA:

1/3 cup lightly toasted blanched almonds (see page 267)
1/3 cup chopped fresh flat-leaf parsley
3 to 4 tablespoons chopped pitted dark olives, such as niçoise or Gaeta
2 tablespoons drained capers
2 medium-size garlic cloves, chopped
1 teaspoon sweet (not smoked) paprika
1 teaspoon coarsely ground black pepper
1 tablespoon best-quality red wine vinegar
1/2 cup light olive oil
1 1/2 teaspoons balsamic vinegar
Coarse salt (kosher or sea)

FOR THE STEAK:
2 pounds skirt steak, cut crosswise into 4-inch pieces
Coarse salt (kosher or sea) and freshly ground black pepper

1. Make the salsa: Place the almonds in a mini food processor and grind them medium-fine (they should have some texture), then transfer them to a bowl. Add the parsley, olives, capers, garlic, paprika, pepper, red wine vinegar, and 2 to 3 tablespoons of the olive oil to the processor. Pulse until all the ingredients are finely chopped but not pureed. Add the parsley mixture to the bowl with the almonds, along with the remaining olive oil and the balsamic vinegar. Stir to combine, season the salsa with salt to taste, and let stand for about 30 minutes for the flavors to develop.

2. Prepare the steak: Light the grill and preheat it to medium-high or heat an oiled, ridged grill pan over medium-high heat until almost smoking.

3. Rub the steaks generously with salt and pepper. Working in two batches, grill the steaks, turning once or twice, until done to taste, 6 to 8 minutes total per batch for medium-rare, depending on thickness. Serve with the salsa. **SERVES 4 TO 6**

CATALAN CUISINE

FROM SOFREGIT TO PICADA

Countless Catalan stews begin with a *sofregit* and end with a *picada,* the two basic elements that, according to Catalan writer Manuel Vázquez Montalbán, define the final flavor of the region's cuisine. An authentic *sofregit* (*sofrito* in Castillian Spanish) is a mixture of onions and often tomatoes, garlic, and parsley, traditionally cooked down for hours until rich and caramelized. *Sofregit* is the base that lends Catalan stews and soups their typical burnished depth. When the dish is nearly ready, it's usually finished with a *picada,* a mortar-pounded paste that both enlivens and thickens it. *Picadas* can be as elemental as a blend of fresh garlic and parsley. Or they can include nuts, fried bread, butter biscuits, chicken or game livers, wine, saffron, even chocolate. Both *sofregit* and *picada* go back to medieval Catalan cooking.

VEAL FRICANDO WITH MUSHROOMS & HAZELNUTS

FRICANDO DE VEDELLA

Veal cooked in a soulful sauce fragrant with wild mushrooms, *fricandó* is Catalan bourgeois home cooking par excellence. It is a preparation that exists in several European cuisines—usually as a fricassee. But the Catalans, who have been making *fricandó* since the eighteenth century, have elevated and enshrined it. The meat, they insist, should be cutlets from a tough economical cut, like shin, which benefits from slow cooking. The classic *fricandó* mushrooms are moixernons, tiny and earthy and available only in the spring. Taking a cue from Carles Abellan, the inventive Barcelona chef who offers tweaked versions of Catalan classics at his restaurant, Comerç 24, I add rosé wine to the sauce and serve the dish sprinkled with some of the ground toasted hazelnuts that go into the *picada* (here, one that also includes a touch of chocolate for extra richness and depth). *Fricandó* is classically served with Spinach with Raisins and Pine Nuts (page 388).

- 1/2 ounce dried porcini mushrooms
- 1 cup boiling chicken stock or broth
- 6 tablespoons extra-virgin olive oil
- 1/2 pound small chanterelles or other delicate wild mushrooms, wiped clean with damp paper towels and chopped if large
- Coarse salt (kosher or sea) and freshly ground black pepper
- 2 pounds veal cutlets (1/3 to 1/4 inch thick) cut from the shoulder or leg
- All-purpose flour, for dusting the veal
- 1 large onion, finely chopped
- 1 medium-size carrot, finely diced
- 6 large garlic cloves, chopped
- 3 medium-size tomatoes, cut in half and grated on a grater, then skins discarded
- 1/2 cup dry but fruity rosé wine, or more if needed
- 1/3 cup hazelnuts, lightly toasted and skinned (page 267)
- 1 tablespoon grated bittersweet chocolate
- 2 tablespoons minced fresh flat-leaf parsley, plus more for garnish

1. Place the dried porcini and the boiling stock in a small heatproof bowl and let soak until softened, 30 minutes. Drain the porcini in a small sieve lined with a coffee filter or cheesecloth, setting aside the soaking liquid. Chop the porcini and set aside.

2. Heat 2 tablespoons of the olive oil in a large, deep skillet over medium-high heat. Add the chanterelles and cook, stirring, until they are lightly browned and release and reabsorb their liquid, 5 to 7 minutes. Season the cooked mushrooms with salt and pepper to taste and set aside. Wipe out the skillet.

3. Season the veal generously with salt and pepper. Spread a thin layer of flour on a large plate and lightly dust the veal in the flour. Add 2 tablespoons olive oil to the skillet and heat over medium-high heat. Working in batches, cook the veal cutlets until lightly browned, about 2 minutes per side, transferring the browned cutlets to a bowl. When all the cutlets have been browned, add the remaining 2 tablespoons olive oil and the onion, carrot, garlic, and the chopped porcini to the skillet. Cook until the vegetables are softened and lightly browned, 5 to 7 minutes. Add the tomatoes, increase the heat to high, and cook until the tomatoes are slightly thickened and reduced, about 5 minutes. Add the ½ cup wine and the reserved mushroom soaking liquid and bring to a boil, scraping the bottom of the skillet to dislodge the brown bits. Add the veal and turn to coat it with the sauce. Cover the skillet, reduce the heat to low, and simmer until the sauce is rich tasting and the meat is extremely tender, about 45 minutes.

4. While the veal is cooking, make the *picada*: Place the hazelnuts in a mini food processor and coarsely grind them. Remove half of the hazelnuts from the food processor and set aside for garnish. Finely grind the remaining hazelnuts. Add the chocolate and the 2 tablespoons parsley and pulse to combine.

5. When the veal is done, transfer the cutlets to a bowl and cover with aluminum foil to keep warm. Add the cooked chanterelle mushrooms to the sauce and cook until warmed through, about 1 minute. If the sauce seems too thick, add more wine. Stir the *picada* into the sauce and cook, stirring, over medium-low heat until the chocolate melts and the sauce is rich and flavorful, about 1 minute. Return the veal to the skillet, turn to coat it in the sauce, and cook until warmed through, 2 to 3 minutes. Transfer the veal to a serving dish, pour the sauce on top, and sprinkle the reserved coarsely ground hazelnuts and the parsley over it. **SERVES 6 TO 8**

VARIATION: *Fricandó* is also delicious made with beef: Use ½-inch-thick chuck or round steaks and cook them for about 1½ hours, adding a little extra stock to keep the sauce moist.

VEAL SHANKS WITH BABY TURNIPS AND PEARS

JARRET DE VEDELLA AMB NAPS I PERES

Veal, turnips, and pears—what could be more Catalan? This deeply delicious dish comes from a small restaurant in Catalonia's Puigcerdà region (close to the border with Andorra), famous for its ungainly looking but fabulously flavorful pears. In typical Catalan fashion, the dish begins with a *sofregit* (a *sofrito*) and ends with a *picada* of ground hazelnuts that enlivens the sauce. If you love osso buco, you'll go nuts for this dish (do make sure to scoop out the delicious marrow and spread it on toast). Rather not tackle veal shanks? Try the recipe with a tied four-pound boneless veal or pork shoulder (if you're using a boneless cut you won't need quite as much liquid).

- 6 meaty crosscut (osso buco cut) veal shanks (about 1 pound each)
- Coarse salt (kosher or sea) and freshly ground black pepper
- 5 tablespoons olive oil
- 1 small onion, chopped
- 1 fat carrot, chopped
- 1 can (14 1/2 ounces) tomatoes, drained and chopped
- 2 cups dry white wine
- 3 cups chicken stock or broth
- 1 fresh rosemary sprig
- 1 fresh thyme sprig
- 1 bay leaf
- 1 small cinnamon stick
- 12 whole baby turnips, or 6 small regular turnips, peeled and halved
- 6 slightly under-ripe small baby pears, such as Forelle or Seckel
- 2 large pinches of sugar
- 12 hazelnuts, toasted and skinned (see page 267)
- 2 medium-size garlic cloves, chopped
- 1 tea biscuit, such as a Maria, or 2 Ritz crackers, broken into pieces
- 2 tablespoons chopped fresh flat-leaf parsley
- 2 tablespoons medium-dry sherry or brandy

1. Preheat the oven to 350°F.

2. Rub the veal generously with salt and pepper. Heat 3 tablespoons of the olive oil in a 5-quart flameproof casserole over medium-high heat until almost smoking. Working in two batches, cook the veal shanks until richly browned, about 7 minutes per side. Transfer the browned meat to a bowl.

3. Add the onion and carrot to the casserole and brown, stirring, for 5 to 7 minutes. Add the tomatoes, reduce the heat to medium, and cook until the tomatoes are thickened and reduced, about 7 minutes, scraping the bottom of the casserole to dislodge any brown bits. Return the veal to the casserole, add the wine, chicken broth, rosemary and thyme sprigs, bay leaf, and cinnamon stick, and bring to a boil, skimming any foam off the surface. Cover the casserole and bake for 1 hour.

4. While the veal is baking, heat the remaining 2 tablespoons olive oil in a large skillet over high heat. Working in two batches if necessary, cook the turnips and pears, adding 1 pinch of the sugar to each batch and stirring, until nicely browned, 8 to 10 minutes. Carefully remove the casserole from the oven and stir the cooked turnips and pears into the pan juices. Cover the casserole, return it to the oven, and continue baking until the meat is very tender, about 1 hour longer.

5. While the veal continues to bake, make the *picada*: Place the hazelnuts, garlic, and tea biscuit in a mini food processor and process until ground. Add the parsley and sherry and process in pulses until the parsley is just minced.

6. When the veal is done baking, using a slotted spoon, transfer the meat to a bowl and cover with aluminum foil to keep warm. Increase the oven temperature to 425°F, remove the herb sprigs, bay leaf, and cinnamon stick, and return the casserole to the oven. Bake, uncovered, until the liquid is nicely reduced, about 15 minutes. Transfer the casserole to the stove top and stir in the *picada.* Return the veal to the casserole, stir to coat with the sauce, and cook over medium heat until warmed through, 2 to 3 minutes. Let the dish rest, covered, for about 5 minutes. Transfer the veal shanks to a large serving platter, spoon the vegetables, pears, and sauce over them, and serve. **SERVES 6**

Nuts, popular in Spanish cooking, show up in dishes from soups to desserts.

MEATBALLS

MEAT

THE MEATBALLS OF MADRID TAPAS BARS

ALBONDIGAS EN SALSA

These are the robust, saucy meatballs served in small earthenware *cazuelas* at old Madrid tapas bars and *tabernas*—the sort of places that transport you to a different era with their long, weathered marble bars, vermouth on tap, and walls plastered with bullfighting photographs. White wine is more commonly used for the sauce, but I prefer red for a more robust color and flavor. The sauce is also delicious served over rice or fried potatoes.

2 slices white sandwich bread, crusts removed
1/3 cup milk
1 pound ground pork (not too lean) or veal
1/2 pound ground beef
1/4 cup grated onion, plus 1 large onion, chopped
2 large eggs, beaten
1 1/4 teaspoons coarse salt (kosher or sea), plus more for the sauce
1 teaspoon freshly ground black pepper
2 to 3 gratings of fresh nutmeg
2 tablespoons minced fresh flat-leaf parsley, plus more for garnish
3 tablespoons olive oil
1 medium-size carrot, diced
3/4 teaspoon sweet (not smoked) paprika
4 to 5 canned peeled tomatoes, drained and chopped, plus 1/4 cup of their juice
3 tablespoons brandy
1 cup dry red wine
1 1/4 cups chicken stock or broth, or more if needed
All-purpose flour, for dusting the meatballs

1. Place the bread and milk in a small bowl and let soak for 5 minutes. Drain, squeeze out the excess liquid, and finely crumble the bread.

2. Place the crumbled bread and the pork, beef, grated onion, eggs, salt, pepper, nutmeg, and parsley in a large bowl. Gently knead the meatball mixture with your hands just until all the ingredients are thoroughly combined; do not overknead. Cover with plastic wrap and refrigerate while you make the sauce, about 40 minutes.

3. While the meatball mixture is chilling, make the sauce: Heat 1 tablespoon of the olive oil in a medium-size saucepan over medium heat. Add the chopped onion and carrot and cook until the vegetables are softened and very lightly browned, about 7 minutes. Add the paprika and stir for a few seconds. Add the tomatoes and their juice and the brandy, increase the heat to high, and cook until the liquid is reduced slightly, about 1 minute. Reduce the heat to medium-low, add the wine and chicken stock, partially cover the pot, and cook until the vegetables are very tender, 30 to 40 minutes. (The sauce can be prepared 1 day ahead up to this point.) Using a slotted spoon, remove about 1 cup of the solids from the sauce and transfer to a blender along with about 1 cup of the liquid. Puree the mixture in pulses until medium-fine. Stir the pureed mixture back into the sauce and add a little more chicken stock if it seem too thick. Keep the sauce warm while you finish making the meatballs.

4. Spread a thin layer of flour on a large plate. Wet your hands, then break off a piece of the meatball mixture and shape it into a ball the size of a large walnut (about 1¼ inches in diameter). Roll the meatball in the flour, shaking off the excess, then gently toss it between cupped hands to give it shape. Repeat with the remaining meatball mixture, placing the floured meatballs on a small baking sheet.

5. Heat 1 tablespoon of the olive oil in a large skillet, preferably nonstick, over medium-high heat. Add half of the meatballs and brown all over, 3 to 5 minutes. Using a slotted spoon, transfer the browned meatballs to a bowl. Add the remaining 1 tablespoon olive oil to the skillet and cook the remaining meatballs in the same fashion.

6. Add about ⅓ cup water to the skillet and cook for about 1 minute, scraping the bottom of the pan to dislodge the brown bits. Stir this liquid into the sauce. Gently stir the browned meatballs and any accumulated juices into the sauce and bring to a simmer. Reduce the heat to low, cover the pan, and cook until the meatballs are completely cooked through, 5 to 7 minutes. Remove the meatballs from the heat and let cool for about 5 minutes. Sprinkle with parsley just before serving. **SERVES 8 AS A TAPA, 4 AS A MAIN COURSE OVER RICE OR FRIED POTATOES**

CATALAN MEATBALLS

ALBONDIGAS CON MANZANAS Y SETAS

Meatballs, *albóndigas,* have been elevated to an art form in Spain, served at tapas bars in earthenware *cazuelas,* passed around at cocktail parties, and enjoyed at home. While I'm pretty addicted to the robust Madrid-style meatballs (see page 265), I'd be the first to admit that the Catalans are the true *albóndiga* masters. Take these, for example. They are juicy and light, with the veal and pork mixture rendered extra special by

At crowded tapas bars, such as Alhambra in Madrid, meatballs are a favorite snack.

the addition of applesauce, wild mushrooms, and some pancetta for juiciness. They are compulsively edible on their own as a tapa, perhaps with *allioli* or *romesco* sauce (see page 44 or 210) on the side, or finished in the Almond and Saffron Sauce that follows. If you're serving the meatballs in the sauce, have plenty of crusty bread on hand for mopping it up.

FOR THE MEATBALLS:

3 tablespoons olive oil
3/4 cup finely chopped white onion
1 very large portobello mushroom (about 4 ounces), wiped clean with a damp paper towel and finely chopped
2 slices white sandwich bread, crusts removed
1/3 cup milk
10 ounces ground veal
10 ounces ground pork
2 to 3 ounces sliced pancetta, minced (see Note)
1 large egg, beaten
3 tablespoons unsweetened applesauce
3 tablespoons minced fresh flat-leaf parsley, plus chopped parsley for garnish
1 1/2 teaspoons sweet (not smoked) paprika
2 teaspoons freshly ground black pepper
1 1/2 teaspoons coarse salt (kosher or sea), or more to taste
All-purpose flour, for dusting the meatballs
Crusty bread, for serving

FOR THE ALMOND AND SAFFRON SAUCE (OPTIONAL):

3 tablespoons olive oil
1/2 cup finely chopped white onion
Reserved chopped portobello mushroom (see Step 1)
1 medium-size ripe tomato, cut in half, peeled, and seeded
2 tablespoons medium-sweet sherry, or 1 large pinch of sugar
1/4 cup dry white wine
1/2 cup chicken stock or broth
1 slice (about 3 inches round and 1/2 inch thick), baguette, cubed
2 medium-size garlic cloves, coarsely chopped
8 toasted almonds (see below), coarsely chopped
2 tablespoons finely chopped fresh flat-leaf parsley
1 small pinch of saffron, pulverized in a mortar and steeped in 2 tablespoons very hot water

TOASTING NUTS

Toasting nuts and seeds brings out their nuttiness and intensifies their flavor. If you're using nuts often, you can toast them in batches larger than you'll need for a single recipe and store them in an airtight container. To prevent nuts from turning rancid, I suggest keeping them on the lowest shelf of the refrigerator.

To skillet-toast almonds, pine nuts, or sesame seeds, heat a medium-size skillet without oil over medium heat (do not use a nonstick skillet for this). Add the nuts and cook them, stirring, until golden and fragrant, about 4 minutes for almonds, two minutes for pine nuts, and slightly less for sesame seeds.

To toast nuts in the oven (which is preferable for larger amounts), place them in a single layer in a small rimmed baking sheet. Bake in a 350°F oven until they're golden and fragrant, 5 to 8 minutes, shaking the pan once or twice. Do not let the nuts burn—start checking after about three minutes.

To toast and skin hazelnuts, place them in a single layer in a small rimmed baking sheet. Bake them in a 350°F oven until the skins are several shades darker and look blistered, about 10 minutes. Wrap the nuts in a kitchen towel and let them stand for about 5 minutes. Rub the nuts vigorously in the towel to loosen their skins, then discard the skins (don't worry if not all the skins come off).

1. Make the meatballs: Heat 1 tablespoon of the olive oil in a medium-size skillet over medium heat. Add the onion and cook until translucent, about 4 minutes. Add 2 cups of the chopped mushroom, reserving the rest for the sauce, if making. If not making the sauce, add all the chopped mushroom here. Cook, stirring, until it releases and reabsorbs some of its liquid, about 5 minutes. Let the mushroom mixture cool.

2. Place the bread and milk in a small bowl and let soak for 5 minutes. Drain, squeeze out the excess liquid, and finely crumble the bread.

3. Place the crumbled bread and the veal, pork, pancetta, egg, applesauce, parsley, paprika, pepper, salt, and the mushroom mixture in a large bowl. Gently knead the meatball mixture with your hands just until all the ingredients are thoroughly combined; do not overknead.

4. Spread a thin layer of flour on a large plate. Wet your hands, then break off a piece of the meatball mixture and shape it into a 1-inch ball. Dust the meatball in the flour, shaking off any excess, then gently toss it between cupped hands to give it shape. Repeat with the remaining meatball mixture, placing the floured meatballs on a small baking sheet.

5. Heat 1 tablespoon of the olive oil in a very large skillet, preferably nonstick, over medium-high heat. Add half of the meatballs and brown all over, shaking the skillet so that the meatballs brown evenly. If you plan to serve the meatballs in the sauce, cook them for 3 to 4 minutes. If serving without sauce, cook them until cooked through, about 7 minutes, adjusting the heat so that the meatballs don't burn. Using a slotted spoon, transfer the meatballs to a bowl. Add the remaining 1 tablespoon of olive oil to the skillet and cook the remaining meatballs in the same fashion. If serving the meatballs without the sauce, let them cool for 5 to 10 minutes, then sprinkle with the chopped parsley and serve with crusty bread. If you are making the sauce, don't clean out the skillet.

6. Prepare the sauce: Heat 1 tablespoon of the olive oil in the skillet over medium heat. Add the onion and cook until translucent, 2 to 3 minutes. Add the reserved chopped mushroom and cook for 2 minutes. Add the tomato and cook, stirring, until it begins to caramelize, 6 to 7 minutes. Add the sherry and wine, increase the heat to high, and cook for 1 to 2 minutes. Add the chicken stock, stir, then stir in the meatballs. Reduce the heat to very low, cover the skillet, and cook for 10 minutes.

7. Meanwhile make the *picada:* Heat the remaining 2 tablespoons olive oil in a small skillet over medium heat. Add the bread cubes and cook until they begin to brown, about 2 minutes. Add the garlic and almonds and cook until fragrant and just beginning to brown, about 1½ minutes. Using a slotted spoon, transfer the bread, garlic, and nuts to a mini food processor. Add the parsley and saffron and pulse until the mixture is ground.

8. Gently stir the *picada* into the skillet with the sauce. Cook until the sauce is flavorful, 2 to 3 minutes. Remove the skillet from the heat and let cool, 5 to 10 minutes. Garnish with additional parsley, if desired, and serve with crusty bread. **SERVES 8 TO 10 AS A TAPA, 4 TO 6 AS A LIGHT MAIN COURSE**

NOTE: Freezing the pancetta for 20 minutes will make it easier to mince.

MINTED LAMB MEATBALLS

ALBONDIGAS DE CORDERO

The tiny *calle* Gamazo is my favorite street in Seville. Not for its landmarks, architecture, or shops, but for what has to be the city's highest concentration of first-rate tapas bars. Each one specializes in something particular, and you can make a full meal by zipping from place to place. The thing to order at Enrique Becerra is a *cazuela* of these juicy meatballs smothered in a rich tomato sauce. Most Spanish meatball recipes are based on pork or beef, but these taste quite Moorish with their combination of lamb and mint. In my adaptation of the recipe, I add fresh mint to the meatballs and dried to the sauce, as it stands up better to slow simmering.

2 slices white sandwich bread, crusts removed
1 1/2 pounds lean ground lamb (see Note)
2 tablespoons finely chopped fresh mint
2 large garlic cloves, crushed with a garlic press
Coarse salt (kosher or sea) and freshly ground black pepper
1 large egg, beaten
3 tablespoons olive oil
1 medium-size onion, chopped
1 cup chopped canned tomatoes with some of their juice
1/4 cup dry sherry
1 cup chicken stock or broth
2 teaspoons finely crumbled dried mint

1. Place the bread in a bowl, add cold water to cover, and soak for 5 to 10 minutes. Drain and squeeze out the excess liquid, then finely crumble the bread.

2. Place the crumbled bread and the lamb, fresh mint, garlic, 1½ teaspoons salt, 1 teaspoon pepper, and the egg in a large bowl. Gently knead the meatball mixture with your hands just until all the ingredients are thoroughly combined; do not overknead. Wet your hands, then break off a piece of the meatball mixture, shape it into a 1-inch ball, gently tossing it between cupped hands to give it shape. Repeat with the remaining meatball mixture, placing the meatballs on a small baking sheet.

3. Heat the olive oil in a deep, 10-inch skillet over medium-high heat. Add half of the meatballs and brown all over, 3 to 4 minutes, shaking the skillet so that the meatballs brown evenly. Using a slotted spoon, transfer the browned meatballs to a bowl. Repeat with the remaining meatballs.

4. If the meatballs have released too much fat, drain off all but 2 to 3 tablespoons. Add the onion and cook over medium-low heat until soft and lightly browned, 5 to 7 minutes. Add the tomatoes and cook, stirring, until they are thickened and reduced, about 7 minutes. Add the sherry and the chicken stock and cook to blend the flavors, 6 to 7 minutes. Let the sauce cool a little, then puree it in a food processor.

5. Return the sauce to the skillet, season it with salt and pepper to taste, and stir in the dried mint. Return the meatballs and any accumulated juices to the skillet and turn to coat with the sauce. Simmer over low heat, partially covered, until the meatballs are cooked through and the sauce has reduced a little, 5 to 7 minutes. Transfer the meatballs and sauce to an earthenware *cazuela* or another rustic serving dish, let cool for 5 to 10 minutes, then serve. **SERVES 6 TO 8 AS A TAPA, 4 AS A MAIN COURSE**

NOTE: If the only ground lamb you can find is fatty, use half lamb and half lean ground beef.

Frutos Secos Caramelos

ES EL MEJOR
DE VENTA AQUI

POULTRY AND GAME

Aves (poultry) has historically occupied an important place at the Spanish table. Medieval and Renaissance cookbooks abound in chicken recipes, many of which would startle modern palates with their extravagant use of sugar and spice. "Confections" such as *manjar blanco* of chicken breast mixed with almond milk, sugar, and rose water; or chicken *mirrauste,* in a thick, sweet sauce of nuts, lemon, ginger, and wine were clearly of Arabic inspiration. White chicken meat even found its way into marzipan! And hens figured prominently in recipes for the sick.

Iberian chicken recipes have gotten much less baroque over the centuries. And if today they aren't particularly plentiful, that's because in the countryside,

Top left: Festive stenciled tables and chairs stand at the ready; *Top right:* A proud display of plumage decorates these beautifully crafted tiles; *Bottom left:* Dried fruits and nuts are often deliciously paired with poultry, especially in Catalonia. *Bottom right:* A Valencian chef, sleeves rolled up, readies himself for dinner service.

away from palace kitchens, the egg always came first—meaning that hens were more valued for *huevo* production than they were for their meat. With the egg as the symbolic center of the Spanish culinary universe, chicken has come to be regarded as a bit of an afterthought. But what a delicious afterthought, as you'll see here. The famous *pollo al ajillo*—bite-size pieces of chicken fried in olive oil with plenty of garlic—is impossible not to love. Another classic is *gallina en pepitoria,* hen in a medieval sauce of almonds, saffron, and eggs. In this chapter, you will also find a cider-braised bird from the *sidra*-mad northern Asturias region, a Basque chicken with cured ham and sweet peppers, and an irresistible Catalan recipe for *pollo* smothered in a delicious eggplant and zucchini ragout. And don't miss Ferran Adrià's chicken with dried fruit and pine nuts, which shows what wonders can be done with a take-out rotisserie bird. Duck? Few poultry dishes can match the depth and the satisfying complexity of chef Jaume Vidal's duck legs braised with olives and prunes.

Hunting remains one of Spain's favorite sports, and at restaurants game is a treat far more common than chicken. What luck! The Spanish knack for game shows in recipes like quail slowly baked in a warm vinaigrette and the marvelous Catalan rabbit stew with a surprising accent of chocolate. As for turkey, introduced from the Americas in the early sixteenth century, it proved to be an almost instant hit with the Spaniards; today it graces most Christmas tables. I haven't included partridge recipes here; these exquisite game birds are out of reach of most cooks. But I do often daydream about sitting in my favorite restaurant in Toledo, picking every morsel of white delicate meat off the bone of *perdiz roja,* the prized red-legged partridge, in *escabeche.* For some things, you just have to travel to Spain.

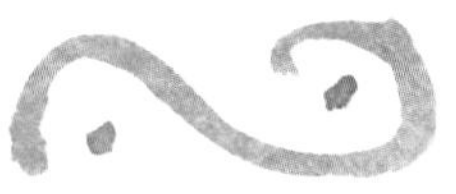

ROSA'S ROAST CHICKEN AND WILD MUSHROOM CASSEROLE WITH RED WINE

POLLO AL HORNO CON SETAS

Rosa Vilaseca is a perfectionist cook who has developed a vocal following for her robust Catalan country cooking at Sant Ferriol, a small spa hotel in the Catalan countryside. This chicken is a big hit with her guests, and Rosa puts it on the menu in autumn when the forests are buzzing with mushroom pickers. The chicken, Rosa explains, should be placed on top of the vegetables so that it roasts rather than stews; the red wine lends extra body to the dark, rich, deeply flavorful sauce. Rosa is also pretty adamant about using a real country chicken (*pollo del país*), so try to find a good organic bird or, failing that, a kosher or a Chinese one. (The recipe can also be made with two three-pound chickens.)

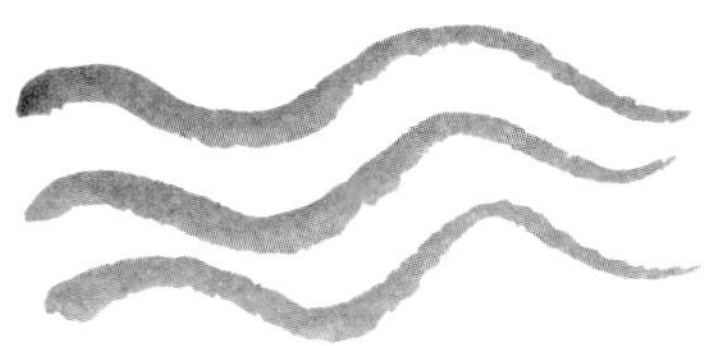

1 roasting chicken ($6^1/_2$ to 7 pounds), rinsed well, patted dry, and trimmed of excess fat
Coarse salt (kosher or sea) and freshly ground black pepper
2 teaspoons crumbled dried rosemary
2 teaspoons crumbled dried thyme
3 tablespoons olive oil, plus more for brushing the chicken
2 fresh rosemary sprigs
2 dried thyme sprigs
1 bay leaf
$^1/_2$ cup chopped onion
1 small carrot, chopped
1 small red bell pepper, cored, seeded, and chopped
8 whole unpeeled medium-size garlic cloves, lightly smashed, plus 2 garlic cloves, finely minced
2 cups full-bodied dry red wine
About 2 cups chicken stock or broth
1 pound assorted wild mushrooms, such as chanterelles, cèpes, morels, and/or trompettes-de-la-mort or a combination of wild and cultivated mushrooms (see Note)
3 tablespoons finely minced fresh flat-leaf parsley

1. Preheat the oven to 425°F.

2. Rub the chicken generously with salt, black pepper, and the crumbled rosemary and thyme and brush it with a little olive oil. Place the rosemary and thyme sprigs and the bay leaf in a double layer of cheesecloth and tie it closed.

3. Heat 1 tablespoon of the olive oil in a heavy 12-inch ovenproof skillet or a flameproof baking dish of similar size over medium-high heat. Add the onion, carrot, red pepper, and 8 whole garlic cloves and cook until richly browned, 5 to 7 minutes. Add

1 cup of the wine and 1 cup of the chicken stock and bring to a boil. Tuck the cheesecloth bag of herbs into the vegetables, then place the chicken on top. Roast the chicken until it is cooked through, about 1 hour and 35 minutes; an instant-read meat thermometer inserted into the thickest part of a thigh (but not so it touches a bone) should register about 180°F. As the chicken roasts, replenish the wine and stock in the skillet every 20 minutes or so (you may not need to use all of the wine or stock).

4. Clean the mushrooms with a damp paper towel. Leave small mushrooms whole and coarsely chop the rest. Heat the remaining 2 tablespoons olive oil in a medium-size skillet over medium-high heat. Add the mushrooms and cook until they release and reabsorb their liquid and are lightly browned, 6 to 7 minutes. Season the mushrooms with salt and pepper to taste, then set them aside.

5. When the chicken is done, transfer it to a cutting board, tilting it slightly as you remove it from the skillet to let the juices in the body cavity run out. Cover the chicken loosely with aluminum foil to keep it warm as it rests.

6. Skim as much fat as possible from the pan juices. If you have any wine or stock left, add it to the skillet. Bring the pan juices to a boil over medium-high heat and cook until reduced, 2 to 3 minutes. Remove and discard the cheesecloth bag. Press the solids through a fine sieve back into the skillet, fold in the mushrooms, and cook until the sauce is heated through. Stir in the parsley and minced garlic and cook for another 30 seconds.

7. Carve the chicken and arrange it on a serving platter. Spoon a little of the sauce over the chicken and pass the rest separately in a deep bowl. Serve at once. **SERVES 6**

NOTE: If wild mushrooms aren't readily available, you can use a mixture of dried porcini and oyster mushrooms. Just soak an ounce of dried porcinis in hot water for half an hour, chop them up, and toss them in the skillet with the oyster mushrooms, adding a little of the mushroom soaking liquid to the chicken's pan juices.

GARLICKY ROAST CHICKEN WITH APPLE AND QUINCE COMPOTE

POLLO ASADO CON COMPOTA DE MANZANAS Y MEMBRILLO

With its seductively sweet fragrance and Arabic heritage, quince has a special place on the Spanish table, most notably as *membrillo,* the dark fruit paste usually eaten with cheese. Here the quince works magic with chicken, a combination that harks back to medieval Moorish-Spanish cuisine. If you're serving a larger crowd, I recommend roasting two chickens. As some quince can be as bland as potatoes, choose carefully, making sure the fruit is deep yellow and very aromatic.

Coarse salt (kosher or sea) and freshly ground black pepper
15 large garlic cloves; 10 crushed with a garlic press, 5 lightly smashed
1 tablespoon dried rosemary, crumbled, plus 1 large pinch of rosemary for the compote
1 tablespoon sweet (not smoked) paprika
About 3 tablespoons extra-virgin olive oil, plus more for the quince compote
1 chicken (about 4 pounds), rinsed well, patted dry, and trimmed of excess fat
About 3 cups chicken stock or broth, or more if needed
1/3 cup dry white wine
1 large quince, peeled and cut into 1-inch chunks (see Note)
1 small Granny Smith apple, peeled, cored, and cut into 1-inch chunks
1 small onion, cut into 1/2-inch chunks

1. Preheat the oven to 425°F.

2. Place 2 teaspoons salt, 1 teaspoon pepper, the 10 crushed garlic cloves, the crumbled rosemary, paprika, and 3 tablespoons olive oil in a small bowl and stir until a paste forms. Set about 1 tablespoon of this paste aside for the quince compote. Rub the rest of the paste all over the chicken and under the skin. Season the cavity with salt and pepper. Cover the chicken loosely with plastic wrap and let stand while you prepare the next step.

3. Place 1½ cups of the chicken stock and the wine and quince in a medium-size saucepan, stir to mix, and bring to a boil over medium-high heat. Reduce the heat to low and simmer until the quince is softened, 10 to 12 minutes. Drain the quince, setting aside the poaching liquid. Place the quince in an 8-inch-square baking dish along with the apple, onion, and the 5 slightly smashed garlic cloves. Using your hands, toss the quince mixture with the reserved 1 tablespoon spice paste, season with more salt and pepper, and drizzle enough olive oil on top to lightly coat the compote.

4. Place the chicken breast side up on a rack set over a roasting pan. Place the chicken and the compote in the oven and bake both for 20 minutes. Then, add the reserved quince poaching liquid to the compote and about 1½ cups water to the roasting pan holding the chicken. Continue roasting, checking the water level in the roasting pan and the stock in the compote (every 20 minutes) and adding more, as necessary. The chicken is done when its skin is crisp and golden and an instant-read meat thermometer inserted into the thickest part of a thigh (but not so that it touches a bone) registers about 180°F, 40 minutes more (1 hour total cooking time). The fruit in the compote should be very tender. If it isn't, continue baking while the chicken rests.

5. Transfer the chicken to a cutting board and let it rest, covered loosely with aluminum foil, for w10 minutes. Strain the juices from the roasting pan through a sieve into the compote. Carve the chicken and arrange it on a serving platter. Transfer the compote to a bowl and serve it with the chicken. **SERVES 4**

NOTE: Quince can be difficult to cut; cut it into thick slices around the center, then dice it.

POTTED CHICKEN WITH CHORIZO AND CHICKPEAS

COCIDO DE POLLO CON CHORIZO Y GARBANZOS

Here's my all-chicken version of Spain's famous *cocido* (boiled dinner), a dish not dissimilar to the French *poule-au-pot* but made with the typically Iberian chorizo and chickpeas. Because the chicken flavor here is rather unmasked, using a quality bird—organic, kosher, or Chinese—makes all the difference. The refreshing sauce of parsley and slightly under-ripe tomatoes is the perfect counterpoint to a hearty, wintry, one-pot meal. You can either save the broth the chicken cooks in for another use or serve it as the Spanish do, as a first course, afloat with cooked pasta shells or fine vermicelli. Another option is to spoon the chicken, chorizo, and all the veggies into large, deep bowls together with the broth, rather than serving the chicken and vegetables on separate plates.

FOR THE CHICKEN, CHORIZO, AND VEGETABLES:

1 chicken (about 3 1/2 pounds), rinsed, patted dry, and trimmed of excess fat
Coarse salt (kosher or sea) and freshly ground black pepper
6 cups chicken stock or broth
1 medium-size onion
1 small garlic head, top trimmed off, outer layer of skin removed
1 bay leaf
1 celery rib
2 fat carrots, cut into 3-inch-long pieces
4 smallish boiling potatoes, cut into wedges
10 ounces sweet Spanish-style chorizo sausages
2 cups canned chickpeas (garbanzo beans), drained (from two 15-ounce cans)

FOR THE PARSLEY SAUCE:

1 cup chopped fresh flat-leaf parsley
2 slightly under-ripe plum tomatoes, peeled and chopped
1/4 cup minced white onion
3 medium-size garlic cloves, crushed with a garlic press
3 tablespoons best-quality red wine vinegar
1/4 cup extra-virgin olive oil
Coarse salt (kosher or sea) and freshly ground black pepper

Flaky sea salt, such as Maldon, for sprinkling

1. Rub the chicken inside and out with salt and pepper and let stand at room temperature for 30 minutes or refrigerate it for several hours, then let it come to room temperature before cooking.

2. Place the chicken breast side down in a heavy 6-quart pot that can hold it snugly. Add the chicken stock and enough water to come almost level with

CHOOSING CHICKEN

Like any other developed country, Spain has its share of mass-produced chickens. But when you buy a *pollo del corral* (free-range bird) at a market or order it at a good restaurant, the flavor comes as a revelation: taut, rather lean, and full of taste that is supremely chickeny. For the recipes in this chapter, an organic bird from a reputable producer is ideal. Before you splurge, however, consider the following, less pricey, options. Empire Kosher chickens taste deliciously moist because they are soaked in salt brine to remove all of the blood. Salt also draws out the flavor (even a regular chicken tastes infinitely better when rubbed with salt and refrigerated for a few hours before cooking). Another excellent non-boutique option is Chinese poultry, labeled "Buddhist style" by the USDA. Found at any good Chinese grocery, these chickens often come with the head and feet still attached and white metal tags on their ankles. The Chinese are obsessive about their poultry, and their chickens, fed on soybeans and corn and slaughtered according to precise and ingenious methods, tend to be very fresh. They are also inexpensive and although not as plump chested as American-style birds, they usually have a nicely firm texture and a clean, healthy flavor.

Don't be fooled by poultry advertised as "all-natural," "fresh," or "young"—these terms are nearly meaningless. To be labeled free-range by the USDA, the chicken must have "been allowed access to the outside" for at least part of its life. This isn't saying much and doesn't necessarily mean better flavor if you don't consider other criteria, such as breed and feed. Equally, organic can be a rather fuzzy term, referring to chickens that have been certified as such by a certifying entity. At best this means the birds were reared on organic feed—grain grown in pesticide-free soil—without the usual antibiotics, supplements, or tranquilizers. But it is important to read any fine print and look for the words "certified organic by so-and-so" on the label and buy from a reputable producer. Good chickens take more care and time to raise—eight to nine weeks compared to the six weeks for regular poultry—and that's what you are paying for. If you really like chicken, it's worth it.

the top of the chicken. Add the onion, garlic head, bay leaf, and celery and bring to a boil over high heat. Thoroughly skim any foam off the top, reduce the heat to low, cover the pot, and simmer the chicken for 10 minutes. Add the carrots and potatoes, bring the broth to a simmer, and continue simmering for another 15 minutes.

3. Bring a pot of water to a boil. Cook the chorizo for 2 minutes, then drain it. Add the chorizo and the chickpeas to the pot with the chicken. Cover the pot again and continue simmering over low heat until the chicken is cooked through and is very tender, about 20 minutes. Occasionally skim any foam off the top.

4. While the chicken is cooking, make the parsley sauce: Place the parsley and the tomatoes in a food processor and add ⅓ cup of the chicken poaching liquid. Pulse the processor until the tomatoes are crushed but not pureed, scraping down the side of the processor bowl several times. Scrape the parsley mixture into a bowl and add the onion and garlic. Whisk in the vinegar and the olive oil and season the sauce with salt and pepper to taste. Let the sauce stand while the chicken finishes cooking.

5. To serve, using a slotted spoon, transfer the chicken to a cutting board, cover it with aluminum foil, and let rest for 5 to 10 minutes. Transfer the chorizo to a cutting board. Carve the chicken and slice the chorizo into thick slices and arrange both on a serving platter. Moisten the chicken and chorizo with some of the cooking broth and sprinkle with the flaky salt. Using a slotted spoon, transfer all of the vegetables and chickpeas to another platter, discarding the onion, celery, garlic head, and bay leaf. Moisten the vegetables generously with some of the broth. Serve the chicken, chorizo, and vegetables accompanied by the parsley sauce, and by a bowl of broth on the side for sprinkling. Set the remaining broth aside for another use. **SERVES 4 TO 6**

LEMON CHICKEN WITH HONEY AND SAFFRON

POLLO A LA MIEL

Here's an old Andalusian recipe that enticingly displays the influence of the Moorish cuisine of Al-Andalus (the Arabic name for Andalusia). Despite the presence of honey, the dominant flavors here are tart, rather than sweet, and sour. The chicken needs to marinate for at least two hours, so plan ahead. Sautéed spinach would make a good accompaniment.

1 chicken (about 4 pounds), quartered, backbone removed, rinsed, patted dry, and trimmed of excess fat
Coarse salt (kosher or sea)
1/2 teaspoon ground cumin
1/2 teaspoon ground ginger
1/2 teaspoon ground coriander
1/2 cup fresh lemon juice
6 teaspoons light honey, such as orange flower
1 large pinch of saffron, pulverized in a mortar and steeped in 1 tablespoon very hot water
1 large onion, quartered and thinly sliced
1 tablespoon olive oil
2 tablespoons lightly toasted sesame seeds (see page 267)

1. Place the chicken in an earthenware *cazuela* that will hold it in one layer, or in an attractive enamel or glass baking dish. Rub the chicken all over with salt and the cumin, ginger, and coriander. Let stand for 15 minutes.

2. Place the lemon juice, 5 teaspoons of the honey, and the saffron in a small bowl and whisk to mix. Pour the mixture over the chicken. Prick the chicken all over with the tines of a fork, cover it with plastic wrap, and refrigerate for 2 to 6 hours, turning several times. Let the chicken come to room temperature before cooking.

3. Preheat the oven to 400°F.

4. Transfer the chicken to a bowl, then scatter the onion in the *cazuela*. Place the chicken on top of the onion and brush it with the remaining 1 teaspoon honey and the olive oil. Bake the chicken for 20 minutes. Reduce the oven temperature to 350°F and continue baking the chicken until it is cooked through, 30 to 40 minutes longer. (To avoid overcooking the breast halves, remove them after 30 minutes.) Stir in the sesame seeds, return the breast halves to the *cazuela,* and bake for 5 minutes longer. Serve the chicken straight from the *cazuela.* **SERVES 4**

SMOTHERED CHICKEN WITH VEGETABLE JAM

POLLASTRE AMB SAMFAINA

Similar to Provençal ratatouille, *samfaina* is an autumnal Catalan vegetable mélange eaten on its own or cooked with meats (I love it with pig's feet). Along with *escalivada* (mixed grilled vegetables), it constitutes one of the foundations of Catalan cooking. While the French cook the vegetables together into a kind of jam, many Catalan cooks insist that *samfaina* requires each vegetable to be fried separately over a lively heat, then cooked together briefly. It takes a little extra effort, but this way the vegetables retain their shape and character (to save time, while one vegetable cooks, I dice the next one). *Samfaina,* of course, is also great without the chicken, cooled to room temperature and served as a spread for grilled bread. And you can combine it with almost any meat in a stew or spoon it over grilled chicken or fish.

Don't be put off by the large quantity of olive oil—it's healthy stuff and much of it is drained off. Roasted or boiled new potatoes are the best accompaniment for this saucy dish, which is also great cold or at room temperature.

- 1/2 cup extra-virgin olive oil, or more if needed
- 1 small eggplant (12 to 14 ounces), peeled and cut into 1/2-inch dice
- 3 small zucchini, cut into 1/2-inch dice
- 1 large, sweet onion, such as a Vidalia, diced
- 4 medium-size garlic cloves, finely chopped
- 3 medium-size, ripe tomatoes, cut in half and grated on a box grater, skins discarded
- 1 pinch of sugar, or more if needed
- 3 large roasted red bell peppers (see page 385), diced
- 1 teaspoon minced fresh rosemary
- 1 teaspoon minced fresh thyme
- Coarse salt (kosher or sea) and freshly ground black pepper
- 3/4 cup pitted small oil-cured black olives, such as Gaeta or niçoise
- 1 chicken (about 3 1/2 pounds), cut into 8 pieces, rinsed, patted dry, and trimmed of excess fat
- 1/3 cup dry white wine
- Best-quality white wine vinegar (optional)
- Minced fresh flat-leaf parsley, for garnish
- Roasted or boiled new potatoes, for serving

1. Heat the olive oil in a 12-inch skillet, preferably nonstick, over medium-high heat until hot but not smoking. Add the eggplant and cook until lightly browned, about 7 minutes. (The eggplant will absorb all the oil, then release it once browned.) Using a slotted spoon, transfer the eggplant to a sieve set over a bowl and let the oil drain off. Add the zucchini to the skillet and cook until lightly browned, adjusting the heat as necessary so that it doesn't burn. Using a slotted spoon, transfer the zucchini to the sieve with the eggplant.

2. If there seems to be too much oil left in the skillet, pour out all but about 2 tablespoons. Add the onion and garlic, reduce the heat to very low, and cook until the onion is very soft but not browned, about 10 minutes, adding a little water if the skillet looks dry. Add the tomatoes and sugar and cook until most of the tomato liquid has evaporated and the tomatoes are thickened and reduced, 5 to 7 minutes. Return the drained eggplants and zucchini to the skillet (setting aside the drained oil) and stir in the roasted peppers, rosemary, and thyme. Season with salt and black pepper to taste. Add ⅓ cup water, cover the skillet, and cook the *samfaina* over very low heat to blend the flavors, about 10 minutes. (If you will be serving the *samfaina* on its own, continue cooking it for another 10 to 15 minutes.) Stir in the olives.

3. Preheat the oven to 350°F.

4. Rub the chicken with salt and pepper. Heat 2 tablespoons of the reserved drained olive oil in a wide ovenproof casserole over medium heat (add more oil if there isn't 2 tablespoons). Working in batches, brown the chicken lightly on all sides, transferring all of the browned pieces to a bowl.

5. Spread half of the *samfaina* on the bottom of the casserole, add the browned chicken, top it with the remaining *samfaina,* and add the wine. Bake the chicken, covered, until it is very tender, about 45 minutes, turning it once.

6. When the chicken is done, taste the sauce. If the flavors don't seem lively enough, stir in a little vinegar and another pinch of sugar. Let the dish cool for 10 to 15 minutes, then spoon off and discard the oil on top. Serve the chicken and *samfaina* sprinkled with parsley, with the potatoes on the side.

SERVES 4

FERRAN ADRIÀ'S ROTISSERIE CHICKEN

POLLO CON FRUTOS Y FRUTAS SECAS

As this recipe demonstrates, Ferran Adrià, the alchemist chef of El Bulli, is as practical as he is inventive. It's adapted from the cookbook he dedicated to quick recipes that can be made with supermarket ingredients, and it features a store-bought rotisserie chicken that's deliciously doctored with a sauce of dried fruit, pine nuts, and port wine. Though you can whip the dish up in less than half an hour, the flavors are sophisticated enough for a fancy dinner party. If you'd like to roast your own chicken, so much the better.

Ferran Adrià's Rotisserie Chicken

FERRAN ADRIA GOES TO THE SUPERMARKET

Ferran Adrià, the Catalan chef of El Bulli restaurant, likes to experiment with liquid nitrogen and calcium chloride. He fashions paella out of Rice Krispies, entraps quail eggs in cages of gold-tinted caramel, and turns foie gras into frozen dust. He's been featured on *Time* magazine's list of the hundred most influential people of our time and touted by the press as an alchemist and a genius. A thirty-course tasting menu at El Bulli is closer to interactive performance art than anything most of us know as dinner.

So what's the guy doing doctoring a take-out rotisserie chicken?

When I came across Adrià's cookbook *Cocinar en Casa* (*Cooking at Home*), it seemed like a volume in which Einstein explains fractions to school children. Yet for a man portrayed by the press as a mad scientist, Adrià emerges from the pages as surprisingly practical. Done in collaboration with the Caprabo supermarket chain and featuring step-by-step photos and quick recipes based on common ingredients, the book combines El Bulli's playful *esprit* (gazpacho Popsicles, mojito foam made in a whipped cream maker), stylish suggestions on what to do with take-out fried rice (serve it with a soy sabayon), and realistic advice on everything from the virtues of Microplane graters to how to produce ice creams without an ice cream maker (just whizz some frozen berries and cream in a food processor).

Adrià has also produced a series of DVDs called *La Cocina Fácil* (*Easy Cuisine*), in which menus and recipe demos are themed around occasions such as candlelit cold supper, a Japanese dinner, or eating with an empty fridge. Here is Adrià making a quick meal for himself from a package of pasta, grated Parmesan, and the surprising addition of vanilla seeds—a brilliant idea! There he is improvising a *tortilla de patata,* Spain's famous potato omelet, using a bag of potato chips, a creation he says he's particularly fond of (see page 143 for more). Now, he's calling for a take-out rotisserie chicken, which he finishes in a lusty Catalan sauce of dried fruit and pine nuts (see this page for the recipe). One of my favorite simple salad ideas is this: Open a bag of mesclun and place it in a bowl. Toss it with a few raspberries, a handful of mint leaves, pine nuts, coarsely chopped hazelnuts and macadamias, and shaved Parmesan. Dress it with a quick olive oil and sherry vinegar vinaigrette that includes a small pinch of cinnamon. Adrià calls it *ensalada de contrastes.* I say delicious.

1 tablespoon extra-virgin olive oil
1/2 cup pitted prunes
1/2 cup dried apricots
1/4 cup pitted dried sour cherries
2 tablespoons pine nuts
1 strip orange zest (4 inches), white pith removed
1 strip lemon zest (4 inches), white pith removed
1/2 cup tawny port
1 small cinnamon stick
2/3 cup chicken stock or broth
1 store-bought rotisserie chicken (about 3 1/2 pounds), cut into 8 pieces, juices reserved

1. Preheat the oven to 425°F.

2. Heat the olive oil in a large skillet over medium heat. Add the prunes, apricots, cherries, pine nuts, and orange and lemon zests and cook, stirring, until the pine nuts turn golden and the fruits are browned in spots, 3 to 5 minutes. Add the port and cinnamon stick and cook until syrupy, about 5 minutes. Add the chicken stock and the chicken juices. Increase the heat to high, bring the sauce to a boil, and cook until reduced, about 5 minutes.

3. Place the chicken pieces in a baking dish that can hold them snugly. Pour the sauce over them, scraping up all the fruit and liquid from the bottom of the skillet and turning the chicken to coat it with the sauce. Bake the chicken until it is warmed through and the sauce is further reduced, about 10 minutes. Transfer to plates and serve at once. **SERVES 4**

CHICKEN IN ALMOND AND SAFFRON SAUCE

POLLO EN PEPITORIA

"Silly," said my friend Gabriela, as we pored over glossy magazine spreads dedicated to the glitzy wedding of Spain's crown prince Felipe. "Why did they have to do that dumb roasted capon, for sixteen hundred people? Why didn't they do something real and truly Spanish, like *pollo en pepitoria?*" she wondered, referring to the famous dish of chicken (or hen, actually) stewed with a mortar-pounded mixture of fried almonds and garlic and tinted with saffron. In addition to being delicious, *pepitoria* is one of the oldest Spanish recipes around, one that dates back to thirteenth-century Hispanic-Moorish cooking. It's mentioned by Cervantes himself. They should have served *that* at the royal wedding.

- 1 chicken (about 3 1/2 pounds), cut into 12 pieces, rinsed, patted dry, and trimmed of excess fat
- Coarse salt (kosher or sea) and freshly ground black pepper
- 1/2 cup extra-virgin olive oil
- 3/4 cup whole blanched almonds
- 6 whole medium-size garlic cloves
- 6 black peppercorns
- 2 tablespoons minced fresh flat-leaf parsley, plus more for garnish
- 2 small onions, finely chopped
- 1 small cinnamon stick
- 3/4 cup dry white wine
- 1 1/4 cups chicken stock or broth
- 1 large pinch of saffron, pulverized in a mortar and steeped in 3 tablespoons very hot water
- 1 medium-size pinch of ground cloves
- 10 very thin lemon slices, cut in half, seeds removed
- 2 hard-cooked eggs
- Toasted slivered almonds or almond flakes (see page 267), for garnish

1. Rub the chicken with salt and pepper and let stand while preparing the next step.

2. Meanwhile, heat the olive oil in a large flameproof casserole over medium heat. Add the blanched almonds and cook until they take on some color, about 2 minutes. Add the garlic and cook until the almonds and the garlic are golden brown, about 2 minutes more. Using a slotted spoon, transfer the almonds and garlic to a plate lined with paper towels to drain; leave the oil in the casserole.

3. Place the browned almonds, garlic, peppercorns, and parsley in a mini food processor and pulse to a paste, then set aside.

4. Heat the casserole over medium-high heat. Working in two batches, brown the chicken well all over, about 5 minutes per side. Transfer the browned chicken to a bowl.

5. Drain off all but about 2 tablespoons of the oil from the casserole, reduce the heat to medium-low, add the onions and the cinnamon stick, and cook until the onions are very soft, about 10 minutes. Return the chicken to the casserole, add the wine and chicken stock, increase the heat to medium-high, and bring to a simmer. Add the almond paste to the casserole, then rinse out the processor bowl with a little of the cooking liquid and add this as well. Stir in the saffron and cloves. Season with salt to taste, reduce the heat to medium-low, cover the casserole, and cook until the chicken is very tender, about 40 minutes, turning the pieces several times. Stir the lemon slices into the cooking liquid and cook for 10 minutes more.

6. Remove the yolks from the hard-cooked eggs. Finely chop the whites and set aside for garnish. Place the yolks in a small bowl, mash them thor-

SAFFRON: THE SPANISH GOLD

There are few kitchen tasks I find more rewarding than pounding a good pinch of La Mancha saffron to a fine powder in my weathered stone mortar. I splash in a few tablespoons of hot water and let it steep for a while. Then, I swirl the bright-orange liquid into a stew or a soup, watching as the dish takes on a hue of twenty-four-karat gold, plus that faint but instantly recognizable exotically bitter scent. From the Arabic *za' farán* (yellow), saffron has been venerated since antiquity, utilized as a spice, dye, and medicine. Introduced to the Iberian peninsula by the Moors in the tenth century, today it is cultivated in the region of Castilla–La Mancha, where the fickle crocuses flourish despite harsh winters and arid, hot summers. "An arrogant flower that is born at sunrise and dies at dark," is how a nineteenth-century Spanish lyric referred to the spice.

At forty dollars per ounce, saffron is worth its weight in gold. Those who quibble at the price tag should consider this: The number of crocuses needed to produce a pound of those fragile amber threads is around 70,000. The crocuses flower in the fall, carpeting the fields of La Mancha in purple. In mid-October they are handpicked one by one—an arduous task, as they grow so close to the ground, which must be performed on a dry morning, after the dew has evaporated but before the sun begins to wither the flowers. Each crocus yields only three red stigmas, the female part of the flower. Pulling a pound of these fragile filaments from the flowers can take the quick-fingered *mondadoras* (petal strippers) who perform this task some two hundred hours. Once extracted, the stigmas are spread out in a sieve and toasted until they lose all their moisture. Saffron farmers usually get paid in kind. It's a deal they gladly accept, because a kilo of *azafrán* in the cellar is better than euros in the bank.

oughly, then whisk in a few tablespoons of the cooking liquid.

7. Transfer the chicken to a bowl and cover with aluminum foil to keep warm. Heat the casserole over medium-high heat and cook until the liquid is reduced slightly, about 5 minutes. Stir in the mashed egg yolks, reduce the heat to medium-low, and cook to thicken the sauce slightly, another 5 minutes. Return the chicken to the casserole, turn to coat it with the sauce, and cook for another 5 minutes. Transfer the chicken to a serving dish, spoon the sauce on top, and garnish with slivered almonds, chopped egg whites, and some parsley. **SERVES 4**

GARLIC CHICKEN

POLLO AL AJILLO

What fried chicken is to the American South, *pollo al ajillo* is to central Spain. And as with fried chicken, arguments over how to make it best never end. Some insist on marinating the chicken in garlic, others add garlic at the very end, so that it doesn't burn. Some fry the chicken in oil alone until it's rather crunchy, others add wine and/or vinegar to the sauce, as in this recipe. The only consensus is that *pollo al ajillo* is best with french fries and a cool, frosty glass of beer. And like American fried chicken, the preferred bird is a young, tender, small one that will cook quickly. It's also important that the chicken be cut into fairly small nuggets of a uniform size, a task that's probably best left to your butcher. If you can only get supermarket chicken, hack it into the smallest pieces you can manage. A Chinese cleaver works well for this.

- 1 chicken (about 3 1/2 pounds), cut into 16 to 18 pieces of roughly equal size, rinsed, patted dry, and trimmed of all fat (see Note)
- Coarse salt (kosher or sea)
- Olive oil, for frying
- All-purpose flour, for dusting the chicken, plus 1 teaspoon for the sauce
- 12 whole unpeeled medium-size garlic cloves, lightly smashed, and 10 large garlic cloves, sliced
- 1/2 dried small red chile, such as arbol, crumbled
- 2/3 cup dry white wine
- 1/3 cup chicken stock or broth
- 2 teaspoons best-quality red wine vinegar, or more to taste
- 3 tablespoons minced fresh flat-leaf parsley

1. Place the chicken in a bowl and rub it generously with salt. Let stand for about 30 minutes.

2. Preheat the oven to 425°F.

3. Pour olive oil to a depth of ½ inch in a heavy ovenproof 12-inch skillet and heat it over medium-high heat until almost smoking. Lightly dust the chicken pieces with flour, shaking off the excess. Add the 12 whole garlic cloves to the skillet and stir to coat with the oil, 1 minute. Working in two batches, cook the chicken until somewhat crisp and richly browned all over, 8 to 10 minutes per batch, adjusting the heat so that the oil doesn't burn. Using a slotted spoon, transfer the browned chicken pieces to a 12-inch earthenware *cazuela* or a baking dish of similar size.

4. Discard the whole garlic cloves. If the oil doesn't seem clean enough, pour it off, wipe the skillet, and add 2 to 3 tablespoons fresh olive oil. If the cooking oil seems fine, pour off all but 3 tablespoons of it. Heat the skillet over low heat, add the 10 sliced garlic cloves, and cook until very fragrant and just beginning to color, about 2 minutes. Add the chile and stir for a few seconds. Add the 1 teaspoon flour and stir for about 20 seconds. Add the wine and chicken stock and bring to a boil, stirring. Season the sauce with salt to taste and pour it over the chicken. Bake the chicken until it is cooked through, about 15 minutes. Stir in the vinegar and the parsley, coating the chicken evenly with sauce, and serve. **SERVES 4**

NOTE: If you don't have a butcher who can help you out and you don't own a cleaver, substitute 2½ pounds of boneless chicken thighs.

Imaginative tilework, here Moorish in design, can be found in restaurants throughout Spain.

GRILLED CHICKEN WITH PIQUILLO GAZPACHO SAUCE

POLLO A LA BRASA CON SALSA DE GAZPACHO

Colorful, flavorful, and thoroughly modern, this recipe shows off the versatility of gazpacho, a soup that contemporary Spanish chefs don't hesitate to turn into sauces or sorbets. Here's a kind of showy restaurant-style dish that can be made at home with great ease. The sauce and the presentation—with a touch of basil-scented oil—also work wonders on cold poached chicken or grilled fish or vegetables.

FOR THE PIQUILLO GAZPACHO SAUCE:

1 slice white sandwich bread, crusts removed
1 large ripe tomato, seeded and chopped
1/3 cup piquillo pepper strips (from a can or jar; if unavailable, substitute pimientos), with a little of their liquid
1/4 cup chopped Italian (frying) pepper
1/4 cup chopped red onion
3 medium-size garlic cloves, crushed with a garlic press
1 pinch of ground cumin
1 small pinch of cayenne, or more to taste
1 pinch of sugar
3 tablespoons fragrant extra-virgin olive oil
3 tablespoons sherry vinegar, preferably aged
Coarse salt (kosher or sea) and freshly ground black pepper

FOR THE CHICKEN:

6 boneless chicken breast halves (each about 8 ounces) either skinless or with the skin, rinsed and patted dry
Coarse salt (kosher or sea) and freshly ground black pepper
Olive oil
Fresh Basil Oil (recipe follows), for serving
Flaky sea salt, such as Maldon, for serving
Small fresh mint leaves, for garnish

1. Make the piquillo pepper gazpacho sauce: Place the bread in a small bowl, add cold water to cover, and let soak for 5 minutes. Drain and squeeze out the excess liquid.

2. Place the soaked bread and the tomato, piquillo pepper strips and liquid, Italian pepper, onion, garlic, cumin, cayenne, sugar, olive oil, and vinegar in a food processor and puree until completely smooth. Season the sauce with salt and black pepper to taste and more cayenne, if desired. Scrape the sauce into a bowl and let stand until the flavors develop, at least 30 minutes.

3. Make the chicken: Light the grill and preheat it to high or preheat the broiler.

4. Rub the chicken generously with salt and pepper and brush it with olive oil. Grill or broil the chicken, turning it once and brushing it again with olive oil, until lightly charred and cooked through, 6 to 8 minutes per side.

5. Transfer the chicken to a cutting board and let rest for about 5 minutes, then slice it on the diagonal. To serve, spread a few tablespoons of the gazpacho sauce on dinner plates and fan the chicken slices on top. Drizzle some basil oil around the sauce and over the chicken, sprinkle flaky salt lightly on top, and garnish with mint leaves. Serve at once. **SERVES 6**

FRESH BASIL OIL

ACEITE DE ALBAHACA

A great way to add a splash of color and herbal flavor, basil oil features in many contemporary Spanish dishes. If using the oil right away, you can skip blanching the basil. If storing it, blanching helps prevent the basil from discoloring.

1 1/2 cups packed basil leaves
1/2 extra-virgin or light olive oil
Coarse salt (kosher or sea)

1. Bring a medium-size saucepan of water to a boil over high heat and prepare a bowl of ice water.

2. Blanch the basil in the boiling water just until it turns bright green, 10 to 15 seconds. Drain and plunge it into the ice water. Drain the basil again, pressing it against the sieve to extract as much water as possible.

3. Place the basil in a blender, add the olive oil, and puree until completely smooth. Transfer the mixture to a bowl, season with salt to taste, and let stand for at least 30 minutes before using. (If you'd like to have the bright green oil without the basil puree, strain the oil through a fine-mesh sieve into a clean bowl.) The oil will keep in the refrigerator for 1 week. Bring it to room temperature before using. **MAKES ABOUT 1/2 CUP**

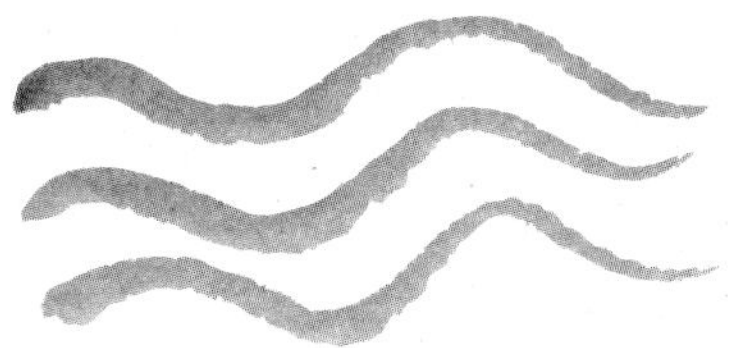

GRILLED CHICKEN WITH FRESH FIG SALSITA

POLLO A LA BRASA CON SALSITA DE HIGOS

There is tradition and there is innovation. And in between? For a taste of modern Spanish cuisine, I scour local food publications and the recipe supplements of popular women's magazines. "Spanish women," says my friend Toni Monné, editorial director of a Barcelona-based magazine group that publishes the wildly popular *Cocina Fácil,* "are no different from women all over the world. They work, they play, they tend to their families. When they cook, they want something attractive, healthy, and easy. Spanish for sure, but also worldly and modern." The recipe here, which I adapted from one of his magazines, captures this spirit.

The *salsita*—a kind of uncooked compote of sliced figs and onion, steeped in sherry and vinegar and tossed at the last moment with mint and almonds—is so yummy, consider making an extra batch. It also works great made with sliced plums.

8 to 9 smallish, ripe but firm fresh purple figs, trimmed and cut into thin wedges
1/2 small red onion, very thinly sliced
3 tablespoons medium-dry sherry
2 tablespoons sherry vinegar, preferably aged, or more to taste if figs are very sweet
3 tablespoons fragrant extra-virgin olive oil
3 large garlic cloves, chopped
1 tablespoon chopped fresh rosemary
Coarse salt (kosher or sea)
1/2 teaspoon freshly ground black pepper
3 boneless chicken breast halves (each 8 ounces) either skinless or with the skin, rinsed and patted dry
1/4 cup lightly toasted slivered almonds (see page 267)
1/4 cup finely slivered fresh mint

1. Place the figs, onion, sherry, vinegar, and 1 tablespoon of the olive oil in a bowl and toss to mix. Let the *salsita* stand for 30 minutes.

2. Light the grill and preheat it to high or preheat the broiler.

3. Place the garlic, rosemary, 1 teaspoon salt, and the pepper in a mortar and, using a pestle, mash them to a paste. Whisk in the remaining 2 tablespoons olive oil. Brush the chicken with some of the garlic paste. Grill or broil the chicken until lightly charred and cooked through, 6 to 8 minutes per side, turning it once and brushing it a few times with the remaining garlic paste.

4. Transfer the chicken to a cutting board and let rest for about 5 minutes. Slice the chicken on the diagonal into thick slices and arrange on a serving platter. Add the almonds and mint to the *salsita* and toss to mix. Season the *salsita* lightly with salt, then transfer it to a serving dish. Serve the chicken at once, accompanied by the *salsita.* **SERVES 4**

CHICKEN FLAMENQUIN

FLAMENQUINES DE POLLO

Classic *flamenquines* (Andalusian fried pork and serrano ham rolls) tend to be a bit pig-intensive and hefty. Not this updated chicken version, which I tasted in the Andalusian city of Osuna. Normally the rolls are layered with only ham and chopped parsley and garlic, but here they are made brighter and moister by the addition of piquillo peppers and luscious melting cheese. Sliced, the rolls turn into delicious, colorful pinwheels that can be served as a tapa or a light luncheon dish.

- 4 thinly sliced skinless, boneless chicken breast halves (scaloppine-cut, about 1 pound total)
- 2 tablespoons coarsely chopped fresh flat-leaf parsley
- 3 fat garlic cloves, coarsely chopped
- Coarse salt (kosher or sea)
- 4 wide, thin slices serrano ham or prosciutto (1 to 2 ounces)
- 4 piquillo peppers (from a can or jar), split and opened like a book, or 2 roasted red bell peppers (see page 385), cut in half
- 4 logs easy-melting cheese, such as Fontina, each about 3 inches long by 1 inch wide by 1/2 inch thick
- About 1 cup dry white bread crumbs, or more if needed
- 1 large egg, beaten in a shallow bowl
- Olive oil, for frying

1. Place a chicken scaloppine between two pieces of waxed paper or in a large, sturdy zipper-top bag and pound it with a kitchen mallet or heavy skillet until very thin, taking care not to tear the meat. Repeat with the remaining cutlets.

2. Place the parsley and garlic on a chopping board and, using a chef's knife, finely mince them together.

3. Place a pounded chicken scaloppine on a work surface and lightly sprinkle it with salt. Top with a slice of ham, trimming it to fit. Sprinkle some of the parsley mixture over the ham, then top with a piquillo pepper, trimming it to fit if necessary. Place a log of cheese across the shortest end of the cutlet, about 1 inch from the edge. Starting at this end, roll the scaloppine into a compact roll. Secure the end with a toothpick. Repeat with the remaining chicken.

4. Place the bread crumbs in a shallow bowl. Dip the chicken rolls in the beaten egg, then roll them in the bread crumbs. Make sure to thoroughly bread the short ends of the rolls, so the cheese can't leak out.

5. Line a large plate with a double layer of paper towels. Pour olive oil to a depth of ¾ inch in a medium-size skillet and heat over medium-high heat to 360°F; when hot, a piece of bread placed in the oil will sizzle on contact. Fry the chicken rolls until golden brown and cooked through on all sides, 7 to 8 minutes total, adjusting the heat so that the rolls don't burn. Using a slotted spoon, transfer the rolls to the paper towels to drain. When just cool enough to handle, transfer the rolls to a cutting board and cut them crosswise into thick slices. Serve at once. **SERVES 6 TO 8 AS A TAPA, 4 AS A LIGHT MAIN COURSE**

BASQUE CHICKEN WITH PEPPERS

POLLO A LA VASCA

The taste of sweet bell peppers is one of the quintessential flavors in the cooking of the País Vasco (Basque Country). Slowly sautéed and enriched with bits of *jamón,* they become a delectable sauce for chicken. In this recipe, given to me by Txuno Etxaniz—a cooking teacher and cookbook author from San Sebastián—the chicken is partially roasted then flambéed and baked in the pepper sauce. Roast potatoes are a classic accompaniment.

- 4 medium-size chicken legs (about 2 1/2 pounds total), separated into drumsticks and thighs, rinsed, patted dry, and trimmed of excess fat
- Coarse salt (kosher or sea) and freshly ground black pepper
- 1 large pinch of sweet (not smoked) paprika
- 3 tablespoons extra-virgin olive oil, or more if needed, plus more for brushing the chicken
- 1 medium-size onion, finely chopped
- 1 piece (3 to 4 ounces) serrano ham or prosciutto, finely diced
- 2 medium-size red bell peppers, cored, seeded, and finely diced
- 1 medium-size green bell pepper, cored, seeded, and finely diced
- 3 large garlic cloves, crushed with a garlic press
- 2 medium-size, ripe tomatoes, peeled, seeded, and chopped
- 2 to 3 tablespoons dry white wine
- 1/4 cup chicken stock or broth
- 1/4 cup brandy

1. Preheat the oven to 375°F.

2. Rub the chicken with salt, black pepper, and the paprika. Arrange the chicken in one layer in a wide earthenware *cazuela,* shallow casserole, or deep flameproof baking dish. Brush the chicken lightly with olive oil and bake until almost cooked through, about 35 minutes.

3. While the chicken is baking, heat the 3 tablespoons olive oil in a large skillet over medium-low heat. Add the onion and cook until limp but not browned, about 5 minutes. Add the ham and cook, stirring, until it just begins to brown, 1 to 2 minutes. Add the red and green peppers, reduce the heat to low, and cook, stirring occasionally, until the peppers soften, about 10 minutes. Add the garlic and stir for 30 seconds. Stir in the tomatoes, wine, and chicken stock, cover the skillet, and cook the pepper sauce until the vegetables are very soft, 10 to 12 minutes. Season with salt and pepper to taste.

4. Remove the *cazuela* from the oven and carefully spoon off the fat (leave the oven on). Place the *cazuela* over medium heat, add the brandy, and bring to a boil. Remove the pan from the heat and carefully ignite the brandy with a match, standing back until the flames subside.

5. Reduce the oven temperature to 325°F. Pour the pepper sauce evenly over the chicken and return the *cazuela* to the oven. Bake the chicken until it is very tender and the sauce thickens, about 15 minutes. Let the chicken cool for 10 to 15 minutes before serving. **SERVES 4**

ANDALUSIAN CHICKEN WITH GREEN OLIVES AND BITTER ORANGES

POLLO CON ACEITUNAS Y NARANJAS AGRIAS

Flavored with the briny olives and bitter oranges that are so ubiquitous in Seville, this Moorish-Andalusian recipe is refreshing and zesty, full of easy sophistication. To heighten the orange theme, I add orange segments to the sauce right before serving. Save some leftovers—this chicken is wonderful at room temperature.

4 medium-size chicken legs (about 2 1/2 pounds total), separated into drumsticks and thighs, rinsed, patted dry, and trimmed of excess fat
Coarse salt (kosher or sea) and freshly ground black pepper
2 tablespoons extra-virgin olive oil
1 large white onion, quartered and thinly sliced
2 large garlic cloves, minced
1/4 teaspoon ground cumin
1/4 cup medium-dry sherry
1/2 cup strained fresh bitter orange juice (see Note)
1/4 cup strained fresh regular orange juice
1 tablespoon minced orange zest
2 ripe plum tomatoes, peeled, seeded, and chopped
3/4 cup pitted green olives, such as picholine or Nafplion
3 tablespoons minced fresh flat-leaf parsley
2 medium-size tart juice oranges
2 tablespoons slivered fresh mint

1. Rub the chicken with salt and pepper and let stand for 10 minutes.

2. Place 1 tablespoon of the olive oil in a heavy, shallow flameproof casserole or sauté pan that can hold the chicken in a single layer and heat over medium-high heat. Working in two batches, brown the chicken all over, about 5 minutes per side. Transfer the browned chicken to a bowl.

3. Add the remaining 1 tablespoon olive oil to the casserole and reduce the heat to medium-low. Add the onion and cook, stirring occasionally, until it is limp but not browned, 5 to 7 minutes. Add the garlic and cumin and stir for 30 seconds. Add the sherry, increase the heat to high, and cook until the sherry is

Andalusian Chicken with Green Olives and Bitter Oranges

slightly reduced, about 1 minute. Add the bitter and regular orange juices and bring to a simmer. Return the chicken to the casserole, cover it, reduce the heat to low, and simmer for 15 minutes.

4. Add the orange zest, tomatoes, olives, and parsley to the casserole. Continue to cook the chicken over low heat, covered, turning it once or twice, until very tender, about 25 minutes.

5. Meanwhile, peel the oranges with a small, sharp knife, removing all the white pith. Working over a sieve set over a bowl, cut in between the membranes to release the orange sections. Carefully stir the orange sections into the stew and cook until heated through, about 5 minutes.

6. Transfer the chicken to a serving bowl, spoon the pan juices and olives over it, sprinkle the mint on top, and serve. **SERVES 4**

NOTE: Bitter oranges (aka Seville or sour oranges, or *naranjas agrias*) have a thick, slightly bumpy skin and can be found at many Hispanic groceries. If you can't find them, use ½ cup fresh lemon juice instead.

CHICKEN AND APPLES BRAISED IN HARD CIDER

POLLO A LA SIDRA

The population of Asturias is hooked on hard apple cider. Whatever isn't drunk ends up in a *cazuela* for braising smoky chorizo (see page 51), sardines, or hake, or this deliciously homey *pollo al sidra.* Asturian cider isn't sweet—in fact it can be diabolically acidic—so don't substitute regular apple cider or nonalcoholic sparkling cider. If you can't find dry imported hard cider at a specialty food shop or good liquor store, try using a cup of *cava* and two tablespoons of clear apple juice.

- 8 to 10 chicken thighs (3 to 3 1/2 pounds total) with skin, rinsed, patted dry, and trimmed of excess fat
- Coarse salt (kosher or sea) and freshly ground black pepper
- 3 to 4 tablespoons olive oil
- 2 slices best-quality smoky bacon or 1 slice pancetta, chopped (optional)
- 2 large onions, cut in half and sliced
- 1 cup dry hard cider
- 1 small bay leaf
- 1 tablespoon unsalted butter
- 1 large green apple, such as Granny Smith, peeled, cored, and sliced
- 1 tablespoon good apple cider vinegar, or more to taste

1. Preheat the oven to 375°F.

2. Rub the chicken generously with salt and pepper and let stand for 15 minutes.

3. Heat 1 tablespoon of the olive oil in a large flameproof casserole over medium-high heat. Working in two batches, brown the chicken all over, about 5 minutes per side, adding a little more olive oil if necessary. Using a slotted spoon, transfer the browned chicken to a bowl. Add the bacon, if using, to the casserole and cook, stirring, until it begins to render its fat, 2 minutes. Transfer the bacon to the bowl with the chicken. Add 2 more tablespoons olive oil and the onions to the casserole and cook until they begin to soften, about 5 minutes. Add 2 tablespoons of the cider, reduce the heat to low, cover the casserole, and cook until the onions are very soft, about 10 minutes. Add the remaining cider to the pan and boil over high heat until it is reduced by one-third, 5 minutes. Return the chicken to the casserole, placing it skin side up, stir in the bacon, and tuck in the bay leaf. The liquid should come no more than halfway up the chicken; if there is too much, spoon some liquid off. Bake the chicken, uncovered, until it is almost tender, about 40 minutes.

4. While the chicken is baking, melt the butter in a large skillet over medium heat. Add the apple and cook, stirring, until it softens, about 5 minutes.

5. Remove the casserole from the oven and carefully transfer the pieces of chicken to a plate. Add the apples and the vinegar to the cooking liquid and return the chicken to the casserole, skin side up. Increase the oven temperature to 425°F and bake the chicken, uncovered, until it is well browned and the cooking liquid is reduced, about 15 minutes. Serve at once. **SERVES 4**

SIDRA, SIDRA!

In the region of Asturias, Spain's answer to the Scottish Highlands, cider consumption is a highly ritualized activity. You enter a dim rustic tavern called a *chigre* and call out your order. The barman uncorks an unlabeled green bottle the size of a bottle of wine. To your great surprise, he stretches his arm high above his head and, holding the bottle at a slight angle, pours about an inch of *sidra* into a thin, wide pint-size glass held way below his waist. Good *esacanciadores* (pourers) can pour from great heights without as much as looking; virtuosos can even pour holding the glass behind their back. These guys aren't just showing off. The procedure—called "throwing" the cider—oxygenates and fizzes it up, reinforcing the natural fermentation and the *sidra's* apple bouquet. Tradition dictates that you swallow your aerated inch quickly, leaving some in the glass and splashing the dregs right onto the sawdust-covered floor. The same tradition tells you to beware of cider drinkers who seem to aim at your shoes. After the first round, you take a bite of chorizo (usually braised in cider) or Cabrales cheese (often mashed up with, what else . . . cider), and start over. The alcohol content may be low—usually between 4 and 6 percent—but after about four glasses, you suddenly realize that your legs can barely carry you home. An average Asturian male is said to consume some ten liters of cider a day. *Que vida.*

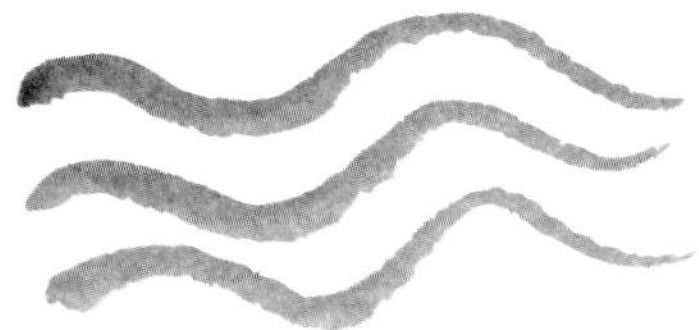

CATALAN CHRISTMAS TURKEY

GALL DINDI FARCIT

Turkey or capon graces Christmas tables in many regions of Spain, but in Catalonia it's a holiday must, normally accompanied by a delicious stuffing of dried fruit, pine nuts, and the subtly spiced pork sausage called *butifarra*. No reason this regal dish can't be translated to American Thanksgiving. And if you'd like to Americanize the stuffing a little, add two or three cups of plain bread stuffing to the dried fruit and sausage mixture. Gravy isn't a particularly Spanish concept, but feel free to thicken the yummy sherry-flavored pan juices with flour. Using good-quality, preferably organic dried fruit in the stuffing will make all the difference.

FOR THE TURKEY:

12 medium-size garlic cloves, coarsely chopped
1 tablespoon crumbled dried rosemary
1 tablespoon crumbled dried thyme
2 bay leaves, crumbled
4 1/2 teaspoons coarse salt (kosher or sea)
1 tablespoon black peppercorns
1 1/2 teaspoons olive oil
1 fresh turkey (12 to 14 pounds), preferably kosher, rinsed and patted dry, neck and giblets reserved for making stock or another use

FOR THE STUFFING AND SAUCE:

2 cups dry sherry
1 pound mixed dried fruit, such as apricots, apples, peaches, and/or prunes, larger pieces cut in half or quarters
1 1/2 cups dried cherries or cranberries
1 pound fresh mild pork sausage links (if using Italian sausage, use one without fennel)
2 tablespoons olive oil
2 medium-size onions, chopped
1 large Granny Smith apple, peeled, cored, and chopped
1 teaspoon crumbled dried rosemary
1 teaspoon dried thyme
1 small cinnamon stick
Coarse salt (kosher or sea) and freshly ground black pepper
About 1/2 cup chicken stock or broth, if needed
1 cup lightly toasted pine nuts (see page 267)

1. Prepare the turkey: Place the garlic, the rosemary and thyme, and the salt, peppercorns, and olive oil in a mini food processor and process to a paste. Rub this mixture all over the turkey, including inside the cavities. Cover the turkey loosely with plastic wrap and let stand while you make the stuffing.

2. Make the stuffing: Place 1 cup of the sherry in a small saucepan and bring to a boil over medium-high heat. Place the dried fruit and the cherries in a heatproof bowl, pour the hot sherry over them, and let stand for 30 minutes. While the fruit is soaking, cook the sausage in boiling water for 2 minutes, drain, and cut into thick slices.

3. Heat the olive oil in a very large skillet over medium heat. Add the onions and cook until barely softened, about 5 minutes. Add the apple and cook, stirring, until it begins to soften, 5 minutes. Add the

sausage and cook, stirring, until it is lightly browned, another 2 to 3 minutes. Stir in the dried fruit and their soaking liquid, the rosemary and thyme, and the cinnamon stick. Season with salt and pepper to taste. Cook the stuffing, stirring occasionally, until the sausage is cooked through and the fruit is soft, about 8 minutes, lowering the heat if it seems to be browning too much. If you'd like the stuffing a little moister, add a little chicken stock. Transfer the stuffing to a bowl, stir in the pine nuts, and let cool to room temperature.

4. Preheat the oven to 450°F.

5. Right before roasting, loosely stuff the main cavity of the turkey with some of the stuffing. Tie the legs together with kitchen string, or if you prefer, secure the legs together with a skewer. Spoon some stuffing into the neck cavity and tuck the excess skin under the turkey. Place the remaining stuffing in a 1½- to 2-quart baking dish, cover it with aluminum foil, and set aside. Place the turkey breast side up in a large roasting pan and bake for 40 minutes. Reduce the oven temperature to 350°F, add 1 cup water to the roasting pan, and bake until an instant-read meat thermometer inserted into the inner thigh (but not so that it touches a bone) registers about 180°F, about 3 hours longer. As the turkey roasts, add 1 cup water to the pan every hour. (The total roasting time will be about 3 hours and 40 minutes.)

6. Transfer the turkey to a cutting board, cover it loosely with aluminum foil to keep warm, and let rest for 35 to 40 minutes. Skim the fat off the pan juices, and set it aside if you want to make gravy.

7. Moisten the remaining stuffing with about ½ cup of the turkey pan juices and bake, covered with aluminum foil, while the turkey rests.

8. To make the sauce, add the remaining 1 cup sherry to the roasting pan. Set the pan over medium-high heat on 2 burners and scrape the bottom to dislodge the brown bits. Cook the pan juices until they are reduced by about one fourth, 5 to 7 minutes. (If you'd like to make gravy, add 3 to 4 tablespoons of flour to 3 to 4 tablespoons of skimmed fat and whisk until a paste forms. Whisk the flour mixture 2 tablespoons at a time into the pan juices and cook until the sauce thickens to your liking, 3 to 5 minutes.)

9. Carve the turkey and arrange it on a serving platter. Serve with the reduced pan juices or gravy and the stuffing from the turkey and the baking dish. **SERVES 8 TO 10**

The streets of Barcelona put on a particularly festive show at Christmastime.

DUCK LEGS WITH PRUNES AND OLIVES

ANEC AMB PRUNES I OLIVES

Say Ampurdan to the Catalans, and they'll start smacking their lips, gleefully recalling the specialties of this inland region north of Barcelona, where the earthy, homey cuisine revolves around rich duck stews, meat and dried fruit combinations, snails, wild mushrooms, and game. This quintessential Ampurdán recipe is from Jaume Vidal, a great chef and hotelier whose small, lovingly decorated inn—La Plaça, in Madremanya—is one of Spain's great little secrets. The combination of the sweet prunes and briny olives lends the sauce a very special complexity. As with many Catalan dishes, the final layer of flavor comes from the *picada,* a mixture of garlic, parsley, and nuts. This isn't exactly a throw-it-in-the-pot-and-forget-it affair, but the resulting dish is truly sensational, well worth a little extra effort.

FOR THE DUCK:

6 large, meaty duck legs (about 4 1/2 pounds total)
Coarse salt (kosher or sea) and freshly ground black pepper
1 large leek, white part only, trimmed and thinly sliced
1 medium-size onion, chopped
1 medium-size carrot, cut into 1/2-inch dice
3 medium-size ripe tomatoes, chopped
1 1/4 cups full-bodied dry red wine
3 1/2 cups chicken stock or broth, or more if needed
1 small bay leaf
1 fresh or dried thyme or rosemary sprig
1 cup halved pitted prunes
3/4 cup pitted green olives, such as picholine, cut in half

FOR THE PICADA:

1 tea biscuit, such as a Maria, or 2 Ritz crackers, crumbled
2 tablespoons chopped lightly toasted hazelnuts or almonds (see page 267)
2 tablespoons toasted pine nuts (see page 267), plus 1/4 cup for garnish
2 medium-size garlic cloves, chopped
3 tablespoons chopped fresh flat-leaf parsley
1/4 cup sweet white wine, such as muscatel, or 1/4 cup medium-sweet sherry

1. Preheat the oven to 325°F.

2. Prepare the duck: Trim the excess fat from the duck legs, setting aside about 1 tablespoon fat. Rinse the duck, pat it thoroughly dry with paper towels, and season it with salt and pepper. Heat the 1 tablespoon duck fat over medium-high heat in a heavy casserole large enough to hold the duck legs in a single layer. Working in two batches, cook the legs, skin side down, until richly browned, about 10 minutes per batch. Turn the legs and cook them until browned on the other side, about 3 minutes. Transfer the duck to paper towels to drain. Carefully spoon off the excess fat before browning the second batch.

3. Once the second batch of duck is browned, pour off all but 2 tablespoons fat from the casserole. Add the leek, onion, and carrot and cook over medium-high heat, stirring, until richly browned, about 10 minutes. Add the tomatoes and cook until they are softened, about 5 minutes. Add ¾ cup of the wine, the chicken stock, bay leaf, and thyme and bring to a simmer, skimming any foam off the surface. Return the duck to the casserole, then cover it. Bake the duck until it is very tender, 1¾ to 2 hours.

4. While the duck is cooking, place the prunes and the remaining ½ cup wine in a microwave-safe bowl and microwave on high power for 1½ minutes. Let stand until the prunes soften, about 10 minutes.

5. When the duck legs are done, transfer them, using tongs, to a plate and cover with aluminum foil to keep warm. Spoon off as much fat as possible from the braising liquid. (The dish can be prepared up to a day ahead to this point. Gently reheat it before proceeding.) Strain the braising liquid and the vegetables through a fine sieve, pressing down on the vegetables to extract all the liquid. Then discard the vegetables and return the liquid to the casserole. Add the prunes with their soaking liquid and the olives and season with salt and pepper to taste. Cook over low heat, covered, for 15 minutes, skimming any foam off the surface if necessary.

6. Meanwhile, make the *picada*: Place the tea biscuit, hazelnuts, 2 tablespoons pine nuts, the garlic, and parsley in a mini food processor and pulse just until the biscuit and nuts are ground. Add the muscatel and pulse to combine. Stir the *picada* into the sauce and simmer until the flavors blend, about 3 minutes, stirring. If the sauce seems too thick, add a little more stock or some water. Return the duck legs to the casserole, spooning the sauce on top so that they are covered. Cook over low heat until the flavors meld, about 3 minutes. You can serve the duck and sauce directly from the casserole or transfer it to a serving dish. Sprinkle the remaining ¼ cup pine nuts on top before serving. **SERVES 6**

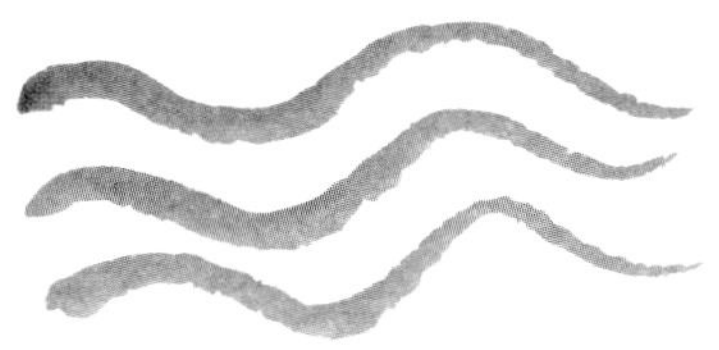

HUNTER'S-STYLE BAKED QUAIL IN ESCABECHE

CODORNIZ ASADA EN ESCABECHE

Slowly baking quail completely covered with an *escabeche* of olive oil, vinegar, white wine, and herbs produces exceptionally moist birds, deliciously suffused with the tang of the marinade and so tender that the meat easily slips off the bones. Served hot or warm, the quail is delicious over lentils, with some marinade on the side. Cold, it's wonderful over an astringent frisée salad. This preparation is usually reserved for partridge, the "it" game in Spain, but quail, as well as Cornish hen or small chickens, are also exceptionally tasty made this way.

Don't worry about the generous amount of olive oil here; the birds are drained before serving. Just don't use a heavy oil for this dish, as it would drown out other flavors. (For more about *escabeche*, see page 298.)

ESCABECHE

The Mediterraneans have a delicious tradition of pickling cooked fish or fowl in a mixture of vinegar and olive oil, typically perfumed with bay leaves, herbs, and plenty of garlic. Known as *escabeche* in Spain and *scapece* in Sicily, the technique was introduced to the area by the Arabs (the word is possibly derived from the Persian *sikbaj,* meaning vinegar stew). In pre-refrigeration days, *escabeches* constituted a basic but ingenious way of preserving food. The ancient Romans were on to this pickling method as well. To preserve fried fish, Apicius instructs, "the moment they are fried and taken out of the pan, pour hot vinegar over them." Not only did food conserved in oil and vinegar last almost forever, it was also delectable: The vinegar kept it tender; the oil made it luscious and moist; the long pickling time left it permeated with the flavor of garlic and spices. According to historical sources, as long ago as the fourteenth century, Spain had roving *escabeche* merchants who packed fish in the marinade in port cities, then transported their wares to the landlocked interior, where fresh fish would never otherwise make it without spoiling. Sixteenth- and seventeenth-century Spanish cookbooks offer plenty of recipes for *escabeches,* usually extravagantly spiced with saffron, bay leaves, and cloves and often including honey and orange juice, as well as mashed-up raisins and pounded nuts and bread.

Though the need for preservation is long gone, *escabeches* continue to captivate Spanish taste buds (this is, after all, a country crazy for conserves). Most popular *escabeches* involve fish, such as tuna, sardines, or anchovies, but the method is even more delicious with poultry and game, such as quail, rabbit, and especially partridge. You'll find an *escabeche* recipe for quail on this page and for fish on page 57.

6 jumbo quail (6 to 8 ounces each; see Note), rinsed well and patted dry
Coarse salt (kosher or sea) and freshly ground black pepper
2 tablespoons plus 1 cup light extra-virgin olive oil
3 large shallots, chopped
1 cup tarragon vinegar or best-quality white wine vinegar
3/4 cup dry white wine
3 medium-size garlic heads, tops trimmed off and outer layer of skin removed
2 bay leaves
2 fresh rosemary sprigs
2 fresh thyme sprigs
1 teaspoon black peppercorns
Chicken stock or broth (optional)

1. Preheat the oven to 325°F.

2. Season the quail generously inside and out with salt and pepper. Heat the 2 tablespoons olive oil over medium heat in a large flameproof casserole that can accommodate all of the birds in one layer. Working in two batches, brown the quail on all sides, about 7 minutes. Transfer the quail to a bowl, add the shallots to the casserole, and cook until soft and lightly colored, about 5 minutes.

3. Return the quail to the casserole, arranging them breast side down. Add the vinegar, wine, garlic, bay leaves, rosemary, thyme, and peppercorns. If there isn't enough liquid to completely cover the quail, add enough chicken stock or water to cover. Bring to a simmer, then carefully transfer the casserole to the oven. Bake the quail, uncovered, until they are extremely tender (the legs should wiggle easily in the joints), about 1¼ hours. Remove the casserole from the oven and let cool for about 15 minutes. Remove and discard the bay leaves.

4. To serve, remove the quail from the cooking liquid and wipe off the excess. If serving the quail hot or warm, make a quick sauce by boiling some of the strained cooking liquid over medium-high heat until it reduces by one third, about 10 minutes. Transfer the quail to serving plates and pass the sauce alongside. If serving the quail cold, transfer it and the cooking liquid to a bowl and let cool. The quail will keep, covered, in the refrigerator for up to 1 week. Bring to room temperature before serving. **SERVES 6**

NOTE: Look for quail at Chinese groceries and supermarkets, where they cost a fraction of what you'd pay at a fancy butcher. Try to find birds labeled jumbo or extra-large.

GRILLED QUAIL WITH MUSHROOMS AND HONEY-COFFEE VINAIGRETTE

CODORNIZ A LAS BRAVAS CON SETAS Y VINAGRETA DE MIEL Y CAFE

This dish was inspired by Josep Maria Boix, a great Michelin-starred chef at the Torre del Remei hotel in the Catalan Pyrenees. Boix's secret ingredient, coffee, adds an interesting note to the sauce, accenting the earthiness of the mushrooms and the smokiness of the grilled quail. At his restaurant, Boix serves quail legs as a dainty appetizer on top of frisée leaves. My adaptation, featuring halved birds, will serve four as a light main course or eight as an appetizer. If you're serving it for eight, you'll need to increase the amount of the frisée and the mushrooms slightly.

FOR THE HONEY-COFFEE VINAIGRETTE:

5 tablespoons strong brewed coffee
5 tablespoons sherry vinegar, preferably aged
2 teaspoons honey
1 large shallot, minced
1 teaspoon coarsely ground coffee beans
1/2 cup extra-virgin olive oil
Coarse salt (kosher or sea) and freshly ground black pepper

FOR THE QUAIL:

1/4 cup extra-virgin olive oil, or more if needed
4 large garlic cloves, crushed with a garlic press
1 teaspoon crumbled dried rosemary
1 teaspoon crumbled dried thyme
Coarse salt (kosher or sea) and freshly ground black pepper
4 partially boned quail (about 4 ounces each), cut in half lengthwise through the breast (ask your butcher to do this; see Note), rinsed, and patted dry
1 pound mild mushrooms (chanterelles, cèpes, shiitake caps, small cremini), wiped clean with a damp paper towel, larger ones coarsely chopped, small ones left whole
8 cups frisée, rinsed and dried

1. Make the vinaigrette: Place the brewed coffee, vinegar, honey, shallot, and ground coffee in a small bowl and whisk to mix well. Gradually whisk in the olive oil. Season the vinaigrette with salt and pepper to taste, then set it aside.

2. Prepare the quail: Place 2 tablespoons of the olive oil, half of the garlic, the rosemary, thyme, and ½ teaspoon each of salt and pepper in a small bowl and stir to mix. Rub this paste all over the quail and let stand while you prepare the mushrooms.

3. Heat the remaining 2 tablespoons olive oil in a large skillet over medium-high heat. Add the mushrooms and the remaining garlic and cook, stirring, until the mushrooms are lightly browned and tender, about 6 minutes, adding a little more olive oil if the skillet looks dry. Add about 2 tablespoons of the vinaigrette to the mushrooms and cook until heated through, about 1 minute.

4. Light the grill and preheat it to medium.

5. Grill the quail on a well-oiled grate about 5 inches above the glowing coals until the skin is nicely browned and charred in spots and the breast meat is pink, about 3 minutes per side. (The quail can also be broiled or cooked on the stove top in a well-oiled ridged grill pan.)

6. To serve, place the frisée in a large bowl and toss it with just enough of the vinaigrette to coat the leaves lightly, then season with salt and pepper to taste. Divide the frisée among 4 dinner plates, placing it to one side. Spoon some mushrooms on each plate and top them with two quail halves. Serve with the remaining vinaigrette on the side. **SERVES 4 AS A LIGHT MAIN COURSE**

NOTE: Many butchers carry partially boned quail with the rib cage removed, but the legs and wing bones still intact. They weigh about 4 ounces (boned weight). If you can't find them at your local market, they may be mail-ordered from www.dartagnan.com.

RABBIT STEW WITH A TOUCH OF CHOCOLATE

CONEJO CON CHOCOLATE RODRIGO MESTRE

Cooking meat, chicken—even crustaceans—in a dark, intense sauce tinged with chocolate is a culinary tradition that never fails to surprise and delight visitors to Catalonia. As with Mexican moles, chocolate contributes complexity and intrigue to the sauce without overpowering it. This exceptional rabbit recipe comes from my friend, Rodrigo Mestre, a legendary Catalan bon vivant and author of sixteen cookbooks. Adding chocolate to savory dishes, Rodri says, became fashionable in Catalonia during the boom in chocolate trade with the Antilles. For the cooking wine, he suggests a good Priorat red, but as that's not a cheap proposition, feel free to use any full-bodied red with a lively acidity. Adding orange zest is Rodri's secret touch, of which he is justifiably proud. He suggests following the dish with a salad of curly endive, torn into small pieces and dressed with good olive oil, lemon juice, and a generous pinch of salt. Spinach with Raisins and Pine Nuts (page 388) is always a fine accompaniment.

- 1 rabbit (2 1/2 to 3 pounds), cut into 8 pieces, rinsed well and patted dry
- Coarse salt (kosher or sea) and freshly ground black pepper
- 2 cups full-bodied dry red wine
- 1 large carrot, diced
- 1 large yellow onion, coarsely chopped
- 6 medium-size garlic cloves, peeled and lightly crushed
- 1 fresh thyme sprig
- 1 fresh rosemary sprig
- 1 small bay leaf
- 6 black peppercorns
- 1 small cinnamon stick
- All-purpose flour, for dusting the rabbit
- 3 tablespoons olive oil
- 1/4 cup brandy
- 1 1/2 cups chicken stock or broth
- 1 ounce bittersweet chocolate, grated or finely chopped
- 2 teaspoons grated orange zest

1. Rub the rabbit generously with salt and pepper, then place it in a glass dish large enough to hold the pieces in a single layer. Add the wine, carrot, onion, and garlic. Cover the dish and refrigerate the rabbit for about 4 hours, turning the pieces occasionally.

2. Meanwhile, place the thyme, rosemary, bay leaf, peppercorns, and cinnamon stick in a double layer of cheesecloth and tie it closed. Set the cheesecloth bag aside.

3. Remove the rabbit from the marinade and pat dry with paper towels. Strain the marinade, setting aside the liquid and the vegetables separately. Blot the vegetables dry with paper towels.

4. Spread a thin layer of flour on a large plate and lightly dust the rabbit with it. Heat 2 tablespoons of the olive oil in a heavy 4- to 5-quart flameproof casserole over medium-high heat. Working in two batches, cook the rabbit until nicely browned all over, about 7 minutes per batch, then transfer it to a bowl.

5. Heat the remaining 1 tablespoon olive oil in the casserole over medium-high heat, add the vegetables from the marinade, and cook until softened and lightly browned, about 7 minutes. Add the brandy and boil for 30 seconds, scraping up the brown bits from the bottom of the casserole. Add the reserved liquid from the marinade and the chicken stock and bring to a simmer, skimming any foam off the surface and scraping up any more brown bits. Return the rabbit to the casserole and tuck the cheesecloth bag of herbs under it. If there isn't enough liquid to just cover the rabbit, add a little water. Cover the casserole and simmer over low heat, skimming off the foam occasionally and turning the rabbit pieces, until the rabbit is tender, about 1 hour.

6. Using a slotted spoon, transfer the rabbit to a bowl and cover with aluminum foil to keep warm. Increase the heat to high and cook the sauce until it is reduced by one third, 5 to 7 minutes. Remove and discard the cheesecloth bag. Reduce the heat to low and add the chocolate, stirring constantly and scraping the bottom of the casserole, until the chocolate melts. Add the orange zest and simmer, stirring, for 1 minute longer. Taste for seasoning, adding more salt and/or pepper as necessary. Return the rabbit to the casserole and cook over very low heat until the flavors meld, 5 to 10 minutes. **SERVES 4 TO 6**

BEANS AND POTATOES

RUSTIC ELEGANCE

Spanish cuisine presents a delicious dichotomy. On the one hand it's all Mediterranean lightness; on the other, it's defined by big-flavored stews starring potatoes and legumes. Because the bean pot is central to

From left to right: Spanish beans and legumes tend to be of exceptional quality; Spain is the world's largest producer of olive oil, and most of it comes from groves like this one, in Andalusia; A riot of comestibles tempts shoppers at a market in Barcelona; Beauties in flamenco costumes enjoy hot dogs (of all things!) and beer at a raucous fair in Jeréz, Andalusia.

traditional Spanish cooking, no other country treats legumes with so much finesse and respect. Chickpeas, lentils, and favas have been relished in Spain since antiquity. Another bean species, *Phaseolus vulgaris* (which includes kidney beans), hails from the New World and was originally cultivated and popularized in Spain by the monks. Historically cheap, tasty, nutritious, and easy to grow, legumes form the backbone of the most important family of Spanish dishes: *potajes, guisos, ollas, potes, pucheros, cocidos*. These bracing stews, soups, and casseroles normally combine pulses and vegetables with meat or, during Lent, bacalao. Once the pillar of *cocina pobre*—poor man's cuisine—today best-quality legumes can be as expensive as seasonal vegetables, and top-grade charcuterie likewise isn't cheap. No matter. Bean cuisine continues to flourish in Spain—in homes, at humble roadside *tabernas,* and at Michelin-starred restaurants where an ethereal emulsion of white beans or chickpeas might come topped with *cigalas* (langoustines) or sautéed foie gras.

Spanish cooks treat legumes in a manner that borders on fetishistic. That's because their beans, lentils, and chickpeas are precious jewels compared to those of most other countries. The best kinds are awarded prizes and afforded prestigious denomination of origin status, like fine wines or boutique olive oils. All over Spain, there are bean-harvesting fiestas and bean-cooking contests. At markets, reputable vendors will often advertise the age of their beans, lest you suspect them to be old and grainy.

Bean preparation is taken seriously here. The cooking liquid is kept at the merest of simmers, and cold water is regularly splashed into the pot to lower the temperature (a nifty technique that keeps beans meltingly tender yet completely intact). The sausages are often precooked separately to cast off excess fat. The resulting bean stews come out tasting pure, noble, and improbably light.

And the potato? Scorned and neglected for almost three centuries after its introduction to Spain in the 1570s, today *la patata* forms a whole subgenre of Spanish gastronomy. The litany of evocatively titled potato dishes is long enough to fill many chapters. Recipe names like *patatas a lo pobre* (poor man's potatoes) and *patatas viudas* (widowed potatoes) hint at their frugal simplicity. But there are heartier dishes, too, such as *patatas a la riojana* with chorizo and peppers; the saucy Basque potatoes in *salsa verde*; a wondrous *zorongollo* from Extremadura—sautéed potatoes and roasted peppers bathed in roasted tomato sauce.

Substantial potato dishes are often featured as the main course at lunch. In this chapter, potatoes also appear stuffed with salt cod *brandada*; sliced and layered with an unusual *picadillo* of minced chorizo and dates; cooked in salt and served with a piquant *mojo* in the style of Canary Islands; and gratinéed with a garlicky Catalan *allioli.* Though the poverty is long gone, *cocina pobre* staples continue to captivate Spanish taste buds. They'll do the same for yours.

BEANS

FABADA
THE ASTURIAN CASSOULET

FABADA

What paella is to Valencia, *fabada* is to the misty, mountainous Asturias region: a one-dish masterpiece that gourmands from all over Spain will happily travel to eat. Along with Brazilian *feijoada* and French cassoulet, *fabada* deserves pride of place in the pantheon of the world's greatest bean dishes. And while even the best cassoulet can be somewhat sludgy and over-rich—not to mention staggeringly time-consuming—a well-prepared *fabada* will taste light and beautifully restrained.

Scrupulous cooking and the quality of Asturian *embutidos* (charcuterie) is what makes a good *fabada* so special. The legumes are the stark white, enormous oblong beans called *fabes de la granja,* which boast their own denomination of origin. The meats that go into *fabada* are collectively called *campagno,* meaning comrade or complement. These always include artisanally produced Asturian chorizo and blood sausage, and sometimes pancetta or bacon, and/or *lacon,* the pink salt-cured ham that needs to be soaked in cold water. To avoid the dish being overly smoky and greasy, perfectionist chefs usually blanch the meats. They also insist that the *fabada* has to be cooked long and slow, with the liquid barely bubbling. At many restaurants, *fabada* is served in two courses—first the beans, as a soup, followed by the *campagno.*

1 piece (1/2 pound) pancetta
3/4 pound sweet Spanish-style chorizo sausage
1/2 pound morcilla or other blood sausage
2 medium-size onions; 1 cut in half, 1 finely chopped
4 large fresh flat-leaf parsley sprigs
3 medium-size garlic cloves, smashed
2 small bay leaves
4 cups (about 1 1/2 pounds) Asturian fabes (see Note) or white cannellini beans, soaked overnight or quick-soaked (see page 308) and drained
1 piece (1 1/2 pounds) good smoky ham, preferably with a bone
About 1 1/2 cups cold chicken stock or broth, or more if needed
2 tablespoons extra-virgin olive oil, plus more if needed
1 teaspoon smoked sweet Spanish paprika, or more if needed
1 large pinch of saffron, pulverized in a mortar and steeped in 2 tablespoons very hot water
Coarse salt (kosher or sea) and freshly ground black pepper

1. Bring a medium-size pot of water to a boil. Add the pancetta, chorizo, and *morcilla* and cook for 2 to 3 minutes. Drain, setting the *morcilla* aside separately.

BEAN FUSS

The primal place of legumes on the Spanish table today is understandable when you consider the quality of the raw material. Catalans go nuts for the small, smooth white Santa Pau beans from the volcanic Garrotxa region, so delicious with grilled *butifarra* sausage. Castilians are willing to pay through the nose for the large, buttery *judiones de la Granja,* white beans grown near Segovia that are slowly simmered with a whole assortment of pig parts. Any good *cocido* restaurant in Madrid has a secret supplier in León or Salamanca that provides artisanal chickpeas with the thinnest skins and the texture of velvet. Asturians fuss over their huge white oval *fabes,* which star in *fabada,* the region's answer to French cassoulet. Rioja and Navarra are famed for *pochas,* fresh white beans from the vine stewed together with anything from quail to partridge to bacalao to blood sausage to clams. Lentils come in several varieties, from creamy green *castellanas* to the small, nutty *pardinas,* which remain remarkably firm as they cook.

Most recipes in this chapter will be delicious made with supermarket dried chickpeas or beans (I recommend the Goya brand). For something better than good, seek out best-quality organic legumes, or, better still, order boutique Spanish beans (see page 461 for sources). Twelve bucks for a pound isn't too much—not when you consider that these are the Champagne of beans.

2. Place the onion halves, parsley, garlic, and bay leaves in a double layer of cheesecloth and tie it shut.

3. Place the beans, ham, pancetta, and chorizo in a 6-quart pot and add cold water to cover by 2 inches. Bring to a boil over high heat, thoroughly skimming off the foam, and add the cheesecloth bag of aromatics. Reduce the heat to low, cover the pot, and cook for 1 hour, skimming the foam off occasionally and adding 3 to 4 tablespoons of the cold chicken stock every 20 minutes. The cooking liquid should barely bubble.

4. Heat the olive oil in a medium-size skillet over medium heat. Add the chopped onion and cook until soft but not browned, 6 to 7 minutes. Remove the skillet from the heat and stir in the paprika. Stir the onion mixture into the bean pot along with the *morcilla* and saffron. Cook until the beans are completely tender and creamy but not falling apart, about 45 minutes to 1 hour longer, adding some cold chicken stock every 20 minutes to maintain the level of liquid.

5. To serve, remove the cheesecloth bag from the pot and discard it. Using a slotted spoon, transfer the ham, pancetta, chorizo, and *morcilla* to a cutting board. If there are any bean skins floating on top of the cooking liquid, skim them off. Remove about ¼ cup of the beans from the pot, mash them up coarsely with a fork, and stir them back into the beans. Cut the meats into chunks and slice the sausages, then carefully stir them into the beans. Taste the stew; if you'd like it a little redder and smokier, heat a little more olive oil in a small skillet over low heat, add about 1 teaspoon paprika, and stir the paprika mixture into the beans. Ladle the stew into soup bowls and serve. **SERVES 10 TO 12**

NOTE: *Fabes,* the huge, tender beans used for *fabada,* are available by mail order (see page 461). While not cheap, they'll make the dish extra special. However, you can still create an excellent *fabada* with regular white beans, such as cannellini. Some like their *fabada* thicker, some thinner; the texture is easily regulated by mashing the desired amount of the beans and stirring them into the pot.

LENTIL AND PUMPKIN STEW WITH ROASTED GARLIC

POTAJE DE LENTEJAS Y CALABAZA

This nourishing *potaje* flavored with fresh *and* roasted garlic makes a terrific vegetarian entrée. If you prefer it more full-bodied, however, use chicken broth instead of water and feel free to add a handful of chopped pancetta to the *sofrito* in Step 4. You can serve the dish as a soupy first course or over rice.

1 large garlic head, plus 4 minced garlic cloves
3 tablespoons extra-virgin olive oil, plus more for brushing the garlic
2 medium-size onions; 1 cut in half, 1 finely chopped
1 fresh thyme sprig
1 bay leaf
1 1/2 cups green or brown lentils, rinsed and picked over
8 to 9 cups water or chicken broth, or more as needed
2 Italian (frying) peppers, cored, seeded, and chopped
2 large ripe tomatoes, peeled and chopped
1/2 pound pumpkin or butternut squash, cut into 3/4-inch cubes
1/2 teaspoon sweet or smoked paprika
Coarse salt (kosher or sea) and freshly ground black pepper
2 tablespoons minced fresh flat-leaf parsley
1 medium-size pinch of saffron
2 tablespoons sherry vinegar, preferably aged, or best-quality red wine vinegar, or more to taste

1. Preheat the oven to 400°F.

2. Cut the top off the head of garlic and discard it. Brush the cut edge of the garlic with olive oil, place it in a small baking dish, and bake until soft, 25 to 30 minutes. When the garlic is cool enough to handle, place it in a double layer of cheesecloth along with the onion halves, thyme, and bay leaf and tie the cheesecloth shut.

3. Place the lentils in a 4-quart pot, add 8 cups water, and bring to a boil over medium-high heat. Skim any foam off the surface, then add the cheesecloth bag, 1 tablespoon of the olive oil, half of the

Inexpensive daily menus fuel diners at many homey Spanish restaurants.

Italian peppers, and half of the tomatoes. Reduce the heat to low, cover the pot, and simmer for 20 minutes. Add the pumpkin and cook until it is almost tender, 20 minutes.

4. While the lentils are cooking, heat the remaining 2 tablespoons olive oil in a small skillet over medium-low heat. Add the chopped onion and remaining Italian pepper and cook, stirring, until soft but not browned, 5 to 7 minutes. Add the paprika and the remaining tomato and cook until the tomato is softened and reduced, 5 minutes. Add the onion mixture to the lentils. If the lentils seem too thick, add some or all of the remaining water. Season the lentils with salt and black pepper to taste and simmer until the lentils and pumpkin are very soft, about 10 minutes longer (it's all right if the pumpkin begins to disintegrate a bit).

5. Remove the cheesecloth bag from the lentils and discard all but the garlic head. Squeeze the flesh from the roasted garlic and chop it finely or coarsely mash it with a fork. Place the raw minced garlic, the parsley, saffron, and a small pinch of salt in a mortar and, using a pestle, mash them to a paste. Add the roasted garlic and mash until combined. Add 2 tablespoons very hot water to the mortar and let sit for 2 to 3 minutes. Stir the garlic mixture into the lentils. Add the vinegar. Taste for seasoning, adding more salt, pepper, and/or vinegar as necessary. Let the lentils cool for 5 to 10 minutes, then serve.

SERVES 4 TO 6

QUICK-SOAKING BEANS

Good-quality legumes in Spain tend to be dried for a longer period of time than those dried in the States. So, Spanish cooks always insist on an overnight soak. Beans available in the States, however, often cook to a firmer, smoother texture when quick-soaked. To quick soak 2 cups of beans or chickpeas, bring about 3 quarts of water to a boil in a large pot over high heat. Add the beans and let boil for 2 to 3 minutes. Take the beans off the heat, cover the pot, and let the beans stand for 1 hour. Drain the beans before using.

LENTIL AND WILD MUSHROOM HASH WITH POACHED EGGS

LENTEJAS CON SETAS Y HUEVOS ESCALFADOS

The earthy combination of lentils, dusky mushrooms, and slightly runny poached egg is nothing if not inspired. Syrupy balsamic vinegar and good olive oil drizzled around the edges lend special savor and elegance. Serve it as a brunch dish or a first course for a winter meal. Without the eggs, the lentil and mushroom hash makes a delicious side dish. Though supermarket brown lentils are fine, the best legumes for the job are firm, high-quality lentils, such as Spanish *pardinas,* French du Puy, or Italian lentils from Umbria.

- 3/4 cup lentils (see Note), rinsed and picked over
- 2 medium-size garlic cloves, smashed, plus 3 large cloves, minced
- 1 small bay leaf
- Coarse salt (kosher or sea)
- 5 tablespoons extra-virgin olive oil
- 9 to 10 ounces assorted wild mushrooms or a mixture of wild and cultivated mushrooms (chanterelles, cèpes, morels, trompettes-de-la-mort, oyster, and/or cremini), wiped clean with a damp paper towel and coarsely chopped
- 2 tablespoons dry sherry
- Freshly ground black pepper
- 3 tablespoons minced fresh flat-leaf parsley, plus more for garnish
- 4 to 6 large eggs (1 egg per serving)
- 3 tablespoons syrupy aged balsamic vinegar, or 1/3 cup thin balsamic vinegar reduced over medium-high heat to 3 tablespoons
- 1/2 tablespoon sherry vinegar, preferably aged
- Fragrant extra-virgin olive oil, for drizzling

1. Place the lentils in a medium-size saucepan and add cold water to cover by 2 inches. Bring to a boil over high heat, stirring. Skim any foam off the surface, then add the smashed garlic and bay leaf. Season with salt to taste. Reduce the heat to low and simmer, partially covered, until the lentils are just tender but still firm, 20 to 35 minutes, depending on the type of lentils. Drain the lentils, discarding the bay leaf and garlic.

2. While the lentils are cooking, heat 4 tablespoons of the olive oil in a large skillet over medium-high heat. Add the minced garlic and stir until fragrant, about 30 seconds. Add the mushrooms and stir for 5 minutes. Add the sherry and cook until the mushrooms are tender and the liquid is absorbed, 2 to 3 minutes longer. Season with salt and pepper to taste. Add the drained lentils, gently stirring to combine, and cook until the flavors meld, 1 to 2 minutes. Taste for seasoning, adding more salt and pepper as necessary, and stir in the 3 tablespoons of parsley. Remove from the heat and cover to keep warm.

3. Poach the eggs following the instructions on page 000. Place the balsamic vinegar and the sherry vinegar in a small bowl and whisk to mix.

4. To serve, place a portion of lentils in a very small bowl to shape them. Invert the lentils onto a soup plate or a dinner plate. Repeat with the remaining lentils. Top each serving with a poached egg. Drizzle the vinegar mixture and fragrant olive oil around the lentils and sprinkle parsley on top. Serve at once. **SERVES 4 TO 6**

NOTE: If you are using Spanish *pardinas,* soak them overnight before cooking; Goya brand *pardinas* don't need soaking, despite what it says on the package.

Chickpea Stew with Chorizo and Meatballs

CHICKPEA STEW WITH CHORIZO AND MEATBALLS

GARBANZOS CON CHORIZO Y ALBONDIGAS

The origin of this recipe has dissolved under a stain of red wine in my notebook. There was a village bar. There was a bowl of these chickpeas, strewn with tiny meatballs and smoky from the *pimentón.* There was a recipe jotted down, which I have since made often. Perhaps it was in Castile or Andalusia or Extremadura—all regions where these ingredients would be used. What ultimately matters is the homey, comforting taste.

The meatballs add a special touch to the stew, but it is also delicious with the chorizo alone. Just skip the meatballs part and increase the amount of chorizo to ten to twelve ounces.

FOR THE CHICKPEAS:

1 cup dried chickpeas (garbanzo beans), soaked overnight or quick-soaked (see page 308)

1 bay leaf

6 ounces sweet Spanish-style chorizo sausage

FOR THE MEATBALLS:

2 slices white sandwich bread, crusts removed

10 ounces ground pork (not too lean)

1/4 cup grated onion

1 small egg, lightly beaten

1 teaspoon coarse salt (kosher or sea)

1/2 teaspoon freshly ground black pepper

Olive oil

FOR FINISHING THE STEW:

2 tablespoons extra-virgin olive oil

1 medium-size onion, finely chopped

1 medium-size carrot, finely diced

4 medium-size garlic cloves, minced

2 large ripe tomatoes, chopped

1 teaspoon smoked sweet Spanish paprika

3 tablespoons finely chopped fresh flat-leaf parsley

Coarse salt (kosher or sea)

1. Prepare the chickpeas: Place the chickpeas in a heavy 4- to 5-quart pot, add cold water to cover by 2 inches, and bring to a boil over high heat. Add the bay leaf, reduce the heat to low, and simmer, partially covered, for 1 hour, periodically replenishing the liquid with more water.

2. After 1 hour, cook the chorizo in boiling water for 2 minutes and drain it. Add the chorizo to the chickpeas and continue cooking until the chickpeas are tender but still a little al dente, about 30 minutes longer, adding more water to maintain the level of liquid.

3. While the chickpeas are cooking, make the meatballs: Place the bread in a small bowl, add cold water to cover, and let soak for 5 minutes. Drain and squeeze out the excess liquid, then finely crumble the bread. Place the bread, pork, onion, egg, salt, and pepper in a bowl. Gently knead the meatball mixture with your hands just until all the ingredients are thoroughly combined. If the mixture is too moist to form into meatballs, refrigerate it for 30 minutes to 1 hour.

4. Preheat the oven to 425°F.

5. With oiled hands, shape the mixture into meatballs the size of a cherry tomato. Arrange the meatballs on a baking sheet and bake, shaking the pan once or twice, until they are lightly browned and firm to the touch, about 12 minutes. Set aside until ready to use.

6. To finish the stew: Heat the olive oil in a medium-size skillet over medium-low heat. Add the onion, carrot, and half of the garlic and cook until soft but not browned, about 5 minutes. Add the tomatoes, cover the skillet, and cook for about 5 minutes. Add the paprika, stir for a few seconds, then stir the tomato mixture into the chickpeas. Cook the stew until the chickpeas are very tender, 15 to 20 minutes longer.

7. Using a slotted spoon, transfer the chorizo to a cutting board. Cut it into ½-inch slices and return them to the pot. Gently stir in the meatballs and simmer them in the stew for about 5 minutes.

8. Place the remaining garlic, the parsley, and a pinch of salt in a mortar and, using a pestle, crush them to a paste. Stir the parsley mixture into the stew and let it cook until all the flavors meld, about 5 minutes. Let the stew cool for about 5 minutes, then ladle it into bowls and serve. **SERVES 4 OR 5**

CHICKPEA & SHRIMP SAUTE

GARBANZOS SALTEADOS CON GAMBAS

It is quite common in Spain to combine humble legumes with luxury items, like foie gras, partridge, or fancy crustaceans. At La Castela tapas bar in Madrid, one of the most sought-after dishes is chickpeas sautéed with the much-prized langoustines called *cigalas.* The dish is divine, thanks to the small, creamy, pedigreed chickpeas, the sweet, delicate langoustines, and the gentle kick of wild garlic shoots. Though you don't find these ingredients in the States, I've devised a simple yet excellent version using shrimp, scallions, and canned chickpeas. The important thing here is to use a well-reduced crustacean stock to infuse the chickpeas with a nice marine flavor. Serve them as a substantial tapa or a light main course; a touch of *allioli* is most welcome.

Albaicin, the most Moorish and evocative of all neighborhoods in Granada, Andalusia

4 tablespoons fragrant extra-virgin olive oil
5 medium-size garlic cloves; 2 smashed, 3 minced
1/2 pound medium-size or large shrimp, shelled and deveined, shells and tails reserved
1 1/2 cups Fish Stock (page 108), or 1 cup bottled clam juice diluted with 1/2 cup water
3 cups drained canned chickpeas (garbanzos; from 2 cans, each about 15 ounces)
2 slender garlic shoots, trimmed and sliced, or 3 scallions, trimmed, with 1 1/2 inches of green, cut into 1-inch lengths
1/2 small dried chile, such as arbol, crumbled
1/2 teaspoon sweet (not smoked) paprika
Coarse salt (kosher or sea) and freshly ground black pepper
3 to 4 tablespoons minced fresh flat-leaf parsley
Allioli (page 44; optional), for serving

1. Heat 1 tablespoon of the olive oil in a medium-size saucepan over medium heat. Add the smashed garlic cloves and the shrimp shells and tails and cook until they turn pink and fragrant, about 1 minute. Add the Fish Stock, increase the heat to high, and cook until reduced to about ¾ cup, about 12 minutes. Strain the stock, discarding the solids, and return it to the pot. (The stock can be prepared up to 1 day ahead. Store, covered, in the refrigerator.)

2. Add the chickpeas to the strained stock. Cook over medium heat until the chickpeas are very tender but not mushy and most of the liquid has been absorbed, about 10 minutes. If there are too many loose chickpea skins in the pot, skim them off.

3. Heat the remaining 3 tablespoons of olive oil in a medium-size skillet over medium-low heat. Add the minced garlic and stir until very fragrant but not browned, 1 to 2 minutes. Add the shrimp, garlic shoots, and chile and cook until the shrimp just begin to turn pink but are not quite cooked, 1 to 2 minutes. Stir in the paprika and the chickpeas with their cooking liquid and cook until the shrimp are just cooked through and the flavors meld, about 2 minutes. Season with salt and black pepper to taste and stir in the parsley. Serve at once, with *allioli* on the side, if you wish. **SERVES 4 TO 6 AS A TAPA, 2 AS A LIGHT MAIN COURSE**

WHITE BEAN AND CLAM CASSEROLE

POCHAS CON ALMEJAS

Traditionally during Lent when meat was prohibited, beans were paired with clams or salt cod rather than chorizo or salt pork. The bean-and-clam combination proved so addictive that these days it's a year-round staple at seafood restaurants along the Cantabrian coast in the north. I order the dish whenever I can, and when I can't, I make it at home because this is one of my one-pot favorites.

- 1 medium-size onion, cut in half, plus 1 small onion, finely chopped
- 3 whole medium-size garlic cloves, smashed, plus 6 garlic cloves, crushed with a garlic press
- 1 small bay leaf
- 1 3/4 cups small dried white beans, such as cannellini or navy, soaked overnight or quick-soaked (see page 308) and drained
- 1 large carrot, diced
- 4 tablespoons extra-virgin olive oil
- 1 large Italian (frying) pepper, or 1 small green bell pepper, cored, seeded, and diced
- 1/2 red bell pepper, cored, seeded, and diced
- 1/2 small dried chile, such as arbol, crumbled, or 1/4 teaspoon crushed red pepper flakes
- 1/2 teaspoon smoked sweet Spanish paprika
- 1 large tomato, peeled, seeded, and chopped
- 1/3 cup bottled calm juice
- 1/4 cup dry white wine
- 2 pounds small clams, such as littlenecks or cockles, scrubbed
- 1/4 cup minced fresh flat-leaf parsley

1. Place the onion halves, whole smashed garlic cloves, and bay leaf in a double layer of cheesecloth and tie it shut.

2. Place the beans in a heavy 4- to 5-quart saucepan and add enough water to cover by 1 inch. Bring to a boil over high heat, skimming any foam off the surface. Add the carrot and the cheesecloth bag. Cover the saucepan, reduce the heat to low, and simmer until the beans are tender but still a little al dente, about 1¼ hours, adding a little cold water every 20 minutes to keep the beans from bursting and to maintain the level of liquid.

3. While the beans are cooking, heat 2 tablespoons of the olive oil in a medium-size skillet over medium-low heat. Add the chopped onion, Italian pepper, and red bell pepper and cook until very soft but not browned, about 10 minutes, lowering the heat if necessary. Add half of the crushed garlic and the chile and paprika and stir for a few seconds. Add the tomato and cook until it softens and reduces, 5 to 7 minutes. Stir the pepper mixture into the beans and continue cooking, partially covered, until the beans are very tender but not bursting, about 15 minutes.

4. Heat the remaining 2 tablespoons olive oil in a large, wide pot over low heat. Add the remaining crushed garlic and stir for about 1 minute. Add the clam juice and wine, increase the heat to medium-high, and bring to a boil over high heat. Add the clams, cover the pot, and cook until the clams open, 5 to 8 minutes depending on their size, shaking the pot occasionally. Discard any clams that don't open.

5. Remove and discard the cheesecloth bag. Add the clams and their cooking liquid to the beans and stir very gently, taking care not to crush the beans. Stir in the parsley, ladle the stew into bowls, and serve. **SERVES 4 TO 6**

POTATOES

BASQUE POTATOES IN SALSA VERDE

PATATAS EN SALSA VERDE

An everyday Basque classic for which every cook has a favorite recipe, these potatoes are so saucy that they border on soup. Normally they are served in bowls as a first course or as a lunch dish with lots of bread. Some like them plain, others might add peas, bacalao, or a broth made with the head of *merluza,* or hake. (A few clams thrown in at the end are lovely as well.) If you reduce the amount of liquid a little and increase the flour to 1½ tablespoons, the potatoes can serve as a side dish. Add more liquid and you'll have a great soup. This recipe is from my friend Oscar Alberdi, whose Bilbao restaurant is considered a temple of bacalao and other traditional Basque specialties. Oscar's savory trick is to add the slightly briny liquid from canned artichokes or Spanish white asparagus to the parsley-flecked sauce instead of (or in addition to) broth. If you don't have any on hand, use all broth.

2 pounds medium-size all-purpose boiling potatoes, peeled
5 tablespoons fragrant extra-virgin olive oil
4 large garlic cloves, minced
5 tablespoons minced fresh flat-leaf parsley
1 tablespoon all-purpose flour
1/4 cup dry white wine
1 cup liquid from canned artichokes or asparagus (optional; you will need two 14-ounce cans)
2 cups chicken stock or broth (use 3 cups if not using the vegetable liquid)
Coarse salt (kosher or sea) and freshly ground black pepper
Crusty bread, for serving

1. Cut the potatoes in half and slice each half into 4 to 6 wedges. Pat the wedges dry with paper towels so they don't stick when cooked. Heat the olive oil in a heavy 3-quart saucepan over medium heat. Add the potatoes and cook until they begin to soften and take on some color, 5 to 7 minutes, stirring often so they don't stick to the bottom. Using a slotted spoon, transfer the potatoes to a bowl.

2. If there seems to be too much oil in the pan, pour off all but 2 tablespoons. Reduce the heat to low, add the garlic and 1 tablespoon of the parsley, and cook until the garlic is very fragrant but not browned, about 1 minute. Add the flour and cook, stirring, to form a paste, about 30 seconds. Gradually add the wine and the vegetable liquid or 1 cup of the chicken stock, increase the heat to medium, and stir until the sauce thickens. Slowly add the 2 cups chicken stock and bring the liquid to a simmer.

3. Return the potatoes to the saucepan and season with salt and pepper to taste. Cover the saucepan and reduce the heat to low. Simmer, stirring occasionally and scraping the bottom of the pot, until the potatoes are extremely tender and some begin to fall apart, 25 to 30 minutes. Stir in the remaining 4 tablespoons parsley and cook about 1 minute. Taste for seasoning, adding more salt and/or pepper as necessary. Serve in soup bowls, accompanied by crusty bread. **SERVES 4 TO 6**

RIOJAN POTATOES WITH CHORIZO AND CHILE

PATATAS CON CHORIZO A LA RIOJANA

Tasting the sweet, fleshy potatoes from La Rioja, one understands why they are so central to this region's cuisine: Even humble french fries here somehow taste like ambrosia. Much of the region's potato production is concentrated around the picturesque Romanesque town of Santo Domingo de la Calzada. While some of these potatoes are destined for chips and other "industrial" uses all over Spain, locals keep the best varieties, such as Desiree or Marfona, for themselves. In this stew, chorizo is a flavoring rather than the main ingredient, and the dish can be served as a soupy first course or as a main course for lunch, with good bread and an astringent green salad.

- 1 large dried pimiento choricero or ancho chile, stemmed, seeded, and torn into pieces
- 3 pounds Yukon Gold potatoes
- 2 tablespoons extra-virgin olive oil, or more if needed
- 1 medium-size onion, quartered and sliced
- 1 small red bell pepper, cored, seeded, and thinly sliced
- 1 small green bell pepper, cored, seeded, and thinly sliced
- 6 to 8 ounces sweet Spanish-style chorizo sausage, cut into 1/2-inch slices
- 2 medium-size garlic cloves, chopped
- 1/2 teaspoon smoked sweet Spanish paprika, or 1/2 teaspoon unsmoked sweet paprika
- 1/2 cup white Rioja or another crisp, dry white wine
- 1 bay leaf
- About 2 cups chicken stock or broth or water
- Coarse salt (kosher or sea) and freshly ground black pepper
- Minced fresh flat-leaf parsley, for garnish

1. Soak the *pimiento choricero* in ½ cup very hot water until softened, about 30 minutes. Place it and the soaking liquid in a blender and puree until smooth.

2. Cut the potatoes into irregular chunks by inserting the tip of a small, sharp knife into a potato and twisting it until a 1½-inch chunk comes out. Repeat until the entire potato is cut up, then continue with the remaining potatoes; set aside.

3. Heat the olive oil in a 4-quart flameproof casserole over medium-low heat. Add the onion and red and green bell peppers and cook, stirring, for 5 minutes. Add the chorizo and cook until the vegetables are soft but not browned, about 5 minutes, adding a little more olive oil if necessary. Add the potatoes and garlic and cook, stirring, for 2 to 3 minutes. Add the paprika and stir for a few seconds. Add the wine and bay leaf, the pureed *pimiento,* and enough chicken stock to barely cover the potatoes. Season with salt and black pepper to taste. Increase the heat to medium-high and bring to a boil, skimming any foam off the surface, if necessary. Cover the casserole, reduce the heat to low, and cook until the potatoes are very tender and some chunks are just beginning to fall apart, 20 to 30 minutes. Transfer 2 or 3 potato chunks to a bowl, mash them, whisk in 2 to 3 tablespoons of the cooking liquid, and stir back into the casserole. Let the stew rest, covered, for 10 minutes. Remove and discard the bay leaf. Spoon the stew into bowls and serve, sprinkled with parsley. **SERVES 6**

BEHOLD THE ROTTEN POT

Cocidos, pucheros, potajes, potes . . . these über-Spanish soup/stews all come out of the proverbial *olla podrida,* or rotten pot, a dish that occupies a mythical place in the Spanish culinary consciousness. It's been long held that the word *podrida* (rotten) refers to the semi-disintegrated state of ingredients left to simmer, sometimes for days. Revisionist scholarship, however, suggests that *podrida* might be a corruption of *poderida,* from *poderoso*—powerful—an allusion either to the sustaining might of the dish or to the fact that, complete with multiple meats, the *olla* could only be enjoyed by the rich and the powerful.

The progenitor of *olla podrida* is thought to be a Sephardic casserole called *adafina* (from the Arab word *dafana,* to cover). A Sabbath dish of beans, chickpeas, chicken, raisins, and hard-boiled eggs, *adafina* was put to simmer on a Friday so it could be enjoyed on Saturday, when no cooking was allowed. The Spanish appropriated the dish around the sixteenth century, adding a whole roster of pork stuffs, so as to catholicize it. Or, it could have been the Marranos (converted Jews) who first added pork to the *adafina,* in their effort to convince Christian neighbors of their faith and avoid the Inquisition. Some scholars speculate that *olla podrida* has its roots in a thirteenth-century Arabic dish called *sinhaji,* a slow-simmered mélange of different meats, chickpeas, meatballs, and spices.

In any case, the classic imperial *olla podrida* was nothing if not epic. A late sixteenth-century recipe calls for many pounds of pork gullet, hock, snout, and ears; wild boar, sausage, and lamb; calf's kidneys and beef; capons, chickens, pigeons, and hindquarters of hare; pheasants, mallards, thrushes, partridges; chickpeas and red beans; garlic, onion, chestnuts, and cabbages—all served arranged in three tiers. So baroque was the dish that it soon disappeared from the repertoire, replaced by more sensible *cocidos, pucheros, potajes,* and *potes.* But the myth lives on.

PYRENEAN POTATO AND KALE CAKE

TRINXAT DE LA CERDANYA

I love this quintessential winter dish of Cerdanya, a section of the Catalan Pyrenees where Barcelonans escape to breathe mountain air, pick wild mushrooms, or just lose themselves rambling on the back roads among wild goats and ramshackle Romanesque churches. There, *trinxat* is prepared with potatoes and *col de invierno,* a local variety of winter cabbage. With its curly dark leaves, *col de invierno* is actually closer to our kale. Josep Maria Boix, a renowned local chef and owner of the exquisite Torre del Remei hotel, tells me that the stalks of this cabbage can grow as high as a person and that it tastes best after the first frosts. To make *trinxat,* home cooks just shake the snow and ice off the leaves and take them to their pans. The potatoes Boix uses are also special. Called *buffet,* "they are ugly as sin with all those eyes" but incredibly buttery (Yukon Golds make an adequate, if not quite perfect, substitute). In Cerdanya, *trinxat* is shaped into a cake the size of a skillet and served cut into wedges. If you prefer, it can also be shaped into smaller pancakes and fried on both sides.

2 1/2 pounds Yukon Gold potatoes, peeled and cut into 1-inch chunks
Coarse salt (kosher or sea)
1 pound kale, stemmed and chopped medium-fine
3 tablespoons olive oil, plus more for brushing the trinxat
2 ounces sliced pancetta, finely chopped
1/2 cup finely chopped white onion
3 medium-size garlic cloves, minced

1. Place the potatoes in a large pot, add enough cold salted water to cover by 2 inches, and bring to a boil over medium-high heat. Reduce the heat to medium and cook the potatoes until they are almost tender, about 15 minutes. Add the kale, pushing it down to submerge it in the liquid, and cook until the kale and the potatoes are tender, about 7 minutes. Drain thoroughly in a colander and transfer to a bowl. Mash and toss the vegetables together with a fork until the potatoes are half mashed.

2. Heat 1 tablespoon of the olive oil in a medium-size skillet over medium heat. Add the pancetta and cook for 1 minute. Add the onion and garlic and cook, stirring, until the onion is soft but not browned, about 5 minutes. Add the onion mixture to the potatoes and stir until well combined.

3. Preheat the oven to 450°F.

4. Heat the remaining 2 tablespoons olive oil in a 10-inch ovenproof skillet over medium-high heat. Add the potato and kale mixture, spreading it out into a cake the size of the skillet. Cook until the underside is golden, about 5 minutes.

5. Brush the top of the *trinxat* with a little olive oil and bake until the top is lightly browned, 10 to 15 minutes. Cut into wedges and serve. **SERVES 8**

POTATOES AND RED PEPPERS WITH ROASTED TOMATO SAUCE

ZORONGOLLO

This potato dish from the Extremadura region is unspeakably scrumptious! Depending on where you are and who's doing the cooking, *zorongollo* takes slightly different guises. However, the dish normally features roasted red peppers and tomatoes. Here, they are combined with sliced potatoes in a delightful cross between a casserole and a salad, eaten warm or at room temperature. Sautéing potato slices in lots of extra-virgin olive oil makes them especially plush and not at all greasy, since the oil is drained off. However, to save time and oil, the potatoes can be boiled. *Zorongollo* is good as a light luncheon, with a salad; as a substantial tapa; or as an accompaniment to grilled lamb chops or fish.

1 1/4 cups olive oil for frying the potatoes, plus more for brushing the vegetables
4 meaty red bell peppers, cored, cut in half, and seeded
2 medium-size ripe tomatoes, cut in half
1 small garlic head, outer layer of skin removed, top trimmed
1/4 cup fragrant extra-virgin olive oil, for the dressing
3 tablespoons best-quality red wine vinegar
Coarse salt (kosher or sea) and freshly ground black pepper
2 pounds large Yukon Gold potatoes of uniform size, peeled, cut in half, and thinly sliced
2 fat scallions, trimmed, with about 3 inches of the green, thickly sliced

1. Preheat the oven to 425°F.

2. Line a large baking sheet with aluminum foil and oil it lightly. Gently crush the red peppers to flatten them. Place the peppers and tomatoes on the baking sheet, cut side up, along with the garlic head. Brush the vegetables with a little olive oil and bake until tender and lightly charred, 35 to 40 minutes. Transfer the tomatoes and garlic to a bowl. Transfer the peppers to another bowl, cover it with plastic wrap, and let stand for 15 minutes. Peel the peppers and tear them into strips, setting them and their accumulated liquid aside separately. Remove and discard the tomato skins and chop the tomatoes coarsely. Squeeze out 5 roasted garlic cloves from the head, setting the rest aside for another use.

3. Place the tomatoes, garlic cloves, and the reserved pepper juices in a mini food processor and pulse until pureed. Transfer the puree to a bowl and whisk in the ¼ cup extra-virgin olive oil and the vinegar. Season the sauce with salt and black pepper to taste, then let stand until ready to use. (The tomato sauce can be prepared up to 1 day ahead; refrigerate, covered. Reheat before using.)

4. Heat the 1¼ cups olive oil in a large skillet over high heat. Add the potato slices, separating them with a spatula and sprinkling them generously with salt. Cook for 5 minutes, stirring gently. Reduce the heat to low, cover the skillet, and cook the potatoes until tender, 15 to 20 minutes, turning them once or twice. Using a slotted spoon, transfer the potatoes to a colander set over a bowl and let drain for 10 to 15 minutes. The olive oil can be strained and reused.

5. Place half of the potatoes on the bottom of a round earthenware *cazuela,* about 12 inches in diameter, or another attractive deep rustic dish.

Sprinkle the potatoes lightly with salt and top with half of the red peppers and half of the scallions. Cover with the remaining potatoes, then season with salt. Scatter the remaining red peppers and scallions on top. Pour the tomato sauce over the potatoes and let stand for 10 to 15 minutes. The dish is best while the potatoes are still slightly warm. Cut the *zorongollo* into squares or wedges and serve.
SERVES 6

VARIATION: To make *zorongollo* with boiled potatoes, do not peel or slice them first. Boil the potatoes until they feel just tender when pierced with a skewer, about 30 minutes. When the potatoes are just cool enough to handle, peel and cut them into thin slices, then continue with Step 5.

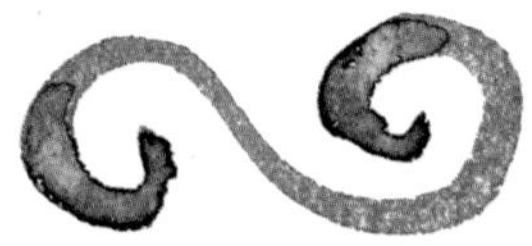

POTATO AND ONION GRATIN WITH ALLIOLI

PATATAS PANADERAS CON ALLIOLI

You don't have to be Catalan to agree that pretty much everything tastes better with *allioli,* the bold, garlicky mayonnaise that brings to life so many of the region's dishes. *Patatas panaderas* (the classic Spanish baked sliced potatoes) are great on their own. But add a cup of *allioli* and you've got a treat. Serve the potatoes with simple roasts that could use a garlicky kick or with saucy dishes, such as Seafood Stew in Romesco Sauce (page 210) or Meaty Oxtail Stew Torero Style (page 257).

3 tablespoons extra-virgin olive oil, plus more for oiling the pan
2 medium-size onions, cut in half and thinly sliced
3 pounds baking potatoes of uniform size, peeled, rinsed, and patted dry
Coarse salt (kosher or sea) and freshly ground black pepper
3/4 cup chicken stock or broth
About 1 1/2 cups Allioli (page 44)

1. Heat the olive oil in a large skillet over medium heat. Add the onions and cook, stirring, until softened and lightly browned, 10 to 12 minutes, adjusting the heat as necessary.

2. Using a mandoline, the slicing disk of a food processor, or a sharp knife, slice the potatoes into 1/8-inch-thick rounds.

3. Preheat the oven to 375°F.

4. Generously oil a heavy, shallow 12- by 9-inch baking dish, preferably earthenware or cast-enamel, or an oval gratin dish (you can also use a cast-iron skillet). Arrange some of the potatoes in one overlapping layer on the bottom of the baking dish, then season them generously with salt and pepper. Scatter half of the cooked onions on top. Arrange another layer of potatoes on top of the onions and season them with salt and pepper. Scatter the remaining onions over the potatoes and top with another layer of potatoes (you might not need all of the potato slices). Press the layers down to compact them. Pour the stock over the potatoes.

5. Cover the baking dish with aluminum foil and bake the potatoes until they feel tender when pierced with a knife, about 50 minutes. Uncover the baking dish, brush some olive oil on the potatoes, and bake for another 10 to 15 minutes.

6. Change the oven setting to broil. Being careful not to burn yourself, remove the baking dish from the oven and spread the *allioli* generously over the top. Broil until the top is browned in spots, 2 to 3 minutes. Let cool for a few minutes, cut into squares, and serve. **SERVES 6 TO 8**

VARIATION: Potato gratins lend themselves to many variations. Instead of the *allioli*, you can top the gratin with Cabrales cheese, as might be done in Asturias. You can add sautéed bell peppers or Italian (frying) peppers and some chopped tomatoes or sautéed wild mushrooms to the layers of sautéed onions. Brushing the potato layers with a little saffron-infused oil is nice too.

POTATO HITS THE NEW WORLD

Of provisions, besides maize, there are two other products which form the principal food of these Indians. One is called potato, and is a kind of earth nut which, after it has been boiled, is as tender as a cooked chestnut, but it has no more skin than a truffle, and it grows under the earth in the same way.

—Pedro Cieza de León, *Chronicle of Peru,* 1553

A band of gold-seeking conquistadors led by Jiménez de Quesada "discovered" potatoes in what is now Colombia in 1537. They mistook them for truffles, describing them as "floury roots of good flavor, a gift very acceptable to Indians and a dainty dish even for a Spaniard." This early endorsement didn't help much in the long run. No one knows exactly when potatoes were first planted in Spain, but in 1573 records from a hospital in Seville indicate that sacks of potatoes were ordered for provisions. However, initial curiosity for this botanical novelty was soon replaced with scorn and disdain. The tuber—a member of the largely poisonous nightshade family long associated with witchcraft—was generally deemed unfit for human consumption and relegated to the role of animal fodder and sustenance for the starving. In Spain, large-scale cultivation of potatoes didn't take off until the mid-eighteenth century, pioneered in Galicia and the Canary Islands. But once Spaniards finally fell in love with it, there was no looking back. Today, Spain boasts more different potato recipes than any country I know, most of them scrumptious.

POTATO "LASAGNA" WITH CHORIZO AND DATES

"LASAÑA" DE PATATAS CON CHORIZO Y DATILES

The combination of chorizo and dates is truly ingenious; the dried fruit tempers the bold flavors of the sausage and contributes an unexpected sweet touch. Throw in potatoes and piquillo peppers and you have a small masterpiece. This layered dish is my riff on a recipe I came across in a cookbook from La Rioja dedicated to modern cooking. You can serve it as a luncheon main course, with a green salad, or as a hearty appetizer. Accompanied by poached or fried eggs, it makes a stellar brunch dish. The chorizo and date mixture is also excellent as a filling for pastry puffs or small empanadas.

- 2 1/2 pounds Yukon Gold potatoes, peeled
- Coarse salt (kosher or sea)
- 2/3 cup chicken stock or broth
- 7 large pitted dates, finely chopped
- 5 tablespoons extra-virgin olive oil
- 12 to 14 ounces sweet Spanish-style chorizo sausage, casings removed
- 2 medium-size garlic cloves, crushed with a garlic press
- Freshly ground black pepper
- 9 to 10 piquillo peppers (from a can or jar), or 3 to 4 large roasted pimientos, cut into strips
- 1/2 teaspoon smoked sweet Spanish paprika

1. Place the potatoes in a large pot, add enough cold salted water to cover by 2 inches, and bring to a boil over medium-high heat. Reduce the heat to medium-low and cook, partially covered, until the potatoes feel almost tender but still offer a little resistance when pierced with a skewer, 20 to 30 minutes, depending on their size. Drain and let cool until manageable.

2. While the potatoes are cooking, place ⅓ cup of the chicken stock in a small saucepan and bring to a boil. Remove from the heat, add the dates, and let soak for about 30 minutes.

3. Heat 1 tablespoon of the olive oil in a large skillet over high heat. Add the chorizo, mashing it up thoroughly with a sturdy fork. Cook the chorizo, breaking it up, until it is no longer raw, 5 to 6 minutes. As you cook, tilt the skillet and spoon off and discard the fat and liquid. Add the dates and their soaking liquid, reduce the heat to medium-high, and continue stirring until the soaking liquid is almost absorbed, about 2 minutes. Using a slotted spoon, transfer the chorizo mixture to a food processor and puree until medium-fine.

4. Preheat the oven to 375°F.

5. Generously brush a 10-inch cast-iron skillet or a similar-size baking dish with olive oil. Place the remaining 4 tablespoons olive oil in a small bowl and stir in the garlic. Using a long, sharp knife, slice the potatoes as thin as you can, dipping the knife in cold water for easier slicing. Arrange half of the potato slices in slightly overlapping concentric circles on the bottom of the skillet. They should cover it completely. Lightly season the potatoes with salt and black pepper and brush them generously with some of the garlic oil. Scatter half of the piquillo pepper strips over the potatoes and spread the chorizo mixture evenly on top. Arrange the remaining potatoes in a layer on the chorizo, brush generously with some of the garlic oil, and season with salt and pepper. Decorate the top with the remaining piquillo peppers. Pour the remaining ⅓ cup chicken stock over the potatoes, cover them tightly with aluminum foil, and bake until the potatoes are very tender, 20 minutes.

6. Increase the oven temperature to 450°F. Stir the paprika into the remaining garlic oil. Uncover the potatoes and brush them with the paprika oil, taking care not to disturb the arrangement of peppers. Bake the "lasagna" until the top is lightly browned, about 10 minutes. Let the "lasagna" cool for about 5 minutes, cut it into wedges, and serve.
SERVES 6

SMOKY MASHED POTATOES FROM EXTREMADURA

PATATAS REVOLCONAS

The word *revolconas* means tumbled, or rolled over, and here it probably refers to the act of mashing up the potatoes. The dish is a specialty of Extremadura (as well as parts of Castile), where the potatoes are mixed with oil flavored with garlic and the local paprika, *pimentón de la Vera* (see page 84). This gives the dish a rusty hue and an addictively dusky taste. Bacon or chorizo bits are sometimes mixed in as well. After being mashed, the potatoes are shaped into a cake and served as an appetizer (or a poor man's main dish), though they definitely make a welcome side dish. Smoked *pimentón* is essential here; it is available at better food shops and by mail order (see page 461).

2 pounds Yukon Gold potatoes, peeled and cut into chunks
1 whole dried ñora pepper or ancho chile
1 bay leaf
Coarse salt (kosher or sea)
About 1/2 cup fragrant extra-virgin olive oil
1 small onion, finely chopped
4 large garlic cloves, crushed with a garlic press
2 to 3 teaspoons smoked sweet Spanish paprika
Freshly ground black pepper
Strips of roasted red pepper (optional; see page 385), for garnish

1. Place the potatoes, ñora pepper, and bay leaf in a saucepan, add cold salted water to cover by 2 inches, and bring to a boil over medium-high heat. Reduce the heat to medium and cook, partially covered, until the potatoes feel completely tender when pierced with a skewer, about 20 minutes. Drain the potatoes, setting about ⅓ cup of the cooking liquid aside and discarding the ñora pepper and bay leaf.

2. While the potatoes are cooking, heat ¼ cup of the olive oil in a small skillet over low heat. Add the onion and cook until soft but not browned, about 7 minutes, stirring occasionally. Add the garlic and cook, stirring, for another minute. Stir in the paprika and immediately remove the skillet from the heat so that the garlic doesn't burn.

One of the pleasures of driving through Spain is a landscape dotted with ancient castles, like Belvis in Extremadura.

3. Transfer the drained potatoes to a bowl and mash them coarsely with a fork or a potato ricer, gradually stirring in the onion and oil mixture, the reserved potato cooking liquid, and the remaining olive oil to taste. Season the potatoes with salt and black pepper. Mold the mashed potatoes into a round cake on a serving plate and serve hot or warm, decorated with roasted pepper strips, if desired. **SERVES 6**

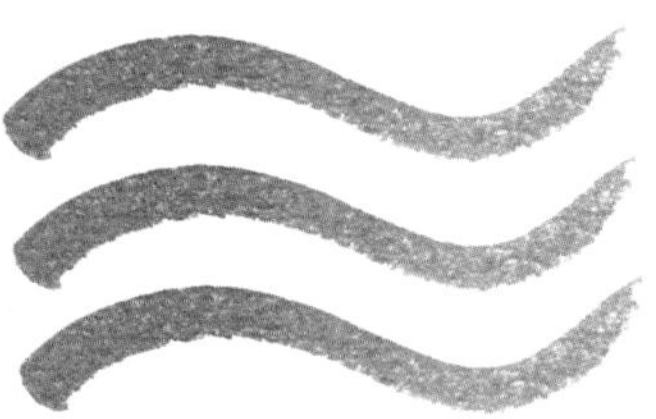

BOILED POTATOES AND GREEN BEANS WITH GARLIC

PATATAS CON JUDIAS VERDES

To accommodate the realities of working women, more and more stalls at Barcelona's La Boqueria market are devoting space to prepared foods. The perennial local favorite is waxy yellow potatoes mixed with a green vegetable, such as beans or Swiss chard, and dressed with aromatic olive oil. The dish is very tasty and so easy to make; I have never understood why it needs to be purchased. The only prerequisites are wonderful olive oil and good potatoes.

1/3 cup fragrant extra-virgin olive oil
2 small garlic cloves, crushed with a garlic press
3 large Yukon Gold potatoes (about 1 1/2 pounds total), peeled
Coarse salt (kosher or sea)
6 to 8 ounces green beans, trimmed and cut into 1 1/2-inch lengths
Freshly ground black pepper

1. Place the olive oil and garlic in a small bowl, whisk to mix, and let stand while you prepare the vegetables.

2. Cut the potatoes into irregular chunks by inserting the tip of a small, sharp knife into a potato and twisting it until a 1½-inch chunk comes out. Repeat until the entire potato is cut up, then continue with the remaining potatoes.

3. Place the potatoes in a large saucepan, add enough cold salted water to cover by 2 inches, and bring to a boil over medium-high heat. Reduce the heat to low and simmer until the potatoes feel almost tender but still offer a little resistance when pierced with a skewer, about 20 minutes. Increase the heat to medium and bring the water back to a boil. Add the green beans and cook, partially covered, until the beans and potatoes are tender, 5 to 7 minutes. Drain the vegetables (the potatoes will be slightly "crushed").

4. Transfer the vegetables to a shallow serving dish, sprinkle with salt and pepper, and drizzle the garlic olive oil evenly over the top. Let cool for 10 to 15 minutes, then serve. **SERVES 4**

WRINKLED POTATOES WITH SPICY CHILE MOJO

PATATAS ARRUGADAS CON MOJO PICON

A specialty of the Canary Islands, this dish uses one of the niftiest techniques for cooking potatoes. Boiled with a large amount of salt—originally sea water was used—the potatoes are drained, then returned to the pot to be cooked some more. This makes them a bit wrinkled and lightly coated with residual salt, for a flavor that's punchy but not overly salty. The classic accompaniment is a ruddy *mojo* of pounded chiles, herbs, and vinegar. It's addictive as a tapa or a side dish for a simple grill.

FOR THE MOJO PICON:

6 medium-size garlic cloves, chopped
1 small dried red chile, such as arbol, crumbled
2 teaspoons sweet (not smoked) paprika
3/4 teaspoon dried oregano
1 teaspoon cumin seeds
1 tablespoon chopped fresh flat-leaf parsley
1 large pinch of coarse salt (kosher or sea)
1/2 cup extra-virgin olive oil
6 tablespoons best-quality red wine vinegar, or more to taste

FOR THE POTATOES:

1 1/2 pounds small white new potatoes, well rinsed
2/3 cup coarse salt (kosher or sea)

1. Make the *mojo picon*: Place the garlic, chile, paprika, oregano, cumin seeds, and parsley in a mortar and, using a pestle, mash to a paste, adding the salt and a little of the olive oil. Scrape the *mojo* into a bowl and stir in the remaining olive oil, the vinegar, and 2 tablespoons water. Taste for seasoning, adding more vinegar or salt if necessary, then set the *mojo* aside. (The texture is preferable when made in a mortar, but the ingredients can also be coarsely pureed in a mini food processor; add the 2 tablespoons water at the beginning.)

2. Prepare the potatoes: Place the potatoes in a large, wide pot. Add the salt and cold water to cover by 3 inches. Bring to a boil, reduce the heat to low, and simmer, partially covered, until just tender when tested with a skewer, about 15 minutes. Drain the potatoes, leaving them slightly damp, and return them to the pot. Cook the potatoes, uncovered, over medium-low heat, shaking the pan frequently, until they are dry and lightly wrinkled, 10 to 12 minutes, lowering the heat if necessary. The potatoes will be slightly white from the salt. Arrange the potatoes on a platter and serve with the *mojo* on the side. **SERVES 4 TO 6**

All kinds of exotic vegetation flourish on Spain's Canary Islands.

BAKED POTATOES STUFFED WITH BRANDADA

PATATAS RELLENAS DE BRANDADA DE BACALAO

This recipe is my trophy from a saint's day fair in the Catalan Pyrenees. Anywhere in the world you go these days, you find baked potatoes with toppings. But these, prepared by a group of village women, were in a class of their own. Stuffed with salt cod and potato puree, and capped with *allioli,* the Catalan garlic mayonnaise, the result was earthy and wonderful. I like to use small to medium-size baking potatoes and serve them as a substantial tapa or as part of a buffet. Larger potatoes would make an excellent luncheon main course.

- 6 smallish baking potatoes (about 6 ounces each), scrubbed and patted dry
- 8 ounces salt cod, soaked and cooked (see page 198), then drained
- 1 cup whole milk
- 1/4 cup extra-virgin olive oil
- 2 medium-size garlic cloves, crushed with a garlic press
- About 1/4 cup Allioli (page 44)
- 1/2 cup plain bread crumbs or Parmesan cheese, or 1/4 cup of each, for topping the potatoes

1. Preheat the oven to 425°F.

2. Prick the potatoes all over with a fork, wrap each one in aluminum foil, and place on a baking sheet. Bake until the potatoes feel completely tender when pierced with a skewer, about 1¼ hours. Let cool in the aluminum foil just until cool enough to handle. Increase the oven temperature to 475°F.

3. Meanwhile, tear the salt cod into small pieces, removing and discarding any bones and hard bits.

4. Heat the milk, olive oil, and garlic in a small saucepan over medium-high heat until it's just simmering, or microwave it on high power for 2 minutes.

5. Place the salt cod and the hot milk in a food processor and pulse until a medium-smooth puree forms. Scrape the puree into a bowl.

6. Unwrap the potatoes, cut them in half lengthwise, and carefully remove the flesh, leaving the skin intact. Mash about half of the potato pulp and stir it into the salt cod mixture. Taste the mixture and if you would like it a little more "potatoey," mash a little more potato and stir it in. The flavors of salt cod and potatoes should be nicely balanced (set the remaining potato flesh aside for another use).

7. Fill the potato shells with the salt cod mixture, smear some *allioli* on each potato, and lightly sprinkle 2 teaspoons bread crumbs, Parmesan, or a mix of both over each. Arrange the potatoes on a baking sheet and bake until the tops are nicely golden, 10 to 15 minutes. If you like, brown the tops more under the broiler. Let cool to warm and serve. **SERVES 12 AS A TAPA, 6 AS A MAIN COURSE**

"In a village of la Mancha,
the name of which I don't wish to recall,
there lived not long ago one of those gentleman who always had
a lance in the rack, an aged shield,
a worn-out horse, and a greyhound for running."

—DON QUIXOTE

QUIXOTE'S CUISINE

Thus begins *Don Quixote,* Miguel de Cervantes' tale about the misadventures of a delusional knight and his squire, Sancho Panza. First published in 1605, *Don Quixote* is considered by most literary scholars as the first modern novel. Among the book's countless virtues are detailed descriptions of seventeenth-century Castilian food. In fact, from the book's second sentence we learn that three quarters of Quixote's income was consumed by the following diet:

- "An *olla,* or stew, of rather more beef than mutton" (mutton was considered more tender and prized at the time)
- *"Salpicón"* (cold beef salad presumably made with leftover meat from the *olla* and seasoned with onions and vinegar) "on most nights"
- "*Duelos y quebrantos* on Saturdays" (the dish, which translates as pain and sorrow, baffles Cervantes scholars, but it was most likely an omelet filled with brains, brains being one of the animal parts permitted to be eaten on Saturdays, a day of semiabstinence)
- "Lentils on Fridays, and a pigeon or so extra on Sundays"

To anyone living in Cervantes' time, Quixote's eating regimen was an indication of the knight's modest means. References to food—much of it comically dire—abound in the novel. Some literary critics suggest that malnutrition and perpetual hunger might well have been the cause of Quixote's hallucinations. One gastronomic highlight, however, is a wedding feast attended by Quixote and Sancho. The first thing Sancho sees is an entire ox spitted on a whole elm tree. There are also vast wineskins filled with generous wines, hares and fowls hanging from tree branches (to keep them cool), a wall made of cheese, and giant cauldrons of oil from which fritters are taken out with two mighty shovels. "Of cooks and cook-maids there were over fifty, all clean, brisk, and blithe," Cervantes recounts. In the capacious belly of an ox hide a dozen soft little suckling pigs, sewn up inside to give them flavor and tenderness.

Not able to bear the sight of these temptations, gluttonous Sancho approaches one of the cooks and begs permission to soak a bread in one of the pots. The magnanimous cook responds by skimming off three hens and two geese for him.

POTATO GYPSY'S ARM

BRAZO DE GITANO DE PATATA

Brazo de gitano, or gypsy's arm, is the picturesque Spanish term for a jelly roll. Most are sponge cake–based sweets, but there are some deliciously savory versions. In this recipe, a mashed potato roll encloses all kinds of things dear to the Spanish palate: anchovies, good canned tuna, red peppers, and olives. The dish is a tad kitschy—the Spanish equivalent of a tuna casserole or *vitello tonnato*—but so good, it's impossible not to love. Serve it as a substantial tapa or a light main course at an alfresco luncheon.

FOR THE POTATOES:

2 pounds medium-size Yukon Gold potatoes, unpeeled
3 tablespoons milk
2 tablespoons extra-virgin olive oil
Coarse salt (kosher or sea)

FOR THE ROLL:

6 ounces imported solid oil-packed tuna, or 1 can (6 ounces) Bumble Bee tonno in olive oil, drained and flaked
1 medium-size tomato, finely chopped
1/3 cup sliced pimiento-stuffed olives, plus more for decorating the roll
6 to 7 piquillo peppers (from a can or jar), or 3 to 4 pimientos, drained and slivered, plus more slivers for decorating the roll
8 to 10 best-quality oil-packed anchovy fillets, drained and chopped
1/4 cup minced fresh flat-leaf parsley
Coarse salt (kosher or sea) and freshly ground black pepper
1 1/2 tablespoons sherry vinegar, preferably aged
1/2 cup mayonnaise (preferably Hellmann's)
1 tablespoon extra-virgin olive oil
1 tablespoon fresh lemon juice
1 large garlic clove, crushed with a garlic press

1. Make the potatoes: Place the potatoes in a medium-size saucepan, add enough cold water to cover by 2 inches, and bring to a boil over high heat. Reduce the heat to medium and simmer, partially covered, until the potatoes feel completely tender when pierced with a skewer, about 30 minutes. Drain the potatoes. When just cool enough to handle, peel the potatoes, add the milk and olive oil, and mash until fairly smooth. Season with salt to taste.

El Rocio festival in Andalusia—during which a lot of sherry is drunk!

2. Prepare the roll: Place a 15-inch piece of waxed paper on a large baking sheet and oil it lightly. Spread the mashed potatoes on the waxed paper in a thin rectangle approximately 15 by 12 inches. Evenly scatter the tuna, tomato, olives, piquillo peppers, anchovies, and parsley all over the rectangle. Season with salt and pepper, then sprinkle the vinegar on top. Starting at a long end, roll the potatoes up jelly-roll fashion, using the waxed paper to shape the roll without catching the edge of the waxed paper in it. When the roll is finished, slide the waxed paper out from under it. If the potatoes tear in places, mend the holes by pinching the potatoes back together.

3. Place the mayonnaise, olive oil, lemon juice, and garlic in a small bowl. Whisk to mix, then season with salt to taste. Spread the mayonnaise all over the roll and decorate it with piquillo pepper slivers and olive slices. Place the roll in the refrigerator and chill for 2 to 3 hours. To serve, cut the roll into thick slices. **SERVES 4 TO 6**

RICE AND PASTA

Rice has been grown on the Mediterranean shores for more than two millennia, having been introduced by soldiers returning from Alexander the Great's expedition to India in 327 B.C. Yet Spain's rice consumption truly took off only when Arabs conquered the country's southeastern coast in the eighth century A.D. Applying their legendary agricultural skills to rice cultivation, the Muslim invaders planted the grain in the fertile soil around Valencia, irrigating the paddies with a brilliantly complex network of dikes and canals. These ingenious Arab watercourses still irrigate the picturesque wetlands around Albufera, a freshwater lagoon south of Valencia, where much

Top left: Colorful houses with charming grillwork and bamboo shades line the streets of Villajoyosa, a fishing village on the Costa Blanca; *Top right:* Cooking several paellas at the same time is hard work; *Bottom left:* The abundant fields of Valencia ensure plenty of rice for its classic dish, paella; *Bottom right:* A mosaic doorway in Cabanyal, Valencia.

of Spain's rice production is concentrated. The Spanish word for rice, *arroz,* comes from the Arabic *al-ruzz.* "For Islam, agriculture had a religious sense," notes paella authority Lourdes March. "Water was the symbol of life and the earth the symbol of fertility and every product extracted from it would multiply in Paradise." Rice would flourish in this environment.

Rice-based cuisine continues to thrive in the Levante—the land where the sun rises—a stretch of Spain's eastern coast that encompasses the provinces of Castellón, Valencia, Alicante, and Murcia. Of these, Valencia is synonymous with Spain's most famous rice dish: paella. "Paella is Valencia itself—the city's symbolic representation," declares Valencian food critic Antonio Vergara. And cooks there can be so fundamentalist on the subject that the issue of whether it's permissible to add red pepper to paella was supposedly brought before the Valencian parliament.

Once the Valencian paella police recite to you the recipe for the one and only true *paella valenciana* with rabbit and snails, they usually relent and admit that there are as many paellas as there are cooks and that the definition, ingredients, and technique vary every five miles in Valencia province alone. Moving south to Alicante, you encounter truly creative and magnificent rice preparations not regulated by Valencian strictures. You also learn that paellas represent just a fraction of the Levante's astonishingly varied rice cuisine. Three elements are usually spelled out when a rice dish is described: the ingredients flavoring it, the receptacle in which it's cooked, and the consistency of the rice. Paella-style rices are *seco* (dry), cooked until the liquid is completely absorbed. Equally popular are *meloso* rices—a little creamy, with syrupy liquid still clinging to the grains. Wonderful too are *caldoso* (brothy) *arroces,* which are prepared in a pot and have a texture halfway between a rice soup and a risotto. In winter, nothing beats an *arroz al horno,* rice baked in an earthenware *cazuela.* Flavorings? The sky's the limit.

I can spend weeks calling on all my favorite rice restaurants in the Levante, each of which specializes in a particular dish. Casa Carmina near Valencia draws crowds with its folksy *arròs amb fesols i naps.* A soupy rice full of rustic oomph, it teems with bits of braised wild Albufera duck, white beans, turnips, pork, and blood sausage. The stunningly picturesque lakeside Casa Salvador in Cullera is the place for lobster rice and a *meloso* rice with skate and wild garlic shoots. At the stylish Monastrell in the city of Alicante, my friend María José San Román prepares a succulent *arroz meloso* with morels and spring vegetables. Mari Carmen Vélez at La Sirena (see page 217) is the queen of *arroz a banda,* a fishermen's rice cooked in an insanely powerful fish broth and traditionally served with fish on the side. At Ca'Sento in Valencia, superstar chef Raúl Aleixandre fashions an iconoclastic paella from puffed-up fried rice (imagine Rice Krispies from the fourth dimension).

And now about Casa Paco. The restaurant is located in Pinoso, an ugly hamlet set amid the achingly drab, arid countryside of inland Alicante, miles from civilization. The service is rude, the décor nonexistent. None of this stops paella fanatics from driving for hours to get there. Their prize? A rabbit and snail paella that qualifies as an existential eating experience. Prepared over live flames so high they seem to shoot straight up to the ceiling, the rice is almost crunchy in texture, as smoky as a good barbecue, and layered so thin in the pan that an eighteen-inch paella feeds only two. Or one, if you *really* love paella.

Nobody can reproduce Casa Paco's paella, but the recipes in this chapter capture the regional spirit. Here you'll find a true *paella valenciana* with rabbit that will please even the toughest Valencian critics, as well as a robust winter paella from Alicante with potatoes and pine nut–studded meatballs. With relatively little effort, you'll be able to reproduce the coastal seafood paellas, such as dramatic jet-black paella made with squid ink, a Catalan seafood rice flavored with a delicious *romesco* broth, and the classic mixed seafood paella one enjoys at *chiringuitos,* the beloved beachside restaurants. There's a sensational Basque smoked cheese risotto, too, and an intriguing couscous from Alicante.

As for the pasta recipes, they'll be a revelation to anybody who thinks pasta belongs only to Italy. A seafood paella prepared with fideo noodles instead of rice is one of the world's greatest and niftiest dishes. And from Barcelona, where Italian cuisine was fashionable in the eighteenth century, come luscious cannelloni and baked macaroni laced with pork and wild mushrooms that can compete with the best pasta creations from Italy.

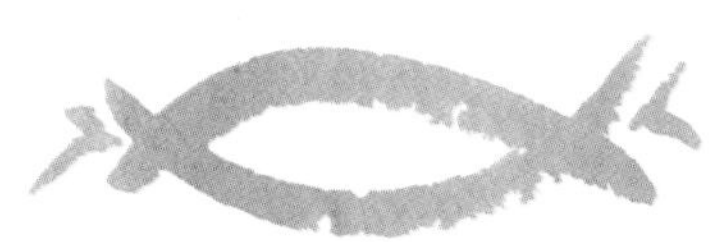

PAELLAS AND OTHER RICE DISHES

CLASSIC VALENCIAN PAELLA

PAELLA VALENCIANA

Here is the classic *paella valenciana,* the only dish that, according to Valencian traditionalists, can be legitimately called paella. It consists of rice, rabbit (and sometimes chicken or duck), land snails, green beans, butter beans, perhaps artichokes, and a simple *sofrito* of tomatoes and garlic. A well-prepared paella is one of the world's greatest dishes. For a simpler version, use only chicken—four or five skinless, boneless thighs. And, you can also legitimately add a few slices of sautéed pork sausage or chorizo. Snails lend an air of funky authenticity to the dish, but a sprig of rosemary is a traditionally acceptable substitute, although nobody is sure exactly why.

1 pound skinless, boneless chicken thighs, rinsed, patted dry, and cut into 1 1/2-inch chunks
1 1/2 pounds rabbit, rinsed, patted dry, and cut into small pieces
Coarse salt (kosher or sea) and freshly ground black pepper
1 1/2 teaspoons smoked sweet Spanish paprika
8 large garlic cloves, crushed with a garlic press
About 6 cups chicken stock or broth (more if using bomba rice)
1 large pinch of saffron, pulverized in a mortar
5 tablespoons extra-virgin olive oil
3/4 cup green beans (preferably Italian flat beans), trimmed and cut into 1 1/2-inch lengths
1 cup frozen butter beans or baby lima beans, thawed
1 package (9 ounces) frozen artichoke hearts, thawed and patted dry with paper towels
2 large ripe tomatoes, cut in half and grated on a box grater, skins discarded
1 pinch of cayenne, or more to taste
2 cups short- to medium-grain rice (see page 338)
12 snails (see Note), or 1 sprig fresh rosemary
1 roasted red bell pepper (optional; see page 385), cut into strips, for garnish

YES, BUT IS IT A REAL PAELLA VALENCIANA?

"Valencians," remarks the famous Catalan writer Manuel Vázquez Montalbán, "believe that God himself revealed the paella recipe to them and to them alone."

And exactly what might that recipe be? Well, for starters, paella *must* be prepared with the squat local rice in the flat two-handled paella pan that both defines the dish and lends it the name. An authentic *paella valenciana* contains chicken, rabbit, sometimes duck, and the land snails called *vaquetes,* for which a rosemary sprig can be substituted. Seafood *and* chorizo? You've got to be kidding. The only permissible flourishes include flat green beans, artichokes, and *garrofón,* or butter beans. Rice and rice again is the true star of the dish.

The list of regulations continues. A true *paella valenciana* has to be cooked outdoors, over a fire fuelled with vine branches or orange tree shoots, enhanced by an aromatic *sofrito* of tomatoes, garlic, saffron, and *pimentón.* Die-hard paella buffs may also tell you that paella is a man's job because only men know how to handle fire . . . that the key to its success is the hard calcium-rich Valencian water . . . that paella is only for lunch, *never* for dinner . . . that tourist paellas that mix shellfish and meat are a crime punishable by imprisonment . . . that any dish that isn't strictly speaking a *paella valenciana* with rabbit and chicken must be called simply *arroz con,* or "rice with." And then they'll wax lyrical about how paella is served.

In the nineteenth century, paella was a celebratory weekend feast cooked in *el campo* (the country) and eaten straight from the pan. The dish evolved from a range of simpler rices prepared by laborers in the Levantine rice paddies and *huertas* (vegetable plots) with whatever could be hunted and gathered: eel, wild duck, rabbit, artichokes, beans—even water rats—and yes, seafood in the fishing communities along the coast. A local newspaper first referred to it as *paella valenciana* in 1840.

The word *paella* continues to carry a ritualistic connotation. "Paella is an activity rather than a particular dish," a rice farmer in Albufera said when I asked him to define the difference between a paella and an *arroz.* "It's what you do on a Sunday, with the whole family gathered around an enormous paella pan set on the fire."

1. Place the chicken and rabbit in a bowl and rub generously with salt, pepper, ½ teaspoon of the paprika, and half of the garlic. Let stand for 10 to 15 minutes.

2. Place the chicken stock in a medium-size saucepan and bring to a simmer. Add the saffron and keep the stock at a simmer until ready to use.

3. Place 4 tablespoons of the olive oil in a 15- or 16-inch paella pan set over a single burner and heat over medium until it starts to smoke. Add the chicken and rabbit and brown, turning several times, for 6 to 7 minutes. Add the green beans, butter beans, and artichokes and stir until the vegetables begin to brown, 2 to 8 minutes. Push everything to the edge of the pan, where it's not as hot.

PAELLA PANS

Strictly speaking, paella is not paella unless it's prepared in the round, shallow, flat-bottomed, two-handled pan that gives it its name. Lourdes March, author of *El Libro de la Paella Arroces,* argues that Valencians got the name from *patella,* a Roman word originally describing ceremonial chalices, which later came to be used for all manner of cooking vessels. Paella pans are relatively thin, made from carbon or stainless steel, which reacts quickly to fluctuations in temperature. The wide, shallow shape allows the largest area of rice to come in contact with the bottom of the pan, where all the flavor is concentrated. It also helps liquid rapidly evaporate. (Because the rice cooks uncovered, there's no steam to cook the top layer.)

Paella pans expand in diameter rather than depth so that the layer of rice is always thin, ideally never more than a half inch thick. While you can use a huge skillet, nothing quite matches a proper paella pan, both for cooking and presentation. You should have no trouble finding paella pans at a good cookware shop or through mail order. The most useful size is fifteen to sixteen inches, which will make a main-course paella for four to six. Carbon-steel paella pans are more traditional and cook the rice better than fancier stainless-steel ones. However, they do tend to rust. After each use, scrub the pan gently with a soft brush, dry it completely, rub it thoroughly with an oiled paper towel, and keep it away from moisture. Like any good traditional pan, *la paella* gets better as it becomes seasoned from use.

4. Add the remaining 1 tablespoon olive oil to the center of the paella pan. Add the remaining garlic and cook until fragrant, about 30 seconds. Add the tomatoes to the center of the pan, reduce the heat to low, and cook, stirring the tomatoes several times, until they are thickened and reduced, 5 to 7 minutes. Using two wooden spoons, push the meat and the vegetables toward the center of the pan and mix them up with the tomatoes. Add the remaining 1 teaspoon paprika and the cayenne and stir for a few seconds.

5. Preheat the oven to 425°F.

6. Add the rice to the paella pan and stir it gently to coat with the pan mixture. Pour in 4 cups of the simmering stock (6 cups if you are using bomba rice), keeping the remaining stock simmering in case it is needed later. Set the paella pan over two burners, stir in the snails or the rosemary, and shake the pan gently to distribute the rice evenly. Cook over medium heat until the cooking liquid is almost level with the rice but the rice is still rather soupy, about 7 minutes. Periodically move and rotate the pan so that the liquid boils evenly. If the liquid is absorbed too fast and the rice still seems too raw, sprinkle on some more stock.

7. Transfer the paella pan to the oven and bake until the rice is tender but still a little al dente, about 15 minutes. Check the paella a few times and sprinkle more stock over the rice if it seems too al dente. Remove the paella from the oven, cover it with aluminum foil, and let stand for 5 minutes. Uncover the pan and let stand for another 10 minutes (the rice gets better as it stands). Garnish with the roasted peppers and serve. **SERVES 8 AS A FIRST COURSE, 6 AS A MAIN COURSE**

NOTE: Cans or jars of snails can be found at specialty food shops.

Chiringuito Seafood Paella (page 340)

PAELLA PERFECTA

Paella might just be the world's most perfect company dish—from the drama of presenting the giant pan at the table, to the beautifully seasoned, addictively flavorful rice. Once you get the knack of it, the paella recipes in this chapter are not at all complicated or time-consuming and can be prepared with supermarket ingredients. They are also infinitely tastier and more authentic than anything you might have encountered as paella at American restaurants. This said, paella is a dish that relies on a specific technique that demands a wee bit of understanding and practice. Here's some guidance.

THE RICE Whether *biryani,* risotto, or sushi, a rice-based dish is only as good as the quality of the rice. For paellas and other traditional *arroces,* cooks in the Levante and Catalonia rely on short- to medium-grain local varieties that are valued for their ability to absorb other flavors and deliver a texture that's miraculously spongy *and* firm all at once. A fashionable rice these days is the boutique *arroz bomba* that grows in the nitrogen-rich soil around Calasparra, a region in the province of Murcia. A low-yield heirloom variety, bomba is extremely dehydrated and absorbs more than three times its weight in liquid, expanding in width like an accordion, rather than in length. Despite its cachet, I'm not a huge fan of bomba, finding it tricky to work with, overly firm, and not as open to absorbing flavor as some other rices. Many Valencian rice cooks who initially embraced bomba share my feelings and are increasingly switching back to humbler but more flavorful strains, such as the smaller-grained senia and bahía. If you do use bomba, remember that it soaks up three to three and a half cups of liquid per cup of rice. I don't recommend linen sacks of rice simply labeled Calasparra without the word *bomba* on the package; these contain the lesser balilla x sollana variety, expensive but unremarkable.

My favorite rice for paella happens to be Italian: vialone nano from the Veneto, traditionally used for risotto. Recommended to me by Raúl Aleixandre, the genius chef at Ca'Sento restaurant in Valencia, it soaks up a ton of flavor, has just the right texture, and cooks faster than bomba, requiring less liquid. (Genetically, vialone nano is almost identical to the traditional Valencian senia and bahía strains, which are unavailable in this country.) Among readily available brands, Beretta vialone nano is quite tasty. While less perfect, arborio risotto rice—preferably good-quality imported—is also acceptable for paella. As is Goya's medium-grain rice, which, like risotto rices, requires about two cups of liquid for one cup of rice. Regular long-grain rice or Oriental short-grain are not suitable for paella.

If you buy a short- to medium-grain Spanish or Italian rice you are not familiar with, start by adding two cups of liquid per cup of rice, then add more liquid later if the rice still feels raw when most of the liquid has been absorbed. Paella is not pilaf or risotto; the rice is never washed and barely stirred. See "The Spanish Pantry" (page 461) for information on finding these rices.

THE FLAVORINGS The boost of flavor in most paellas comes from *sofrito,* a mixture of aromatics cooked down until dark and intense. Catalans will use a jammy, long-cooked *sofregit* of onions and tomatoes. In Valencia, *sofritos* tend to be lighter, consisting of garlic and grated tomatoes. In Alicante, fleshy dried ñora peppers are often added. Other seasonings might include herbs, as well as saffron and paprika for color. While unsmoked paprika from Murcia is more traditional, a dash of smoked *pimentón de la Vera* is a great way to simulate the smokiness of a wood-fired grill, the classic way of cooking paella. And then there are the ingredients particular to each paella—rabbit, chicken, pork, artichokes, seafood—their flavors intensified and caramelized by the intense heat of the thin steel paella pan. Don't neglect salt: If your meats, seafood, or vegetables aren't amply seasoned, the paella will come out bland.

THE LIQUID For cooking paellas, Valencians swear by their hard, lime-rich water. Obsessive cooks even carry water with them when planning to cook paella away from home. Well, the business about hardness or softness of water turns out to be a bit of an old wives' tale. At least according to my friends the brilliant Michelin-starred Alicantine chef Quique Dacosta and the Valencian rice scientist Santos Ruiz, who are collaborating on an iconoclastic rice cookbook meant to debunk this and other rice-cooking myths.

The best liquid for flavoring the rice is a simple but tasty broth: chicken for poultry and meat paellas; and fish or shrimp shell stock for seafood rices. And I've seen many a paella cook crumble a bouillon cube into their liquid. It works!

THE TECHNIQUE Like risotto, paella is all about method. First, the ingredients that will flavor the rice are sautéed over lively heat in a paella pan. Once the rice and liquid are added, the grain cooks for a few minutes at a fast uninterrupted boil over high heat; this "opens up the pores" of the rice, as local cooks say. The heat is then reduced, and the rice continues to simmer until the kernels become plump and somewhat firm, though never fluffy or overtly al dente. The surface of a properly cooked paella should look compact and beautifully caramelized. The rice is fluffed only when the paella is served.

HOW MUCH LIQUID TO ADD Ah, the million-dollar question. The accepted wisdom is two cups of liquid per one cup of rice. This ratio tends to be foolproof when the rice is covered and cooked by absorption. When the grain cooks uncovered in a shallow paella pan, liquid tends to evaporate more rapidly, at a rate that will vary slightly each time you cook. The exact amount of liquid also depends on the rice, how thickly it's layered, and the diameter of the pan. For rices other than bomba, begin with the two-to-one ratio, setting aside an extra cup of liquid for each cup of rice. Before the rice goes into the oven, taste it. If it feels raw, sprinkle on about a half cup of liquid. As the rice bakes, check it a couple more times, splashing on more liquid if the rice still refuses to give. As you check for doneness, taste the bottom or middle layer of rice, not the top. And keep in mind that the rice should come out of the oven somewhat al dente, so it can finish cooking off the heat. As with the amount of liquid, cooking times may vary slightly depending on the variety of rice and the rate it absorbs liquid. Your best guides are feel, look, and taste. After a few trials and errors, you'll get it perfect each time.

SERVING Now, the fun stuff. Proudly carrying the paella pan to the table is definitely part of the drama, a climactic reward for your work. Set the pan in the middle of the table and let guests scoop the rice out onto their plates with a wooden spoon. Traditionally, you start at the edge of the pan, working your way toward the center. A good paella should be flavorful enough to eat on its own, but lemon wedges and/or *allioli* are always welcome, especially with seafood-flavored rices. Most authentic paellas come unadorned; if you'd like a splash of color, decorate the paella with roasted pepper strips.

CHIRINGUITO SEAFOOD PAELLA

PAELLA A LA MARINERA

Come summer, the Spanish flock to the water with the determination of fish. Awaiting them on the beach are *chiringuitos,* humble seaside establishments that are to the Spanish coast what clam shacks are to New England. There is usually a pretty *terraza* with a view of the sea and a menu that revolves around salt-baked fish, lacy fried baby squid, clams in *salsa verde,* and, invariably, a simple but irresistible mixed seafood paella, such as this one. Feel free to play with the seafood assortment here, substituting mussels for the clams and small scallops for the monkfish, but keeping the proportions pretty much constant.

A good seafood paella is a minimalist affair, with few other ingredients besides seafood and rice. As the flavor depends on a good rich fish stock, I strongly recommend using Shrimp Shell Stock or another well-reduced flavorful fish or seafood stock. And don't skip the *allioli* for serving.

About 5 cups Shrimp Shell Stock (page 356), or 3 1/2 cups clam juice diluted with 1 1/2 cups water (more if using bomba rice)
1 large pinch of saffron, pulverized in a mortar
5 tablespoons extra-virgin olive oil
1/2 pound monkfish or other firm-fleshed fish, cut into 1-inch chunks
Coarse salt (kosher or sea)
4 to 6 ounces cleaned squid, bodies and tentacles cut into 1-inch pieces
10 medium-size garlic cloves; 8 crushed with a garlic press, 2 minced
2 large, ripe tomatoes, cut in half and grated on a box grater, skins discarded
1 1/2 teaspoons sweet (not smoked) paprika
1 3/4 cups short- to medium-grain rice (see page 338)
1/2 cup minced fresh flat-leaf parsley
12 small littleneck clams, scrubbed
12 jumbo shrimp, shelled and deveined
2 lemons, cut into wedges, for serving
Allioli (page 44), for serving

1. Place the shrimp stock in a medium-size saucepan and bring to a simmer over medium heat. Add the saffron and keep the stock at a simmer until ready to use.

2. Place 3 tablespoons of the olive oil in a 15- or 16-inch paella pan set over a single burner and heat on medium until it starts to smoke. Add the monkfish and cook until barely seared, about 1 minute, seasoning it lightly with salt. Using a slotted spoon, transfer the fish to a bowl. Cook the squid, stirring, until just seared, about 2 minutes, seasoning it with salt.

3. Push the squid to the edge of the paella pan, where it's not as hot. Add 1 tablespoon of the olive oil to the center of the pan. Add the crushed garlic and cook until fragrant, about 30 seconds. Add the tomatoes to the center of the pan, reduce the heat to low, and cook, stirring the tomatoes several times, until they are thickened and reduced, 5 to 7 minutes. Using two wooden spoons, push the squid toward the center of the pan and mix it up with the tomatoes. Add the paprika and stir for a few seconds.

4. Preheat the oven to 425°F.

5. Add the rice to the paella pan and stir it gently to coat with the pan mixture. Pour in 3½ cups of the simmering stock (5 cups if you are using bomba rice), keeping the remaining stock simmering in case it is needed later. Set the paella pan over two burners, stir in the parsley, and shake the pan gently to distribute the rice evenly. Cook over medium heat for 5 minutes. Periodically move and rotate the pan so that the liquid boils evenly.

6. Press the clams and the monkfish into the top of the rice and cook until the cooking liquid is almost level with the rice but the rice is still rather soupy, another 2 to 3 minutes. If the liquid is absorbed too fast and the rice still seems too raw, sprinkle on some more stock.

7. Transfer the paella pan to the oven and bake until the clams open and the rice is tender but still a little al dente, about 15 minutes. Check the paella a few times and sprinkle more stock over the rice if it seems too al dente. Remove the paella from the oven and discard any clams that have not opened. Cover the pan with aluminum foil, and let stand for 5 minutes. Uncover the pan and let stand for another 5 minutes (the rice gets better as it stands).

8. While the rice is standing, heat the remaining 1 tablespoon olive oil in a large skillet or wok over high heat. Stir-fry the shrimp, a few at a time, adding some of the minced garlic to each batch, until the shrimp are bright pink and just cooked through, 2 to 3 minutes per batch. Transfer the shrimp to a bowl and keep warm.

9. To serve, arrange the lemon wedges around the edge of the paella and decorate the top with the shrimp. Serve the paella straight from the pan, along with the *allioli,* for stirring into the rice. **SERVES 6 AS A FIRST COURSE, 4 AS A MAIN COURSE**

BLACK PAELLA WITH SQUID, MUSSELS, AND PEAS

ARROS NEGRE

For sheer drama, few dishes can beat the sensational Spanish seafood paellas tinted jet black with squid ink. Enjoyed along Spain's eastern coast from Catalonia to Alicante, black paellas are pretty easy to make at home, provided you can get your hands on packets of squid ink, which will save you the trouble of extracting your own. As the intensity of the ink varies, you'll need to use enough to color the broth completely black (otherwise the color of the finished dish will be gray). Serve the paella with either plain or Roasted Garlic Allioli.

1 dried ñora pepper or ancho chile, stemmed, seeded, and torn into pieces
About 4 1/2 cups Shrimp Shell Stock (page 356), or 3 1/2 cups clam juice diluted with 1 cup water (more if using bomba rice)
5 to 6 packets (each 4 grams/.14 ounce) squid ink (see page 220 and Note)
12 large garlic cloves, crushed with a garlic press
1/2 cup minced fresh flat-leaf parsley
5 tablespoons extra-virgin olive oil
1/2 pound medium-size shrimp, shrimp and deveined
Coarse salt (kosher or sea)
1/2 pound cleaned squid, bodies cut into 1/2-inch dice, tentacles chopped, if large
2 large ripe tomatoes, cut in half and grated on a box grater, skins discarded
1 1/2 cups short- to medium-grain rice (see page 338)
12 mussels, scrubbed and debearded right before cooking
3/4 cup fresh peas, or 1 cup frozen peas, thawed
Allioli or Roasted Garlic Allioli (pages 44 and 45), for serving

1. Place the ñora pepper in a small bowl, add very hot water to cover, and let soak until soft, about 30 minutes. Transfer the pepper and ½ cup of the soaking liquid to a blender and puree it, then set aside.

2. Place the shrimp stock in a medium-size saucepan and bring to a simmer over medium heat. Using a small spoon or the tip of a dinner knife, scrape the squid ink from 5 packets into a small bowl. Whisk in about ½ cup of the simmering broth and pour the mixture into the remaining broth. It should be jet black. If it is not, repeat with the remaining packet of ink. Add one third of the garlic and the parsley and keep the stock at a simmer until ready to use.

3. Place 3 tablespoons of the olive oil in a 15- or 16-inch paella pan set over a single burner and heat on medium until it starts to smoke. Add the shrimp and half of the remaining garlic and stir until the shrimp just turn pink, about 1 minute, seasoning them lightly with salt. Using a slotted spoon, trans-

HAIL TO THE WATER COURT

Visitors to Valencia who find themselves outside the city's cathedral on a Thursday get to witness a curious spectacle. Promptly at noon, a crowd gathers around as eight elderly men dressed in black convene with great pomp outside the Gothic doorway of the cathedral. This is Valencia's renowned *Tribunal de las Aguas,* or Water Court. Dating back to the tenth century, the tribunal is Europe's oldest surviving court. Its purpose? To settle disputes concerning the distribution of water. Today, few serious disagreements are actually brought before the old men in black. Usually, they just meet, ask anyone with a water dispute to come forward, and when no one does, promptly disband. Yet the very presence of this archaic judicial body is symbolic of the importance of irrigation here in the epicenter of Spanish rice production.

When the Arabs began planting rice in the rich agricultural hinterlands outside the city, they set up a complicated network of dikes and canals that channeled river water from the mountains into the rice paddies. They also established a system of communal government for water rights, a setup still intact today as rice growers administer the irrigation of each area on the principle of equal shares. These days the Comunidad de Regantes Acequia (Association of Water Users) is doing a pretty good job at settling their own disputes. But Valencia just wouldn't be the same if the Water Court didn't solemnly meet every Thursday at noon outside the cathedral.

fer the shrimp to a bowl. Add half of the squid to the pan and cook until just seared, about 2 minutes, seasoning it with salt. Transfer the seared squid to the bowl with the shrimp, then repeat with the remaining squid, adding it to the bowl.

4. Add the remaining 2 tablespoons olive oil to the paella pan. Add the remaining garlic and cook until fragrant, about 30 seconds. Add the tomatoes, reduce the heat to low, and cook, stirring several times, until the tomatoes are thickened and reduced, 5 to 7 minutes. Add the pureed ñora pepper and cook, stirring, until the flavors meld, 2 to 3 minutes.

5. Preheat the oven to 425°F.

6. Add the rice to the paella pan and stir it gently to coat with the pan mixture. Pour in 3 cups of the simmering stock (4½ cups if you are using bomba rice), keeping the remaining stock simmering in case it is needed later. Set the paella pan over two burners and shake it gently to distribute the rice evenly. Cook over medium heat for 5 minutes. Periodically move and rotate the pan so that the liquid boils evenly.

7. Gently stir the shrimp, squid, mussels, and peas into the rice, shake the pan again to flatten the top of the rice, and cook until the cooking liquid is almost level with the rice but the rice is still rather soupy, another 2 to 3 minutes. If the liquid is absorbed too fast and the rice still seems too raw, sprinkle on some more stock.

8. Transfer the paella pan to the oven and bake until the mussels open and the rice is tender but still a little al dente, about 15 minutes. Check the paella a few times and sprinkle more stock over the rice if it seems too al dente. Remove the paella from the oven and discard any mussels that have not opened. Cover the pan with aluminum foil and let stand for 5 minutes. Uncover the pan and let stand for another 5 minutes (the rice gets better as it stands).

9. Serve the paella straight from the pan, along with the *allioli,* for stirring into the rice. **SERVES 6 AS A FIRST COURSE, 4 AS A MAIN COURSE**

NOTE: If the squid ink seems a little congealed, warm the packets in a bowl of hot water.

VALENCIAN PAELLA WITH VEGETABLES & PORK

ARROZ CON VERDURAS Y MAGRO

Here is a robustly flavored vegetable and pork paella from the inland *huertas* (vegetable plots) of Valencia and Alicante, a rice dish as delicious and classic as the seafood and chicken versions. The bouquet of vegetables here includes chard, cauliflower, artichokes, red peppers, and green beans. Feel free to add whatever else looks good and seasonal—peas, fava beans, small cubes of eggplant—while maintaining the same proportion of rice to vegetables, since a paella should never be overloaded with too many ingredients. If you know a place to get garlic shoots, they would be more than welcome here.

PAELLA 101

1. Don't experiment: Paella making is an art honed by decades, and like any great rice dish it loves continuity: same pan, same kind of rice, same stove, same proportions. When you've mastered the basic technique and can produce perfect rice in your sleep, start taking creative license. The only secret to a great paella is the same as how you get to Carnegie Hall: practice.

2. Avoid overloading paella with extraneous stuff: Paella is about rice and rice again. The great Spanish gastronome Rafael García Santos decries paellas with too many ingredients as "pointless baroque exhibitionism." Besides being an affront to tradition, too much food in the pan smothers the rice and prevents it from cooking evenly. While the recipes in this chapter are open to substitutions, try not to alter the proportion of rice to the other ingredients.

3. Don't attempt to double the serving size in a particular pan. Paella pans are designed for specific amounts of ingredients; the layer of rice should always be rather thin. If you're planning on making paella often, get pans in two sizes: a 15-inch pan for four people and an 18-inch one to serve six to eight.

4. Place a paella pan over two burners, if it's more than 13 inches in diameter. As you cook, keep turning and moving the pan every few minutes, gently shaking it as you rotate it. If you're really into paellas, consider getting the appropriate paraphernalia, such as a special gas burner and a tripod to help the paella cook evenly without baking. See "Sources" (page 461) for where to find these.

5. Have everything chopped, measured, and ready to go before you start cooking, just as you would with stir-frying. Because paella pans tend to get very hot, the ingredients cook quickly and organization is crucial. With a little advance prep, assembling and cooking paella is a relative breeze.

6. If you see the rice cooking unevenly, sprinkle some water over the "raw" spots or gently stir the undercooked bits in the bottom of the pan. Valencians insist that the rice should never be stirred—agitating the starches makes the rice gummy—but some gentle fiddling is perfectly fine. If the rice is getting soft before the liquid is absorbed, raise the heat to cook down the liquid. If the top of the rice is undercooked while the bottom is soft and ready, remove the pan from the heat, cover it with a damp kitchen towel, and leave it for about ten minutes.

7. Always let the paella rest after cooking, as the rice continues to absorb moisture away from the heat. Standing for ten to fifteen minutes, covered with a kitchen towel or aluminum foil, is standard. However, when tardy guests once forced me to leave the paella sitting for forty-five minutes, I was amazed at how much the texture improved upon standing. (Some Valencian paella junkies even suggest that paella is at its best at room temperature the following day!) If you're letting paella stand for more than fifteen minutes, tent it very loosely with aluminum foil or cover it loosely with paper towels, so that it doesn't continue steaming.

8. The paella can be prepared ahead of time up to the point the liquid is added. Letting the rice stand once it's been coated with the pan mixture is actually good for its flavor. Advance preparation can be done a few hours ahead, with the rice cooked right before the guests arrive. Figure on

Rice dishes aren't just from Valencia; here a Basque chef is overseeing his creamy creation.

about forty minutes from the time you add water to the time you serve. Most of this is hands-off. (Note: If the paella contains artichokes, do not let them sit in the pan or they will blacken. Remove the artichokes from the pan while the paella sits and return them to it when you add the liquids.)

9. Be sure the cooking liquid is at a simmer before adding it to the rice, but don't allow it to boil. Besides affecting flavor, boiling liquid causes it to evaporate and you will lose track of the proportions.

10. Leftover paella—in the utterly unlikely event you'll have any—is delicious the following day. Just don't leave the rice in the paella pan overnight, as it will take on a metallic flavor. Reheat the rice briefly in a microwave until it's quite warm but not piping hot.

12 ounces boneless pork loin or shoulder, cut into 1-inch pieces
Coarse salt (kosher or sea) and freshly ground black pepper
2 teaspoons dried oregano
2 1/2 teaspoons sweet (not smoked) paprika
2 large dried ñora peppers or ancho chiles, stemmed, seeded, and torn into pieces
About 6 cups chicken stock or broth (more if using bomba rice)
1 large pinch of saffron, toasted and pulverized in a mortar
5 tablespoons extra-virgin olive oil
3/4 cup green beans, trimmed and cut into 1-inch lengths
1 cup small cauliflower florets
1 small ripe red bell pepper, cut into large dice
5 to 6 ounces frozen artichoke hearts, thawed and patted dry with paper towels
2 1/2 cups (tightly packed; from 1 small bunch) slivered Swiss chard or spinach
8 medium-size garlic cloves, crushed with a garlic press
3/4 cup canned crushed tomatoes
2 cups short- to medium-grain rice (see page 338)

1. Rub the pork generously with salt, black pepper, the oregano, and 1 teaspoon of the paprika. Let stand at room temperature for 30 minutes or refrigerate, covered, for about 2 hours.

2. Place the ñora peppers in a small bowl, add very hot water to cover, and let soak until soft, about 30 minutes. Transfer the peppers and ½ cup of the soaking liquid to a blender and puree them, then set aside.

3. Place the chicken stock in a medium-size saucepan and bring to a simmer over medium heat. Add the saffron and keep the stock at a simmer until ready to use.

4. Place 2 tablespoons of the olive oil in a 15- or 16-inch paella pan set over a single burner and heat on medium until it starts to smoke. Add the pork, increase the heat to high, and brown, tossing and turning it, for 3 to 4 minutes. Push the pork to the edge of the pan, where it's not as hot. Add 2 more tablespoons olive oil to the pan and the green beans, cauliflower, and red bell pepper. Cook the vegetables, stirring, until they begin to brown, 5 to 7 minutes. Add the artichokes and cook for another 1 to 2 minutes. Add the chard and stir just until it wilts. Season the vegetables with salt and pepper, then, using a slotted spoon, transfer the vegetables and pork to a large bowl.

5. Add the remaining 1 tablespoon olive oil and the garlic to the paella pan and stir for a few seconds. Add the remaining 1½ teaspoons paprika and stir for another few seconds. Add the tomatoes and the pureed ñora peppers, reduce the heat to low, and cook, stirring, until the sauce is thickened and reduced, 5 to 7 minutes. Return the vegetables and pork to the pan and stir to mix.

6. Preheat the oven to 425°F.

7. Add the rice to the paella pan and stir it gently to coat with the pan mixture. Pour in 4 cups of the simmering stock (6 cups if you are using bomba rice), keeping the remaining stock simmering in case it is needed later. Set the paella pan over two burners and shake it gently to distribute the rice evenly. Cook over medium heat until the cooking liquid is almost level with the rice but the rice is still rather soupy, about 7 minutes. Periodically move and rotate the pan so that the liquid boils evenly. If the liquid is absorbed too fast and the rice still seems too raw, sprinkle on some more stock.

8. Transfer the paella pan to the oven and bake until the rice is tender but still a little al dente, about 15 minutes. Check the paella a few times and sprinkle more stock over the rice if it seems too al dente. Remove the paella from the oven, cover it with aluminum foil, and let stand for 10 minutes. Uncover the pan and let stand for another 5 minutes (the rice gets better as it stands). Serve the paella straight from the pan. **SERVES 8 AS A FIRST COURSE, 6 AS A MAIN COURSE**

PAELLA WITH PINE NUT MEATBALLS, SAUSAGE, AND POTATOES

ARROS AMB MANDONGUILLES

On a chilly night, few things hit the spot better than this rib-sticking paella from Alicante, which teams rice with pine nut–studded meatballs, potatoes, tomato quarters, chunks of chicken or pork, and slices of *morcilla* (blood sausage). If *morcilla* isn't your thing, use another sausage, such as chorizo or fresh pork sausage. The meatballs take only minutes to prepare (make them before you start the paella), but feel free to omit them and increase the amount of chicken or pork.

½ pound skinless, boneless chicken thighs, or boned country-style pork ribs, cut into 1-inch chunks
3 very small all-purpose boiling potatoes (about 2 inches in diameter), peeled and halved, then each half cut into 4 wedges
1 large red bell pepper, cored, seeded, and cut into 1-inch dice
Coarse salt (kosher or sea) and freshly ground black pepper
1½ teaspoons smoked sweet Spanish paprika
About 4½ cups chicken stock or broth (more if using bomba rice)
1 large pinch of saffron, pulverized in a mortar and steeped in 2 tablespoons very hot water
5 tablespoons extra-virgin olive oil
4 ounces fully cooked morcilla without rice or other blood sausage (see Note), cut into thick slices
6 medium-size plum tomatoes; 3 quartered, 3 cut in half and grated, skins discarded
1 small onion, chopped
8 medium-size garlic cloves, chopped, plus 1 whole small garlic head, outer layer of skin removed
1 large pinch of cayenne
1½ cups short- to medium-grain rice (see page 338)
1 fresh rosemary sprig
3 tablespoons minced fresh flat-leaf parsley
Pine Nut–Studded Meatballs (recipe follows)

1. Place the chicken, potatoes, and red bell pepper in a bowl, rub generously with salt and black pepper and ½ teaspoon of the paprika, and let stand until ready to use.

2. Place the chicken stock in a medium-size saucepan and bring to a simmer over medium heat. Add the saffron and keep the stock at a simmer until ready to use.

3. Place 3 tablespoons of the olive oil in a 15- or 16-inch paella pan set over a single burner and heat on medium until it starts to smoke. Add the sausage, increase the heat to medium-high, and brown quickly on both sides, about 2 minutes total. Using a slotted spoon, transfer the browned sausage to a bowl. Add the tomato quarters to the pan and sear quickly all over, about 1 minute. Transfer the tomato quarters to another bowl. Add the chicken, potatoes, and red pepper to the pan. Reduce the heat to medium-low and cook, stirring, until nicely browned, 5 to 7 minutes. Push everything to the edge of the pan, where it's not as hot.

4. Add the remaining 2 tablespoons olive oil to the center of the paella pan. Add the onion and the chopped garlic and cook, stirring in the center of the pan, until the onion softens, about 5 minutes. Add the grated tomatoes, reduce the heat to very low, and cook, stirring in the center several times, until the tomatoes are thickened and reduced, 5 to 7 minutes. Using two wooden spoons, push the meat and vegetables toward the center of the pan and mix them with the tomatoes. Return the sausage to the pan. Add the remaining 1 teaspoon paprika and the cayenne and stir for a few seconds.

5. Preheat the oven to 425°F.

6. Add the rice to the paella pan and stir it gently to coat with the pan mixture. Pour in 3 cups of the simmering stock (4½ cups if you are using bomba rice), keeping the remaining stock simmering in case it is needed later. Place the whole garlic head, pointy side up, in the middle of the pan. Set the pan over two burners, stir in the rosemary and parsley, and shake the pan gently to distribute the rice evenly. Cook over medium heat until the cooking liquid is almost level with the rice but the rice is still rather soupy, about 7 minutes. Periodically move and rotate the pan so that the liquid boils evenly. Gently press the meatballs and the tomato

quarters, cut side up, into the top of the rice and cook for 2 to 3 minutes longer. If the liquid is absorbed too fast and the rice still seems too raw, sprinkle on some more stock.

7. Transfer the paella pan to the oven and bake until the rice is tender but still a little al dente, about 15 minutes. Check the paella a few times and sprinkle more stock over the rice if it seems too al dente. When the rice is done, change the oven setting to broil. Pass the paella under the broiler until the top of the rice looks darkened and caramelized, 2 to 3 minutes.

8. Cover the paella with aluminum foil and let stand for 10 minutes. Uncover the pan and let stand for another 5 minutes (the rice gets better as it stands). Serve the paella straight from the pan. **SERVES 4 OR 5 AS A MAIN COURSE**

NOTE: You can substitute 4 ounces chorizo or fresh pork sausage (preferably without fennel) for the blood sausage. If you're using fresh pork sausage, blanch it first in boiling water, then cut it into thick slices and continue with Step 3 of the recipe.

VARIATION: This kind of rice is also frequently prepared *al horno*—baked in an earthenware *cazuela*—which is wonderful too. If you're baking the rice in a dish deeper than a paella pan, you won't need more than 3 cups liquid (4½ for bomba rice).

PINE NUT–STUDDED MEATBALLS

ALBONDIGAS CON PINONES

These Alicantine meatballs are also terrific without the rice, cooked in a light tomato sauce for a few minutes after they're baked. Or try them with Almond and Saffron Sauce (page 283).

- 1 slice white sandwich bread, crusts removed
- 6 ounces ground pork
- 4 ounces fresh pork sausage (preferably without fennel), casings removed, meat mashed with a fork
- 1 teaspoon sweet (not smoked) paprika
- 1/2 teaspoon coarse salt (kosher or sea)
- 1/2 teaspoon freshly ground black pepper
- 1/2 teaspoon dried oregano
- 1 small pinch of ground cinnamon
- 1 large garlic clove, crushed with a garlic press
- 2 heaping tablespoons pine nuts
- 1 large egg
- Olive oil, for shaping the meatballs

1. Preheat the oven to 425°F.

2. Place the bread in a small bowl, add water to cover, and let soak for 2 to 3 minutes. Drain, squeeze out the excess liquid, and finely crumble the bread.

3. Place the crumbled bread and the pork, sausage, paprika, salt, pepper, oregano, cinnamon, garlic, pine nuts, and egg in a large bowl. Gently knead the meatball mixture with your hands just until all the ingredients are thoroughly combined; do not overknead.

4. Lightly oil your hands, then break off a piece of the meatball mixture and shape it into a 1¼-inch ball and place it on a rimmed baking sheet. Repeat with the remaining meatball mixture. Bake the meatballs, shaking the baking sheet once or twice, until they are lightly browned and firm to the touch, about 12 minutes. (The meatballs can be prepared up to a day ahead and refrigerated, covered.) **MAKES 10 TO 12 MEATBALLS**

RICE WITH TUNA AND ROMESCO BROTH

ARROZ MELOSO CON ATUN AL ROMESCO

This wonderful recipe is adapted from the Catalan chef David Solé i Torné, the great *romesco* sauce specialist from the city of Tarragona. Studded with shrimp and cubes of fresh tuna, the rice gets its special character from the ruddy *romesco* broth enriched with pureed roasted tomatoes, peppers, and garlic. The texture of the rice is *meloso,* which is to say slightly creamy, rather like a risotto. Once you've tried the original recipe, you can experiment, adding sautéed artichokes, pieces of scallions, fava beans or peas, and shellfish like mussels or scallops.

FOR THE ROMESCO BROTH:

2 dried ñora peppers or ancho chiles, stemmed, seeded, and torn into pieces
2 large red bell peppers, cored, cut in half, and seeded
1 large ripe tomato, quartered
1 small garlic head, outer layer of skin removed, top cut off
Olive oil, for brushing the vegetables
16 toasted almonds (see page 267)
1 1/2 teaspoons sweet (not smoked) paprika
1/2 cup dry white wine
4 cups Shrimp Shell Stock (page 356) or store-bought fish stock, or 3 cups bottled clam juice diluted with 1 cup water

FOR THE RICE:

3 tablespoons extra-virgin olive oil
3/4 pound fresh tuna, cut into 3/4-inch cubes
1/2 pound medium-size shrimp, shelled and deveined
Coarse salt (kosher or sea)
6 large garlic cloves, minced
1 1/2 cups short- to medium-grain rice (see page 338)
1/4 cup minced fresh flat-leaf parsley

1. Make the broth: Preheat the oven to 400°F.

2. Place the ñora peppers in a small bowl, add 1 cup very hot water, and let soak until soft, about 30 minutes.

3. Arrange the red bell peppers, tomato, and garlic head on a small baking sheet and brush lightly with olive oil. Bake the vegetables until they are soft and lightly charred, 30 to 40 minutes. Transfer the red peppers to a bowl, cover them with plastic wrap, and let stand for 15 minutes. Then, peel and coarsely chop the peppers and the tomato. Squeeze the flesh out of the cloves of the garlic head.

4. Transfer the ñora peppers and their soaking liquid to a blender. Add the chopped red peppers, tomato, roasted garlic cloves, almonds, paprika, wine, and 1 cup of the shrimp stock. Puree until very smooth. Transfer the pepper mixture to a medium-size saucepan and add the remaining 3 cups shrimp stock (you should have about 6 cups of *romesco* broth). Bring the broth to a simmer over medium heat and cook until the flavors meld, about 5 minutes. (The broth can be prepared up to a day ahead and refrigerated, covered. When you're ready to use it, bring the broth back to a simmer.)

5. Make the rice: Heat 2 tablespoons of the olive oil in a wide medium-size casserole or a deep 12-inch skillet over medium-high heat. Add the tuna and sear until lightly browned on all sides, about 1 minute. Using a slotted spoon, transfer the tuna to a bowl. Add the shrimp to the casserole and stir until they just turn pink, about 1 minute. Transfer the shrimp to the bowl with the tuna and season with salt.

6. Add the remaining 1 tablespoon olive oil to the casserole and raise the heat to high. Add the minced garlic and stir until very fragrant, about 30 seconds. Add the rice and toss to coat with the oil. Add 3 cups of the simmering *romesco* broth, reduce the heat to medium-low, and cook until most of the liquid has been absorbed, about 12 minutes, stirring occasionally so the rice doesn't stick to the bottom. Add the remaining broth, stir, and continue cooking, stirring occasionally, until the rice is almost tender but still al dente, about 7 minutes longer. Stir in the parsley and the tuna and shrimp and cook for another 2 minutes, or until the rice is done to your liking. The rice should have the consistency of a slightly soupy risotto, though it will be a little less creamy. If the broth is absorbed too quickly as the rice cooks, keep adding a little water so the rice stays moist. Serve the rice at once. **SERVES 6 AS A FIRST COURSE, 4 AS A MAIN COURSE**

AMPURDAN BAKED RICE WITH RABBIT AND MUSHROOMS

ARROZ AL HORNO CON CONEJO Y SETAS

Ampurdán is a Catalan region renowned for its lusty autumnal cuisine, which often combines wild mushrooms and game. They team up beautifully in this baked rice dish from the charmed Hotel La Plaça in Madremanya. If you don't have rabbit, substitute chicken. The best dish to cook this in is an earthenware *cazuela* with straight sides—one that can be carried right to the table. Lacking a *cazuela,* use a wide, flameproof casserole. Much of the dish can easily be prepared ahead; cook the rice right before you're ready to serve.

- 5 tablespoons extra-virgin olive oil, or more if needed
- 2 medium-size onions, finely chopped
- 1 large ripe red bell pepper, cored, seeded, and cut into medium-size dice
- 1 rabbit (about 2 1/2 pounds), cut into 12 pieces, or 2 1/2 pounds chicken (8 to 10 pieces), rinsed and patted dry
- Coarse salt (kosher or sea) and freshly ground black pepper
- 1/2 pound fresh sweet pork link sausages (preferably without fennel)
- 1 pound assorted wild mushrooms or a mixture of wild and cultivated mushrooms (chanterelles, cèpes, morels, oyster, cremini, and/or portobellos), wiped clean with a damp paper towel; larger mushrooms coarsely chopped, small ones left whole
- 6 medium-size garlic cloves; 4 crushed with a garlic press, 2 minced
- 1 1/4 teaspoons sweet (not smoked) paprika
- 1/2 cup dry white wine
- 1/3 cup best-quality canned tomato sauce
- 1 medium-size pinch of sugar
- 3 cups chicken stock or broth (more if using bomba rice)
- 3 tablespoons minced fresh flat-leaf parsley
- 1 1/2 cups short- to medium-grain rice (see page 338)

1. Heat 3 tablespoons of the olive oil in a deep earthenware *cazuela* or a wide (12- to 14-inch diameter) flameproof casserole over low heat. Add the onions and red pepper and cook, stirring from time to time, until the pepper is very soft and the onions are beginning to reduce to a jamlike consistency, about 30 minutes (about as long as it takes to prepare the rabbit, sausages, and mushrooms in Step 2). As the vegetables cook, periodically add a little water to the pan when it looks dry.

2. Rub the rabbit with salt and black pepper. Prick the sausages all over with a fork. Heat the remaining 2 tablespoons olive oil in a large skillet over medium heat. Working in two batches, cook the rabbit until nicely browned all over, about 10 minutes per batch, adding more olive oil if necessary. Transfer the rabbit to a large bowl, add the sausages to the skillet, and brown all over, about 5 minutes. Transfer the sausages to the bowl with the rabbit. Cook the mushrooms in the fat from the sausages until they are lightly browned, about 7 minutes. Transfer the mushrooms to the bowl with the rabbit. (As you cook the meats and the mushrooms, keep an eye on the onion mixture.)

3. Once the onions have cooked down, add the crushed garlic to them and cook, stirring, for 1 minute. Add the paprika and stir for a few seconds. Add the wine, increase the heat to high, and cook until the liquid has reduced somewhat, 2 to 3 minutes. Add the tomato sauce and sugar, reduce the heat to low, and simmer, stirring, until the sauce is thickened, 5 to 7 minutes longer. (The onion mixture and the rabbit, sausages, and mushrooms can be prepared ahead up to this point and refrigerated, separately, for 6 hours. Let them return to room temperature before continuing with the recipe.)

4. Preheat the oven to 400°F.

5. Cut the sausage into thick slices and add it, the rabbit, and mushrooms to the *cazuela* with the onion mixture. Add the chicken stock, the minced garlic, and the parsley and bring to a boil. Season with salt and pepper to taste. Add the rice and bring back to a boil. Carefully transfer the *cazuela* to the oven and bake, uncovered, until the rice is tender but still a little al dente and the liquid has been absorbed, 22 to 25 minutes. Remove the casserole from the oven, cover with aluminum foil, and let stand for 15 minutes before serving. **SERVES 6 AS A FIRST COURSE, 4 AS A MAIN COURSE**

CREAMY BASQUE SMOKED CHEESE RISOTTO

ARROZ CREMOSO CON IDIAZABAL

Like the rest of the world, Spain has eagerly embraced Italian dishes, especially risotto, which is quite similar in texture to *caldoso-* or *meloso-*style soupy Spanish rice dishes. In the Basque Country, where tastes run to mild comfort food, a delicious risotto enriched with the local smoked Idiazábal cheese is one of the favorite restaurant staples. This recipe, from the Cuchara de San Telmo tapas bar in San Sebastián, is absolutely sensational—better than most of the risottos I have had in Italy. Sometimes, the chefs drizzle green herb oil and old balsamic vinegar on their tapas-scaled portions; on other occasions they add Catalan *allioli* for a garlicky kick. The dish is great as a first course or as a bed for seared scallops or other fish. If smoked Idiazábal cheese (see page 170) is not available, substitute another smoked cheese, such as Gouda or mozzarella.

1 1/2 tablespoons olive oil
1/2 cup finely sliced scallions, including a bit of the green
2 large garlic cloves, minced
1 1/2 cups best-quality risotto rice, preferably carnaroli
1/2 cup dry white wine
5 1/2 to 6 cups chicken stock or broth, kept at a simmer
1/3 cup heavy (whipping) cream
1 cup shredded smoked cheese, such as Idiazábal or Gouda
1/3 cup freshly grated Parmesan cheese, preferably Parmigiano-Reggiano
2 to 3 tablespoons Parsley Oil (recipe follows)
3 tablespoons syrupy aged balsamic vinegar, or 1/3 cup thin balsamic vinegar reduced over medium-high heat to 3 tablespoons

1. Heat the olive oil in a heavy wide 3-quart saucepan, over medium-low heat. Add the scallions and cook, stirring, until soft but not browned, about 5 minutes. Add the garlic and stir for 30 seconds. Add the rice and stir for about 1 minute. Increase the heat to medium, add the wine, and stir vigorously until the wine is absorbed, 2 to 3 minutes.

2. Add 3 cups of the simmering stock, about 1 cup at a time, stirring constantly with a wooden spoon until each addition of liquid is absorbed. Continue adding the remaining stock, ½ cup at a time, stirring after each addition. Cook until the rice is tender but a little al dente, about 20 minutes total.

3. Add the cream, smoked cheese, and Parmesan and stir vigorously until the cheese melts, 1 to 2 minutes. Immediately spoon the risotto into serving bowls and drizzle some of the Parsley Oil and balsamic vinegar over each portion. Serve at once. **SERVES 4 TO 6**

PARSLEY OIL

ACEITE DE PEREJIL

Parsley oil brightens the appearance and flavor of many dishes—gazpachos, risottos, grilled fish, or cream soups, such as Garbanzo Cream with Ham Cracklings (page 83).

- 1/3 cup extra-virgin olive oil
- 1/2 cup chopped fresh flat-leaf parsley

Place the olive oil and the parsley in a blender and puree until bright green and completely smooth. Let the oil stand at room temperature for at least 15 minutes or up to 2 hours, then strain it through a fine-mesh sieve into a bowl. The oil can be prepared up to several hours ahead. **MAKES ABOUT 1/4 CUP**

PASTA AND COUSCOUS

NOODLES WITH WHITE BEANS, CHORIZO, AND CLAMS

CAZUELA DE FIDEOS CON ALUBIAS BLANCAS, CHORIZO Y ALMEJAS

In northern Spain, baked pastas are almost as beloved as rice, whether prepared with thin vermicelli-like *fideos* (noodles) or the sturdier ones reminiscent of our macaroni. This is one of my favorite pasta *cazuelas,* a dish I've been serving for years, always to raves. Once you've tried it, play around with the recipe, substituting diced potatoes for the beans, nuggets of pork sausage for the chorizo, mussels for the clams, and macaroni for the *fideos.* It tastes good every which way.

2 tablespoons extra-virgin olive oil
4 to 5 ounces sweet Spanish-style chorizo sausage, diced
1 1/2 cups canned small white beans, such as cannellini, drained
6 medium-size garlic cloves, minced
1 teaspoon sweet (not smoked) paprika
Crushed red pepper flakes
2 medium-size tomatoes, cut in half and grated on a box grater, skins discarded
About 10 ounces fideo noodles or thin spaghetti, broken into 2-inch lengths
3 cups bottled clam juice diluted with 2 cups water
18 to 20 small littleneck clams, scrubbed
1/4 cup minced fresh flat-leaf parsley, plus more for garnish
Coarse salt (kosher or sea) and freshly ground black pepper

1. Preheat the oven to 425°F.

2. Heat the olive oil in a 12-inch earthenware *cazuela* or a large, deep ovenproof skillet over medium heat. Add the chorizo and brown, stirring, for 2 to 3 minutes, then add the beans and garlic and gently stir for 1 minute. Add the paprika, season with red pepper flakes to taste, then add the tomatoes and cook, stirring, until they thicken and reduce, 5 to 7 minutes.

3. Add the noodles and stir to coat with the pan mixture. Stir in 4 cups of the diluted clam juice and bring to a boil. Cook over medium heat, gently stirring occasionally, until the liquid is level with the noodles and the noodles are half cooked, about 8 minutes. Add the remaining 1 cup clam juice and bring to a boil. Stir in the clams and ¼ cup of parsley, burying the clams in the noodles. Cover the *cazuela,* reduce the heat to low, and cook until the clams just open, 4 to 7 minutes. Discard any clams that don't open. Season with salt and black pepper to taste.

4. Transfer the *cazuela* to the oven and bake until the top looks fairly dry and the noodles underneath are tender and still a little soupy, about 8 minutes. Remove the casserole from the oven and let stand for 5 minutes. Sprinkle parsley over the casserole and serve it straight from the *cazuela.* **SERVES 6 AS A FIRST COURSE, 4 AS A MAIN COURSE**

TOASTED PASTA "PAELLA" WITH SHRIMP

ROSSEJAT DE FIDEUS

Whenever I ask Spanish friends for their favorite party recipe, they always mention a scrumptious Catalan and Valencian dish of toasted noodles cooked in a paella pan with some manner of seafood. This Catalan version gets a flavor boost from *sofregit*—a mixture of slowly cooked onions and tomatoes (see page 357). The dish uses small shrimp, which cook with the pasta until they're very soft, and jumbo ones to decoratively top the noodles.

6 tablespoons extra-virgin olive oil
About 1 pound fideo noodles or thin spaghetti, broken into 2-inch lengths
6 cups Shrimp Shell Stock (page 356), or 4 cups bottled clam juice diluted with 2 cups water
1 medium-size pinch of saffron, pulverized in a mortar
2 tablespoons finely minced garlic
1 pound small shrimp, shelled
2 teaspoons sweet (not smoked) paprika
Sofregit (recipe follows or see Note)
3 tablespoons minced fresh flat-leaf parsley
12 to 16 jumbo shrimp, shelled and deveined
Lemon wedges, for serving
Allioli (page 44), for serving

1. Toast the noodles: Heat 3 tablespoons of the olive oil in a 15- or 16-inch paella pan or a very large skillet over medium heat. Add half the noodles and cook, stirring, until nicely browned, 4 to 5 minutes. Watch the noodles closely, as they tend to burn in no time. Using a slotted spoon, transfer the noodles to a large bowl, making sure none remain in the pan. Add 1 tablespoon of the olive oil to the pan and toast the remaining noodles in the same fashion, transferring them to the bowl when browned. Wipe the paella pan clean. (The noodles can also be toasted in a 425°F oven without oil: Just spread them on two large-rimmed baking sheets and toast them until nicely browned, stirring often, about 5 minutes. Either way, the noodles can be browned up to 1 day ahead and stored at room temperature, covered with aluminum foil.)

2. Place the shrimp stock in a medium-size saucepan and bring to a simmer. Add the saffron and keep at a simmer until ready to use.

3. Preheat the oven to 425°F.

PASTA PAELLA, ANYONE?

Could anything be more delicious than a seafood paella made with short-grained Valencian rice? Well, perhaps *fideuá,* the same dish prepared with noodles. Enjoyed all over the Levante and well beyond, *fideuá* is believed to have originated in the coastal resort of Gandía in Alicante. The myths of its invention are many. Some say that back in the 1960s, a fisherman aboard a trawler was getting ready to prepare a seafood paella and, upon discovering that he was out of rice, improvised with dried noodles. Others credit the creation of the dish to various chefs in Gandía, a city where *fideuá* is honored with an international competition each June. In truth, thin *fideo* noodles have been used along Spain's Mediterranean coast since the Middle Ages, and the idea of combining them with local seafood is hardly original. In Catalonia and parts of Valencia, for example, one can feast on scrumptious pasta paellas prepared with toasted noodles and a strong flavorful *sofregit.* On Paseo Neptuno, a beach promenade in Valencia densely lined with seafood establishments, a restaurant called La Rosa prepares spectacular black *fideo* with squid and its ink. And on Spain's northern Cantabrian coast, noodle and clam casseroles are a common treat. Just don't mention this to folks in Gandía.

4. Heat 1 tablespoon of the olive oil in the paella pan over medium-high heat. Add half of the garlic and stir until fragrant, about 30 seconds. Add the small shrimp and stir until they turn opaque, 1 to 2 minutes. Add the paprika and stir for a few seconds. Add the *sofregit* and cook until it is warmed through. Add the toasted noodles and stir to coat with the pan mixture. Pour in 3 cups of the simmering stock,

SHRIMP SHELL STOCK

For cooking seafood-flavored rices and pastas, my favorite liquid is a store-bought fish stock or clam juice I've enhanced with the toasty nuttiness of sautéed shrimp shells. If you can get shrimp with their heads on (try Chinese or other ethnic markets), they will intensify the stock's flavor still further. Whenever you are peeling shrimp or cooking a lobster, save the shells; keep them in a zipper-lock bag in the freezer so you can make stock at whim.

1 tablespoon olive oil
4 whole garlic cloves, unpeeled and smashed
Shells (and heads, if available) from 1 pound shrimp
1 tablespoon tomato paste
10 cups store-bought fish stock, or 7 cups clam juice diluted with 3 cups water
3 fresh flat-leaf parsley sprigs

Heat the olive oil and garlic in a large saucepan over medium heat. Add the shrimp shells and heads, if using, and cook, stirring, until pink and very aromatic, 2 to 3 minutes. Add the tomato paste and stir until darkened, about 30 seconds. Add the fish stock and parsley, increase the heat to medium-high, bring to a boil, and cook until reduced to 6 to 7 cups, 15 to 20 minutes. Strain the stock, discarding the solids. The stock can be refrigerated, covered, for 2 to 3 days or frozen for up to 1 month. **MAKES 6 TO 7 CUPS**

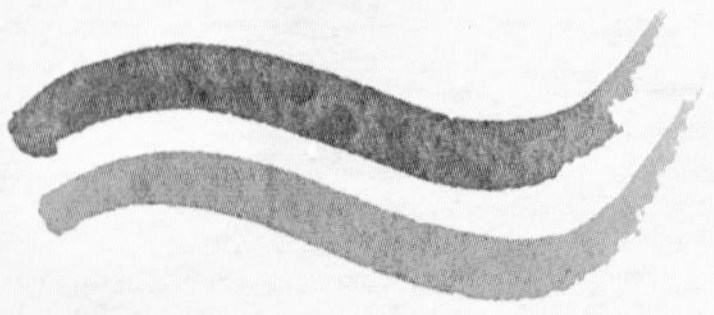

keeping the remaining stock simmering. Set the paella pan over two burners and stir in the parsley. Reduce the heat to medium and cook, stirring occasionally, until most of the liquid has been absorbed and the noodles begin to soften, about 5 minutes. Periodically move and rotate the pan so that the liquid boils evenly. Add another 2 cups of the stock and continue cooking in the same fashion until most of the liquid is absorbed and the noodles are cooked but a little al dente, another 5 to 6 minutes. If the liquid is absorbed too fast and the noodles are still hard, add some or all of the remaining 1 cup stock. Transfer the paella pan to the oven and bake until the noodles are soft and the liquid in the pan is syrupy, 7 to 8 minutes.

5. While the noodles are baking, heat the remaining 1 tablespoon olive oil in a large skillet or wok over high heat. Stir-fry the jumbo shrimp, a few at a time, adding some of the remaining garlic to each batch, until bright pink and just cooked through, about 3 minutes per batch. Transfer the shrimp to a bowl and keep warm.

6. When the noodles are done, change the oven setting to broil. Pass the noodles under the broiler until the noodles on top are lightly toasted, 2 to 3 minutes. Let the noodles stand for about 5 minutes. Arrange the jumbo shrimp decoratively over the noodles. Serve the dish straight from the pan, accompanied by lemon wedges and *allioli*. **SERVES 8 AS A FIRST COURSE, 6 AS A MAIN COURSE**

NOTE: If you're in a hurry, you can make a quicker *sofregit* by cooking 1 chopped medium-size onion and 4 cloves crushed garlic in 2 tablespoons olive oil in the paella pan for 7 to 8 minutes. Add 1 large grated tomato and cook the *sofregit* until it is darkened and reduced, about 5 minutes.

SOFREGIT

Sofregit, a Catalan *sofrito* of onions and tomatoes, is the perfect flavor base for many Spanish-Mediterranean dishes, especially rices. A real Catalan *sofregit* can be time-consuming, as the onions have to cook for hours to caramelize properly. After experimenting with various shortcuts, I arrived at a rather unconventional solution: adding a little dried onion flakes and sun-dried tomatoes to simulate the intense onion and tomato flavors without spending all day by the stove. The *sofregit* can be made ahead and will keep for up to a week. It will greatly enhance any paella recipe in this chapter.

- 6 medium-size sun-dried tomatoes
- 2 dried ñora pepper or ancho chiles, stemmed, seeded, and torn into pieces
- 2 tablespoons dried onion flakes
- 2 tablespoons olive oil
- 2 medium-size onions, finely chopped
- Coarse salt (kosher or sea)

1. Place the sun-dried tomatoes, ñora peppers, and onion flakes in a small heatproof bowl. Add 1 cup very hot water and let soak until the peppers soften, about 30 minutes. Puree the chiles and tomatoes with their soaking liquid in a blender. Set the tomato puree aside.

2. Heat the olive oil in a medium-size skillet over medium-high heat, add the onions, and cook until they begin to brown, about 8 minutes. Reduce the heat to very low, cover the skillet, and cook until the onions are soft, about 15 minutes, adding a little water to the pan if it looks dry. Add the tomato puree and continue cooking, stirring occasionally, until the *sofregit* is thickened and reduced, about 10 minutes. Season with salt to taste. Let the *sofregit* cool, scrape it into a jar, and refrigerate until ready to use (it can be refrigerated for up to 1 week).

MAKES ABOUT 1 CUP

SPAGHETTI AND CLAMS IN A SKILLET

ESPAGUETIS CON ALMEJAS

This pasta dish combines three influences: the Spanish-Mediterranean pasta paella called *fideuá,* Italian spaghetti *alle vongole* (with clams), and superchef Ferran Adrià, who featured this recipe in his cookbook *Cocinar en Casa.* Adrià says that the clever idea of cooking pasta in a skillet with a flavorful liquid that it absorbs was suggested to him by Moreno Cedroni, a hyper-creative Italian chef (and himself an Adrià acolyte). Lightly toasted and full of marine flavors, the pasta is easy to make and compulsively edible.

3 tablespoons extra-virgin olive oil
About 12 ounces fideo noodles or thin spaghetti, broken into large pieces
4 medium-size garlic cloves, minced
1 medium-size pinch of crushed red pepper flakes, or more to taste
3 cups bottled clam juice diluted with 1 cup water
Coarse salt (kosher or sea)
3 dozen littleneck clams, scrubbed
1/4 cup finely chopped fresh flat-leaf parsley

Heat the olive oil in a large deep skillet with a tight-fitting lid over medium heat. Add the noodles and cook, stirring constantly, until golden brown, 3 to 5 minutes. Add the garlic and red pepper flakes and cook until fragrant, about 1 minute. Add the diluted clam juice and bring to a boil. Season with salt to taste, cover the skillet, and cook until the pasta is barely al dente, about 8 minutes. Add the clams, nestling them into the pasta, cover the skillet, and cook until the pasta is al dente and the clams have opened, 4 to 7 minutes longer, adding a few tablespoons of water if the pasta looks dry. Discard any clams that haven't opened, stir in the parsley, and serve at once. **SERVES 4**

INMA'S BAKED MACARONI

MACARRONI CON SETAS Y MAGRO DE CERDO

Mercé Navarro and Inma Crosas are the chef-owners of Roig Robí, a great Barcelona restaurant and the source of several outstanding recipes in this book. Among other things, the restaurant is famous for Inma's Monday special of baked macaroni laced with wild mushrooms and thin ribbons of pork. It's a simple dish, but the bosky mushroom perfume makes it luxurious. The Italian pastas—macaroni and cannelloni—have been part of bourgeois Catalan cooking since the nineteenth century. Because it can be hard to find extremely aromatic wild mushrooms, I recommend adding dried porcini for depth of flavor. The dish can easily be prepared ahead and baked right before serving.

1 ounce dried porcini mushrooms (optional)
6 tablespoons extra-virgin olive oil, or more if needed
6 ounces boneless center-cut pork chops, cut into thin strips
1 pound assorted wild mushrooms or a mixture of wild and cultivated mushrooms (chanterelles, cèpes, morels, oyster, cremini, and/or portobellos), wiped clean with a damp paper towel; larger mushrooms coarsely chopped, small ones left whole
4 medium-size garlic cloves, minced
1 medium-size onion, finely chopped
1 large tomato, cut in half and grated on a box grater, skin discarded
2/3 cup heavy (whipping) cream (see Note)
Coarse salt (kosher or sea) and freshly ground black pepper
1 pound penne pasta
2 cups grated Gruyère or Emmental cheese
3/4 cup freshly grated Parmesan cheese, preferably Parmagiano-Reggiano

1. If using the dried porcini mushrooms, soak them in 1 cup very hot water for 30 minutes. Drain, straining the soaking liquid through a sieve lined with a coffee filter or a paper towel, and set the liquid aside. Finely chop the mushrooms.

2. Heat 1 tablespoon of the olive oil in a large skillet over high heat. Add half of the pork and stir-fry until lightly browned, about 1 minute. Using a slotted spoon, transfer the browned pork to a large bowl. Add 1 tablespoon olive oil to the skillet and stir-fry the remaining pork the same way, then transfer it to the bowl.

3. Add 3 tablespoons olive oil and the chopped porcini, if using, to the skillet, reduce the heat to low, and cook for 2 minutes, stirring. Add the fresh mushrooms, increase the heat to high, and cook until the mushrooms have released and reabsorbed their liquid and are lightly browned, about 7 minutes, adding a little more olive oil if the skillet looks dry. Add half of the garlic to the skillet and cook until fragrant, about 1 minute. Transfer the mushrooms and garlic to the bowl with the pork. Wipe out the skillet.

4. Heat the remaining 1 tablespoon olive oil in the skillet over medium-low heat. Add the onion and cook until very soft and light golden, about 10 minutes. Add the remaining garlic, stir for 1 minute, then add the tomato. Cook, stirring, until the mixture is thickened and reduced, about 5 minutes. Add the cream and ½ cup of the reserved mushroom soaking liquid, if using, or ½ cup more of cream and bring to a boil. Cook the sauce until it thickens a little, about 2 minutes. Add the sauce to the bowl with the mushrooms, stir to mix, and season generously with salt and pepper to taste. (The sauce can be prepared up to 6 hours ahead. Reheat it gently before tossing it with the pasta.)

5. Preheat the oven to 425°F.

6. Bring a large pot of salted water to a boil and cook the pasta until tender but still slightly firm to the bite, 1 to 2 minutes less than the instructions on the package. Drain the pasta, then place it in a large mixing bowl. Add the mushroom sauce and half of the Gruyère and toss to coat evenly. Place the pasta in a lightly buttered 13- by 9- by 2-inch baking dish and sprinkle the remaining Gruyère and the Parmesan evenly over it. Bake until the top is browned and bubbly, about 15 minutes. Serve at once. **SERVES 8 AS A FIRST COURSE, 6 AS A MAIN COURSE**

NOTE: If you are not using the dried porcini mushrooms, you will need an additional ½ cup cream.

CANNELLONI WITH SPINACH, RAISINS, AND PINE NUTS

CANELONS D'ESPINACS

Their origins might be Italian, but today cannelloni are something of a Catalan national dish. The cannelloni-eating tradition there goes back to the eighteenth century, when many restaurants in an increasingly worldly and bourgeois Barcelona hired Italian chefs. Eschewing the tomato sauce and ricotta of the Italian version, classic Catalan *canelons* can be filled with anything from seafood or salt cod, to ground roast meat, to the wildly popular spinach. Though I've used a touch of *jamón* in this recipe to enrich the filling, vegetarians can omit it. The best option for noodles is fresh egg pasta squares, which are available at many specialty food stores. Otherwise, you can use

Cannelloni with Spinach, Raisins, and Pine Nuts

no-boil lasagna noodles; they will have somewhat different dimensions, but there won't be that much difference in the overall shape of the cannelloni.

- 2 packages (each 10 ounces) fresh spinach, or 2 medium-size bunches spinach, coarse stems discarded
- 3 tablespoons extra-virgin olive oil
- 2 medium-size garlic cloves, minced
- 1/4 cup pine nuts
- 7 to 8 tablespoons golden or dark raisins
- 2 to 3 ounces sliced serrano ham or prosciutto (optional), torn into slivers
- Coarse salt (kosher or sea) and freshly ground black pepper
- 3 1/2 tablespoons unsalted butter
- 2 1/2 tablespoons all-purpose flour
- 2 cups whole milk
- 1 medium-size pinch of freshly grated nutmeg
- 8 squares (about 6 by 6 inches) fresh egg pasta, or 8 no-boil lasagna noodles (7 by 4 inches), without curly edges
- 1 1/4 cups freshly grated Parmesan cheese, preferably Parmagiano-Reggiano, or more to taste

1. Rinse the spinach but do not drain it. Cook the spinach, covered, in a large saucepan over medium heat in the water clinging to its leaves until wilted, 4 to 5 minutes, stirring a few times. Transfer the spinach to a colander and drain. When cool enough to handle, squeeze out the excess moisture by pressing small handfuls in your hands. Finely chop the spinach.

2. Heat 2 tablespoons of the olive oil in a large skillet or wok over low heat. Add the garlic, pine nuts, raisins, and ham, if using, and cook until the pine nuts and garlic are light golden, 3 to 5 minutes. Add the chopped spinach and cook for about 1 minute, stirring to distribute all the ingredients evenly. Season the spinach with salt and pepper to taste, transfer it to a bowl, and set aside.

3. Melt the butter with the remaining 1 tablespoon olive oil in a heavy, medium-size saucepan over medium-low heat. Whisk in the flour and cook, whisking, for about 2 minutes. Add the milk in a steady stream, whisking, and bring to a boil over high heat, whisking constantly. Reduce the heat to low and simmer, whisking occasionally, until the sauce thickens, about 2 minutes. Stir in the nutmeg and season with salt and pepper to taste. Set about ½ cup of the spinach mixture aside. To finish the filling, stir ⅔ cup of the sauce into the remaining spinach; set the rest of the sauce aside.

4. Preheat the oven to 400°F. Lightly butter a 12- by 9-inch gratin dish or a shallow ceramic baking dish.

5. Bring 5 to 6 quarts salted water to a boil over high heat. Place a large bowl of ice water next to the pot. Working in two batches, boil the sheets of pasta, stirring to separate them, until al dente, about 2 minutes for fresh pasta and about 6 minutes for no-boil lasagna noodles. Using tongs, transfer the noodles to the ice water to stop the cooking. Lift the noodles from the water, shaking off the excess, and lay them flat on dry linen kitchen towels. Repeat with the remaining pasta, bringing the water back to a rolling boil before adding the second batch. Pat the pasta dry with paper towels before filling it.

6. Place about ¼ cup of the spinach filling close to one end of a noodle (a long end, if you're using lasagna noodles), shaping it into a compact log. Starting with a long end, roll up the noodle, then cut it in half crosswise. Place the filled noodles seam side down in the prepared gratin dish. Repeat with the remaining noodles and filling. The filled noodles should fit in the dish snugly and in a single layer.

7. Stir the reserved ½ cup of spinach (and any of the filling that you might have leftover) into the reserved sauce and spread evenly over the cannelloni. Sprinkle the cheese evenly on top. Bake the cannelloni until they are hot and the top is browned and bubbly, about 25 minutes. If you'd like the top to be more browned, pass the dish under the broiler for a few minutes. Let the cannelloni cool for a few minutes, then serve them straight from the baking dish. **SERVES 8 AS A FIRST COURSE, 4 AS A MAIN COURSE**

DAY-AFTER-CHRISTMAS CANNELLONI

CANELONS DE CARN

It's December 26 and Catalans are still feasting, gathering around the table again for Sant Esteve. The centerpiece of the saint's day meal are these luscious cannelloni, filled with the ground meat of the *rostit* (roast) and *escudella* (multimeat boiled dinner) left over from the festivities of the previous two days. Although I've given instructions for making the roast meat filling from scratch—it takes some time but not much work—you can certainly improvise with your own holiday leftovers. Use four to five cups of leftover roast or stewed pork, roast turkey, or skinned rotisserie chicken, mixed with one sautéed onion and a few sautéed chicken livers and some beef or chicken broth to moisten it. Grind everything together as directed in Step 3. When making the béchamel sauce, use two full cups of milk.

2 medium-size bone-in, skinless chicken thighs
8 to 10 ounces veal shoulder or beef chuck, cubed
8 to 10 ounces pork shoulder, cubed
Coarse salt (kosher or sea) and freshly ground black pepper
3 tablespoons olive oil
1 medium-size onion, chopped
4 medium-size garlic cloves, peeled and lightly smashed
1 medium-size tomato, chopped
1/4 cup medium-dry sherry
About 3 cups chicken stock or broth, or more if needed
4 large chicken livers
About 1 cup whole milk
3 1/2 tablespoons unsalted butter
2 1/2 tablespoons all-purpose flour
8 squares (about 6 by 6 inches) fresh egg pasta, or 8 (7 by 4 inches) no-boil lasagna noodles without curly edges
1 1/4 cups freshly grated Parmesan cheese, preferably Parmagiano-Reggiano, or more to taste

1. Preheat the oven to 450°F.

2. Make the filling: Place the chicken, veal, and pork in a medium-size roasting pan, rub them with salt and pepper, and toss with 2 tablespoons of the olive oil. Roast until the meats begin to brown, about 45 minutes, stirring once or twice. Add the onion, garlic, and tomato and roast for another 15 minutes. Add the sherry and ½ cup of the chicken stock to the pan, reduce the oven temperature to 350°F, and continue roasting, stirring occasionally, until the meats are very tender, about 15 minutes longer for the chicken and about 1¼ hours for the veal and the pork (remove the chicken and set it aside while the veal and pork finish roasting). As the meats roast, periodically add a few tablespoons of stock to the pan. After the meats have roasted for a total of 1 hour and 55 minutes, stir in the

chicken livers. (The chicken livers should roast during the last 20 minutes of the meats' roasting time.)

3. Remove the meat from the oven, add 1 cup of the chicken stock to the roasting pan, and scrape the brown bits off the bottom. Strain the meats, reserving the pan juices separately. When the meats are cool enough to handle, grind them medium-fine in a food processor together with the chicken thighs and ¼ cup of the chicken stock. Season the filling with salt and pepper to taste. (The filling can be prepared up to a day ahead to this point; refrigerate it, covered.)

4. Measure the pan juices and add enough milk to make 2 cups total. Melt the butter with the remaining 1 tablespoon olive oil in a heavy, medium-size saucepan over medium-low heat. Whisk in the flour and cook, whisking, for about 2 minutes. Add the pan juice and milk mixture in a steady stream, whisking, and bring to a boil over high heat, continuing to whisk. Reduce the heat to low and simmer, whisking occasionally, until the sauce thickens, about 2 minutes. Season with salt and pepper to taste, then set the sauce aside.

5. Preheat the oven to 400°F. Lightly butter a 12- by 9-inch gratin dish or shallow ceramic baking dish.

6. Bring 5 to 6 quarts salted water to a boil. Place a large bowl of ice water next to the pot. Working in two batches, boil the sheets of pasta, stirring to separate them, until al dente, about 2 minutes for fresh pasta and about 6 minutes for no-boil lasagna noodles. Using tongs, transfer the noodles to the ice water to stop the cooking. Lift the noodles from the water, shaking off the excess, and lay them flat on dry linen kitchen towels. Repeat with the remaining pasta, bringing the water back to a rolling boil before adding the second batch. Pat the pasta dry with paper towels before filling it.

7. Add 2 to 3 tablespoons of the sauce to the meat filling, plus a couple of tablespoons of chicken stock if it doesn't seem moist enough. Taste for seasoning, adding more salt and/or pepper as necessary. Place about ¼ cup of the filling close to one end of a noodle, shaping it into a compact log. Starting with a long end, roll up the noodle, then cut it in half crosswise. Place the filled noodle seam side down in the prepared gratin dish. Repeat with the remaining noodles and filling. The filled noodles should fit in the dish snugly and in a single layer.

8. Spread the remaining sauce evenly over the cannelloni. Sprinkle the cheese evenly on top. Bake the cannelloni until they are hot and the top is brown and bubbly, about 25 minutes. If you'd like the top to be more browned, pass the dish under the broiler for a few minutes. Let the cannelloni cool for a few minutes, then serve them straight from the baking dish. **SERVES 8 AS A FIRST COURSE, 4 AS A MAIN COURSE**

LAMB AND VEGETABLE COUSCOUS FROM POLOP

CUSCUS DE POLOP

From historic references we know that *al-cuzcuz* was quite common in Andalusia during the Muslim rule. After the Moors were expelled in the fifteenth century and the country was thoroughly Catholicized, couscous seems to have disappeared from Spanish cuisine. In a book dedicated to the cuisine of Alicante, my friend Angeles Ruiz includes the following couscous recipe from the town of Polop. In the early twentieth century, Angeles says, Polop's inhabitants spent half the year working in Tunisia and Algiers (which are just a short ferry ride away), bringing recipes back and incorporating them into the cuisine—a delicious example of modern Spanish–North African fusion.

3 pounds boneless lamb shoulder, cut into 1 1/2-inch chunks
Coarse salt (kosher or sea) and freshly ground black pepper
1 tablespoon sweet (not smoked) paprika, plus more for rubbing on the lamb
2 tablespoons unsalted butter
1 tablespoon olive oil
2 large onions, quartered and sliced
2 large tomatoes, peeled, seeded, and quartered
2 teaspoons dried thyme
2 teaspoons ground cumin
1 large pinch of cayenne, or more to taste
1 large pinch of saffron, pulverized in a mortar and steeped in 2 tablespoons very hot water
10 fresh flat-leaf parsley sprigs, tied together
2 fat carrots, scraped, quartered lengthwise, and cut into 2-inch pieces
2 medium-size turnips or boiling potatoes, peeled and quartered
3 fat celery ribs, cut into 2-inch pieces
4 medium-size artichokes, pared down to the heart (see page 370) and quartered, or 1 1/2 cups frozen artichoke hearts, thawed
2 large zucchini, cut in half lengthwise, then cut into 2-inch pieces
2 cups frozen baby lima beans, thawed
Steamed Couscous (recipe follows)
Store-bought harissa or another pure chile paste (optional), for serving

1. Place the lamb in a large bowl and rub it generously with salt, black pepper, and paprika. Heat the butter and olive oil in a large, heavy stockpot over medium heat. Add the onions and cook, stirring, until they begin to soften, about 5 minutes. Add the lamb and cook, stirring, until it is very lightly browned, about 7 minutes. Add the tomatoes, thyme, cumin, cayenne, saffron, parsley, and 10 cups water and bring to a boil over high heat, skimming. Season with salt and pepper to taste and more cayenne, if desired. Cover the pot, reduce the heat to low, and simmer until the lamb is very tender, 1½ to 1¾ hours.

2. Add the carrots, turnips, and celery to the pot, increase the heat to bring to a simmer, then lower the heat to medium-low and cook for 10 minutes. Add the artichokes, zucchini, and lima beans, increase the heat to return to a simmer, then reduce the heat to low. Cook the vegetables until they are all very tender but not mushy, 15 to 20 minutes.

SLOW DOWN

If you are only familiar with quick-cooking couscous from a box, I urge you to try couscous made the traditional way: prepared with loose couscous, soaked, raked by hand, and steamed twice. The process is soothing and pleasurable, and the results are a hundred times lighter and fluffier than the instant kind. To time the dish properly, make sure to read the couscous recipe before you begin cooking. If you're making instant couscous from a box, use two and a half cups and cook it according to the instructions on the package. To make it tastier, you can use half water and half broth from the stew for the liquid.

3. To serve, mound the couscous on a large platter. Make a big well in the middle of the couscous and spoon some of the vegetables from the broth into it. Arrange some of the lamb around the mound of couscous. Moisten the couscous with about 1 cup of the cooking liquid. Serve the remaining stew in a large deep bowl with *harissa* on the side, if desired. **SERVES 8 TO 10**

STEAMED COUSCOUS

CUSCUS TRADICIONAL

To prepare couscous the authentic way, first you moisten the dried (long-cooking) semolina pellets with water, letting them swell. Then you rake and rub them with your fingers to get rid of lumps. The couscous is steamed, then the whole process is repeated. Although it sounds complicated and time-consuming, it isn't. Making couscous is one of my favorite kitchen chores, and the results are so marvelous you'll find it hard to go back to instant couscous again.

4 cups (1 1/2 pounds) fine or medium couscous (not instant), preferably sold loose at a Middle Eastern specialty food store
Olive oil, as needed
1 teaspoon coarse salt (kosher or sea)
2 tablespoons unsalted butter, cut into small pieces

1. Place the couscous in a fine sieve. Place the sieve under cold running water and thoroughly wet the couscous. Spread it out in a very large rimmed baking sheet or roasting pan and let stand until it absorbs the moisture, 10 to 15 minutes.

2. Evenly sprinkle about 2 tablespoons olive oil over the couscous and work the oil into the grains with your fingers. Take a small handful of grains and rub them between your thumb and two middle fingers to get rid of all the little lumps. Let the grains drop back into the baking sheet, repeating with the remaining couscous. Alternatively, you can work over a bowl to give yourself more space and keep track of what's been raked through.

3. Using an oiled paper towel, oil the perforated top of a large, wide steamer. Pour water to a depth of 4 to 5 inches in the steamer bottom and bring to a rolling boil over high heat. If there is a lot of steam escaping through the seam between the top and bottom of the steamer, wrap it with aluminum foil. When a good deal of steam starts rising, transfer the couscous to the top of the steamer (don't worry, it won't fall through the steamer holes). Steam the couscous, uncovered, for 15 to 18 minutes.

4. Return the couscous to the baking sheet and spread it out again, breaking up the lumps with a fork. Let the couscous cool just until you can handle it. Place 1½ cups water in a measuring cup and stir in the salt. Gradually sprinkle the salted water evenly over the couscous, working the water in with your fingers. Spread the couscous out again and let stand for 10 to 15 minutes. Oil your hands and repeat the raking procedure in Step 2 but don't add any more olive oil.

5. Repeat the steaming process, letting the couscous cook for about 20 minutes. The grain will be fluffy and separated and taste slightly al dente compared to instant couscous. Turn off the heat, leaving the couscous in the steamer, and carefully stir in the butter, using a fork to break up any lumps that might have formed. (The couscous can be steamed once and raked up to 6 hours ahead. Let it sit, uncovered, at room temperature until continuing with Step 5.) **SERVES 8 TO 10**

VEGETABLES
LUXURIOUSLY PERFECT

As she approached my table with a plate of tomatoes, Paquita Rexach, co-owner of Hispania, a legendary Catalan country restaurant, stated, "the seasonal is sacred." They were raw, cut into wedges, barely dressed, and at first glance, not much to look at: pinkish rather than blazing red, irregularly shaped, with a hollow where one normally expects flesh. But the flavor . . .

From left to right: Spanish shoppers are notoriously picky when choosing vegetables; An olive farmer is clearly pleased with his pick; Fresh artichokes with tightly closed leaves, perfect in springtime; Future chefs at the famous Luis Irizar cooking school in San Sebastián.

intensely aromatic and possessing the perfect balance between sweetness and acidity, they reminded me of what a true tomato should taste like. At Hispania, tomatoes aren't a side dish, or—perish the thought—garnish. They're a stand-alone seasonal treat, meant for the diners to worship and pay dearly for. And while Hispania has many great things on its menu, what everyone mentions when they talk about the restaurant are those amazing *tomates de Montserrat,* the tiny white ganxet beans, the sweet peas grown in the nearby town of Llavaneras.

And yet tourists accustomed to a meat-and-three-veggie mentality often quip that Spanish restaurants don't serve enough vegetables. What they don't realize is that on Spanish menus vegetables tend to be their own category, not a free filler that justifies the high price of an entrée. (Spaniards generally are not big on side dishes.) And because vegetables are frequently eaten as a first course or a light meal, the preparations are often rather substantial: the tumbet of Mallorca, with its autumnal layering of potatoes, eggplants, zucchini, and a bright-red tomato sauce; the menestras of La Rioja, stews that combine both braised and batter-fried vegetables; the vegetable ollas (pots) of the Mediterranean Alicante region; the Castilian braised green beans bolstered with smoky cured ham.

Anyone who doubts the importance of vegetables to Spanish cuisine should visit a good local market to admire the shrinelike displays of purple-tipped artichokes, slender wild asparagus, and fuzzy baby zucchini with their yellow flowers attached. I'll never forget being berated by a burly *verduras* vendor at the Mercado de la Brecha in San Sebastián. She screamed long and hard (and in Basque, so to this day I have no clue what she said), flailing her arms, shaking her head, and pointing to her precious leeks, peas, and lettuces. My offense? Apparently I handled her wares in a way that she found disrespectful.

That same day, the three-star Michelin chef Juan Mari Arzak invited me to share a staff lunch around a long marble table in the back of his restaurant. When I came in, everyone from the dishwasher to Arzak himself was eating peas. This was their meal—just peas, briefly cooked and topped with poached eggs. "Why eat all the fancy stuff in the main dining room," Arzak chuckled, "when the first peas of the season are such a *maravilla?*"

Dinner that night was at Mugaritz, a restaurant nestled in the hills outside San Sebastián, among haystacks and fat cows that graze on rich local grasses. Mugaritz is the domain of the experimental young chef Andoni Luis Adúriz, whose menus are mainly centered on vegetables. The pièce de résistance of my meal was, again, peas, in a dish called *lágrimas de guisantes,* or tears of peas. Caught in fleeting transition between sprout and legume, the peas were smaller than lentils, and snapped in the mouth with the freshness of spring. Coated in a veil of ginger gelée and strewn with tiny wildflowers, the dish was heart-stoppingly lyrical. "Perfect vegetables," said Andoni, "are the world's greatest luxury."

It is in this spirit that I invite you to dig into the dishes in this chapter. While they will taste fine made with supermarket vegetables, when prepared with the seasonal spoils of a trip to a farmers' market they will truly shine.

BATTER-FRIED ARTICHOKES

ALCACHOFAS FRITAS

During artichoke season, Spanish restaurants and bars usually serve a starter of these crisp artichoke slices fried in a simple batter of flour and eggs. They are so good that one order is never quite enough, and a main dish seems almost redundant. If you can get your hands on tender baby artichokes, you don't need to cut down to the heart: Just trim off the tops and the leaf tips, and quarter the artichokes (you will need six or seven). Though these are normally served without sauce, feel free to offer any of the *allioli* recipes in this book alongside (see pages 44 and 45).

- 4 medium-size artichokes, pared down to the heart (see box, page 370)
- 1 lemon, cut in half
- About 1 1/2 cups all-purpose flour, for coating the artichokes
- Olive oil, for frying
- 2 large eggs, beaten in a shallow bowl
- Coarse salt (kosher or sea), for sprinkling the artichokes

1. Drain the acidulated water from the prepared artichokes and cut each heart crosswise into thin slices, including the stems. Rub the slices with the cut side of a lemon half. Cut the remaining lemon half into wedges and set aside for serving.

2. Place the flour in a medium-size bowl. Place a few artichoke slices in the flour and toss well, scooping under the artichoke to make sure the slices are generously coated. Place the floured artichoke slices in a sieve over the flour bowl and shake off any excess flour. Repeat with the remaining artichoke slices.

3. Pour olive oil to a depth of 1½ inches in a heavy, medium-size saucepan and heat it over medium-high heat to 360°F. When the olive oil reaches 360°F, dip 5 or 6 artichoke slices in the beaten egg, then gently shake off the excess. Fry the slices in the hot oil, turning once, until golden brown, 2 to 3 minutes. Using a slotted spoon, transfer the fried slices to a plate lined with a double thickness of paper towels to drain. Repeat with the remaining artichoke slices, adjusting the temperature so that they don't burn. Place the artichokes on a serving plate, sprinkle them with salt, and serve with lemon wedges. **SERVES 4 TO 6 AS A TAPA OR APPETIZER**

ROASTED BABY ARTICHOKES WITH COGNAC

ALCACHOFAS ASADAS CON COÑAC

Roasted vegetables are a great specialty at Quim de la Boqueria, my favorite breakfast counter in Barcelona. Asparagus with white wine, baby artichokes with a dash of cognac—extremely

PREPARING ARTICHOKE HEARTS

Most people think of trimming artichokes down to the heart as a cumbersome chore, but it needn't be. To remove all the extraneous leaves in one spiral motion—as Spanish chefs do—all you need is a sharp knife and a little practice. For best results, select very fresh, unblemished artichokes with tightly closed leaves.

Choose as many artichokes as you need, then cut two lemons in half. Partially fill a bowl with water and add the juice from one of the lemons. Drop the squeezed lemon halves into the water. Working with one artichoke at a time, remove about half of the outer leaves by pulling them away from the artichoke until they snap off. Using a sharp knife, cut off and discard the top half of the artichoke. Place the artichoke on its side on a cutting board and firmly grab onto the stem with one hand. Holding a sharp, serrated knife in the other hand and cutting away from you, remove all but the tender, yellow-green inner leaves, following the contour of the artichoke and leaving only the heart. Using a spoon, scoop out the choke and the small purple leaves from the center. Trim all but a half inch off the stem. Using a sharp knife or a vegetable peeler, trim off the tough, fibrous parts around the base of the artichoke. Scrape the remaining stem with a vegetable peeler. As you work, keep rubbing the cut parts of the artichoke with the cut side of one of the remaining lemon halves to prevent the artichoke from discoloring. Place the artichoke heart into the lemon water until ready to use.

simple and always incredibly satisfying. Roasting the artichokes intensifies their flavor, bringing out their nuttiness. While tender baby artichokes with edible chokes are best, regular artichoke hearts cut into wedges will work also. Serve these as part of a tapas spread, with toothpicks and one of the *alliolis* or as a side dish with roast chicken or lamb. The artichokes are also great mixed with other vegetables, such as roasted potatoes or the baked cherry tomatoes on page 390.

About 1 1/2 pounds baby artichokes, or 6 or 7 regular artichokes pared down to the heart (see box, this page)
1/4 cup fragrant extra-virgin olive oil
2 tablespoons cognac or brandy
2 tablespoons minced fresh flat-leaf parsley
Flaky sea salt, such as Maldon, for serving
1 lemon, cut into wedges, for serving (optional)
Allioli, for serving (optional; pages 44 and 45)

1. Preheat the oven to 400°F.

2. Drain the acidulated water from the prepared artichokes and pat them dry with paper towels. Cut the baby artichoke hearts in half lengthwise. If using regular artichokes, cut each heart into 6 wedges.

3. Place the artichokes and 2 tablespoons of the olive oil in a large bowl and toss to coat. Arrange the artichokes in a baking dish that can fit them snugly in a single layer and sprinkle the cognac over them. Place a round of waxed paper on top of the artichokes and seal the baking dish tightly with aluminum foil. Bake the artichokes until they are tender, 25 to 30 minutes.

4. Increase the oven temperature to 450°F. Drizzle the remaining 2 tablespoons olive oil over the artichokes, then bake, uncovered, stirring once or twice, until the artichokes are nicely browned,

Spring Artichoke Ragout with Ham and Sherry (page 372)

BREAKFAST AT LA BOQUERIA

There is nothing like spending the morning with your nose pressed against the cases of Quim de la Boqueria, a tiny dining stand at Barcelona's most famous market. Behind the small glass vitrines, anchovies glimmer like silver dollars soon to be gently heated with garlic and olive oil. Arrayed on ice, the extravagantly priced *cigalas*—langoustines—are alive and so pretty it seems improbable that someone could be cruel enough to toss them on a cast-iron griddle. Quim, the owner, takes roast artichokes and asparagus out of the oven, then arranges vegetable-filled omelets on platters. What will my breakfast be, he wants to know. I point to the aromatic pile of chanterelles and cèpes on the counter. He nods. Do I want them with a bit of foie gras? I shake my head, no. He scratches his head, then turns to his frying pan. A few minutes later I receive a lavish timbale of mushrooms and lentils (see page 308). It's crowned with a fried egg with a bright orange yolk and decorated with drizzles of syrupy aged balsamic vinegar. My friend is having the tiniest, sweetest baby squid in a garlicky puddle of olive oil. Soon we're on our third round of *cava*. I look at my watch. It's eight o'clock in the morning. At the counter beside us, market vendors are finishing their morning papers and hastily gulping rations of *pan con tomate* and *café con leche,* getting ready to return to their stalls and battle the crowds.

10 to 15 minutes longer. Serve the artichokes warm or at room temperature, sprinkled with the parsley and sea salt and accompanied by lemon wedges and/or *allioli.* **SERVES 4 TO 6 AS A TAPA OR SIDE DISH**

SPRING ARTICHOKE RAGOUT WITH HAM AND SHERRY

GUISO DE ALCACHOFAS Y JAMON

Spring in Spain brings many pleasures, not the least of which is this delicious stew. There are as many versions as there are cooks: Some add peas, others potatoes. The stew can be flavored with the smoky notes of *jamón* or a touch of pounded fried almonds. In any case, the stew's sweet essence of spring remains the same. Feel free to substitute leeks for the onions and fresh shelled peas and/or sliced asparagus for the fava beans (tender asparagus and peas should be added in the last ten minutes of cooking). You can also use six to eight tender baby artichokes instead of the larger ones. There's no need to pare them; just trim off the stems and the leaf tips. If you use baby artichokes, cook the stew about ten minutes less.

This isn't your bright-green, flash-cooked al dente California version of the Mediterranean. To be really good, sweet, and authentic, the vegetables have to braise for quite some time. What's lost in color is gained in taste. Serve the stew on its own as a first course, as a light lunch, or as a side dish with roast lamb, chicken, or fish.

- 1 1/2 cups shelled fresh fava beans (about 1 1/2 pounds unshelled), or 1 1/2 cups soybeans or peas, thawed if frozen
- 4 medium-size artichokes, pared down to the heart (see box, page 370)
- 1 lemon, cut in half
- 5 tablespoons fragrant extra-virgin olive oil
- 1 medium-size onion, quartered and thinly sliced
- 1 piece (3 to 4 ounces) serrano ham or prosciutto, finely diced
- 4 large garlic cloves, minced
- 1 medium-size Yukon Gold potato, peeled and cut into 1/2-inch dice
- 3 to 4 ounces green beans (preferably Italian flat beans), trimmed and cut into 1 1/2-inch lengths
- 1/3 cup dry sherry
- 1 1/4 to 1 1/2 cups chicken stock or broth, or water
- Coarse salt (kosher or sea) and freshly ground black pepper
- 2 tablespoons minced fresh flat-leaf parsley
- 1 squeeze of fresh lemon juice (optional)

1. Bring a pot of water to a boil, then add the fava beans and cook until just tender, 2 to 4 minutes. Drain the fava beans in a colander and place it under cold running water until the beans are cool enough to handle. Gently peel the skins off the beans. Set the beans aside.

2. Drain the acidulated water from the artichokes and cut each heart crosswise into ¼-inch-thick slices, including the stems. Rub the slices with the cut side of the lemon halves to prevent discoloring, then set aside.

3. Heat the olive oil in a heavy 4-quart saucepan over medium heat. Add the onion and ham and cook, stirring, until the onion is limp, about 5 minutes. Add half of the garlic and the sliced artichokes and cook, stirring, for about 1 minute. Partially cover the pan and continue cooking until the artichokes are almost tender, 5 to 7 minutes, adjusting the heat so that the artichokes cook without browning. Add the potato and green beans and cook for 1 minute, stirring. Add the sherry, increase the heat to high, and cook until slightly reduced, about 1 minute. Add enough stock to barely cover the vegetables and season with salt and pepper to taste. Reduce the heat to very low and simmer the stew, partially covered, until all the vegetables are tender, about 20 minutes. Add the fava beans and cook until tender, about 5 minutes longer.

4. Place the parsley and the remaining garlic in a mortar and, using a pestle, mash them to a paste. Add the parsley mixture to the stew. Taste for seasoning, adding more salt and/or pepper as necessary and the lemon juice if desired. Cook the stew until the flavors meld, another minute or so. Let the stew cool to warm and serve. **SERVES 4 TO 6 AS A FIRST COURSE**

GRILLED ASPARAGUS WITH HONEY AND SHERRY VINEGAR

ESPARRAGOS CON MIEL Y VINAGRE DE JEREZ

This is one of those Spanish dishes that leaves you wondering how something so elemental—little more than asparagus, vinegar, and honey—

can taste so memorable. It also makes you appreciate the transformational effects of good salt. Here I recommend a delicate flaky variety, such as Maldon, beloved by Spanish chefs. Make this in the spring when the asparagus is fat but tender. If you don't have a grill, asparagus is just as delicious broiled.

- 2 pounds beautiful fat asparagus, trimmed
- 4 tablespoons fragrant extra-virgin olive oil
- 1 1/2 teaspoons honey
- 3 tablespoons sherry vinegar, preferably aged
- Coarse salt (kosher or sea) and freshly ground black pepper
- Flaky sea salt, such as Maldon, for sserving

1. Light the grill and preheat it to medium or preheat the broiler.

2. Using a vegetable peeler, scrape off the tough outer skin from the lower stalks of the asparagus. Rinse the asparagus, pat it dry with paper towels, and toss with 1 tablespoon of the olive oil.

3. Place the honey, vinegar, and the remaining 3 tablespoons olive oil in a small bowl and whisk to mix. Season lightly with coarse salt and pepper and set aside.

4. Grill or broil the asparagus until tender and only lightly charred, turning once, about 3 minutes per side.

5. Arrange the asparagus on a serving plate, toss with the sauce, and sprinkle flaky sea salt on top. Serve at once. **SERVES 4 TO 6**

ASPARAGUS WITH TANGERINE AND PISTACHIOS

ESPARRAGOS CON CITRICOS Y PISTACHOS

I tasted this simple and arresting dish at an idyllic restaurant in Alicante, and to me it perfectly captures the Moorish-Mediterranean essence of the region's cuisine. It is so lovely that I prefer to serve it as a first course rather than as a side dish, where it tends to get lost in the shuffle. Try it with fat, perfect asparagus and the most fragrant green olive oil you can find. If you don't have a steamer large enough for the asparagus, just cook it in a little water and pat it dry before serving.

- 1/4 cup fresh tangerine juice
- 2 tablespoons fresh lemon juice
- 2 teaspoons sherry vinegar, preferably aged, or best-quality white wine vinegar, or more to taste
- 2 tablespoons fragrant extra-virgin olive oil
- 1 tablespoon grated tangerine zest
- Coarse salt (kosher or sea) and freshly ground black pepper
- 1/3 cup lightly toasted unsalted shelled pistachios (see page 267)
- 1 1/2 pounds beautiful fat asparagus, trimmed

1. Place the tangerine juice in a small saucepan over medium-high heat and cook until reduced to about 2 tablespoons, about 5 minutes. Let cool completely.

ASPARAGUS

As wild as the Spanish are about artichokes, eggplants, and peppers, *the* springtime treat is a plate of perfect asparagus. Spain is one of Europe's largest asparagus producers. Much of it grows in the vegetable *huertas* of Aranjuez—a palace town not far from Madrid also known for its strawberries—as well as in the fertile plots of Navarra and La Rioja. The reverence for asparagus in these central regions, where it's often consumed as a delicious conserve, is summed up by a popular joke. A man from Navarra goes to Bilbao. Upon seeing Frank Gehry's titanium-sheathed Guggenheim Museum, he exclaims: "Wow, if this is the can, I can't wait to taste the asparagus!"

The Phoenicians are widely credited with introducing asparagus to the Mediterranean. But it was the Arabs' belief in the vegetable's aphrodisiac properties (blame it on the phallic shape) that was responsible for its widespread appreciation on the Iberian peninsula. Spanish asparagus comes in more than just one, pale-green variety. Topping the list is the wild *triguero* asparagus, which traditionally grow amid *trigo,* or wheat. Not much thicker than a wooden skewer and with an incomparably wild bitterish flavor, *espárragos trigueros* are best when folded into a simple *revuelto,* or added to vegetable stews. White asparagus, produced mainly in the Navarra region, is another Spanish delicacy. The pale porcelain color isn't the result of a particular plant variety but is due to the fact that the asparagus doesn't see daylight while the tender shoots are sprouting (the shoots are covered with loosely packed earth until they're picked). Fat and buttery, white asparagus is delicious when poached and allowed to cool slightly, then served in a simple vinaigrette or, perhaps, with a shaving of truffles or a drizzle of truffle oil. It's also one of the best canned products around. As for *espárragos verdes,* I've enjoyed it in Spain fried and roasted, grilled and braised, plain or with rather elaborate sauces. In season, there have been times when I ate green asparagus with every meal—a treat, indeed.

2. Place the reduced tangerine juice, the lemon juice, and vinegar in a medium-size bowl. Whisk in the olive oil. Stir in the tangerine zest and season with salt and pepper to taste and more vinegar, if desired. Set the vinaigrette aside. (The vinaigrette is best prepared a couple of hours ahead so it can infuse with the zest.)

3. Place the pistachios in a mortar and, using a pestle, lightly crush them. Set the pistachios aside.

4. Bring water to a boil in the bottom of a large, wide steamer. Using a vegetable peeler, scrape off the tough outer skin from the lower stalks of the asparagus. Rinse the asparagus, then place it in the steamer. Cook the asparagus until bright green and just tender, 5 to 6 minutes.

5. Transfer the steamed asparagus to a serving dish. Whisk the pistachios into the vinaigrette and pour the dressing over the warm asparagus. Toss and serve at once. **SERVES 4 AS A FIRST COURSE**

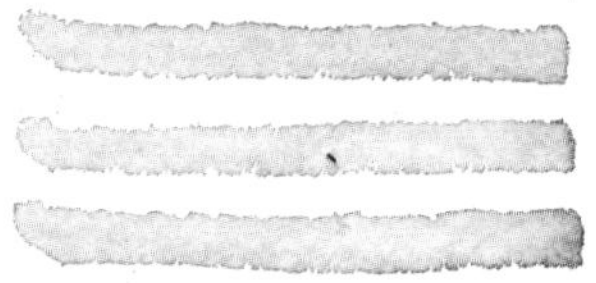

GARLICKY BRAISED BEANS WITH JAMON

JUDIAS VERDES CON JAMON

Vegetables cooked al dente may be fashionable and pretty to look at, but often they can't compare to the sweet, fully realized flavor of vegetables slowly cooked. Green beans, parboiled and gently braised with garlic and smoky bits of *jamón,* are pretty fundamental to Spanish cooking. They're eaten more often than not as a first course or even as a light meal—fantastic topped with a fried egg! If you can find them, Italian flat beans would actually be a more authentic choice here.

1 1/4 pounds string beans or broad green beans (Italian flat beans), trimmed (if using broad green beans, cut them into 2-inch lengths)
3 to 4 tablespoons fragrant extra-virgin olive oil
1 small onion, quartered and thinly sliced
1 piece (3 ounces) serrano ham or prosciutto, finely diced
3 large garlic cloves, minced
1/4 teaspoon smoked or sweet paprika
2 tablespoons dry sherry
1 medium-size ripe tomato, cut in half and grated on a box grater, skin discarded
1/2 cup chicken stock or broth, or water
Coarse salt (kosher or sea) and freshly ground black pepper
2 tablespoons minced fresh flat-leaf parsley, for garnish

1. Bring a large pot of salted water to a boil. Add the beans and cook until just al dente, 3 to 4 minutes. Drain thoroughly.

2. Heat the olive oil in a large earthenware *cazuela* or a deep skillet over medium-low heat. Add the onion and cook until soft but not browned, about 5 minutes. Add the ham and garlic and stir for 1 minute. Add the boiled beans and the paprika and stir to coat with the olive oil. Add the sherry, tomato, and chicken stock. Season with salt and pepper to taste, cover the *cazuela,* and cook the beans, stirring occasionally, until they are extremely tender and sweet and the liquid has been absorbed, about 20 minutes. Let the beans cool for about 5 minutes, then sprinkle with the parsley and serve.

SERVES 4 AS A SIDE DISH

CHRISTMAS RED CABBAGE

LOMBARDA A LA SAN QUINTIN

Besides baked *besugo* (bream), and roast turkey or capon, the traditional *madrileño* Christmas feast always includes *lombarda,* the delicious red cabbage slowly braised with apples and smoky salt pork until all the flavors meld. Some versions of the dish include diced potatoes; others have raisins and pine nuts, so feel free to play around with the ingredients. Pancetta makes a good substitute for Spanish salt pork, but for a vegetarian dish you can skip it. This cabbage is excellent with roast pork, turkey, or game.

1 tablespoon olive oil
1 medium-size onion, chopped
2 to 3 ounces sliced pancetta, chopped
6 to 7 cups thinly sliced red cabbage (from 1 large head)
2 medium-size Golden Delicious or Jonagold apples, peeled, cored, cut into wedges, and sliced
3/4 cup chicken stock or broth, or water
1/4 cup dry red wine
1 tablespoon sherry vinegar, apple cider vinegar, or red wine vinegar, or more to taste
Coarse salt (kosher or sea) and freshly ground red pepper
1 bay leaf
1 pinch of sugar, or more to taste (optional)

1. Preheat the oven to 350°F.

2. Heat the olive oil in a heavy flameproof casserole over medium-low heat. Add the onion and pancetta and cook, stirring, until the onion is soft but not browned, 5 to 7 minutes. Add the cabbage and apples, increase the heat to medium-high, and cook, stirring, until the cabbage begins to wilt, about 5 minutes. Add the chicken stock, wine, vinegar, and salt and pepper to taste and bring to a boil.

3. Tuck in the bay leaf, cover the casserole, and bake until the cabbage is very tender, about 50 minutes, stirring once or twice.

4. Taste the cabbage and add sugar and/or a little more vinegar, if desired. If the cabbage is too liquid, cook it over medium-high heat for a couple of minutes. Let cool for about 5 minutes before serving. **SERVES 6 TO 8 AS A SIDE DISH**

BABY CARROT AND CHARD STEW FROM GABRIELA'S GARDEN

ZANAHORIAS CON ACELGAS DE LA HUERTA DE GABRIELA

My friend Gabriela was squatting in the vegetable patch of her sprawling farm, digging baby carrots from the moist soil and inhaling greedily. "Smell this," she said, swooning from the sweet perfume. Once we filled our basket with carrots, we moved on to the chard and the onions. Figuring out what to do with our booty was a no-brainer. As Gabi's farm is in Extremadura, she prepared the vegetables like the locals, braised with a few dried chiles, a good dose of smoky *extremeño* paprika, and a *majado,* a pounded mixture of garlic, parsley, and peppercorns. While the dish tastes fine with supermarket vegetables, seasonal baby carrots and chard from the farmers' market will make it truly special.

- 1/3 cup plus 1 1/2 teaspoons fragrant extra-virgin olive oil
- 1 small white onion, quartered and thinly sliced
- 5 medium-size garlic cloves; 2 sliced, 3 chopped
- 1 pound whole trimmed farm-fresh baby carrots, or 1 pound slender young carrots, trimmed, cut in half, then cut into 1 1/2-inch chunks
- 1 small whole dried ñora pepper or ancho chile, stemmed, seeds shaken out
- 1 medium-size bunch Swiss chard (leaves only), sliced (3 1/2 to 4 cups)
- 1/2 teaspoon smoked sweet Spanish paprika
- 3 tablespoons chopped fresh flat-leaf parsley
- 1/4 teaspoon whole black peppercorns
- Coarse salt (kosher or sea)
- 1/2 teaspoon best-quality red wine vinegar
- Boiled new potatoes or rice, for serving

1. Heat ⅓ cup of the olive oil in a wide, heavy flameproof 4-quart casserole over medium heat. Add the onion and the sliced garlic and cook until wilted but not browned, about 5 minutes. Add the carrots and the ñora pepper and cook, stirring occasionally, until the carrots are almost tender, about 7 minutes, reducing the heat if they're browning. Add the chard and cook, stirring and tossing, until wilted, about 2 minutes. Add the paprika and stir for a few seconds; then add ½ cup water. Cover the casserole, reduce the heat to low, and cook the vegetables until they are very tender, about 15 minutes.

2. Place the chopped garlic cloves and the parsley, peppercorns, a large pinch of salt, and the remaining 1½ teaspoons olive oil in a mortar and, using a pestle, mash them to a paste. Stir the parsley mixture into the casserole. Rinse out the mortar with a few tablespoons of the vegetable cooking liquid, then add this as well. Add the vinegar and cook, uncovered, until the flavors meld, about 5 minutes. Let the stew cool to warm, transfer it to a bowl, and serve with boiled new potatoes or rice. **SERVES 4 AS A FIRST COURSE OR SIDE DISH**

EGGPLANT "FRIES" WITH HONEY DRIZZLES

BERENJENAS FRITAS CON MIEL

Combining eggplant with either sugar, honey, or cane syrup (which offset its slight bitterness) is an Arab legacy, encountered frequently in both Catalan and Andalusian cooking. (Eggplant jam is quite common in Spain.) These ethereal eggplant "fries" with a light drizzle of honey are one of the most inspired examples of this pairing. The recipe is from Santiago López, chef at La Gaviota, a lovely little bistro off the tourist trail in Granada.

The secret to flawless frying is coating the eggplant in a slightly coarse wheat flour or semolina, being scrupulous about shaking off the excess—

and using the best-quality olive oil, at just the right temperature. An instant-read thermometer is indispensable.

8 to 10 ounces slender Asian eggplant (about 1 1/2 eggplants), stemmed
Olive oil, for frying
About 1 1/2 cups semolina, preferably coarse or medium ground, or a mixture of half all-purpose flour and half medium-ground cornmeal
Coarse salt (kosher or sea)
2 to 3 tablespoons honey

1. Peel the eggplants with a vegetable peeler and cut them into sticks that are approximately 4 inches long and ½ inch thick.

2. Pour olive oil to a depth of 1½ inches in a deep, heavy skillet and heat it over medium-high heat to 360°F. As the oil heats, sift the semolina and 2 teaspoons salt into a medium-size bowl. Place 6 to 8 eggplant sticks in the semolina and toss well, scooping under the eggplant to make sure the pieces are thoroughly coated. Place the coated eggplant in a fine sieve over the flour bowl and shake off the excess semolina.

3. When the olive oil reaches 360°F, fry the eggplant sticks until crisp and golden brown, 2 to 3 minutes total. Using a slotted spoon, transfer the fried eggplant to paper towels to drain. Repeat with the remaining eggplant sticks, working in batches of 6 to 8.

4. Place the fried eggplant sticks on a serving platter, sprinkle them with salt, lightly drizzle honey over them, and serve at once. **SERVES 2 OR 3 AS AN APPETIZER**

Lush vines add mystery to this Spanish doorway.

EGGPLANT GRANADA

GRANADA DE BERENJENAS

Here's another classic eggplant recipe from Mallorca as rendered by the great local chef Joan Torrens. *Granada* (no relation, I suppose, to the Andalusian town) is a kind of delicate eggplant flan bound with milk and eggs and baked in a mold. The hint of sweet spices suggests an Arabic provenance. Like the *tumbet,* it is eaten with a bright, compotelike tomato sauce made with red-ripe seasonal tomatoes. I suggest using the slender Asian eggplants that don't need salting.

Serve *granada* as an elegant first course, a brunch dish, or a vegetarian main course. To gild the lily, try adding drizzles of Fresh Basil Oil (page 287) right before serving. And don't worry about the amount of olive oil—the eggplants are drained well after cooking.

$^2/_3$ cup plus 2 tablespoons olive oil
1 large onion, chopped
2 medium-size garlic cloves, minced
1 small bay leaf
1 $^1/_2$ pounds slender Asian eggplants, trimmed, peeled with a vegetable peeler, and cut into small dice
5 large eggs
1 cup whole milk
4 to 5 tablespoons plain dry bread crumbs
1 medium-size pinch of ground cinnamon
1 dash of freshly grated nutmeg
Coarse salt (kosher or sea) and freshly ground white pepper
Joan's Tomato Compote (page 386)
Fresh marjoram leaves or tiny mint leaves, for garnish

1. Heat 2 tablespoons of the olive oil in a medium-size skillet over medium-low heat. Add the onion, garlic, and bay leaf and cook, stirring, until the onion is very soft but not browned, about 10 minutes. Remove and discard the bay leaf. Set the onion mixture aside.

2. Heat the remaining ⅔ cup olive oil in a very large skillet over medium-high heat. Add the eggplant and cook, stirring, for 3 to 4 minutes. Reduce the heat to low, cover the skillet, and cook the eggplant until the cubes are very soft but still hold their shape, 15 to 20 minutes. If the skillet looks dry, add a little water. Using a slotted spoon, transfer the eggplant to a sieve set over a bowl and let it cool completely. (The eggplant can be prepared up to 3 hours ahead.)

3. Preheat the oven to 350°F and bring a kettle of water to a boil.

4. Place the eggs and milk in a large bowl and whisk until smooth. Add the onion mixture, the cooked eggplant, and 3 to 4 tablespoons of the bread crumbs. Stir well to combine evenly. Add the cinnamon and nutmeg and season with salt and pepper to taste.

5. Line a 9- by 4- by 2½-inch loaf pan with a piece of aluminum foil, leaving an overhang on two sides. Oil the aluminum foil and generously sprinkle the remaining bread crumbs in the bottom. Scrape the eggplant mixture into the prepared loaf pan and set it in a larger baking pan. Carefully pour enough boiling water into the baking pan to come halfway up the sides of the loaf pan. Transfer the loaf pan in the water bath to the oven and bake until a toothpick inserted into the *granada* comes out clean, about 1 hour.

6. Remove the loaf pan from the water bath and let cool to warm or to room temperature. Invert the *granada* onto a plate and remove the foil, then cut it into thick slices and place on serving plates. Spoon some tomato compote around each portion. Garnish with marjoram and serve at once. **SERVES 8 AS A FIRST COURSE OR BRUNCH DISH**

VARIATION: Once you've tried Joan's version, feel free to experiment with other vegetables, such as a combination of sautéed diced zucchini, cooked diced potatoes, and red bell peppers or cooked sliced artichoke hearts and blanched fresh fava beans.

EGGPLANT HAM AND CHEESE "SANDWICHES"

BERENJENAS REBOZADAS CON JAMON Y QUESO

Frying in olive oil in a plush batter of flour and egg is one of the most basic and popular ways to prepare vegetables in Spain. At tapas bars in the Basque Country, Navarra, and La Rioja, battered veggies are often fancied up with a stuffing of ham, cheese, shrimp, or béchamel sauce. Oozing cheese, these eggplant "sandwiches" are positively luscious. They are great as a tapa, a sit-down first course, or for brunch. Gruyère would be the first choice in Spain, but you can use an easy-melting cheese such as Munster. *Jamón York* (boiled ham) in Spain, tends to be of excellent quality and saltier than it is here; try to get ham that isn't too sweet.

1 medium-size eggplant, about 3½ inches in diameter and not too tapered, trimmed
Coarse salt (kosher or sea)
8 thin slices boiled ham
8 thin slices Gruyère or Munster cheese
All-purpose flour, for coating the eggplant
2 large eggs, beaten in a shallow bowl
Olive oil, for frying

1. Cut 16 round slices of eggplant, slightly thinner than ¼ inch. Sprinkle salt lightly on both sides. Cut the ham and cheese into rounds slightly smaller than the eggplant slices. Place a round each of ham and cheese on an eggplant slice, season it very lightly with salt, and top with another eggplant slice. Repeat with the remaining eggplant, ham, and cheese.

2. Spread flour on a large plate and dip the "sandwiches" in it on both sides, shaking off the excess.

3. Line a small baking sheet with a double layer of paper towels. Pour olive oil to a depth of about ¾ inch in a medium-size skillet and heat it over medium-high heat to 360°F; when hot, a small bread cube placed in the oil will sizzle and brown on contact. Working in two batches, dip the eggplant "sandwiches" in the beaten egg on both sides and place them in the oil. Fry the "sandwiches" until the batter is deep golden and the eggplant is soft, about 2 minutes per side, adjusting the heat so the oil doesn't burn. Using a slotted spoon, transfer the "sandwiches" to paper towels to drain. Let the "sandwiches" cool for 3 to 4 minutes, then serve. **MAKES 8 "SANDWICHES"**

ENDIVE & FENNEL GRATIN WITH ALMONDS

GRATINADO DE ENDIVIAS Y HINOJO CON ALMENDRAS

Here is my adaptation of *cardos con almendras,* a wonderful vegetable preparation popular at Christmas time in Navarra and Aragon. *Cardos* are cardoons, a vegetable that looks like oversize celery and tastes like artichokes. As cardoons are hard to find in this country, I use fennel and endives, which deliver a rather similar flavor. This is a fabulous dish to serve with a Christmas roast.

- 3 tablespoons fresh lemon juice
- 5 medium-size Belgian endives (about 1 1/2 pounds), trimmed but with the root ends left intact
- 1 medium-size fennel bulb (about 1 pound), stalks trimmed
- 1 1/2 cups chicken stock or broth
- 4 tablespoons olive oil
- 1 large pinch of sugar
- Coarse salt (kosher or sea)
- 1/3 cup minced onion
- 3 large garlic cloves, minced
- 3 tablespoons minced fresh flat-leaf parsley
- 5 teaspoons all-purpose flour
- 3/4 cup whole milk
- 1 1/4 cups sliced blanched almonds; 1 cup coarsely ground in a food processor, 1/4 cup left sliced
- Freshly ground black pepper

A bridge spans the Ebro river in Navarra, a region renowned for its vegetables.

1. Fill a large bowl with cold water and add 2 tablespoons of the lemon juice. Quarter the endives lengthwise and add them to the lemon water. Cut the fennel bulb in half lengthwise and cut each half into 4 wedges. Add the fennel wedges to the lemon water.

2. Drain the endives and fennel and arrange them in 2 overlapping layers in a wide, heavy pot. Add ¾ cup of the chicken stock, 2 tablespoons of the olive oil, the remaining 1 tablespoon of lemon juice, and the sugar. Place a round of waxed paper directly on top of the vegetables. Bring to a boil, then reduce the heat to very low, cover the pot, and cook the vegetables until just tender, about 20 minutes. Drain the vegetables well in a colander, then arrange them in a single layer in a 12- by 9-inch gratin pan or shallow baking dish and season lightly with salt. (The vegetables can be prepared a few hours ahead to this point.)

3. Preheat the oven to 450°F.

4. Heat 2 tablespoons olive oil in a heavy, medium-size saucepan over medium-low heat. Add the onion and cook until soft but not brown, about 5 minutes. Add the garlic and parsley and cook until fragrant, about 1 minute. Stir in the flour and cook, stirring constantly, for 1 minute. Increase the heat to medium, add the milk and the remaining ¾ cup chicken stock and cook, stirring constantly, until the mixture thickens, 3 to 5 minutes. Stir in the ground almonds and cook for another minute. Season the almond sauce with salt and pepper to taste.

5. Spread the almond sauce evenly over the vegetables. Bake until the top of the gratin is brown and bubbly, 20 to 25 minutes. Sprinkle the sliced almonds evenly over the gratin and bake for 5 minutes longer. Let cool for about 10 minutes, then serve. **SERVES 6 TO 8 AS A SIDE DISH**

SAUTEED WILD MUSHROOMS WITH HAM AND ALLIOLI

SETAS SALTEADAS CON JAMON Y ALLIOLI

A creamy, garlicky drizzle of the Catalan *allioli* mayonnaise adds a delicious accent to a classic dish of sautéed wild mushrooms spiked with smoky cured ham. These are incredible served on a slice of grilled or toasted peasant bread, a kind of Spanish bruschetta. Or serve them for breakfast on toast topped with a poached or fried egg. Use delicate mushrooms here, preferably not the dark-spored cremini or portobellos.

- 3 tablespoons fragrant extra-virgin olive oil, or more if needed
- 3 large cloves garlic, minced
- 1 piece (3 ounces) serrano ham or prosciutto, finely diced
- 12 ounces assorted delicate wild mushrooms (chanterelles, cèpes, and oyster mushrooms), or 12 ounces oyster mushrooms (caps only), wiped clean with a damp paper towel and sliced if large
- Coarse salt (kosher or sea) and freshly ground black pepper
- 2 to 3 tablespoons finely minced fresh flat-leaf parsley
- About 1/3 cup Allioli (page 44), thinned with 2 to 3 teaspoons water if it seems too thick to drizzle
- Grilled bread or toast, for serving (optional)

1. Heat the olive oil in a large skillet over medium-low heat. Add the garlic and ham and cook, stirring, until the garlic is very fragrant but not browned, about 2 minutes. Increase the heat to medium-high, add the mushrooms, and cook, stirring, until the mushrooms have released and reabsorbed their liquid and are lightly browned, 6 to 7 minutes, adding more olive oil if the skillet looks dry. Season with salt and pepper to taste, then stir in the parsley.

2. Transfer the mushrooms to a serving plate or grilled bread or toast, if desired. Generously drizzle the *allioli* over them. Serve at once. **SERVES 4 ON ITS OWN AS A TAPA, 6 TO 8 AS A CANAPE**

ROAST GREEN PEPPERS WITH FRIED GARLIC CHIPS

PIMIENTOS VERDES ASADOS CON AJO FRITO

Red peppers, with their color and sweet, meaty flesh, tend to get all the attention. But as any Basque or Catalan will attest, roasted green pimientos have just as much character. Moistened with good olive oil and vinegar and sprinkled with garlic chips, these are one of life's great little pleasures. Serve them with simple roast chicken or lamb, with a grill, or as a tapa. I prefer the more delicate green Italian (frying) peppers, but green

PICK A PEPPER

When tomatoes were introduced to Spain from the Americas, they were thought to be poisonous. As for potatoes, they weren't even deemed fit for pigs. Compared to other New World foodstuffs, which sometimes took centuries to become commonplace, the pepper was a hit from the onset. This despite Columbus's confusing moniker for the spicy chiles he encountered in the Caribbean. *Pimientos* is what he called them, a word almost identical to *pimienta, Piper nigrum* or black peppercorns, the prized spice he was so eager to find. It took botanists centuries to figure out that *pimientos* (capsicum peppers) and *pimienta* are entirely different botanical species.

Today, Spaniards are prodigious *pimiento* consumers. Dried, smoked, and ground, it becomes *pimentón,* the indispensable ruddy-hued Spanish paprika. The pointy *pimientos de piquillo* (see page 34) make the world's best conserve. There is no *romesco* sauce without the aromatic dried Catalan *romesco* pepper. No *chilindrón* dishes and no *bacalao a la vizcaína* without the meaty, dried *pimientos choriceros.* The small, hot guindilla chile is what lends subtle heat to dishes sautéed with garlic and olive oil. Spain's greatest peppers, however, are all but impossible to find in this country. I'm talking about the small, green, thin-skinned *pimientos de padrón,* so venerated in their native Galicia that they're honored with their own fiesta, at which a lot of albariño gets drunk. When fried in olive oil and sprinkled with coarse salt, *pimientos de padrón* are the most ambrosial of capsicum species, even if eating them is a bit of Russian roulette: Occasionally you get one so hot that not even a sea of bottled water and seven big bread loaves can stop your mouth from burning. Then again, it's all part of the thrill.

bell peppers will also work nicely. As in so many cases, good flaky sea salt is what brings the dish to life.

8 to 10 Italian (frying) peppers, or 6 large, meaty green bell peppers, cored, cut in half, and seeded
1/3 cup fragrant extra-virgin olive oil, plus more for brushing the baking sheet and peppers
6 large garlic cloves, thinly sliced
1 tablespoon best-quality red wine vinegar
Flaky sea salt, such as Maldon

1. Preheat the oven to 425°F.

2. Line a large baking sheet with aluminum foil and brush it with olive oil so the peppers won't stick. Place the peppers on the baking sheet skin side up and brush them with a little olive oil. Bake the peppers until they are tender and blistered in parts, about 20 minutes for Italian peppers, longer for bell peppers.

3. While the peppers are baking, heat the 1/3 cup olive oil and the garlic in a small skillet over low heat for about 2 minutes. Increase the heat to medium and cook, stirring, until the garlic just begins to brown and crisp, 2 to 3 minutes longer. Using a slotted spoon, transfer the garlic to a plate. Set the garlic oil aside.

4. If necessary, peel the peppers. The skin on the Italian peppers is delicate, so peeling is optional.

Bell peppers will need to be peeled. To do this, transfer the peppers to a bowl, cover it with plastic wrap, let stand for 15 minutes, then peel the peppers. Arrange the peppers on a serving plate, drizzle the vinegar and a little of the garlic oil over them, and scatter the garlic chips on top. Serve warm.

SERVES 6 AS A TAPA OR SIDE DISH

MALLORCAN EGGPLANT AND POTATO CASSEROLE

TUMBET

This version of *tumbet,* the famous Mallorcan vegetable casserole, is adapted from Joan Torrens of the restaurant Es Baluard in Palma. Rather unconventionally, Joan adds bell peppers to the tomato sauce, rather than layering them in the casserole with the other vegetables. What you'll find here is a full, proper *tumbet* recipe—each vegetable is fried separately in olive oil, as it should be. The results are incomparable, even if the dish does take a bit of time and olive oil. If you prefer, the following shortcuts are possible: The potatoes can be parboiled, rather than fried; the eggplant and zucchini can be generously brushed with olive oil and broiled; and this peppers can be roasted following the instructions in the box on this page.

One last thing: Peeling the peppers might seem somewhat obsessive and can certainly be omitted. However, it's very easy (using one of those snazzy serrated vegetable peelers) and eliminates the annoying skin that tends to stick in your teeth. It's the small details that make food taste outstanding rather than merely good.

ROASTING PEPPERS

Roasted peppers are essential to Spanish cuisine. They can be prepared in either the oven or the broiler with equally good results, but you must start with peppers that are fresh and very red or beautifully green.

Red or green bell peppers as needed, cored, cut in half, and seeded
Olive oil, for brushing the peppers

TO ROAST PEPPERS IN THE OVEN: Preheat the oven to 425°F. Line a baking sheet with aluminum foil and lightly brush it with olive oil. Push down gently on the peppers to flatten them and place them on the baking sheet skin side up. Brush the peppers with a little olive oil and roast until they are tender and lightly charred, about 35 minutes. Transfer the peppers to a large bowl, cover with plastic wrap, and let stand for 15 minutes. Peel the peppers and use as directed in the individual recipes.

TO ROAST PEPPERS IN A BROILER: Prepare the peppers as directed above, then arrange them skin side up on a well-oiled broiling tray and broil about 3 inches from the heat until tender and lightly charred, 15 to 20 minutes. Let stand and peel as directed above.

2 medium-size firm purple eggplants (about 2 1/2 pounds total), trimmed and cut lengthwise into 1/3-inch slices
Coarse salt (kosher or sea)
1/2 cup fragrant extra-virgin olive oil, or more if needed
2 medium-size yellow bell peppers, peeled with a vegetable peeler, cored, seeded, and diced
2 medium-size ripe, fleshy red bell peppers, peeled with a vegetable peeler, cored, seeded, and diced
1 pinch of sugar (optional)
1 splash of vinegar (optional)
3 medium-size Yukon Gold potatoes (about 1 1/2 pounds), peeled and cut into 1/8-inch-thick slices
2 thick, medium-size zucchini, cut in half crosswise, then cut lengthwise into 1/4-inch-thick slices
Joan's Tomato Compote (recipe follows)

1. Rub the slices of eggplant generously with salt and place them in a colander. Let stand for 30 minutes. Rinse well and pat dry thoroughly with paper towels.

2. While the eggplants are standing, heat 2 tablespoons of the olive oil in a large skillet, preferably nonstick, over medium-high heat. Add the yellow and red peppers and cook, stirring, until they begin to soften, 5 minutes. Reduce the heat to low, cover the skillet, and cook the peppers until they are very tender, about 20 minutes, stirring occasionally. Taste the peppers; if the flavor is not vibrant enough, add the sugar and vinegar, then season with salt to taste. Increase the heat to high and cook until the liquid is reduced a little bit, 1 to 2 minutes. Set the peppers aside.

3. Heat the remaining 6 tablespoons olive oil in another large skillet over medium heat. Working in two batches, cook the potato slices until light golden and almost soft, about 4 minutes per side. Don't overcrowd the skillet. Using a slotted spoon, transfer the fried potatoes to paper towels to drain. Then, using the same skillet and working in batches, cook the eggplant until golden brown on both sides, about 3 minutes per side. Transfer the fried eggplant to paper towels to drain. Cook the zucchini slices in the same fashion until light golden, 2 to 3 minutes per side, adding more olive oil to the skillet if necessary.

4. When you are ready to assemble the *tumbet,* preheat the oven to 350°F.

5. Place the cooked peppers and the tomato compote in a large bowl and stir to mix. Arrange the potatoes in a layer on the bottom of a 12- by 9- by 2-inch baking dish. Sprinkle them lightly with salt and dab a little of the tomato compote on top. Arrange the zucchini in a layer over the potatoes, sprinkle it with salt, and dab some sauce on top. Arrange the eggplant in a layer over the zucchini and sprinkle it with salt. Spread the remaining compote on top and bake until the flavors meld, 15 to 20 minutes. *Tumbet* is delicious warm, at room temperature, or cold. To serve, cut it into squares. **SERVES 8 AS A FIRST COURSE OR SIDE DISH**

JOAN'S TOMATO COMPOTE

COMPOTA DE TOMATES

A vibrant sauce from the reddest ripe tomatoes perfectly complements the other vegetables in a *tumbet.*

TUMBET: AN ODE TO MALLORCAN VEGETABLES

As enchanted Mallorca, an island off the eastern coast of mainland Spain, falls prey to blond German sun-seekers, finding true local flavors is becoming more and more of a challenge. Which is why I'm so grateful for chefs like Joan Torrens, who zealously preserves the island traditions at his restaurant Es Baluard, in Palma. Els Baluard is a modest place, with marble tables and tiled floors. All the excitement is on the plates, and most of these feature vegetables in one form or another. Joan oven-braises thick, meaty grouper fillets with peppers, tomatoes, and chard, letting the slow, patient cooking coax out their natural sugars. He fashions eggplants into a wonderful *granada de albergines,* a lightly sweetened, subtly spiced flan. He gratinées salt cod with a smoky *allioli* prepared from grilled eggplant. And he makes a stupendous *tumbet*!

Tumbet, as any Spaniard will tell you, is the most famous dish of Mallorca, a layered casserole of potatoes, eggplant, zucchini, and peppers accompanied by a vibrant tomato sauce. To show off the ingredients that fuel his kitchen, Joan took me to his neighborhood market. There, at a breakfast counter, I learned that the greatest surprise of Mallorcan cuisine is the bold juxtapositions of the sweet and the savory. "Purely Arab," Joan said, handing me an *ensaimada* (the signature Mallorcan coiled pastry), which contained both candied fruit and *sobrasada,* a local chorizo spread; startling and completely delicious, in a perverse kind of way. Then, Joan whisked me around the produce stalls, which were ablaze with plumlike tomatoes still on their vines; firm, sweet local eggplants; tiny strawberries with a complex floral fragrance; and peppers so bright and luminous I wondered how they could be real. Seeing these raw ingredients, I understood why a simple vegetable dish like *tumbet* is so glorified on Mallorca.

The word *tumbet* means something like flattened, and, as Joan explained, its function at a Mallorcan table is pretty flexible: What's called a *plato unico*—a dish that stands by itself—the basic casserole is made in a huge pan to be enjoyed for the rest of the week. *Tumbet* can be eaten on its own for lunch or supper, served as an accompaniment, or used as a base for grilled or baked fish. It tastes good cold, warm, or at room temperature.

1 tablespoon extra-virgin olive oil
2/3 cup finely chopped white onion
1 medium-size garlic clove, minced
2 pounds very ripe tomatoes, peeled, seeded, and chopped
1/4 cup dry white wine
1 pinch of sugar
1 splash of vinegar
Coarse salt (kosher or sea)

Heat the olive oil in a deep, medium-size skillet over low heat. Add the onion and cook until soft but not brown, about 5 minutes. Add the garlic and stir for 30 seconds. Add the tomatoes, increase the heat to medium-high, and cook, stirring, until they release their liquid, 3 to 4 minutes. Add the wine, sugar, and vinegar and season with salt to taste. Cook the compote until the tomatoes are soft but still hold their shape, about 5 minutes longer. If the compote is too liquid, increase the heat to high and cook until reduced, 1 to 2 minutes. Let the compote cool to warm before using.

MAKES ABOUT 2 CUPS

SPINACH WITH RAISINS AND PINE NUTS

ESPINACS A LA CATALANA

An addictive mélange of spinach, garlic, raisins, pine nuts, and good olive oil, this is one of the best-known Catalan dishes. Its uses in the Catalan kitchen are many—in croquettes (see page 65) or egg tortillas, as a topping for *cocas* (flat breads), as a filling for savory turnovers or cannelloni, or as a base for baked fish. As a side dish, it goes with just about anything, and nothing beats it in the morning on toast, topped with poached eggs. The recipe is also great made with other wilted greens, such as chard or escarole.

- 5 to 6 tablespoons golden or dark raisins
- 2 packages (each 10 ounces) fresh spinach, or 2 medium-size bunches spinach, tough stems discarded
- 3 to 4 tablespoons fragrant extra-virgin olive oil
- 6 to 8 whole small peeled garlic cloves, lightly smashed
- 5 tablespoons pine nuts
- Coarse salt (kosher or sea) and freshly ground black pepper

1. Place the raisins in a small bowl, add very hot water to cover, and soak until plump, 10 to 15 minutes. Drain well and pat dry with paper towels, then set aside.

2. Rinse but do not drain the spinach. Place the spinach in a large saucepan over medium heat and cover the pan. Cook the spinach in the water that clings to its leaves until wilted, 4 to 5 minutes, stirring a few times. Transfer the spinach to a colander and squeeze out the excess moisture by pressing on the spinach with the back of a spoon. Chop the spinach coarsely. (The spinach can be prepared a few hours ahead up to this point.)

3. Heat the olive oil in a large skillet or wok over low heat. Add the garlic, pine nuts, and soaked raisins and cook until the nuts and the garlic are light golden, 3 to 5 minutes. Increase the heat to medium, add the chopped spinach, and cook for about 1 minute, stirring to combine evenly. Season with salt and pepper to taste, transfer to a serving bowl, and serve. **SERVES 4 AS A SIDE DISH**

ANDALUSIAN SPINACH WITH CHICKPEAS

ESPINACAS CON GARBANZOS

I don't think there is a tapas bar in Seville that doesn't serve *espinacas,* the classic Arab-influenced specialty of cooked spinach braised in olive oil together with chickpeas and spices. This dish is an example of the Sevillian predilection for *tapas de cuchara* (tapas eaten with a spoon), which is to say stewy things served in miniature *cazuelas.* I'm actually not convinced that the saucy spinach functions best as a nibble—although who am I to argue with tradition?—which is why I've included it in the vegetable chapter. When served as a *tapa,* the spinach is usually accompanied by bread, deliciously fried in olive oil. As a side dish, it's great over rice.

- 2 packages (each 10 ounces) fresh spinach, or 2 medium-size bunches spinach, tough stems discarded
- 3 tablespoons extra-virgin olive oil, plus more for frying the optional bread
- 4 large garlic cloves, chopped
- 1 teaspoon sweet (not smoked) paprika
- 1 small pinch of crushed red pepper flakes
- 3/4 teaspoon ground cumin
- 1 teaspoon dried oregano
- 1 large pinch of freshly grated nutmeg
- 1 small pinch of ground cinnamon
- 4 plum tomatoes, chopped
- 1 can (about 15 ounces) chickpeas, with their liquid
- 1 medium-size pinch of saffron, pulverized in a mortar and steeped in 2 tablespoons very hot water
- 1 small pinch of sugar
- Coarse salt (kosher or sea) and freshly ground black pepper
- 2 teaspoons red wine vinegar
- 6 slices (each 1/4 inch thick) baguette (optional)

1. Rinse but do not drain the spinach. Place the spinach in a large, wide saucepan over medium heat and cover the pan. Cook the spinach in the water that clings to its leaves until wilted, 4 to 5 minutes, stirring a few times. Transfer the spinach to a colander and squeeze out the excess moisture by pressing on the spinach with the back of a spoon. When just cool enough to handle, chop it medium-fine.

2. Heat the 3 tablespoons of olive oil in a 10-inch earthenware *cazuela* or a large skillet, over medium-low heat. Add half of the garlic and cook, stirring, until fragrant, about 1 minute. Add the paprika, red pepper flakes, cumin, oregano, nutmeg, and cinnamon and stir for a few seconds. Add the tomatoes and cook, stirring, until the mixture is slightly thickened and reduced, about 5 minutes. Add the spinach and the chickpeas with their liquid and bring to a simmer. Add the saffron, sugar, and salt and black pepper to taste and cook the spinach, uncovered, stirring once or twice, until the spinach is very tender and has absorbed some of the liquid, 8 to 10 minutes.

3. While the spinach is cooking, place the remaining garlic in a mortar and, using a pestle, crush it to a paste. Add the vinegar to the mortar and stir the garlic mixture into the spinach. Cook until the flavors meld, 2 to 3 minutes. Let the spinach cool to warm, about 15 minutes, before serving.

4. If serving the spinach with the fried bread, pour olive oil to a depth of about ½ inch into a small skillet. Heat it over medium-high heat until a piece of bread placed in the hot oil sizzles on contact. Working in two batches, fry the bread until golden and crisp, about 45 seconds per side. Using a slotted spoon, transfer the bread to drain on paper towels.

5. To serve the spinach, spoon it into a shallow serving dish. Arrange the fried bread slices around the spinach, and serve. **SERVES 4 TO 6 AS A TAPA OR SIDE DISH**

BAKED CHERRY TOMATOES WITH GARLIC AND SAFFRON OIL

TOMATES ASADOS AL ACEITE DE AZAFRAN

Inspired by a dish I had in La Mancha, where saffron and paprika rule, these tomatoes make a fantastic side dish or a condiment for grilled chicken, lamb, or fish. If you increase the amount of olive oil to a half cup and toss in some diced serrano ham or prosciutto, you have a great, easy pasta sauce.

- 1/3 cup extra-virgin olive oil
- 1 medium-size pinch of saffron, pulverized in a mortar
- 2 pints cherry or grape tomatoes
- 4 fat garlic cloves, slivered
- 1/2 teaspoon smoked sweet Spanish paprika
- 1 small pinch of crushed red pepper flakes
- 2 fresh thyme sprigs
- 1 small bay leaf
- Flaky sea salt, such as Maldon
- 2 to 3 tablespoons minced fresh flat-leaf parsley, for serving

1. Preheat the oven to 400°F.

2. Heat the olive oil and saffron over low heat in an earthenware *cazuela* or a flameproof baking dish that can hold the tomatoes in one layer. Add the tomatoes and garlic and cook for 1 minute. Remove the *cazuela* from the heat, stir in the paprika and red pepper flakes, and scatter the thyme and bay leaf on top. Sprinkle salt over the tomatoes and bake until they are plump and tender and are just beginning to split, about 20 minutes.

3. Let the tomatoes cool for about 5 minutes. The tomatoes can be served straight from the *cazuela* or carefully transferred to a serving dish. Remove and discard the thyme sprigs and bay leaf, sprinkle parsley on top, and serve. **SERVES 6 TO 8 AS A SIDE DISH**

TOMATO JAM

MERMELADA DE TOMATES

The surprising bright accent of sweetness in this popular modern Catalan relish makes it an ideal counterpoint to savories such as anchovies, pungent cheese, or smoked ham. Normally, the tomatoes are slowly baked or cooked on top of the stove with sugar syrup, but my quick microwave version is delicious and simple. The tomatoes will splatter as they are microwaved, so choose a deep bowl with sides at least three inches tall.

- 2 pounds medium-size ripe tomatoes, blanched, peeled, and chopped medium-fine
- 3 tablespoons sugar
- 2 tablespoons light corn syrup
- 1 tablespoon fresh lemon juice
- Coarse salt (kosher or sea)
- Olive oil, for storing the jam

1. Place the tomatoes in a fine sieve set over a bowl and let the juices drain for a few minutes.

2. Place the tomatoes in a deep microwave-safe bowl, add the sugar, corn syrup, and lemon juice, and toss to combine. Season with salt to taste, then microwave on high for 5 minutes. Using oven mitts, remove the bowl from the microwave, stir the tomatoes, and return them to the microwave. Microwave until the tomatoes are completely soft and their juices have thickened, another 6 minutes. Remove the tomatoes from the microwave and let them cool completely. If there seems to be too much liquid, transfer the jam to a sieve and drain again for about 1 minute. Spoon the jam into a clean jar and pour a thin layer of olive oil on top. It will keep in the refrigerator for about 1 week. **MAKES ABOUT 1 1/4 CUPS**

ZUCCHINI "BOATS" WITH TUNA AND ROASTED TOMATOES

CALABACINES RELLENOS DE ATUN

When I saw this recipe demonstrated at the Congreso Lo Mejor de la Gastronomía, a showcase for Spanish chefs held in San Sebastián, I instantly wanted to try it. Its creator is Mari Carmen Vélez, one of my favorite chefs in Spain, who cooks at the produce-driven La Sirena restaurant in Alicante. Uncomplicated and infinitely tasty, the dish features lightly steamed zucchini "boats" filled with a tuna and roasted tomato mixture that is then gratineed. Mari Carmen uses *atún en salazón,* the pungent salt-brined tuna so fundamental to the coastal cuisine of Alicante. While a good canned tuna lacks the *atún's* pungent kick, it is still delicious when you add the oomph of *allioli,* the potent garlic mayonnaise. The tuna filling is also great on its own, spread on crusty grilled bread; feel free to add some chopped black olives to the stuffing mixture. Serve the zucchini as a tapa or a light luncheon dish.

Zucchini "Boats" with Tuna and Roasted Tomatoes

3 medium-size ripe tomatoes, quartered and seeded
Extra-virgin olive oil, for brushing the tomatoes
4 large zucchini (choose ones that are not too tapered), stemmed and cut in half lengthwise
Coarse salt (kosher or sea)
12 ounces imported solid oil-packed tuna, or 2 cans (each 6 ounces) Bumble Bee tonno in oil, drained and flaked into bite-size chunks
1/2 cup plus 2 tablespoons Allioli (page 44)
About 1/2 cup plain dry bread crumbs

1. Preheat the oven to 450°F.

2. Arrange the tomatoes on a small baking sheet, brush them with olive oil, and bake until soft, about 35 minutes. Leave the oven on.

3. While the tomatoes are baking, using a small knife or a grapefruit spoon, scoop out and discard the pulp of the zucchini, leaving shells that are just a little more than ⅛ inch thick. You will have 8 "boats." Steam the zucchini in a wide steamer set over boiling water until just softened, 3 to 4 minutes. Do not overcook. When the zucchini is cool enough to handle, blot it dry with paper towels and sprinkle the insides with salt.

4. When the tomatoes are cool enough to handle, slip the skins off and coarsely chop the tomatoes. Place the tuna, chopped tomatoes, and about 2 tablespoons of the *allioli* in a mixing bowl and toss to mix. Fill the zucchini "boats" with the tuna mixture. Spread the top of each with 1 tablespoon of the remaining *allioli* and sprinkle about 1 tablespoon of the bread crumbs on top of each. Set the stuffed zucchini on a baking sheet and bake until the tops are lightly browned, about 10 minutes. Cut each "boat" in half crosswise and serve warm or at room temperature. **SERVES 8 TO 10 AS A TAPA, 4 TO 6 AS A LIGHT LUNCHEON DISH**

GYPSY POT

OLLA GITANA

The *olla* is a typical *potaje,* which is to say a soupy legume stew served as a first course or a main dish for lunch. In some versions wheat berries are added to the pot. Other renditions include white beans, Swiss chard, potatoes, or eggplant. This *olla,* so representative of the vegetable cooking of Murcia and Alicante, is called *gitana*—gypsy—because of its seemingly anarchic roster of ingredients. True, the mixture of legumes and pears is a little unusual, but it results in an incredibly flavorful and original stew. Grilled or toasted country bread and a refreshing vegetable salad are the best accompaniments, but the *olla* is also great over couscous (page 365) or rice.

1 cup dried chickpeas (garbanzo beans), soaked overnight and drained (see Variation)
1 fat carrot, cut into 1-inch dice
9 to 10 cups chicken stock or broth, or vegetable stock
1 pound pumpkin or butternut squash, cut into 1-inch chunks
10 ounces green beans, trimmed and cut into 1-inch lengths
2 small slightly under-ripe Anjou pears, peeled, cored, and cut into 1-inch chunks
Coarse salt (kosher or sea) and freshly ground black pepper
2 tablespoons extra-virgin olive oil
3 large garlic cloves, chopped
8 whole blanched almonds
3/4 cup chopped white onion
1 teaspoon sweet (not smoked) paprika
2 medium-size ripe tomatoes, finely chopped

THE SIREN OF ALICANTE

I first fell for Mari Carmen Vélez at a high-profile chefs' conference in San Sebastián, where Spain's avant-garde toques gathered to demonstrate their latest experiments. One chef delivered a presentation about working with a liver transplant institute to improve his foie gras—for real! Another demonstrated a futuristic vacuum distiller that can extract colorless flavor essences from ingredients. Among these alchemists, Mari Carmen was the only woman, and there was something disarmingly down-to-earth about her discussion of *allioli,* the indispensable Spanish-Mediterranean mayonnaise. And her croquettes, filled with *allioli* in flavors like blood orange and almonds, were such a tour de force I vowed to make a pilgrimage to her restaurant, La Sirena, in the Mediterranean region of Alicante.

La Sirena is located in Elda, a town utterly nondescript but flush from being the center of Spain's shoe production. Waiting for a table, my friend and I perched at a polished-wood bar arrayed with an aquarium's worth of crab, langoustines, and bright red prawns. Then, between bites of gratinéed zucchini with tuna, crisp salt cod fritters, and artichoke hearts stuffed with foie gras, we noticed something utterly strange. Every patron who came into the restaurant was wearing an outlandish costume. Suddenly we were surrounded by a carnival crowd of turbaned Moors, warriors in shiny plastic armor, characters dressed as crusaders, and concubines in frilly skirts. The reason? *Moros y Cristianos,* a raucous fiesta, which celebrates the 1276 victory battle of the Christians over the Moors, an event that led to the Reconquista—the reconquest—of Spain. Returning from their parade and mock battle, the revelers were streaming into the restaurant, hungry for Mari Carmen's famous seafood paella.

The masquerade was completely absorbing, but when the food arrived, everything else faded into insignificance. Each dish that came out of Mari Carmen's kitchen was full of elegance and Mediterranean luster. There was a sparkling sea bass carpaccio, minimally accessorized with olive oil, tiny bits of caramelized red pepper, and a scoop of tart apple granita. There was a thin crumbly flat bread layered with silvery anchovies and marinated wild berries. Seared scallops were redolent of citrus juice and candied lemon; tuna *escabeche* was reinvented with exotic spices like cardamom and Szechuan peppercorns. The pièce de résistance was *suquet,* a fish stew that smacked of the sea, accompanied by Mari Carmen's signature almond *allioli.* It was the kind of dish that could only be prepared by a fisherman's daughter (which Mari Carmen happens to be). When we were finishing the hazelnut cream with bitter chocolate, Mari Carmen finally came out of the kitchen. She was exhausted, wiping beads of sweat from her forehead. "The Moors and the Christians are driving me nuts," she complained. "Imagine, making a paella for a rowdy table of thirty." She was clearly glad that *Moros y Cristianos* battle in Elda only once a year.

1 medium-size pinch of saffron, pulverized in a mortar and steeped in 3 tablespoons very hot water
2 teaspoons best-quality red wine vinegar, or more to taste
2 tablespoons slivered fresh mint, or 1 large pinch of dried mint
Grilled or toasted country bread, cooked couscous (page 365), or rice, for serving

1. Place the chickpeas and carrot in a 5-quart pot, add 6 cups of the chicken stock, and bring to a boil over high heat. Skim any foam off the surface, reduce the heat to low, cover the pot, and cook until the chickpeas are tender, about 1¼ hours.

2. Add about 3 more cups of the chicken stock to the pot—enough to cover the chickpeas by about

2 inches. Stir in the pumpkin, green beans, and pears and season with salt and pepper to taste. Increase the heat to medium and bring to a simmer. Reduce the heat to low and simmer, partially covered, until the vegetables have softened, 15 to 20 minutes.

3. Meanwhile, heat the olive oil in a medium-size skillet over medium heat. Add the garlic and almonds and cook, stirring, until golden, about 2 minutes. Using a slotted spoon, transfer the garlic and almonds to a bowl and set aside. Add the onion to the skillet and cook until softened, about 5 minutes. Add the paprika and stir for a few seconds. Add the tomatoes and a few tablespoons of the cooking liquid and cook until the tomatoes soften and reduce, about 7 minutes.

4. Gently stir the tomato mixture and the saffron into the pot with the chickpeas. Continue cooking until all the vegetables are very soft and the pumpkin is almost falling apart, 5 to 7 minutes longer, adding some of the remaining chicken broth if the stew seems too thick.

5. Meanwhile, place the fried garlic and almonds in a mini food processor and process just until ground (you can also grind the garlic and almonds in a mortar using a pestle). Stir the ground garlic mixture and the vinegar into the pot with the chickpeas. Taste for seasoning, adding more salt, pepper, and/or vinegar as necessary. Let the stew cool for about 10 minutes. Garnish with mint and serve with bread or over couscous (page 365) or rice. **SERVES 6 TO 8 AS A FIRST COURSE**

VARIATION: Dried chickpeas, of course, are the authentic deal, but you can substitute canned chickpeas to speed up the recipe. You'll need two 15-ounce cans. Place the drained chickpeas and carrot in a 5-quart pot, add enough chicken broth to cover the chickpeas by about 1½ inches, and bring to a boil. Reduce the heat to low, add the pumpkin, green beans, pears, and salt and pepper as directed in Step 2, and continue with the recipe.

MALLORCAN VEGETABLE STEW WITH BROWN BREAD

SOPES MALLORQUINES

Sopes mallorquines, or Mallorcan sops, is a dish as wonderful as it is curious. A kind of "dry soup" of many vegetables and dark bread, it's a fundamental part of the island's cuisine. The bread used for the dish is *pan moreno,* completely unseasoned, unsalted dense loaves designed to soak up other flavors. While cabbage features in most versions, the assortment of vegetables is entirely flexible, dictated by what's local and seasonal. Feel free to add to or make substitutions in the selection here. Chopped chard, peas, thin asparagus cut into segments, and Italian peppers or, in the winter, potatoes would all be good. During *matanza* (pig-slaughter) season, pork goes into the pot as well.

The idea is to braise the vegetables very slowly with little liquid; this renders them mild and almost startlingly sweet. The stew is then layered over stale bread, which soaks up the delicious juices. Traditionally, *sopes* are eaten accompanied by halved black olives and marinated capers. There are *a lot* of great veggies here, but despite the long ingredient list the stew is a cinch. Serve it as a luncheon or a vegetarian meal.

- 10 to 12 ounces (a medium-size loaf) sturdy unseasoned whole-wheat bread from a bakery, cut into 1/4-inch slices
- 6 tablespoons extra-virgin olive oil, plus 1/4 cup for finishing the stew, and a little extra for serving
- 1 medium-size white onion, quartered and thinly sliced
- 1 medium-size leek, white and some pale green parts, cut in half lengthwise, rinsed thoroughly, and sliced
- 6 medium-size garlic cloves, sliced, plus 3 large cloves, chopped
- 1 red bell pepper, cored, quartered, seeded, and sliced
- 3 1/2 cups chopped green cabbage
- 6 ounces string beans, trimmed and cut into 1-inch lengths
- 6 fat scallions with about 3 inches of green, trimmed and cut into 1-inch lengths
- 4 1/2 teaspoons sweet (not smoked) paprika
- 1 small bay leaf
- 1/2 dried small hot chile, such as arbol
- 3 medium-size ripe tomatoes, chopped
- 3 medium-size artichokes, pared down to the heart (see page 370) and quartered, or 1 package (9 ounces) frozen artichoke hearts, thawed
- 2 cups small cauliflower florets
- 1 cup plus 2 tablespoons chopped fresh flat-leaf parsley
- Coarse salt (kosher or sea)

1. Place the bread in a single layer on a large baking sheet and let it dry on a countertop for 4 to 6 hours, turning once. (Alternatively, the bread can be dried by baking in a 300°F oven for about 20 minutes.)

2. Heat the 6 tablespoons olive oil in a heavy 5-quart pot over medium heat. Add the onion, leek, and sliced garlic and cook, stirring, until softened but not browned, 6 to 7 minutes. Add the red bell pepper, cabbage, string beans, and scallions and cook, stirring, until the cabbage wilts, 5 to 7 minutes, adjusting the heat so that the vegetables don't brown. Add the paprika and stir for a few seconds. Add the bay leaf, chile, tomatoes, and 1 cup water and raise the heat to bring to a boil. Place a round of waxed paper directly on the surface of the stew, reduce the heat to low, cover the pot, and simmer for 15 minutes. Stir in the artichokes, cauliflower, the 1 cup parsley, and ½ cup water and let the stew return to a simmer. Season with salt to taste, cover the stew again with waxed paper, and cook, covered, over very low heat, until the vegetables are very soft, 25 to 30 minutes.

3. While the vegetables are cooking, place the chopped garlic, the remaining 2 tablespoons parsley, and a large pinch of salt in a mortar. Using a pestle, mash to a paste, then add the remaining ¼ cup olive oil.

4. Preheat the oven to 450°F.

5. Place a layer of dried bread slices on the bottom of an 11- or 12-inch earthenware *cazuela* or a deep ceramic baking dish of similar size. Sprinkle the bread lightly with salt and brush with some of the garlic-parsley mixture. Spoon half of the vegetable stew over the bread. Top with another layer of bread, brush the slices with the remaining garlic-parsley mixture, and spoon the remaining stew and its liquid on top. Bake until the flavors meld, about 10 minutes. Let stand for a few minutes before serving. Invite each guest to drizzle his or her portion with a little olive oil. **SERVES 6 TO 8 AS A LIGHT MAIN COURSE**

EL OBRADOR DEL
Charcutería

PASTAS ALIMENTICIAS
BOMBONS

DESSERTS

INNOVATIVE FINALES

Spanish restaurant desserts today often offer an exhilarating ride on the wild side. El Celler de Can Roca's pastry chef, Jordi Roca, makes sweets that reproduce the aromas of popular fragrances. It's uncanny! First, diners are handed a paper swatch scented with perfume. Then comes Roca's composition of loquats, apricot sorbet, and warm peaches, layered with notes of honey, roses, lilac, and mallow, which perfectly matches the flowery fragrance of the Lancôme Trésor on the paper swatch. A mélange of eucalyptus, orange blossoms, nutmeg, and mint tastes like granita from heaven and smells like Ralph Lauren's Polo. At Arzak restaurant in San Sebastián, a strawberry shake explodes in an extravagant cascade of pink bubbles, thanks to dry ice that

Top left: Lingering over a hot chocolate with a window on the rest of the world; *Top right:* An outdoor ice-cream cart attracts passers by; *Bottom left:* A gorgeously ornate *fin de siècle* confectionery shop—the source of many sweet treats; *Bottom right:* A fresh Valencian Orange Tart (see page 402).

chemically reacts with the milk. At El Bulli I ate a dessert that smelled like a pound cake, looked like a pound cake, and arrived in a loaf pan. One bite revealed a tromp l'oeil: a cake fashioned from frozen "air" that dissolved on the tongue—pastry station meets chemistry lab meets performance art.

Compared to this avant-garde alchemy, classic Spanish confections belong to an entirely different world: a rich sugary blend of Roman, Sephardic, Arab, and Catholic traditions. The Moors introduced sugar cane and sophisticated methods of refining its juice into sugar. Soon after the Muslim conquest of Spain in the eighth century, acres of sugary reeds were planted in the Andalusian countryside. In just a few centuries, there were dozens of sugar mills in the region—no small feat considering that elsewhere in medieval Europe sugar was still a scarce luxury. Almonds, another defining flavor in Spanish sweets, were first planted in Spain by the Phoenicians. Arabs kept on cultivating the nuts, singing praises

SWEET SCIENCE

I'm contemplating my dessert at El Celler de Can Roca, Catalonia's most innovative restaurant after El Bulli. In front of me is a gossamer caramel bubble the size of a grapefruit, with the pearlescent silvery sheen of a vintage Tiffany vase. "Puncture it," the waiter instructs. I comply, watching in utter amazement as sweet-fragrant wisps of olive-wood smoke emerge from inside. When I break the bubble completely, I discover a lush scoop of smoke-tinged porcini ice cream. Underneath lurks a layer of porcini carpaccio bathed with olive oil and scattered with pine nuts, not sweet but not quite savory. Puzzling, magical, and a technical miracle—smoke is trapped in a bubble handblown like glass from high-tech sugar derivatives—the dessert is like Cirque du Soleil for the taste buds. It is also proof that some of the most exciting culinary innovations these days are coming out of Spain's pastry stations.

The revolution began in the late 1990s, when Dalíesque chef Ferran Adrià of El Bulli and his pastry-whiz brother, Albert, first began dismantling boundaries between sweet and savory kitchens. Olive oil, vinegars, spices, herbs—even foie gras and truffles—were boldly incorporated into desserts. Techniques normally confined to the pastry station—mousses, ice creams, gelatins, granitas—were grafted onto tapas and main courses, each new dish a delicious slap in the face of convention. Adrià's obsession with textures led to a vocabulary of groundbreaking methods now common among Spanish chefs: airy *espumas* (foams whipped in a canister of nitrous oxide), hot and cold gelées set with such unusual jelling agents as agar agar, bubbly "airs," *crujientes* (gossamer brittles), intriguing iced powders. Other pastry provocateurs have followed suit. All but banishing flour and butter from their repertoire, they wow diners instead with daring juxtapositions of flavors and textures.

to the beauty of the almond trees that covered Andalusian valleys in pinkish white lace when they blossomed.

Turrón and marzipan, Spain's most famous almond confections, date back to the time when Arabs held sway. So does the repertoire of sugary fritters, candied fruit, sweets bathed in syrup, and stove-top puddings and custards, such as *arróz con leche* and *natillas* (a kind of crème anglaise). When Arabs and Jews were expelled in 1492, convent nuns took over Spain's pastry kitchens, perfecting the art of cookies, fritters, sponge cakes, and marmalades. One striking feature of traditional Spanish sweets—an excessive reliance on egg yolks—is a holdover from the days when egg whites were used to clarify sherry and leftover yolks were donated to Andalusian nuns.

When Catholicism led to a premium on eating pig, another ingredient, lard—which lends an inimitable crumbliness to Spanish holiday cookies—became fundamental. The French contributed the caramel so essential to making flan. And these days even the nuns are keeping up with the times (just try the stylish banana and hazelnut tart from the Clarisa Sisters on page 405). Playing tradition against innovation, the desserts in this chapter offer the best of both worlds: an apple and nut tart updated with rosemary, dramatic chocolate treats, imaginative granitas and ice creams, and intriguing Ferran Adrià–inspired whimsies, like the gorgeous parfait that daringly combines yogurt, rose water, and . . . beets. Welcome to the New Spanish pastry kitchen!

TARTS AND CAKES

ROSEMARY-SCENTED APPLE AND NUT TART

TARTA DE MANZANA PERFUMADA CON ROMERO

Xavier Canal, the favorite baker of Barcelona's smart set, is a great master of apple tarts. In this one, he fills a crumbly tart shell with pine nut and almond custard and tops it with diced apples briefly cooked in rosemary syrup. The rosemary accent is faint but intriguing; if you want to intensify the herbal flavor, add a little finely minced rosemary to the apples. Once you've made this version, Xavier suggests trying a saffron-infused pastry cream (see facing page). The tart can be prepared ahead and put together before serving.

2 large eggs
1/2 cup plus 1/3 cup sugar
1/2 cup lightly toasted pine nuts (see page 267)
1/4 cup lightly toasted slivered almonds (see page 267)
3 tablespoons all-purpose flour
8 tablespoons (1 stick) unsalted butter, at room temperature
Rosemary-Scented Tart Shell (recipe follows)
2 large fresh rosemary sprigs, twisted and smashed
4 medium-size Granny Smith apples, peeled, cored, and cut into small dice
Cocoa powder, for dusting the tart

1. Position a rack in the center of the oven and preheat the oven to 375°F.

2. Place the eggs and ¼ cup of the sugar in a small bowl and whisk to mix.

3. Place the pine nuts and almonds in a food processor and process until finely ground. Add the flour and ¼ cup sugar and pulse until well combined. Add 6 tablespoons (¾ stick) of the butter and pulse briefly until the mixture begins to form moist clumps. With the motor running, gradually add the egg mixture, processing just until all the ingredients are well combined.

4. Scrape the almond mixture into the tart shell, spreading it evenly (you may have more than will fill the shell). Bake until the filling is set and the top is light golden, about 35 minutes. Transfer the tart to a rack to cool completely.

5. Meanwhile, prepare the apples: Place the remaining ⅓ cup sugar, the rosemary, and ½ cup water in a microwave-safe dish and heat on high power for 2 minutes (microwaving releases rosemary flavor better than boiling). Let the rosemary syrup stand for 30 minutes, then strain it.

6. Melt the remaining 2 tablespoons butter in a large nonstick skillet over medium-high heat. Add the apples and cook, stirring, until they begin to release their juice, about 3 minutes. Add the rosemary syrup, cover the skillet, and cook until the apples soften, about 5 minutes. Uncover the skillet and cook, stirring gently a few times, until the apples are soft and most of the liquid has evaporated, about 5 minutes. The apples should be moist and intact, not mushy. Let cool completely.

7. To assemble the tart, arrange the apples evenly in the tart shell. Using a sifter, lightly dust the top of the tart with cocoa powder and serve. **MAKES ONE 9-INCH TART**

ROSEMARY-SCENTED TART SHELL

PASTA QUEBRADA CON ROMERO

The lovely hint of rosemary in this pastry is a marvelous complement to the apple filling on the previous page, as well as the Saffron Pastry Cream below. Think of it, too, for fruit tarts—especially pear, plum, and peach.

SAFFRON PASTRY CREAM

You can also fill the Rosemary-Scented Tart Shell (this page) with a saffron-hued pastry cream. The cream is delicious and striking topped with the rosemary-scented apples or with fresh berries, such as blueberries, raspberries, or a combination.

3 large egg yolks
2/3 cup sugar
1 medium-size pinch of saffron, pulverized in a mortar and steeped in 2 tablespoons very hot water
3 tablespoons all-purpose flour
1 1/2 cups half-and-half

1. Place the egg yolks, 1/3 cup of the sugar, and the saffron mixture in a medium-size bowl and whisk until thick and pale yellow. Whisk in the flour.

2. Place the half-and-half in a heavy medium-size saucepan over medium-low heat and bring to a simmer. Gradually whisk 1/2 cup of the hot half-and-half into the egg mixture. Whisk the egg mixture into the saucepan of half-and-half, increase the heat to medium-high, and bring to a boil, whisking constantly. Reduce the heat to low and cook, whisking, until it thickens, 3 to 5 minutes. Scrape the pastry cream into a small bowl. Press a piece of plastic wrap directly onto the surface of the pastry cream and let cool completely, then refrigerate it for 1 hour. Spread the pastry cream evenly in a prebaked tart shell and continue with Step 5 of the Rosemary-Scented Apple and Nut Tart (see facing page). **MAKES ABOUT 1 1/2 CUPS**

1 1/4 cups all-purpose flour
1/2 cup confectioners' sugar
1 teaspoon minced fresh rosemary
8 tablespoons (1 stick) unsalted butter, chilled and cut into small pieces
4 to 6 tablespoons ice water

1. Place the flour, confectioners' sugar, and rosemary in a food processor and pulse 6 or 7 times to crush the rosemary just a bit. Add the butter and pulse until the mixture resembles coarse meal.

2. Transfer the dough to a bowl, sprinkle on 4 tablespoons ice water, and stir until it is evenly distributed. Pinch a piece of dough between your fingers. If it doesn't hold together, add more ice water. Gather the dough into a ball. Lightly flour a work surface, then flatten the ball into a disk, wrap it in plastic, and refrigerate for at least 2 hours. (The pastry can be prepared up to 2 days ahead.)

3. Place the disk of dough between two pieces of lightly floured parchment paper, and roll it out to an 11-inch circle. Transfer the dough to a 9-inch tart pan with a removable bottom, press it into the side of the pan, and trim the overhang. Freeze, covered with aluminum foil, for 20 minutes.

4. While the pastry is chilling, position a rack in the center of the oven and preheat the oven to 400°F.

5. Without removing the aluminum foil, fill the tart pan with pie weights or dried beans, then bake it on the center rack for 20 minutes. Remove the pie weights and the foil and continue baking until the pastry is light golden and baked through, 8 to 10 minutes longer. Let cool completely in the pan on a rack before filling. **MAKES ONE 9-INCH TART SHELL**

VALENCIAN ORANGE TART

TARTA DE NARANJAS VALENCIANA

Once a source of immense wealth for the city, oranges are a symbol of Valencia. They feature in this citrus-intensive, not-too-sweet tart, which is just the ticket after a filling meal. Since the orange slices decorating the tart are not peeled, be sure to use thin-skinned juicy California oranges; thick-skinned oranges will not work. Blood oranges or a combination of orange and lemon slices make a nice variation. For an extra jolt of citrus, serve the tart with the refreshing Tangerine Sorbet (page 442), Agua de Valencia Granita (page 444), or a good store-bought citrus sorbet.

4 medium-size thin-skinned California oranges, scrubbed well
2 1/2 cups fresh orange juice
1 cup sugar, plus more for caramelizing the tart
1 tablespoon grated orange zest
2 teaspoons orange flower water (optional)
About 1 cup best-quality orange marmalade
Prebaked Tart Pastry (recipe follows)

Valencian Orange Tart

1. Cut off and discard a thick slice from each end of the oranges. Using a sharp knife, cut the oranges into ⅛-inch-thick slices. Place the orange juice, sugar, grated orange zest, and orange flower water, if using, in a wide pot and bring to a simmer over medium-high heat, stirring until the sugar dissolves. Add the orange slices; if they are not submerged in liquid, add a little water. Reduce the heat to low and let the oranges simmer, partially covered, for 15 minutes. Let the orange slices cool in the cooking liquid, then drain them and gently pat them dry with paper towels. Cut the orange slices in half.

2. Position a rack in the center of the oven and preheat the oven to 375°F.

3. To assemble the tart, spread the marmalade evenly in the bottom of the tart shell and arrange the halved orange slices on top in concentric circles, overlapping slightly. Bake it on the center rack until the oranges are very soft and lightly browned, 30 minutes.

4. Preheat the broiler. When the tart is just cool enough to handle, wrap aluminum foil around the edge of the crust so that it doesn't burn when the tart is caramelized. Sprinkle sugar in a thin, even layer over the tart and broil until the sugar is caramelized, 4 to 7 minutes, depending on the heat of the broiler, being very careful not to let the tart burn (you can also use a kitchenware blowtorch to caramelize the tart). Let the tart cool to room temperature before serving. **MAKES ONE 9-INCH TART**

PREBAKED TART PASTRY

PASTA QUEBRADA

This basic pastry suits all manner of tarts, including the one on page 408, filled surprisingly with blue cheese.

- 1½ cups all-purpose flour
- ⅔ cup confectioners' sugar
- 1 medium-size pinch of salt
- 10 tablespoons (1¼ sticks) unsalted butter, chilled and cut into small pieces
- 1 large egg yolk beaten with 2 tablespoons chilled heavy (whipping) cream
- 1 tablespoon ice water, if needed

1. Place the flour, confectioners' sugar, and salt in a food processor and pulse 5 or 6 times, just to combine. Add the butter and pulse until the mixture resembles coarse meal.

2. Transfer the flour mixture to a bowl and, using two forks, stir in the egg yolk mixture until it is evenly distributed. Pinch a piece of dough between your fingers. If it doesn't hold together, stir in the ice water. Gather the dough into a ball. Lightly flour a work surface, then flatten the ball into a disk, wrap it in plastic, and refrigerate for at least 2 hours. (The pastry can be prepared up to 2 days ahead.)

3. Place the disk of dough between two pieces of lightly floured parchment paper and roll it out to an 11-inch circle. Transfer the dough to a 9-inch tart pan with a removable bottom, press it into the side of the pan, and trim the overhang. Freeze, covered with aluminum foil, for 20 minutes.

4. While the pastry is chilling, position a rack in the center of the oven and preheat the oven to 400°F.

5. Without removing the aluminum foil, fill the tart pan with pie weights or dried beans, then bake it for 25 minutes. Remove the pie weights and the foil and continue baking until the pastry is light golden and baked through, 8 to 10 minutes longer. Let cool completely in the pan on a rack before filling. **MAKES ONE 9-INCH TART SHELL**

THE CLARISA NUNS' BANANA & HAZELNUT TART

TARTA DE PLATANOS Y AVELLANAS HERMANAS CLARISAS

Of all the Spanish cookbooks I own, one of my favorites is *Repostería Monacal de las Hermanas Clarisas*—a mouthwatering volume full of sweets compiled from various convents of the St. Clara order. Nuns are recognized in Spain as master bakers, and conventual cookbooks are incredibly popular. What's striking about this tome is that, in addition to the usual *yemas* (egg yolk sweets) and *mantecadas* (crumbly lard cookies), it contains some seriously sophisticated desserts, demonstrating that the good sisters are keeping up with the times. This tart is a terrific example: sweet triumph from the sisters at the fifteenth-century convent of Nuestra Señora de la Esperanza in Alcalá de Henares, a town close to Madrid. It consists of a pastry shell filled with a tangy pineapple cream, topped with pineapple-macerated bananas and baked under a hazelnut streusel. The pastry, the filling, and the nut topping can all be prepared ahead and the tart assembled and baked at your leisure. Divine, indeed.

FOR THE PASTRY SHELL:

- All-purpose flour, for dusting the work surface
- 1 sheet puff pastry (from a 17 1/4-ounce package), thawed

FOR THE HAZELNUT TOPPING:

- 1/4 cup chopped skinned hazelnuts (see page 267)
- 3 tablespoons all-purpose flour
- 3 tablespoons light brown sugar
- 3 tablespoons chilled unsalted butter, cut into small pieces
- 1/2 teaspoon ground cinnamon

FOR THE BANANA AND CREAM FILLING:

- 3 large bananas, cut on the diagonal into medium-thin slices
- 1 1/2 cups pineapple juice
- 2 tablespoons fresh lemon juice
- 1/3 cup sugar
- 1 1/2 tablespoons cornstarch
- 3 large egg yolks
- 2 tablespoons unsalted butter, at room temperature

1. Prepare the pastry shell: Flour a work surface, then, using a floured rolling pin, roll out the puff pastry to a roughly 12-inch square. Cut out an 11-inch circle by tracing around a plate or an 11-inch tart pan with the tip of a paring knife. Transfer the pastry circle to a 9-inch tart pan with a removable bottom and press it against the side of the pan. Prick the pastry all over with the tines of a fork, cover it with plastic wrap, and freeze for 30 minutes.

2. While the pastry is chilling, position a rack in the center of the oven and preheat the oven to 375°F.

3. Remove and discard the plastic wrap from the pastry, then bake it on the center rack until light golden, about 20 minutes. When cool enough to handle, press gently on the bottom to deflate it. Let the pastry cool until ready to use. (The pastry shell can be baked up to a day ahead. Store at room temperature, covered loosely with aluminum foil.)

4. Make the hazelnut topping: Place the hazelnuts, flour, brown sugar, butter, and cinnamon in a mini food processor and process until moist crumbs form. Scrape the topping into a bowl and refrigerate it, covered, while you prepare the filling.

SWEET BLESSINGS

Walking up to the small, discreet window at a convent's entrance, I ring the bell and place a few euros on a wooden tray. The thin, black-cuffed hand of a cloistered nun hands me a box; a voice offers a blessing. Overcome by sweet piety, I walk away, slowly unwrapping bundles of cinnamon-dusted cookies, the insanely rich candied egg yolks called *yemas,* and confections shaped like the bones of a saint. High on sugar, I imagine the bakers sequestered behind convent walls skinning almonds, blanching orange peel, and patiently beating eggs laid by the convent hens.

Nuns have been guardians of Spain's sweet traditions for more than five centuries. Although the idea of sisters who bake like angels is decidedly Catholic, many of their confections are actually of Muslim heritage—a sweet irony. When Moors were expelled from Spain in the fifteenth century after some eight hundred years of domination, recipes for their pastries rich in honey, almonds, and sesame seeds were preserved and perfected at convents. "Their products are often the culmination of centuries of tradition, and are made from jealously guarded recipes transmitted from one abbess to another in secret handwritten notebooks," writes Xavier Domingo in *The Taste of Spain.* For the sisters, confectionary was more than simply a hobby that killed time between prayers. With sugar considered a status-laden luxury, sweet gifts were their way of currying favors from visiting dignitaries and repaying noble families at holiday times for endowments. In the nineteenth century, as support for religious orders waned, some convents began relying on confection sales as their main source of income. These days *repostería conventual* makes up a small industry, flourishing in some two hundred convents all over Spain.

The repertoire of conventual sweets is vast. There are the ubiquitous lard cookies, such as *polvorones* and *mantecadas;* anise ring cookies called *roscos;* and *borrachuelos,* dainty cakes soaked in syrup or wine. There are dense nut confections, airy sponge cakes, and a long litany of marmalades and candied fruit. Whenever I'm in Toledo I visit the church of Santo Tomé—not to admire El Greco's *The Burial of the Count of Orgaz,* but to stock up on the amazing marzipans made by its nuns. I never leave Seville without a box of *yemas* prepared by the cloistered Augustinian sisters of the San Leandro convent according to a fifteenth-century recipe. In fact, I don't think I've ever passed a convent in Spain without emerging with a parcel of sweets. It's reassuring to know that God will forgive me for this little indulgence.

5. Make the banana and cream filling: Place the bananas in a bowl, add the pineapple and lemon juices, and let stand for about 20 minutes. Strain the soaking liquid into a medium-size saucepan. Set the bananas aside.

6. Bring the soaking liquid to a simmer over medium-high heat. Place the sugar and cornstarch in a medium-size bowl and whisk to mix, then beat in the egg yolks. Gradually whisk ½ cup of the hot soaking liquid into the egg mixture, then whisk it into the saucepan with the remaining hot liquid. Cook over medium heat, whisking constantly, until the custard is thickened and just beginning to bubble around the edges, 3 to 4 minutes. Strain the custard into a bowl and let cool slightly. Whisk in the butter, press a piece of plastic wrap directly onto the surface of the custard, and let cool to warm. It will keep for 4 hours at room temperature or overnight in the refrigerator.

7. Position a rack in the center of the oven and preheat the oven to 425°F.

8. To assemble the tart, spread the custard evenly in the pastry shell. Arrange the bananas on top of the custard in concentric circles and sprinkle the hazelnut topping evenly over them. Bake the tart on the center rack until the top is brown and bubbly, 20 to 25 minutes. Let cool in the pan on a rack and serve at room temperature. **MAKES ONE 9-INCH TART**

FRESH FIG TARTS

TARTAS DE HIGOS

Not even the most devoted Catalan gourmands know about Fonda Xesc, a gem of a haute rustic restaurant hidden away on a small winding road too obscure for most people to find. What a shame. My recent meal there included a sublime *coca* with fresh figs and foie gras, a squid and artichoke rice for the ages, and these delicious caramelized fig tarts. I count the days until I can make it back to Fonda Xesc, and in the meantime, I make these tarts whenever fresh figs are in season. For an unusual grace note, you can sprinkle a few fresh rosemary leaves instead of the cinnamon on each tart before baking. I love these with Honey and Cinnamon Ice Cream.

All-purpose flour, for dusting the work surface
2 sheets (one 17 1/4-ounce package) frozen puff pastry, thawed
1 1/2 tablespoons unsalted butter, chopped, plus more for greasing the baking sheet
2 tablespoons honey, preferably rosemary or orange blossom
4 teaspoons plus 2 tablespoons sugar
16 to 20 ripe purple figs (about 1 1/2 pounds), trimmed and cut lengthwise into 1/4-inch-thick slices
Ground cinnamon, for dusting the tarts
Honey and Cinnamon Ice Cream (page 439) or store-bought vanilla ice cream (optional), for serving

1. Lightly flour a work surface, then, using a floured rolling pin, roll out a sheet of puff pastry to a roughly ⅛-inch-thick rectangle. Using a small plate as a template, cut out two 6-inch rounds and wrap each one in plastic. Repeat with the remaining sheet of puff pastry, cutting out 2 more rounds and wrapping them in plastic. Refrigerate the puff pastry rounds for at least 1 hour.

2. Position a rack in the upper third of the oven and preheat the oven to 400°F. Lightly butter a large baking sheet.

3. Place the butter and honey in a microwave-safe bowl and heat on high power until the butter is melted, 15 seconds, then stir to mix.

4. Unwrap the puff pastry rounds and arrange them on the baking sheet; sprinkle 1 teaspoon of the sugar over each. Fold in the edge of each round to form a ½-inch border. Arrange the fig slices on the pastry rounds in concentric overlapping circles. Brush each tart generously with some of the honey and butter mixture and sprinkle cinnamon very lightly on top. Bake the tarts in the upper third of the oven until the figs are tender and the pastry is golden, about 25 minutes.

5. Change the oven setting to broil. Sprinkle each tart with 1½ teaspoons of the remaining sugar and caramelize it under the broiler, taking care not to burn the pastry, about 2 minutes. (You can also use a kitchen blowtorch, if you have one, to caramelize the sugar.) Let the tarts cool on a rack for about 10 minutes. Serve warm, accompanied by ice cream, if desired. **MAKES 4 TARTS**

BLUE CHEESE & PEAR TART

TARTA DE QUESO AZUL CON PERAS

Anyone who likes pears with blue cheese will love this worldly, surprising tart with its smooth, mousselike cheese filling and a topping of sliced, wine-poached pears. The recipe was passed on to me by María Jesús Gil de Antuñano, one of Spain's premiere food writers and recipe developers, who writes a weekly recipe column in *El País,* the country's most widely read newspaper. While Cabrales would seem like the authentic choice of cheese, Roquefort is equally, if not more, popular in Spain and is recommended by María Jesús. Gorgonzola or Danish blue will also work, and you can vary the proportions of blue cheese and cream cheese according to the pungency you desire. Start ahead to give the tart sufficient time to set.

FOR THE BLUE CHEESE FILLING AND PASTRY:

1 3/4 cups half-and-half
3 teaspoons unflavored gelatin (from 2 envelopes)
6 ounces Roquefort or another blue cheese, at room temperature, crumbled
6 ounces cream cheese, at room temperature
1/4 cup sugar
Prebaked Tart Pastry (page 404)

FOR THE PEAR TOPPING:

4 large firm Bartlett pears, peeled, cored, and cut in half lengthwise
2 cups full-bodied dry red wine
2/3 cup sugar
1 medium-size cinnamon stick

1. Make the blue cheese filling: Pour the half-and-half into a medium-size bowl. Place the gelatin and ¼ cup water in a small heatproof bowl and let sit until the gelatin softens, about 10 minutes. Place the bowl with the gelatin in a small skillet of barely simmering water and stir until the gelatin dissolves, about 2 minutes. Remove the bowl from the water, pour ½ cup of the half-and-half into the gelatin mixture, stirring it well, then gently whisk the gelatin mixture into the remaining half-and-half until well blended.

2. Place the cream mixture, Roquefort, cream cheese, and sugar in a food processor and process until completely smooth. Scrape the cheese mixture into the tart shell and smooth the top with the back of a spoon. Cover the tart loosely with plastic wrap, making sure it doesn't touch the top of the filling, and refrigerate until set, at least 6 hours or overnight.

3. While the tart is chilling, prepare the pear topping: Place the pear halves and wine in a medium-size saucepan that will hold them snugly (if the wine doesn't cover the pears, add a little water). Bring to a simmer over medium-high heat, then add the sugar and cinnamon stick, stirring gently to dissolve the sugar. Reduce the heat to low and simmer, covered, turning the pears once, until they feel tender when pierced with a skewer, about 20 minutes. Let the pears cool in the poaching liquid, then, using a slotted spoon, transfer them to a bowl to cool. Cook the poaching liquid over high heat until it is reduced to about ⅓ cup, about 12 minutes. Cool it to room temperature.

4. To assemble the tart, slice the pears lengthwise into medium-thin slices. Remove the tart from the

Huge hunks of Cabrales and Picon, two of the world's great blue cheeses.

refrigerator. Arrange as many pear slices as will comfortably fit on top of the filling in concentric circles. Spoon a little of the reduced poaching liquid on and around the pears, and to make slicing easier, place the tart in the freezer for about 20 minutes before serving. **MAKES ONE 9-INCH TART**

BASQUE CREAM AND CHERRY TART

PASTEL VASCO

The *pastel vasco* is a symbol of Basqueness every bit as much as the *txapela* or games of jai alai. Mark Kurlansky devotes a whole chapter to it in his *The Basque History of the World.* The sweet, Kurlansky notes, was likely created in the eighteenth century, when it was known as *bistochak* and was rather breadlike. While enjoyed on both sides of the border, the tart is actually more of a cult (and a little bit tastier) on the French side, where it's called *gâteau basque.* Traditionally, the crumbly, nutty pastry is filled with either pastry cream or with preserves made from the local black cherries (this version is similar in taste to linzer torte). In some circles mixing the two fillings would be considered heretical, but the results are so wonderful I find it hard to resist tampering with tradition.

Fresh, sweet cherries in abundance at market in San Sebastián.

FOR THE PASTRY:

3/4 cup slivered almonds
1 cup confectioners' sugar
2 3/4 cups all-purpose flour
1 teaspoon baking powder
10 tablespoons (1 1/4 sticks) unsalted butter, at room temperature
1 large egg
1 large egg yolk
1 teaspoon vanilla extract
1/2 teaspoon almond extract
4 1/2 teaspoons anise liqueur, such as Spanish anís dulce or sambuca

FOR THE FILLING:

1 1/2 cups whole milk
3 large egg yolks
1/3 cup granulated sugar
2 tablespoons plus 1 1/2 teaspoons flour
1 teaspoon vanilla extract
1/2 teaspoon almond extract
1 tablespoon anise liqueur
1/3 cup finely ground almonds

3/4 cup best-quality cherry preserves
1 egg yolk whisked with 1 teaspoon milk, for the glaze

1. Make the pastry: Place the almonds, 2 tablespoons of the confectioners' sugar, and the 2 tablespoons of flour in a food processor and process until the almonds are finely ground. Add the remaining flour and the baking powder and process just to blend.

2. Place the butter, the remaining confectioners' sugar, the egg and egg yolk, vanilla and almond extracts, and liqueur in a large mixing bowl and, using an electric mixer at low speed, cream until creamy and fluffy. Using a rubber spatula, fold in the almond mixture until completely combined. Divide the dough in half, shape each half into a ball, wrap in plastic, and refrigerate for 30 minutes.

3. While the dough is chilling, make the filling: Heat the milk in a medium-size saucepan over medium heat until it is hot but not boiling and begins to bubble around the edges. Remove the milk from the heat. Place the 3 egg yolks, the sugar, and flour in a bowl and whisk until completely blended (the mixture will be very thick). Gradually whisk in the hot milk. Pour the milk mixture into the saucepan and cook over medium heat, whisking constantly, until it thickens and boils, 3 to 5 minutes. Strain the pastry cream through a sieve into a bowl and whisk in the vanilla and almond extracts, liqueur, and the ground almonds. Place a piece of waxed paper directly on top and let cool to room temperature, about 1 hour.

4. Meanwhile, flatten each ball of dough into a disk. Press one of the disks into the bottom and up the side of a 9-inch tart pan with a removable bottom. Cover with plastic wrap. Lightly flour the other disc on both sides, place it between two pieces of waxed paper, and roll it out to a 10-inch circle. Refrigerate both pieces of dough for at least 1 hour.

5. Position a rack in the center of the oven and preheat the oven to 350°F.

6. Spread the cherry preserves on the bottom of the tart. Spread the pastry cream over the preserves, making sure it is evenly distributed. Place the top crust over the tart and pinch the top and bottom edges together, being very careful not to tear the pastry. Brush the top of the tart with the egg yolk glaze and, using a sharp knife, make several slits in the top for the steam to escape. Place the tart pan on a sturdy baking sheet and bake on the center rack until golden brown, about 45 minutes.

7. Transfer the tart to a rack and let cool in the pan completely, at least 2 hours, before serving.

MAKES ONE 9-INCH TART

GRANDMOTHERS OF SILS' APPLE AND YOGURT CAKE

COCA DE POMAS DE ABUELAS DE SILS

One of my trophies from the cooking session with the Grandmothers of Sils (see page 412) was the recipe for this moist, satiny apple cake flavored with lemon yogurt and ratafia, a brown herbal liqueur. Since ratafia is a rarity outside Catalonia, the *abuelas* suggest substituting an anise liqueur. Cointreau or an apple brandy, like Calvados, are also good options. The cake is rustic and unadorned, delicious for breakfast, *merienda* (a late-morning snack), or afternoon coffee or tea. It's best when made a day ahead.

THE GRANDMOTHERS OF SILS

The Grandmothers of Sils are a phenomenon in Catalonia—as famous as superchef Ferran Adrià. Some ten years ago, a dozen old ladies in the drowsy Catalan hamlet of Sils (population 3,000) decided to form a cooking club. Their idea was to exchange and record traditional recipes that would otherwise disappear with their generation. Today the club is sixty grandmothers strong, and when *las abuelas de Sils* recently published a cookbook, it struck such a chord that the volume is now in its eighth printing. And more books are on the way. The grandmothers, meanwhile, are busy appearing on television, being photographed with dashing celebrity chefs, and flying all over Spain to demonstrate their homey dishes in places like the Hotel Ritz in Madrid. Grandmothers in the rest of the country are green with envy.

A TV camera greeted me at the door when I arrived in Sils to have lunch with the grandmothers. A young independent producer was recording every detail of the grandmothers' lives for a reality show. Inside the musty old home of one of the women, a TV news crew was filming yet another program about the *abuelas* of Sils. I felt as if I had walked into a celebrity wedding. Unfazed by it all, the grandmothers, who were sprightly and impeccably coiffed, just kept on cooking. In a vast kitchen with a live hearth and an antique stove, an octogenarian named Rosario was busy stirring a frugal soup of bread, mint, and olive oil. Around the table, a clutch of old ladies sat arguing about how to improve stewed chicken with salsify, their signature dish. Did it need a ground almond *picada* or not? A commotion ensued when it was time to caramelize the *crema catalana,* a custard with a burnt-sugar topping. One grandmother stuck a long-handled flat iron into the hearth. The reporters rushed in. Lights, camera, action . . . With a dramatic swoosh, the red-hot iron branded the sugar. "Encore," the producers demanded.

Finally, we sat down to lunch. The *abuelas'* dishes were straightforward and appropriately grandmotherly, full of the deep rustic flavors one no longer finds in cities these days. Long-simmered pig's feet were improbably paired with snails, an example of the Catalan penchant for combining *mar i muntanya* (sea and mountain). That stewed barnyard chicken flavored with salsify, a deliciously fleshy root traditional in Catalan country cooking, was offered. "People almost stopped using salsify," one grandmother noted, "but we feel it deserves to be resurrected." She rushed back to the kitchen, emerging with *cazuelas* of robust baked macaroni with pork ribs and veal stewed with wild mushrooms. Everyone agreed that the *crema catalana* turned out very fine. As did the big fluffy apple cake flavored with ratafia, an herbal liqueur (you'll find the recipe on the facing page).

For days after my visit, people in Barcelona kept stopping me on the street. "Hey, haven't I see you somewhere?" "Weren't you the one on TV with the famous Grandmothers of Sils?" This was my own five minutes of Catalan fame.

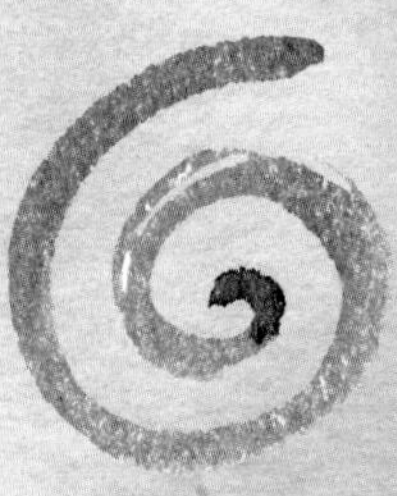

Unsalted butter, for greasing the pan
2 1/4 cups all-purpose flour, plus more for dusting the pan
1 1/4 teaspoons baking powder
4 large eggs
1 1/4 cups granulated sugar
1 cup lemon yogurt
1/4 cup anise liqueur, such as Sambuca
1/2 cup plus 2 tablespoons light olive oil
3 cups finely diced or shredded peeled and cored baking apples, such as Granny Smith or Jonagold, or a combination
Confectioners' sugar, for dusting the cake
Crème fraîche, for serving (optional)

1. Position a rack in the center of the oven and preheat the oven to 350°F. Butter and flour a 9-inch springform pan.

2. Sift the flour and baking powder together in a bowl. Place the eggs and granulated sugar in a large mixing bowl and, using an electric mixer, beat until fluffy and pale yellow, about 1 minute. Beat in the yogurt and liqueur until completely smooth. Working in batches, beat in the sifted flour, alternating it with the olive oil. Gently but thoroughly fold in the apples.

3. Scrape the batter into the prepared springform pan, tap it on a counter to level the batter, then smooth the top with an offset spatula. Bake the cake on the center rack until the top is golden, a cake tester or toothpick inserted in the center comes out clean, and the cake springs back when you touch it, 55 to 65 minutes. Let the cake cool on a rack.

4. Run a thin knife around the side of the cake to loosen it. Remove the side and the bottom of the pan, then place the cake on a cake platter. (The cake can be baked up to 3 days ahead.) Wrap it loosely in plastic until ready to use. Serve the cake sprinkled with confectioners' sugar, accompanied by crème fraîche, if desired. **MAKES ONE 9-INCH CAKE**

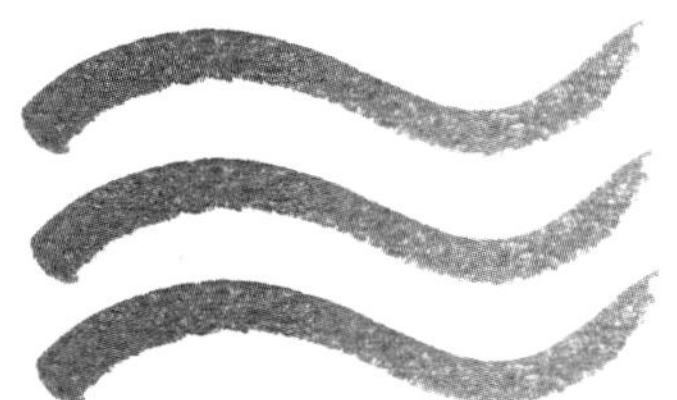

LAURA'S CHEESECAKE WITH PINE NUT GLAZE

TARTA DE QUESO CON FRUTOS SECOS

The Casa Robles restaurant is as famous a landmark in Seville as the Moorish Giralda tower. In charge of desserts here is Laura Robles, the proprietor's daughter, whose sweets winningly combine tradition and innovation. With its glasslike glaze of pine nuts and white raisins, Laura's cheesecake is as luscious as it is dramatic to look at. A mixture of cream cheese and ricotta is a good approximation of the creamy San Millán cheese Laura uses. And while she suggests a clear apple juice for the glaze, a light white dessert wine, such as a muscat or sweet riesling, would be another interesting option. If you're not in the mood to make the glaze, just stir the pine nuts into the cheesecake batter. As the cake bakes, the nuts will rise up, forming a natural topping.

FOR THE CHEESECAKE:

Unsalted butter, for greasing the pan
1 pound (two 8-ounce packages) cream cheese
15 to 16 ounces ricotta
6 tablespoons heavy (whipping) cream
1 1/2 cups sugar
3 1/2 tablespoons all-purpose flour
6 large eggs
2 large egg yolks
2 tablespoons fresh lemon juice
1/2 teaspoon orange flower water (optional)
Grated zest of 1 large lemon
Grated zest of 1 medium-size orange

FOR THE GLAZE:

1/3 cup golden raisins
1/3 cup sweet or medium-dry sherry, or 1/3 cup sweet white wine
2 1/4 teaspoons (1 envelope) unflavored gelatin
1 cup clear apple juice or light white dessert wine
3/4 cup lightly toasted pine nuts (see page 267)

1. Make the cheesecake: Position a rack in the center of the oven and preheat the oven to 350°F. Bring a kettle of water to a boil. Line the bottom of a 10-inch springform pan with aluminum foil to seal it, fold the edges underneath, then assemble the pan. Butter the sides of the pan.

2. Place the cream cheese, ricotta, cream, and sugar in a large mixing bowl and, using an electric mixer, beat at medium speed until well blended and fluffy, about 2 minutes. Beat in the flour until incorporated. Gradually add the eggs and the egg yolks, beating well after each addition and scraping down the side of the bowl. At low speed, beat in the lemon juice, orange flower water, if using, and the lemon and orange zests. (Alternatively, the batter can be mixed in a food processor; add the eggs one at a time through the feed tube.)

3. Scrape the batter into the prepared springform pan and give it a light tap on the counter to level the batter. Set the pan in a large baking dish and pour in enough hot water to come halfway up the sides of the springform pan. Bake the cheesecake until the top looks set but the cake still jiggles when you tap the pan, about 55 minutes. Leave the cake in the oven for 1 hour with the door ajar. Transfer the cake to a rack and let cool for another hour. Drape plastic wrap over the cake and refrigerate for 6 hours or overnight.

4. Make the glaze: Place the raisins and sherry in a small microwave-safe bowl and microwave for 1 minute on high power, or heat in a small saucepan over medium-high heat until the sherry is very hot. Off the heat, let the raisins soak for about 30 minutes. Drain the raisins and pat thoroughly dry with paper towels.

5. Place the gelatin in a small saucepan, sprinkle 2 tablespoons of the apple juice over it, and let stand for 5 minutes. Add the remaining apple juice and heat over medium-low heat, stirring, until the gelatin is completely dissolved. Pour the gelatin mixture into a metal bowl and place it in the freezer until it just begins to thicken but is still completely pourable, 15 to 25 minutes. Start checking the gelatin after 15 minutes and do not leave it in the freezer too long; it sets very quickly.

6. To glaze the cheesecake, first lightly press the raisins and pine nuts into the top, distributing them evenly. They should completely cover the cake. Using a tablespoon, dab the gelatin mixture over the cake until it is covered in a thin, even layer (you will probably not need all of the gelatin mixture.) Refrigerate the cake, uncovered, until the glaze is completely set, about 2 hours.

7. Run a thin knife around the sides of the cake to loosen it, then remove the side of the pan. Transfer the cheesecake to a platter and serve. **MAKES ONE 10-INCH CAKE**

CATALAN COCA WITH CUSTARD & CANDIED FRUIT

COCA DE SANT JOAN

In Catalonia, the summer solstice fiesta of Sant Joan is celebrated with this sweet, spongy *coca* topped with a lush smear of pastry cream and a colorful scattering of candied fruit and nuts. Although historically the bread was round (as an homage to the sun), today the *coca* is shaped into a rectangle and accompanied by sips of sweet muscatel wine. Spectacularly delicious, it's now as popular for Christmas as it is for Sant Joan.

The base of the cake consists of an airy, buttery *brioix* (brioche) dough that's quite similar to the French original but less tricky to make. Because the dough is too soft to knead by hand, you'll need a mixer with a dough hook attachment.

Cut into dainty rectangles, this enormous *coca* is ideal for a large holiday party. To serve a smaller group, don't attempt to halve the dough recipe, make the whole batch, use what you need to make a smaller *coca,* and freeze the rest for later (covered with plastic wrap, the dough will keep for about 2 months). This is one of my all-time favorite festive sweets.

2 packed teaspoons fresh yeast, or 1 package active dry yeast (2 1/2 teaspoons)
1/2 cup warm whole milk (about 115°F)
4 tablespoons sugar, plus 1/3 cup sugar for decorating the cake
1/2 teaspoon fine sea salt
2 1/3 cups all-purpose flour, plus more for sprinkling on the dough
3 large eggs
1 teaspoon aniseed, crushed in a mortar
1 teaspoon almond extract
1 tablespoon orange flower water
14 tablespoons (1 3/4 sticks) unsalted butter, cut into small pieces, at room temperature
Pastry Cream (recipe follows)
1/2 cup chopped mixed candied fruit (see Note)
1/3 cup pine nuts, or more to taste

1. Place the yeast, milk, and 1 tablespoon of the sugar in a warmed medium-size bowl and stir until the yeast dissolves. Let stand until foamy, about 5 minutes. Stir in the salt and ⅓ cup of the flour. Set the sponge in a warm place, cover it with plastic wrap, and let rise for 1½ hours.

2. Place the eggs, 3 tablespoons of the sugar, and the aniseed, almond extract, and orange flower water in the warmed bowl of a stand mixer fitted with a paddle attachment and beat at medium speed until the eggs are pale yellow. (This can also be done with a handheld mixer.) Scrape the risen sponge into the mixer bowl and beat briefly. With the mixer running, add the butter, 2 or 3 pieces at a time, beating for 2 to 3 minutes at medium speed (the butter

DESSERTS

won't be completely melted). Beat in the remaining 2 cups flour, ½ cup at a time. Exchange the beater for a dough hook. Knead the dough until it is smooth and elastic and easily pulls away from the bowl, about 8 minutes. The dough will be very soft, almost like butter.

3. Lightly sprinkle a large warmed bowl with flour and scrape the dough into it. Sprinkle a little more flour evenly on top to prevent the dough from drying, cover it with plastic wrap, and set in a warm place. Let rise until doubled in bulk, about 1½ hours.

4. Deflate the dough by lifting it by the edges and dropping it back into the bowl. Sprinkle the top with flour, cover the bowl again with plastic wrap, and refrigerate for 2 to 3 hours. It will rise slightly. (The dough can be prepared up to this point a day ahead.)

5. Let the dough come to room temperature (about 20 minutes), then place it on a very large baking sheet and pat it into a rectangle about 16 by 8 inches. Cover with a clean linen kitchen towel and let rise in a warm place for about 45 minutes.

6. Position a rack in the center of the oven and preheat the oven to 425°F.

7. Smear the dough generously with the Pastry Cream, leaving a ½-inch border on all sides (you may not need all of the Pastry Cream). Scatter the candied fruit and pine nuts decoratively on top. Bake the *coca* on the center rack for exactly 10 minutes.

8. While the *coca* is baking, place the remaining ⅓ cup sugar in a bowl and sprinkle 2 teaspoons cold water over it. Using your hands, work the water into the sugar until it forms clumps (if the clumps are too moist, add a couple more tablespoons of sugar). Remove the *coca* from the oven and lower the oven temperature to 350°F. Working very quickly and gently, so as not to deflate the dough, pat the sugar clumps all over the top of the *coca.* Bake the *coca* until the edges are golden brown and a cake tester or toothpick inserted in a part not covered with Pastry Cream comes out clean, about 15 minutes.

9. Transfer the *coca* to a rack to cool. Cut it into rectangles (3 by 1¼ inches is a nice size) and arrange on a plate. Alternatively, serve the *coca* on a large wooden board and let your guests cut their own.

NOTE: Catalans use bright-red cherries and gaudy green candied melon, along with sugared fruit such as pineapple, citron, and orange peel. Improvise with what you can easily get, as long as the topping will look colorful and the fruit is of respectable quality. Some recipes call for soaking the fruit in sweet wine before baking; if you can spare some muscatel, give it a try. **MAKES ONE 16- BY 8-INCH FLAT BREAD**

PASTRY CREAM

CREMA PASTELERA

Basic pastry cream gets a delicious whiff of cinnamon and lemon zest.

1 1/2 cups whole milk
Zest from 1 lemon, in 1 piece
1 medium-size cinnamon stick
3 large egg yolks
1/2 cup sugar
2 1/2 tablespoons all-purpose flour

1. Place the milk, lemon zest, and cinnamon stick in a heavy medium-size saucepan and bring to a simmer over medium heat. Remove the saucepan from the heat and let steep for about 30 minutes. Strain and reheat the milk until it is hot but not boiling and begins to bubble around the edges. Remove the saucepan from the heat.

2. Place the egg yolks, sugar, and flour in a bowl and whisk until completely blended (the mixture will be very thick). Gradually whisk in the hot milk. Transfer the milk mixture to the saucepan and cook over medium heat, whisking constantly, until it thickens and boils, 3 to 5 minutes. Strain the pastry cream through a sieve into a bowl and place a piece of waxed paper directly on the surface. Let cool to room temperature, about 1 hour. **MAKES ABOUT 2 CUPS**

LOCO FOR CHOCOLATE

CHOCOLATE CUSTARDS WITH A CITRUS CLOUD

NATILLAS DE CHOCOLATE CON NATA Y CITRICOS

The pairing of dark chocolate and citrus is unbeatable, which is why I'm so in love with this recipe from the legendary Basque chef Juan Mari Arzak. Taking off on *natillas*—the thin custard that the Spanish adore—he flavors it with chocolate and tops it with a foamy cream whipped with citrus-infused syrup and lightened with beaten egg whites. The play of textures and flavors is to die for.

4 large egg yolks
9 tablespoons sugar
2 cups whole milk
6 ounces best-quality bittersweet chocolate, grated or very finely chopped, plus a little grated chocolate, for garnish
2 tablespoons fresh orange juice
Grated zest of 1 lemon
Grated zest of 1 large orange
Grated zest of 1/2 pink grapefruit
1 cup heavy (whipping) cream, chilled
2 large egg whites, chilled (see Note)
Small mint leaves, for garnish

1. Place the egg yolks and 5 tablespoons of the sugar in a large bowl and whisk until well blended.

2. Place the milk in a heavy medium-size saucepan and bring to a simmer over medium heat. Gradually whisk the hot milk into the egg yolk mixture. Return the egg mixture to the saucepan and stir over medium heat until the custard thickens enough to lightly coat the back of a spoon, about 12 minutes. (It should have the consistency of a thin crème anglaise.) Do not let the custard boil, or it will curdle. Off the heat, add the chocolate, stirring constantly in one direction until it is melted and smooth. Strain the custard into a bowl, let it cool a little, then divide among 6 or 7 dessert glasses or small wineglasses. Cover the glasses with plastic wrap and refrigerate for at least 2 hours.

3. Meanwhile, place 3 tablespoons sugar and the orange juice in a small saucepan and bring to a simmer over medium heat, stirring until the sugar dissolves. Add the citrus zests and simmer for another minute. Remove the citrus syrup from the heat and let stand while the mousses chill.

4. When ready to serve, whip the cream until medium-stiff peaks form. Scrape the citrus syrup into the cream and fold until well combined. Using clean, dry beaters, beat the egg whites with the remaining 1 tablespoon sugar until they are shiny and form stiff peaks. Fold half of the whites into the whipped cream mixture, then thoroughly fold in the rest.

5. To serve, top each glass of chocolate cream with a generous amount of citrus cream and garnish with a little grated chocolate and a mint leaf. To eat, dig into the bottom of the glass to combine the chocolate and the foam in one spoonful. **SERVES 6 OR 7**

NOTE: The egg whites in this recipe remain uncooked. Be sure to use the freshest refrigerated eggs from a top-quality purveyor.

ADOLFO'S WARM CHOCOLATE SOUFFLE CAKES

PASTELES DE CHOCOLATE DE ADOLFO

A signature dessert at the Adolfo restaurant in Toledo, these airy individual chocolate cakes are almost as spongy and soft as soufflés. Adolfo Muñoz, the chef-proprietor, serves them with house-made vanilla ice cream infused with fresh thyme. You can make your own Thyme Ice Cream or use store-bought ice cream scattered with thyme leaves. Make sure the ramekins are buttered and dusted well with sugar; otherwise the cakes will stick. (For more about Adolfo, see page 241.)

4 tablespoons (1/2 stick) unsalted butter, cut into pieces, plus 1 tablespoon at room temperature for buttering the ramekins
3/4 cup confectioners' sugar, sifted, plus more for dusting the ramekins
4 1/2 ounces bittersweet chocolate, grated or finely chopped
6 large eggs, separated
1 small pinch of fine sea salt
1/4 cup all-purpose flour
Thyme Ice Cream (page 437), or 1 pint store-bought vanilla ice cream plus 4 teaspoons coarsely chopped fresh thyme leaves

1. Position a rack in the center of the oven and preheat the oven to 425°F.

2. Generously butter the bottom and the sides of eight 1-cup ramekins with the 1 tablespoon of softened butter and line the bottoms with rounds of parchment paper. Butter the paper and dust the sides of the ramekins with confectioners' sugar.

3. Place the chocolate and remaining 4 tablespoons butter in a microwave-safe bowl and melt it on high power, checking it every 10 seconds. Stir the chocolate mixture until smooth.

4. Place the egg whites with a pinch of salt in a large mixing bowl and, using a handheld electric mixer, beat them on medium speed until soft peaks form. Add ¼ cup of the confectioners' sugar, 1 tablespoon at a time, beating well after each addition. Increase the speed to high and beat until the whites are glossy, 3 to 4 minutes.

5. Place the egg yolks and the remaining ½ cup confectioners' sugar in another large bowl and whisk until pale yellow and fluffy. Whisk the chocolate mixture into the egg yolks, then gradually whisk in the flour. Using a large rubber spatula, fold one third of the beaten whites into the yolk mixture, then fold in the rest until no white streaks remain.

6. Spoon enough batter into each of the prepared ramekins to reach three fourths of the way up the side. Set the ramekins on a large baking sheet and bake on the center rack until the cakes are puffed and just set in the middle, about 15 minutes (see Note). Leave the oven on.

7. Let the cakes cool in the ramekins until the edges of the cakes begin to pull away from the sides of the ramekins, about 5 minutes. Invert the cakes onto a large baking sheet, then peel off the parchment paper and set the cakes right side up on the baking sheet. Reheat the cakes in the oven for 2 minutes. Transfer the cakes to plates and serve with the ice cream. **MAKES 8 SMALL CAKES**

NOTE: The cakes can be prepared ahead through Step 6 and stored in the ramekins at room temperature for up to 3 hours. Before serving, invert the cakes as directed in Step 7, peeling off the parchment paper, and reheat them for 3 to 4 minutes in a 425°F oven.

WHITE CHOCOLATE MOUSSE WITH PASSION FRUIT GELEE

MOUSSE DE YOGUR Y CHOCOLATE BLANCO CON GELATINA DE FRUTA DE PASSION

The very first time I visited the Guggenheim in Bilbao, I'm not sure what impressed me more, Frank Gehry's titanium extravanganza or the fittingly avant-garde lunch prepared by the museum restaurant's former chef Bixente Arrieta. The meal ended with a battery of miniature futuristic desserts, stylishly arranged in shot glasses, on skewers, and on porcelain spoons. Among them were glasses of sensational white chocolate mousse trapped under a cap of passion fruit gelée. Bixente has since left, and I never did get the recipe. But my version comes pretty close. While I normally find white chocolate too cloying, when paired with the tartness of yogurt and passion fruit, it tastes just right.

2 cups plain whole-milk yogurt
7 to 8 ounces best-quality white chocolate, finely chopped or grated
1/4 cup heavy (whipping) cream
2 1/4 teaspoons (1 envelope) unflavored gelatin
1 cup strained fresh passion fruit juice, or 1 cup thawed frozen passion fruit puree (see Note)
1/3 to 1/2 cup sugar

1. Place the yogurt in a sieve lined with cheesecloth and set over a bowl. Let the yogurt drain for about 2 hours. Stir well before using.

2. Place the white chocolate and cream in the top of a double boiler, set over simmering water, and stir until the chocolate is completely melted, 3 to 5 minutes. Scrape the mixture into a large bowl. Let stand until cool and just beginning to thicken, about 30 minutes, stirring occasionally. Using a spatula, thoroughly stir the drained yogurt into the chocolate mixture until completely combined.

3. Divide the chocolate mousse among 6 small squat glasses, martini glasses, or glass bowls and refrigerate, covered, until slightly set, 30 minutes.

4. Meanwhile, place the gelatin in a small saucepan, sprinkle 2 tablespoons of the passion fruit juice over it, and let stand for 5 minutes. Add the remaining passion fruit juice and heat over medium-low heat, stirring, until the gelatin completely dissolves. Add ⅓ cup sugar, stirring until it dissolves. Taste the passion fruit mixture; if it seems too tart, add the remaining sugar. Let the passion fruit mixture cool to room temperature.

5. Remove the mousse from the refrigerator and slowly pour about 2½ tablespoons of the passion fruit mixture over each, being careful not to mix the passion fruit with the mousse. Cover the glasses with plastic wrap and chill until set, about 2 hours. Then serve. **MAKES 6 MOUSSES**

NOTE: Frozen passion fruit puree is available at many Hispanic markets and specialty food stores.

White Chocolate Mousse with Passion Fruit Gelée

CHOCOLATE MOUSSE WITH OLIVE OIL AND FLAKY SALT

MOUSSE DE CHOCOLATE CON ACEITE DE OLIVA Y SAL MALDON

This thrilling Dalíesque marriage of flavors—dark chocolate and fruity olive oil, with a strange and wonderful accent of salt—seems to spell out *nueva cocina.* But actually, Catalan chocolate–olive oil desserts go back further in time. As historians have told me, after World War II, when luxury ingredients such as chocolate were strictly rationed, Catalans would melt a piece of chocolate, spread it on toast, and sprinkle olive oil and a bit of salt on top for a sweet-savory treat (you'll find the recipe on page 167). Avant-garde chefs took the idea and ran with it.

As you serve this sweet, prepare for drama: Some people go wild over it, others raise their eyebrows, but either way, it will be the talk of the evening. While the mousse is easy to make, good ingredients are essential: the best, darkest chocolate with at least 70 percent cacao content; an extra-fruity, slightly peppery olive oil that can stand up to the chocolate; and the flaky British sea salt called Maldon (look for it at specialty food shops). Because the dessert is so explosively flavorful and unusual, serve tiny scoops of it in stylish glasses or glass bowls. And only to your most adventurous friends.

SEPARATION ANXIETY

This chocolate mousse consists of ganache, a simple, classic emulsion of chocolate and cream used for truffles. While the cooking method, suggested to me by the test kitchen team of the *Los Angeles Times,* is fairly foolproof, emulsions are fragile things and sometimes they do break. You will know if it does—it's when the mixture looks oily or slightly curdled. To repair the ganache, use the following method from the chocolate diva, Alice Medrich: Heat one quarter cup heavy (whipping) cream to a simmer, transfer it to a medium-size bowl, and begin whisking in the broken ganache, bit by bit, as if making mayonnaise. It will come together.

1 cup heavy (whipping) cream
9 ounces best-quality bittersweet chocolate (at least 70 percent cacao), finely chopped or coarsely ground in a food processor
Best-quality fruity, peppery extra-virgin olive oil
Flaky sea salt, such as Maldon
Very thin unflavored Italian bread sticks, for serving (optional)

1. Place the cream in a small, heavy saucepan and heat it over medium heat until it is hot but not boiling and begins to bubble around the edge. Place the chocolate in a metal bowl and pour the hot cream over it all at once. Let the cream stand for 2 to 3 minutes while the chocolate melts. Using a rubber spatula, slowly stir the chocolate mixture in a circular motion, starting at the center of the bowl and working your way out to the side. Be careful not to stir too vigorously, or you will add too much air to the ganache. Keep stirring until all the chocolate is melted and completely blended with the cream. Scrape the mixture into a bowl, cover it with plastic wrap, and let sit at room temperature for at least 4 hours. The mixture will firm as it sits.

2. To serve, using a melon baller, scoop balls of the mousse into small wide tumblers, or "minimalist" glass bowls. Pour 2 to 3 teaspoons of the olive oil around but not over the mousse and judiciously sprinkle salt on top. If desired, serve with very thin breadsticks for dipping into the mousse. **MAKES 6 TO 8 SMALL SERVINGS**

HOT CHOCOLATE WITH MERINGUE STARS

CHOCOLATE CON CROCANTES DE ALMENDRA

Adapted from a dessert of Josean Martínez Alija, the very young but astonishingly talented chef at the Guggenheim Museum restaurant in Bilbao, this is perfect to serve during the winter holidays. Josean's cutting-edge version features an extremely concentrated unsweetened chilled cocoa soup touched with salt and afloat with meringue stars and a scoop of house-made Star Anise Ice Cream. I opted for something cozier, adding solid chocolate to the cocoa powder for a richer texture, serving it hot, and skipping the iconoclastic salt. You can make Star Anise Ice Cream yourself or use store-bought ice cream—vanilla or coffee—sprinkling the dessert with a little cinnamon, grated nutmeg, or freshly ground star anise.

FOR THE MERINGUES:

- 2 large egg whites, chilled
- 1 small pinch of fine sea salt
- 1/2 cup minus 1 tablespoon superfine sugar
- 1/3 cup finely ground lightly toasted almonds (see page 267)

FOR THE CHOCOLATE:

- 1 1/4 cup best-quality unsweetened cocoa powder, such as Valrhona
- 2 tablespoons instant espresso or coffee powder (see Note)
- 1 cup heavy (whipping) cream
- 8 ounces best-quality bittersweet chocolate, grated or finely chopped
- Star Anise Ice Cream (page 437), or 1 pint store-bought vanilla or coffee ice cream

1. Make the meringues: Position a rack in the center of the oven and preheat the oven to 250°F. Line two baking sheets with parchment paper (or better yet, Silpat pan liners).

2. Place the egg whites and salt in a mixing bowl and, using an electric mixer, beat them on medium speed until soft peaks form. Add the superfine sugar, 1 tablespoon at a time, beating well after each addition. Increase the speed to high and continue beating until the whites are stiff and glossy, 2 to 3 minutes. Using a wooden spoon, carefully fold the ground almonds into the egg white mixture.

3. Spoon the meringue into a pastry bag fitted with a ⅜-inch plain tip. Pipe out star shapes on the prepared baking sheets, spacing them evenly. Bake the meringues on the center rack until they are dry, about 1 hour, switching the position of the baking sheets halfway through the cooking. Let cool in the oven with the door ajar for 30 minutes. Then carefully peel the stars off the parchment paper and transfer them to a rack to cool completely, about 1 hour. (The meringues can be stored in an airtight container for up to 3 days.)

4. Make the chocolate: Place 2 cups water in a heavy medium-size saucepan and bring to a simmer over medium heat. Stir in the cocoa and coffee powders and cook, stirring, for 2 to 3 minutes. Add the cream and bring to a simmer. Stir in the chocolate, reduce the heat to medium-low, and cook, stirring in one direction, until completely melted.

5. Pour the hot chocolate into wide glasses or big, pretty cups. Top each with a small scoop of ice cream and a meringue star. Serve at once. **SERVES 12 TO 14**

NOTE: You can use ¼ cup brewed espresso in place of the instant. Reduce the water to 1¾ cups.

HEALING WITH CHOCOLATE

It is of the greatest benefit, when made with the necessary purity of ingredients, for the stomach and the chest; it maintains and restores the natural warmth of the body; it nourishes; it dissipates and destroys malignant humors; and fortifies and maintains the voice.

—Juan de la Mata, *Arte de Repostería* (The Art of Confectionary), 1747

MARICEL'S 17TH-CENTURY HOT CHOCOLATE

CHOCOLATE CALIENTE DE MARICEL, SIGLO XVII

My friend Maricel Presilla is amazing. A brilliant chef and restaurateur with a PhD in medieval Spanish history, she is an expert in the cuisines of Latin America and one of the world's preeminent chocolate scholars, as evident in her erudite tome *The New Taste of Chocolate*. Adapted from a recipe in her book, this hot chocolate—spiced with achiote, dried rose buds, vanilla, cinnamon, and chile, among other things—is the closest you'll ever come to a taste of the drink as it might have been enjoyed by the Spanish nobility in the Age of Discovery. Maricel's inspiration was the first European treatise on chocolate, written by Antonio Colmenero de Ledesma in 1644, some 125 years after the Spaniards had encountered the potent pairing of chocolate and spices in Mexico. The potion is completely bewitching. One sip, and you'll understand why hot chocolate was deemed so addictive as to be dangerous.

8 cups water or whole milk
1/4 cup achiote (annatto) seeds
12 blanched almonds
12 toasted hazelnuts (see page 267), skinned
2 plump vanilla beans, preferably Mexican
1/4 ounce dried rose buds (rosa de Castilla) (see box, this page)
1 tablespoon aniseed
2 medium-size cinnamon sticks, preferably canela (Ceylon cinnamon)
2 whole dried arbol or serrano chiles
8 ounces best-quality bittersweet chocolate, finely chopped
1 medium-size pinch of salt
1 tablespoon orange flower water (optional)
Sugar

1. Place the water or milk and the achiote seeds in a heavy 3-quart saucepan and bring to a low boil over medium heat, stirring frequently. Reduce the heat to very low and simmer until the achiote colors the liquid bright orange, about 10 minutes.

2. Meanwhile, finely grind the almonds and hazelnuts in a mini food processor.

3. Strain the achiote liquid, discarding the solids; return the liquid to the saucepan. Cut the vanilla bean in half lengthwise and, using the tip of a small knife, scrape the seeds into the saucepan. Add the vanilla bean pods and the ground nuts, rose buds, aniseed, cinnamon sticks, and chiles. Bring the liquid to a boil over high heat, reduce the heat to low, and simmer until infused with the spices, about 10 minutes. Add the chocolate and salt and stir until the chocolate melts, 1 to 2 minutes. Remove the saucepan from the heat and add the orange flower water, if using. Taste for sweetness, adding sugar to taste. Strain the hot chocolate through a fine sieve into a tall narrow pot.

4. Froth the chocolate until foamy using a Mexican wooden *molinillo* (chocolate beater), a cappuccino frother, or an immersion blender. Or whisk the hot chocolate vigorously with a wire whisk. Serve at once. **SERVES 8 TO 10**

OLD FLAVORS

If you can't find dried rose buds for this special hot chocolate, substitute a quarter teaspoon of rose water or omit them. All the other ingredients can be easily found at Hispanic groceries and some supermarkets. For best results Maricel suggests using chocolate made with Venezuelan cacao beans (such as El Ray Gran Saman or Chocovic Ocumare), which would have been the likely choice in seventeenth-century Spain. For a more chocolaty taste, use all water; for a softer, more luscious drink, use milk.

LIQUID GOLD

In the seventeenth century, Spaniards flavored their hot chocolate with aniseed, dried rosebuds, nuts, chiles, and achiote. In the twenty-first century, adventurous Spanish pastry chefs are spiking their dark, sumptuous creations with balsamic vinegar, jasmine, pink peppercorns, even smoke! Are Spanish taste buds reverting to type?

In 1502, Columbus encountered chocolate off the coast of present-day Honduras, where he was accompanied by his son Ferdinand. The pair intercepted a Mayan trading canoe stocked with cacao and observed the Indians drop a few almondlike beans to the ground. Ferdinand later wrote that the Indians panicked so utterly, he thought "an eye had fallen from their head." Columbus might not have realized that cocoa beans carried the status of currency in that part of the world (sacks of beans were even considered an acceptable form of tax payment). However, chocolate's value and ceremonial significance weren't lost on the Spanish colonizers in Mexico, who reported back of Aztec nobility drinking frothy bitter cacao from golden vessels.

Probably introduced to Spain in 1544 by a group of Kekchi Maya chaperoned by Dominican friars, chocolate became an instant sensation—helped along by rumors of its aphrodisiac properties that trickled in from the New World. Bernal Díaz del Castillo, author of *History of the Conquest of New Spain,* reported that chocolate was served to the emperor Montezuma from goblets of fine gold before he went to visit his wives. Other accounts credited it with magical healing powers or medicinal properties. Initially suspicious of chocolate, Spanish clergy engaged in endless debates about whether it was liquid or solid and thus permissible—or not—during Lent. But soon, even the church gave in, falling under chocolate's dark sensuous spell. According to historical documents, the Grand Inquisitor himself indulged in huge cups of hot chocolate, prepared for him by the nuns at his service.

While Mayan and Aztec aristocrats took their chocolate cold and usually bitter (or occasionally sweetened with honey), Spaniards got the bright idea of mixing in another colonial product: sugar cane. Spanish missionary nuns in Mexico were probably the first to sweeten the bitter ground cocoa with sugar; apparently, the sisters amassed small fortunes selling this potion to the chocolate-craving colonial elite. The Spaniards in Mexico (particularly ladies and clergy) became so addicted to chocolate that "their strength failed them if they did not have it at their accustomed hour," according to one report. The Spanish further perfected the art of chocolate drinking by frothing it with a nifty wooden beater called a *molinillo,* an improvement on the Aztec technique of pouring it from vessel to vessel. From the early seventeenth century on, hot chocolate was de rigueur in Spain, a treat especially enjoyed by noble *señoras,* who would throw afternoon parties, serving the drink with sweet dainties like candied fruit, sponge cakes, and nougat.

Spaniards' affection for hot chocolate has never waned. Every *madrileño* who ever partied until *madrugada* (the wee hours of dawn) knows the address of Chocolatería San Ginés, an ancient café in Madrid conveniently located near most of the major nightclubs. At 7 A.M. lines snake around the block as revelers wait to be revived with a cup of puddinglike chocolate so thick, rich, and dense it can qualify as an alternative energy source. The classic accompaniment is a *churro,* a crisp fried cruller for dipping.

If you haven't dunked *churros* in chocolate at dawn, you haven't been to Spain.

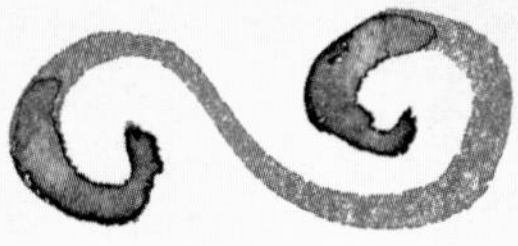

CHOCOLATE-COVERED ALMOND CAKE

TORTA DE ALMENDRAS CON TRUFA DE CHOCOLATE

Almond cakes are so ubiquitous in Spain that after a while you stop noticing them—too much of a good thing. This one, however, frosted with a dark chocolate ganache, is in a league of its own.

FOR THE ALMOND CAKE:

8 ounces (slightly more than 1 1/2 cups) blanched whole almonds, preferably marcona, lightly toasted (see page 267)
1 cup sugar
4 large eggs, at room temperature
1/3 cup all-purpose flour
1/4 cup light olive oil
1/4 cup whole milk
2 teaspoons grated lemon zest
1/2 teaspoon ground cinnamon
Unsalted butter, for greasing the pan

FOR THE RUM SYRUP:

3/4 cup dark rum
1/2 cup sugar

FOR THE CHOCOLATE GANACHE:

1/2 cup heavy (whipping) cream
6 ounces best-quality bittersweet chocolate (at least 70 percent cacao), grated in a food processor

1. Make the almond cake: Place the almonds and ½ cup of sugar in a food processor and process until very finely ground.

2. Place the eggs in a warm mixing bowl and, using an electric mixer, beat them until fluffy, about 1 minute. Add the remaining ½ cup sugar and continue beating at high speed until the eggs are pale yellow and approximately triple in volume, 3 to 4 minutes. Working in batches, beat in the almond mixture and the flour, alternating with the olive oil and milk. Stir in the lemon zest and cinnamon.

3. Position a rack in the center of the oven and preheat the oven to 350°F. Line the bottom of a 9-inch springform pan with a circle of waxed paper. Generously butter the paper and the sides of the pan.

4. Scrape the batter into the prepared springform pan and tap it on a counter to level the batter. Bake the cake on the center rack until a cake tester or toothpick inserted in the center comes out clean, about 45 minutes. Let the cake cool on a rack for about 20 minutes.

5. While the cake is cooling, make the rum syrup: Place the rum and sugar in a small saucepan. Add ½ cup water and heat, stirring, over medium heat until the sugar is completely dissolved, about 2 minutes.

6. Run a thin knife around the side of the cake to loosen it, then remove the side of the pan. Invert the cake onto a plate and remove the bottom of the pan and the waxed paper. Prick the cake all over with a fork and generously brush it with the rum syrup, waiting for the syrup to be absorbed before brushing on more. Cover the cake loosely with plastic wrap and let stand for about 1 hour to fully absorb the syrup.

7. Make the chocolate ganache: Place the cream in a small, heavy saucepan and heat it over medium heat until it is hot but not boiling, and begins to bubble around the edge. Place the chocolate in a metal bowl and pour the hot cream over it all at once. Let the cream stand while the chocolate melts, 2 to 3 minutes. Using a rubber spatula, slowly stir the chocolate mixture in a circular motion, starting at the center of the bowl and working your way out to the side. Be careful not to stir too vigorously, or you will add too much air to the ganache. Keep stirring until all the chocolate is melted and completely blended with the cream. (If by some chance the ganache "breaks"—begins to look oily or slightly curdled—you can fix it following the instructions on page 422.) Let the ganache stand at room temperature until thickened but spreadable, about 1 hour.

8. Place the cake on a cake platter, spread the ganache generously over the top and the sides, and chill for 30 minutes to 1 hour before serving. **MAKES ONE 9-INCH CAKE**

MOUSSES, CUSTARDS & CUPS

HAZELNUT MOUSSE WITH ESPRESSO GRANITA

MOUSSE DE AVELLANAS CON GRANIZADO DE CAFE

So utterly magical is the combination of hazelnuts, caramel, and strong coffee it seems that every modern restaurant in Spain offers some kind of riff on this dessert. Granitas are a cinch to make, but if you're pressed for time, top the hazelnut mousse with a small dollop of good store-bought chocolate sorbet. For a different texture you can add some broken amaretti, pieces of pound cake, or macaroons to the bottom of each glass.

- 1/2 cup plus 1/3 cup sugar
- 1/3 cup heavy (whipping) cream at room temperature, plus 3/4 cup chilled cream, or more if needed
- 1/4 cup brewed espresso or strong black coffee
- 1/4 cup hazelnut liqueur, dark rum, or brandy
- 5 large eggs
- 1 cup toasted hazelnuts (see page 267), skinned and finely ground
- Espresso Granita (page 446)
- 2 tablespoons grated dark chocolate, for serving

1. Place the ½ cup sugar and 3 tablespoons water in a heavy medium-size saucepan and bring to a simmer over medium-high heat, stirring until the sugar dissolves. Once the sugar is dissolved, cook the caramel without stirring until it begins to bubble and color, about 5 minutes. At it cooks, swirl the pan gently and brush down the sides with a wet pastry brush to remove the sugar crystals. Continue cooking until the caramel turns dark amber, 1 to 2 minutes longer, swirling the pan carefully and watching that the caramel doesn't burn. As soon as the syrup is dark amber, turn off the heat and add the ⅓ cup cream and the espresso, standing back, as the mixture will sputter vigorously. Using a wooden spoon, stir the caramel thoroughly, then cook it over low heat, stirring, until it is smooth, 1 minute. Let the caramel cool to room temperature, stirring occasionally.

2. Place the liqueur, the remaining ⅓ cup sugar, and the eggs in a metal mixing bowl and whisk to mix. Keep whisking until the eggs are well beaten and the mixture is frothy.

3. Set the mixing bowl over a saucepan of barely simmering water, without letting the bottom of the bowl touch the water. Whisk and stir the custard until it is thick enough to coat the back of a spoon (it will register 160°F on a candy thermometer), 6 to 8 minutes. Remove the custard from the heat, let cool for about 5 minutes, then stir in the hazelnuts. Transfer the custard mixture to a blender, add the caramel, and blend until very smooth, adding a little cold cream if the mixture seems too thick to blend and scraping down the sides of the blender container. Scrape the custard mixture into a bowl and let cool to room temperature.

4. Whip the ¾ cup chilled cream until stiff peaks form. Set aside about ½ cup of the whipped cream and refrigerate it, covered. Gently but thoroughly fold the remaining whipped cream into the custard until completely blended. Cover the mousse with plastic wrap and chill for 2 to 4 hours. (It won't be as thick as mousses containing gelatin.)

5. To serve, place some coffee granita in a parfait glass or other tall, slender glass. Top with some of the hazelnut mousse, then with more granita. Spoon a dollop of the reserved whipped cream on top and sprinkle it with grated chocolate. Repeat with the remaining granita, mousse, and whipped cream, working quickly so that the granita doesn't melt. Serve at once. **SERVES 6 TO 8**

CREMA DE YOGUR CON GELATINA DE MIEL

At a recent meal at Roig Robí, a Barcelona restaurant I adore, I fell in love with this dessert from the mother-daughter chef team of Mercé Navarro and Inma Crosas. It consisted of a pretty glass bowl filled with thick yogurt, which was topped with squares of honey gelée and a dollop of mandarin sorbet that practically burst with citrus flavors. The sweet felt as healthy and virtuous as it was delicious. Homemade sorbets add a special touch and are a simple proposition, if you own an ice-cream maker. However, if you have a source for high-quality mandarin or orange sorbet, feel free to substitute. This dessert is extremely easy, but everything needs to be made ahead, so plan accordingly.

- 1 1/2 teaspoons (1 envelope) unflavored gelatin
- 2/3 cup honey, preferably orange blossom
- 4 cups plain goat's milk yogurt, or Greek yogurt or other good-quality whole-milk yogurt, preferably organic
- Tangerine Sorbet (page 442), or 1 pint store-bought tangerine sorbet

1. Place the gelatin in a small saucepan, sprinkle 2 tablespoons water over it, and let stand for 5 minutes. Add the honey and ⅓ cup water and bring to a simmer over medium-low heat, stirring until the honey liquefies and the gelatin dissolves. Pour the mixture into an 8-inch-square baking pan and refrigerate, covered, until set, 2 to 3 hours.

2. Meanwhile, place the yogurt in a sieve lined with cheesecloth and set over a bowl (if you are using Greek yogurt it is not necessary to drain it). Let the yogurt drain in the refrigerator for about 2 hours. Stir well before serving.

3. To serve, using a sharp knife, cut the honey gelée into roughly 1½-inch diamonds or squares. Spread about ½ cup of the drained yogurt in each of 8 pretty glass serving bowls, then top with a dollop of sorbet and a few pieces of gelée. Serve at once.

SERVES 8

ROSE WATER GELEE WITH YOGURT & BEET GRANITA

GELATINA DE ROSAS CON YOGUR Y GRANIZADO DE REMOLACHA

Ethereally light and completely unusual, here's a sweet guaranteed to end a meal with a bang. It's adapted from the guru of avant-garde Spanish cooking, Ferran Adrià. The first time I served it for a dinner party, I wasn't sure how my guests would react to such a cutting-edge confection. They went wild, and I've been making it ever since. Serve it in small glasses as a palate cleanser before a more substantial dessert.

- 8 sweet fragrant strawberries, hulled and chopped
- 2 tablespoons sugar
- 1 1/2 teaspoons (1 envelope) unflavored gelatin
- 3 to 4 teaspoons rose water
- 2 1/2 cups plain whole-milk yogurt
- 1 tablespoon confectioners' sugar
- Beet and Strawberry Granita (page 444)

1. Place the strawberries, sugar, and 1¼ cups water in a small saucepan and bring to a boil over high heat, stirring, until the sugar dissolves. Reduce the heat to low, cover the saucepan, and simmer until the liquid is well infused with strawberry flavor, about 20 minutes.

2. Meanwhile, place the gelatin in another small saucepan, sprinkle 2 tablespoons water over it, and let stand for 5 minutes. Strain the hot strawberry

liquid into the saucepan with the softened gelatin, discarding the solids. Place the saucepan over medium-low heat and cook, stirring, until the gelatin completely dissolves. Stir in the rose water. Divide the gelée among 8 very small glasses, cover with plastic wrap, and refrigerate until set, 2 to 3 hours.

3. Meanwhile, place the yogurt in a sieve lined with cheesecloth and set over a bowl. Let the yogurt drain in the refrigerator for about 2 hours. Transfer the drained yogurt to a bowl, add the confectioners' sugar, and stir until smooth.

4. To serve, spoon a dollop of yogurt on the gelée in each glass and top with some granita. Serve at once. **MAKES 8 SMALL SERVINGS**

MY CHRISTMAS BREAD PUDDING

BUDIN DE PAN

One winter, the year that I was renting a flat in Madrid, a friend bestowed an enormous *roscón de reyes* on me—a Christmas ring cake adorned with sugar and candied fruit. We picked and nibbled for days, and when it got stale, I baked the leftovers into tasty pudding. As American bakeries don't usually carry *roscón,* at home I've made a delicious version with panettone, the Italian Christmas cake. If you can't find panettone, this will also be good made with brioche. Just increase the amount of sugar to two thirds of a cup and toss in some diced candied fruit.

1 pound panettone (available at Italian bakeries and some markets), cut into 1-inch cubes
4 large eggs
2 large egg yolks
1/2 cup sugar
1 1/2 cups milk
1 1/2 cups heavy (whipping) cream
4 tablespoons (1/2 stick) unsalted butter, cut into small pieces

1. Position a rack in the center of the oven and preheat the oven to 400°F.

2. Spread the panettone cubes on a large rimmed baking sheet and bake on the center rack, stirring once, until lightly toasted, about 10 minutes. Turn the oven off.

3. Place the eggs, egg yolks, sugar, milk, and cream in a large bowl, and whisk until completely smooth. Place the toasted panettone in a round earthenware *cazuela* 10 to 12 inches in diameter or a 2-quart shallow baking dish. Pour the egg mixture over it and let stand for 1 hour, stirring occasionally. (The bread pudding can be refrigerated, covered with plastic wrap, for several hours before baking.)

4. Preheat the oven to 350°F.

5. Dot the top of the bread pudding with butter and bake until puffy and golden and the custard is set, about 1 hour. Let cool for about 30 minutes, then serve. **SERVES 6 TO 8**

FRUIT TREATS

BAR PINOTXO FRUIT SALAD

MACEDONIA DE FRUTAS, BAR PINOTXO

There are few food rituals in Barcelona more revered than a late, post-shopping breakfast at Bar Pinotxo, the venerable food counter by the entrance to La Boqueria market. By 11 A.M. the feeding frenzy is on, with vendors and shoppers thronging the stools. But my favorite time to hang out there is around eight in the morning, when I can observe the cooks at work. One familiar sight is a young girl dicing fruit for Pinotxo's signature *macedonia,* a fruit salad that, depending on the season, will contain apples, pears, kiwis, mangos, and ruby pomegranate seeds. Like everything at Pinotxo, the salad is simple and no-nonsense but wonderful, relying on the bounty of the produce surrounding the tiny kitchen. It makes a pretty and easy dessert, but I like it best as part of a brunch buffet or even as a late-afternoon snack, with a dollop of organic yogurt. Feel free to vary the fruit and to add berries, slivered mint, and/or a dash of liqueur, such as Grand Marnier.

1 cup fresh orange juice
2 tablespoons fresh lemon juice, or more to taste
1 1/2 tablespoons sugar, preferably superfine, or more to taste
1 large apple, peeled, cored, and diced
1 large ripe but firm Bosc pear, peeled, cored, and diced
2 ripe but firm mangoes, peeled and diced
5 kiwis, peeled and diced
Seeds from 1 large pomegranate
Yogurt or sorbet, for serving (optional)

1. Place the orange and lemon juices and the sugar in a bowl and whisk to mix.

2. Place the apple, pear, mangoes, kiwis, and pomegranate seeds in a large bowl, add the orange juice mixture, and toss to mix. Taste for sweetness, adding more lemon juice or sugar as necessary. Let the salad stand until the fruit is nicely macerated in the orange juice, about 2 hours at room temperature. The fruit salad can be refrigerated, covered, for up to 6 hours. Serve the salad in pretty glasses or glass bowls, with a dollop of yogurt or sorbet, if desired. **SERVES 6**

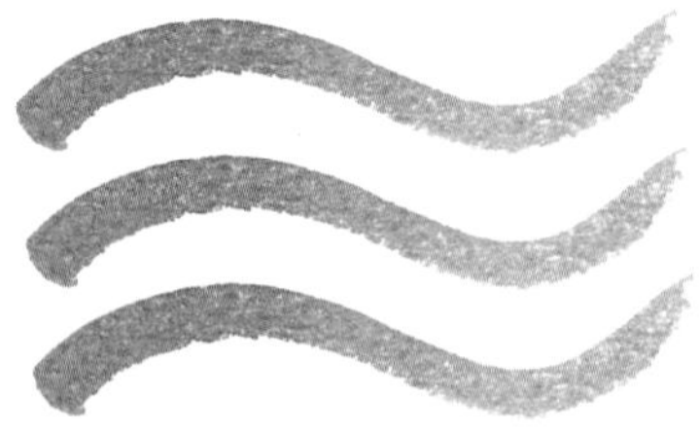

FRUIT MERINGUE BROCHETTES

CHUPA CHUPS JULIO VERNE

Fantastical lollipops, often in outrageously outré flavor combinations, are a signature at El Bulli, Ferran Andrià's temple of experimental cuisine. Coming down to earth for his book dedicated to home cooking, Adrià devised these easy and entertaining meringue-coated fruit skewers. *Chupa Chups Julio Verne,* or Jules Verne lollipops, is what he calls them, no doubt because their look resembles something out of old-fashioned science fiction. Apple halves serve as a base so the skewers can stand upright in the oven. For serving, the "cloud-covered" fruit skewers look dramatic stuck into an unpeeled half pineapple.

2 large egg whites
1/2 cup sugar
1 large apple, cut in half
8 small strawberries
8 cubes (each 1 inch) pineapple
8 cubes (each 1 inch) mango
8 slices (each 1 inch thick) ripe but firm banana

1. Position a rack in the lower third of the oven, then preheat the broiler.

2. Place the egg whites in a mixing bowl and, using an electric mixer, beat them on medium speed until soft peaks form. Add the sugar 1 tablespoon at a time, beating well after each addition. Increase the speed to high and continue beating until the whites are stiff and glossy, 2 to 3 minutes. Spoon the meringue onto a plate.

3. Place the apple halves cut side down on a baking sheet. Place 2 pieces of fruit on each of 16 small skewers, mixing up the combinations. Using a wide knife, spread the meringue evenly all over the fruit. Poke one end of each skewer into an apple half. Broil the brochettes in the lower third of the oven until the meringue is golden and caramelized in spots, about 30 seconds. (You can also use a kitchen blowtorch, if you have one, to brown the meringue.) Serve at once. **MAKES 16 SKEWERS**

CHRISTMAS COMPOTE WITH SPICED RIOJA

COMPOTA NAVIDEÑA

When I spent the holiday season in Madrid, I kept overhearing ladies exchange recipes for this classic Christmas compote, which combines dried and fresh fruit with red wine infused with vanilla and spices. Dried fruit in Spain—figs, peaches, cherries—is of exceptional quality, so seek out excellent organic dried fruit for the compote. If the prunes are very soft, add them along with the fresh fruit. Adjust the amount of sugar depending on the sweetness of the apple and pear; the liquid shouldn't be syrupy sweet. The compote is wonderful on its own or with a scoop of Honey and Cinnamon Ice Cream (page 439) and/or pound cake. If you're serving the compote over ice cream or cake, you might want to strain it. Set aside the fruit, then cook the poaching liquid until it is reduced by half.

2 medium-size cinnamon sticks
6 cloves
1 vanilla bean, cut in half lengthwise
8 black peppercorns
1 long strip fresh orange peel without white pith
1 bottle (750 milliliters) red Rioja wine (3 1/4 cups)
1/4 cup brandy
1/2 cup sugar, or more to taste
6 dried Calimyrna figs, cut in half lengthwise
3/4 cup dried apricots, preferably Californian, cut in half
1 cup dried cherries or peaches (cut in half), or a combination of the two
8 to 10 prunes, cut in half
1 medium-size Granny Smith apple, peeled, cored, and cut into 1-inch chunks
1 medium-size, ripe but firm Bosc pear, peeled, cored, and cut into 1-inch chunks
1/2 cup seedless dark grapes, cut in half
1 handful of pomegranate seeds, for garnish
1/4 cup lightly toasted pine nuts (see page 267), for garnish

1. Place the cinnamon sticks, cloves, vanilla bean, peppercorns, and orange peel on 2 layers of cheesecloth and tie the cheesecloth shut.

2. Place the wine, brandy, sugar, and the cheesecloth bag in a 3-quart saucepan. Add ½ cup water and stir to mix. Bring to a boil over high heat, stirring until the sugar dissolves. Add the figs, apricots, cherries, and prunes. Reduce the heat to low, cover the saucepan, and simmer until the fruit begins to soften, 10 minutes.

3. Add the apple and pear to the saucepan and stir very gently to distribute the fruit evenly in the liquid. Cover the saucepan again and simmer for another 10 minutes. The apple and pear should be quite soft. Add the grapes and simmer until all the fruits are tender, about 5 minutes. Let cool completely, then serve in glass bowls, garnished with the pomegranate seeds and pine nuts. **SERVES 6**

Plump figs are just as good on their own as they are baked into a tart or cooked in a compote.

COOL COMFORTS

LOURDES'S LUSCIOUS STRAWBERRY ICE CREAM

HELADO DE FRESAS DE LOURDES

My elegant Madrid friend Lourdes Plana is the ultimate foodie. A former editor of *Restauradores* (a restaurant magazine) and a recipe columnist for a very popular women's weekly called *Mía,* she now organizes Madrid-Fusión, a high-profile food conference that draws the world's greatest chefs. She is the kind of cook who can turn something as basic as strawberry ice cream into a sensational treat. Unlike most strawberry ice creams, which rely on an egg-based custard, this one is just pure berries mixed with whipped cream. The berry flavor is particularly vivid, and the texture is somewhere between parfait and gelato. Make it in strawberry season when the berries are at their fragrant best. Lourdes suggests serving this freshly churned, or at least not frozen solid.

1 pound fragrant ripe strawberries, hulled and chopped (about 2 3/4 cups)
5 tablespoons fresh lemon juice
1 cup sugar
1 1/3 cups heavy (whipping) cream, chilled

1. Place the strawberries, lemon juice, and sugar in a food processor and puree.

2. Place the cream in a large bowl and whip it until medium-stiff peaks form. Thoroughly fold in the pureed strawberries. Refrigerate the strawberry mixture until chilled, then freeze it in an ice-cream maker following the manufacturer's instructions.
MAKES ABOUT 1 QUART

PEACH ICE CREAM WITH MINTED PEACH COMPOTE

HELADO DE MELOCOTON CON COMPOTA DE MELOCOTON

In this delightful recipe, the great Catalan chef Carme Ruscalleda of the Michelin two-star Restaurant Sant Pau proves that you don't need an ice-cream maker to have a frozen treat prepared *al momento.* Diced peaches macerated in muscatel infused with mint complement a no-fuss ice cream made of cream cheese and frozen peaches. Ripe white peaches are lovely in the compote.

AROMATIC ICE-CREAM FLAVORS: BEYOND VANILLA

A basic ice cream custard is the little black dress of frozen desserts, infinitely adaptable to flavors beyond the predictable vanilla. As Spanish chefs will attest, herbal ice creams are wonderful with warm tarts and fall fruit desserts, particularly those made with apples; tea-flavored ice creams add a touch of adventure to chocolate desserts; and pepper ice creams pair beautifully with both berries *and* chocolate.

The Basic Custard you'll find here can be infused with any of the flavors that follow. Just bring the milk mixture to a boil with the desired seasoning and let it stand. Heating the milk mixture in a microwave oven is a neat trick, as microwaving releases the fragrance of the aromatics better than cooking on a stove top does. For a lighter, more vividly flavored ice cream, double the amount of milk and omit the cream.

BASIC CUSTARD

2 cups whole milk
2 cups heavy (whipping) cream
Ice-cream flavoring (suggestions follow)
8 large egg yolks
2/3 cup sugar
1 small pinch of salt

1. Place the milk and cream in a large, heavy saucepan and bring just to a boil over medium-high heat with the flavoring of your choice. Or place the milk, cream, and flavoring in microwave-safe container and microwave on high power for 3 minutes. Let stand, covered, for as long as directed for the particular flavoring and strain if necessary, then bring back to a boil and turn off the heat.

2. Place the egg yolks, sugar, and salt in a medium-size bowl and whisk until very smooth. Pour about a quarter of the hot cream mixture into the eggs, stirring constantly and vigorously. Stir another quarter of the hot cream into the egg mixture, then whisk it into the saucepan with the remaining cream.

3. Cook the custard over medium-low heat, stirring constantly (make sure to stir around the bottom and side of the pan), until it thickens enough to coat the back of a spoon, about 5 minutes. Never let the custard boil or the eggs will curdle. (If the custard does curdle a little, a whiz in a blender should fix it.) As soon as the custard thickens, immediately pour it through a fine sieve set over the bowl. Cover the bowl with aluminum foil and refrigerate the custard until chilled, at least 4 hours. (The custard can be made up to 2 days ahead.)

4. Freeze the chilled custard in an ice-cream maker following the manufacturer's instructions. **MAKES ABOUT 1½ QUARTS**

VARIATIONS: BEYOND VANILLA

BAY LEAF: Use 6 large fresh bay leaves or 4 dried bay leaves. Let stand for 2 hours. Strain before making the custard. This ice cream is sensational with *tarte tatin* and other warm apple desserts.

BERGAMOT: Heat the milk mixture and 1/4 cup loose Earl Grey tea leaves in a saucepan until it just begins to boil. Cover the pan and let steep for 15 minutes. Or add 5 Earl Grey tea bags to the hot milk mixture. Strain the milk mixture, pressing on the tea leaves or bags to extract as much liquid as possible, then make the custard.

JASMINE: Heat the milk mixture and 1/2 cup loose jasmine tea leaves in a saucepan until it just begins to boil. Cover the pan and let steep for 15 minutes. Or add 7 jasmine tea bags to the hot milk mixture. Strain the milk mixture, pressing on the tea leaves or bags to extract as much liquid as possible, then make the custard.

LEMON AND LAVENDER: Use 1/3 cup dried lavender leaves and the zest of 2 lemons cut into long strips. Let stand for 1 hour. Strain before making the custard.

PEPPER: For **white pepper** ice cream, use 1 1/2 teaspoons crushed white peppercorns along with the seeds and pod of 1 vanilla bean. Let stand for 1 hour. Strain before making the custard.

For **pink peppercorn** ice cream, use 1/4 cup lightly crushed pink peppercorns. Let stand for 30 minutes. Strain before making the custard.

ROSEMARY AND ORANGE: Use 2 large, gently bruised fresh rosemary sprigs and the zest of 1 orange cut into long strips. Let stand for 1 hour. Strain before making the custard.

SAFFRON: Use 1 large pinch of saffron, pulverized in a mortar and steeped in 2 tablespoons hot milk, along with the seeds and pod of 1 vanilla bean. Let stand for 30 minutes. Strain before making the custard.

STAR ANISE: Use 4 large star anise, broken into points, and 1 medium-size cinnamon stick. Let stand for 1 hour. Strain before making the custard.

THYME: Use 4 large, gently bruised fresh thyme sprigs along with the seeds and pod of 1 vanilla bean. Let stand for 2 hours. Strain before making the custard.

FOR THE PEACH COMPOTE:

- 4 ripe aromatic peaches, blanched, peeled, pitted, and diced
- 1 1/4 to 1 1/2 cups white dessert wine, such as Spanish white muscatel, Italian moscato, or American muscat
- 2 large fresh mint sprigs

FOR THE ICE CREAM:

- 1 pound frozen peaches, chopped
- 4 ounces cream cheese (see Note)
- 1/2 cup evaporated milk, chilled (see Note)
- 1 tablespoon fresh lemon juice
- 1/2 cup confectioners' sugar

1. Make the peach compote: Place the peaches in a bowl and add just enough wine to cover. Twist and bruise the mint sprigs slightly and nestle them in the compote. Let stand for 30 minutes. Remove the mint and let the peaches macerate in the wine for another 30 minutes.

2. Make the ice cream: Place the peaches, cream cheese, evaporated milk, lemon juice, and confectioners' sugar in a food processor and pulse until medium-smooth, scraping the side of the bowl occasionally. If the peaches thaw too much as you work, transfer the ice cream to a bowl and freeze for about 20 minutes. Otherwise, serve the ice cream immediately, topped with the peach compote. **SERVES 6 TO 8**

NOTE: For the best results, chill the cream cheese and evaporated milk in the freezer for about 30 minutes before using.

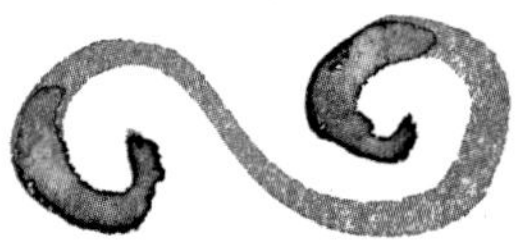

RICE PUDDING ICE CREAM WITH CARAMEL-COFFEE SAUCE

HELADO DE ARROZ CON LECHE CON SALSA DE CARAMELO AL CAFE

Rice pudding finds its way into all kinds of exciting desserts in modern Spanish kitchens. It's turned into ethereal creams and foams, set with gelatin and used as a filling for tarts, and transformed into a frozen treat, as here. For anybody who loves rice pudding *and* ice cream, this is heaven. (Of course, the rice pudding is also delicious on its own, unfrozen.) The ice cream is best served soft and freshly churned; when frozen too long it tends to solidify and becomes somewhat grainy. If you're making it ahead, let it sit at room temperature for about twenty minutes before serving. The caramel and coffee sauce is a perfect foil, but I also love this ice cream with a tart fruit puree or with drizzles of sweet, raisiny Pedro Ximénez sherry. I thank María Jesús Gil de Antuñano, one of Spain's most prolific and popular recipe developers, for allowing me to adapt her recipe.

4 cups whole milk
1/3 cup short-grain rice, either Spanish or arborio
1/4 cup plus 1/3 cup sugar
1 medium-size cinnamon stick
1 long piece of lemon zest
2 cups evaporated milk
3 large egg yolks
1 small pinch of salt
Caramel-Coffee Sauce (recipe follows)

1. Place the milk, rice, 1/4 cup of the sugar, the cinnamon stick, and lemon zest in a heavy, medium-size saucepan over medium-high heat and bring to a boil, stirring. Reduce the heat to medium and simmer, stirring often, until the rice is tender and the mixture is thick, about 35 minutes. Discard the cinnamon stick and the lemon zest.

2. While the rice is cooking, heat the evaporated milk in a heavy, medium-size saucepan over medium heat until it is hot but not boiling and bubbles appear around the edges.

3. Place the egg yolks, the remaining 1/3 cup of sugar, and the salt in a bowl and whisk until very smooth. Pour about a quarter of the hot evaporated milk into the egg mixture, stirring constantly and vigorously. Stir in another quarter of the hot milk, then whisk the yolk mixture into the saucepan with the remaining milk.

4. Cook the custard over medium-low heat, stirring constantly (make sure to stir around the bottom and side of the pan), until it thickens enough to coat the back of a spoon, about 5 minutes. Never let the custard boil or the eggs will curdle. (If the custard does curdle a little, a whiz in a blender should fix it.) As soon as the custard thickens, immediately pour it through a fine sieve set over a bowl.

5. When the rice is ready, let it cool for about 5 minutes, then stir it thoroughly into the custard. Let the mixture cool for about 10 minutes, then puree it to medium-fine in a blender. Scrape the pureed mixture back into the bowl, place a round of waxed paper directly on top, and refrigerate until chilled.

6. Freeze the chilled custard in an ice-cream maker following the manufacturer's instructions. **MAKES A LITTLE MORE THAN 1 QUART**

CARAMEL-COFFEE SAUCE

SALSA DE CARAMELO AL CAFE

This sauce is delicious over a number of sweets, from simple vanilla ice cream to regular rice pudding or the bread pudding on page 431.

- 1/2 cup heavy (whipping) cream
- 1/4 cup espresso or strong-brewed coffee
- 2 tablespoons brandy
- 1/2 cup sugar
- 2 tablespoons light corn syrup
- 2 tablespoons unsalted butter

1. Place the cream, espresso, and brandy in a microwave-safe bowl and stir to combine. Microwave on high power for 1 minute. Set aside.

2. Place the sugar, corn syrup, and ¼ cup water in a heavy, medium-size saucepan and bring to a simmer over medium-high heat, stirring, until the sugar dissolves. Once the sugar is dissolved, cook the caramel without stirring until it begins to bubble and color, about 6 minutes. As it cooks, swirl the pan gently and brush down the sides with a wet pastry brush to remove the sugar crystals. Continue cooking until the caramel turns dark amber, 1 to 2 minutes longer, swirling the pan carefully and watching that the caramel doesn't burn. As soon as the syrup is dark amber, turn off the heat and add the cream and coffee mixture and the butter, standing back, as the mixture will sputter vigorously. Using a wooden spoon, stir the sauce thoroughly, then cook it over low heat, stirring, until the sauce is completely smooth, about 1 minute. Let the sauce cool to room temperature, stirring a few times. It will thicken as it stands. The sauce will keep for 1 day, covered, in the refrigerator. Stir before serving.

MAKES ABOUT 1 CUP

HONEY AND CINNAMON ICE CREAM

HELADO DE MIEL Y CANELA

With its smooth, silky texture and warm autumnal flavors, this ice cream makes a lovely accompaniment to anything from a simple pound cake to tarts and bread pudding.

- 3 medium-size cinnamon sticks, broken in half
- 1 plump vanilla bean
- 2 cups heavy (whipping) cream
- 2 cups whole milk
- 1/3 cup light, floral honey, such as orange blossom
- 8 large egg yolks
- 2/3 cup sugar
- 1 small pinch of salt

1. Place the cinnamon sticks in a skillet (do not use a nonstick skillet) over medium heat and cook until fragrant, 2 to 3 minutes.

2. Cut the vanilla bean in half lengthwise and, using the tip of a small knife, scrape the seeds into a large saucepan. Add the vanilla bean pod, toasted cinnamon sticks, cream, milk, and honey and bring to a boil over medium-high heat, stirring to dissolve the honey. Turn off the heat and let the mixture infuse for 2 hours (or longer if you'd like a stronger cinnamon flavor).

SPANISH ICE CREAM: THE LATEST IN COOL

Combining ice with food or drink goes back millennia, to China, Mesopotamia, Greece, and Rome. Credit for Spain's love affair with *helado* can be traced to Moorish caliphs sweltering in Granada who had ice hauled down from the cool peaks of the Sierra Nevada to make sherbets—refreshing slushes of fruit, honey, and ice. In the 1560s Basilius Villafranca, a Spanish physician living in Rome, produced the first solid cream-based chilled dessert, employing ice sprinkled with saltpeter. By the seventeenth century, Spain's ice trade was booming; muleteers transported it from mountain tops to big cities, where it was stored in vast underground ice houses called *pozos de nieve*. Though Spain is as fond of ice cream as any hot Mediterranean country, its *helados* were delicious but not especially memorable. Until, that is, Ferran Adrià and his pastry-chef brother Albert came along.

I will never forget my first tasting menu at Adrià's restaurant in 1997. Among other avant-garde provocations—smoked water mousse, sardines with raspberry foam—I sampled a stunning Parmesan ice-cream sandwich, a thrillingly outlandish sorbet of caramelized eggplant, a celestial savory scoop of frozen *ajo blanco* (almond gazpacho), and a crunchy caramel tube filled with an intriguing smoked bacon ice cream. I've never looked at vanilla ice cream again.

Blurring boundaries between hot and cold and sweet and savory became one of Adrià's signature trademarks, soon copied by young chefs all over Spain. No longer confined to dessert status, ice creams, sorbets, and granitas appear on modern menus in shot glasses as tapas or as cool counterpoints to fish, meat, or vegetables. White asparagus with truffle ice cream, anyone? Or how about raw oysters with a cool dollop of soft fennel ice cream and a flourish of spicy orange granita? Thanks to powerful emulsifying machines like the Thermomix and to secret alchemical formulas that include converted sugars and high-tech stabilizers, Spain's techno ice creams are smoother and airier than anything you might have tasted before. The flavors are bright and attention grabbing, ranging from sweet (smoked chocolate, caramelized quince, rice pudding) to savory (cèpes, artichokes, foie gras, sea urchins) to savory-sweet (cheese, olive oil, sherry vinegar). A space-age contraption called a Paco Jet, which aerates frozen mixtures at very high speed, allows Spanish chefs to garnish dishes with *polvo helado* (frozen dust) of, say, cheese, smoked potato, or chiles. The latest sensation? Liquid nitrogen: a gas that flash-freezes at negative 196°C. A substance dipped in the vaporous nitro bath can emerge solid on the outside yet liquid within; it can even be both cold *and* hot. Ice creams and sorbets freeze in an instant, with all the ingredients perfectly integrated and softly gelled. Not to stop there, Adrià is playing with a teppan nitro, his sci-fi take on the Japanese-style teppanyaki griddle—it freezes instead of heating.

An old-fashioned stand selling ice cream and *horchata* (a creamy Valencian drink) seems worlds away from new-wave frozen treats.

3. Strain the infused cream into a clean saucepan, discarding the cinnamon sticks and vanilla bean, and bring it back to a boil. Turn off the heat.

4. Place the egg yolks, sugar, and salt in a medium-size bowl and whisk until very smooth. Pour about a quarter of the hot cream into the egg mixture, stirring constantly and vigorously. Stir another quarter of the hot cream into the egg mixture, then whisk it into the saucepan with the remaining cream.

5. Cook the custard over medium-low heat, stirring constantly (make sure to stir around the bottom and side of the pan), until it thickens enough to coat the back of the spoon, about 5 minutes. Never let the custard boil or the eggs will curdle. (If the custard does curdle a little, a whiz in a blender should fix it.) As soon as the custard thickens, immediately pour it through a fine sieve set over a bowl. Cover the bowl with aluminum foil and refrigerate the custard until chilled, at least 4 hours. (The custard can be made up to 2 days ahead.)

6. Freeze the chilled custard in an ice-cream maker following the manufacturer's instructions. **MAKES ABOUT 1½ QUARTS**

ROQUEFORT ICE CREAM WITH PEARS

HELADO DE ROQUEFORT CON PERAS

Combining the cheese and dessert courses into one delicious package, cheese ice creams are featured on many modern Spanish menus. Blue cheese ice cream in particular is a tasty and terrific idea. While pears make perfect sense, the ice cream can also be paired with other fruit, especially figs, either fresh, roasted, or in a quick compote. Instead of Roquefort, you can substitute Gorgonzola. And try making the ice cream with a mild or aged goat cheese, too.

FOR THE ROQUEFORT ICE CREAM:

2½ cups half-and-half
2 tablespoons light corn syrup
6 ounces Roquefort, finely crumbled
3 large egg yolks
⅓ cup sugar
1 small pinch of salt

FOR THE PEAR COMPOTE:

1¼ cups dry white wine
5 tablespoons sugar
1 vanilla bean
1 large strip of lemon zest
4 medium-size, ripe but firm Bartlett pears, peeled, cored, and cut into small dice
1 to 3 teaspoons fresh lemon juice

1. Make the Roquefort ice cream: Place the half-and-half, corn syrup, and Roquefort in a heavy medium-size saucepan and heat over medium-low heat, stirring, until the cheese is completely melted, 5 to 7 minutes. Do not let the half-and-half boil. If the mixture doesn't quite seem smooth enough, strain it into a clean saucepan.

2. Place the egg yolks, sugar, and salt in a medium-size bowl and whisk until very smooth. Pour about a quarter of the hot half-and-half mixture into the egg mixture, stirring constantly and vigorously. Stir another quarter of the half-and-half into the egg mixture, then whisk it into the saucepan with the remaining half-and-half.

3. Cook the custard over medium-low heat, stirring constantly (make sure to stir around the bottom and side of the pan), until it thickens enough to coat the back of a spoon, about 5 minutes. Never let the custard boil or the eggs will curdle. (If the custard does curdle a little, a whiz in a blender should fix it.) As soon as the custard thickens, immediately pour it through a fine sieve set over a bowl. Cover the bowl with aluminum foil and refrigerate the custard until chilled, at least 4 hours. (The custard can be made 2 days ahead.)

4. Freeze the chilled custard in an ice-cream maker following the manufacturer's instructions, then transfer it to a container and freeze it briefly, about 1 hour. The ice cream is best freshly churned. If making ahead, let it sit at room temperature for 10 to 15 minutes before serving.

5. Make the pear compote: Place the wine, sugar, and ¾ cup water in a 2-quart saucepan and bring to a simmer over medium heat. Cut the vanilla bean in half lengthwise and, using the tip of a small knife, scrape the seeds into large saucepan. Add the vanilla bean pod and the lemon zest and simmer to infuse the wine mixture, 5 minutes. Add the pears and a little more water if there doesn't seem to be enough liquid in the pan and bring the liquid back to a simmer. Reduce the heat to low, cover the pan, and simmer the pears until they are very soft but still hold their shape, about 20 minutes. Add lemon juice to taste and transfer the compote to a bowl. Refrigerate, covered, until chilled, 1 to 2 hours.

6. To serve, remove and discard the lemon zest and the vanilla bean pod from the compote. Place some compote in small wide glasses or glass bowls and top with a scoop of Roquefort ice cream. **SERVES 8**

TANGERINE SORBET

SORBETE DE MANDARINA

This intensely citrusy sorbet is ultrarefreshing. Serve it with the Yogurt Cream with Honey Gelée (page 429) or on its own to offset rich chocolate desserts. Look for plump, juicy tangerines rather than clementines, which will take forever to juice.

1 1/4 cups sugar
1/3 cup light corn syrup
3 cups tangerine juice (from about 10 medium-size tangerines)
1/3 cup fresh lemon juice
2 tablespoons finely grated tangerine zest

Place the sugar, corn syrup, and ¼ cup water in a small saucepan and bring to a boil over high heat, stirring until the sugar dissolves. Reduce the heat to medium and cook until a fairly thick syrup forms, 2 to 3 minutes. Transfer the syrup to a heatproof pitcher or large bowl, add the tangerine and lemon juices and the tangerine zest, and stir well to mix. Refrigerate the sorbet mixture until chilled, then freeze it in an ice-cream maker following the manufacturer's instructions. **MAKES ABOUT 1½ QUARTS**

GREAT GRANITAS

Moorish nobility in medieval Andalusia chilled down with sherbets made with ice transported from the mountains. In present-day Spain, *granizados* (granitas) shine in contemporary desserts and even in appetizers and entrées. A breeze to prepare and requiring no fancy equipment other than a metal pan and a sturdy fork, the unusual *granizados* here, both sweet and savory, are perfect summer refreshers.

To make a granita, pour the mixture into a shallow metal dish, such as a 13- by 9- by 2-inch baking pan or a 9-inch metal pie plate (the shallower the dish, the faster the granita will freeze). Cover the granita with aluminum foil and place it on a level shelf in the freezer. Freeze until ice crystals begin to form on the sides and the bottom of the pan, about 30 minutes, then stir it with a fork and

A little romance, a little dessert—a popular scene at local Spanish bars.

return it to the freezer. Keep stirring and mashing the granita as the ice crystals continue to form, about every 30 minutes or so, until all the liquid has been completely frozen. This should take about 3 hours for most flavors, longer for granitas containing alcohol. Then, fluff and mash the granita one final time and leave it in the freezer for another 20 minutes or so before serving. If you're making the granita ahead of time, transfer it to a plastic container and keep it frozen for as long as you need. Fluff with a fork before serving.

How much sugar you add to the recipes that follow will depend on your taste. Keep in mind, however, that the sweetness fades once the granita is frozen.

AGUA DE VALENCIA GRANITA

GRANIZADO "AGUA DE VALENCIA"

Valencia's signature cocktail, *Agua de Valencia* is an enticing blend of freshly squeezed orange juice, *cava,* and a liqueur. Each bar has its "secret" recipe. Transformed into granita, it's a treat with sliced strawberries soaked in a bit of Cointreau or alongside a chocolate or citrus dessert, such as Valencian Orange Tart (page 402).

2 cups fresh juice from sweet oranges
3 tablespoons superfine sugar, or more to taste
1/3 cup cava
2 tablespoons orange liqueur, such as Cointreau

Place the orange juice, sugar, *cava,* and orange liqueur in a bowl and stir until the sugar dissolves. Taste and add more sugar, if desired. Freeze as instructed on page 443. **SERVES 4 TO 6**

BEET & STRAWBERRY GRANITA

GRANIZADO DE FRESAS Y REMOLACHA

The natural sugar and striking ruby-red color of beets make them a natural in a pastry kitchen—a fact not lost on chef Ferran Adrià, who plays with beets endlessly. As a dessert, serve this in the Adrià-inspired Rose Water Gelée with Yogurt and Beet Granita (page 430). Or if you omit the strawberries, the beet granita can be a stand-in for borscht, with a dollop of crème fraîche or frozen yogurt and a garnish of diced cucumber and dill. If serving as borscht, double the recipe and increase the amount of lemon juice to taste.

1 medium-size beet (about 12 ounces), peeled and diced
8 to 10 sweet fragrant strawberries, hulled and chopped
1/4 cup sugar
2 teaspoons fresh lemon juice

Place the beet, strawberries, sugar, and 2 cups water in a medium-size saucepan and heat over medium-high heat, stirring until the sugar dissolves. Reduce the heat to medium-low and cook, uncovered, until the liquid has reduced to about

1 cup, 20 to 25 minutes. Strain into a bowl, pressing on the solids to extract as much liquid as possible. Stir in the lemon juice and let cool completely. Freeze as instructed on page 443. **SERVES 4 TO 6**

BLOODY MARY GAZPACHO GRANITA

GRANIZADO DE GAZPACHO A LA "BLOODY MARY"

Serve this zesty granita as a summertime appetizer, scooped into martini glasses or hollowed-out tomatoes and topped with poached or grilled shrimp. Or, spoon it on raw oysters or clams.

- 1 pound ripe tomatoes, blanched, seeded, and chopped
- 1/4 cup chopped Italian (frying) pepper
- 2 tablespoons chopped celery
- 1 large garlic clove, chopped
- 1 tablespoon sherry vinegar, preferably aged
- 4 1/2 teaspoons light corn syrup
- 1/4 teaspoon Tabasco sauce, or more to taste
- 1 teaspoon grated horseradish
- 1/2 teaspoon freshly ground black pepper
- Coarse salt (kosher or sea)
- Marjoram leaves, for garnish

Place the tomatoes, Italian pepper, celery, garlic, vinegar, corn syrup, Tabasco sauce, horseradish, and black pepper in a food processor and process until smooth. Taste for seasoning, adding salt to taste. Refrigerate until the flavors develop, about 1 hour. Freeze as instructed on page 443. Serve garnished with marjoram leaves. **SERVES 6**

CAMPARI & BLOOD ORANGE GRANITA

GRANIZADO DE CAMPARI Y NARANJA SANGRINA

This granita is divine spooned over raw oysters or sliced raw scallops marinated in citrus juices, as a between-course or predessert palate cleanser, or as an accompaniment to buttery pound cakes or dark chocolate cakes. When blood oranges are out of season, try it with the freshly squeezed juice of Seville oranges, tangerines, or ruby grapefruits.

- 3 cups fresh blood orange juice
- 1 1/2 tablespoons finely grated blood orange zest
- 1/4 cup sugar, or more to taste
- 1/3 cup Campari, or more to taste

Place the orange juice, zest, and sugar in a medium-size saucepan over medium-high heat, stirring until the sugar dissolves. Cook until reduced to about 2½ cups, about 7 minutes. Let cool completely, then stir in the Campari. Taste and add more sugar or Campari. Freeze as directed on page 443. **SERVES 6**

ESPRESSO GRANITA

GRANIZADO DE CAFE ESPRESSO

A dark coffee granita is the perfect bitter counterpoint to many sweets, especially the Hazelnut Mousse on page 428. It's also great on its own, served in a glass with a dollop of unsweetened whipped cream and a grating of chocolate (try it for brunch with toasted brioche).

- 1 3/4 cups espresso
- 1/2 cup sugar, or more to taste

Place the espresso and sugar in a small saucepan and heat over medium-high heat, stirring until the sugar dissolves. Taste, and if it seems too bitter, add a little more sugar (keep in mind that if you are serving it with the Hazelnut Mousse, the bitterness of the granita should contrast with the caramel sweetness of the mousse). Let cool to room temperature, then chill completely in the refrigerator. Freeze as instructed on page 443. **SERVES 4 TO 6**

Coffee fuels the Spanish mornings, afternoons, and evenings.

GIN & TONIC–SPIKED GRANITA WITH LYCHEES

GRANIZADO DE GIN Y TONIC CON LYCHEES

Gin and tonic, Spain's favorite cocktail, inspires many of the country's playful modern dessert chefs. Serve this granita in martini glasses as a surprise "aperitif," accompanied by savory skewers of green olives, anchovies, and pimiento chunks.

- 2 cups tonic water, preferably Schweppes
- 2/3 cup gin
- 2 tablespoons fresh lime juice
- 2 teaspoons grated lime zest
- 1/4 cup superfine sugar, or more to taste
- Freshly peeled lychees or drained canned lychees, for garnish

Place the tonic water, gin, lime juice and zest, and sugar in a blender and wait for the bubbles in the tonic to subside, about 10 minutes. Blend briefly, until the sugar is just combined. Taste and add more sugar, if needed. Freeze as instructed on page 443. Serve garnished with lychees. **SERVES 4 TO 6**

MINTY GRANITA

GRANIZADO DE MENTA

This herbal granita is refreshing with just about anything, sweet or savory. I especially like it as a cool, contrasting topping for the gazpacho recipes in this book. You can also make the granita with basil.

2 1/2 cups fresh mint leaves
Boiling water
Ice water
1/2 cup sugar
2 tablespoons fresh lemon juice

1. Place the mint leaves in a colander and slowly pour boiling water over them to blanch them so they don't discolor. Immediately dunk them in a bowl of ice water to refresh.

2. Place the sugar and 2 cups water in a small saucepan and bring to a boil over high heat, stirring until the sugar dissolves. Let cool completely.

3. Drain the mint, then place it, the sugar water, and the lemon juice in a blender and puree until fine. If the mixture is too frothy, let it stand for a few minutes or spoon off some of the froth. Freeze as instructed on page 443. **SERVES 4 TO 6**

SPICED RED WINE GRANITA

GRANIZADO DE VINO TINTO PICANTE

Try this spicy granita as a topping for the White Chocolate Mousse (page 420), instead of the passion fruit gelée called for in the recipe. Or serve it in a shot glass alongside a steamed pudding or a rich fruitcake or spooned over poached pears, berries, sliced peaches or figs, or lemon sorbet.

1 1/2 cups dry red wine, preferably Rioja
1/3 cup sugar
1 long strip of orange zest
1 long strip of lemon zest
1 medium-size cinnamon stick
1 bay leaf
4 or 5 cloves
1 star anise
1 teaspoon lightly crushed black peppercorns
1 1/2 tablespoons best-quality red wine vinegar

Place the wine, sugar, and ¾ cups water in a medium-size saucepan and heat over medium-high heat, stirring until the sugar dissolves. Add the orange and lemon zests, cinnamon stick, bay leaf, cloves, star anise, and peppercorns, reduce the heat to medium-low, and cook for 10 minutes. Remove from the heat and let stand until the wine infuses with the spices, about 2 hours. Strain, discarding the solids, and stir in the vinegar. Freeze as instructed on page 443. **SERVES 6**

MUSCATEL & GREEN GRAPE GRANITA

GRANIZADO DE MOSCATEL Y UVAS

I love serving shot glasses of this refreshing granita as a palate cleanser with a cheese course. If you can't find muscatel, a sweet riesling will also be great. As a variation, try this with red grapes and red dessert wine.

- 1 pound seedless green grapes
- 1/2 cup white dessert wine such as Spanish white muscatel, Italian moscato, or American muscat
- 2 tablespoons fresh lemon juice
- 2 tablespoons superfine sugar, or more to taste

Place the grapes in a food processor and puree until smooth, then let stand for 30 minutes. Strain the grapes through a fine sieve into a bowl, pressing on the solids with the back of a large spoon and scraping the bottom of the sieve; discard the solids. Add the muscatel, lemon juice, and sugar and stir well. Freeze as instructed on page 443. **SERVES 4 TO 6**

CONFECTIONS & COOKIES

ORANGE & PISTACHIO MAGDALENAS

MAGDALENAS DE NARANJA Y PISTACHOS

The irresistible tea cakes called *magdalenas* are Spain's answer to French madeleines or American muffins. Their fluffy, light texture resembles madeleines, but *magdalenas* are shaped like cupcakes or muffins and contain the healthier olive oil instead of butter. This version comes from Barcelona's master baker Xavier Canal, who has contributed other terrific sweets to this book. The Moorish-inspired flavors—orange, nuts, and a touch of orange flower water—are particularly enticing. For a variation, Xavier suggests flavoring half of the batter with orange and pistachios (use half the amounts indicated) and the other half with anything from dark chocolate chips to whole raspberries or blueberries to almond extract. While the *magdalenas* do keep nicely, they are best warm. Baked in mini muffin tins, they are great for coffee breaks or breakfast or as after-dinner petits fours. Don't use olive oil that is too assertive or peppery.

1 cup cake flour (not self-rising)
1/2 cup all-purpose flour
1 small pinch of salt
3/4 teaspoon baking powder
3 large eggs, at room temperature
1 1/3 cups confectioners' sugar, sifted, plus more for dusting the cakes
1/3 cup heavy (whipping) cream
1/4 cup fresh orange juice
1/2 cup light olive oil
1/3 cup lightly toasted pistachios (see page 267), coarsely chopped
1 tablespoon finely grated orange zest, or more to taste
2 teaspoons orange flower water
1 tablespoon unsalted butter, at room temperature, for buttering the muffin tins

1. Sift the cake and all-purpose flours, salt, and baking powder together in a mixing bowl.

2. Place the eggs in a large warm mixing bowl (see Note) and, using an electric mixer, beat them until fluffy, about 1 minute. Add the 1⅓ cups confectioners' sugar and continue beating at high speed until the eggs are pale yellow and approximately triple in volume, about 5 minutes. Working in three batches, beat in the sifted flours, alternating with the cream, orange juice, and olive oil. Stir in the pistachios, orange zest, and orange flower water. Cover the batter with plastic wrap and let rest at room temperature for about 30 minutes. Stir the batter well before proceeding.

3. Position a rack in the center of the oven and preheat the oven to 375°F. Generously butter the cups and top of the tin of one 24-cup mini muffin tin or two 12-cup mini muffin tins; the cups should be 2 inches in diameter.

4. Fill the prepared muffin cups almost full with the batter (you might have a little left over). Bake the *magdalenas* on the center rack until they are light golden and a cake tester or toothpick comes out clean, 20 to 23 minutes, switching the position of the tins after 10 minutes. Do not let the *magdalenas* overbake; they dry out in an instant. Let the *magdalenas* cool on a rack for about 20 minutes, then remove them from the tin(s). Serve the *magdalenas* warm, sprinkled with confectioners' sugar. **MAKES 24 SMALL CAKES**

CHOCOLATE TURRON

TURRON DE CHOCOLATE

Here is an easy but absolutely irresistible chocolate version of *turrón* (nougat), an essential Spanish Christmastime sweet. Adapted from a recipe on the back of a Spanish chocolate box, this *turrón* features an enticing and unmistakably Iberian combination of orange, almonds, and chocolate. Serve thin slices of it with coffee after a festive meal, or take it as a gift to your friends—in Spain no one would ever show up for a holiday meal without bearing *turrón*.

CHRISTMAS: TIME FOR TURRON

In Spain, there is no better way to say "Feliz Navidad" than with a gift of *turrón,* a confection too exquisite to be simply called nougat or fudge. Come Christmas time, the lines at Casa Mira, Madrid's antique *turrón* house, are so long, matronly salesladies dispense small tastes to shoppers to sweeten the wait. Whenever I'm in Madrid during the winter holidays I always join the queue—especially to snag some free samples and get a few Christmas recipes from the ladies in line.

Turrón these days can get pretty baroque, ranging in flavor from candied egg yolk to coconut, praline, truffle, and glacé fruit. Purists, however, swear by the two "original" kinds: the soft luscious *turrón* from Jijona and the deliciously brittle Alicante *turrón,* both produced in the Levante, where *maestros turroneros* have been plying their trade for over five centuries. The word is possibly from the Latin *torrere,* to toast, while *turrón's* ingredients—honey and nuts—point to the Arabic heritage of the sweet.

The *turrón* production season starts in September and lasts until early winter, when the Christmas and Epiphany fiestas are finally over and everybody has pretty much overdosed on the confection. The defining ingredient is the locally grown marcona almonds, which are toasted, crushed and mixed with egg whites, and heated with sugar and wild orange blossom and rosemary honey. After a long, thorough grinding and blending, *turrón* is shaped into blocks and cut into the characteristic slabs, the sight of which make Spanish mouths water. The country consumes over 35,000 tons of *turrón* a year, most of it during Christmas. *Feliz Navidad!*

4 large navel oranges
1 cup granulated sugar
12 ounces best-quality bittersweet chocolate, finely chopped or grated
4 tablespoons (1/2 stick) cold unsalted butter, cut into tablespoons
1 2/3 cups lightly toasted slivered almonds (see page 267), finely ground in a food processor
1/3 cup Grand Marnier
Confectioners' sugar, for dusting

1. Using a sharp knife, remove the zest from the oranges in long strips, taking care not to include any of the bitter white pith; set the oranges aside. Cook the orange zest strips in boiling water for 2 minutes, then drain and rinse them under cold running water. Using a small, sharp knife, cut the strips of zest crosswise into slivers.

2. Set a small sieve over a measuring cup and squeeze ½ cup of juice from the oranges. Place the granulated sugar and the orange juice in a medium-size saucepan and bring to a simmer over medium heat, stirring until the sugar dissolves and skimming any foam, if necessary. Add the orange zest, cover the saucepan, reduce the heat to as low as possible, and simmer to candy the zest, 45 minutes. Strain the orange syrup, setting the orange zest and the syrup aside separately.

3. Place a stainless-steel mixing bowl over a pot of simmering water, add the chocolate and the orange syrup, and stir until the chocolate melts completely, about 5 minutes. Add the butter, 1 tablespoon at a time, whisking until the mixture is glossy. Remove the bowl from the heat and vigorously fold in the orange zest, almonds, and Grand Marnier. The chocolate mixture will be fairly thick, almost like dough.

4. Line a small loaf pan with aluminum foil, leaving an overhang on both sides and making the foil as smooth as possible. Scrape the chocolate mixture into the pan and smooth the top with the back of a wet spoon. Fold the overhang loosely over the *turrón* and refrigerate until the chocolate is solid, 4 to 6 hours. To serve, invert the *turrón* on a plate and remove the foil. Sift a little confectioners' sugar over the top, cut the *turrón* into thin slices, and serve. *Turrón* will keep, wrapped in plastic, for up to 3 days at room temperature. **SERVES 10 TO 12 AS A POST-DESSERT SWEET**

PISTACHIO AND SAFFRON SHORTBREAD LA MELISSA

GALLETAS AL PISTACHO Y AZAFRAN DE MELISSA

Anything baked by my friend the food writer Melissa Clark is outstanding, but shortbread is her particular forte. Admiring the intriguingly flavored crumbly cookies she so effortlessly whips up for parties, I asked her to devise shortbread with a Spanish theme. Her response was this recipe, so delicious and easy I now bake these practically every week. The shortbread is a perfect match for Sauternes, accentuating the honey and saffron notes in the wine.

- 3/4 cup shelled unsalted pistachios
- 2 cups all-purpose flour
- 1/3 cup granulated sugar
- 1/4 cup confectioners' sugar, plus more for dusting the shortbread (optional)
- 1/2 teaspoon coarse salt (kosher or sea)
- 1 cup (2 sticks) unsalted butter, chilled and cubed
- 1 large pinch of saffron, pulverized in a mortar, steeped in 2 tablespoons very hot water, and cooled
- 1 tablespoon full-flavored honey, such as wildflower

1. Position a rack in the center of the oven and preheat the oven to 350°F.

2. Spread the pistachios on a rimmed baking sheet and toast on the center rack until fragrant, 5 to 7 minutes. Let the pistachios cool. Reduce the oven temperature to 300°F.

The breathtakingly intricate entrance to the Forn des Teatre bakery on Mallorca.

3. Place the flour, granulated and confectioners' sugars, and salt in a food processor and pulse to combine. Add the butter, saffron, honey, and toasted pistachios and pulse until the dough just begins to come together. Transfer the dough to a 9-inch-square baking pan and pat it out to cover the bottom of a pan. Smooth the top with an offset spatula.

4. Bake the shortbread on the center rack, rotating the pan halfway through the cooking time, until the dough is lightly golden and firm to the touch, about 40 minutes. Place the pan on a wire rack and let cool for about 20 minutes. While the shortbread is still warm, using a long sharp knife, cut it into 6 strips lengthwise, then crosswise. Let the shortbread cool completely and serve lightly sprinkled with confectioners' sugar, if desired. **MAKES ABOUT 3½ DOZEN**

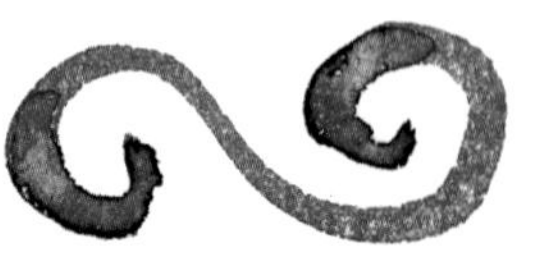

CHOCOLATE-DIPPED ALMOND-STUFFED FIGS

HIGOS RELLENOS DE ALMENDRAS EN CHOCOLATE

I became obsessed with chocolate-covered figs on a recent visit to the lush Jarandilla de la Vera section of Extremadura, stopping at every shop to taste just a few more. They are so luscious and proved so easy to make at home I often have a hard time convincing myself to make any other dessert. Double or triple the recipe for holiday giving—your *amigos* will love you.

- ¾ cup brandy
- 16 soft plump dried Calimyrna figs
- 16 lightly toasted blanched almonds (see page 267), preferably marcona
- 10 ounces best-quality bittersweet chocolate (at least 70 percent cacao), finely chopped or coarsely ground in a food processor
- 2 tablespoons unsalted butter, chopped

1. Place the brandy in a small microwave-safe bowl and microwave on high power until very hot, 1 minute. Place the figs in a bowl that will hold them snugly. Pour the hot brandy over the figs and let soak for about 30 minutes, stirring several times. Drain the figs thoroughly and pat dry with paper towels. (If you'd like, the brandy can be reused in baking or to plump dried fruit.)

2. Using the tip of a small, sharp knife, make a deep incision in the bottom of a fig and push an almond inside. Repeat with the remaining figs and almonds. (Calimyrna dried figs often come tightly pressed together in round packages. If this is the case, once the figs are stuffed, pat and squeeze them lightly between your fingers to restore their round shape.)

3. Place the chocolate in a small stainless-steel mixing bowl set over a pot of simmering water or in the top of a small double boiler (over simmering water) over low heat and stir until it melts completely, about 5 minutes. Whisk in the butter and stir until the chocolate mixture is glossy, then remove from the heat. The melted chocolate mixture needs to be at least 1½ inches deep to cover the figs. If the level in the mixing bowl or double boiler is too shallow, scrape about half of it into a 1-cup measure, replenishing it as needed.

4. Line a small baking sheet or a large plate with aluminum foil or use a Silpat pan liner, if you have one. Holding a fig by the stem, dip it in the chocolate mixture, turning to coat it completely and letting the excess drip off. If the stem is not long enough to hold, you can skewer the fig on a toothpick. Place the chocolate-dipped fig on the baking sheet. Repeat with the remaining figs.

5. Refrigerate the figs until the chocolate is completely set, about 2 hours. After an hour, use a thin spatula or knife to gently separate the figs from the aluminum foil or pan liner so they don't stick. **MAKES 16 FIGS**

APPROXIMATE EQUIVALENTS

1 STICK BUTTER = 8 tbs = 4 oz = ½ cup

1 CUP ALL-PURPOSE PRESIFTED FLOUR OR DRIED BREAD CRUMBS = 5 oz

1 CUP GRANULATED SUGAR = 8 oz

1 CUP (PACKED) BROWN SUGAR = 6 oz

1 CUP CONFECTIONERS' SUGAR = 4½ oz

1 CUP HONEY OR SYRUP = 12 oz

1 CUP GRATED CHEESE = 4 oz

1 CUP DRIED BEANS = 6 oz

1 LARGE EGG = about 2 oz or about 3 tbs

1 EGG YOLK = about 1 tbs

1 EGG WHITE = about 2 tbs

Please note that all conversions are approximate but close enough to be useful when converting from one system to another.

WEIGHT CONVERSIONS

US/UK	METRIC	US/UK	METRIC
½ oz	15 g	7 oz	200 g
1 oz	30 g	8 oz	250 g
1½ oz	45 g	9 oz	275 g
2 oz	60 g	10 oz	300 g
2½ oz	75 g	11 oz	325 g
3 oz	90 g	12 oz	350 g
3½ oz	100 g	13 oz	375 g
4 oz	125 g	14 oz	400 g
5 oz	150 g	15 oz	450 g
6 oz	175 g	1 lb	500 g

LIQUID CONVERSIONS

U.S.	IMPERIAL	METRIC
2 tbs	1 fl oz	30 ml
3 tbs	1½ fl oz	45 ml
¼ cup	2 fl oz	60 ml
⅓ cup	2½ fl oz	75 ml
⅓ cup + 1 tbs	3 fl oz	90 ml
⅓ cup + 2 tbs	3½ fl oz	100 ml
½ cup	4 fl oz	125 ml
⅔ cup	5 fl oz	150 ml
¾ cup	6 fl oz	175 ml
¾ cup + 2 tbs	7 fl oz	200 ml
1 cup	8 fl oz	250 ml
1 cup + 2 tbs	9 fl oz	275 ml
1¼ cups	10 fl oz	300 ml
1⅓ cups	11 fl oz	325 ml
1½ cups	12 fl oz	350 ml
1⅔ cups	13 fl oz	375 ml
1¾ cups	14 fl oz	400 ml
1¾ cups + 2 tbs	15 fl oz	450 ml
2 cups (1 pint)	16 fl oz	500 ml
2½ cups	20 fl oz (1 pint)	600 ml
3¾ cups	1½ pints	900 ml
4 cups	1¾ pints	1 liter

OVEN TEMPERATURES

°F	GAS MARK	°C	°F	GAS MARK	°C
250	½	120	400	6	200
275	1	140	425	7	220
300	2	150	450	8	230
325	3	160	475	9	240
350	4	180	500	10	260
375	5	190			

Note: Reduce the temperature by 20°C (68°F) for fan-assisted ovens.

THE SPANISH PANTRY

While many of the recipes in this book can be prepared with simple supermarket ingredients, there are some flavors particular to Spain that will render the dishes authentic and extra special. Luckily, most of the ingredients you'll find described here—Spanish paprika, chorizo, serrano ham, sherry vinegar, and Spanish olive oil—are becoming easier to find at specialty markets. For others, see "Sources" on page 461 for mail-order information.

ALMONDS: Almonds show up in myriad Spanish dishes from tapas to desserts. Good-quality regular ones will do fine in recipes that call for a small amount. For dishes that feature almonds prominently, it's worth seeking out the remarkable marcona almonds grown along Spain's Mediterranean coast. Flat, almost round, with a sort of crunch and a complex nuttiness, marconas are positively habit forming. You can find them at specialty food stores, such as Whole Foods or see "Sources" (page 461).

ANCHOVIES: Salt curing fish has been a major industry in Spain since Roman times, and anchovies remain something of an addiction there—particularly the fatty, silky anchovy fillets cured in L'Escala in Catalonia or in the Basque portion of the Cantabrian coast. Look for good Spanish anchovies at better markets or order them by mail (see page 461). Some brands of imported Italian oil-packed anchovies are also outstanding. If supermarket anchovies are your only option, taste them before using; if they seem too salty, soak them in milk for about 30 minutes, then drain and rinse them, and toss with a little olive oil. If you're not going to use the anchovies right away, cover them with olive oil. I don't recommend using salt-packed anchovies—

they are too much of a bother to clean.

The mild-flavored white Spanish anchovies called *boquerones,* which are cured in vinegar rather than in salt, are another treat. Ditto fresh anchovies. If you spot them at a fish market, grab them. Rinse the fish thoroughly and clean them as you would sardines (see page 53) but without boning. Cook fresh anchovies gently in olive oil, using the Fresh Sardines with Garlic and Parsley recipe (page 200) as your blueprint.

BEANS, CHICKPEAS & LENTILS: Spanish dried beans and chickpeas are exceptional—creamy, firm, and supremely flavorful when cooked. Yes, they are expensive and must be ordered by mail (see "Sources," page 461), but once you taste them it's hard to go back to the supermarket variety. Try the big white beans called *judiones* or the Asturian *fabes de la granja,* which are so essential for making *fabada* (page 305). Otherwise, I recommend seeking out good-quality organic dried beans and chickpeas. For canned beans and chickpeas, I like Goya's. (You'll find more about Spanish beans on page 306.)

Lentils in Spain come in several varieties, including the flat *castellanas,* which become creamy when cooked, and the small firm *pardinas.* Imported pardinas are super dried and need to be soaked overnight, but Goya's *pardina* lentils don't really need soaking, despite what the package says. French du Puy lentils are another good choice when you want firm cooked lentils.

BREAD: From gazpachos to stews to sauces, many Spanish dishes are thickened with bread. When bread doesn't go into a dish, it usually accompanies it. Look for good country loaves from a bakery. You want one with a rather dense crumb. For most of the canapé recipes in this book a good-quality French baguette will do just fine.

CHEESE: Thankfully, markets in the United States are carrying more and more Spanish cheese, even if Manchego remains the most common kind. In recipes that call for aged Manchego, Parmesan or Romano can be substituted. (For information about specific Spanish cheeses see page 171.)

CHILES: *Spicy* isn't a word one associates with Spanish cuisine, but mild, fleshy dried peppers are frequently used to add flavor and color to dishes. Spanish dried red pepper varieties include the dark, roundish ñoras, *romesco* peppers, and *pimientos choriceros.* Ñora peppers can be mail ordered (see page 461), or you can substitute dried ancho or New Mexico chiles, although the latter have quite tough skins. Pieces of small dried red guindilla peppers often impart a subtle accent of heat to garlicky dishes sautéed in olive oil, such as Sizzling Garlic Shrimp (page 49). Mexican arbol chiles are a good stand-in. Mild green guindilla peppers packed in vinegar make an addictive Basque pickle and are essential to the briny skewer called the Gilda (page 26); they are carried by Spanish markets (see "Sources," page 461).

CHORIZO & OTHER SAUSAGES: Chorizo is one of Spain's most famous comestibles, a fabulous brick-colored sausage prepared with slight variations in various parts of the country. Normally, chorizo is made with pork (although venison or wild boar versions are also common), fat, and *pimentón,* which lends it its characteristic color and smokiness. In this country, chorizo comes in three varieties. Fully cured, dry chorizo, with a texture similar to pepperoni, is best for slicing and eating uncooked (the Palacios brand imported from Spain is excellent).

Semicured, fully cooked soft chorizo, with a consistency similar to kielbasa, is what I recommend in most recipes. Fresh chorizo is raw, uncooked sausage, usually Mexican. While you shouldn't substitute fresh chorizo for semicured, dry chorizo can be used in its place if this is all you can locate. If possible, use chorizo labeled Spanish or Spanish style; otherwise, use another type, such as the Goya brand, which is quite adequate and relatively easy to find. All the recipes in this book call for sweet Spanish-style chorizo sausage.

Blood sausage (*morcilla*) has a wonderfully earthy flavor that is adored in Spain. *Morcilla* comes in two varieties: *morcilla de Burgos,* with rice; and *morcilla de cebolla,* with onions, which is the kind called for in this book. Spanish *morcilla* can be mail ordered (see "Sources," page 461), or you can use another blood sausage, such as *boudin noir.*

HAM: Spanish cured ham is one of the world's greatest ingredients. While the amazing ham from the *ibérico* pig is still unavailable in the United States at the time of publication, *jamón serrano* is becoming quite common at specialty food stores. For cooking, Italian prosciutto may be substituted. (For more about Spanish ham, see page 237.)

OLIVES: Spain boasts a huge range of table olives, yet the choice in America remains quite limited. The variety most commonly found are the fat, green manzanillas. They are sold loose or in jars or cans. Manzanilla olives stuffed with pimientos or anchovies are delicious. You might also be able to find the small, delicate greenish-brown jarred arbequina olives. Otherwise, use Mediterranean olives, such as the black niçoise or Gaeta olives; and green olives like Napflion, picholine, or lucque. Fat purple-black Greek olives, like kalamatas, don't taste particularly Spanish.

OLIVE OILS: Spain is the world's largest producer of olive oil (see page 126 for more). And its varieties are reaching American markets in ever-increasing amounts. How to chose? First, determine your needs: sautéing, dressing a salad, baking, deep-frying, and/or drizzling on dishes as a garnish. For basic cooking needs, like sautéing, go with a tasty but inexpensive Spanish or Spanish-style extra-virgin oil, such as the Borges, Carbonell, or Goya brands. For deep-frying, many of the sturdier, inexpensive extra-virgin oils are perfectly fine. If you're unsure, look for an oil simply labeled "olive oil" (without the words *virgin* or *extra-virgin*) or dilute extra-virgin olive oil with a vegetable oil such as canola; 60 percent olive oil and 40 percent vegetable oil is a good proportion.

In dishes where the particular flavor of olive oil is integral to the overall taste (in recipes calling for fragrant extra-virgin olive oil), make an effort to use a fine, fruity extra-virgin. Often, these will be delicate oils, not suitable for cooking, especially at high temperatures. Some of the bottles you'll find in American markets will specify a particular olive varietal, such as the Catalan arbequina or Andalusian hojiblanca. Among the boutique olive oils available in the States that I especially like are Gasull, Soler Romero, Nuñez de Prado, Columela, and Siurana. But I urge you to experiment with different kinds to discover the range and flavor nuances of Spanish olive oils for yourself. Fine, delicate olive oils are best stored in a cool dark place.

The words *light* or *extra-light* on a bottle refer to the oil's color and mildness of flavor. These are usually neutral-flavored, light-textured oils made with an extremely fine filtration process. I call for light oil in dishes where I don't want a pronounced olive oil flavor; if you don't have a bottle on hand, you can always blend extra-virgin oil with some canola or peanut oil.

PAPRIKA: Smoked paprika (*pimentón de la Vera*) from Extremadura is one of the small glories of Spanish cuisine, imparting a special color and dusky earthiness to a great number of dishes. *Pimentón de la Vera* comes in three categories: *dulce,* or sweet; *agridulce,* or bittersweet; and *picante,* or hot. Because *pimentón dulce* is the easiest to find, this is what I suggest in most recipes. If you come across *pimentón picante,* buy that, too, and use it in dishes to add both smoke and heat. La Chinata *pimentón,* sold in red tins, is my favorite brand. Sweet unsmoked paprika (normally from Murcia) is likewise used widely in Spanish cuisine. As *pimentón de la Vera* has a very distinctive smoky aroma, don't substitute it in recipes that call for unsmoked paprika. If you can't find *pimentón,* use regular paprika. (To learn more about *pimentón de la Vera,* see page 84.)

PEPPERS: When buying fresh bell peppers, look for ones that are fleshy and deep colored—the redder the sweeter. Some recipes call for Italian (frying) peppers, which are pale green and have delicate skins. You should be able to find them easily at most markets. Piquillo peppers are the extraordinary, small pointy red peppers from Navarra. They are roasted over wood fires and packed in jars or cans, either slivered or whole. As demand for piquillo peppers grows, more and more specialty food stores are carrying them. Peppers from Lodosa (you'll see it on the label) are best. (For more about piquillo peppers, see page 34.)

RICE: For paellas and other rice dishes, Spanish cooks normally rely on short- to medium-grain varieties grown in Valencia and Alicante. Such boutique Spanish rices as bomba can be found at some specialty markets or by mail order (see page 461), or you can use good-quality imported risotto rice, such as vialone nano or arborio. Long-grained rice is not very common in Spain. (For more about rice, see page 339.)

SAFFRON: Saffron is the gold of Spanish cuisine—and priced accordingly. However, if you choose saffron well and treat it right, a little goes along way. Some of the world's best saffron is grown in La Mancha; Iranian saffron is excellent too. Buy saffron in threads rather than powdered, from a good producer, and keep it in a tightly closed container in a dry place away from sunlight.

Good saffron threads should be brittle; if yours seem limp or a little damp, wrap a pinch of saffron in a flat packet of aluminum foil and toast it in a dry skillet over medium heat for about 45 seconds per side. To extract maximum color and flavor from saffron, pulverize it into a powder with a mortar using a pestle (or crush it in a small cup with the back of a wooden spoon). Then, steep the saffron in a little very hot liquid for several minutes. You can always just crumble a few threads into the cooking liquid, but the results aren't quite the same.

For the saffron measures in this book:

- A large pinch is a scant ¼ teaspoon of crumbled loosely packed threads
- A medium-size pinch is about ⅛ teaspoon
- A small pinch is 8 to 10 threads

SALT: As a basic seasoning I recommend coarse salt, either kosher or sea. For sprinkling over finished dishes—even desserts—to create a textural accent, Spanish chefs love the flaky sea salt called Maldon. This salt is actually British; it comes in fabulous flat crunchy light flakes. Maldon salt is a bargain compared to the fancy French *fleur de sel* and can be found at such specialty food stores as Williams-Sonoma. Don't miss it.

SHERRY FOR COOKING: Most recipes in this book that include sherry call for dry (fino) sherry. While cooking sherry doesn't need to be extra special, I don't recommend cooking with sherry you wouldn't want to drink (the same goes for cooking wine). If you happen to have some dry oloroso or amontillado on hand, you are welcome to use those in the recipes. Avoid cheap sweet sherries. (For more about sherry, see page 58.)

SQUID INK: Dishes tinted black with squid ink are dramatic and memorable. While extracting your own ink from squid is a bother, the packaged squid ink available at some better fish stores or by mail makes life much easier. Usually squid ink comes in four-gram clear plastic packages (.14 ounce). If the squid ink inside the package looks congealed, warm the package in a bowl of very hot water before opening it, then scrape the ink out with the tip of a dinner knife or a tiny coffee spoon. Packaged squid ink is inexpensive and keeps forever. I suggest buying more than you need to keep some for later. I store squid ink in the refrigerator.

CANNED TUNA: Even Michelin-starred chefs in Spain are hooked on canned tuna. When you taste top-grade Spanish *ventresca* (tuna belly), you'll understand why. For the recipes in this book, look for canned tuna imported from Spain or Italy in specialty food stores or order Spanish tuna by mail (the Ortiz brand is excellent). Otherwise, use better-grade domestic tuna, such as Bumble Bee *tonno* in olive oil, Cento solid-pack light tuna, or Genovo light *tonno*. (For more about canned tuna, see page 114.)

VINEGAR: Sherry, red, and white wine vinegars are all used in Spanish cooking. When buying sherry vinegar look for one labeled *reserva* (aged); some bottles will even indicate the number of years the vinegar has been aged (for more about sherry vinegar, see page 128). For red wine vinegar, I recommend seeking out a good imported kind, especially when making sauces and salads. White wine vinegar in Spain is aromatic and mild; if yours is very sharp, use less or combine it with a little rice vinegar. Syrupy aged balsamic vinegar from Modena has become very popular among Spanish chefs, especially for drizzling over dishes before serving. True Modenese *aceto balsamico* is beautifully viscous, complex, and concentrated, a product drastically different from supermarket-style imitations. I strongly recommend investing in a bottle of the real stuff, to be used sparingly. However, you can reduce thin balsamic vinegar to achieve the syrupy consistency called for in the recipes here.

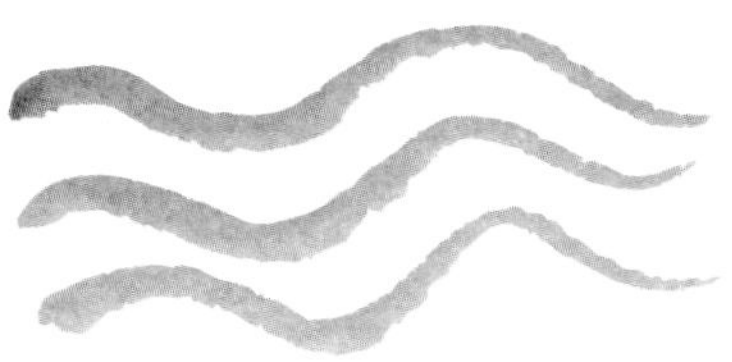

UTENSILS

You will need very little in the way of special equipment to make Spanish dishes at home. There are, however, a few indispensable items. Here are the essentials.

MORTAR AND PESTLE: Nothing releases the flavors of aromatic ingredients—garlic, spices, herbs, nuts—better than an old-fashioned mortar and pestle. Spanish cooks use their *morteros* constantly: for pulverizing saffron or nuts, for emulsifying sauces, such as *allioli* and *romesco,* for making *picadas* and *majados* (pounded mixtures added to dishes at the last minute to enliven their flavor). The ceramic yellow and green Spanish mortars with wooden pestles are pretty to look at, but I prefer a sturdier mortar and a heavier pestle. Marble is my favorite; granite and stoneware are also good options. Mortars are carried by most good kitchenware stores as well as many ethnic groceries.

MINI FOOD PROCESSOR: For pounding a quantity of ingredients too large for a mortar but too small for a regular food processor, a mini food processor is indispensable. These are also useful for mincing such ingredients as parsley and garlic. Cuisinart is a good brand.

CAZUELA: Brown earthenware *cazuelas,* glazed on the inside, have been used in Spanish cooking for centuries and remain a most popular kitchen item. *Cazuelas* are available at stores specializing in Spanish products (see "Sources," facing page) and at some kitchenware shops. They come in many different sizes; if you only buy one, I recommend a round one that's 12 to 13 inches in diameter. Before using a *cazuela* for the first time, soak it in cold water overnight, then dry it thoroughly. When a *cazuela* is properly treated it can be used both in the oven and on a stove top, and it is very attractive for presenting at table. To prevent cracking, don't put a *cazuela* over a high flame; heat it gradually and avoid sudden changes in temperature.

PAELLA PANS: A paella is not really a paella unless it's made in a paella pan. Available at many cookware shops, paella pans come in a variety of sizes. The most useful is about 16 inches in diameter. Thin carbon-steel pans are best. To prevent rusting, dry the paella pan *thoroughly* after washing it and always rub it lightly with olive oil. If the pan does rust, just rub the rust off with steel wool. (For more about paella pans, see page 336.)

SOURCES

A wide variety of Spanish products—from *pimentón* to chorizo to cheeses, serrano ham, rice, piquillo peppers, olive oils, sherry vinegars, boutique anchovies, and canned tuna—are available by mail order. Here are some reliable sources. Despaña Brand Foods and La Española are particularly good for sausages and other meat products. La Tienda and the Spanish Table are excellent bets for utensils, such as earthenware *cazuelas* and paella pans. Spanish comestibles can also be found at gourmet and cookware stores, such as Whole Foods and Dean & Deluca.

SPANISH PRODUCTS

Despaña Brand Foods
www.despanabrandfoods.com
86-17 Northern Boulevard
Jackson Heights, New York 11372
(718) 779-4971

The house-cured chorizo and *morcilla* (blood sausage) are particularly excellent.

La Española Meats
www.laespanolameats.com or
www.donajuana.com
25020 Doble Avenue
Harbor City, California 90710
(310) 539-0455

From Spain
www.fromspain.com
542 Westport Avenue
Norwalk, Connecticut 06851
(866) 846-4113, toll-free, or
(203) 846-4113

The Spanish Table
www.spanishtable.com or
www.tablespan.com
1427 Western Avenue
Seattle, Washington 98101
(206) 682-2827

Besides its flagship in Seattle, the Spanish Table also has stores in Berkeley and Santa Fe.

La Tienda
www.tienda.com
3601 La Grange Parkway
Toano, Virginia 23168
(888) 472-1022, toll-free, or
(757) 566-9606

This catalog and Internet-only store is constantly updating its inventory.

Zingerman's
www.zingermans.com
620 Phoenix Drive
Ann Arbor, Michigan 48108
(888) 636-8162, toll-free, or
(734) 663-3354

One of America's greatest sources for boutique products, Zingerman's always carries interesting Spanish cheeses, olive oils, piquillo peppers, and especially vinegars, such as Puig's incomparable Forum cabernet and chardonnay vinegars. It also has vialone nano risotto rice, which is excellent for paella.

ARTISANAL SPANISH CHEESES

Igourmet.com
www.igourmet.com
(877) 446-8763
This Internet-only store carries a near comprehensive selection of Spanish cheeses.

Murray's Cheese
www.murrayscheese.com
254 Bleecker Street
New York, New York 10014
(888) 692-4339, toll-free, or (212) 243-3289
This famous cheese store is another source for great Spanish cheeses.

BEEF

Lobel's of New York
www.lobels.com
1096 Madison Avenue
New York, New York 10028
(877) 783-4512

GAME BIRDS, ORGANIC POULTRY, AND MEATS

D'Artagnan
www.dartagnan.com
280 Wilson Avenue
Newark, New Jersey 07105
(800) 327-8246;
fax (973) 465-1870

Web sites with more information about Spanish products:

CHEESE
www.cheesefromspain.com

OLIVE OIL
www.oliveoilfromspain.com

PIQUILLO PEPPERS
www.piquillopepper.com

SERRANO HAM
www.consorcioserrano.com

WINES
www.winesfromspain.com

PHOTO CREDITS

All food photography by Susan Goldman except the following:

FRONT COVER: bottom: Jan Baldwin/ Narratives, top: Instituto Espanol de Comercio Exterior

BACK COVER: (third from top): Jan Baldwin/ Narratives; Author photo: Katie Dunn

page ii (top left): Travelstock44, (top right): Ace Stock Limited, (bottom left): David Sanger, (bottom right): Jean Dominique Dallet. page iv: Jan Baldwin/Narratives; page ix (left and middle): Atlantide S.N.C./ Age fotostock; page x (middle): Bartomeu Amengual/Age fotostock, (right): Instituto Espanol de Comercio Exterior; page xi (left): Ken Welsh/Alamy, (right): Javier Larrea/Age fotostock; page xii (right): Pablo Galan Cela/Age fotostock, (middle): Ken Walsh/ Age Fotostock, (right): Paco Ayala/Age fotostock, page xiv (left): Carles Martorell/ Age fotostock, (right): Javier Larrea/ Age fotostock.

REGIONS OF SPAIN: page 4: P. Narayan/ Age fotostock; page 7: Age fotostock; page 9: Wojtek Buss/Age fotostock; page 10: J. D. Dallet/Age fotostock; page 11: Bjorn Svensson/Age fotostock; page 14: Charlie Dass/Age fotostock; pages 3, 5, 6, 7, 8, 12, 13, 15: Instituto Espanol de Comercio Exterior.

THE NEW SPANISH TABLE (PART TITLE): page 16: (left top and right bottom): San Rostro/Age fotostock, (right top): Atlantide S.N.C./Age fotostock, (left bottom): Westend61/Alamy Images Inc.

TAPAS: page 18 (left): Atlantide S.N.C./ Age fotostock, (right): Santiago Yaniz/Age fotostock; page 19 (left): Jan Baldwin/ Narratives; (right): Javier Larrea/Age fotostock; page 42: Jan Baldwin/Narratives; page 47: Digital Vison Ltd/Age fotostock; page 51: Instituto Espanol de Comercio Exterior; page 52: Javier Larrea/Age fotostock; page 61: Juan Carlos Munoz/ Age fotostock.

SOUP: page 74 (bottom right): Oliver Strewe/Lonely Planet Images, (top right): Pat Justis, (bottom left): P. Narayan/Age fotostock, (top left): Atlantide S.N.C./Age fotostock; page page 81: Instituto Espanol de Comercio Exterior; page 85: Michael Juno/Alamy Images; page 89: Juan Carlos Munoz/Age fotostock; page 101: Oliver Strewe/Lonely Planet Images; page 105: Pat Justis.

SALAD: page 111 (right): Gonzalo Azumendi/Age fotostock; pages 110 (left and right), 111 (left), 119, 132: Instituto Espanol de Comercio Exterior; page 127: Jan Baldwin/Narratives.

EGGS: page 136 (bottom left): Bartomeu Amengual/Age fotostock; page 136 (top left): Juan Carlos Munoz/Age fotostock; page 136 (top right): Zurbar/Age fotostock; page 136: Instituto Espanol de Comercio Exterior.

EMPANADAS: page 158 (left): Pat Justis; page 159 (right): Jean Dominique Dallet/ Age fotostock; pages 158 (right), 159 (left), 170, 174: Instituto Espanol de Comercio Exterior.

SEAFOOD: page 184 (bottom right): Pat Justis, (top right): Carles Martorell/Age fotostock, (top left): PhotoBliss/Alamy Images, (bottom left): Instituto Espanol de Comercio Exterior; page 189: Ken Welsh/ Alamy Images; page 204: J. D. Dallet/Age fotostock; page 214: Narratives.

MEAT: page 229 (right): G.V.P./Age fotostock; page 246: Javier Larrea/Age fotostock; page 250: Ian Dagnall/Alamy Images; pages 228 (left and right), 229 (left), 257, 264, 266: Instituto Espanol de Comercio Exterior; page 254: Jan Baldwin/ Narratives.

POULTRY: page 270 (bottom left): Instituto Espanol de Comercio Exterior, (top left): Paco Ayala/Age fotostock, (top right): Ken Welsh/Alamy Imagespage, (bottom right): Jan Baldwin/Narratives; page 286: Pat Justis; page 295: Isifa Image Service/ s.r.o/Alamy.

BEANS & POTATOES: page 302 (right): Rex Butcher/Age fotostock, page (left): Instituto Espanol de Comercio Exterior; page 303 (left): Peter Phipp/Age fotostock, (right): Pedro Coll/Age fotostock; page 307: Ken Walsh/Age fotostock; page 312: Wojtek Buss/Age fotostock; page 323: Pablo Galan Cela/Age fotostock; page 325: Marcro Cristofori/Age fotostock; page 328: Grant Rooney/Alamy Images.

RICE & PASTA: page 330 (bottom left): Atlantide S.N.C./Age fotostock, (top left): J.D. Dallet/Age fotostock, (botom right): Matthew Hranek/Art + Commerce Anthology INC.; page 345: Doug Scott/ Age fotostock.

VEGETABLES: page 366 (right): J. D. Dallert/Age fotostock, (left): Oliver Strewe/Lonely Planet Images; page 367 (right): Javier Larrea/Age fotostock, (left): Jan Baldwin/Narratives; page 382: Instituto Espanol de Comercio Exterior; page 379: Pat Justis; page 382: Instituto Espanol de Comercio Exterior.

DESSERTS: page 396 (bottom left): Instituto Espanol de Comercio Exterior, (top right): Travel-Shots/Alamy, (top left): Jan Baldwin/Narratives; page 409: Ken Welsh/Age fotostock; page 410: Javier Larrea/Age fotostock; page 434: Jan Baldwin/Narratives; page 440: Instituto Espanol de Comercio Exterior; page 443: San Rostro/Age fotostock; page 446: Jan Baldwin/Narratives; page 451: Ruddy Gold/Age fotostock.

INDEX

Page references in *italic* refer to photographs.

INDEX

C

M

N

O

P

Q R

T